The Secret Diplomacy of the Vietnam War

The Secret Diplomacy of the Vietnam War
The Negotiating Volumes of the Pentagon Papers

EDITED BY GEORGE C. HERRING

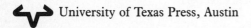 University of Texas Press, Austin

Photocopies of the volumes were photographed for this edition; the quality of reproduction varies according to that of the original material.

Library of Congress Cataloging in Publication Data

Pentagon Papers. Negotiating volumes.
  The secret diplomacy of the Vietnam War.

  Includes bibliographical references and index.
  1. Vietnamese Conflict, 1961–1975—Diplomatic history.   2. Vietnamese Conflict, 1961–1975—Peace.   I. Herring, George C., 1936–
DS557.7.P43   1983   959.704'32   82-21960
ISBN 0-292-77573-3

Contents

Introduction

The materials printed in this volume comprise a small but highly significant portion of that larger body of documents and analysis known as the *Pentagon Papers*. Authorized in the spring of 1967 by Secretary of Defense Robert S. McNamara, who had become progressively disillusioned with the war that had once borne his name, the Pentagon study sought to answer fundamental questions of how the United States had become bogged down in a seemingly endless war in Vietnam. McNamara later claimed that his principal purpose was to compile for future scholars the essential raw materials for historical analysis of the war. It seems likely, however, that he was also seeking immediate answers to the questions that so perplexed him in 1967, and he may have hoped to use the results to alter a policy he felt had proven bankrupt.

Although McNamara's instructions called for an "encyclopedic" review of American policy in Vietnam, the study assumed proportions he had not foreseen. The original timetable called for completion in three to six months by a staff of six people. Assigned to a task force headed by Morton Halperin and under the immediate supervision of Leslie Gelb in the Pentagon's International Security Affairs division, the study in fact required the efforts of thirty-six people, along with numerous other part-time consultants and collaborators. It was not completed until early 1969, nearly a year after McNamara had left office. The finished product comprised some forty-seven volumes, more than seven thousand pages, and an estimated two and one-half million words. Comprehensive in coverage and based on extensive research in official records, it provided detailed analysis of American involvement in Vietnam from the end of World War II until 1967, with particular emphasis on the Kennedy-Johnson years, and included voluminous supporting documents.[1]

Originally designed as an in-house study and routinely classified "Top Secret," the papers would also attain a notoriety that McNamara had not intended. Upon leaving the Pentagon in 1969, Gelb and Halperin placed a set in the RAND Corporation, a private think tank with long and close ties to the Defense Department. There they came under the scrutiny of Daniel Ellsberg, an economist and former Marine officer who had once firmly supported the war, had spent some time in Vietnam working for the Defense Department, and

---

1. For background on the Pentagon Papers project, see Sanford J. Ungar, *The Papers and the Papers* (New York: E. P. Dutton & Co., 1972), pp. 20–41, and Harrison E. Salisbury, *Without Fear or Favor: The New York Times and Our Times* (New York: Times Books, 1980), pp. 57–60. George McT. Kahin, "The Pentagon Papers: A Critical Evaluation," *American Political Science Review* 69 (June 1975): 675–684, and H. Bradford Westerfield, "What Use Are Three Versions of the Pentagon Papers?," ibid., pp. 685–696, assess the strengths and weaknesses of the several editions of the papers as historical sources.

had compiled one section of the Pentagon study. Now a RAND consultant, Ellsberg secured access to the papers for a study of the lessons of Vietnam, and he found in them evidence that heightened his increasingly passionate disenchantment with the war. Persuaded that something must be done to end a conflict he had come to regard as futile and immoral, he and another RAND worker, Anthony Russo, without the knowledge of their superiors, photocopied the documents on a machine belonging to a friend. In the spring of 1970, Ellsberg passed them to Senator J. William Fulbright in hopes that the leading Senate "dove" could be persuaded to conduct a series of public hearings on them. Fulbright insisted that he would use the study only with official clearance, however, and he was unable to secure such authorization from Secretary of Defense Melvin Laird. Ellsberg later decided that more drastic measures must be taken, and in February 1971 he turned the volumes over to *New York Times* reporter Neil Sheehan, who had spent considerable time in Vietnam and had gone through a similar process of conversion from "hawk" to "dove." After weeks of heated internal debate and close consultation with a battery of lawyers, the *Times* on Sunday, June 13, 1971, published the first installment of a projected series based on the *Pentagon Papers*.[2]

From Ellsberg's standpoint, the timing could not have been more propitious. The United States had been involved in full-scale war in Vietnam for six years, and despite President Richard M. Nixon's promises of peace and his commitment to a phased withdrawal of American forces, there was little indication by the summer of 1971 that the conflict was nearing an end. Polls showed a dramatic rise in public frustration and disillusionment with the war. Domestic protest, which had quieted in Nixon's first year in office, was again on the increase, a massive demonstration in Washington in the spring provoking one of the worst riots in the city's history. Well aware of the risks it was taking in publishing still-classified documents, the *Times* cautiously downplayed its initial story. What Sheehan aptly described as a "thermonuclear vial" would quickly explode, however, producing a classic confrontation between government and the press, adding to popular disillusionment with the war and provoking Nixon to take steps that would eventually force his resignation.

Although the *Pentagon Papers* exposed the policy failures of his predecessors, Nixon moved quickly to stop their publication. In his view, government could not function effectively without complete secrecy, and from the day he had taken office he had been obsessed with the chronic leakage of official secrets. The massive leak of the *Pentagon Papers* enraged him. Long distrustful of the *Times* and the press in general, he concluded that he could not permit

2. For Ellsberg, see Ungar, *Papers*, pp. 42–84. The internal deliberations at the *Times* preliminary to publication are recounted at great length in Salisbury, *Without Fear or Favor*, pp. 80–124, 165–206.

newspapers to decide what classified material should be made public. He first attempted to dissuade the *Times* from further publication of the papers. This failing, he took the unprecedented step of obtaining from the courts a temporary restraining order preventing the newspaper from publishing additional materials from the Pentagon study.[3]

Nixon's dramatic move failed to suppress the *Pentagon Papers*. On June 30, 1971, by a vote of six to three, the Supreme Court rejected the government's request for a permanent restraining order. The much publicized clash between the government and the press probably gave the papers more attention than they would have received otherwise, and the Supreme Court decision opened the floodgates. The *Times* resumed publication of its series and gave the papers prominent play over a period of several weeks. The *Washington Post*, which had also secured a set of the papers, published its own series, and excerpts from the McNamara study appeared in newspapers across the nation. By the end of the year, moreover, the papers had been published in book form in three separate editions. The *Times* published a 677-page version, which included extensive documents and the summaries of the original studies put together by its own reporters. Senator Mike Gravel of Alaska, another Senate "dove," arranged with Beacon Press to print a much more complete four-volume edition, and the government released its own twelve-volume version, which contained most of the original study.

It remains difficult even after eleven years to assess the impact of the *Pentagon Papers*. Most commentators agreed that they contained few real bombshells, and while the original studies by the Pentagon analysts frequently questioned the means being employed in Vietnam, only rarely did they question the larger purposes of the war. The papers did, however, seem to confirm what critics of the war had long been saying and what increasing numbers of Americans had come to believe: that Kennedy and Johnson had secretly committed the nation to war in Vietnam while publicly denying such intentions and that they had repeatedly misled the public in their optimistic reports of progress. It seems reasonable to conclude that publication of the papers contributed to increased opposition to the war and a rising distrust of government among the nation's articulate public.[4]

Although the greatest portion of the *Pentagon Papers* had been released by the end of 1971, four volumes remained unavailable and generally unknown to the public. Published here for the first time, these so-called negotiating vol-

3. For Nixon's response to publication of the papers, see Salisbury, *Without Fear or Favor*, pp. 231–243, and Richard M. Nixon, *RN: The Memoirs of Richard Nixon* (New York: Grosset & Dunlap, 1978), pp. 508–515.

4. Floyd Abrams, "The Pentagon Papers: A Decade Later," *New York Times Magazine*, June 7, 1981, pp. 22–26, 76–95, attempts to weigh the impact of the papers from the vantage point of 1981.

umes deal with the diplomacy of the war between 1964 and 1968.[5] Compiled
by Gelb and Richard Moorsteen and based on the classified files of the Department of State, they comprise more than eight hundred pages of analysis and
documents. They provide a wealth of detail on the evolution of American policies toward a negotiated settlement, the sporadic diplomatic contacts between
the United States and North Vietnam, and the persistent and unsuccessful
efforts of numerous third parties to bring the two antagonists to the conference
table. They assess with considerable candor the way in which the Johnson administration responded to domestic and international pressures for negotiations, the sincerity of its professed commitment to a negotiated settlement,
and the reasons why the various peace initiatives failed.

From their inception, the negotiating volumes stood apart from the rest of
the Pentagon study. Because they dealt with ongoing and unresolved issues,
they were compiled differently. Rejecting the standard historical narrative and
interpretation approach used in the other sections of the papers, Gelb and
Moorsteen put together for each of the thirteen different initiatives or contacts
a brief introductory summary and analysis followed by a lengthy "chronology" recounting the events of that particular affair on a day-to-day basis. Because the matters they dealt with aroused heated controversy in the United
States and abroad, involved numerous other nations, including some of America's closest allies, and concerned unsettled issues of fundamental importance,
the volumes were treated as especially sensitive, only three or four people having access to them. The studies were compiled on the assumption that they
might be used as background papers should negotiations materialize. They
were in fact completed after negotiations had actually begun in Paris in June
1968 and were immediately sent there for the use of the American delegation.
After assuming office as Nixon's national security adviser in January 1969,
Henry Kissinger used the volumes as a basis for developing policy, and Gelb
has claimed that the negotiating strategy eventually employed by Kissinger in
the secret talks derived at least in part from recommendations contained in a
study based on the negotiating volumes.[6]

The subsequent history of the volumes is as intriguing and, in places, as
confusing as the events described in them. For reasons that will probably
never be entirely clear, Ellsberg decided to withhold them from the *New York
Times*. "I didn't want to get in the way of diplomacy," he later explained. "I
wanted to get in the way of bombing and killing."[7] By this, he apparently
meant that he feared leakage of these materials might damage the prospects of

5. A much more heavily "sanitized" collection of the negotiating volumes was made
available on microfiche through the Declassified Documents Reference System in 1975.
6. Interviews with Leslie H. Gelb, July 15, 31, 1981.
7. Quoted in Ungar, *Papers*, pp. 83–84.

a negotiated settlement of the war. The logic of his explanation may be questioned—the Paris peace talks had been hopelessly deadlocked since 1968, and he might as easily have concluded that release of the volumes would increase pressures on the United States to compromise. There seems no reason to question his sincerity, however, and he may also have felt that leakage of the negotiating volumes, because of their special sensitivity, would damage his cause by making him appear irresponsible.

Sheehan and the *Times* did not contest Ellsberg's decision. Sheehan concluded that withholding this material might lessen the danger that the newspaper would be charged with a major breach of security. Fully aware of the risk they were taking by publishing the rest of the papers, the *Times'* editors agreed. During subsequent hearings on the papers before the Supreme Court, government attorneys adamantly insisted that the negotiating volumes contained information that must remain classified, reinforcing the *Times'* concern about their special sensitivity. Apparently satisfied with what it had accomplished and uneager to take on the government again, the newspaper made no effort to secure the remaining volumes.[8]

While the rest of the *Pentagon Papers* were splashed across the pages of the nation's press in the summer of 1971, the negotiating volumes languished in obscurity until the trial of Daniel Ellsberg nearly a year later. Quickly pinpointing Ellsberg as the source of the leak, the government indicted him and, subsequently, Russo for theft and espionage, and after a long delay the trial finally got underway in Los Angeles in the spring of 1972. The trial attracted almost as much attention as the event that had precipitated it. It opened in a highly charged political atmosphere, paralleling the initial stages of the presidential campaign, Nixon's dramatic escalation of the war against North Vietnam, and the Moscow summit meeting. It posed the fundamental issue of government secrecy against the public's right to know. On the part of both major contestants, it assumed the form of a vendetta. Certain that Ellsberg was part of a much larger and more sinister conspiracy against his administration and determined not merely to convict but to destroy him, Nixon had ordered a secret operations group in the White House to use any means necessary to discredit his foe. On the other hand, the defendants and their attorneys hoped to convert the trial into a public forum on government secrecy and the morality and legality of the Vietnam War. Although the proceedings in Los Angeles at times took on a carnival atmosphere and the results were both inconclusive and anticlimactic, chief defense attorney Leonard Boudin only slightly exaggerated in terming the affair the "political trial of our time."[9]

8. Salisbury, *Without Fear or Favor*, pp. 121, 301, 318–319.
9. Quoted in Kenneth W. Salter, *The Pentagon Papers Trial* (Berkeley: Editorial Justa, 1975), p. 2.

Ironically, although Ellsberg had cautiously withheld the negotiating volumes, they assumed a central role at his trial. The government indicted him and Russo for removing the *Pentagon Papers* from the RAND Corporation and for photocopying them, rather than for transmitting them to the *Times*, and the indictment listed the four negotiating volumes along with the others. The Justice Department early concluded, moreover, that the four volumes were vital to the prosecution of Ellsberg and Russo. Fingerprints on one of them seemingly clinched the case for theft. More important, Defense Department "damage reports" on the rest of the papers raised serious doubts that their leakage in 1969 could be proven to have harmed the national security, significantly weakening the government's case for espionage. Because the negotiating volumes dealt with especially sensitive issues, they seemed to meet most closely the tests provided by the Espionage Act. Attorney General John Mitchell insisted that they were "essential to a successful prosecution" and privately conceded that without them "there is serious doubt that we can obtain a conviction of Ellsberg and Russo."[10]

Adding even greater irony, the government's determination to convict the defendants ran afoul of the system of secrecy they had challenged and it was so vigorously defending. From the outset, the State Department vehemently protested the use of the negotiating volumes in a public trial. Pointedly emphasizing that Ellsberg himself had refused to leak these "most sensitive documents," Secretary of State William Rogers warned that if the government took the initiative in disclosing their contents it would seriously weaken its own case for their special sensitivity. Rogers further warned that public use of the volumes could do untold harm to American foreign relations. Echoing Ellsberg's expressed fears, he cautioned that revelations about earlier Vietnam negotiations could disrupt the Paris peace talks and hinder efforts to secure release of the American prisoners of war. Disclosures of the role of third parties, Rogers continued, might antagonize the other nations involved and limit their future willingness to assist the United States. Ominously alluding to matters then given top priority by the Nixon administration (and about which the State Department itself had not been kept fully informed), the Secretary admonished that release of the negotiating volumes could damage negotiations with the Soviet Union and China "during the critically important phase of our relations with these governments in the months immediately ahead."[11]

The State Department eventually acquiesced to Mitchell, but only on condition that he take every step legally available to protect the negotiating volumes from public disclosure. The Justice Department agreed to request that

---

10. Robert W. Mardian to William B. Macomber, Jr., December 22, 1971, and John Mitchell to William Rogers, February 4, 1972, both in Morton Halperin File on the Pentagon Papers and the Ellsberg Trial, Center for National Security Studies, Washington, D.C.
11. Rogers to Mitchell, February 10, 1972, ibid.

during testimony on the volumes all spectators would be required to leave the courtroom and the press would be prohibited from publishing the testimony. It would attempt to keep the documents and testimony related to them sealed until the court should order otherwise. It would do everything possible to keep the volumes out of the hands of the defendants, and if the court insisted on access it would seek a protective order preventing disclosures except as required by the trial.[12]

The prosecution got considerably less than it wanted. Defense attorneys vigorously protested that evidence treated with confidentiality violated the defendants' right to a public trial and that approval by the court of special means to protect the confidentiality of the volumes conceded the prosecution's point that they were vital to the national security. "The government has to make the hard choice between making these documents public and not using them in court," defense attorneys insisted. The presiding judge, William Matthew Byrne, Jr., in general sided with the defense, concluding that since the volumes were being used as evidence they must be made available to the defendants. To satisfy the prosecution's concerns at least partially, however, he did add a protective order preventing the defense from making the volumes public and requiring it to provide a full list of all consultants and witnesses to whom they were made available. The judge's ruling temporarily appeased the State Department, but it also opened the way for continued intragovernmental feuding over control of the volumes and created considerable later confusion as to their status.[13]

Several months after the judge had ordered that the volumes be made available to the defense, moreover, columnist Jack Anderson began publishing a series of articles based on them. The series ran from June 9 to June 23, 1972, and throughout Anderson carefully disguised his source, referring only to "background papers" or a "top secret analysis" of American efforts to open negotiations with North Vietnam. He divulged some of the choicest tidbits from the volumes, recounting the Soviet Union's mysteriously shifting role as a would-be mediator between the United States and North Vietnam, revealing that the British had passed to the United States intercepts of phone conversations between Leonid Brezhnev and Alexei Kosygin during the latter's 1967 visit to London, and reporting then private citizen Henry Kissinger's role as a go-between in a contact in Paris later that year. Anderson usually related his revelations to topics of current interest, such as Nixon's recent summit meeting in Moscow and the ongoing attempts to negotiate a Vietnam peace settle-

12. Rogers to Mitchell, February 10, 1972, and Charles Brower to John Davitt, February 25, 1972, ibid.
13. Peter Schrag, *Test of Loyalty: Daniel Ellsberg and the Rituals of Secret Government* (New York: Simon & Schuster, 1974), pp. 176–177, and protective order issued by Byrne, April 25, 1972, Halperin File.

ment. His columns were unsensational in tone, moreover, and they carefully refrained from criticism of Johnson's diplomacy. Ironically, in view of the columnist's well-deserved reputation as a political gadfly and a persistent critic of the Nixon administration, these columns warmly praised the President and Kissinger's skillful handling of recent negotiations with the Soviet Union and China.[14]

Despite the restraint exercised by Anderson, the government seized on the columns to broaden its attack on Ellsberg and Russo. Explicitly identifying Anderson's source as the negotiating volumes, the Justice Department accused the defendants of leaking material that was "still highly classified" and contained vital information relating to a "communications intelligence system." In Los Angeles, the prosecution speculated that the defense had publicized the volumes in a desperate attempt to affect the outcome of the trial and charged that the press was cooperating with the lawbreakers. The chief prosecuting attorney, David Nissen, demanded to see the confidential list of consultants and witnesses given access to the volumes and asked the judge to undertake a full investigation of the leak.[15]

The defense responded in kind. Attorneys for Ellsberg and Russo labeled the charges "scurrilous," "absolutely false," and "demeaning to the process of justice" and suggested that the government itself may have leaked the material in an effort to win a case the American people were "coming more and more to recognize as a hoax." Arguing that the government had "purposely and vindictively" attacked the defendants "to deprive them of their right to a free trial," Russo's attorneys moved for a dismissal of the charges on the grounds that the most recent accusations had resulted in prejudicial pretrial publicity.[16]

The source of the leak remains a mystery. The defense certainly had every reason to avoid anything so risky at this stage of the trial, but the events of 1972 were not always governed by rationality. The defendants, their attorneys, or defense witnesses might have decided to display their contempt for government secrecy or to prove their essential point—that the *Pentagon Papers* contained nothing damaging to the national security—by leaking them to Anderson. On the other hand, it is not inconceivable that the government may have leaked the volumes in a crude effort to frame Ellsberg and Russo. The White House "plumbers" group, which included Watergate conspirators E. Howard Hunt and G. Gordon Liddy, had already burglarized Ellsberg's psychiatrist's office to find evidence to discredit the defendant, and it is entirely possible that they, or some other government official, may have arranged the leak. It is also possible, of course, that the leak was unrelated to the trial. Someone with ac-

14. See especially *Washington Post*, June 10, 1972.
15. Ibid., June 23, 1972.
16. Ibid., and *Los Angeles Times*, June 28, 1972.

cess to the volumes might have given them to Anderson to protest Nixon's escalation of the war or for some other unknown reason.

While lawyers sparred in Los Angeles, Anderson shed his earlier caution. In a column on June 26, he admitted having a copy of those sections of the *Pentagon Papers* that Ellsberg had "carefully withheld" from the press. Since President Nixon had made public information much more sensitive and since the Justice Department was using the material against Ellsberg, he argued, there was "no legitimate reason" for continuing the secrecy. Shifting to an attack on the administration's foreign policy, he noted that the volumes contained some "painful lessons" that "still seem to be disregarded in the quest for a Vietnam peace." The papers made clear, he concluded, that Johnson's attempts to bludgeon North Vietnam into negotiating on his terms by bombing had produced the opposite effect in Hanoi, a point that seemed to be lost on Nixon and Kissinger.[17]

Anderson followed the next day with a much harsher column entitled "The Government Secrecy Syndrome." Chortling that the "custodians of government secrets are gnashing their teeth again over our access to the still-secret portions of the *Pentagon Papers*," he proceeded to attack the system that had kept the volumes from the public. He noted that President Johnson had published in his memoirs carefully selected excerpts from the volumes to prove "how right and reasonable he had been," and he went on to charge that the power to classify information "is nothing less than the absolute authority of the government to make a secret of whatever it wishes." The "divine right" to classify had been abused beyond all reason, Anderson added, permitting the government to cover up its blunders and embarrassments. Echoing a theme that had dominated response to the leakage of the *Pentagon Papers* a year earlier, he concluded that Vietnam had proven the "fateful consequences of allowing any president to exercise power in splendid isolation behind the double walls of executive privilege and official secrecy." Breathing defiance, he vowed that he would continue to publish information that the government "seeks to hide from the public by classifying."[18]

To underscore his disdain for government secrecy, Anderson turned over the still-classified volumes to the *Washington Post* and *New York Times*, each of which gave them immediate and prominent one-day coverage. The *Post* ran two front-page stories, Murray Marder highlighting the major revelations from the volumes and Don Oberdorfer detailing Kissinger's role in the abortive 1967 peace contact. On an inside page, veteran Asian correspondent Stanley Karnow critically analyzed Johnson's handling of the various peace initiatives. The *Times* printed a front-page story by Bernard Gwertzman on the

17. *Washington Post*, June 26, 1972.
18. Ibid., June 27, 1972.

Soviet role in Vietnam peace moves, published a full page of documents, most of them relating to Kissinger's unofficial diplomacy, and ran an inside story by Sheehan, which assessed in broad-brush fashion the contents of the negotiating volumes.

The treatment accorded by both newspapers was unsensational in tone and cautious in judgment. The writers conceded the absence of shocking new revelations and only mildly criticized Johnson's diplomacy. They did note that the volumes conclusively proved what the 1971 installments had hinted, that the various bombing pauses were designed primarily to prepare American and world opinion for further escalation of the war. Karnow also observed that the Johnson administration's handling of the peace contacts was as "confused, disorganized, and aimless as the war itself." With the possible exception of Kissinger, he added, the various go-betweens not only "lacked clear concepts of the issues at stake, but, in many cases were mainly striving to promote their own interests." Karnow, Marder, and Sheehan all agreed, however, that diplomacy failed between 1964 and 1968 primarily for reasons of substance. The papers provided ample evidence of bungling diplomacy and of misperceptions on both sides, and there were probably lost opportunities along the way. More than anything else, however, the utter irreconcilability of the negotiating positions staked out by both sides rendered a settlement impossible. "The mating dance described in the Pentagon documents, and the maneuvers that have gone on since," Karnow concluded, "may therefore prove that, in the Vietnam conflict, diplomacy is only war by other means." [19]

Compared to the uproar of 1971, the leak of the negotiating volumes attracted little attention. After initial publication, the *Times* and *Post* all but ignored them. The story did not make the major newsweeklies, and other newspapers gave the volumes little coverage. Even the *Los Angeles Times*, published at the site of the Ellsberg trial, printed only a brief wire-service report buried deep inside the first section. To minimize further the impact of the story, the *Times* added a paragraph stating that the volumes contained little that had not been disclosed about the peace contacts in the investigative reporting of Stuart Loory and David Kraslow printed in its own pages in 1968. [20]

The Anderson leaks did, however, reopen the intragovernmental struggle over handling of the negotiating volumes at the trial. The flap over the leak itself quickly subsided. Byrne peremptorily rejected both the defense motion for a dismissal of charges and the prosecution request for a formal investigation into the source of the leak. Pointing to the information disseminated by Anderson as an example of the dangers from unrestricted use of the volumes in an open court, the prosecution then dredged up its old request for con-

19. Ibid.; *New York Times*, June 28, 1972.
20. *Los Angeles Times*, June 28, 1972.

fidential treatment of the documents in the trial. Byrne again rejected the proposal, reiterating his stand that evidence used in a public trial must be made public. When the trial finally began in January 1973 after a long delay occasioned by a defense appeal to the Supreme Court on another court ruling, the judge ordered the negotiating volumes, along with the other evidence, placed in the clerk's office, where they were open to public scrutiny.

New revelations broke almost immediately. On January 30, 1973, three days after the signing of the treaty ending American participation in the Vietnam War, *Washington Post* reporter Sanford Ungar announced the availability of the documents and printed previously unpublished excerpts. Citing evidence for the alleged callousness of the United States—and its allies—he quoted at length from a top secret cable on May 15, 1964, in which Ambassador to South Vietnam Henry Cabot Lodge, Jr., had warned President Johnson that the "total annihilation" of North Vietnam would leave nobody upon whom the United States could "put pressure." Ungar also summarized documents that indicated that Canadian Prime Minister Lester Pearson, subsequently a Nobel Peace Prize winner, had supported Johnson's 1965 decision to bomb North Vietnam upon receiving assurances that nuclear weapons would not be used.[21]

Byrne's decision and the Ungar story brought to the surface the long-simmering conflict between the requirements of the judicial process and those of diplomacy. An outraged State Department protested that the repeated leaks from the trial were damaging American foreign relations. Britain and Canada had recently complained about the publication of materials that concerned them directly, and the Pearson story had been particularly embarrassing because Canada had just agreed to help supervise the Vietnam cease-fire. In most undiplomatic language, State questioned Byrne's authority to declassify official documents, claimed that his recent ruling was "totally inconsistent" with his April 27, 1972, protective order, blasted the prosecution's "totally insufficient" efforts to protect the volumes, and demanded that the Justice Department do something to prevent further "adverse repercussions" to American foreign policy.[22] Dutifully responding to the State Department's protests, the prosecution in Los Angeles pointed out the seeming contradiction between the judge's two rulings and offered new proposals to safeguard the confidentiality of the volumes.

The struggle ended in a curious standoff that left the status of the papers at best murky. Byrne stood his ground, explaining that the April protective order applied only during pretrial preparation, not after the materials went into evidence. Admitting that his actions did not constitute formal declassification, he

21. *Washington Post*, January 30, 1973.
22. Charles Brower to William Olson, February 7, 1973, Halperin File.

continued to insist on public availability.[23] The State Department could not change Byrne's ruling, but it insisted with equal vehemence that the documents were still classified top secret. Standing by its self-proclaimed "obligation to preserve the integrity of the diplomatic process and to protect the sanctity of confidential exchanges with other governments," it flatly rejected Fulbright's request to declassify a Foreign Relations Committee study based on the volumes.[24] The papers thus remained in a sort of limbo, still officially classified despite the fact that a federal judge had made them available to the public.

When testimony in the Ellsberg trial finally began in the spring of 1973, the negotiating volumes again attained a great deal of notoriety. As the complex legal issues were framed by attorneys on both sides and by the court, the case hinged on the basic question of whether release of the *Pentagon Papers* in 1969 would have adversely affected the security interests of the United States or given advantage to a foreign power. The negotiating volumes, which were generally conceded to contain the most sensitive information, were central to the case for both prosecution and defense.[25]

The prosecution took the broad position that the information in the *Pentagon Papers* as a whole, rather than any specific part, could have been used to the detriment of the national interest, but prosecution witnesses frequently singled out the negotiating volumes for special emphasis. Arguing that the *Papers* in their entirety would have been an "intelligence windfall" for a foreign government, chief prosecution witness General Paul Gorman, who had himself worked on them, went on to contend that release of the negotiating volumes in 1969 would have been highly injurious to the cause of peace in Vietnam, American foreign relations in general, and U.S. intelligence operations. The North Vietnamese had repeatedly warned that negotiations must be conducted in absolute secrecy, Gorman stressed, and leakage of details about earlier contacts might have provoked them to break off the Paris talks. Information regarding the initiatives undertaken by third parties might have damaged those nations' relations with the United States or reduced their effectiveness as potential intermediaries. For example, Gorman noted, revelations about British wiretaps of Kosygin's telephone might have embarrassed the British government and compromised its position as co-chairman of the Geneva Conference. Disclosures of the names of intermediaries and other information contained in the papers could have drastically undermined the intelligence-

23. Transcript of Ellsberg Trial, February 16, 1973, ibid.
24. Marshall Wright to J. William Fulbright, March 2, 1973, ibid.
25. The complex issues at stake in the trial are clearly set forth in Morton H. Halperin and Daniel N. Hoffman, *Top Secret: National Security and the Right to Know* (Washington: New Republic Books, 1977), pp. 115–123.

gathering operations of the United States and provided other governments the means to cut off major sources.[26]

The defense vigorously challenged the prosecution's arguments. Defense attorneys and witnesses attempted to show that neither the volumes in their entirety nor any specific part of them met the tests of espionage as defined by the law. The defense further contended that, even if the information contained in the papers could be proven to relate to the national security, it made no difference in this case because the information was already in the public domain. The defense paraded across the stand an impressive array of witnesses, including former Kennedy adviser McGeorge Bundy, who dismissed the *Pentagon Papers* as the "first cut of history," less useful to a foreign government than the *Congressional Record*.[27] Using the work compiled by a small army of researchers, many of them student volunteers who had joined Ellsberg's crusade against the government and the war, the defense produced excerpts from books, newspapers, and unclassified government documents to show that the information in the *Pentagon Papers* was already available to the public.

The defense took considerable pains to refute specific arguments related to the negotiating volumes. Witness Allen Whiting, a scholar who had worked in State Department intelligence in the 1960s, testified that these volumes would provide nothing more than a "learning experience" for foreign analysts. The greatest danger to intelligence operations from leaks was the betrayal of sources, Whiting observed, and information that would make this possible did not appear in these volumes. Whiting also curtly dismissed the significance of the much discussed wiretap of Kosygin's telephone. The Russians most probably knew of the tap, he speculated, and may even have used it to convey to the British and Americans their good faith as intermediaries. "This is not an unusual way of one Government getting information to another," he concluded.[28]

Canadian diplomat Chester Ronning, who had been an intermediary between the United States and North Vietnam in 1966, denied that revelations from the volumes were potentially damaging to America's relations with its allies. One of the most colorful of the many witnesses, the avuncular Ronning created a stir upon appearing in the courtroom by ostentatiously proceeding to the bench and shaking hands with the judge before taking the stand. Conced-

26. Schrag, *Test of Loyalty*, pp. 221–224, 241–243; *Los Angeles Times*, January 24–27, 1973. To some extent, as Schrag has suggested, the government's own "Byzantine system of secrecy" frustrated its efforts to prosecute those who had breached it. Either the State Department, which was presumably best qualified to evaluate the sensitivity of the diplomatic volumes, refused to testify or the prosecution, knowing its opposition to use of the volumes in the trial, declined to request its help.

27. Schrag, *Test of Loyalty*, p. 285.

28. *New York Times*, March 15, 1973.

ing that his trips to Hanoi were supposed to have been conducted in secrecy, he noted that the details appeared in the *New York Times* shortly after he returned. As a result, he concluded, the disclosures in the negotiating volumes "were of damage to no one." The prosecution made Ronning read an excerpt from the volumes in which Secretary of State Dean Rusk had questioned the sincerity of Canada's stated motives in proposing the Ronning mission and pointedly asked the diplomat whether such revelations might not be offensive to Canadians and therefore harmful to Canadian-American relations. Pulling himself forward in the witness chair and speaking in a clear and firm tone, Ronning responded without hesitation: "Canadians would know that's not true."[29]

Journalist Stuart Loory testified that most of the information in the negotiating volumes had already been revealed to the public, among other places in the book *The Secret Search for Peace in Vietnam*, which he and co-author David Kraslow had published in 1969. To make his case, Loory flashed documents from the volumes on a large screen in the courtroom while reading portions of his book. Loory went on to note that he and Kraslow had obtained much of their information from U.S. government officials, thus supporting a major defense argument that the government itself was the source of most leaks to the media. When the cross-examiner countered that the book did not contain the actual documents, Loory insisted that this was not true, although he produced only broadcasts from Radio Hanoi to prove his point.[30]

Unquestionably, the most flamboyant defense witness was Tom Hayden, founder of the Students for a Democratic Society and long-time radical activist opponent of the war, whose unauthorized mission to Hanoi had caused a furor in the United States. Before a packed courtroom, with his wife, actress Jane Fonda, in the front row, Hayden testified as an "expert" on diplomacy. Ignoring the issues central to the trial, he launched a vicious attack on Johnson's handling of the peace initiatives. The negotiating volumes proved, he affirmed, that "a lot of diplomacy on the part of the United States was stage managed to create the image that the United States was seeking peace" when in fact it was not. The Johnson administration was determined to impose a settlement by force, Hayden claimed, and its bargaining position was consistently more rigid than that of North Vietnam. The President had eventually agreed to hold talks with the North Vietnamese in Paris only because of the success of the Communist Tet offensive and Eugene McCarthy's showing in the New Hampshire primary.[31]

The Ellsberg trial ended anticlimactically without resolving the basic issues

29. Ibid.
30. Ibid., March 30, 31, 1973.
31. Schrag, *Test of Loyalty*, pp. 310–311; *New York Times*, April 6, 1973.

raised by the leak of the *Pentagon Papers*. As the lawyers were presenting their final arguments, the proceedings in Los Angeles suddenly became entwined with the simultaneous Watergate investigation of abuses of power in the Nixon administration, which, ironically, the leak of the *Pentagon Papers* had helped to set in motion. In late April, the Watergate investigators turned up the sensational revelation that the plumbers group that had attempted to bug the headquarters of the Democratic National Committee had also broken into the office of Ellsberg's psychiatrist. Disclosures soon followed that records of wiretaps possibly relevant to the Ellsberg case had mysteriously disappeared from FBI files and that the White House had attempted to influence Judge Byrne by offering him a top-level government position. Ruling that these "bizarre events have incurably infected the prosecution of this case," Byrne on May 11, 1973, dismissed the charges against the defendants.[32]

It would take an additional four years of legal wrangling to resolve the status of the four negotiating volumes. Shortly after the trial ended, the volumes were removed from the clerk's office in Los Angeles and returned to the custody of the Department of State. In March 1974, Morton Halperin took action under the Freedom of Information Act to secure their release. Halperin had been responsible for the Pentagon Papers project while serving as Deputy Assistant Secretary of Defense under McNamara and had been a consultant for the defense at the Ellsberg trial. At this time working for the American Civil Liberties Union, he based his claim on the grounds that since the volumes had been available for public scrutiny during the trial their release now could not "reasonably be expected to cause damage to the national security."[33]

Halperin's request initiated a prolonged struggle over the disposition of the volumes. In March 1975, after more than a year's delay, the State Department declassified some 498 of the original 886 pages. An additional 118 pages were released with some deletions, and 270 pages were withheld. Adhering firmly to the position it had taken throughout the Ellsberg trial, the department insisted that disclosure of the information that had been withheld would "damage the ability of the United States to conduct its foreign affairs." Citing criteria traditionally used to classify diplomatic documents, it maintained that the documents that had not been released were papers originated by foreign governments, U.S. records that contained quotations and close paraphrases of confidential conversations in which foreign officials had been involved, and U.S. documents that discussed the activities of foreign diplomats who were still in office.[34]

A subsequent appeal by Halperin pried loose small additional amounts of

32. Schrag, *Test of Loyalty*, p. 355.
33. Halperin to Martin R. Hoffman, March 21, 1974, Halperin File.
34. Elritt N. Nettles to Halperin, March 10, 1975, ibid.

material. Halperin argued that some of the documents withheld had been read into the record of the Ellsberg trial and were therefore already available to the public. In ensuing months, the State Department released to him some additional documents that met this test, but it continued to hold back roughly one-third of the material in the volumes, insisting that these documents involved other governments and could only be declassified with their permission.[35]

Branding the State Department's continued attempts to classify parts of the volumes "arbitrary, capricious, and without basis in fact," a persistent Halperin took the government to court in June 1976 to secure release of the remaining pages. After more than a year of deliberation, the suit was finally settled out of court. The State Department provided Halperin a copy of the negotiating volumes that contained some deletions it still insisted were necessary to protect the interests of the United States. Halperin agreed not to challenge the propriety of these deletions. In October 1977 all but about sixty pages of the controversial volumes were in the public domain.[36]

When viewed against the backdrop of their turbulent history, the negotiating volumes may seem at first glance surprisingly bland. They contain no real bombshells, and many of their more dramatic revelations appeared in the press at the time of the Ellsberg trial. Although Stuart Loory grossly exaggerated in claiming that the volumes contained little he had not written about earlier, most of the events covered in them were indeed described in some detail and with remarkable accuracy in contemporary newspaper accounts and in such books as Kraslow and Loory's *Secret Search for Peace in Vietnam*. The bureaucratic language employed in the documents masks the intense emotions of the period, moreover, and at times seems to reduce the participants to colorless actors on a vast impersonal stage.

The negotiating volumes nevertheless constitute an invaluable record of a convulsive era in world history. They cover the critical period from mid-

35. Halperin to Assistant Secretary of Defense, April 8, 1975, and John E. Reinhardt to Halperin, December 12, 1975, ibid.

36. The negotiating volumes are reproduced here just as they were found in the archives, including typographical errors, misspellings, and blank spaces and pages showing material that is still classified. The handwritten designations in the margins (XGDS-1 and XGDS-3) indicate that the deleted material was "exempted under the general declassification system" under categories 1 and 3 of Section 5(B) of Executive Order 11652. Category 1 includes "classified information or material furnished by foreign governments or international organizations and held by the United States on the understanding that it be kept in confidence." Category 3 includes "classified information or material disclosing a system, plan, installation, project or specific foreign relations matter the continuing protection of which is essential to the national security." Roughly three-fifths of the deleted material in the negotiating volumes was exempted under category 1, the bulk of it Canadian material from the Seaborn and Ronning sections of VI.C.1.; British material from VI.C.3., SUNFLOWER; and Swedish and Norwegian material from VI.C.4.

1964—when the confrontation between North Vietnam and the United States began to take form—until the eve of Lyndon Johnson's March 1968 decision to curtail the bombing and withdraw from the presidential race. During this time, the conflict in Vietnam evolved from a relatively low-level guerrilla struggle supported by North Vietnam and the United States to a full-scale war pitting large regular armies against each other and including a bombing campaign on a scale exceeding that of World War II. By the late 1960s, Vietnam had become the dominant event of world politics, attracting the concern and involvement of large nations and small. For the United States, it was the most divisive issue of a tumultuous era.

The negotiating volumes deal with some of the most controversial issues of a war that generated enormous controversy. Critics at the time and since have charged that, although the North Vietnamese evinced a repeated willingness to negotiate, the Johnson administration was interested in peace only on its own terms; that the much publicized bombing pauses were meaningless gestures designed primarily to appease domestic opponents of the war and lay the basis for future escalation; and that the administration's rigid bargaining position effectively precluded substantive negotiations, and U.S. officials either bungled or deliberately sabotaged several promising peace initiatives. The administration naturally denied such charges, and in his memoirs Johnson went to great lengths to refute them. He conceded that he undertook the various pauses reluctantly but insisted that he was sincerely committed to a negotiated settlement. He claimed to have diligently followed up more than seventy peace overtures, and he argued that the United States significantly modified its position in a futile attempt to bring about negotiations, but his efforts produced nothing more than angry replies from North Vietnam. The quest for a negotiated peace failed, he concluded, because the "North Vietnamese were not ready to talk with us." [37]

The negotiating volumes provide new and rich documentation on the futile, behind-the-scenes search for peace that was an integral part of this phase of the war. The first volume (VI.C.1.) [38] opens with Canadian Blair Seaborn's several missions to Hanoi, during the course of which each nation in effect announced its belligerency to the other. The individual subsections then cover in

37. For representative statements of the "dove" critique of Johnson's handling of the peace initiatives, see David Kraslow and Stuart Loory, *The Secret Search for Peace in Vietnam* (New York: Random House, 1968), and Gareth Porter, *A Peace Denied: The United States, Vietnam, and the Paris Agreement* (Bloomington: Indiana University Press, 1975), pp. 47–62. Johnson's rejoinder is in Lyndon B. Johnson, *The Vantage Point: Perspectives on the Presidency* (New York: Holt, Rinehart, & Winston, 1970), especially pp. 250–252.

38. The designations for the negotiating volumes (VI.C.1–VI.C.4.) come from the outline format used to organize the entire Pentagon Papers project. A copy of the original outline is included on p. xxvii to show the relationship of these volumes to the rest of the study.

sequence the first American bombing pause (MAYFLOWER) in the spring of 1965; the mysteriously titled and long-secret XYZ contact in Paris that summer; and the Johnson administration's noisy, early 1966 "peace offensive," which resulted in a brief, direct contact between U.S. and North Vietnamese diplomats in Rangoon. VI.C.1. concludes with the first major third-party initiative, Canada's dispatch of Chester Ronning to Hanoi in 1966, an exercise in futility that starkly revealed the extent to which the two belligerents had embarked on courses from which there would be no easy turning back.

The second and third volumes chronicle two of the most intriguing and controversial peace moves. VI.C.2. concerns the affair code-named MARIGOLD, an initiative undertaken by Poland in mid-1966 whose origins and denouement remain shrouded in mystery. Since it dealt with more substantive issues than most of the other initiatives and allegedly produced a North Vietnamese commitment to engage the United States in direct talks in Warsaw, MARIGOLD has frequently been viewed as offering singular hope. It terminated abruptly in December 1966, however, provoking angry Polish-American recriminations and subsequent charges that the United States was guilty of gross diplomatic ineptitude or calculated sabotage. SUNFLOWER, covered in VI.C.3., came in the immediate aftermath of the MARIGOLD imbroglio. It involved a direct U.S. approach to North Vietnam in Moscow, as well as a parallel attempt on the part of British Prime Minister Harold Wilson and Soviet Premier Alexei Kosygin to bring the two belligerents together. Like MARIGOLD, it failed, and a seemingly incredible breakdown in communications between Washington and London placed enormous strains on the Anglo-American "special relationship," evoking comparisons to the Suez debacle slightly more than a decade earlier, and produced additional charges of American bungling or double-dealing.

The final volume (VI.C.4.) covers a series of peace moves in the period between early 1967 and early 1968. Norway, Sweden, Rumania, and Italy took turns at playing the role of intermediary, and private citizen Henry Kissinger, on the initiative of the U.S. government, attempted to arrange talks with North Vietnam through two French go-betweens. The documents in VI.C.4 indicate the problems the various third parties met in trying to maneuver between the two belligerents and the difficulties encountered by Hanoi and Washington in trying to communicate through sometimes overzealous and frequently unreliable third parties. The failure of all these initiatives makes clear the continuing intractability of the basic issues of the war. As the climactic events of Tet 1968 approached, however, the belligerents were forced to make some tactical concessions, and the Rumanian and Italian contacts may have played a part in their 1968 decisions to go to the conference table without abandoning their fundamental objectives. Thus, as the volumes close, the formal negotiations that each side had long professed to want were near to becoming a reality, although the ultimate goal of a negotiated settlement was still five years away.

As a historical source, these volumes, like the rest of the *Pentagon Papers*, have certain notable deficiencies. In putting together their story, Gelb and Moorsteen relied almost exclusively on cable traffic drawn from State Department files. The documents printed here therefore represent only a tiny and highly selective portion of the overall record. By its very nature, the cable traffic is operational in substance. It shows what is being done but only rarely goes into the background of and motivation for major policy decisions. The absence of White House files means that little light is shed on the thinking of President Johnson and his top advisers. In part because of the sources used, in part because of the oft-noted tendency of the administration to compartmentalize the various aspects of the war, the peace moves sometimes appear to be occurring in a vacuum. Only infrequently are they discussed in the larger context of simultaneous strategic decisions and military and political developments. The volumes tend also to be one-dimensional. They focus heavily on the United States and provide little more than tantalizing glimpses into the policies and methods of operation of the many other actors.

Because of the way these volumes were put together and because of their subject matter, the analysis in them, even more than that in the published sections of the papers, must be used with caution. As noted earlier, each section and subsection consists of a brief introductory summary and analysis, followed by a "chronology." As a result they tend to be less interpretive and lack the unity of theme that characterized other sections of the *Pentagon Papers*. The authors were dealing with problems that showed no signs of resolution at the time they wrote, and the analysis necessarily is more speculative and tentative than in many of the other volumes. The questions raised, while frequently affording important hints into the principal concerns of the policy makers of the 1960s, are not always those that loom most significant from the longer historical perspective. Inasmuch as the volumes develop an overriding thesis, it is that diplomacy failed because each nation refused to give way on the basic issues, an argument at once more balanced than the official view and "dove" critique and less satisfying as an explanation of the breakdown of the numerous individual initiatives.

These caveats aside, the negotiating volumes represent a major contribution to the ongoing documentation of one of the most controversial and destructive events in recent history. When used with the rest of the *Pentagon Papers* and other sources, they shed much new light on the Johnson administration's conduct of the war. They tell a great deal about the formulation of American strategy and the American diplomatic style. They reveal much about the way the

United States dealt with its adversaries and its allies. They show how the war became a football of international politics by the late 1960s. In their own right, they provide a fascinating case study in what Stanley Karnow called the "mating dance" of diplomacy, the manner in which two nations of vastly different cultures, historical backgrounds, and ideologies engaged in a bloody war, responded to various pressures, sought to communicate with each other, and attempted to manipulate each other and other nations to gain ends that were mutually irreconcilable. Until the records of the Department of State and the presidential libraries become available, these volumes will be the indispensable source for studying the secret diplomacy of the Vietnam War.

In editing the volumes, I have attempted merely to make them easier to use and more useful without impairing their original form or intruding on the potential user's prerogative to interpret them. I have compiled a glossary of terms to help the reader penetrate the mysteries of bureaucratic jargon, acronyms, and abbreviations, and a glossary of names to identify the positions of the hundreds of individuals mentioned in the text. My own annotations, indicated by boldface note numbers, have been placed at the end to maintain the original integrity of the papers and to keep them separate from the footnotes in some sections of the original. Their purpose is to explain or clarify textual matters that seemed obscure or confusing and to provide references to documents mentioned but not included and cross-references to documents included in other places in the volumes. The introductions to the individual sections or subsections are intended to place the peace moves in their larger context, update the text in terms of information not available to the authors in 1968, raise questions that do not occur in the original, and offer some interpretations of my own. I have done these things in the hope that they will be of value to the reader but with full knowledge that the ultimate worth lies in the original documents themselves.

OSD Vietnam Task Force Outline of Studies

I. **Vietnam and the U.S., 1940–1950**
   A. U.S. Policy, 1940–1950
   B. The Character and Power of the Viet Minh
   C. Ho Chi Minh: Asian Tito?

II. **U.S. Involvement in the Franco–Viet Minh War, 1950–1954**
   A. U.S., France, and Vietnamese Nationalism
   B. Toward a Negotiated Settlement

III. **The Geneva Accords**
   A. U.S. Military Planning and Diplomatic Maneuvers
   B. Role and Obligations of State of Vietnam
   C. Viet Minh Position and Sino-Soviet Strategy
   D. The Intent of the Geneva Accords

IV. **Evolution of the War**
   A. U.S. MAP for Diem: The Eisenhower Commitments, 1954–1960
      1. NATO and SEATO: A Comparison
      2. Aid for France in Indochina, 1950–1954
      3. U.S. and France's Withdrawal from Vietnam, 1954–1956
      4. U.S. Training of Vietnamese National Army, 1954–1959
      5. Origins of the Insurgency
   B. Counterinsurgency: The Kennedy Commitments, 1961–1963
      1. The Kennedy Commitments and Programs, 1961
      2. Strategic Hamlet Program, 1961–1963
      3. The Advisory Build-up, 1961–1967
      4. Phased Withdrawal of U.S. Forces in Vietnam, 1962–1964
      5. The Overthrow of Ngo Dinh Diem, May–November 1963
   C. Direct Action: The Johnson Commitments, 1964–1968
      1. U.S. Programs in South Vietnam, November 1963–April 1965: NSAM 273—NSAM 288—Honolulu
      2. Military Pressures against NVN
         a. February–June 1964
         b. July–October 1964
         c. November–December 1964
      3. ROLLING THUNDER Program Begins: January–June 1965
      4. Marine Combat Units Go to DaNang, March 1965
      5. Phase I in the Build-up of U.S. Forces: March–July 1965
      6. U.S. Ground Strategy and Force Deployments: 1965–1967
         a. Volume I: Phase II, Program 3, Program 4

Glossary of Abbreviations, Acronyms, and Cable Designations

ADM   Admiral
AFP   Agence France-Presse (French news agency)
AMEMB   American Embassy
AP   Associated Press
ARVN   Army, Republic of Vietnam (South Vietnam)

CANFONMIN   Canadian Foreign Minister
CAS   Saigon Office, U.S. Central Intelligence Agency
CHICOM   Chinese Communist
CIA   U.S. Central Intelligence Agency
CINCPAC   Commander-in-Chief, U.S. Pacific Forces
CJCS   Chairman, U.S. Joint Chiefs of Staff
COB   Close of Business
COMUSMACV   Commander, U.S. Military Assistance Command, Vietnam
CONF   Confidential
CONFID   Confidential
CPSU   Communist Party, Soviet Union
CPR   Peoples Republic of China
CSDI   Center for the Study of Democratic Institutions

DCM   Deputy Chief of Mission
DEPCIRTEL   State Department Circular Telegram
DEPTEL   State Department Telegram
DIRGEN   Director General
DMZ   Demilitarized Zone
DOD   U.S. Department of Defense
DRNVN   Democratic Republic of North Vietnam
DRV   Democratic Republic of Vietnam

EMBTEL   Embassy Telegram
EXDIS   Exclusive Distribution (designates extremely limited distribution at
   high levels)
EXTAFF   Department of External Affairs, Canada
EYES ONLY   Document to be read only by individuals with a need to know

FAO   United Nations Food and Agriculture Organization
FBIS   Foreign Broadcast Information Service
FE   Office of Far Eastern Affairs, Department of State
FLASH   The most urgent of all cable indicators, used only in the event of war
   or when the outbreak of war is imminent

FM   Foreign Minister or Foreign Ministry
FONMIN   Foreign Minister
FONOFF   Foreign Office
FONSEC   Foreign Secretary
FORNMIN   Foreign Minister or Foreign Ministry
FYI   For Your Information

GDRV   Government of the Democratic Republic of Vietnam
GMT   Greenwich Mean Time
GOC   Government of Canada
GOF   Government of France
GOI   Government of India
GOJ   Government of Japan
GON   Government of Norway
GOP   Government of Poland
GOR   Government of Rumania
GOS   Government of Sweden
GVN   Government of Vietnam (South Vietnam)

ICC   International Control Commission
ICRC   International Committee, Red Cross
ICSC   International Commission for Supervision and Control
IMMEDIATE   Second to flash in terms of importance, this indicator means that the message requires the immediate attention of the recipient
INFO   Information

JCS   U.S. Joint Chiefs of Staff

KGB   Komitet Gossudarstvennoi Bezopastnosti (Committee on State Security, Soviet Secret Police)

LIMDIS   Limited distribution, meaning very limited distribution or dissemination
LITERALLY EYES ONLY   Level of classification designating very restricted readership

MACV   Military Assistance Command, Vietnam
MAP   Military Assistance Program
MEMCON   Memorandum of Conversation
MIG   Mikoyan and Gurevich, designation for Soviet aircraft formed from the names of the designers

NATO   North Atlantic Treaty Organization
NFLSV   National Front for the Liberation of South Vietnam
NLF   National Liberation Front

NODIS   No distribution beyond addressee
NOFORN   No foreign dissemination
NSA   U.S. National Security Agency
NSAM   National Security Action Memorandum
NVA   North Vietnamese Army
NVN   North Vietnamese

OSD   Office of the Secretary of Defense

PARAS   Paragraphs
PAVN   Peoples Army of [North] Vietnam
PERM REP   Permanent Representative to the United Nations
PM   Prime Minister
POL   Petroleum, oil, and lubricants
PRIORITY   Below flash and immediate in terms of importance, a priority message is to be considered above the vast flow of routine cable traffic but does not require immediate action
PW   Prisoners of war

QTE   Quote

RDVN   Democratic Republic of Vietnam (French abbreviation)
RECCE   Reconnaissance
REF   Reference
REFTEL   Reference Telegram
REUR   Regarding your telegram
RGUB   Revolutionary Government of the Union of Burma
RPT   Repeat
RT   ROLLING THUNDER
RVN   Republic of [South] Vietnam

S   Secret
SAM   Surface-to-air missile
SEA   Southeast Asia
SEATO   Southeast Asia Treaty Organization
SECTO   Cable identifier, from Secretary of State to addressee
SEPTEL   Separate telegram
SVN   South Vietnam
SYG   Secretary General

TASS   Telegraphnoye Agentstvo Sovyetskovo Soyuza (Telegraphic Agency of the Soviet Union, Soviet News Agency)
TCC   Troop Contributing Countries (allies providing troops in support of the United States in Vietnam)

TELECON   Telephone Conversation

TS   Top Secret

UAR   United Arab Republic

UK   United Kingdom

UN   United Nations

UNQTE   Unquote

UNR   Groupe de l'Union pour la Nouvelle Republique (French political party)

URTEL   Your telegram

USA   U.S. Army

USDEL   U.S. Delegation to the United Nations

USG   U.S. Government

USIB   U.S. Intelligence Board

USN   U.S. Navy

USSR   Union of Soviet Socialists Republics

USUN   U.S. Delegation to the United Nations

VC   Vietcong

VEHDOP   Vehicle depots

VN   Vietnam or Vietnamese

VNA   Vietnamese National Army (South Vietnam)

VNA   Vietnam News Agency (North Vietnam)

VNAF   Vietnam National Air Force (South Vietnam)

Z   Zulu Time (Greenwich Mean Time)

Glossary of Names

Akalovsky, Alexander. First Secretary, U.S. Embassy, Moscow.

Algard, Ole. Norwegian Ambassador to the People's Republic of China.

Arkas-Duntov, Urah. Mutual fund executive; intermediary in the XYZ contact.

Armstrong, Sam G. U.S. Consul-General, Hong Kong.

Ashmore, Harry S. Executive Vice-President, Center for the Study of Democratic Institutions.

Aubrac, Raymond. Director of the U.N. Food and Agriculture Organization and friend of Ho Chi Minh; intermediary in the PENNSYLVANIA contact.

Baggs, William. Editor, *Miami News*; director, Center for the Study of Democratic Institutions.

Ball, George W. U.S. Undersecretary of State, 1961–1966.

Belfrage, Leif A. L. Permanent Undersecretary of State, Swedish Foreign Ministry.

Bergstrom, R. Hichens. Director of Political Affairs, Swedish Foreign Ministry.

Bogdan, Corneliu. Rumanian Ambassador to the United States.

Boun Oum, Prince. Right-wing leader and head of U.S.-backed government in Laos before 1962, replaced by General Phoumi Nosavan in coalition government.

Bovey, John Alden, Jr. U.S. Consul-General, Oslo.

Boye, Thore A. Secretary General, Norwegian Foreign Ministry.

Brezhnev, Leonid. Secretary General of the Central Committee, Communist Party, Soviet Union.

Brimelow, Thomas. British Ambassador to Poland.

Brown, George. Secretary of State for Foreign Affairs, United Kingdom.

Brown, Winthrop. U.S. Ambassador to South Korea.

Bruce, David K. E. U.S. Ambassador to the United Kingdom.

Buffum, William B. Deputy U.S. Representative to the United Nations.

Bui Diem. South Vietnam's Ambassador to the United States.

Bundy, McGeorge. Assistant to the U.S. President for National Security Affairs, 1961–1966.

Bundy, William P. U.S. Assistant Secretary of State for Far Eastern Affairs, 1966–1969.

Burchett, Wilfred. Australian journalist with close ties to the North Vietnamese leadership.

Butterworth, W. Walton. U.S. Ambassador to Canada, 1962–1968.

Byroade, Henry A. U.S. Ambassador to Burma, 1963–1968; key figure in the Rangoon contact.

Cabot, John Moors. U.S. Ambassador to Poland, 1962–1965.

Cameron, Turner C., Jr. U.S. Consul-General, Stockholm.

Canham, Dr. Erwin D. Journalist, editor-in-chief, *Christian Science Monitor*; actively involved in United Nations' affairs.

Ceausescu, Nicolae. Secretary General, Communist Party of Rumania.

Chalfont, Lord. Arthur Gwynne Jones, Baron Chalfont, Minister of State, British Foreign Office.

Ch'en Yi. Foreign Minister, People's Republic of China.

Chou En-lai. Premier, People's Republic of China.

Chung Hee Park. President, South Korea.

Clement, Carl John. Intelligence Research Specialist, U.S. Department of State.

Clifford, Clark M. U.S. Secretary of Defense, 1968–1969.

Colvin, John. British Consul, Hanoi.

Cooper, Chester L. Special Assistant to U.S. Ambassador-at-Large W. Averell Harriman.

Davidson, Daniel. Special Assistant to U.S. Ambassador-at-Large W. Averell Harriman.

Davies, Harold. Parliamentary Secretary, British Ministry of Pensions and National Insurance; close friend of Harold Wilson and acquaintance of Ho Chi Minh.

Dean, David. Officer in Charge, Bureau of Mainland China Affairs, U.S. Department of State.

Dean, Sir Patrick. British Ambassador in Washington.

de Besche, Hubert W. Swedish Ambassador to the United States.

Devillers, Philippe. French historian and expert on Vietnam; author of *Histoire du Viet-Nam de 1940 à 1952* and other works.

Diefenbaker, John G. Former Prime Minister of Canada and leader of the opposition, 1965–1967.

Dillon, C. Douglas. U.S. Secretary of the Treasury, 1961–1965.

Dobrynin, Anatoly. Soviet Ambassador to the United States.

D'Orlandi, Giovanni. Italian Ambassador to South Vietnam.

Doty, Paul M., Jr. Professor of Chemistry, Harvard University; active in promoting disarmament and international cooperation.

Drndic, Ljubomir. Yugoslavian Ambassador to Burma.

Duong Van Minh. Chief of State, South Vietnam, 1963–1965; in exile, 1965–1968.

Fanfani, Amintore. Italian Foreign Minister.

Farace di Villapresta, H. E. Alessandro. Deputy Director General for Political Affairs, Italian Foreign Ministry; Italian Ambassador to Canada.

Feld, Bernard. Professor of Physics, Massachusetts Institute of Technology.

Fenoaltea, Sergio. Italian Ambassador to the United States.

Finger, Seymour M. Senior Adviser to the U.S. Representative to the United Nations.

Firyubin, Nikolai. Deputy Soviet Foreign Minister.

Forrestal, Michael V. Member of White House National Security Staff, 1962–1965.

Fulbright, J. William. U.S. Senator (D. Ark.).

Gleysteen, Culver. Senior Officer, Political Section, U.S. Embassy, Paris.

Glitman, Maynard G. International Relations Officer, U.S. Department of State.

Goldberg, Arthur J. U.S. Representative to the United Nations, 1965–1969.

Gore-Booth, Sir Paul Henry. Permanent Undersecretary of State, British Foreign Office.

Gromyko, Andrei. Foreign Minister, Soviet Union.

Gronouski, John. U.S. Ambassador to Poland, 1965–1968.

Gullion, Edmund. Retired Foreign Service officer; unofficial U.S. envoy in the XYZ contact, 1965.

Guthrie, John C. Deputy Chief of Mission, U.S. Embassy, Moscow.

Habib, Philip. Minister, U.S. Embassy, Saigon.

Harriman, W. Averell. U.S. Undersecretary of State for Political Affairs, 1963–1965; after March 1965, Ambassador-at-Large; after summer 1966, given primary responsibility for following up peace contacts.

Hauret, Robert. French legislator and representative to the Assembly of the Council of Europe.

Ha Van Lau. Head of the North Vietnamese Liaison Office with the ICC.

Heath, William W. U.S. Ambassador to Sweden, 1967–1969.

Ho Chi Minh. President of Democratic Republic of Vietnam.

Ignatieff, George. Permanent Representative of Canada to the United Nations.

Iliescu, Marin. First Secretary, Rumanian Embassy in Washington.

Isham, Heyward. Member of U.S. State Department working group on Vietnam with primary responsibility for watching peace initiatives.

Jacobsen, Frithjof. Norwegian Undersecretary of State.

Jacobson, Harold W. Director, Bureau of Asian Communist Affairs, U.S. Department of State.

Janczewski, Zbigniew. Polish Foreign Ministry Official.

Jenkins, Walter. Deputy Chief of Mission, U.S. Embassy, Warsaw.

Johnson, U. Alexis. U.S. Deputy Undersecretary of State, 1961–1964; Deputy Ambassador to South Vietnam, 1964–1965; Deputy Undersecretary of State for Political Affairs, 1965–1966.

Kaiser, Philip M. Deputy Chief of Mission, U.S. Embassy, London.

Katzenbach, Nicholas deB. U.S. Undersecretary of State, 1966–1969.

Kissinger, Henry A. Professor of Government, Harvard University; principal figure in the PENNSYLVANIA contact.

Klaus, Josef. Chancellor of Austria.

Kohler, Foy D. U.S. Ambassador to the Soviet Union, 1962–1966.

Kornienko, Georgi M. Head of American Department, Soviet Foreign Ministry.

Kosygin, Alexei. Chairman of the Council of Ministers, Soviet Union.

Kreisberg, Paul H. Officer-in-Charge, Mainland China Affairs Branch, U.S. Department of State.

Kulebiakin, N. P. Member of the Soviet delegation to the United Nations.

Kuznetsov, Vasily V. Deputy Foreign Minister, Soviet Union.

LaPira, Giorgio. Italian law professor; conveyor of peace feeler from Hanoi, November 1965.

Le Chang (or Le Trang). Minister-Counsellor, North Vietnamese Embassy, Moscow.

Le Duan. Secretary General of the Communist Party of North Vietnam.

Le Duc Tho. Member of the Politburo of North Vietnam.

Lewandowski, Januscz. Polish Representative to the ICC; prime mover in the MARIGOLD initiative.

Lin Piao. Minister of Defense, People's Republic of China.

Lodge, Henry Cabot, Jr. U.S. Ambassador to South Vietnam, 1963–1964, 1965–1967.

Lucet, Charles. Director of Political Affairs, French Foreign Ministry.

Lyng, John. Norwegian Minister for Foreign Affairs.

McCloskey, Robert. Information Officer, U.S. Department of State.

McGhee, George C. Aide to U.S. Secretary of State Dean Rusk.

MacLellan, K. W. Commissioner, Canadian Delegation to the ICSC, Laos.

McNamara, Robert S. U.S. Secretary of Defense, 1961–1968.

Macovescu, Gheorghe. Rumanian First Deputy Foreign Minister, 1967–1969.

McPherson, Harry C. Member of President Johnson's White House Staff.

Mai Van Bo. Chief of the North Vietnamese Commercial Delegation in Paris and the top-ranking DRV diplomat in the non-Communist world, a key figure in the XYZ contact and the source of several apparent North Vietnamese peace feelers.

Manac'h, Etienne. Director of Asian Affairs, French Foreign Ministry.

Manescu, Corneliu. Foreign Minister of Rumania.

Mann, Thomas. U.S. Assistant Secretary of State for Inter-American Affairs.

Marcovich, Herbert. Professor of Microbiology at the University of Paris; intermediary in the PENNSYLVANIA contact.

Martin, Paul. Canadian Secretary of State for External Affairs.

Maurer, Ion Gheorghe. Chairman of the Council of Ministers, Rumania.

Meloy, Francis E., Jr. Deputy Chief of Mission, U.S. Embassy, Rome.

Mendenhall, Joseph A. Director of U.S. State Department working group on Vietnam, 1963–1964.

Menzies, Sir Robert Gordon. Prime Minister of Australia.

Michalowski, Jerzy. Director-General, Polish Foreign Ministry.

Miller, Robert H. Deputy Director, U.S. Departent of State working group on Vietnam.

Millionshchikov, Mikhail D. Applied physicist; Vice-Chairman, Soviet Academy of Science.

Moore, Victor. Canadian Representative on the Vietnam ICC.

Murray, Donald F. Counsellor, British Diplomatic Service; specialist on Vietnam affairs.

Ngo Dinh Diem. President of South Vietnam, 1955–1963.

Ngo Loan. North Vietnamese Ambassador to the People's Republic of China.

Nguyen Cao Ky. Vice Air Marshal and Commander of the South Vietnamese Air Force; Prime Minister of South Vietnam, 1965–1967; Vice-President, 1967–1971.

Nguyen Chanh Thi. South Vietnamese army general; commander of forces in the northern provinces.

Nguyen Duy Trinh. Foreign Minister and Vice-Premier of North Vietnam.

Nguyen Khanh. Prime Minister of South Vietnam, 1964; President, 1964; Chairman, Armed Forces Council, 1965.

Nguyen Tho Chan. North Vietnamese Ambassador to the Soviet Union.

Nguyen Van Binh. Archbishop of Saigon.

Nguyen Van Chi. Unofficial Vietminh representative in Paris during the First Indochina War.

Nguyen Van Kinh. North Vietnamese Ambassador to the Soviet Union.

Nguyen Van Thieu. Chief of State, South Vietnam, 1965–1967; President, 1967–1975.

Nilsson, Torsten. Foreign Minister of Sweden.

Nkrumah, Kwame. President of Ghana.

Oberg, J. C. S. First Secretary, Political Division, Ministry of Foreign Affairs of Sweden.

Ortona, Egidio. Italian Ambassador to the United States.

Palliser, Arthur Michael. Private Secretary to British Prime Minister Harold Wilson.

Parsons, James G. U.S. Ambassador to Sweden, 1961–1967.

Pearson, Lester B. "Mike." Prime Minister of Canada.

Pedersen, Richard. Deputy U.S. Representative to the United Nations.

Peter, Janos. Foreign Minister of Hungary.

Petri, Lennart. Swedish Ambassador to the People's Republic of China.

Pham Ngoc Thach. North Vietnamese Minister of Health.

Pham Van Dong. Premier of North Vietnam.

Phan Huy Quat. Minister for Foreign Affairs, South Vietnam, 1964; Prime Minister, 1965.

Phan Van Su. North Vietnamese Ambassador to Czechoslovakia.

Phoumi Nosavan. Second Vice-Premier and Minister of Finance, Laos; representative of right-wing forces in coalition government.

Podgorny, Nikolai. Chairman of the Praesidium, Supreme Soviet, U.S.S.R.; titular head of state.

Porter, William J. Deputy U.S. Ambassador to South Vietnam.

Quaison-Sackey, Alex. President of the United Nations General Assembly, 1964–1965; Foreign Minister of Ghana, 1965–1966.

Quintanilla, Don Luis. Mexican scholar-diplomat, one-time Ambassador to the Soviet Union and the United States, and professor at the University of Mexico; helped arrange the Baggs-Ashmore mission and accompanied the two men to Hanoi.

Raborn, Admiral William F. Director, U.S. Central Intelligence Agency, 1965–1966.

Radhakrishnan, Sarvepalli. President of India.

Ranard, Donald Louis. Consul-General, U.S. Embassy, Rangoon.

Rapacki, Adam. Foreign Minister of Poland.

Read, Benjamin H. Executive Secretary, U.S. Department of State.

Reddy, Leo. Second Secretary, U.S. Embassy, Rangoon.

Reinhardt, Frederick G. U.S. Ambassador to Italy.

Reston, James "Scotty." Washington columnist, *New York Times*.

Robinson, H. Basil. Minister-Counsellor, Canadian Embassy, Washington.

Ronning, Chester A. Retired Canadian diplomat who undertook missions to Hanoi in March and June 1966.

Rostow, Walt W. Assistant to the U.S. President for National Security Affairs, 1966–1969.

Rusk, Dean. U.S. Secretary of State, 1961–1969.

Sainteny, Jean. Former French colonial official in Indochina who maintained close ties with Ho Chi Minh and brought back a vague peace feeler from Hanoi in July 1966.

Salinger, Pierre. Former Press Secretary to Presidents Kennedy and Johnson; President of Fox Overseas Corporation.

Salisbury, Harrison E. *New York Times* correspondent.

Saragat, Giuseppe. President of Italy.

Scott, Joseph W. Minister, U.S. Embassy, Ottawa.

Seaborn, J. Blair. Canadian Delegate to the ICC.

Segonzac, Adalbert. French journalist for *France Soir*.

Shelepin, Alexandr N. Secretary, Central Committee, Communist Party, Soviet Union.

Sieverts, F. A. Special Assistant to the U.S. Undersecretary of State.

Sisco, Joseph. Assistant U.S. Secretary of State for International Organization.

Smirnovsky, Mikhail. Soviet Ambassador to the United Kingdom.

Smith, Arnold Cantwell. Canadian Deputy Undersecretary of State for External Affairs.

Smith, Walter Bedell. U.S. Undersecretary of State and head of unofficial U.S. delegation to Geneva Conference, 1954.

Soe Tin, U. Permanent Secretary, Ministry of Foreign Affairs of Burma.

Souphanouvong, Prince. Pathet Lao leader; Vice-Premier, Laotian coalition government.

Souvanna Phouma, Prince. Neutralist leader; head of the coalition government of Laos.

Stevenson, Adlai E. U.S. Representative to the United Nations, 1961–1965.

Stewart, Sir Michael. Minister, British Embassy in Washington, 1964–1967.

Sturm, Paul. Retired U.S. Foreign Service officer; "Y" in the XYZ contact of 1965.

Sullivan, William. Special Assistant to W. Averell Harriman and chairman of an interagency committee on Vietnam; U.S. Ambassador to Laos.

Swank, Emory C. U.S. Consul-General, Vientiane.

Taylor, Maxwell D. U.S. Ambassador to South Vietnam, 1964–1965.

Thant, U. Secretary General, United Nations, 1962–1971.

Thi Han, U. Minister of Foreign Affairs and National Planning, Burma.

Thompson, Llewellyn E. U.S. Ambassador-at-Large, 1962–1967; Ambassador to the Soviet Union, 1967–1969.

Tibbets, Margaret Joy. U.S. Ambassador to Norway.

Tomorowicz, Bohdan. Permanent Representative of Poland to the United Nations.

Topping, Seymour. *New York Times* correspondent, Hong Kong.

Tran Van Do. Minister for Foreign Affairs, South Vietnam, 1966–1969.

Trend, Sir Burke. Secretary to the British Cabinet.

Truong Dinh Dzu. Runnerup to Nguyen Van Thieu in the South Vietnamese presidential election of 1967.

Unger, Leonard. Deputy Assistant U.S. Secretary of State for Far Eastern Affairs.

Vo Nguyen Giap. Defense Minister and Commander-in-Chief, Armed Forces, North Vietnam.

Vo Van Sung. Second ranking official in North Vietnamese Embassy, Paris.

Vu Huu Binh. North Vietnamese Consul-General in Rangoon; principal in the Rangoon contact.

Wachtmeister, Count Wilhelm H. F. Swedish Foreign Office Political Director, 1965–1966; Ambassador to Algeria, 1966–1968.

Walker, Patrick Gordon. British Secretary of State for Foreign Affairs, 1964–1965.

Waller, John Keith. Australian Ambassador to the United States.

Wallner, Woodruff. Deputy Chief of Mission, U.S. Embassy, Paris.

Walsh, J. P. Deputy Executive Secretary, U.S. Department of State.

Wang Kuo-chuan. People's Republic of China Ambassador to Poland.

Warnke, Paul. Assistant U.S. Secretary of Defense for International Security Affairs.

Westmoreland, General William C. Commanding Officer, U.S. Military Assistance Command, Vietnam.

Wheeler, General Earle G. Chairman, U.S. Joint Chiefs of Staff.

Williams, G. Mennen. Assistant U.S. Secretary of State for African Affairs.

Winiewicz, Josef. Polish Vice-Minister for Foreign Affairs.

Wylie, Laurence W. Cultural Attaché, U.S. Embassy, Paris.

Xuan Thuy. Minister of Foreign Affairs, North Vietnam, 1963–1965; Minister without Portfolio and Representative to the Paris Peace Talks, 1968.

Zinchuk, Alexandr. Counsellor, Soviet Embassy in Washington.

Zorthian, Barry. Minister-Counsellor for Information, U.S. Embassy, Saigon.

The Negotiating Volumes of the Pentagon Papers

UNITED STATES - VIETNAM RELATIONS

1945 - 1967

VI. C.1

Settlement of the Conflict

History of Contacts

Negotiations, 1965- 1966 By JK (img),

VIETNAM TASK FORCE

OFFICE OF THE SECRETARY OF DEFENSE

Sec Def Cont Nr. X- 0205

VI. C. I.

SETTLEMENT OF THE CONFLICT

History of Contacts

Negotiations, 1965 - 1966

NEGOTIATIONS, 1965-1966

This book includes five negotiating tracks:

(1) Seaborn Missions (Canadian ICC Delegate Periodic
     Visits to Hanoi), June 1964 - June 1965.

(2) Project Mayflower (the First U.S. Bombing Pause),
     May 12-18, 1965.

(3) XYZ (U.S. Contacts with Mai Van Bo in Paris),
     May 19, 1965 - May 6, 1966.

(4) Pinta-Rangoon (the Second U.S. Bombing Pause),
     December 24, 1965 - January 31, 1966.

(5) Ronning Missions (Canadian Ambassador Extraordinary
     Visits to Hanoi), March and June, 1966.

Each section has a summary and analysis followed by a chronology
(except Project Mayflower, which is told narratively).

VI.C.1., The Seaborn Mission to Hanoi, June 1964–June 1965

The Pentagon study opens with the 1964–1965 missions of Canadian diplomat J. Blair Seaborn to Hanoi, the first American attempt to communicate with North Vietnam through a third party.

The decision to use Seaborn as an intermediary reflected the dilemma in which American officials found themselves by the spring of 1964. Since the overthrow of Ngo Dinh Diem in November 1963, the political situation in South Vietnam had become increasingly chaotic, and the Vietcong insurgents, supported by growing assistance from North Vietnam, had effectively exploited the political and military weakness of the Saigon government. U.S. intelligence warned that if the adverse trends could not be corrected South Vietnam might soon fall. Frustrated by their inability to deal with the turmoil in Saigon or to strike back at North Vietnam, some American officials began pushing for large-scale air operations against the North to boost morale in the South and limit Hanoi's ability to support the insurgency. Uneager to lose South Vietnam, but unwilling at this point to commit U.S. forces directly to the war, President Lyndon B. Johnson desperately groped for alternatives. He significantly increased the volume of economic and military aid and the number of American advisers, while pressing the government of Nguyen Khanh to take measures to restore political stability. He also expanded covert operations against North Vietnam to signal Hanoi that it could not continue to support the insurgency with impunity.

To head off pressures for more drastic steps, Johnson also approved Ambassador Henry Cabot Lodge's proposal to send an emissary to North Vietnam. The major purposes of the mission, as conceived by Lodge, would be to explore North Vietnamese attitudes toward the conflict in the South and to make clear to the Hanoi regime the determination of the United States to maintain an independent, non-Communist South Vietnam. Lodge proposed for the mission J. Blair Seaborn, an experienced and trusted Canadian diplomat with whom he had worked at the United Nations. Seaborn had recently been appointed Canadian representative on the International Control Commission established to supervise the 1954 Geneva Agreements, an assignment that gave him ready access to North Vietnamese leaders. The United States advised Seaborn to inform the North Vietnamese that it did not seek an expanded war, but also to warn them that it was determined to preserve the independence of South Vietnam and was prepared to use force against them if necessary. He was also to dangle a carrot in front of them by indicating that the United States was prepared to live in peace with North Vietnam and would provide economic assistance when peace became a reality.

Seaborn made five trips to Hanoi between June 1964 and June 1965, on several occasions talking directly with top leaders and each time reporting in detail to the U.S. government. It remains difficult to evaluate the missions. The full records of Seaborn's conversations remain classified,[1] and here, as elsewhere, it is virtually impossible to probe beneath the subtle and frequently ambiguous rhetoric employed by the North Vietnamese leaders and uncover their motives and intentions. It seems clear that Hanoi did not shut the door to negotiations. In June and again in August, immediately after the Tonkin Gulf incident and the first American air strikes against North Vietnam, they expressed willingness to negotiate, a message also conveyed to U.N. Secretary General U Thant through the Soviets in September 1964. They appear to have regarded negotiations primarily as a means of offering the United States a face-saving exit from Vietnam, however, and, inasmuch as peace terms were discussed with Seaborn, it is evident that the two sides were far apart from the outset. The United States insisted that North Vietnam must respect the independence of South Vietnam and put an end to the insurgency it presumably controlled. North Vietnamese leaders vaguely spoke of a neutral South Vietnam but insisted that a "just solution" would require eventual reunification. They also insisted upon an American withdrawal from Vietnam and maintained that the political future of South Vietnam must be determined by the South Vietnamese themselves with the National Liberation Front playing a major role.

The most important result of the Seaborn missions was probably to afford an additional reason, if one were needed, for subsequent American escalation of the war. Seaborn's reports seemed to indicate that Hanoi was not only unyielding but also confident of eventual success. Administration officials thus dismissed out of hand U Thant's proposals for peace talks. The presidential election safely past and the situation in South Vietnam still chaotic, Johnson decided early in 1965 to take the war directly to North Vietnam. The Seaborn initiative represented less a peace move than an attempt by each side to indicate to the other its determination to prevail. "To the extent they believed each other," the Pentagon analyst correctly concluded, "the two sides were amply forewarned that a painful struggle lay ahead."—*Ed.*

1. In response to the leak of the *Pentagon Papers* in June 1971, the Canadian government issued a report on Seaborn's missions to Hanoi. The report is in Canadian House of Commons, *Proceedings*, June 17, 1971, pp. 6803–6805, and is a useful supplement to the documents printed here.

THE SEABORN MISSION TO HANOI, JUNE 1964-JUNE 1965

This paper considers US/DRV communications passed via the Canadian ICC Delegate, J. Blair Seaborn. It is in three parts: (1) a discussion of principal topics; (2) a summary description of Seaborn's main visits to Hanoi; and (3) a more detailed chronology extracted from cables, reports and memoranda. Part 3 contains the references underlying part 1; they are keyed in Part 1 by dates, in brackets.

Discussion

The messages carried by Seaborn were unusually substantive and dramatic. Possible (but quite different) settlement terms were sketched by both sides, but the main subject stressed repeatedly by each was its determination to do and endure whatever might be necessary to see the war to a conclusion satisfactory to it.

To the extent they believed each other, the two sides were amply forewarned that a painful contest lay ahead. Even so, they were not inclined to compromise their way out. They held very different estimates of the efficacy of US military might. We thought its pressures could accomplish our goals. The Communists did not.

Resolution to Win

Both sides gave strong warnings as early as June 1964. On Seaborn's first visit to Hanoi, he conveyed US determination "to contain the DRV to the territory allocated it" at Geneva 1954 and to see the GVN's writ run throughout SVN. US patience was running thin. If the conflict should escalate, "the greatest devastation would of course result for the DRV itself."[a] He underlined the seriousness of US intentions by reminding his principal contact, Pham Van Dong, that the US commitment to SVN had implications extending far beyond SE Asia. (6/20/64)

---

[a] As reported in another study, Seaborn's was not the only warning given the DRV that June. Dillon also told the French Finance Minister, on the presumption it would be relayed to Hanoi, that we would use military force against the North if necessary to attain our objectives in SVN.

Pham Van Dong laughed and said he did indeed appreciate the problem. A US defeat in SVN would in all probability start a chain reaction extending much further. But the stakes were just as high for the NLF and its supporters, hence their determination to continue the struggle regardless of sacrifice. (6/20/64)

He did not specifically deny that there was DRV intervention in the South and said of the war in SVN, "We shall win." (Emphasis added.) But he also said "the DRV will not enter the war . . . we shall not provoke the US." (6/18/64) Perhaps he drew a distinction between existing levels of DRV intenvention and "entering the war." He also warned that "if the war were pushed to the North, 'nous sommes un pays socialiste, un des pays socialistes, vous savez, et le peuple se dressera.'" (6/18/64) This is quite ambiguous, but does threaten further consequences should the DRV itself come under attack.

Although he clearly did not consider the DRV under attack at that time, he complained that "US military intervention" in Laos in the wake of the April 1964 coup was spilling over the frontier.[1] "There are daily incursions of our air space across the Laotian border by overflights of military aircraft and by commando units bent on sabotage." (6/18/64)

Their positions stiffened after Tonkin. When Seaborn saw Pham Van Dong on August 13, he transmitted a blunt US refutation of the DRV's Tonkin Gulf account and an accusation that DRV behavior in the Gulf saught to cast the US as a paper tiger or to provoke the US.

Pham Van Dong answered angrily that there had been no DRV provocation. Rather, the US had found "it is necessary to carry the war to the North in order to find a way out of the impasse . . . in the South." He anticipated more attacks in the future and warned, "Up to now we have tried to avoid serious trouble; but it becomes more difficult now because the war has been carried to our territory . . . If war comes to North Vietnam, it will come to the whole of SE Asia. . ." (8/13/64)

He was thus ambiguous about whether he considered the war already carried to the North or yet to come and of course about that the consequences would be. As indicated in another study, however, it is now believed that the first organized NVA units infiltrated into SVN were dispatched from the DRV in August, 1964. (These units were being readied as early as April 1964. The date of the decision to dispatch them is, of course, unknown.) Meanwhile, Seaborn observed the North Vietnamese to be "taking various precautionary measures (air raid drills, slit trenches, brick bunkers, etc. and, reportedly at least, preparation for evacuation of women and children.)" (8/17/64)

2

The DRV position stiffened further after Pleiku.[2] Seaborn returned to Hanoi in December, 1964, but at our request did not actively seek appointments with ranking leaders. He was to leave the initiative to them, but they did not seek him out either and he returned to Saigon without significant contact.

When he visited again, March 1-4, 1965, he was given a US message to convey to Pham Van Dong. The latter was "too busy", and he had to settle for Col. Ha Van Lau, NVA liaison to the ICC, who received him March 4. (3/5/65)

From Lau and others, he gathered that Hanoi was not seriously concerned by the US air strikes, considering them an attempt to improve US bargaining power at a conference the US strenuously desired. Hanoi's interpretation, he believed, was that the US realized it had lost the war and wanted to extricate itself; hence it was in Hanoi's interest to hold back -- a conference then might, as in 1954, deprive it of total victory. (3/7/65) DRV interest in Seaborn as a channel of communication with the US seemed to him virtually to have vanished, whereas it had been underlined by Pham Van Dong both in June and August. (3/5/65) On March 3, Mai Van Bo told the Quai in Paris that "while previously the DRV had been ready to consider negotiation of some sort, US actions had changed the situation. Negotiations (were) no longer a matter for consideration at this time." (3/4/65)

The May 1964 Bombing Pause brought no softening.[3] The US/DRV impasse was again reflected in Seaborn's May 31-June 6 (1964)5 visit to Hanoi. On the one hand, Embassy Saigon expressed reservations about a passage in his instructions because it might "lead us towards a commitment to cease bombing simply in return for a cessation or reduction in VC armed actions in SVN." (5/28/65) On the other, Seaborn returned from Hanoi persuaded that the "DRV is not now interested in any negotiations." (6/7/65)

Opposing Proposals for Settling the War

The toughness of the two sides was reflected by large differences in their proposals for settling the war. The US wanted Hanoi to bring an end to armed resistance to the GVN in SVN. In exchange, it was willing to co-exist peacefully with the DRV, extending to it the possibility of economic and other beneficial relations enjoyed by Communist countries such as Poland and Yugoslavia. The US sought neither military bases in the region nor the overthrow of the regime in Hanoi. (6/1/64)

Pham Van Dong replied that a "just solution" in Indochina required (1) US withdrawal from Indochina; (2) the affairs of SVN to be arranged by the SVN people, with NLF participation; (3) "peace and neutrality for SVN, neutrality in the Cambodian manner"; and (4) reunification. He said that the idea of coalition government was snow-balling in SVN and that the Laos pattern of 1962 should serve as a guide for SVN.[4]

When Seaborn expressed the fear that the NLF would take over any coalition in which it participated, Pham Van Dong said "there was no reason to have such fears." He also said that neutrality for SVN need not be considered only as a first step toward reunification. SVN would remain neutral as long as the "people of SVN" wished. (6/18/64)

These opening positions, sketched by the two sides during Seaborn;s June 1964 visit, were swamped then and subsequently by the discussion of military measures and their possible consequences. The two sides were never close in their proposals, though in both cases their initial language was sufficiently flexible to permit subsequent bargaining and compromise. But their differing estimates of what would be accomplished in battle kept them from focusing the Seaborn exchanges on settlement terms, and no reduction in their differences over settlement occurred after the first visit.

The Laotian Problem

Seaborn expressed US concern at DRV intervention in Laos on his June 1964 visit. Pham Van Dong replied, "We do not send units to the Pathet Lao." He leveled charges of US military intervention there and demanded a "return to the situation which existed prior to the April coup." To restore peace and neutrality in Laos, "a new conference of the 14 parties is necessary. . . . Only the 14 nation conference is competent to deal with the Laos situation."[5]

The problem of Laos was not pursued in subsequent contacts.

4

Summary

1964 Seaborn Conversations [a]

June 1964. In his (June 18, 1964) meeting with Pham Van Dong
(which took place with no one else present) Seaborn communicated a
US message (a) emphasizing US determination to contain the DRV to
the territory allocated it by the Geneva Agreements (1954), (b) reassuring the DRV that the US did not seek to overthrow the DRV or
want military bases in SVN, (c) noting that the US was aware of
Hanoi's control over the Viet Cong, (d) indicating that the US stake
in resisting a DRV victory in SVN was increased by the relevance of
this type of struggle to other areas of the Free World, (e) noting
that US patience was growing thin, and (f) hinting at the benefits
of "peaceful coexistence" to other Communist regimes.

Pham Van Dong clearly understood the message but declined "at
present" to send any formal reply. He emphasized the key points in
a "just·solution" for the DRV were (a) a US withdrawal from SVN,
(b) the establishment of a neutral "Cambodian-style" regime in SVN,
in accordance with the NFL program, and (c) NFL participation in the
determination of the fate of SVN when SVN was ready for negotiations.
Pham emphasized the DRV's determination to continue with the struggle
if the US increased its aid to the GVN and that the ultimate success
of the Viet Cong was not in question. Pham denied that SVN's neutrality
was only a first step, stating this was up to the people of the region.
Pham did not specifically challenge Seaborn's observation that,
while the NFL would have to be in a SVN coalition government, it
did not represent all or even a majority of South Vietnamese. Pham
added that there was no reason to fear that the NFL would take over
a coalition government.

Pham told Seaborn that the DRV would not "force" or "provoke"
the US. He concluded by stating that he looked forward to further
talks with Seaborn and that the next time Seaborn could also see
Ho Chi Minh.

Seaborn concluded from the conversation that one could not count
on war weariness, factionalism, or the prospect of material benefits
to bring the DRV to an accommodation with the US. He emphasized
Pham's confidence in ultimate victory and conviction that military
action could not bring the US success.

[a]
This paper was drafted for State Department use by P.H.Kreisberg
November 20, 1965.

- 2 -

Comment: My impression is that the general tone of the conversation did appear to offer some grounds for believing that at a
subsequent discussion additional progress might be made toward preliminaries for concrete discussions. It should be noted that neither
our message nor Pham's remarks raised the question of any direct
contact or discussions between the US and the DRV.

August 1964. The key theme at the next meeting between Seaborn
and Pham Van Dong on August 13, 1964 (this time in the presence of
two other DRV observers) was the Tonkin Gulf incident. The US message
conveyed by Seaborn rejected the DRV version of the incident, charged
the DRV with deliberately planning the attack, and stated that as a
result the US was increasing its military forces in SVN. The message
also once more referred to possible economic and other benefits for
the DRV if it halted its expansionism.

Pham's reaction was extremely angry. He said the US was seeking
a way out by expanding the war to North Viet-Nam and that the US election
campaign was also responsible for the stronger US line. He stressed the
"very dangerous" nature of the situation, said the US might be led
to "new acts of aggression", and warned that the DRV would fight a
war if it came and that this would spread to all SEA and possibly
further. He referred to support from other countries including
Peking and Moscow. At the same time he said the DRV had tried for
peace but the US did not want it. He urged the ICC to take a more
important role and seek a solution "on the basis of the Geneva Agreements." He emphasized that he found the Seaborn link useful and wanted
to keep the channel open.

Seaborn commented on the meeting that Pham Van Dong's reaction
was not surprising in view of the blunt US rebuttal of the official
DRV position and that the DRV might actually believe there was a
chance of new US attacks. He found no evident DRV concern over the
firmness of the US message, however, and noted that Pham's reaction
had been one of anger rather than of seeking a way out. Seaborn was
encouraged by Pham's desire to keep the channel of communication open
but thought Pham continued to be "genuinely convinced" that things
were going the DRV's way and there was no need to compromise.

Comment: The negotiating content of this meeting was totally
barren as a result of its timing and its complete focus on the events
immediately preceding it rather than on broader issues as had been
adumbrated at the June meeting. Pham made no effort to develop his
remarks in June or to bring Seaborn together with Ho. The participation
of other DRV observers, including a note taker, in the meeting may also
have forced an increased formality, coldness, and rigidity in Pham Van
Dong's remarks as compared with those in June. There is no question,

- 3 -

however, that there was no indication of "give" in Pham's position
and that the only note of "encouragement" was his continuing desire
to keep lines of communication open.

December 1964. On Seaborn's visit to Hanoi in December he carried
no US message, it having been agreed that it was now up to Hanoi to
take some initiative. Seaborn did not actively seek appointments
with any ranking DRV leaders but did make it clear that he was available
if anyone he had seen earlier wished to see him again. He saw Pham Van
Dong informally at a social gathering but Pham did not use the opportunity
to discuss substantive matters or seek a further appointment with him.
Seaborn was told other DRV leaders were away or unavailable. Seaborn
told junior DRV officials of continued US firmness and of the possibility
that further US counteraction might be taken.

Comment: The complete aridity of this visit suggests that the
DRV had changed its mind about using Seaborn as a channel of communication, was not prepared to make any new or forward proposals on negotiations, or--contrary to our own conclusion--believed the initiative to
make some new offer lay in the US court and that if Seaborn was carrying
no new message there was no point in carrying on the exchange at that
time.

Over-all Comment: I believe that the August and December meetings
support the tenor of your memorandum to Mr. Ball but that this is less
certain in the case of the June conversation. I also believe specific
note should be taken of the fact that Seaborn did not specifically
request an interview at a high level in December. It might be put
that Hanoi made no effort in December when Seaborn was there to renew
its discussions or put forward any new proposal for negotiations or
meetings.

The Seaborn Approach to Hanoi [b]

March 1965: At our request, Blair Seaborn, Chief Canadian
representative on the International Control Commission in Vietnam,
gave the Hanoi authorities on March that portion of Ambassador Cabot's[6]
February 24 statement to WANG Kuo-chuan in Warsaw dealing with Vietnam.
We hoped thus to convince the North Vietnamese that the United States
has no designs on their territory nor any desire to destroy them.
Seaborn, at our suggestion, sought an appointment with the Prime
Minister, but was obliged to settle for a meeting with the chief of
the North Vietnamese Army's Liaison Section, to whom he read the

[b] This paper was prepared for State Department use. Its date of preparation and drafter are not indicated. Sub-headings have been supplied.

- 4 -

statement. This officer commented that it contained nothing new and
that the North Vietnamese already received a briefing on the Warsaw
meeting from the Chicoms. The Canadian Government publicly noted in
April that Seaborn had two important conversations with DRV officials
in recent months, but did not go into details.

June 1965. In May we again asked Seaborn to seek an appointment
with Phan Van Dong and on our behalf reiterate the March message and
U.S. determination to persist in the defense of South Vietnam, to regret
that Hanoi had not responded positively to the various recent initiatives,
including the bombing pause, and to state that, nevertheless, the
United States remained ready "to consider the possibility of a solution
by reciprocal actions on each side." If the Vietnamese brought up Pham
Van Dong's four points,[7] Seaborn was authorized to endeavor to establish
whether Hanoi insisted that they be accepted as the condition for
suspension, that we planned to inform Hanoi separately, and that we
expected Hanoi would find easily detectable means of displaying that it
understood the message.

May 1, 1964

STATE 1821 (S/EXDIS), Priority, to AmEmbassy Saigon, Sent 1 May 1964.

FOR THE AMBASSADOR FROM THE SECRETARY

    I flew up to Ottawa yesterday to talk with Mike Pearson and Martin concerning the Canadian presence in Hanoi. . . .

    . . .

    They readily agreed that Seaborn should plan to spend much more time in Hanoi than have his predecessors in this assignment.

X G<u>D</u>S - 1

    Following are some of the matters which we roughed out in Ottawa and which I will have further developed here. . . .

    2. Seaborn should get across to Ho and his colleagues the full measure of US determination to see this thing through. He should draw upon examples in other parts of the world to convince them that if it becomes necessary to enlarge the military action, this is the most probable course that the US would follow.

    3. Seaborn should spread the word that he is puzzled by Hanoi's intentions. The North Vietnamese should understand that the US wants no military bases or other footholds in South Viet Nam or Laos. If Hanoi would leave its neighbors alone, the US presence in the area would diminish sharply.

    4. The North Vietnamese should understand that there are many examples in which the Free World has demonstrated its willingness to live in peace with communist neighbors and to permit the establishment of normal economic relations between these two different systems. We recognize North Viet Nam's need for trade, and especially food, and consider that such needs could be fulfilled if peaceful conditions were to prevail.

Pearson also agreed to instruct Seaborn and his people in general to work more actively on trying to break the Poles off from constant and active espousal of North Vietnamese aggression.[8] He felt, however, that the Poles are playing something of a middle role in Sino-Soviet matters these days and doubted that there would be much profit in this.

Sullivan/RUSK

May 15, 1964

AmEmb Saigon 2212 (S/Nodis), Rec'd 15 May 64, 7:2 A.M.

FOR THE PRESIDENT FROM LODGE

. . .

. . .

3. If prior to the Canadian's trip to Hanoi there has been a terroristic act of the proper magnitude, then I suggest that a specific target in North Viet Nam be considered as a prelude to his arrival. The Vietnamese Air Force must be made capable of doing this, and they should undertake this type of action.

4. I much prefer a selective use of Vietnamese Air power to an over U.S. effort perhaps involving the total annihilation of all that has been built in North Viet Nam since 1954, because this would surely bring in the Chinese Communists, and might well bring in the Russians. Moreover, if you lay the whole country waste, it is quite likely that you will induce a mood of fatalism in the Viet Cong. Also, there will be nobody left in North Viet Nam on whom to put pressure. Furthermore, South Viet Nam's infrastructure might well be destroyed. What we are interested in here is not destroying Ho Chi Minh (as his successor would probably be worse than he is), but getting him to change his behavior. That is what President Kennedy was trying to do in October with Diem and with considerable success.

. . .

6. This is a procedure the intensity of which we can constantly control and bring up to the point to which we think the Communist reaction would cease to be manageable. It should be covert and undertaken by the Vietnamese, but, of course, we must be clear in our own minds that we are ready and able to take care of whatever reaction there may be.

7. It is easy for us on the one hand to ignore our superiority as we did at the time of Berlin in 1948 (when we still had sole possession of the atomic bomb). It is also a relatively simple concept to go out and destroy North Viet Nam. What is complicated,

but really effective, is to bring our power to bear in a precise
way so as to get specific results.

8. Another advantage of this procedure is that when, as and
if the time ever came that our military activities against the North
became overt, we would be in a strong moral position both with
regard to U.S. public opinion, the U.S. Congress, and the U.N. I
say this because we would then have a record to show that we had
given Ho Chi Minh fair warning to stop his murdrous interference
in the internal affairs of Viet Nam. Not only would we have given
him fair warning, but we would have given him honest and valuable
inducements in the way of some withdrawal of American personnel
and in the way of economic aid, notably food. . . .

    . . .

LODGE

May 22, 1964

STATE 2049 to AmEmb SAIGON (TS/NODIS), Priority, Sent 22 May 64, 7:40 P.M.

LITERALLY EYES ONLY FOR AMBASSADOR FROM SECRETARY

    . . .

2. . . . in light of present Canadian attitudes we tend to
see real difficulty in approaching the Canadians at this time with
any message as specific as you suggest, i.e., that Hanoi be told by
the Canadians "that they will be punished."[9] But we are keeping
this in mind and will see whether we can go further when we consult
them next week than the more general type of message stated in my
1821. As you can see, the more specific message might lead us
into a very difficult dialogue with the Canadians as to just what
our plans really were.

3. On the othe question, whether initial substantial attacks
could be left without acknodledgement, it is our present view
here that this would simply not be feasible. . . . Once such
publicity occurred, I think you can see that the finger would
point straight at us and that the President would then be put in
perhaps a far more difficult position toward the American public
and the Congress.

4. Thus, we are using a GVN- or US-acknowledged enterprise
rc part of our main planning track at the present time, although
we do recognize that something a little stronger than the present
OPLAN 34-A might be carried on on the basis you propose.[10]

    . . .

BUNDY

May 25, 1964

AmEmbassy SAIGON 2305 (TS/Nodis), Rec'd 25 May 64, 5:22 AM.

LITERALLY EYES ONLY FOR THE SECRETARY FROM LODGE

1. It is not rpt not at all necessary that the Canadians either agree or disagree. What is important is that the Canadian transmit the message and be willing to do that and report back accurately what is said. . . .

2. The Communists have a great advantage over us in that they do things and never talk about them. We must not rpt not let them continue to have this advantage. . . .

. . .

LODGE

May 26, 1964

AmEmbassy SAIGON 2318 (TS/Nodis), Rec'd 26 May 64, 3:30 A.M.

LITERALLY EYES ONLY FOR THE SECRETARY FROM LODGE

1. . . .

2. I am coming to the conclusion that we cannot reasonably and prudently expect a much better performance out of the GVN than that which we are now getting unless something new of this kind is brought into the picture. . . .

LODGE

May 30, 1964

STATE 2133 to Amembassy SAIGON (TS/Exdis), Priority, Sent 30 May 1964, 10:40 A.M.

FOR THE AMBASSADOR FROM THE ACTING SECRETARY

President and Mac Bundy met May 28 in New York with Canadian Prime Minister Pearson. Simultaneously Sullivan met in Ottawa with Foreign Minister Martin, Deputy Under Secretary Smith, and ICC Commissioner-Designate Seaborn.

President told Pearson that he wishes Hanoi to know, that while he is a man of peace, he does not intend to permit the North Vietnamese to take over Southeast Asia. He needs a confidential and responsible interlocutor to carry the nessage of US attitudes to Hanoi. In out-lining the US position there was some discussions of QTE carrots and sticks UNQUOTE.

Pearson, after expressing willingness to lend Canadian good offices to this endeavor. indicated some concern about [11]

In Ottawa Sullivan found much the same disposition among Canadian officials. While Foreign Minister Martin seemed a little nervous about the prospect of QTE expanding the war UNQTE, External Affairs officials readily assented to the use of Seaborn as an interlocutor. . . .

Seaborn, who struck Sullivan as an alert, intelligent and steady officer, readily agreed to these conditions and has made immediate plans for an accelerated departure. . . .

. . .

BALL

June 1, 1964

Memo To: G - Mr. U. Alexis Johnson, from S/VN - Joseph A. Mendelhall, dated June 1, 1964 (TS)

Subject: Instructions for Canadian Interlocutor with Hanoi.

I am enclosing a copy of the "Outline of Subjects for Mr. Seaborn" which Bill Sullivan prepared prior to departure for Honolulu. He gave a copy of this general paper of instructions to Mr. Robinson, Minister-Counselor of the Canadian Embassy, on May 30.

At your request I have prepared and am enclosing a draft of a further outline in specific terms of the message which we would expect the Canadian interlocutor to get across in Hanoi. This further outline is based on the assumptions that (a) a U.S. decision has been taken to act against North Viet-Nam and (b) we plan to use "carrots" as well as a "stick" on Hanoi. I believe that we would probably not wish to hand this further outline to the Canadian Government pending the initial soundings of the Canadian interlocutor in Hanoi pursuant to Mr. Sullivan's original set of instructions.

. . .

Enclosures:
1. Outline of Subjects for Mr. Seaborn.
2. Further Outline for Mr. Seaborn.

OUTLINE OF SUBJECTS FOR MR. SEABORN

1. The President wishes Hanoi to understand that he is fundamentally a man of peace. However, he does not intend to let the North Vietnamese take over all of Southeast Asia. He wishes to have a highly confidential, responsible interlocutor who will deliver this message to the authorities in Hanoi and report back their reaction.

2. The messages which may be transmitted through this channel would involve an indication of the limitations both upon US ambitions in Southeast Asia and upon US patience with Communist provocation. The interlocutor of his Government need not agree with not associate themselves with the messages that are passed. The only requirement is that there be faithful transmittal of the messages in each direction.

3. Mr. Seaborn should arrive in Hanoi as soon as possible and establish his credentials as a political personality who can and will deal with senior representatives of the Hanoi regime.

4. Mr. Seaborn should also, by listening to the arguments and observing the attitudes of the North Vietnamese, form an evaluation of their mental outlook. He should be particularly alert to (a) differences with respect to the Sino-Soviet split, (b) frustration of war weariness, (c) indications of North Vietnamese desire for contacts with the West, (d) evidences of cliques or factions in the Party or Government, and (e) evidence of differences between the political and the military.

5. Mr. Seaborn should explore the nature and the prevalence of Chinese Communist influence in North Viet Nam; and perhaps through direct discussions with the Soviet representatives, evaluate the nature and influence of the Soviets.

6. Mr. Seaborn should stress to appropriate North Vietnamese officials that US policy is to see to it that North Viet Nam contains itself and its ambitions within the territory allocated to its administration by the 1954 Geneva Agreements. He should stress that US policy in South Viet Nam is to preserve the integrity of that state's territory against guerrilla subversion.

7. He should state that the US does not seek military bases in the area and that the US is not seeking to overthrow the Communist regime in Hanoi.

8. He should stipulate that the US is fully aware of the degree to which Hanoi controls and directs the guerrilla action in South Viet Nam and that the US holds Hanoi directly responsible for that action. He should similarly indicate US awareness of North Vietnamese control over the Pathet Lao movement in Laos and the degree of North Vietnamese involvement in that country. He should specifically indicate US awareness of North Vietnamese violations of Laotian territory along the infiltration route into South Viet Nam.

9. Mr. Seaborn should point out that the nature of US commitment in South Viet Nam is not confined to the territorial issue in question. He should make it clear that the US considers the confrontation with North Vietnamese subversive guerrilla action as part of the general Free World confrontation with this type of violent subversion in other lesser developed countries. Therefore, the US stake in resisting a North Vietnamese victory in South Viet Nam has a significance of world-wide proportions.

10. Mr. Seaborn can point to the many examples of US policy in tolerance of peaceful coexistence with Communist regimes, such as Yugoslavia, Poland, etc. He can hint at the economic and other benefits which have accrued to those countries because their policy of Communism has confined itself to the development of their own national territories and has not sought to expand into other areas.

11. Mr. Seaborn can couple this statement with the frank acknowledgement that US public and official patience with North Vietnamese aggression is growing extremely thin.

12. Insofar as Mr. Seaborn considers it might be educational he could review the relative military strengths of the US, North Viet Nam, and the available resources of Communist China in Southeast Asia.

13. In sum, the purpose of Mr. Seaborn's mission in North Viet Nam would be as an interlocutor with both active and passive functions. On the passive side, he should report either observations or direct communications concerning North Vietnamese attitude toward extrication from or escalation of military activities. On the active side, he should establish his credentials with the North Vietnamese as an authoritative channel of communications with the US. In each of these functions it would be hoped that Mr. Seaborn would assume the posture that the decision as to the future course of events in S outheast Asia rests squarely with Hanoi.

FURTHER OUTLINE FOR MR. SEABORN

1. The U.S. objective is to maintain the independence and territorial integrity of South Viet-Nam. This means that the South Vietnamese Government in Saigon must be able to exercise its authority throughout the territory south of the 17th Parallel without encountering armed resistance directed and supported by Hanoi.

2. We know that Hanoi can stop the war in South Viet-Nam if it will do so. The virtually complete cease-fires which have obtained at Tet time for the past two years demonstrate the ability of Hanoi to control all Viet Cong operations in South Viet-Nam if it has the will to do so.

3. In order to stop the war in South Viet-Nam the United States is prepared to follow alternative courses of action with respect to North Viet-Nam.

(a) Unless Hanoi stops the war within a specified time period (i.e., ceases all attacks, acts of terror, sabotage or armed propaganda or other armed resistance to government authority by the VC), the United States will initiate action by air and naval means against North Viet-Nam until Hanoi does agree to stop the war.

(b) If Hanoi will agree to stop the war, the United States will take the following steps:

(1) Undertake to obtain the agreement of Saigon to a resumption of trade between North Viet-Nam and South Viet-Nam, which would be helpful to North Viet-Nam in view of the complementarity of the two zones of Viet-Nam and the food difficulties now suffered by North Viet-Nam.

(2) Initiate a program of foodstuffs assistance to North Viet-Nam either on a relief grant basis under Title II of Public Law 480 or on a sales for local currency basis under Title I PL-480 (as in Poland and Yugoslavia).

(3) Remove U.S. foreign assets controls from the assets of North Viet-Nam and reduce controls on U.S. trade with North Viet-Nam to the level now applicable to the USSR (i.e., strategic items only).

(4) Recognize North Viet-Nam diplomatically and, if Hanoi is interested, undertake an exchange of diplomatic representatives.

(5) Remove U.S. forces from South Viet-Nam on a phased basis, winding up with a reduction to the level of 350 military advisors or trainers as permitted under the Geneva Accords. (This was the number of U.S. military personnel in Viet-Nam when the Geneva Accords were signed in 1954.)

4. If Hanoi stops resistance in South Viet-Nam, the United States and South Vietnamese Governments will permit Hanoi to withdraw any Viet Cong personnel whom it may wish from South Viet-Nam. The Government of South Viet-Nam will also make a clear public announcement of full amnesty for all rebels who discontinue armed resistance to the authority of the Government.

5. If Hanoi agrees to cease resistance, the order from Hanoi to the Viet Cong units and personnel can be issued, if Hanoi prefers, either publicly or confidentially through the communications channels from Hanoi to the Viet Cong. The test the U.S. will apply will be whether or not all armed resistance to the authority of the Government at Saigon actually stops.

6. Timetable for these actions:

(a) All hostilities must cease within one week of the approach to the authorities at Hanoi. If they have not stopped within that time, the U.S. will immediately initiate air and naval action against North Viet-Nam.

(b) If agreement is reached between the U.S. and North Viet-Nam on the cessation of resistance in South Viet-Nam, the cessation of hostilities will be preceded by a general GVN amnesty announcement.

(c) If the DRV desires to repatriate Viet Cong from South Viet-Nam, this can be done over whatever period the DRV desires.

(d) If the DRV desires to announce an agreement publicly with the United States, the entire package of measures on both sides can be announced within three days of the complete cessation of hostilities. If the DRV does not desire a public announcement of its agreement to have the Viet Cong cease resistance, then the United States measures of concession to North Viet-Nam can be announced only over a phased period starting one week from the complete cessation of hostilities. Announcement of all steps taken by the U.S. as concessions to North Viet-Nam would be completed by three months from the cessation of hostilities.

(e) U.S. forces would be removed from South Viet-Nam on a phased basis over a period of one year from the data of cessation of resistance to the Government of South Viet-Nam. At the end of one year U.S. military personnel would be down to the 350 permitted by the Geneva Accords.

June 8, 1964

STATE 2205 to Amembassy Saigon (TS/Exdis), Priority, Sent Jun 7, 64 7:55 PM

REF: Embtel 2434

Seaborn has been given condensed outline version May 22 Talking Paper drafted by Sullivan. Believe it might be confusing if original paper itself also given Seaborn and would suggest you cover substance orally in order indicate general concurrence Washington-Saigon views this subject.

RUSK

June 18, 1964

STATE 115 to Amembassy SAIGON (TS/Exdis), Sent Jul 11, 1964, 5:19 P.M.

Embtel 74.

As requested final paragraph reftel, texts first two Seaborn messages sent Ottawa follow:

The DRVN realize that the "loss" of SVN for the Americans would set off (what was the atomic expression?) a chain reaction which would extend much further. The USA is in a difficult position, because Khanh's troops will no longer fight. If the war gets worse, we shall suffer greatly but we shall win. If we win in the South, the people of the world will turn against the USA. Our people will therefore accept the sacrifice, whatever they may be. But the DRVN will not enter the war.

If the war were pushed to the North, "nous sommes un pays socialiste, vous savez et le peuple so dressera". But we shall not force the USA, we shall not provoke the USA.

As far as the ICC is concerned, we are very glad to have you here. But don't put too many items on the agenda, don't give yourself too much work to do.

August 8, 1964

STATE 169 to Amembassy OTTAWA, STATE 383 to Amembassy SAIGON, Immediate, (TS/Exdis), Sent 8 Aug 64, 4:41 P.M.

Follwing message was handed directly to Canadian Embassy here for transmittal to Seaborn by fastest channel. This is for your information only.

QUOTE Canadians are urgently asked to have Seaborn during August 10 visit make following points (as having been conveyed to him by US Government since August 6):

A. Re Tonkin Gulf actions, which almost certainly will come up:[14]

        1. . . . Neither the MADDOX or any other destroyer was in any way associated with any attack on the DRV islands.

        2. Regarding the August 4 attack by the DRV on the two US destroyers, the Americans were and are at a complete loss to understand the DRV motive. . . . About the only reasonable hypothesis was that North Viet-Nam was intent either upon making it appear that the United States was a INNER QUOTE paper tiger END INNER QUOTE or upon provoking the United States.

        3. The American response was directed solely to patrol craft and installations acting in direct support of them. As President Johnson stated : INNER QUOTE Our response for the present will be limited and fitting. END INNER QUOTE

        4. In view of uncertainty aroused by the deliberate and unprovoked DRV attacks this character, US has necessarily carried out precautionary deployments of additional air power to SVN and Thailand.

B. Re basic American position:

. . .

9. Mr. Seaborn should conclude with the following new points:

a. That the events of the past few days should add credibility to the statement made last time, that INNER QUOTE US public and official patience with North Vietnamese aggression is growing extremely thin. END INNER QUOTE

b. That the US Congressional Resolutions was passed with near unanimity, strongly re-affirming the unity and determination of the US Government and people not only with respect to any further attacks on US military forces but more broadly to continue to oppose firmly, by all necessary means, DRV efforts to subvert and conquer South Viet-Nam and Laos.[15]

c. That the US has come to the view that the DRV role in South Viet-Nam and Laos is critical. If the DRV persists in its present course, it can expect to continue to suffer the consequences.

d. That the DRV knows what it must do if the peace is to be restored.

e. That the US has ways and means of measuring the DRV's participation in, and direction and control of, the war on South Viet-Nam and in Laos and will be carefully watching the DRV's response to what Mr. Seaborn is telling them. UNQUOTE.

RUSK

August 9, 1964

STATE 389 to Amembassy SAIGON (TS/Exdis) Flash, Sent 9 Aug 64, 6:42 A.M.

REF Saigon 362, repeated Info as Saigon 8 to Ottawa

. . . request you immediately contact Seaborn with view to deleting two words QUOTE to continue UNQUOTE from last sentence paragraph 9 c.

RUSK

August 18, 1964

SAIGON 467 to SecState (TS/Exdis) Priority, Rec'd 18 Aug 64, 2:07 P.M.

Deptel 383

Seaborn called on Sullivan August 17 to show him copies his reports (which presumably Dept has seen) concerning his recent visit to Hanoi. As Dept probably aware, Seaborn was under instructions omit last two points reftel in his ciscussions with Pham Van Dong, but otherwise feels he made all points practically verbatim.

Principal observation which Seaborn expressed re his conversation was sense satisfaction that Phan Van Dong, despite his angry reaction to Seaborn presentation, was unhesitating in his statement that channel of communication to US should stay open and that Seaborn should continue to bear US messages, no RPT no matter how unpleasant they may be.

· · ·

TAYLOR

August 19, 1964

MEMORANDUM FOR: The Secretary

FROM: S/VN - Michael V. Forrestal

THROUGH: S/S

Herewith the second installment of the Seaborn talks.

The verbatim account of the conversation still remains to come from Ottawa.

Attachment

SEABORN

December 3, 1964

STATE 1210 to Amembassy SAIGON, STATE 645 to Amembassy OTTAWA, Immediate, (Top S/Exdis), Sent 3 Dec 64, 6:51 P.M.

The following message has been handed directly to Canadian Embassy here for transmittal to Seaborn through fastest channel. This is for your information only.

Quote: Canadians are asked to have Seaborn take following position during his next visit to Hanoi which, we understand, is currently scheduled for December 7th or 10th (Embtel 1618).

The United States has nothing to add to the points made by Seaborn on his last visit to Hanoi in August. All the recent indications from Washington, however, point to a continued and increasing determination on the part of the US to assist the South Vietnamese in their struggle. Although he has no specific message on this trip, Seaborn has noted from its public statements increased US concern at DRV role in direct support of Viet Cong, and this together with reported high-level meetings Washington makes him feel that time is ripe for any new message Hanoi may wish to convey.

Seaborn should convey attitude of real personal concern over the growing possibility of direct confrontation between GVN and DRV. End quote.

FYI: Purpose of this approach is to probe for any new DRV reactions.

HARRIMAN

SEABORN

January 29, 1965

AmEmbassy PARIS 4295 to SecState (Limdis/Noforn/S), Rec'd 29 Jan 65, 2 P.M.

EmbOff has been shown in strictest secrecy large portions of record conversations on Viet Nzm held here between ranking officials of Quai on one hand and separately with Chinese Charge Sung and North Vietnamese delegate Mai Van Bo on other. Conversation with Bo took place December 22 and was renewed again last week. . . .

In addition to discussion of international conference along Geneva lines, conversation with North Vietnamese XHIKXQK,* essentially to three questions put by French (1) Would Hanoi accept and join in guarantees for neutral and completely independent South Vietnam? (2) Would Hanoi agree to knock off political and military subversion in SVN? (3) Would Hanoi accept some control mechanism more serious and with wider powers than present ICC? Total ineffectiveness of latter and paralysis through veto demonstrated, especially in Laos.

Mai Van Bo showed considerable interest in (1) and (3) and spoke of settling on basis 1954 Geneva Accords but was obviously embarrassed and evasive on (2), since affirmative response would have constituted confession. French told Bo frankly they could not accept Vietnamese protestations that there was only American intervention and that French were convinced of Hanoi subversive role. If Hanoi did not wish to own up, would they at least undertake guarantee not to engage in such activities in future?

At second meeting in January above questions explored further and French said that in order to discuss meaningfully, Bo should obtain precise answers from Hanoi on above three points. No answer yet received.

. . .

*As received, will service upon request.

February 27, 1965

STATE 942 to Amembassy OTTAWA (S/Exdis) Immediate, Sent 27 Feb 65, 4:11 P.M.

We have passed to Canadian Embassy here text of that portion of Ambassador Cabot's presentation at latest Warsaw talks dealing with Viet-Nam situation. Text as follows: QUOTE. I have been instructed to restate United States policy in South Viet-Nam. Our constant policy has been to assist South Viet-Nam in its efforts to maintain its freedom and independence in the face of Communist aggression directed and supported by Hanoi. So long as the Viet Cong, directed

and supported by North Viet-Nam and encouraged by your side,
continues its attacks in South Viet-Nam, the United States will
find it necessary to affort the Government of Viet-Nam such help
as it desires and needs to restore peace. The pressures being
mounted by the North Vietnamese across the frontiers of South
Viet-Nam are intolerable. We must and will take action to stop
them.

    . . .

    . . . It was our hope that the 1954 Geneva arrangements
would allow the Governments in Indochina to exist in peace.

    . . .

We would be satisfied if the Geneva agreements of 1954 were
observed by all parties. . . . Any evidence of willingness on
the part of the DRV to return to these accords would be noted and
welcomed by our side.

    . . . If there is any doubt in Hanoi as to this U.S. position,
I hope that you will convey it to them. UNQUOTE.

We have asked Canadian Embassy here to seek Ottawa's approval
for having Blair Seaborn convey above quoted passage to appropriate
Hanoi authorities in course of next visit.Hanoi. . . .

    . . .

RUSK

SEABORN

March 4, 1965

Amembassy PARIS 5008 to SecState Wash DC (S/Limdis/Noforn), Priority,
Rec'd 4 Mar 65, 2:02 P.M.

Following from Quai IndoChina Chief Brethes:

    Chief DRV Commercial Delegation Mai Van Bo came to Quai
yesterday for discussion of unspecified disagreement over French
Lycee in Hanoi. He took opportunity to remark that while previously
DRV had been ready to consider negotiation of some sort, US actions
had changed situation. Negotiations no longer matter for consideration at this time, and people of North and South Viet Nam were going
to defend themselves. Tone of Bo's comments was very stern and
French concluded he had probably received instructions avoid any
discussion with French on possible political settlement.

        . . .

BOHLEN

March 7, 1965

AmEmbassy SAIGON 2880 to SecState Wash DC (S/Exdis), Rec'd 7 Mar 65, 2PM.

        . . .

    Seaborn also discussed his general impression on which he drafting
separate report. Because of his inability to see any senior official
or have any substantive discussion with any Vietnamese, and discussions
with Eastern Bloc deplomats primary impression is that Hanoi thus far
not seriously concerned by strikes,[16] it being Hanoi's interpretation

of events that strikes are only a limited attempt by us to improve its bargaining position for conference which USG is strenuously. seeking in order to extricate itself from war in SVN which USG now recognizes is lost. Thus Hanoi not very concerned by strikes which have not seriously hurt it and as USG is one urgently seeking conference it is to Hanoi's advantage to continue to hold back on agreeing to any conference which at this time could only,as in 1954, result in depriving DRV of that full victory which it sees in sight as turmoil in SVN continues and pressures on US for withdrawal continue to mount.

TAYLOR

March 27, 1965 [17]

STATE 2718 to Amembassy SAIGON (TS/EXDIS), Immediate, Sent 27 Mar 65, 3:48 P.M.

    We are considering asking Canadians to instruct Seaborn to bear message to Hanoi, when he leaves May 31, for delivery to senior DRV official if and only if his first contacts with his normal liaison contact, in which he would inquire about availability senior officials, meet with forthcoming response and DRV initiative for appointment. . . .

    Proposed presentation Seaborn would make to senior official would be as follows:

    1. In my last visit, I conveyed a statement of US views concerning South Viet-Nam, which followed the lines of what the USG had stated to Peiping representatives at Warsaw. . . .

    2. Since my last visit, the USG has of course further publicly stated its position in President Johnson's speech of April 7 and in the US reply to the note of the 17 non-aligned nations, in which the USG further defined its readiness for unconditional discussions, its objectives, and the sequence of actions that might lead to a peaceful solution of the problem.[18]

    3. The USG has been disappointed to note that actions in the South supported and directed by Hanoi appear to continue without change, and even to be currently intensified. . . .

    4. In addition, the USG informed Hanoi on May 12 that it was undertaking a temporary suspension of bombing attacks for a period of several days.[19] The USG regrets that this action met with no response from Hanoi neither directly not in the form of any significant reductions of armed actions in South Viet-Nam by forces

whose actions, in the view of the USG, can be decisively affected from North Viet-Nam. Accordingly, the USG, in coordination with the Republic of Viet-Nam, was obliged to resume bombing attacks. Nonetheless, the USG continues to consider the possibility of working toward a solution by mutual example.

5. In making these points, the USG again must make it clear that in the absence of action or discussions leading to a political solution it must and will take whatever actions may be necessary to meet and to counter the offensive actions being carried out by North Viet-Nam against South Viet-Nam and against American forces acting to assist the Republic of Viet-Nam.

6. If but only if senior DRV representative gets on to Pham Van Dong four points of April 8, Seaborn would reply that he has no message from USG on this subject. However, his study of four points would indicate that some might be acceptable to USG but that others would clearly be unacceptable. It has also not been clear whether DRV statements should be taken to mean that the recognition of these points was required as, in effect, a condition for any discussions. He would say that the USG appears to have made its position clear, that it would accept unconditional discussions in the full sense, with either side free to bring up any matter, and that he would be personally interested in whether the DRV representative wished to clarify the question of whether their recognition is regarded by the DRV as a condition to any discussions. End proposed text.

. . .

RUSK

May 28, 1965

Amembassy SAIGON 3927 to SecState Wash DC (TS/Exdis), Immediate, Rec'd 28 May 1965, 4:10 A.M. (Passed White House, DOD, CIA, 5/28/65, 4:55 A.M.

Ref DEPTEL 2718

We see no objection to Seaborn seeking in manner set forth first paragraph RefTel to make approach.

With respect to substance, we offer following comments:

Last part third sentence of numbered para one appears to be worded in somewhat more astringent terms than useful or desirable in such private approach, although it is important point be made.

We are concerned by degree to which numbered para four continues to lead us towards commitment to cease bombing simply in return for cessation or even reduction of VC armed actions in SVN. Without laboring point, believe it is important not at this time at least to give away our position on withdrawal of VC. . . .

. . .

TAYLOR   28

June 6, 1965

Amembassy SAIGON 4083 to SecState (Confid/Limdis), Rec'd Jun 7, 1965, 2:06 A.M.

Canadian ICC Commissioner Blair Seaborn told EmbOff this morning results of his latest week-long visit to Hanoi, from which he had returned yesterday.

Seaborn said that he is persuaded from his conversations with diplomats and DRV officials that DRV is not now interested in any negotiations. He said that he was able to see new Foreign Minister Trinh but that discussion had revealed nothing new.[20]

Trinh followed standard line that US offer of unconditional discussion was "deceitful" since US continued build-up in South Vietnam and bombing of North. Seaborn pressed Trinh to elaborate on "Four Points," asking whether points intended to be seen as preconditions to talks or as result of talks or as ultimate goals. Trinh remained deliberately vague and gave no clear answers. . . .

. . . .

TAYLOR

VI.C.1., Project MAYFLOWER—the First Bombing Pause

By the time of Project MAYFLOWER, the second major peace move discussed in the negotiating volumes, the character and magnitude of American involvement in the war had changed drastically. Faced with continuing military and political deterioration in South Vietnam and with evidence of steadily increasing North Vietnamese involvement, the Johnson administration concluded by early 1965 that it had no choice but to expand the war. Responding to Vietcong attacks on a U.S. Army base at Pleiku on February 6, it initiated reprisal bombing raids on North Vietnamese staging areas across the seventeenth parallel. In ensuing weeks, it expanded and regularized the reprisals into the ROLLING THUNDER program of sustained bombing attacks on North Vietnam. The bombing provided justification for the first commitment of U.S. ground combat forces to Vietnam. In early March, Marines were dispatched to guard the air base at Danang. In the weeks that followed, additional troops were sent and their mission was gradually enlarged to permit offensive operations in support of South Vietnamese units.

The administration's dramatic escalation of the war produced mounting pressures at home and abroad for a negotiated settlement. The bombing provoked the first stirrings of a peace movement that would in time assume major proportions. Professors and students conducted teach-ins at several major universities, and in early April thousands of students converged on Washington for the first large-scale protest march against the war. Democratic Senators Mike Mansfield, Frank Church, and George McGovern joined the *New York Times* in protesting the bombing and urging the President to seek a negotiated settlement. Escalation also produced international appeals for restraint. U.N. Secretary General U Thant, alluding to his own abortive peace initiative of the preceding year, pointedly stated that if the American people knew the "true facts" about the war they would reject the administration's contention that a negotiated settlement was impossible. Canadian Prime Minister Lester Pearson, speaking at Temple University, called for a bombing halt as a first step toward peace, and representatives of seventeen nonaligned nations urged negotiations without "delay and condition."

The accumulation of pressures during February and March forced the administration to respond. Aware that its position in South Vietnam was still perilously weak, the United States was not ready for serious negotiations and indeed had not even begun to formulate terms for a settlement. In any event, Johnson and his advisers were certain that the North Vietnamese had no real interest in negotiations at this point. Recognizing that he had to do something to defuse his critics, however, the President matched his tough actions with soothing words. On March 25, he stated publicly that he was "ready to go anywhere at any time, and meet with anyone whenever there is promise of progress toward an honorable peace," characteristically inflated rhetoric that alarmed some of his advisers. In a much publicized speech at Johns Hopkins University on April 7, he stressed American determination to prevail in Vietnam, but he added his willingness to engage in "unconditional discussions" and expanded on the carrot secretly offered Hanoi by Seaborn a year earlier by proposing a billion-dollar economic development program for Southeast Asia in which North Vietnam could participate once peace had been restored.

Although the Johns Hopkins speech silenced his critics temporarily, Johnson soon concluded that an additional conciliatory move would be expedient. North Vietnam responded to the speech by issuing its first formal statement of peace terms. Premier Pham Van Dong's Four Points of April 8 demanded that the United States withdraw its forces from Vietnam and cease its acts of war; called for neutralization of both Vietnams pending unification; proposed a settlement of the internal affairs of South Vietnam in accordance with the program of the National Liberation Front; and insisted that reunification must be arranged by the Vietnamese people without outside interference. American officials took particular exception to point three, which seemed a thinly disguised cover for Vietcong domination of South Vietnam. Some of Johnson's advisers nevertheless felt that the United States should explore with Hanoi the precise meaning of the statement to see if there was any room for compromise, and that Pham's proposal appeared to put the United States on the defensive and required some sort of response.

Like the Johns Hopkins speech, however, MAYFLOWER was designed primarily to silence domestic and international critics. Johnson's military intervention in the Dominican Republic in late April had stirred up a hornet's nest at home, provoking some previously firm supporters, such as Senator J. William Fulbright, into an opposition that quickly spilled over into Vietnam. More important, by early May, the administration was on the verge of escalating the war once again. It had become evident that bombing alone would not force North Vietnam to the conference table, and administration officials shifted to a strategy of ending the war by denying the enemy victory on the ground in South Vietnam. This strategy would obviously require considerable time and additional American troops. Reasonably certain that North Vietnam would not respond positively to any American gesture, the administration concluded that a bombing pause, the step critics had been calling for, would help place the onus for escalation on the enemy.

As the documents that follow make clear, MAYFLOWER accomplished about what had been expected of it. The United States asked Hanoi for a reciprocal scaling down of military operations in South Vietnam, in return for which it vaguely promised to extend the bombing pause. It had difficulty even transmitting the message to North Vietnam through various intermediaries, however, and Hanoi's public response to the pause was hostile and unyielding. Arguing that his gesture had been rudely rebuffed, Johnson resumed the bombing on May 18.

Like the numerous other peace initiatives, MAYFLOWER has been the subject of heated controversy. Critics at the time and since have argued that a five-day pause was too brief to accomplish anything and that the United States offered Hanoi no real inducement to negotiate. They imply, at least, that the North Vietnamese were more willing to negotiate than the United States was prepared to admit and dismiss the pause as a cynical gesture. William Bundy has since conceded that the United States might have handled the initiative better. Officials were preoccupied with the Dominican crisis, he argues, and did not give MAYFLOWER the thought it merited. The American proposal, he concedes, was a "crisp, kind of lawyer's document, with . . . the sharp edges of the document showing." Bundy nevertheless concludes that Hanoi was not interested in negotiations and that a more tactful approach would have produced nothing.[1]

The Pentagon documents fill in the details of the MAYFLOWER initiative, but they leave many of the most important questions unanswered. They make clear that, despite its hostile public reaction, Hanoi did respond to the initiative, although its response came after the pause had ended, an approach taken throughout this period and probably calculated to avoid the appearance of responding under duress. The Seaborn mission documents (above) and the XYZ documents (below) also make clear that the United States responded to Hanoi's vague overtures, probing through the Seaborn visit in June the precise meaning of Pham's Four Points and engaging in extended and eventually fruitless talks in Paris. The Pentagon analyst may be incorrect in accepting the administration's conclusion that North Vietnam had no interest in negotiations. The Paris overture and the reception of Seaborn appear to suggest otherwise. It does seem clear, however, that, while Hanoi kept the door for negotiations slightly ajar, it was interested only in a settlement on its own terms. Hence a stalemate that would persist until 1968 and subsequent drastic escalation of the war.—*Ed.*

1. William Bundy Oral History Interview, Lyndon Baines Johnson Presidential Library, Austin, Texas.

XII.   PROJECT MAYFLOWER -- THE FIRST BOMBING PAUSE [1]

A. The Background

Pressure for some form of bombing halt had mounted steadily throughout April and early May. As early as April 2, Canada's Prime Minister Lester Pearson, on his way to meet with President Johnson, had stopped off to make a speech in Philadelphia in which he suggested that the President should order a "pause" in the bombing of North Vietnam.

Pearson's gratuitous advice was particularly galling to the President because the pause had become the battle slogan of the anti-Vietnam movement. Students had picketed the LBJ Ranch in Texas, demanding a cessation of bombing. A massive teach-in had been scheduled for May 15 in Washington, with academicians who wanted withdrawal of American influence from the Asian mainland, ready to demand as a first step an immediate end of the bombing. Pressure for a pause was building up, too, in Congress among liberal Democrats. 116/ . The U.N. Secretary General was on a continual bombing pause kick, with a proposal for a three month suspension of bombing in return for Hanoi's agreement to cease infiltration in South Vietnam. U Thant had told Ambassador Stevenson on April 24 that he believed such a gesture would facilitate renewed non-aligned pressure upon Hanoi to negotiate.

Evidently, however, the President was not impressed with the widespread clamor that such a gesture would evoke any response from Hanoi. He had responded favorably to the 17-Nation appeal in his April 7th speech,[2] only to be answered with blunt rejection by Hanoi and Peking. The U.S. had responded favorably to the idea of a Cambodian Conference that would provide opportunities for "corridor contacts" with Communist powers on the Vietnam problem, but Peking had apparently blocked that initiative. Encouragement had been given to a UK approach to the Soviets in February looking toward consultations under Article 19 of the 1962 Geneva Accords,[3] but no response from the USSR had been received. The Radhakrishnan proposal for a cease-fire along the 17th parallel, supervised by an "Afro-Asian Force" was being favorably considered by the U.S. only to be denounced as a "plot" by Peking and as an "offense" by Hanoi.[4] Publicly, the President was plaintive:

There are those who frequently talk of negotiations and political settlement and that they believe this is the course we should pursue, and so do I. When they talk that way I say, welcome to the club. I want to negotiate. I would much rather talk than fight, and I think everyone would. Bring in who you want us to negotiate with. I have searched high and wide, and I am a reasonably good cowboy, and I can't even rope anybody and bring them in who is willing to talk and

settle this by negotiation. We send them messages through
allies - one country, two countries, three countries, four
or five countries - all have tried to be helpful. The distinguished British citizen, Mr. (Patrick Gordon) Walker,[5]
has been out there, and they say, we can't even talk to you.
All our intelligence is unanimous in this one point, that
they see no need for negotiation. They think they are
winning and they have won and why should they sit down and
give us something and settle with us. 117/

But while the public clamor persisted and became more and more
difficult to ignore, the President was receiving intelligence assessments from Saigon and from Washington that tended to confirm his reading
of Hanoi's disinterest in negotiations, but that provided him with a
quite different argument for a bombing pause at this time: if the conflict was going to have to be expanded and bombing intensified before
Hanoi would "come to reason," it would be easier and politically more
palatable to do so after a pause, which would afford an opportunity for
the enemy's intentions to be more clearly revealed.

On May 4, in response to an urgent request from Washington, Ambassador Taylor submitted a U.S. Mission "Assessment of DRV/VC Probable
Courses of Action During the Next Three Months." The assessment confirmed the Washington view that Hanoi continued to have a very favorable
view of its prospects for victory:

> ...Tone of statements emanating from Hanoi since /Febru-
> ary and March/ indicate that the DRV has not weakened in its
> determination to continue directing and supporting Viet Cong
> and seeking further intensification of war in the South.
>
> From DRV viewpoint, outlook is probably still favorable
> despite air strikes on North. Although their general
> transportation system in North has been significantly damaged,
> thus somewhat reducing their infiltration capability, Hanoi
> may calculate it can accept level of damage being inflicted
> as reasonable price to pay for chance of victory in South.
> Viet Cong forces in south retain capability of taking local
> initiatives on ground, although they must accept cost of
> heavier losses from tactical air support, and their morale
> possibly has been reduced by recent developments. GVN force
> levels still are not adequate to cope with these Viet Cong
> capabilities. Despite relative longevity of Quat Govt.,[6]
> which marks improvement over previous recent Govts., politi-
> cal situation is still basically unstable. While military
> and civilian morale has risen, rumblings among generals con-
> tinue, suspicion among political and religious groups
> persist and are subject to exploitation by communists. On
> balance, Hanoi probably believes it has considerable basis

for expectation that Viet Cong, who were clearly making progress as recently as February, can regain the initiative and,
by the application of offensive power, can create an atmosphere
in which negotiations favorable to the DRV can be instituted.

Given this situation, the report argued, the most probable course
of action that Hanoi would pursue is to continue its efforts to expand
its military action in the South, "including covert introduction of
additional PAVN units on order of several regiments. This course offers
...the prospect of achieving major military gains capable of offsetting
US/GVN application of air power. Such gains would expand Viet Cong areas
of control and might lead to political demoralization in South Vietnam."
118/

A similarly unencouraging assessment had been submitted to the
President by the Board of National Estimates on April 22. In a "highly
sensitive, limited distribution" memorandum, the leading personalities
of the U.S. intelligence community concurred in the prediction that:

> If present US policies continue without the introduction
> of large additional forces or increased US air effort, the
> Communists are likely to hold to their existing policy of
> seeking victory in the local military struggle in South Viet-
> nam. They will try to intensify that struggle, supporting it
> with additional men and equipment. At the same time, DRV air
> defenses will be strengthened through Soviet and perhaps
> Chinese aid.

If, however, the U.S. deepens its involvement by increasing its
combat role and intensifying its air effort, the intelligence officers
believed:

> ...that the Viet Cong, North Vietnam, and China would
> initially...try to offset the new enemy strength by stepping
> up the insurgency, reinforcing the Viet Cong with the men and
> equipment necessary. They would likely count on time being
> on their side and try to force the piecemeal engagement of
> US troops under conditions which might bog them down in jungle
> warfare, hoping to present the US with a de facto partition of
> the country. The Soviet Union... would almost certainly
> acquiesce in a decision by Hanoi to intensify the struggle. 119/

This lack of any real prospect of "give" on the enemy's part was
also confirmed by Admiral Raborn, shortly after he had succeeded John
McCone as Director of Central Intelligence. On the day of Raborn's
swearing-in (April 28), the President had given him a letter from McCone
(apparently worded along the lines of his memorandum described in
Section IX.E. of this study) which McCone had handed to the President
as his last official act. The President had asked Raborn to prepare

his own comments on McCone's views. Raborn's comments, circulated to
Secretaries Rusk and McNamara on May 6, included the following:

> Our limited bombing of the North and our present ground-
> force build-up in the South are not likely to exert sufficient
> pressure on the enemy to cause him to meet our present terms
> in the foreseeable future. I note very recent evidence which
> suggests that our military pressures are becoming somewhat more
> damaging to the enemy within South Vietnam, but I am inclined
> to doubt that this damage is increasing at a rate which will
> bring him quickly to the conference table.

With particular reference to McCone's recommendation that the US
add much heavier air action against the North to its planned combat
force deployment to the South, Raborn indicated his agreement, and
expressed his belief that such an action would have the following consequences:

> The DRV is, in my view, unlikely to engage in meaningful
> discussions at any time in coming months until US air attacks
> have begun to damage or destroy its principal economic and
> military targets. I thus concur with the USIB's judgment of
> 18 February 1965, that, given such US punishment, the enemy
> would be "somewhat more likely" to decide to make some effort
> to secure a respite, rather than to intensify the struggle
> further and accept the consequent risks.

And then he added the following advice:

> Insofar as possible, we should try to manage any program of
> expanded bombings in ways which (1) would leave the DRV an oppor-
> tunity to explore negotiations without complete loss of face,
> (2) would not preclude any Soviet pressures on Hanoi to keep the
> war from expanding, and (3) would not suddenly produce extreme
> world pressures against us. In this connection, the timing and
> circumstances in which the bombings were extended northward could
> be of critical importance, particularly in light of the fact that
> there have been some indications of differing views between Moscow,
> Peiping, and Hanoi. For example, it would probably be advantageous
> to expand bombings after, not before, some major new VC move
> (e.g., obvious concentration for imminent attack on Da Nang or
> Kontum) <u>and after, not before, any current possibilities of serious
> negotiations have been fully tested.</u> And such bombings should not
> be so regular as to leave no interval for the Communists to make
> concessions with some grace. <u>Indeed, we should keep in mind the
> possibility of a pause at some appropriate time, which could serve
> to test the Communist intentions and to exploit any differences
> on their side.</u> (Emphasis supplied)

One other consideration may have entered into the President's bombing pause calculus at this time. · On April 5, a TROJAN HORSE photography
mission had revealed the first SA-2 SAM site under construction fifteen ·
miles SSE of Hanoi, confirming the long-rumored shipment of Soviet
surface-to-air missiles to North Vietnam. 120/   Moreover, the SAMs ·
were only the most dramatic form of considerably increased quantities
of modern military equipment beginning to be furnished to the DRV by
the Soviet Union. The Soviet Union was now in the process of becoming
visibly committed to assisting North Vietnam in resisting U.S. attacks
on its territory, and a more direct confrontation of US and USSR military
force was rapidly approaching. Indeed, the Joint Chiefs had indicated,
on April 14, their desire to obtain approval for air strikes against the
· sites on short notice as they become operational, had estimated, on
May 6, that the first site construction could be completed by May 15,
and had instructed CINCPAC to commence planning to conduct air strikes
against that site. 121/   A decision involving a major Soviet "flashpoint",
therefore, would soon have to be faced, and the President may well have
wished to provide a prior opportunity for a quiet Hanoi backdown, before
proceeding with more forceful military activity. ·

B. Setting the Stage .   ·   ·   .

On the evening of May 10 the President sent a personal **FLASH**
message to Ambassador Taylor, 122/ informing him that he (the President)
had decided to call a brief halt to air attacks in the North and instructing him to obtain Premier Quat's agreement to the plan. The text of the
message follows:

> .   I have learned from Bob McNamara that nearly all ROLLING
> THUNDER operations for this week can be completed by Wednesday
> noon, Washington time. This fact and the days of Buddha's
> birthday seem to me to provide an excellent opportunity for a
> pause in air attacks which might go into next week and which I
> could use to good effect with world opinion.   ·
>
> My plan is not to announce this brief pause but simply to
> call it privately to the attention of Moscow and Hanoi as soon
> as possible and tell them that we shall be watching closely to
> see whether they respond in any way. My current plan is to
> report publicly after the pause ends on what we have done.
>
> .   Could you see Quat right away on Tuesday and see if you
> can persuade him to concur in this plan. I would like to ·
> associate him with me in this decision if possible, but I
> would accept a simple concurrence or even willingness not to
> oppose my decision. In general, I think it important that he ·
> and I should act together in such matters, but I have no desire
> to embarrass him if it is politically difficult for him to join
> actively in a pause over Buddha's birthday.   ·

We have noted your /recent cables/ but do not yet have
your appreciation of the political effect in Saigon of acting
around Buddha's birthday. From my point of view it is a
great advantage to use Buddha's birthday to mask the first
days of the pause here, if it is at all possible in political
terms for Quat. I assume we could undertake to enlist the
Archbishop and the Nuncio in calming the Catholics. [7]

You should understand that my purpose in this plan is to
begin to clear a path either toward restoration of peace or
toward increased military action, depending upon the reaction
of the Communists. We have amply demonstrated our determination and our commitment in the last two months, and I now
wish to gain some flexibility.

I know that this is a hard assignment on short notice, but
there is no one who can bring it off better.

I have kept this plan in the tightest possible circle here
and wish you to inform no one but Alexis Johnson. After I have
your report of Quat's reaction I will make a final decision and
it will be communicated promptly to senior officers concerned.

Ambassador Taylor promptly relayed the President's plan to Quat,
whose major objection was to the notion of linking the pause in any way
with Buddha's birthday. Taylor reported this objection to Washington
123/ and received the following additional instructions from the
Department in return. 124/

We have decided here to go ahead commencing on Thursday
/May 13/ for period of approximately 5 - 7 days. Orders through
military channels will place stand-down on basis "in order to
observe reaction of DRV rail and road transportation systems"
and will order increase in photo recce of DRV and bombing within
SVN. You should tell Westmoreland true basis for his personal
use only so that you and he and Alex Johnson remain the only
three Americans in Saigon aboard. We have informed Dobrynin
tonight and are instructing Kohler to convey message to Hanoi
through DRV Ambassador in Moscow. I will also be telling
British and Canadian Foreign Ministers personally tomorrow and
we will convey message to Menzies through Embassy here. However, each of these being informed only at highest levels and
their Saigon representatives will not repeat not be witting.

You should take following actions:

1. Inform Quat we are going ahead. You should not specify
period but let us know if he raises question or still insists
on as short a period as 4 - 5 days. Tell him we will definitely

refrain at all times from associating action with Buddha's birthday and that our initial plan will be to refer all press queries to Washington and to hold as long as possible simply to operational factors as explanation. You should raise with him question of what he will tell generals urging in strongest terms that he tell them only what we are saying through military channel and preferably delay even this until question arises. If Quat raises question of what we are saying to Communist side, you will have copies tonight's talk with Dobrynin and instructions to Kohler by septels and may draw generally on these for his personal use only.

2. To deal with any possibility adverse Catholic reaction you should inform Archbishop and/or Nuncio very privately that any variation in actions in forthcoming period will be USG decisions not related in any way to Buddha's birthday or any appeal or issue connected with it. You may of course also reiterate that any such variations have no effect whatever on our determination as clearly shown in recent months. We leave timing this approach to you but believe it should be done earliest before any speculation arises.

3. At appropriate time you should instruct Zorthian to report simply that no operations other than reconnaissance were conducted on each day and to refer press queries, preferably by indirection, to Washington.

A few hours later, Secretary McNamara, with the concurrence of Secretary Rusk and McGeorge Bundy, sent the following FLASH joint State/Defense message through military channels to Ambassador Taylor, CINCPAC and COMUSMACV: 125/

In order to observe reaction of DRV rail and road transportation systems, bombing (including armed recce and other strike operations) of targets within DRV will cease for several days effective 2400 12 May Saigon time. CINCPAC should issue the necessary instructions to US forces and Ambassador should seek to obtain compliance of VNAF.

During the period in which bombing operations are suspended, photo and eyeball reconnaissance flights over DRV, in so far as they can be carried out without flak suppression escorts and within currently approved rules relating to altitudes and latitudes, will be increased to the level required to permit a thorough study of lines of communication. The bombing sorties which would have been directed against the DRV during this period, to the extent practical, will be targeted against appropriate targets in South Vietnam.

ROLLING THUNDER 15 [8] as outlined in JCS 1736 has been approved. It is to be executed upon receipt of appropriate execution orders.

Press guidance for the period during which bombing operations are suspended will be furnished in a separate message.

Acting on these instructions, Taylor saw Quat in Saigon on the morning of May 12, and reported back as follows: 126/

Along with Alex Johnson, I called this morning to convey to Quat the information contained in Department's instructions. I told him that his views with regard to linking the pause with Buddha's birthday had been accepted and that this element had been removed from the plan. I explained that the pause begins tomorrow (Saigon time) and will continue for several days. As he did not raise any question with regard to the precise duration, I did not elaborate. He liked the military justification for the pause as explained in REFTEL and undertook to remain within this language in dealing with his generals. I assured him that General Westmoreland would do the same in his military contacts.

We explained to Quat how the message was being conveyed to the USSR and Hanoi. He had no comment except to express doubt that any detectable change in DRV conduct will take place during the suspension of attacks.

As for comment to the press, he repeated his intention to ward off queries by references to "Operational Requirements."

While securing Quat's support has been somewhat easier than I had anticipated, I am sure that he and his colleagues will become uneasy very quickly if this pause runs beyond the "four to five days" which Quat has indicated to be acceptable from his point of view. I would hope that our purposes can have been fulfilled within the five day period.

With regard to paragraph 2 /of Department's instructions/, Johnson and I feel that it is unnecessary and probably undesirable to approach Archbishop Binh or the Nuncio at this time. We will watch closely the local reaction to the suspension and convey the message to the Catholic leadership, if necessary, at a timely moment.

Much additional attention was lavished by Washington upon maintaining near-absolute secrecy, preserving a plausible front vis-a-vis the press, and other aspects of stage management. On May 12, the operation was given the codeword MAYFLOWER,[9] and all communications on it were thenceforth to be slugged with that indicator. Besides Taylor and Johnson, the only American Ambassadors informed of the political purpose of MAYFLOWER were William Sullivan in Vientiane, Foy Kohler in Moscow, and Winthrop Brown in Seoul -- the latter only for the purpose of informing President Park Chung Hee who was about to embark on a state visit to Washington and who, the Department felt, should be forewarned so that he might more effectively fend off press probings.

On the evening of May 11, Secretary Rusk made two moves designed to inform "the other side" of the fact that a bombing halt was being called and of its political purpose:

1. He sent a cable 127/ to Foy Kohler in Moscow, instructing him to make urgent contact with the DRV Ambassador in Moscow to convey a carefully prepared message to him, as quoted below. The cable set forth the instructions and rationale as follows:

...We are using you as channel to avoid using Soviets as intermediaries and also to insure that message is accurately and directly delivered. We leave appropriate method of arranging contact to you and are not concerned if Soviets should become aware you are making such contact. You should of course make maximum effort avoid any attention by any third party.

Message you should deliver should be oral but confirmed by written piece of paper which you should hand to Ambassador with request he deliver message to Hanoi. Message is as follows:

BEGIN TEXT. The highest authority in this Government has asked me to inform Hanoi that there will be no air attacks on North Viet-Nam for a period beginning at noon, Washington time, Wednesday, May 12, and running into next week.

In this decision the United States Government has taken account of repeated suggestions from various quarters, including public statements by Hanoi representatives, that there can be no progress toward peace while there are air attacks on North Viet-Nam. The United States Government remains convinced that the underlying cause of trouble in Southeast Asia is armed action against the people and Government of South Vietnam by forces whose actions can be decisively affected from North Vietnam. The United States will be very watchful to see whether in this period of pause there are significant reductions in such armed actions by such forces. (The United States must emphasize that the road toward the end of armed attacks against the people and Government of Vietnam is the only road which will permit the Government of Vietnam (and the Government of the United States) to bring a permanent end to their attacks on North Vietnam.)...

In taking this action the United States is well aware of the risk that a temporary suspension of these air attacks may be misunderstood as an indication of weakness, and it is therefore necessary for me to point out that if this pause should be misunderstood in this fashion, by any party, it would be necessary to demonstrate more clearly than ever, after the pause ended, that the United States is determined not to accept aggression without reply in Vietnam. Moreover, the United States must point out that the decision to end air attacks for this limited trial period is one which it must be free to reverse if at any time in the coming days there should be actions by the other side in Vietnam which required immediate reply.

But my Government is very hopeful that there will be no such misunderstanding and that this first pause in the air attacks may meet with a response which will permit further and more extended suspension of this form of military action in the expectation of equally constructive actions by the other side in the future. END TEXT.

2. He summoned Soviet Ambassador Anatol Dobrynin to his office in the State Department and made virtually the same oral statement to him, confirmed by a parallel written version handed to him. Rusk, that same evening described the meeting to Foy Kohler in a second cable, 128/ sent immediately after the message quoted above:

I explained we were not indicating any precise number of days, that we retained freedom of action, and that we would convey similar message to Hanoi. I also said we would make no announcement although we expected press pressures, and made clear our action related only to strikes of any sort and not to continued reconnaissance. (Paper itself makes clear action confined to DRV and does not include Laos or SVN.)

I also said we did not know what to expect but that Hanoi knows what it is doing and can find a way to make its response clear.

Dobrynin noted we were merely informing Soviets and was clearly relieved we not asking them to act as intermediary. Asked about my trip to Vienna and indicated there might be further conversations there Saturday with Gromyko. Asked basically whether action represented any change in fundamental US position.

I replied that it did not and that this should be no surprise.

I reviewed recent indications that Cambodia conference [10] blocked by Peiping despite favorable mention in DRV-Moscow communique and that three-party talks on Laos [11] likewise in

abeyance apparently following Peiping and perhaps Hanoi pressure.
President on April 7 had tried open up discourse but thus far
channels blocked. If attacks on DRV were part of problem, Communist response to present action might open up channels.

Dobrynin said he thought we would get some answer but could
not predict what.

I underscored importance action not be misunderstood in
Hanoi. Hanoi appears to have impression they may succeed, but
US will not get tired or be affected by very small domestic
opposition or by international pressures, Hanoi cannot rely on
Saigon instability. They may have wrong ideas on these points
and important they not misunderstand our action.

Dobrynin responded he saw no danger of misunderstanding but
problem was to find way.

Parallel with the Secretary's diplomatic moves, the President made
a major public address on the first day of the bombing pause, in which
he made no reference to the pause, but in which he urged Hanoi to consider
a "political solution."[12] The speech, embracing the theme of the "three
faces of war" (1. armed conflict, 2. diplomacy and politics, and 3. human
need) contained the following passage:

The second face of war in Viet-Nam is the quest for a
political solution - the face of diplomacy and politics - of
the ambitions and the interests of other nations. We know,
as our adversaries should also know, that there is no purely
military solution in sight for either side. We are ready for
unconditional discussions. Most of the non-Communist nations
of the world favor such unconditional discussions. And it
would clearly be in the interest of North Vietnam to now come
to the conference table. For them the continuation of war,
without talks, means only damage without conquest. Communist
China apparently desires the war to continue whatever the cost
to their allies. Their target is not merely South Viet-Nam;
it is Asia. Their objective is not the fulfillment of Vietnamese nationalism; it is to erode and to discredit America's
ability to help prevent Chinese domination over all of Asia.

In this domination they will never succeed. 129/

C. Transmitting the Messages

Foy Kohler in Moscow, upon receiving the Secretary's instructions,
directed his Deputy Chief of Mission to telephone the North Vietnamese
Embassy on the morning of May 12 to request an urgent appointment for
Ambassador Kohler with the North Vietnamese Ambassador. The latter, however,

declined to receive the American Ambassador "in view of the absence of diplomatic relations between our two countries," and suggested instead that the "important, high level private message" from the US Government which Ambassador Kohler wished to communicate to the NVN Ambassador be sent to the Soviet Government "in its capacity as Co-Chairman of the Geneva Conference."

Kohler felt it would not be productive to press the NVN embassy further, and cabled the Department for instructions as to which of two alternatives he should pursue: "(1) Transmit message by letter via messenger to NVN ambassador; or (2) seek appointment with Acting Foreign Minister Kuznetsov to convey message."130/

The Department's reply was as follows:

Believe you should pursue both alternatives urgently, explaining to Kuznetsov (who will by now have heard from Dobrynin) that you recognize reluctance of Soviets to act as intermediary and are asking solely that Soviets transmit message to DRV Ambassador in accordance with DRV suggestion. 131/

Kohler acted promptly on both alternatives. He transmitted the "oral" communication to the DRV Ambassador under cover of a letter signed by Kohler, which read as follows:

In accordance with the suggestion made by a member of your staff today, I am attempting to reach the Acting Foreign Minister tonight.

Since this may not be possible and because of its importance, I enclose the message I had hoped to be able to convey to you personally earlier today.

However, though hand-delivered by an American embassy employee to a DRV employee, the communication was returned the following morning in a plain envelope addressed simply Embassy of US of A. 132/

At the same time, Kohler sought an urgent appointment with Acting Foreign Minister Kuznetsov (Gromyko being out of town) but Kuznetsov was not available and Kohler was able to see only Deputy Foreign Minister Firyubin. The latter, after some temporizing, flatly refused his government's services as an intermediary and lectured Kohler at length upon the US misconception of the real nature of the conflict in Vietnam. Kohler's account of the conversation follows: 133/

I informed Firyubin that as he must know from report of Dobrynin's conversation with Secretary, US Government has made decision which we hoped would be both understood and not misunderstood. I had been informed by several high

117   TOP SECRET Sensitive

Soviet sources that decision we had taken was precisely what
was called for but none had been in position to predict reaction. Our purpose in reaching this significant decision
was to attempt to ascertain if a way could be found to peaceful solution of current crisis in Southeast Asia. We had
hoped we would be able to deliver oral communication conveying this decision to DRV authorities and I had attempted to
do so today through DRV Ambassador. Unfortunately Ambassador
let it be known that he did not wish to receive me personally
and when his embassy was informed that the message I sought
to deliver was of extreme importance, it was suggested that
we transmit the message through the Soviet Government in its
capacity as Geneva Co-Chairman. It was because of these circumstances that I had found it necessary to disturb
Mr. Firyubin tonight. I pointed out that although DRV
Ambassador had refused to receive me, embassy had succeeded
in delivering a copy of oral communication to employee of
DRV embassy earlier this evening (2015 Local) who agreed to
bring it to attention of Ambassador (communication as set
forth in DEPTEL 3103 then translated in full for Firyubin
with sole interruption being Firyubin's inquiry if cessation
attacks applied only to those from air - which I confirmed.)
After receiving confirmation from me that communication was
of oral nature, Firyubin said he viewed communication as based
on old erroneous conception on which US has proceeded, a conception which precludes US recognizing that the South Vietnamese people are fighting for their freedom and are struggling
against aggression and control by Saigon puppets. Furthermore
it indicated to Firyubin that we continued to view the picture
incorrectly when we referred again to the struggle in South
Vietnam as being organized and directed by the DRV. The
absurdity of this view, he said, is obvious and naturally the
Soviet Government cannot agree with it as it has made clear
in numerous statements. Firyubin could only view the communication as repetition of the threat against the DRV -- now a
threat of renewed and expanded aggression. This was the only
way he could interpret the reference to the risk that a suspension of attacks involved. Obviously we are suffering from
a gross misunderstanding if we think that such aggression will
go unpunished, without response. The only constructive approach
to a peaceful settlement of the situation in South Vietnam was
to end the aggression, recall troops from South Vietnam and give
the Vietnamese people the right to choose their own form of
Government -- a choice which can be made freely only if the
so-called specialists should be withdrawn and their opportunity
of exercising influence on the Vietnamese thus removed. Firyubin
said that he well acquainted with the countries and peoples of
Southeast Asia; he therefore was aware and could understand the
feelings caused by our actions there as well as the reaction in
many other parts of the world.

I told Firyubin I had asked to see him to put a very simple question to him. Does the Soviet Government agree to transmit the oral communication to the DRV? I said this was the whole purpose of my visit.

Firyubin said the DRV embassy had not put such a request to the Soviet Government. I must agree that for Soviets to act as intermediary between us and DRV is very unusual. Naturally he would report my request to his Government and if the DRV should request this service he would not exclude the possibility of transmitting the communication to the DRV Government. Meanwhile he would be interested in knowing just how the DRV embassy had responded to our approach. .

I again described for Firyubin our efforts to deliver the message to the DRV through its embassy in Moscow and told him that the end result was a suggestion by the embassy that we transmit the message through the Soviet Government in its capacity as Geneva Co-Chairman. Firyubin repeated his promise to report my request to his Government and to inform me of the results.

While the conversation continued in this vein, Firyubin had passed a note to a Foreign Office assistant, Kornienko, who attended him, and the latter left the room. After some time, Kornienko reappeared and handed a note to Firyubin, which the latter read carefully. After reading the note, Firyubin said flatly that the Soviet Government would not transmit the U.S. Government's message to the DRV, that the DRV embassy had not requested this service and that it was the U.S. responsibility to find a convenient way of passing the message. Kohler's account continues:

I said I wished to understand him correctly. Was he rejecting my request to transmit the communication to the DRV?

He said this was a correct understanding of the Soviet Government position. We must ourselves find the way.

I said that what I was seeking was the cooperation of the Soviet Government and Firyubin's remarks indicated clearly that the Soviet Government was refusing this. Firyubin said, "I am not a postman" and again said we could find our own ways of transmitting messages.

I pointed out to Firyubin that the cooperation I had requested is a well-known and not unprecedented process in international diplomacy. I had great difficulty in reconciling Soviet Government refusal to cooperate with its declaration in support of peaceful settlement of disputed questions.

Kornienko chimed in that he had recalled statement by both the President and Secretary of State on several occasions that the U.S. Government has channels for transmitting messages direct to Hanoi. On this the conversation ended but it should be noted that Firyubin made no effort to return to me the text of the oral communication which I had handed him at the outset of the conversation.

After further reflection on his meeting with Firyubin, Kohler sent a follow-on message to Washington that afternoon, 134/ in which he sought to present the Soviet position with some sympathy and to promote an understanding of the Soviet rebuff in the light of the "rather strenuous nature" of the document we were asking them to transmit. Kohler's comments were as follows:

> I came away from my meeting with Firyubin last night with mixed feelings. On the one hand, I was annoyed at the apparent Soviet rebuff of an effort to take heat out of admittedly dangerous situation in SEA and impatient with flimsy rationale for Soviet refusal offered by Firyubin. On the other hand, I could understand, if not sympathize with, Soviet sensitivity, given Chicom eagerness to adduce proof of their charges of collusion against Soviets and, frankly, given rather strenuous nature of document they were being asked to transmit to DRV.

> Implicit in latter view, of course, is assumption that Soviets in fact want bombing to stop, are genuinely concerned at possibilities escalation, and are interested in working out some sort of modus vivendi which would take heat out of situation while not undercutting their own position in Commie world as loyal socialist ally. We cannot be sure that this is way Soviets view situation, and it entirely possible they so confident our ultimate defeat in Vietnam that no gesture on our part would meet with encouraging response. Believe at this point, however, we lose nothing assuming Soviets have not completely forgotten lesson Cuba and there is some flexibility in Soviet position which we should seek to exploit.[13]

> I would hope, therefore, we would not regard Firyubin's reaction last night as evidence conscious hardening of Soviet attitude. It may simply be reflection of bind Soviets find themselves in at moment. Meanwhile, we can feel sure message is already in DRV hands -- copies now available thru Dobrynin, Firyubin, and DRV embassy here -- and I would suggest we go through with original plan and be on alert, both here and on the scene for any signs reaction from other side. Seen from here, we would lose nothing by doing so; and we gain at least with our friends and the unaligned.

By this time (1:00 p.m. March 13, Moscow time), though Kohler was not aware of it, the bombing pause had already been in effect for seventeen hours. It had gone into effect as planned at 2400 on March 12,[14] Saigon time, and the Department so informed Kohler. The Department also decided, in spite of Kohler's confidence that the U.S. "oral" communication had reached Hanoi, to make doubly sure by asking the U.K. Government to instruct its Consul in Hanoi to transmit the same message, in writing, to his normal contact in the DRV. Informed by the Department that this step was about to be taken, Kohler expressed his dissatisfaction with the character and tone of the communication by recommending that, in any resubmission, the message be shortened and softened:

> ...I would recommend we shorten and revise wording of "oral" communication to DRV if we plan resubmit through British Consul Hanoi. If cast is present form, I think we are simply inviting rebuff, and exercise-Hanoi would prove as fruitless as our efforts in Moscow. Something along lines following would get essential message across:
>
> BEGIN TEXT. The highest authority in this Government has asked me to inform Hanoi that there will be no air attacks on North Vietnam for a period beginning at noon, Washington time, Wednesday, May 12 and running into next week.
>
> In this decision the United States Government has taken account of repeated suggestions from various quarters, including public statements by Hanoi representatives, that there can be no progress toward peace while there are air attacks on North Vietnam.
>
> The United States Government expects that in consequence of this action the DRV will show similar restraint. If this should not prove to be the case, then the United States Government will feel compelled to take such measures as it feels are necessary to deal with the situation in Vietnam. END TEXT. 135/

Kohler's recommendation was not accepted, and the message was transmitted to the DRV by the British Consul in Hanoi in its original form. As in the Moscow case, the message was shortly thereafter returned to the sender, ostensibly unopened.

As a footnote to the "unopened letter" episodes, it may be worth noting that Canadian ICC Commissioner Blair Seaborn, on an early-June visit to Hanoi, was approached by the Czech Ambassador to the DRV, who recounted to him the story of Kohler's unsuccessful effort to deliver the message to the DRV Ambassador in Moscow, with the message having been returned ostensibly unopened. The Czech Ambassador said "everybody" in Hanoi knew the story. 136/

D. Awaiting a Response

While the Administration expected little in the way of a positive Hanoi response, a watchful eye was kept for any signals or actions
that might suggest North Vietnamese or Soviet receptivity to any further
diplomatic explorations. Such signals as were received, however, were
entirely negative. On May 15 a Hanoi English language broadcast noted
Western news reports of the bombing cessation, terming them "a worn out
trick of deceit and threat..." On the same day, in a conversation with
British Foreign Secretary Michael Stewart in Vienna, Soviet Foreign
Minister Andrei Gromyko indicated the USSR's disinclination to participate in any negotiations on Indochina.

In the meantime, in Saigon, the U.S. Mission was hard at work
trying to clarify its own thinking -- and that of Washington -- on the
persuasive, or rather coercive, possibilities of bombing pauses. In
particular, the Mission was hoping to link the intensity of US bombing
after the resumption closely to the level of VC activity during the
pause. The purpose would be to make it clear to Hanoi that what we were
trying to accomplish with our bombing was to get the DRV to cease directing and supporting the VC and to get VC units to cease their military
activities in the South. In this approach, a downward trend in VC
activities would be "rewarded" in a similar manner by decreasing US
bombing. Thus it was hoped that, during the bombing pause, the DRV
would offer the first step in a series of events which might ultimately
"lead to the termination of hostilities on satisfactory /i.e., U.S./
terms, without engaging in formal negotiations."

Ambassador Taylor described this approach to Washington in a
lengthy cable 137/ concurred in by Deputy Ambassador Johnson and General
Westmoreland. The Ambassador recognized that there were one or two minor
pitfalls in the scheme, but seemed undaunted in his confidence that US
bombing could be designed to have powerful coercive effects. Taylor
admitted that:

Any success in carrying out such a scenario /would/ obviously
depend on a considerable amount of cooperation from the DRV side
based on a conviction arising from self-interest that the DRV
must accept a settlement which excludes the conquest of SVN by
NVN. There is little likelihood that the Hanoi leaders are yet
ready to reach such a conclusion, but a rigorous application of
air attacks at a tempo related to Hanoi/VC activities accompanied by pressure on the ground to compel the VC to engage in
incidents or retreat appears to us to have possibilities. Conceivably, these ground operations might eventually result in
herding VC units into "safe havens"...Whatever its other weaknesses, such a program would eliminate in large measure the
danger which we may now be facing of equating our bombing activity to VC initiated incidents, and of seeming to suggest that
we will stop bombing for good if the VC will simply lie low.

A quite different approach to a settlement was proposed in a rather puzzling informal contact between Pierre Salinger and two somewhat shadowy Soviet officials in Moscow. On the evening of May 11 (i.e., one full day prior to the inauguration of the bombing pause) Salinger, who was in Moscow at the time on private movie production business, was invited to dinner by Mikhail Sagatelyan, whom Salinger had known in Washington during the Kennedy years as the TASS Bureau Chief, and who was at this time assigned to TASS headquarters in Moscow. Salinger reported his conversation to Ambassador Kohler who related it to Secretary Rusk in a cable 138/ as follows:

> Sagatelyan probed Salinger hard as to whether he was on some kind of covert mission and seemed unconvinced despite latter's reiterated denials. In any case, Sagetelyan, protesting he was speaking personally, talked at length about Viet-Nam. He wanted Salinger's opinion on hypothetical formula for solution approximately on following lines:
>
> 1. US would announce publicly temporary suspension of bombing DRV;
>
> 2. DRV or USSR or both would make statement hailing suspension as step toward reasonable solution;
>
> 3. Soviet Union would intercede with Viet Cong to curtail military activities;
>
> 4. De facto cease fire would thus be accomplished.
>
> 5. Conference would be called on related subject (not specifically Viet-Nam). Viet Cong would not be participant but have some kind of observer or corridor status (this followed Salinger's expression of opinion US Government would never accept Viet Cong as participant in any conference).
>
> 6. New agreement would be worked out on Viet-Nam providing for broader-based SVN Government not including direct Viet Cong participation but including elements friendly to Viet Cong.

In a follow-up dinner conversation between Salinger and Sagatelyan two nights later, in which a Foreign Office representative, identified only as "Vassily Sergeyevich" also participated, the Soviet interlocutors generally confirmed the proposal quoted above, modifying points three and four by suggesting that an actual cease fire could take place only after initiation of negotiations and that a cease fire would in fact be the first item on the agenda of any negotiations. 139/ Additional items of interest were reported by Kohler as follows:

Soviet interlocutors talked at length about President
Kennedy's forebearance post-Cuba period and broadly implied
that Soviets now interested in reciprocating such forebearance. It was clear from their remarks that Soviets assume
we would welcome some avenue of withdrawal so long as this
would not involve loss of American prestige.

Soviets informed Salinger that Soviet Government had
received a "Rusk proposal" with regard Vietnam but would not
answer proposal or act on it in any way until Soviet Government had some idea as to how current exercise with Salinger
would turn out...

As to mechanics of carrying on exercise, Sagatelyan
suggested Salinger might convey proposal to US Government
through embassy Paris and he himself would fly immediately
Paris in order receive from Salinger there any official
reaction. Alternatively, if Salinger wished to proceed
direct Washington, contact could be designated there,
probably either Zinchuk (Soviet embassy counselor) or
Vadvichenko (TASS Washington Bureau).

Throughout conversation Soviets made clear to Salinger
that because of sensitive Soviet position any progress
toward political settlement Vietnam problem must be initiated
and carried through, at least in preliminary stages, on basis
unofficial contacts, clear implication being if leak should
occur or if scheme should go awry, Soviet Government would
be in position disavow whole affair. At same time, it was
clear from remarks as well as presence of Foreign Office
representative that proposal by Sagatelyan had official
backing.

Salinger had one further contact with Sagatelyan and Vassily the
following day, where it became apparent that the Soviet officials'
interest in the proposal had waned. By the time Salinger had returned
to Washington and saw Ambassador Thompson at the State Department on
May 18, the Soviet disinterest in any role for themselves during the
current bombing pause had been made clear through other channels, and
Salinger's contacts were not further pursued.

Of these other channels, the most important (and also the most
casual) was a brief Kaffeeklatsch between Secretary Rusk and Foreign
Minister Gromyko at the Austrian Chancellor's residence in Vienna on
May 15. The proceedings are described in a Rusk cable 140/ to
Undersecretary Ball as follows:

Have just returned from Chancellor's lunch for visiting
dignitaries. After lunch Gromyko and I and our wives were
at a small table for coffee. I commented to Gromyko that we

were in something of a dilemma about Southeast Asia. We felt
there might be some value in a serious exchange of views
between our two Governments but that we did not know whether
they themselves wished to discuss it.

He commented with considerable seriousness that the Soviets
will not negotiate about Viet-Nam. He said there were other
parties involved in that situation and that the United States
would have to find ways of establishing contact with them, and
he specifically mentioned the DRV. He said they will continue
to support North Viet-Nam and will do so "decisively." He then
made reference to a fellow socialist country under attack.

I interrupted to point out that the problem was not that a
socialist country was subject to attack but that a socialist
country was attacking someone else. I said that American
military forces are in South Vietnam solely because North Vietnam has been sending large numbers of men and arms into the
South.

He denied these facts in the usual ritual fashion but added
that in any event it was not up to the United States to be the
judge between Vietnamese. I reminded him that he must know by
now that a North Korean attack against South Koreans would not
be accepted merely because both were Korean. He merely commented that there were important differences between those two
situations.

He referred to Dobrynin's talk with me and said that the
temporary suspension of bombing was "insulting." I said I
could not understand this in view of the fact that Hanoi,
Peiping and Moscow have all talked about the impossibility of
discussions while bombing was going on.

At this point Chancellor Klaus joined the table to express
great happiness that Gromyko and I were sitting together.
Neither one of us dispelled his illusion.

I do not know whether Gromyko will pursue the matter
further when the four foreign ministers meet briefly with
Quaison-Sackey this afternoon or when we all assemble for
the opera tonight.

Thompson and I both have the impression that Gromyko's
attitude clearly means that the Salinger talk was of little
substance and that we should now merely consider what kind
of signal we wish to get back by way of Salinger as a part of
the closing out process.

125

I do not believe that we should assume from Gromyko's
remarks that we ourselves should not put to Moscow our own
most serious views of the situation, whether they are willing to discuss them or not. It is quite clear, however,
that Gromyko wanted me to believe that they are not prepared
to work toward a settlement in Hanoi and Peiping and that,
indeed, unless we abandon our effort in South Viet-Nam there
will be very serious consequences ahead.

E. Resuming the Bombing

Having thus been unmistakably rebuffed by Moscow, Hanoi, and
Peking, the President determined on the evening of May 16 that the bombing raids should be resumed, beginning on the morning of May 18 Saigon
time. In addition to the ROLLING THUNDER XV execute message sent by
the JCS to CINCPAC on the 16th, Secretary Rusk sent messages of a political nature to Saigon, London, and Ottawa on May 17, so that the action
could be cleared with Premier Quat (which Taylor promptly accomplished),
and so that the foreign ministers of the Commonwealth countries would
be informed beforehand. 141/

You should see Fon Min immediately to inform that beginning Tuesday morning, Saigon time, bombing of North
Viet-Nam will be resumed by US and South Vietnamese forces,
marking the end of a five-day suspension.

You should convey message from me that we regret that
the reception of the other side to the idea of a pause was
not merely negative but hostile. Gromyko told Rusk that
our message to Dobrynin on subject was "insulting."
Nevertheless we do not exclude possibility of other such
attempts in future.

There will be no public announcement of the resumption
of bombing. When press questions are asked, it will be
pointed out that there have been and may again be periods
when no bombing will take place in response to operational
factors and that we do not discuss these operational
questions.

Ambassador Kohler, upon receiving word of the resumption, suggested
that the US might inform the NATO Council and the 17 non-aligned nations
of our actions, in advance of any resumption, to underline the seriousness of the President's response to the Unaligned Appeal. The Department,
however, responded negatively to Kohler's suggestion: 142/

There will be no official public statement from here concerning suspension or resumption. Decision at highest levels
is to avoid any discussion Project MAYFLOWER, which now

concluded, outside of restricted circle designated when Project begun. Despite disappointing response, we wish to keep open channel with Soviets on this subject and we hope eventually with DRV via Soviets. We feel that use of this channel another time might be precluded if we appear to have carried through Project MAYFLOWER solely for credit it might earn us with third parties and public opinion in general. Therefore we would not now wish inform NATO Council and 17 Non-aligned countries.

Only British, Canadians, Australians, UN Secretary General and Korean President Park (here on state visit) were in fact informed in advance of resumption bombing and also of negative outcome of soundings of other side.

In addition to this limited circle of allied intimates, a larger circle of friendly governments was provided with Ambassadorial briefings on the bombing pause after the resumption. An instruction to this effect went out to American ambassadors in New Delhi, Tokyo, Bangkok, Vientiane, Manila, Wellington, and Paris: 143/

You should take first opportunity see Pri. Minister, Fon Min, or other appropriate high level official to inform him that the U.S. and South Vietnamese Governments suspended bombing against North Viet-Nam for a period of five days which ended on May 18. The initiation of this pause in bombing was accompanied by an approach by us to the Governments of the Soviet Union and North Viet-Nam which took note of repeated calls from that side for cessation of bombing and their statements that discussions could not take place while bombing continued. Unfortunately the reception of our approach was not merely negative but hostile...In view of the complete absence of any constructive response, we have decided the bombing must be resumed. Nevertheless we do not exclude possibility of other such attempts in the future.

You should add that the record of the past several weeks is discouraging in that Communists and particularly Peking appear intent on rejecting every effort from whatever quarter to open up contacts and conversations which might lead to a resolution of the Viet-Nam situation. The rejection of President Johnson's April 7 proposals for unconditional discussions, of the appeal of the Seventeen Non-aligned countries and of President Radhakrishnan's proposal all illustrate the point together with Peking and Hanoi's obvious efforts to obstruct the convening of a conference on Cambodia. We will nevertheless continue to explore all possibilities for constructive discussion, meanwhile maintaining with the Government of South Viet-Nam our joint military efforts to preserve that country's freedom.

On the evening of May 18, the DRV Foreign Ministry issued a statement denouncing the gesture as a "deceitful maneuver designed to pave the way for new U.S. acts of war," and insisted U.S. planes had, since May 12, repeatedly intruded into DRV airspace "for spying, provocative and strafing activities."

Communist China's Foreign Ministry issued a statement May 21 fully endorsing Hanoi's position and denouncing the suspension with characteristic intemperateness.

F. Aftermath

A still somewhat ambiguous diplomatic move was made by Hanoi on May 18, shortly after the bombing had been resumed.

It appears that in Paris, on the morning of May 18, Mai Van Bo, head of the DRV economic delegation there, approached the Asian Direction of the Quai d'Orsay to explain the reasons for the DRV's rejection of the Radhakrishnan proposals (involving a cordon sanitaire by Afro-Asian troops along the 17th parallel). More important, however, Bo explained with text in hand that the Pham Van Dong Four Points, enunciated on April 8, should not be isolated from the declaration that had followed the four points. He then softened the language of that declaration by pointing out that the four points constituted the "best basis" from which to find the "most just" solution, and that recognition of these principles would create favorable conditions for a solution of the problem and would open the possibility of convoking a conference.

When asked if Hanoi recognized that realization of its proposed "principle of withdrawal" of American forces would depend upon the "conclusions of a negotiation," Bo responded "exactly," and indicated that if there were agreement on the "bases," the "ways and means" of application of "principles" would be found and in a peaceful manner; the possibilities were many; a way out (porte de sortie) should be found for the US; "our suggestion humiliates no one."

This happening, which occurred on May 18, was first reported by a Quai official to the US Embassy's Political Counsellor in Paris unofficially on May 19, in a highly glossed version, making it appear that the DRV was clearly responding to the bombing pause by a significant softening of its position on "prior conditions." In the official version that Lucet, the Director of Political Affairs of the French Foreign Office conveyed to the DCM on May 20, however, the continued ambiguity of the DRV position --- as to whether or not recognition of the four points remained a precondition to talks of any sort -- was fully revealed.

This ambiguity was in no sense resolved a few weeks later, when Blair Seaborn raised this question with the DRV Foreign Minister in Hanoi. The U.S. had asked Seaborn in late May to seek an appointment with Pham

Van Dong and on its behalf reiterate the March message and U.S. determination to persist in the defense of South Vietnam, to regret that Hanoi had not responded positively to the various recent initiatives, including the bombing pause, and to state that, nevertheless, the United States remained ready "to consider the possibility of a solution by reciprocal actions on each side." If the Vietnamese brought up Pham Van Dong's four points, Seaborn was authorized to endeavor to establish whether Hanoi insisted that they be accepted as the condition for negotiations. On June 3, Seaborn succeeded in gaining an audience with the DRV Foreign Minister (and concurrent Deputy Premier) Nguygen Duy Trinh, who reluctantly heard him out after stating that the U.S. position was too well known to require restatement. Trinh's reaction to the message was totally negative, and in the exchange preceding its recitation he studiously avoided going beyond the vague statement that Pham Van Dong's four points were the "basis for solution of the Vietnam question."144/

• As there was considerable misunderstanding concerning the Mai Van Bo approach of May 18, and misleading accounts of it were circulating, the State Department informed several U.S. ambassadors (Saigon, Paris, Bonn) of what it considered the true facts in the case. 145/

Facts are that bombing was actually resumed on morning May 18 Saigon time. Subsequently on morning May 18, Paris time, but undoubtedly on antecedent instructions, DRV economic delegate in Paris, Mai Van Bo, approached Quai urgently for appointment. His message was to explain negative Hanoi attitude toward Indian proposal (cessation of hostilities on both sides and Afro-Asian force) but second, and more important, to discuss Pham Van Dong's four points originally stated April 8 and later included in Hanoi statement referring to appeal of 17 Non-aligned nations... Bo repeated four points with slight variations from public statements, apparently softening language by indicating that four points might be "best basis" for settlement and apparently insisting less strongly that their recognition was required as condition to negotiations. During course of conversations, French asked whether withdrawal US forces visualized as prior condition or as resulting from negotiations, and Bo responded that latter was correct.

French passed us this message on May 20 (delaying two days) so that we had in fact resumed well before we heard of it. More important, message still left ambiguity whether recognition of four points remained precondition to talks of any sort. Accordingly, we saw no reason to alter conclusion based on Hanoi propaganda denunciation of pause, plus fact that pace of Hanoi-directed basic actions in South had continued and even increased -- that Hanoi not ready to respond to pause and that we must resume.

Subsequently, Canadian ICC Representative, Seaborn, visited Hanoi commencing May 31. He himself raised same questions with DRV Foreign Minister and response indicated DRV evasive, and in effect negative, apparently taking position recognition four . points, plus some element US withdrawal, were preconditions to any talks.

VI.C.1., XYZ (Mai Van Bo Contacts), May 1965–February 1966

The XYZ contact in Paris is one of the most fascinating and least known of the numerous initiatives discussed in the negotiating volumes. Although it occurred just after the United States had decided to embark upon a full-scale ground war in Vietnam, it appeared for a time to offer solid prospects. It collapsed as abruptly and mysteriously as it had begun, however, for reasons that remain unclear. Of all the contacts, it was the best kept secret. Its existence was not divulged at the time, and the investigative journalists who uncovered most of the other contacts never learned about it. Lyndon Johnson does not even mention it in his memoirs, and the negotiating volumes remain virtually the only available source from which to study it.

The Johnson administration moved to initiate discussions with the North Vietnamese in Paris within days after committing itself to all-out war in Vietnam. Facing once again the possibility of a complete political and military collapse in South Vietnam, the President, after extended internal discussions, decided on July 27 to commit an additional 175,000 U.S. ground troops to Vietnam with the promise of more to come later. The July decision was the closest to a formal decision for war ever taken by the United States in Vietnam. Nevertheless, when an American businessman informed the State Department on July 29 of the possibility for establishing a contact with North Vietnamese diplomat Mai Van Bo in Paris, the administration eagerly seized the opening. Johnson was obviously anxious to pursue any lead in order to counter those critics who accused him of seeking military victory rather than a negotiated settlement. During the discussions on the troop buildup, moreover, Secretary of Defense McNamara and Undersecretary of State George Ball, the latter a leading opponent of escalation, had urged the President to continue to explore the possibility of negotiations to determine if North Vietnam might prefer a peaceful settlement to the prospect of a costly, drawn-out war with the United States.

Unlike many of the other initiatives, the XYZ project was handled with considerable care. The President entrusted it to Ball, who could be counted upon to treat it seriously and pursue it vigorously. The Undersecretary modeled his approach on contacts that had preceded the opening of the 1954 Geneva Conference. He selected for the delicate mission Edmund Gullion, an experienced diplomat who was fluent in French and had served in Vietnam during the early 1950s. By using a private citizen, he hoped to retain maximum flexibility, leaving the government free to disavow the contact if problems developed, while at the same time making clear to North Vietnam that Gullion had the authority to speak for the United States. To ensure maximum secrecy, the contact was revealed only to a handful of top U.S. officials, the code letters X and R were used to designate Gullion and Bo, and communications were handled by "backchannels" and known only to the U.S. ambassador in Paris. The principal purpose of the Gullion mission was to probe into the meaning of Hanoi's private and public statements to determine if there was any room for substantive negotiations. The United States was still determined to negotiate from a position of strength and was unwilling to concede anything on the fundamental issue—the preservation of the South Vietnamese government. The approach devised by Ball was nevertheless more conciliatory in tone and, on the surface at least, more flexible than that taken in earlier initiatives. Gullion was instructed to try to build a basis for negotiations around Pham Van Dong's Four Points without doing anything to compromise the position of South Vietnam.

As the following documents make clear, Gullion and Bo engaged in the most substantive discussions that would take place between 1964 and 1968, and for a time they appeared to be making considerable progress. They more or less agreed that a reconvened Geneva Conference would be an appropriate forum for formal negotiations. There was no mention of stopping the bombing as a precondition to negotiations, and Bo appeared to accept the idea of mutual troop withdrawals. Whether American acceptance of the Four Points remained a precondition to negotiations or would provide the basis for a settlement remained unclear, but Bo at least held out the possibility of full South Vietnamese representation at the conference, seemingly an important concession. U.S. officials were further encouraged by the arrival in Paris of a top-level North Vietnamese delegation, including Le Duc Tho, then virtually an unknown, later to play a prominent role in the final peace settlement.

The contact ended just as it appeared to be on the verge of tangible accomplishments. At a meeting on September 3, Bo took a hard line on the troop withdrawal issue and insisted that the bombing must be ended "unconditionally, immediately, totally, and definitively." Whatever progress had been made seemed to come undone, and Gullion's subsequent efforts to revive the talks were unavailing. Some U.S. officials speculated at the time that American bombing of North Vietnamese dikes and power plants shortly before the September 3 meeting may have so enraged the North Vietnamese that they decided to break off the talks. It seems more likely that the breakdown of the contact reflected North Vietnam's purposes in undertaking it in the first place. Like the United States, it was preparing a major buildup of its own in South Vietnam, and it was willing to negotiate only if it felt it could gain what it wanted by political means. When it became evident that this would not be the case, the North Vietnamese simply broke off the talks.—*Ed.*

SUMMARY and ANALYSIS

1. Ambiguous Beginning

The U.S. contacts with Mai Van Bo, Head of the DRVN Delegation
in Paris, developed in three stages: first, through the French Government; then, through a free-lancing private U.S. citizen; and finally by
means of an authorized but "unofficial" U.S. representative.

The timing of Bo's initial approach to the French and the precise content of his message represent two important and ambiguous points.
With respect to the timing, the French claimed that Bo made a "fairly
pressing approach" to them on the morning of May 18th, just prior to the
resumption of U.S. bombings. In fact, this meeting must have occurred
after the resumption. The earliest that Bo saw the French was probably
9:00 a.m., Paris time. The bombings had resumed at 8:00 a.m., Saigon
time -- in other words, eight hours earlier. There was, then, sufficient
time for Hanoi to cable Bo and tell him not to make the approach. Moreover, it seems clear that the message was probably drafted before the
bombings resumed, with the signal to execute delivery being given after
the resumption.

This technique of delaying response to a bombing pause until
a few hours after the pause ended was repeated in Rangoon on January 31,
after the 37-day suspension.[1] The DRV probably used this gap for two
purposes: propaganda and bargaining. The propaganda value was potentially high -- couldn't the U.S. wait a few more hours before plunging
back to the attack? More importantly, it was a way of cancelling out
the U.S. negotiating blue chip. The DRV would not respond with the
threat of resumption hanging over its head, since this could be read
as a sign of weakness. If it were to enter negotiations, the DRV seemed
bent on doing so only after the threat of bombing resumption had been
minimized (public declaration on cessation?) and only after the U.S.
conveyed a "recognition" of the Four Points.

It was this latter element, the meaning of the Four Points,
that represented the second ambiguity. Since the April 8, 1965 enunciation of the Four Points, the U.S. had been interpreting our acceptance
as a precondition for negotiations. While Pham Van Dong explained their
meaning as the "basis for the soundest political settlement" (underlining
added), the U.S. tended to focus on what followed: "if this basis is
recognized, favorable conditions will be created for the peaceful settlement of the Vietnam problem, and it will be possible to consider the

reconvening of an international conference along the pattern of the
1954 Geneva Conference on Vietnam." Hanoi had done nothing to clarify
this issue. Indeed, when Seaborn, on June 6, 1965, asked Trinh whether
the points were preconditions or ultimate goals, Trinh deliberately
remained vague.

The two slightly contradictory messages conveyed to us by the
French on May 19 (by Asian Director Manac'h) and on May 20 (by Director
of Political Affairs Lucet) did not lift the veil, but they were suggestive. The first message, given in "strict confidence," indicated that
Bo stated that the Four Points "were to be considered not rpt not prior
conditions but rather as working principles for a negotiation which
should, in the DRVN view, represent ultimate goal of settlement in Vietnam." The second message, conveyed officially, stated: "Recognition
these 'principles' would create favorable conditions for solution problem
and would 'open' possibility of convocation conference like Geneva, 1954."
This message also included a bonus from Bo--U.S. troop withdrawal would
depend on the "conclusions of a negotiation." The U.S. did not follow
up this approach to the French, despite an inquiry at the Quai by Bo on
June 14 as to what had happened.[2]

Private enterprise and American ingenuity entered the picture
in July 1965, when Mr. Arkas-Duntov of the Dreyfus Fund applied through
a French journalist friend to see Bo. The first Bo-Duntov meeting took
place on July 16. Bo seemed very forthcoming, making references to self-
determination, delay in the withdrawal of U.S. troops and not making
much of U.S. bombings in the north. Against State Department wishes,
Duntov saw Bo again on August 5. In response to a question, Bo said he
would be prepared to receive a U.S. official if he makes clear the U.S.
acceptance of the Four Points.

At this point, the USG moved in by dispatching Edmund Gullion,
former U.S. DCM in Saigon but now a private citizen, to contact Bo.
Bo (R) and Gullion (X) had four meetings: August 6, 15, 18, and September 3. Bo did not show up for an arranged fifth meeting, scheduled for
September 7. Y, another ex-FSO, saw Bo only once and nothing was said,[3]
and Z never existed. It is obvious that "XYZ" should be renamed "X".

The talks between X and R represent the most serious mutual
effort to resolve matters of substance between the U.S. and the DRV
before and since.

It is striking that the first flirtations, from which the contact
developed, were Bo's approaches to the Quai in May and June of 1965. This
is just the time at which Seaborn returned from Hanoi with the conclusion
that the "DRV is not now interested in any negotiations." Seaborn was turned
off just as Bo apparently began an effort to awaken U.S. interest more
directly in Paris. The Russians, who had tried to foster negotiations about
Vietnam through a conference on Cambodia and in other ways, also expressed
their unwillingness to try further at about this time.

2. X's Guidance -- Flexibility and Pressures

The U.S. was sending X with the intention of seeking peace from a position of U.S. strength. X was to show a desire for ending the conflict along lines "compatible with the Four Points, but he was also to say that the prolongation of the war" is bound to lead to progressively larger U.S. pressures and long-term China control of North Vietnam. X was to convey that pressures in the U.S. to widen the war were growing and that "it would be increasingly harder to exercise restraint."

X took this guidance seriously. At the end of the second meeting when R refused to accept X's formulation of a statement announcing the reconvening of the Geneva Conference, X threatened to call off all future contacts. It was R who demurred and urged the third meeting -- as he had taken the initiative in setting up the second. Except for the last meeting when R grew heated about recent U.S. escalations,[4] R was serious and responsive. Throughout and even at this last meeting, there were no ideological harangues.

3. Convening a Conference

The most basic point to emerge from the X and R contacts with respect to convening a conference was made by R at the August 6 meeting. R said that there was a difference between "discussions" and "settlement." "There could not be settlement without recognition of the principles within the 4 Points." R did not indicate what "recognition" meant. Later, in an August 31 speech (and repeated in the DRV Memorandum of September 23), Pham Van Dong made this point more ambiguous, but did not change it. He stated: "This 4 Point stand must be solemnly accepted by the USG before a political settlement of the Vietnam problem can be contemplated." This formulation, in turn, differed from Ho's demand for "tangible proofs" of U.S. acceptance on the 4 points. In the Dong speech and the DRV memo, U.S. acceptance of the 4 Points is pegged to a "political settlement" and not explicitly to starting negotiations. It is probable, nevertheless, that since DRV viewed the 4 points as "principles" and not, as the Americans called them, "preconditions," the DRV always intended that the U.S. in one way or another give evidence of acceptance prior to serious negotiations. Successful negotiations to the DRV had to be based on these principles. If the United States would not accept the principles prior to negotiations, there could be no strong presumption on the DRV part that the negotiations would be successful.

These were the first of many distinctions that Hanoi was to make among words like contacts, talks, discussions, negotiations, and peace. In June 1966, Ronning learned from Trinh that neither the 4 nor the 5 points were preconditions for "talks" -- a new term at that time.[5] If the U.S. stopped the bombing completely, Trinh told Ronning, the DRV would "talk." Ronning conveyed these distinctions to the USG, but they were lost sight of until the fall of 1967.

3

The U.S. position throughout as enunciated in President Johnson's Johns Hopkins speech of April 1965, was for "unconditional discussions." If, however, the DRV were to demand preconditions, for example, a bombing halt, the U.S. would insist on reciprocity. In other words we would make no preconditions, but if the other side did so, we would have some of our own.

X and R reached agreement at their August 15 meeting on a Geneva Conference forum. R had previously told Duntov (at their second meeting) that Geneva was the "only possible" procedure for negotiations. At this same meeting with Duntov, R said that the UN would be folly since the Chinese are not represented. At the August 6 meeting between X and R, R rejected the UN and other interlocutors, saying that Geneva was a "valid base, since it brought the interested bodies together."

The DRV Foreign Ministry Memo of September 23, however, was less specific on these points. With respect to the UN, it confined its denunciation of the organization to the use of formal UN machinery, declaring only that it will regard as null and void any UN resolution and any "solution" which seeks UN intervention. This memo did not explicitly reject mediation attempts by the UN Secretary General and others in the UN organization. With respect to the Geneva Conference, the memo says that the Vietnam problem falls within the competence of the "participants" of the 1954 Geneva Agreements.

X and R, at their August 15 meeting even went so far as to discuss a statement to announce the reconvening of the Geneva Conference. X offered the following statement: "In order to secure and preserve the fundamental right of the Vietnamese people, etc., as affirmed in the Geneva Accords, a meeting of Geneva conferees would be held which would take up Pham Van Dong's 4 points and other propositions." R expressed agreement with the first part of the sentence, but disagreed with the latter. (The disagreement on the latter could have signalled continued DRV insistence on the need to accept the 4 Points as the basis for negotiations.)

The agreement that a Geneva Conference would be the appropriate forum was clear. What was not clear was the issue of "participants." The U.S. position was that we were prepared to negotiate with "any government," and that all elements of South Vietnamese society could participate in free elections. X was told, in his instructions for the third meeting, that the U.S. was opposed to coalition government now, but that "groups" could attend a peace conference and express their views.

The DRV position was tough but ambiguous. Ho, on August 15, implied that only the NLF could participate in an international conference, and stated that the Saigon authorities were "a creation of the Americans...." On August 31, Dong stated that the Front was the "only genuine representative of the South Vietnamese people," and the "real master of the situation." On September 23, Foreign Ministry Memo stated that there could be no "negotiations on any South Vietnam problem without NFLSV having its decisive say." Later, on May 6, 1966, R said to Segonzac that the NLF was the "only valid negotiator," but that certain groups like the Buddhists which were not dominated by the U.S. could participate. Because the other conditions necessary for convening a conference were never met, it remains unclear how far either side would have departed from its opening position.

With respect to participants other than the GVN and NLF, there was nothing said, but presumably this was not necessary. By virtue of their agreement on the reconvening of a Geneva Conference, it could have been assumed that all former participants in the 1954 conference would attend again.

4. The Bombing Issue

One of the interesting features of the R and X contacts was the relative absence from discussion of the bombing issue -- until their last meeting on September 3. In R's initial meeting with Duntov, he only mentioned the bombings in passing and with mild reproof. When, in the second meeting with R, X brought up the issue of reconvening the Geneva Conference, R did not mention U.S. bombings. At their August 18 meeting, the change began when R revealed to X that the DRV viewed the cessation of the bombings as "tangible evidence" of acceptance in principle of the 4 Points. From the August 31 Dong speech on, however, the issue was brought back to prominence. Dong raised the issue in a rather odd way. He said that the U.S. must "put an end to escalation (emphasis added) in air attacks against North Vietnam," prior to negotiations. In his September 3 meeting with X, R said that the U.S. had intensified bombings in the North and ground actions in the South in the last 15 days as an attempt to force negotiations on the DRV. R added: "Bombings must stop unilaterally, immediately, totally, and definitively. Then, there would be a possibility for negotiations." Again, on January 29, 1966, R indicated: "The pause in bombing is not negotiable...we have always demanded that these bombings stop as a prerequisite of any negotiations...."

In other words, the bombings did not receive any prominence at all until the third meeting when they were indicated as "tangible evidence," and they were not raised as a serious issue in dispute until the 4th and final meeting. One explanation of this may be that the DRV knew that the bombing issue would complicate the discussion of other issues, and it did not want to so complicate the discussions until the U.S. had revealed the full extent of the concessions that it might make. In any event, from this point on, the DRV position was that it would not trade anything for a cessation of the U.S. bombardments in the north. In March, 1966, the DRV made clear to Ronning that the cessation of such bombardments was a prerequisite for "talks."

5. Opposing Settlement Proposals: The DRV's 4 Points and Ours

Both sides' settlement proposals nominally included the four
principles laid down in the DRV's 4 Points (withdrawal of "foreign"
military forces; non-intervention; self-determination for SVN; peaceful
reunification), but they held quite different views on content.

The distance between them is illustrated by another topic they
touched on, cease-fire provisions. Neither side wished an early cease-
fire. Both feared it would permit the other to consolidate its position
prior to the final settlement. In other words, both expected the final
settlement to be much more to their liking than the status quo. (For
the U.S. view, see 8/18/65; for the DRV, see 9/23/65.)

A. Withdrawal of "foreign" forces

The DRV 4 Points demanded the withdrawal of U.S. troops,
military personnel, weapons, bases and alliances with SVN. Nothing was
said publicly about NVA forces in SVN, but neither did DRV declaratory
policy during XYZ specifically deny their presence. In private, when
pressed by X, R did not deny DRV troop presence in SVN (8/18/65), or
even that the 325th NVA Division was in SVN, but claimed it was not then
engaged in military operations (9/3/65).[6] After the contact had ended,
again speaking privately, R said there were no regular northern troops
in SVN, but that northern volunteers might have joined the NLF (1/27/66).
While conceding little, this DRV posture permitted the discussions to
include provisions for mutual troop withdrawal.

On the timing of U.S. withdrawal, X consistently argued that
there would be no problem in the event of an agreement between the two
sides on an internal solution for SVN, though the specifics he envisioned
grew progressively less liberal as the episode went along. He told Duntov
in July that withdrawal would be a technical problem, as easily solved as
with the French in 1954. It could take place over 2 or 3 years (7/16/65).
To X in August, he said that the final settlement should see troop withdrawals completed (8/18/65). By September, R was telling X that U.S.
troops must leave before elections were held (9/3/65). Several months
later, speaking to the journalist Segonzac, he gave this as Hanoi's concept
for U.S. withdrawal:

"It contemplates three stages -- in the first stage, the US
would agree on the principle of their departure before the South
Vietnamese settled by themselves their problems, which cannot
be resolved so long as a foreign army is on their national territory. The second stage is that of negotiation. The third stage
is departure." (5/6/66)

6

The principle that troop withdrawal would have to be mutual was apparently accepted by R at the second meeting with X (8/18/65), and reaffirmed at the third (8/18/65). At the fourth, however, he pulled back completely and denied with agitation that there had been any inconsistency in his successive positions or between them and the official DRV position (9/3/65).

The US accepted in principle all the DRV demands regarding withdrawal at the first meeting with R, stipulating however that they apply to the DRV as well as SVN and that they include regrouping and redeployment of indigenous forces as well as withdrawal of 'foreign military and quasi-military personnel and weapons" (8/6/65). As X later explained, this included all persons with military functions and all support equipment related to the war effort. The regroupment provisions were intended to separate the combatants (8/18/65).

The U.S. did not specify the timing it thought appropriate for withdrawal, except to indicate mutually agreed stages as among the topics for negotiations. X was instructed to give North Vietnamese infiltration of men and supplies as the sole reason for the U.S. presence. If the infiltration stopped, the U.S. would go home (8/9/65). He stressed that withdrawal would have to be "phased" and "balanced" (meaning mutual and at rates to be negotiated between the two sides); R accepted these modifiers without inquiring into their meaning (8/15/65).

B. Non-interference

Although the two sides found different words to express this principle, the issue gave them little difficulty and was scarcely discussed by X and R. The U.S. noted that "a sovereign government should have the right to call for help if necessary in its own self-defense," and in other ways left room for our SEATO commitments to be observed. There is no indication of the DRV response to this reservation.

C. Self-determination for SVN

Before the contact between X and R was established, R had spoken to Duntov of self-determination as "the one basic premise" needed for a solution to the Vietnam problem (7/16/65). At his July 28 press conference, President Johnson said, "we will always insist that the people of SVN shall have the right of choice, the right to shape their own destiny in free elections in the south, or throughout all Vietnam under international supervision...."[7] Duntov urged Bo to see him again, suggesting that this statement had been influenced in some degree by his (Duntov's) report of their first meeting (End July)'.

The possibility of a convergence of views on this issue may have motivated the DRV in permitting the contact between X and R.

As the contact developed, though, US/DRV differences about what constituted self-determination simply came into sharper focus, undermining the
"premise" on which agreement over the conditions for troop withdrawal
might have rested. In the end, troop withdrawal and self-determination
became a chicken-or-the-egg type of conundrum. As R parodied the U.S.
position and rebutted it as follows: The U.S. "will withdraw from
Vietnam 'as soon as the Vietnamese will be left to solve their problems
alone.' In fact, the Vietnamese will be left to solve their problems
alone precisely after the Americans have left." (1/27/65)

        The DRV 4 Points call for "the internal affairs of SVN to be
settled by the SVN people themselves in accordance with the NLF Program...."
This was amplified on many occasions, including Pham Van Dong's National
Day address of August 31, 1965--between the third and fourth contacts--to
mean that the NLF "is now the real master...in SVN. It must have a decisive
say in the settlement of the SVN question." As R had done earlier with
Duntov, Pham Van Dong heaped scorn on the "Saigon Quisling administration...."
Prior to this speech, the issue was apparently passed over lightly by X and
R. At the fourth and last meeting, R took a line similar to Pham Van Dong's
speech and modified his earlier position to require U.S. troop withdrawal
before elections in SVN (9/3/65). Much later, he explained himself to
Segonzac. Without condemning the principle of elections, he asked, "How
can elections be held in a country over which no authority is exercised?"
Did he mean the exercise of authority is decisive, not the electoral process?
No doubt. In which case, the question of who should organize the elections--
the NLF with DRV help, or the GVN with U.S. help--would be the real issue.

        The US envisaged no NLF role "as of right" in SVN (9/8/65),
and would not guarantee a role for it before elections because to do so
would be contrary to "free determination." Individual members of the NLF
could participate in the political process. At most, the future of the
NLF should be a matter for discussion, not something settled in principle
before negotiations began (8/15/65). In the event of a ceasefire, it was
our intention to insist on the GVN's right to operate throughout SVN (9/1/65).

D. Peaceful reunification

        The two sides offered virtually identical wording in their
provisions for peaceful reunification. The U.S. required that reunification come about "on the basis of free determination" (8/6/65), a phrase
absent from the DRV's fourth point, but parallel to an elaboration given
by R at the first meeting (8/6/65). R stated then, as he had previously
and would again, that the DRV was not in a hurry to see reunification
accomplished. Clearly, though, it did expect a settlement that would
insure reunification ultimately, namely the NLF coming to power in SVN
(7/16/65).

6. Ho/Bo Differences?

On the morning of the second meeting, Le Monde published an interview with Ho Chi Minh. Ho essentially reiterated the DRV's 4 Points, insisting at each turn on the NLF as the sole authentic representative of the SVN people and brushing aside the GVN--"there is no question of Saigon authorities, a creation of the Americans...." Thus he was for self-determination, on the basis of the NLF program. He accepted an autonomous SVN for as long as the SVN people desired, noting that reunification would come by free consent, according to the program of the NLF.

When asked a complex question--would the DRV enter discussions with the U.S. on withdrawal if the U.S. affirmed the principles of Geneva, and would an end to U.S. air strikes against the DRV be preconditions for a settlement--Ho replied, "To this end, the USG must give tangible proofs that it accepts the Four Point stand of the DRV...; it must immediately stop the air attacks..., stop forthwith the aggressive war against the south..., and withdraw from there all US troops and weapons" (8/15/65).

This aroused consternation in Washington, which wondered if he was making immediate US troop withdrawal a precondition for an "effort at settlement" (8/17/65). Given the elegance of the French newspaper's question, however, it is not at all clear what Ho meant. He could equally have been laying down preconditions for a termination of the war (rather than the opening of negotiations), or simply leveling a demand without making compliance a precondition for anything. At the third meeting, R assured X that his statements on phasing and balancing troop withdrawals were the accepted DRV position (8/18/65).

7. Why Did the Contact Break Down?

Until the last meeting between X and R, all was proceeding at a better than expected pace. At this September 3rd conversation, R turned cold. He insisted on immediate cessation of U.S. bombings, and he pulled back on his agreement for the staged withdrawal of forces from SVN. Undoubtedly, a decision was made after the third meeting to wipe the slate clean at the fourth--and then, to schedule the fifth just in case something new arose. What happened between August 18 (the third meeting) and September 3? Did, in fact, the breakdown of these conversations have anything to do with the surrounding events, or was it part and parcel of the DRV's negotiating strategy all along? Or, could it have had something to do with events and relations external to the contact itself, such as China?

Could the breakdown of conversations have been related to ground action in South Vietnam? It could have, but the major announcement on U.S. force inputs to this ground action was made by the President on

July 28, that is, well before the initial X and R meeting. If the DRV regarded President Johnson's announced U.S. force increase from 75,000 to 125,000 and his saying that "additional forces will be needed later and they will be sent as requested" as a threat, they might not have allowed the meetings in the first place. But it could also be that the impact of this announcement and the impact of the U.S. forces actually on the ground and fighting in South Vietnam was not felt until a month later.

U.S. bombings in the North is another possible explanation for the breakdown. In his August 31 speech, Dong said: "To achieve these aggressive purposes, the U.S. imperialist further step up the escalation of the war in North Vietnam in an attempt to intimidate the Vietnamese people...and are threatening further escalation!" He accused the U.S. of "bombing and strafing densely populated areas, many hospitals...and public utility installations such as the Ban Thach Dam..." While there is no evidence on our attacking population and hospitals, it is true that we first struck the Ban Thach Hydropower Plant on August 23. Other U.S. first strikes in this period that could have affected Dong's speech were: Lang Bun RR Bridge on July 29, Nam Dinh Thermopower Plant on August 4, and the Bich Phuong Lock on August 23. Measured in sorties or tons, however, overall U.S. air activity in the north in August was not higher than the previous month, July.

Another possible explanation for the breakdown may lie in North Vietnam's relationship to the warring giants of the socialist world-- China and the USSR. It was on September 2, 1965, that Lin Piao gave his famous wars of national liberation speech.[8] Some scholars speculate that this speech surfaced previously existing differences between Hanoi and Peking over how to fight the war in Vietnam (the Chinese arguing for a more prolonged, lower keyed, approach and the Vietnamese for a more militant one) and how to order the political battle (the Chinese arguing for united front tactics and the Vietnamese pushing for social revolution).

It can also be argued that the DRV broke off the contact simply because it had accomplished some purpose. This purpose might have been, by seeming forthcoming and using the right words (e.g., self-determination), to see how far the Americans would go in indicating their fallback positions. Hanoi could have been testing the U.S. position after the bombing pause to see if it had stiffened or softened. To Hanoi, pause and subsequent escalation were signs that the war in SVN was going badly for us. Perhaps they reasoned that these signs would be reflected in new and softer U.S. objectives. Bo did deliver his first message to the French right after the bombing resumed, then inquired in June as to what had happened with it, and it was the U.S. that delayed making contact until August.

Hanoi and Washington had never had a private and direct talk about settlement terms. This may have seemed an easy first way of proceeding. Since the contact was not with an American official, the exchanges were always disownable, and in fact, R ultimately did renege on points of agreement. When it became clear that the U.S. was not about to make far-reaching concessions, Hanoi could have viewed this as a demonstration of clear intransigence and decided to break off.

Because the R and X exchanges were so responsive and productive and because these exchanges were severed so abruptly, no explanation is really satisfying. It seems that this dialogue between Americans and Vietnamese was as mysterious in its ending as it was fruitful and suggestive in its beginnings.

XYZ (MAI VAN BO CONTACTS): MAY 1965 - FEBRUARY 1966

May 19, 1965

French Foreign Ministry Asian Director told U.S. Embassy Political Counselor "in strict confidence" that on May 18, just prior to the resumption of U.S. bombings, Mai Van Bo (head of the DRVN Delegation, Paris) had made a fairly pressing approach to the French.

Bo wanted to understand that Hanoi's four points "were to be considered not rpt not as prior conditions but rather as working principles for a negotiation which should, in DRVN view, represent ultimate goal of settlement in Vietnam." Bo said that he was speaking with authorization, and the French source believed that the Bo approach was responsive to the U.S. suspension of bombing.

(Paris 6582).

May 20, 1965

Lucet, Director of Political Affairs of the French Foreign Office, called on the U.S. DCM in Paris to convey a message from Hanoi--although he said "we were not asked to convey message.."

He went on to deliver a message that substantially differed from the one transmitted by his own Asian Director. According to Lucet, "Bo stressed that the four points should not be 'isolated' from 'declaration' which followed." He went on: "The four points constituted 'best base' from which to find 'most just' solution. Recognition these 'principles' would create favorable conditions for solution problem and would 'open' possibility of convocation conference like Geneva, 1954."

In response to a question on U.S. withdrawal Bo agreed /"exactly"/ that the withdrawal of American forces would depend upon the "conclusions of a negotiation." Bo went on: "If there were agreement on the 'basis', then a 'ways and means' of application of 'principles' would be found and in peaceful manner;...'our suggestion humiliates no one'."

With respect to the discrepancy between this message and the public May 18 Hanoi communique denouncing "so called cessation bombings," Lucet said the latter was "for public consumption."[9]

(Paris 6612).

1

May 22, 1965

State cabled appreciation for the Lucet information and asked that Lucet be told we continued to follow the matter with interest and that he should continue to keep us informed." (State 6056).

June 14, 1965

Bo called on Manac'h. Manac'h told Bo that his message of May 18 had been transmitted to the Americans, and Manac'h said the Americans were "deeply interested."

Bo asked if Manac'h could give him the name of the American diplomat with whom he discussed this matter. Manac'h did not do so.

(Paris 7071).

July, 1965

Mr. Urah Arkas-Duntov, a partner in the Dreyfus Fund, on his own tact, took steps to arrange a meeting with Mai Van Bo. Duntov contacted Messr. M. Parisot, of France Soir, and Parisot, knowing that Eli Maissi, another journalist, had good connections with Bo, asked Maissi to arrange an interview for Duntov. Bo, at first, refused to see Duntov. Later, Maissi convinced Bo that such an interview might be an advantageous way of communicating to the U.S. at no political risk.

July 16, 1965 (First Duntov-Bo meeting)

Maissi and Parisot were present. The following were the main points of the meeting:

"1. Hanoi's Attitude toward Negotiations. Duntov asked why Hanoi would not negotiate. Bo responded that Hanoi did want to negotiate, and that there were ample contacts in which negotiations might take place. However, there must first be a basis for negotiations. Bo first said that the proper basis would be the Geneva Accords of 1954. He then added that these accords are often misinterpreted and misquoted, and that the true interpretation is found in the Four Points laid out by Pham Van Dong. Thus these formed the proper basis for negotiations.

"2. Unification of Viet-Nam. Bo stressed very strongly that Viet-Nam is one country and cannot be divided. When asked whether the US had not made clear its willingness to negotiate unconditionally, Bo replied that the President's Baltimore speech of April 7 was a trap, and that the President was really

laying down conditions by his insistence on the necessity of
an independent South Viet-Nam and guarantees for such a
South Viet-Nam.

"One of the participants asked Bo whether his position
was not in conflict with statements by the National Liberation
Front to the effect that the Front favored an independent
South Viet-Nam. Bo seemed somewhat taken aback by this question, but recovered and said that this would be all right,
since an 'independent' government in South Viet-Nam would
in fact decide to join the north.

"3. Internal Solution in South Viet-Nam. Bo insisted,
somewhat emotionally, that there was one basic premise, self-
determination by the South Vietnamese people, and that if this
was accepted, a solution was possible. He referred at different
times to the phrase, 'self-determination,' and to the Liberation
Front program for the South (insistence on which, of course,
is the third of Pham Van Dong's Four Points). In referring to
'self-determination,' Bo explained that, if this principle was
recognized, an independent government could be formed. However,
he went on to say that no 'traitor' could be included, apparently
meaning by this that at least the present South Vietnamese military leaders would be excluded.

"4. Withdrawal of US Forces. Bo was asked what time schedule
would be required--in the event of an agreement for an independent
South Viet-Nam--on the withdrawal of US forces. Bo replied that
this was no problem and that it was a technical detail that could
be worked out as it had been with the French in 1954. The withdrawal could be discussed and could take place over a two- or
three-year period. Bo related US withdrawal clearly, however, to
acceptance of the principles he had laid down for 'independence'
and 'self-determination' in South Viet-Nam.

"5. Cease-fire or Cessation in Bombings. Bo mentioned the
bombings of the North only in passing and with mild reproof. He
gave no indication that a cessation of bombing was required
before there could be discussions."

Duntov reported all this to the State Department on July 29.

End July

State judged the Bo statements to be in accord with the Nhan Dan
editorial of July 20, 1965.

3

The background for the second Duntov-Bo meeting is quite confused. Duntov's story is that Maissi had phoned him, saying that Bo is very pleased with the President's press conference of July 28, 1965. Maissi asked Bo if there were any point in his seeing Duntov again and Bo said that it would be a good idea. Again, according to Duntov, Maissi then made the arrangements with Bo. Duntov conveyed this to the State Department and was told that "we are very interested in his information but that we would prefer that he hold off at this time." Duntov said that he understood.

Maissi's story is quite different. He said that on 30 July, Duntov telephoned him saying that he had conveyed the report of the first meeting to "certain friends in Washington," that he believed the President's press conference had been influenced to some degree by this report, and that this encouraged him to believe he should meet again with Bo.

August 5, 1965 (Second Duntov-Bo meeting)

Parisot and Maissi were again present.

Duntov told Bo that he had conveyed the results of the first meeting to friends in Washington. Bo said that he was not convinced of U.S. sincerity to negotiate.

Duntov asked Bo if he were prepared to receive an authorized USG official for the purpose of explaining the American position. Bo replied that if such an official will come to Paris, and if he makes it clear that the USG will accept the 4-point program, it would be possible to "halt the war."

Also with respect to the four points, Bo initially insisted that only the NLF should represent SVN in peace negotiations--but subsequently implied this was a matter for the South Vietnamese people to decide.

With respect to the machinery for the negotiations, Bo said that the UN would be folly since the Chinese are not represented. Bo argued that the only possible machinery for negotiations is a revival of the Geneva Accords procedures.

TEXT OF A STATEMENT ON VIETNAM BY PRESIDENT JOHNSON AT HIS PRESS CONFERENCE OF JULY 28, 1965

"WE WILL STAND IN VIETNAM"

"....We have learned at a terrible and brutal cost that retreat does not bring safety and weakness does not bring peace.

"It is this lesson that has brought us to Vietnam. This is a different kind of war. There are no marching armies or solemn declarations. Some citizens of South Vietnam, at times with understandable grievances, have joined in the attack on their own government.

"But we must not let this mask the central fact that this is really war. It is guided by North Vietnam, and it is spurred by Communist China. Its goal is to conquer the South, to defeat American power, and to extend the Asiatic dominion of communism.

"There are great stakes in the balance.

"Most of the non-Communist nations of Asia cannot, by themselves and alone, resist growing might and the grasping ambition of Asian communism.

"Our power, therefore, is a very vital shield. If we are driven from the field in Vietnam, then no nation can ever again have the same confidence in American promise or in American protection.

"In each land the forces of independence would be considerably weakened and an Asia so threatened by Communist domination would certainly imperil the security of the United States itself.

"We did not choose to be the guardians at the gate, but there is no one else.

5

"Nor would surrender in Vietnam bring peace, because we learned from Hitler at Munich that success only feeds the appetite of aggression. The battle would be renewed in one country and then another country, bringing with it perhaps ever larger and crueler conflict, as we have learned from the lessons of history.

"Moreover, we are in Vietnam to fulfill one of the most solemn pledges of the American Nation. Three Presidents-- President Eisenhower, President Kennedy, and your present President--over 11 years have committed themselves and have promised to help defend this small and valiant nation."

. . . .

"What are our goals in that war-stained land?

"First, we intend to convince the Communists that we cannot be defeated by force of arms or by superior power. They are not easily convinced....

"I have today ordered to Vietnam the Air Mobile Division and certain other forces which will raise our fighting strength from 75,000 to 125,000 men almost immediately. Additional forces will be needed later, and they will be sent as requested. This will make it necessary to increase our active fighting forces by raising the monthly draft call from 17,000 over a period of time to 35,000 per month, and for us to step up our campaign for voluntary enlistments.

"After this past week of deliberations, I have concluded that it is not essential to order Reserve units into service now...."

. . . .

"Second, once the Communists know, as we know, that a violent solution is impossible, then a peaceful solution is inevitable.

"We are ready now, as we have always been, to move from the battlefield to the conference table. I have stated publicly and many times, again and again, America's willingness to begin unconditional discussions with any government at any place at any time...."

. . . .

"I made a similar request at San Francisco a few weeks ago,[10] because we do not seek the destruction of any government, nor do we covet a foot of any territory, but we insist and we will

6

always insist that the people of South Vietnam shall have the right of choice, the right to shape their own destiny in free elections in the south, or throughout all Vietnam under international supervision, and they shall not have any government imposed upon them by force and terror so long as we can prevent it.

"This was the purpose of the 1954 agreements which the Communists have now cruelly shattered. If the machinery of those agreements was tragically weak, its purposes still guide our action...."

. . . .

August, 1965 - U.S. Reaction

At this point, Washington decided that Duntov should be kept out of the picture, and that an authorized but disownable U.S. representative should contact Bo directly. The U.S. representative was Edmund Gullion, former U.S. DCM in Saigon.

For purposes of the negotiating track, Gullion is referred to as X and Mai Van Bo is referred to as R.

Initial talking points for X:

1. These were to be simple and vague, but to set limits in which talks can safely take place.

2. X was to show desire for peace, and a free, independent, and unified Vietnam.

3. X was to say that the prolongation of conflict is bound to lead to progressively larger US pressures and long-term China control in NVN.

4. X was to insist that nothing can force the US out. Indeed, X was to say that pressures in the US to a wider war were growing and that it would be increasingly harder to exercise restraint.

5. If R does not seem receptive to a second meeting, then proceed as follows:

Theme: US is flexible to some degree. See, for example, the President's press conference of 28 July.

a. US ready to discuss the four points.

b. People of SVN have a right to peace and to determine

7

their own destiny in free elections in SVN or throughout Vietnam under international supervision.

c. The four points, in some measure, parallel our own. Are we right in assuming these points are not stated as the only basis for starting talks and that other points can be discussed?

d. The four points mention withdrawal of forces. The US says it will do so once SVN "is secure from outside aggression."

e. We did not ask SVN to be our ally or to keep US bases there -- although a "sovereign government should have the right to call for help if necessary in its own self-defense."

f. US is not opposed to unification "at some future time under democratic processes."

Purpose of X's mission:

Primary -- To ascertain whether any serious purpose to negotiate exists and, if so, on what basis? Secondary -- R as possible contact? Third, clarify the four points (prerequisite or best basis, timing on unification and elections, a settlement in accord with NLF program, timing on withdrawal). Fourth -- Collateral intelligence (DRV attitude on the Indian proposal, UN, China, NLF, and the possible use of Laos and Cambodia as a gambit for talks).[11]

August 6, 1965 - First meeting between X and R

1. It was clear to X that R was aware that report of this meeting would go to US officials, and X believed that R spoke and made comments on instructions.

2. R said "convening of discussion should stipulate withdrawal as one of objectives...but confirmed that there would be 'modality' including staging and timing."

3. R rejected any UN intervention and other interlocutors such as France, Ghana, and the Commonwealth countries. Geneva, he said, was a "valid base, since it brought 'the interested bodies' together."

4. On reunification -- R said that it could take a long or short time but only on the basis of "free decision and consultation between Vietnamese people." Pending reunification, R expressed desire for freer movement between the zones, more trade, etc.

5. R said that the NLF was solely qualified to represent the South.

6. R seemed to agree with X's statements about China to the effect that Hanoi should be worried about increasing Chinese influence and control.

7. On the four points, R said that there is a difference between "discussion and settlement." "There could not be settlement without recognition of the principles within the four points." This is the main point in the initial meeting.

8. R wanted to know U.S. reaction to a whole series of questions. R did not get a chance to ask questions since X went on to his pre-planned discussion about the U.S. version of the four points.

9. R says that he wants to ensure understanding of the DRV position and that contacts could be continued. R, himself, then suggested a date for the next meeting.

10. There was no mention whatsoever of US bombing in NVN.

11. X handed R a U.S. version of the four points. It was quite similar to the one we   transmitted to the North Vietnamese in Rangoon in January of 1966.[12]

"Point I - The basic rights of the Vietnamese people to peace, independence, sovereignty, unity and territorial integrity are recognized as set forth in the Geneva Accords of 1954. Obtaining compliance with the essential principles in the Accords is an appropriate subject for immediate, international discussions without preconditions and subsequent negotiations. Such discussions and negotiations should consider, among other things, appropriate means, including agreed stages, for the withdrawal of foreign military and quasi-military personnel and weapons from South and North Viet-Nam; the dismantling of foreign military bases in both areas; the cancellation of military alliances in controvention of the Accords; and the regrouping and redeployment of indigenous forces.

"Point II - Strict compliance with the military provisions of the Geneva Accords must be achieved in accordance with schedules and appropriate safeguards to be agreed upon in the said discussions and subsequent negotiations.

"Point III - The internal affairs of South and North Viet-Nam must be settled by the South and North Vietnamese peoples themselves in conformity with the principles of self-determination without any foreign interference.

"Point IV - The issue of reunification of Viet-Nam must be decided peacefully, on the basis of free determination by the peoples of South and North Viet-Nam without foreign interference."

August 9, 1965 - McGeorge Bundy memo to the President

Talking points for next X meeting with R:

    1. Let R do the talking this time and see if there is any give in his position.

    2. Make clear U.S. interest in "unconditional Geneva Conference."

    3. Instructions:

        a. Purpose -- set stage for formal negotiations if possible.

        b. Seek a no preconditions Geneva Conference and timing thereof.

        c. On NLF -- Throw ball in R's court. What would he suggest, recognizing the U.S. view on negotiations between governments?

        d. Stress that the sole reason for the U.S. presence in SVN is North Vietnamese infiltration of men and supplies. If infiltration stops, the U.S. will go home. This is a matter for Hanoi and no one else. Withdrawal of all forces must be the product of negotiations, not the preliminary.

        e. If R brings up bombing, say that U.S. must view "suspension or cessation in the context of adequate reciprocal actions."

        f. Would R want conference on Vietnam alone, or Vietnam plus Laos and Cambodia? How would he want the conference convened -- by invitation from the co-chairmen, privately, publicly, or by direct US-Vietnamese means?

        g. U.S. envisages no NLF role as of right in SVN. Is this really a precondition of the DRV?

        h. Pick up R's suggestion about greater contacts between the zones.

August 15, 1965 - Ho-Devillers interview in Le Monde

"Question: Does the position of the Government of the Democratic Republic of Vietnam remain that which was defined by

Premier Pham Van Dong on 8 April, namely the South Vietnamese
people must be left to solve their own affairs themselves without foreign interference and on democratic bases?

"Answer: That's right, and this on the basis of the program of
the NFLSV, the sole authentic representative of the South Vietnam
people.

"Question: Is the Democratic Republic of Vietnam ready to accept,
so long as the South Vietnamese people will so desire, the
existence of an autonomous South Vietnam, neutral of course,
but disposed to establish with the north the relations implied
by fraternity and a common nationality?

"Answer: Of course. Along with preparations for the national
reunification of Vietnam which will be carried out through
peaceful means, on the basis of the free consent of the north
and the south, according to the program of the NFLSV and the
program of the Vietnam Fatherland Front, our entire people are now
struggling with their main and might against the U.S. aggression
in our country to defend the DRV, liberate South Vietnam, and
achieve peaceful reunification, highest goal of all the Vietnamese.[13]

"Question: In case the U.S. Government would solemnly reaffirm
its will to respect the basic principles of the Geneva agreements --
namely, unity and independence of Vietnam and prohibition of any
base and any presence of foreign troops on its soil -- would the
Government of the DRV agree to discuss with it the conditions and
guarantees for disengagement which this U.S. declaration would
imply? Also, in your opinion, is an end to the U.S. air attacks
against the DRV territory a sine qua non condition leading to a
settlement of the Vietnam problem?

"Answer: To this end, the U.S. Government must give tangible proofs
that it accepts the four-point stand of the Government of the DRV
which conforms to the essential political and military clauses of
the 1954 Geneva agreement on Vietnam; it must immediately stop the
air attacks against DRV territory, stop forthwith the aggressive
war against the south of our country, and withdraw from there all
U.S. troops and weapons. That is peace in honor; there is no
other way out.

"Question: Do you think, Mr. President, that the solution to
the Vietnam problem depends directly on the Hanoi and Washington
governments -- without the holding of an international conference --
or do you think that it rests essentially with the NFLSV and the
Vietnamese authorities in Saigon to find a settlement?

"Answer: The four-point stand of the Government of the DRV gives
a clear answer to this question, and there is no question of
Saigon authorities, a creation of the Americans which is cursed
by our people, and which nobody in the world takes seriously."

August 15, 1965 - Second meeting between X and R.

1. "R was rigid and even retrograde."

2. R said that Hanoi understood pressures in the US, but he
implied that the American people would be opposed to the continuation
of the war.

3. X asked if R had thoughts on U.S. version of the four points.
R said that the U.S. interpretation was not a "correct solution." R
did not take a clear position on the four points being stipulated or
accepted in advance of the conference. R seemed to reject the U.S.
version of the four points, but not definitively and finally.

4. X and R agreed on a Geneva Conference forum, but their discussion on preconditions was left vague. R tried to argue that the DRV
did not oppose the Cambodian Conference initiative but was merely
accepting Sihanouk's insistence on NLF participation in the government
of SVN.[14] X rebutted this saying that Sihanouk had ended up saying that
both Saigon and the NLF could be represented.

5. R said that "Hanoi had noted President Johnson's reference to
some form of meeting with NLF, but it was up to the US to give concrete
details." He then launched into a tirade against the Saigon government.

6. X returned to the issue of getting the conference started. R
did not mention bombing. R said the US "must leave Vietnam alone to
work out its destiny...claimed that President Johnson recently said
US must remain in Vietnam and could never leave it." X denied this.

7. X went back to the issue of infiltration and the withdrawal
of all forces, saying that the U.S. was ready to put its promise of
six months withdrawal to test. X said that withdrawal would have to
be phased and balanced with a holding back of North Vietnamese forces
as well. R indicated agreement. R then said "these accusations" of
DRV activity in SVN are only recent -- the US has been sabotaging Vietnam since 1954.

8. R asked if X had seen Ho's response to Devillers. X said no,
since he had not read the day's papers yet.

9. X returned to the issue of getting the conference going and
discussed the terms of announcing such conference. X offered the

following statement: "In order to secure and preserve the fundamental right of Vietnamese people, etc., as affirmed in the Geneva Accords, a meeting of Geneva conferees would be held which would take up Pham Van Dong's four points and other propositions." R expressed agreement with first part of sentence, but disagreed with the latter. X then said that maybe there was no use in future meetings. R was eager to set another meeting in case there should be "some change in the points of confrontation."

10. X noted some flexibility on R's part on the issue of troop withdrawal and NLF representation.

Instructions for next meeting

1. X should be tough, indicating that his reading of the Ho-Devillers interview was very discouraging.

2. U.S. will not guarantee role for the NLF before elections because to do so would be contrary to "free determination." However, South Vietnamese citizens in the NLF/VC could participate fully in the political process. Would Hanoi buy this, or, at least, discuss it?

3. Does Ho's interview really mean that the DRV would buy two separate Vietnams as long as South Vietnam desired it? X should suggest more definitive machinery for the free plebescite than existed in 1954.

4. In his interview, Ho asked for "tangible evidence" of U.S. acceptance of the four points. He said prior withdrawal of U.S. forces was required before "effort at settlement." (There is a clear conflict here between Ho's statements and R's.) R had not mentioned bombing -- as Ho most explicitly did in his interview -- or even a cease-fire. He may fear cease-fire effect on NLF just as we fear its effect on GVN legitimacy and control.

August 18, 1965 - Third meeting between X and R

1. This was the most positive meeting to date. R: (a) revealed fall-back position from the Ho interview, and (b) pin-pointed bombing as "tangible evidence" of acceptance in principle of the four points; (c) queried the meaning of X's four points, showing serious consideration thereof, and (d) stressed the desirability of a further meeting.

2. R did not reject the idea that a formula on South Vietnamese representation at the Conference table could be worked out if "other obstacles removed." R tried to get X to make another move on representation.

3. R said reunification could "wait some time." Like X, R insisted on the word "stages." On mechanisms for elections and supervision, R did not object to X's formulations.

4. Bombing issue re-emerges as the key DRV objective.

5. R said that troop withdrawals should be "phased," but that the final settlement should see troop withdrawals completed. X indicated that troop withdrawals must be "balanced" as well. R did not deny DRV troop presence in the South. Contrary to Ho, R insisted that his statements on phasing and balancing of troop withdrawals was the accepted DRV position.

6. R asked for clarification in detail of X's four points:

a. He did not like the word "compliance" and preferred "execution" or "acceptance."

b. Did "quasi military" mean men or weapons, or both? X said it meant all persons with military functions and all support equipment related to the war effort.

c. R asked for the meaning of regrouping and redeployment. X responded that one word was more static than the other, but that the key element was separation of combatants at some stage.

d. R asked about the meaning of the phrase "foreign personnel." X said that meant all foreign personnel.

7. R referred to "separation of combatants." X noted that R's interest in this issue was very tricky and could lead to VC consolidation of territory in the South. R said that this issue was very complicated.

U.S. Talking Points -- Where we stand in the talks and where we go from here

1. Two positive signs -- withdrawal and reunification issue.

a. Hanoi through R is not insisting on prior withdrawal and even envisages DRV balanced and phased withdrawal.

b. Hanoi accepts X's reunification formulation and the idea of phasing.

2. Remaining issues in dispute:

a. DRV insistence on the four points.

b. Conditions for cessation of bombing.

c. NLF representation.

d. Terms of the cease-fire (but this issue is not an obstacle to the inception of the Conference).

14

3. On X's point three, X should press the U.S. self-determination formula -- at least to some sort of verbal agreement.

4. On the bombing issue:

a. Hanoi is clear in its insistence on bombing cessation before the Conference can begin, and

b. We are clear that we will stop only if the DRV ceases infiltration and there is a sharp reduction in military activity in SVN.

5. On the NLF, we should:

a. Reject the Algerian analogy.[15]

b. Say this is a matter for Saigon and the VC to decide.

c. Stick to the no-coalition-now formula, and

d. Make clear that other "groups" could attend the Conference and express their views.

6. On the issue of the full cease-fire, we should insist on the GVN right to operate throughout SVN.

7. In his next meeting with R, X should:

a. Concentrate on his formulation of the four points (which have gained legitimacy by the Rusk TV interview).[16]

b. Ascertain what the DRV would give for cessation of U.S. bombing, and

c. Suggest a formula of reductions in incidents in SVN (like French/Algerian agreement) as a possible DRV response to a bombing cessation.

September 2, 1965 - Pham Van Dong Report at National Day Meeting, 31 August

"But no difficulty whatsoever could force our people
to retreat, and no enemy whosoever could intimidate us.
With seething hatred and undaunted determination, all our
compatriots from north to south rose up like one man and
waged a nationwide and all-sided patriotic war in accordance
with the appeal by our party and President Ho Chi Minh: . . .
We would rather sacrifice everything than lose our independence. We are determined not to be enslaved again.
The hour of struggle for national salvation has struck.

Let us make sacrifices till our last drop of blood in
order to defend our country. In spite of hardships imposed
by the war of resistance, with a spirit of determination to
make sacrifices, our people will certainly win victory.

"Soon after the DRV's founding and even after the outbreak of the resistance war in South Vietnam, we entered
into negotiations with the French colonialists on many
occasions and concluded with them several agreements and a
modus vivendi in an effort to preserve peace. But to the
French colonialists the signing of agreements was only a
move designed to gain time and to prepare military forces
and make plans for further aggression. It was only when
our victories had made it clear to them that they could
never conquer Vietnam and subdue our people and that further
military adventures would only result in still heavier
defeats that peace could be restored on the basis of the
recognition of our national rights: This is a clear lesson
of history, a lesson on relations with the imperialists which
our people will never forget."

. . . .

"The NFLSV, now controlling more than four-fifths of
South Vietnam's territory and over two-thirds of its population, is the only genuine representative of the people of
South Vietnam. The front's international prestige and
influence increase with every passing day. The front is
now the real master of the situation in South Vietnam. It
must have a decisive say in the settlement of the South
Vietnam question. In the meantime, the Saigon quisling
administration has unmasked itself more and more clearly
as the U.S. imperialists' henchman, as traitor to its country.
It is hated by the people and regarded by world opinion as
a puppet unworthy of notice."

. . . .

"....The U.S. aggressors think that by launching air raids
against the north they can intimidate our people both in North
and in South Vietnam and menace the peoples of the socialist
countries and other parts of the world. In reply to this
threat our people both in North and in South Vietnam, far
from flinching, have dealt, are dealing, and will deal ever
stronger blows at the U.S. aggressors and their agents...."

. . . .

16

"The socialist camp is more and more powerful; all
socialist countries are extending wholehearted support and
assistance to our people; close to us, like the lips and
the teeth, are the stanch Chinese people; always side by
side with us are the peoples of the mighty Soviet Union
and the other fraternal socialist countries."

. . . .

"A few years ago the U.S. President and U.S. military
and political circles often made arrogant statements. They
said the Viet Cong must be wiped out, that they are resolved
to pacify South Vietnam, and that the national liberation war
in South Vietnam must be defeated to set a good example for
the world. But now their tone has changed. In his speech
on 28 July President Johnson even began to talk about his
readiness to discuss Hanoi's proposals, to mention the question
of reunifying Vietnam, and the NFLSV. Why is there such a
change? Is that an indication of Washington's willingness
for peace?

"Replying to this question, we must consider not the
statements by the U.S. ruling circles, but their deeds. What have
they done? They have been intensifying the aggressive war in
South Vietnam and stepping up the escalation in the north. They
have decided to dispatch all at once 50,000 more U.S. combat
troops and still more in the future to South Vietnam and at
the same time are making preparations in all fields for expansion
of the war in this area.

"In a word, President Johnson talks about peace in an attempt
to cover up his war schemes; the more he talks about peace the
more he steps up the war...."

. . . .

"In order to expose the U.S. imperialists as aggressors and
warmongers, we call on the world's people, including the American
people, to further push forward the movement demanding that they
stop the aggressive war in South Vietnam, put an end to the
escalation in air attacks against North Vietnam, implement the
Geneva agreements, accept the four-point stand of the DRV Government and the stand expounded in the 22 March 1965 statement of
the NFLSV.[17] Only in this way could there be a genuine and lasting
peace in this area and could peace be safeguarded in other parts
of the world."

. . . .

"....To put an end to the war in Vietnam and deter
similar wars in other parts of the world, it is necessary
to resolutely stay the hands of the U.S. aggressors and
warmongers, the source of all types of unjust wars."

"....To bow down before the threats of the U.S. imperialists or to compromise with them would constitute an act
of encouragement fraught with incalculably serious consequences....
That is why the entire world has unanimously and strongly protested against the U.S. escalation of the war to North Vietnam."

"....The purpose of the Vietnamese people's bold struggle
has been fully embodied in the four-point stand of the DRV
Government.

"This is the sole correct stand of peace which has been
recognized by world public opinion as the only basis for a
settlement of the Vietnam problem. This four-point stand fully
conforms to the most important political and military provisions
of the 1954 Geneva agreements on Vietnam, and the whole world
is now of the view that these agreements must be correctly
implemented. This four-point stand must be solemnly accepted
by the U.S. Government before a political settlement of the Vietnam problem can be contemplated."

. . . .

September 3, 1965 - Fourth meeting between X and R

1. R took a line similar to the Pham Van Dong speech. This was
a retrogression from previous talks in two very important respects:

a. U.S. troops must leave before elections, and

b. U.S. intensification of bombings in the North and ground
actions in the South in the last 15 days was viewed by the DRV as an
attempt to force negotiations on the DRV. R said that the bombings
must stop "unilaterally, immediately, totally, and definitively." Then,
he said, there would be a "possibility for negotiations."

2. R, when pressed, did not deny that the 325th was in SVN, but
claimed it was not now engaged in military operations.

3. X offered a formula of "parallel but ostensibly unlinked"
actions to halt the bombings, possibly synchronized by the third
party. X said that U.S. was showing restraint and has not hit a number
of sensitive targets. R said that thousands in the North were being
killed.

4. R pulled back on "stages" approach to troop withdrawal.

5. X noted that talks with R had taken zig-zag course. R, obviously agitated, demanded confirmation from X that R had always taken a consistent line in these talks and had never deviated from the official DRV position. X did not comply with this request.

September 7, 1965 - Fifth meeting

R does not show up. DRV officials said that he was "sick."

Sum-up Memo:

Even though the talks dissipated in the last meeting, R showed interest in:

a. X's own initiative on U.S. troop withdrawals before elections, and

b. Possible Hanoi responses to a bombing cessation without stipulating DRV counterparts.

September 23, 1965 - DRV Foreign Ministry Memorandum [18]

. . . .

"The 'unconditional discussions' proposal of the U.S. authorities is but an attempt to compel the Vietnamese people to accept their own terms."

"These are: U.S. troops will not withdraw, but will cling on to South Vietnam; the United States always regards South Vietnam as a separate nation, that is to say, it wants the partition of Vietnam to be prolonged indefinitely; it does not recognize the NFLSV, the sole, genuine representative of the people of South Vietnam. As a matter of fact, its scheme is to try to achieve at the conference table what it has been unable to gain on the battlefield. The Vietnamese people will never accept such insolent conditions."

"The 'cease-fire' trick of the U.S. authorities is designed in fact to compel the Vietnamese people in both zones to lay down their arms while U.S. troops continue to be reinforced, to occupy and commit aggression against Vietnam. This is also an attempt to play for time to consolidate the puppet administration and army, to increase forces for further expansion of the war in Vietnam....

"....Now they are saying that they 'will cease bombing the north' if there is some 'response' from Hanoi."

19

"The DRV Government solemnly declares that the U.S.
authorities must stop their criminal war acts against the
DRV. They have no right to impose any condition on the
DRV Government....

"....Yet the U.S. Government refuses to recognize it as the
sole genuine representative of the people of South Vietnam.
It has declared that it does not regard the front as an independent party in negotiations. This further exposes its talks
about negotiations as a mere swindle. There cannot be any
negotiations on the South Vietnam problem without the NFLSV
having its decisive say."

. . . .

"The DRV Government has on repeated occasions delcared that
internationally speaking the consideration of the U.S. Government's war acts against the DRV and the U.S. war of aggression
in South Vietnam falls within the competence of the participants
in the 1954 Geneva conference on Indochina, and not of the United
Nations. Any U.N. resolution in furtherance of the above U.S.
scheme will be null and void and will completely discredit the
United Nations...."

. . . .

"To settle the Vietnam problem it is essential to remove
the roots of the serious situation in Vietnam--U.S. aggression.
Any approach which puts the aggressor and the victim on the
same footing or which does not proceed from the real situation
in Vietnam will fail to bring about a settlement of the Vietnam
problem."

"This stand also proceeds from the legitimate aspirations
of the Vietnamese people in both zones, as embodied in the program
of the Vietnam Fatherl.nd Front and that of the NFLSV; namely,
peace, independence, unity, and democracy."

"The Vietnamese people and the DRV Government earnestly call
on the governments and peoples of the world to resolutely struggle
and demand that the U.S. Government accept the four-point stand
of the DRV Government. The U.S. Government must put an immediate
end to the air war against the DRV and completely stop encroaching
on the latter's sovereignty and security. It must immediately end
the war of aggression in South Vietnam and withdraw all U.S.
troops and weapons from there...."

"The four-point stand of the DRV Government is enjoying an
ever-warmer sympathy and support from the peace-loving governments and peoples all over the world. It is the sole correct

20

basis for a settlement of the Vietnam problem. Any solutions at variance with it are inappropriate and so are any solutions which seek U.N. intervention in the Vietnam situation, because such solutions are fundamentally contrary to the 1954 Geneva agreements on Vietnam."

"The U.S. Government must solemnly declare its acceptance of this four-point stand before a political settlement of the Vietnam problem can be considered."

November 1, 1965 - X introduces Y by letter to R

Instructions for Y: [19]

1. Stress building pressures in the U.S. for escalation -- not a threat but a fact.

2. Take an anti-Chinese tack.

3. Develop theme of Asian economic development and aid.

4. DRV Aide Memoire, September 23, 1965:

    a. Asserts U.S. insists on keeping forces in SVN. With respect to this, pursue the idea of stages.

    b. Asserts U.S. insists on separate Vietnams forever.

    c. Seeming change on point three -- now NLF "must have decisive say."

    d. What is meant by "solemnly declaring acceptance of four points -- stopping all action, withdrawal or agreement to withdraw, bombing cessation?"

    e. Rules out any DRV response to a bombing cessation.

November 18, 1965 - First meeting of Y and R

1. R seemed puzzled Y had no new knowledge to convey.

2. UNR Deputy Hauret tells Wylie (Cultural Attache) that R may have something to communicate to the U.S.

3. On 29 December, R says (unconfirmed) that he would like to meet with Gleysteen, senior officer, Political Section.

December 29, 1965 - Instructions for Y

    1. Y should indicate to R knowledge of Deptel 202/Rangoon.[20]

    2. Y can indicate that possible DRV response to a bombing cessation would be "a clear major reduction in level of VC military activity and terrorism in SVN."

On January 1, 1966, Y tries to contact R and is told that R is sick.

January 3, 1966 - Meeting of Y and Jean (Vo Van Sung), second or third man in DRV delegation

    1. Jean said that the DRV four points "must be basis of solution."

    2. Jean accepted papers (Rangoon and French translation of X's four points), but had no message to transmit.

January 11, 1966 - R report encouraging intermediaries

    1. Senator McGovern

    2. Kingsbury-Smith

    3. Sanford Gottlieb [21]

January 13, 1966 - Meeting of Y and Jean

Nothing transpires.

<u>January 27, 1966</u>

- Bo Conversation with Left-of-Center French Journalist

- Statements by Bo on U.S. Peace Offensive (14 Points) (CSDB 312/ 00280-66) [22]

"2. Asked to comment on the United States peace offensive with regard to Vietnam, Bo replied as follows:

"With their peace offensive the Americans tried
to create a double illusion. First, the illusion that
they had made concessions. In fact, their fourteen
points show absolutely no change of position from
before. Each principle they state is followed by a
condition that makes the principle unworkable, i.e.
that denies the principle. They say that they will
withdraw from Vietnam 'as soon as the Vietnamese
will be left to solve their problems alone.' In fact,
the Vietnamese will be left to solve their problems
alone precisely after the Americans have left. I could
give you more examples of how each of their fourteen
points is a statement of principle coupled with a condition that denies the principle.

"The second illusion created by their peace offensive is that they have 'accepted three of our four
points,' as Dean Rusk said. But let us look at the
remaining point, i.e., point number three. That point
states that South Vietnam should apply the program of
the National Front for the Liberation of South Vietnam
(NFLSV). That program consists of independence, democracy,
neutrality, peace, and peaceful reunion of the two Vietnams. In rejecting point number three, the Americans in
fact reject the three points that they claim to accept.
You see, one must look at the heart of the matter. The
Americans have not budged an inch in their position.
They are not willing to 'give' anything. They want to
hang on to Vietnam. Their bombings have failed. Our
Prime Minister said, 'Nobody, not even children are
afraid of the bombings;' that is the heart of the matter,
that is our victory. Of course, our roads, bridges,
schools, and hospitals are sacred to us, dear to us.
The Americans gambled on that; they thought that we would
rather save them than fight. They failed. Their ground
escalation and ground war have failed. We have downed
200 planes and killed 20,000 Americans. Our victories are
tremendous. So, having failed to bring us to our knees
by bombings and by ground war, they have tried to force
our hand by putting pressure on world opinion in order

to have others put pressure on us and lead us to the
negotiation table--only to accept the American conditions.
That was the meaning of the peace offensive. They wanted
to bring many countries to force us to sit down and accept
the American conditions. That was the 'content' of their
sincerity. When we speak of sincerity we must define the
word, find out what is the 'content' of American sincerity.
They are sincere in wanting to stay in Vietnam and in
wanting us to sit down and accept that as a fact. They
are in an impasse and they are going to sink further and
further into the impasse. We are prepared and we will
wait for them to bomb Haiphong and Hanoi. The price for
this will become higher and higher for them; they will
have to pay more money and suffer more casualties. We
are not going to be deterred by any type of escalation.
Aside from that, while the 'peace offensive went on' the
Americans continued to expand their military and logistic
infrastructure, to prepare the way for a wider, bigger,
wilder, longer war--not for a retreat.

"3. Asked about the bombing pause, Bo stated:

"The pause in bombing is not negotiable. The Americans unilaterally violate the territorial integrity of a
nation and then stop and expect something in exchange for
it? That is mad. We have always demanded that these
bombings stop as a prerequisite of any negotiations but
the stopping of bombing is not enough.

"4. Asked what he would consider as a gesture on the American
side that would show willingness, i.e. 'sincerity with content,'
to negotiate, Bo replied:

"There are several things that they could do: recog-
nizing the Front as the sole representative of the South
Vietnamese people is one; stopping the bombings in the
North and aggression in the South are others.

"5. The interviewer pointed out that many discussions have
taken place about whether North Vietnam wants the United States
to withdraw its troops before any negotiations or whether American
acceptance of the four points in principle, without withdrawal of
its troops, would be sufficient for North Vietnam to negotiate.
He asked what the true North Vietnamese position on this question
was. Bo smiled, appearing slightly embarassed, and replied:

"Each thing in its own good time. We are now faced
with escalation, with more war. If the Americans ever
decide to leave our country and by certain practical

concrete gestures show to us that they mean it, then
we can find ways and means for a settlement for their
departure; then we can solve the problems that will
arise. So why speculate? As for now, the Americans do
not accept our four points and want to stay in Vietnam.
If some day they accept our four points, then we can
look for solutions to the problems that will arise on
how to make their acceptance of the four points concrete.

(Source Comment: This was Bo's way of saying, or of hinting
without stating, that the departure of United States troops was
not a pre-condition to negotiations. I am categorical about that,
i.e. that he tried to convey this impression.)

"6. Asked whether he did not think, as some do, that the
Americans did not want peace but that they wanted to use the
peace offensive to bring about an agreement with Hanoi so as
not to escalate the war on either side, to maintain it within
its present size or perhaps decrease it on both sides, Bo
replied: 'C'est tire par les cheveux' (that is far-fetched).
Bo repeated that the peace offensive was the result of American
failure to bring the NFLSV or Hanoi to their knees and was but
an attempt to bring them to their knees by diplomatic means,
which were as heavy handed as their military ones.

"7. When asked if Aleksandr N. Shelepin's visit to North
Vietnam had been useful, Bo smiled broadly and said, 'Very!'[23]
This contrasted with Bo's comments on Chinese and Soviet help
made at a previous interview on 30 September 1965 when he was
restrained and polite in saying that these countries had helped
North Vietnam. This time, at mention of Shelepin, Bo smiled
broadly and was very dramatic although maintaining his traditional
coolness of manners. Bo said, "The Soviets are giving us substantially increased material and military aid.' Asked if the
North Vietnamese were satisfied with Russian aid, Bo said "very
satisfied" and added, 'Shelepin's trip was but the symbol of the
increase of Russian aid to us.' The interviewer noted that the
Russian communique and the North Vietnamese communique issued
in Hanoi were slightly different and asked if this did not mean
that Shelepin had pressured the Vietnamese to be more moderate
and had indirectly worked for the Americans. Bo smiled and
answered, 'I can only repeat to you that officially and privately,
in name and in fact, the Russians approve of our struggle, back
it, and are increasingly with us.'

"8. When asked if his statements meant that North Vietnam
had missiles capable of destroying Saigon in reprisal if Hanoi
were bombed, Bo smiled--it seemed a secret, happy smile--and
said, 'I cannot go into such details for obvious reasons, but,
yes, the Russians have significantly contributed to our defenses.'

"9. When asked why Soviet missiles did not shoot down as
many American planes as expected, Bo said this was because the
missiles were manned by North Vietnamese. If the North Vietnamese had asked the Soviets to man them, Bo said, they would
have had to ask for Chinese Communist personnel as well, and
the North Vietnamese thought they could handle things by themselves. Bo said that now the North Vietnamese were getting
more experience and training.

"10. Bo would not answer a question as to the presence of
Soviet military personnel in North Vietnam.

"11. To a question as to whether Nguyen Van Chi represented
the NFLSV in France, Bo responded rather contemptuously that
Chi was 'just a Vietnamese gentleman who lives in France' and
represented nobody.

"12. When it was suggested to Bo, to provoke a reaction, that
manifestations of dissent in the United States by students and
others would not persuade President Johnson to stop the war, but
would only serve to provoke indignation and raise prospects of a
new 'McCarthyism' and even fascism in America, Bo showed skepticism.
He said that he did not have a simplistic view of the United States,
and that it was true that progressive action normally brought
about reaction, as in France in 1956,[24] but that he did not believe
that this would lead to fascism in the United States, where the
Government, after all, was obliged to take public opinion into
account. Bo spoke at length on the reasons he did not think that
public opinion would harden in the United States. While he agreed
to a point with statements that there were no proletarians in the
United States and that most of the people were bourgeois and
prosperous and therefore backed the Government to defend their
advantages, he seemed profoundly convinced that public opinion in
the United States is reacting more and more against the war in
Vietnam and that the high cost of the war and loss of American lives
will eventually lead the United States to want to get out of Vietnam.
Bo quoted television commentator David Schoenbrun, a French general,
and others to back up his case. He presented a long argument about
the Americans and the atomic bomb, which he said could kill a lot
of people and was not something to be despised and ignored, but he
said what ultimately counted was man--man's brain. The Americans,
Bo said, rely only on machines, and that is their weakness; Europe
has a solid cultural infrastructure--thousands of years of history--
the Americans do not. Bo said the Americans were not like other
people, and that their blind faith in machinery and mechanical
devices would be their doom. He said the atomic bomb was "not the
end of the world," and that the human factor was more important.
He said that the whole world hated the Americans; they were the
most hated people in history.

26

"13. To a question as to whether Hanoi had pulled some troops back as a result of the American peace offensive, Bo said there were no northern troops in South Vietnam--at least not regular troops. He said that North Vietnam was backing the NFLSV morally and materially and that North Vietnamese volunteers might have joined the NFLSV but that they were fighting on their own."

May 6, 1966 - Bo meeting with Adalbert de Segonzac of France Soir

Bo told Segonzac that "the essential thing is to find out whether or not the Americans are willing to leave." Bo related that the internal situation in North Vietnam had improved greatly over what it was in the first months of the U.S. bombings. In fact, he said: "The country is much better off now than it was before the bombings because it is receiving from the communist countries a flood of foodstuffs and other useful products in much greater quantities than in the past."

Bo gave Segonzac the impression of being intransigent on the question of NLF representation at a conference. To Bo, the Front "is the only valid negotiator." Bo did say, however, that certain groups that are not dominated by the U.S. can also have their say, for example, "the Buddhists are patriots."

Bo showed skepticism about the possibility of holding free elections. "How can elections be held in a country over which no authority is exercised?" Bo did not condemn the principle of elections.

Bo freely admitted that Hanoi was helping the VC, but maintained that the VC were acting independently of Hanoi.

Bo gave the following schedule of particulars of Hanoi's version of a plan for the departure of U.S. forces:

"It contemplates three stages -- in the first stage, the U.S. would agree on the principle of their departure before the South Vietnamese settled by themselves their problems, which cannot be resolved so long as a foreign army is on their national territory. The second stage is that of negotiation. The third stage is departure."

VI.C.1., PINTA: The Rangoon Contact

The PINTA contact emerged from the peace offensive initiated by the Johnson administration in late 1965. By this time, U.S. forces in Vietnam numbered close to 200,000. The bombing and infusion of ground troops had staved off the defeat so widely predicted in the summer, but it was also evident that much more would have to be done before American goals could be attained. Warning of a massive enemy buildup in the South, the Joint Chiefs pressed for a doubling of U.S. forces by the end of 1966 and for a vastly expanded bombing campaign. Although unwilling to go as far as the JCS wished, Secretary McNamara agreed that a major escalation of the war would soon be necessary.

Throughout the last months of 1965, top administration officials debated the merits of preceding the anticipated escalation with another bombing pause accompanied by some kind of peace initiative. McNamara had long advocated such an approach, arguing that it would be a good way to test whether American escalation had produced any tendency toward negotiations in Hanoi. It would also help defuse criticism at home and abroad, he continued, and would "lay a foundation in the minds of the American public and world opinion . . . for an enlarged phase of the war."[1] The Joint Chiefs adamantly opposed anything that would relieve pressure on the enemy even momentarily and expressed concern about the impact of a bombing pause on the still shaky Saigon government. Secretary of State Rusk and National Security Adviser McGeorge Bundy at first expressed strong skepticism, but by December they had been converted to McNamara's position. Journalist Eric Sevareid's revelations about American rejection of the U Thant initiative the preceding year had placed the administration on the defensive, and Bundy and Rusk appear also to have been influenced by hints that the Soviet Union might attempt to use its influence to get Hanoi to negotiate.[2]

Johnson himself reached the same conclusion more slowly and with considerable reluctance. He agreed to a brief holiday truce before going to his Texas ranch for Christmas, but only on December 27, possibly as the result of word passed by the Hungarian Foreign Minister that Hanoi would be receptive, did he commit himself to an extended pause. He later conceded that he had "grave doubts" about McNamara's proposal but that he went along because he "wanted to explore every possible avenue of settlement before we took additional military measures."[3]

1. *The Senator Gravel Edition, The Pentagon Papers*, 4 vols. (Boston: Beacon Press, 1971), IV, 33.
2. Eric Sevareid, "The Final Troubled Hours of Adlai Stevenson," *Look* 30 (November 1965): 81–86. Bundy Oral History Interview, Johnson Library, provides extensive background on the decisions leading to the pause.
3. Johnson, *The Vantage Point*, p. 237.

On his own initiative and clearly reflecting his own personal style, Johnson combined the pause with a noisy "peace offensive." He dispatched such top officials as W. Averell Harriman, Vice-President Hubert Humphrey, and Assistant Secretary of State G. Mennen Williams to capitals across the world to deliver the message that he was prepared to negotiate without condition. He sent personal messages to numerous heads of state and to U.N. Secretary General U Thant underlining his desire for peace and indicating that he was looking for signs of restraint demonstrating that Hanoi too was ready to discuss peace terms. He used old and new private channels, of which PINTA turned out to be the most important, to inform North Vietnam of the bombing halt and to indicate that if it would reciprocate in some way the pause might be extended. At the same time, Secretary of State Rusk released the first formal statement of American peace proposals, what came to be known as the Fourteen Points. They contained little that had not been said before, and on the salient issues conceded nothing. The United States would go no further than state that Hanoi's Four Points "could be discussed along with other points that others might wish to propose." While reiterating support for self-determination in South Vietnam in principle, it conceded nothing regarding the status of the Vietcong beyond Johnson's earlier statement that they "would not have difficulty being represented and having their views represented if for a moment Hanoi decided she wanted to cease aggression."

From the administration's point of view, the peace offensive produced about what had been expected. A statement by the North Vietnamese Foreign Ministry on January 4 did not insist on U.S. recognition of the Four Points as a precondition to negotiations, a possible sign of interest in peace talks, and there were some indications of a decline in North Vietnamese military operations in January. The administration ignored the former and dismissed the latter as of less importance than the fact that North Vietnam had used the pause to rush large quantities of men and supplies into the South. Private channels, including a Polish mission to Hanoi arranged by Harriman apparently in cooperation with the Soviets, turned up nothing. The North Vietnamese public response was harsh and uncompromising. The Foreign Ministry statement denounced the bombing pause as a trick. A letter from Ho Chi Minh to various heads of state broadcast by Hanoi radio on January 28 accused the United States of deceit and hyprocrisy, demnded the withdrawal of U.S. forces, and insisted that the NLF was the "sole representative of the people of South Vietnam." With virtually no debate, the administration resumed the bombing on January 31. William Bundy and others felt that the pause had been worthwhile in terms of mollifying domestic and world opinion, but Johnson was not persuaded. Never really convinced that a pause had been the right thing to do, he concluded that it had been a serious mistake. His views hardened, and he would not even consider another extended halt to the bombing for two years, and then under very different conditions.[4]

Much as with the May bombing pause, the most positive response from Hanoi came immediately after the bombing had been resumed, this time in Rangoon. Within hours after the pause ended, North Vietnamese Consul-General Vu Huu Binh invited U.S. Ambassador Henry Byroade to meet with him. Binh offered nothing new, merely restating familiar positions in response to the message Byroade had delivered in connection with the pause. He did invite Byroade to respond, however, signaling that at least Hanoi was interested in keeping the channel open.

Much like the XYZ contact, PINTA closed abruptly and mysteriously. By the time Byroade responded to Binh's overture on February 19, North Vietnam had apparently lost interest, and Binh simply said that the contact should be terminated. As with XYZ, it is impossible to determine why the channel was opened in the first place and then summarily closed. U.S. officials speculated that North Vietnam was engaging in a pattern of deliberately dangling tantalizing leads to keep them off balance. More may have been involved. It is possible that some Hanoi officials would have preferred at this time a compromise settlement to continuation of the war and would have accepted, at a minimum, a coalition government in South Vietnam. Johnson's meeting with the South Vietnamese leadership in Honolulu in February, which seemed to preclude any possibility of a coalition government, along with the escalation of the war after the pause, may have played into the hands of the hardliners in Hanoi and eliminated any reason to keep the Rangoon channel open.—*Ed.*

4. Bundy Oral History Interview, Johnson Library.

PINTA: THE RANGOON CONTACT

SUMMARY and ANALYSIS

This paper is in three parts: (1) A discussion of the main questions raised by the episode. (2) A brief description of the principal events in Rangoon. (3) A more detailed chronology based on cables, memoranda, etc. Parts 1 and 2 are based on the sources cited in Part 3.

1. Discussion

The U.S. entered the 37-day bombing pause on December 24, 1965, with few illusions that the communists would respond readily by entering negotiations. On December 10, Radio Hanoi denounced the May 1965 pause as "shameful trickery" amounting to "an ultimatum." It noted indications that another halt was in the offing and announced that the U.S. should "harbor no hope that the Vietnamese people would be taken in...." It demanded U.S. recognition of the DRV's 4 Points, a "definite" halt to the bombing and the "war of aggression" in SVN, etc. On December 16, Soviet Embassy Counsellor Zinchuk indicated to Bundy that Hanoi would almost certainly not respond at that time, though a pause could improve the atmosphere for the long run.

In spite of this, the U.S. made a maximum effort to draw the DRV into contact during the pause. A modicum of success was attained in Rangoon, where the DRV Consul General agreed to receive the U.S. Ambassador on December 29 and accept his Aide Memoire.

Timing: Contact While Bombing? No formal DRV reply was received until the evening of January 31, over 12 hours after the bombing had been resumed. The circumstances left unclear whether this timing was coincidential or a delay intended to avoid the appearance that the DRV agreed to the contact out of fear of the bombing. The ambiguity was so well contrived as to suggest that it was intentional. It did not provide a basis for claiming either that the DRV had gone back on its pledge never to talk while being bombed, or that the enticements of a pause in the bombing were sufficient to induce the DRV to enter contact.

A Stab at "Unconditional Discussions"?   The DRV response turned out to be a rebuttal of the U.S. 14 Points.[1] It objected particularly to U.S. troop withdrawal being offered on the condition, it claimed, that the NLF lay down its arms and accept amnesty. This meant keeping the "puppet government" and not recognizing the NLF as the sole genuine representative of the SVN people or negotiating with it. U.S. acceptance of the DRV 4 Points was again demanded. At the end, the DRV representative offered to listen to what the U.S. Ambassador "may wish to expound on the US position."

1

Perhaps this rather stilted beginning was intended as a small move toward unconditional discussions, since the DRV had taken some account of our 14 Points, presented its rebuttal and offered to hear our reply. The substance of the matter was not pursued, however. Instead our representative turned to arrangements, objecting to DRV contentions that its 4 Points should be the exclusive basis for exchanges and asking if "responsible emissaries of our two Governments could meet and talk about all of these things (the 4 Points and our 14 Points) together." This more formal arrangement was firmly rejected.

On February 1, Hanoi published a lengthy article containing essentially the same arguments as the confidential Aide Mémoire. One new point was injected: Raising doubt about U.S. acceptance of neutrality for SE Asia, the article asks "is it not plain enough that... (the Americans) oppose the holding of an international conference guaranteeing the neutrality and territorial integrity of Cambodia?" In fact, the U.S. had earlier urged such a conference in the hopes that Vietnam might be discussed by the way. Was this an involuted DRV probe of U.S. interest in resurrecting the Cambodian conference idea? It seems unnecessarily oblique, and the notion was not tested at the time.

The Channel Stays Open. The Rangoon channel was still open on February 3, when the U.S. delivered a note assuring the DRV that its Aide Memoire was under study.

Opposing Settlement Proposals. The substantive U.S. reply was delivered on February 19 in an Aide Memoire urging that the political future of SVN be settled through truly free elections, without any outside interference. The U.S. would accept the results of such an election, though it would not agree to put the NLF into a coalition government or take it as the sole representative of SVN without an election. U.S. forces would withdraw when peace was restored. The specific proposals passed to the DRV during the XYZ exchanges were offered again.

The issues separating the two sides are fairly clear. The communists demanded assurance of a major role for the NLF as the price for ending the war; and they feared that no such assurance would be valid while U.S. troops remained in Vietnam. The U.S. was unwilling to see such a role for the NLF imposed by force of arms; it wanted the war ended first. It would withdraw its troops only as the DRV withdrew and the NLF gave up the use of force as a means to political power. This would mean accepting the GVN, with such alterations as could be negotiated, as the legitimate government of SVN. In short, the communists were not willing to contend for power peacefully under GVN auspices, whereas we insisted they do so.

The Channel Closes. After accepting the Aide Memoire for transmittal to Hanoi, the DRV representative assailed as acts of war the bombing resumption and the USG/GVN Declaration of Honolulu.[2] Acting under instructions, he then declined to continue the contact, citing the bombing resumption as the reason. Given his willingness to accept a U.S. message on February 3, however, and in view of the DRV's great emphasis on a role

for the NLF and its rejection of the GVN, it seems possible that the
Honolulu Declaration was as much responsible.   Contrary to repeated
communist demands, the Declaration must have read to them as a reaffirmation of U.S. recognition of the GVN as the "sole genuine representative
of the SVN people."

2.   Principal Events in the Rangoon Contact

December 29, 1965. Byroade hands the DRV Consul General, Vu, an Aide-Memoire calling attention to the bombing suspension begun December 24, and expressing the hope that DRV reciprocity would permit it to be extended.

January 4, 1966. The DRV Foreign Ministry issues a blast at "so-called peace efforts" of the US. The statement does not explicitly acknowledge that the bombing has stopped. It objects to numerous other US activities. Its main point is that "a political settlement of the Vietnam problem can be envisaged only when the USG has accepted the 4-Point stand of the DRV, has proved this by actual deeds, has stopped unconditionally and for good its air raids and all other acts of war against the DRV."

January 21, 1966. Byroade calls on Vu to remind him we await a reply to our Aide-Memoire. Vu says he has no instructions yet, but offers his "personal" view that the Aide-Memoire amounted to an ultimatum. He uses the occasion to protest press reports from the White House hinting at their direct contact.

January 24, 1966. Vu sends Byroade a hand-carried Aide-Memoire dated January 21, and repeating, virtually verbatim, Vu's oral remarks of that date.

January 27, 1966. Byroade responds to Vu's January 24 Aide-Memoire with a memo inquiring about a response to his December 29 Aide-Memoire.

January 31, 1966. Some hours (at least 6) after the resumption of air strikes against the DRV, Vu asks Byroade to call. When they meet (more than 12 hours after the resumption), Vu delivers an Aide-Memoire referring to the DRV Foreign Ministry statement of January 4 and adding specific rebuttals of the US 14 Points: (a) the 14 Points and subsequent US statements constitute a refusal to recognize the principles of the 1954 Geneva Accords; (b) the US offers to withdraw its troops from SVN only on its own terms, which means that it really refuses to withdraw them; (c) the US statement that it seeks no military bases in SE Asia is inconsistent with its reiterated commitment to SEATO; and (d) the US demands that the NLF lay down its arms and accept amnesty as a condition for self-determination of the SVN people, which means the US intends to keep the "puppet regime" in power, does not recognize the NLF as the sole genuine representative of the entire SVN people, and will not negotiate with the NLF -- the US rejects Point 3, which amounts to rejecting all 4 Points.

The Aide-Memoire concludes by expressing Vu's willingness to listen to what Byroade "may wish to expound on the US position." Byroade replies by objecting to the 4 Points as an exclusive basis for US/DRV exchanges and asks if "responsible emissaries of our two Governments could meet and talk about all of these things (the 4 Points and our 14 Points) together." Vu says there is no possibility of negotiations unless we accept their 4 Points. However, he also offers to communicate to Hanoi whatever Byroade has to say at any time, and shows Byroade out by a back gate which is indicated as better to use from a security point of view.

February 1, 1966. Hanoi's English service broadcasts a lengthy article from the Vietnam Courier (published only in French and English), listing the US 14 Points and rebutting them with essentially the same arguments used in Vu's January 31 Aide-Memoire. In elaborating on objections to SEATO, it calls the US a "sworn enemy of neutral countries" asking in substantiation "is it not plain enough that...(the Americans) oppose the holding of an international conference guaranteeing the neutrality and territorial integrity of Cambodia?"

February 3, 1966. Byroade delivers a brief memo saying Vu's January 31 Aide-Memoire is under study in Washington. The purpose is to see if Hanoi is willing to maintain the contact, in spite of the bombing resumption.

Meanwhile Bundy, in Washington, concludes that "there appears to be a substantial possibility...that Hanoi even waited till it knew of the resumption before it dispatched (Vu's) instructions...Hanoi may have been unwilling to open any dialogue during the suspension, lest this appear as a sign of weakness." He notes that Hanoi had enough time to call Vu off by a commercial cable simply saying not to carry out prior instructions.

February 16, 1966. State sends Byroade an Aide-Memoire to be handed Vu, without the appearance of urgency. It responds to Vu's January 31 Aide-Memoire, as follows: (a) The US believes the 1954 and 1962 Geneva Accords are an adequate basis for peace in SE Asia. (b) The US is willing to withdraw its troops from SVN when peace is restored. It does not demand to be the sole judge of this condition. DRV violation of the regroupment provisions of the 1954 Accords has made US actions necessary. US withdrawal under international verification would be undertaken in the light of DRV actions in this regard. (c) The US desires neither military bases nor forces in SVN. (d) The DRV's Point 3 would be acceptable if it means only seeking "to achieve independence, democracy, peace and neutrality in SVN and to advance toward peaceful reunification," as paraphrased January 29 by Ho. It would not be acceptable if it meant putting the NLF in a coalition government or accepting the NLF as "sole genuine representative" of the SVN people, prior to and without regard to an election. The political future of SVN should be settled through truly free elections. The US is categorically prepared to accept the results.

2

This statement of the US position is accompanied by a settlement proposal similar to that handed Mai Van Bo in XYZ (q.v.) Byroade is instructed not to amplify on the text, but to note Vu's comments.

February 19, 1966. Byroade delivers the text to Vu, who listens to his interpreter's reading of it, promises to transmit it to Hanoi, but does not comment on its contents. Vu then assails as acts of war the bombing resumption and the USG/GVN Declaration of Honolulu. Noting that he is acting under instructions, Vu says, "Since the US has resumed the bombing, I hold that it is inappropriate to continue our talks at your request."

February 21, 1966. Vu's oral remarks of February 19 are confirmed and elaborated in an Aide-Memoire dated February 19 but hand-carried to Byroade on February 21.

3.   Chronology

December 10, 1965

U.S. PAUSE IN BOMBING OF DRV DECEIVES NO ONE

Hanoi VNA International Service in English 1706 GMT 10 December 1965--B

. . .in an attempt to hoodwink public opinion in the United States and the world and cover up their frenzied efforts to expand and escalate the war in both zones of Vietnam. U.S. President Johnson, State Secretary Dean Rusk and the U.S. delegate to the United Nations, Ambassador Goldberg have once again played their record of uncon- ditional discussions. Worthy of note was that U.S. State Secretary Dean Rusk has been claiming noisily about a so-called second pause in the bombing raids in North Vietnam. At a press conference in the White House on 1 December 1965 he said, I am not now excluding a stop in the bombing as a step toward peace. He also recalled the so-called first pause in May this year and slanderously accused the DRV with not responding to this gesture of the United States. He even threatened that if North Vietnam did not respond the peaceful settlement of the Vietnam question would be delayed.

This trick of the U.S. state secretary is not novelty. It must be recalled that in May this year, Dean Rusk in the name of his government, already sent a message to a number of countries announcing a halt in the bombing of the DRV by U.S. aircraft for a week beginning on 12 May. Making black white, the message slanderously charged North Vietnam with aggression against South Vietnam and threatened that if the South Vietnamese people did not stop their self-deliberation fight, the United States would continue to bomb the north.

In its essence, the message was an ultimatum to the Vietnamese people, urging the South Vietnamese to abandon their patriotic struggle as a condition for a halt in the bombing of the DRV. The message . itself has revealed that the unconditional discussion offer of Johnson is only a bid to make the Vietnamese people lay down arms and submit to their brute force of aggression.

This shameful trickery has failed miserably. Now the U.S. imperialists are having another try at it. . . .

. . .

It also must be pointed out that the U.S. imperialists' deeds never match with their words. In the period of the so-called sus- pension of the bombings over North Vietnam, from 12 to 17 May this year, U.S. aircraft and warships continued to encroach upon the airspace and territorial waters of the DRV for spying, provocative, and raiding activities. Two U.S. F-105 jetfighters were downed over Nghe on 13 and 17 May, respectively. Meanwhile, the United States brought to South Vietnam (?over 1,400) more combat troops and the U.S.-puppets intensified both their ground and air raids against the population. On 14 May alone, U.S.-puppet aircraft flew 186 sorties.

. . .

. . . L. Johnson himself did not hide the true intention of the United States when he declared at his ranch in Texas on 6 December: We will send as many men as necessary to Vietnam. Is it not sufficiently clear that the new decision to halt the bombing in North Vietnam is only a maneuver to prepare for further expansion of the war by the U.S. imperialists?

Let the U.S. imperialists harbor no hope that the Vietnamese people would be taken in by such a shopworn trick of theirs. The United States must declare its recognition of the four-point stand of the DRV and prove it by concrete acts. Concretely speaking they must stop definitely all bombing raids against the DRV, stop their war of aggression against South Vietnam, withdraw all US troops from South Vietnam and let the Vietnamese people decide themselves their own a affairs. Only then can there be genuine peace in Vietnam. As pointed out by President Ho Chi Minh in his reply to questions by Uruguayan journalist Salomon Schvarz Alexandroaith, editor in chief of EL POPULAR, organ of the Uruguayan Communist Party, this stand is the only correct basis for a solution to the Vietnam problem since it conforms with the Geneva agreements, with the practical situation in Vietnam and with the national rights of the Vietnamese people.

December 17, 1965

NOTE TO THE SECRETARY: (TOP SECRET--EYES ONLY)

Subject: Last Thoughts on the Pause Proposal

1. My recommendation would continue to be affirmative, but only if we give ourselves time for real understanding with the GVN, and we were determined to continue it at least for two weeks, not jumping back in at the first predictable counter-blast from Hanoi.

2. I lunched with Zinchuk of the Soviet Embassy yesterday and, for what it is worth, he seemed to be saying that Hanoi almost certainly would not respond this time, but that it would greatly improve the atmosphere for the long run. I got the impression that the Soviets have had recent talks in Hanoi, in which Hanoi has taken pretty much the line reflected in its propaganda broadcasts of December 10 and 11, virtually denouncing a second pause in advance unless we also do something major with respect to the South--which I take to imply the suspension of reinforcements. This I most emphatically do not feel we should do.

. . .

                                        William P. Bundy

la

December 29, 1965

STATE 202 (to Amembassy RANGOON), S/Nodis, Flash, Sent 29 December 1965

EYES ONLY FOR AMBASSADOR FROM SECRETARY

1. President has decided that he wishes defer resumption of bombing for several more days. We are most anxious that word of this action be conveyed directly to DRV, although we are also naturally conveying message to key Communist governments that in touch with Hanoi.

2. Accordingly, you should convey aide memoire in text given below in some manner to DRV Ambassador Rangoon. ...

3. Text of aide memoire is as follows:

BEGIN TEXT:

"1. As you are no doubt aware, there has been no bombing in North Viet-Nam since December 24 although some reconnaissance flights have continued. No decision has been made regarding a resumption of bombings and unless there is a major provocation we would hope that the present stand-down, which is in its fifth day, could extend beyond New Year. If your government will now reciprocate by making a serious contribution toward peace, it would obviously have a favorable effect on the possibility of further extending the suspension.

"2. I and other members of my Embassy staff stand available at any time to receive any communication you may wish to address to me or to us." END TEXT.

RUSK (Drafted by W. P. Bundy)

RANGOON 315 (to SecState), S/Nodis, Immediate, sent 29 Dec 65; Rec'd 0715, 29 Dec 65

EYES ONLY FOR THE SECRETARY

REF: DEPTEL 202; EMBTEL 311

I called upon DRV Consul General at 3 P.M. today. ...

Vu Huu Binh ... received me with slight smile and ready handshake. I told him I was grateful for opportunity to see him personally as my government wished me to convey message directly to him for transmittal to his government. I then handed him the aide memoire. He and his interpreter studied document together with interpreter translating parts thereof into Vietnamese.

After studying document Vu Huu Binh said he would transmit it to his government. . . . I thanked him and told him I planned to keep my visit to him and the subject thereof quite confidential I had come in official U.S. Embassy car but not my own because it was conspicuous. He said that on his part he would also keep matter confidential.

I . . . . would be available in Rangoon anytime of day or night if he should wish to see me. . . .

. . . .

. . . .

BYROADE

RANGOON 316 (to SecState), S/Nodis, Immediate, Sent 29 Dec 65; Rec'd 1334, 29 Dec 65

Eyes Only for the Secretary

Ref: DepTel 202

In an unprecedented evening meeting in the Foreign Office I saw U Thi Han and U Soe Tin together there tonight. . . .

I filled them in on the day's developments, going into substance along lines Deptel 201 only slightly and they did not ask substantive questions. They were obviously delighted that present effort was being made, and that direct contact had been made in Rangoon, and that I had sought to inform them promptly.

U Soe Tin asked if I expected a direct reply. I said I had had personal experience with Far East Communists only of the Chinese variety but, based upon that, I doubted, though I hoped to contrary, that a direct reply would come. He said he thought this correct and that, if Hanoi did in fact decide upon affirmative response, it would be in actions and not in form of reply to us.

. . . .

. . . .

BYROADE

2

January 4, 1966

(Hanoi VNA International Service in English 1749Z 4 Jan 66)

"Statement by Spokesman of DRV Foreign Ministry on So-Called Peace Efforts
Made Recently by the United States"

Text

Hanoi, 4 January--Follows the full text of the statement issued today
by the spokesman of the DRV Foreign Ministry regarding the so-called peace
efforts made recently by the United States:

Recently, the U.S. Government has started a large-scale deceptive
peace campaign coupled with the trick of temporary suspension of air attacks
on North Vietnam as a sign of good will. U.S. President Johnson has
repeatedly stated that the United States is determined to exhaust every
prospect for peace, and will search relentlessly for peace. The U.S.
Government has sent envoys to approach foreign countries, and has put
forward new peace proposals which are actually a mere repetition of old
themes.

The fact is that in spite of repeated military and political defeats,
the U.S. policy of aggression in Vietnam has remained unchanged. The
United States has impudently sabotaged the 1954 Geneva Agreements on
Vietnam which it had undertaken to respect. It still states shamelessly
that it will keep its commitments with the puppet regime rigged up by
itself in Saigon, and this with a view to clinging to South Vietnam and
perpetuating the partition of Vietnam. It still refuses to recognize the
South Vietnam National Front for Liberation, the sole genuine representative
of the people of South Vietnam, and the leader of their struggle against
the U.S. imperialists' war of aggression. The United States still refuses
to allow the people of South Vietnam to settle by themselves their own
affairs in accordance with the program of the South Vietnam National
Front for Liberation.

Moreover, it is frantically using U.S. and puppet troops to burn
down or destroy villages and crops, and massacre the people in South
Vietnam and even arrogantly demanding that the people of South Vietnam
lay down their arms and accept the rotten Saigon puppet regime. The
United States still brazenly gives itself the right to launch air attacks
on the Democratic Republic of Vietnam, an independent and sovereign country.
It talks about respecting the 1954 Geneva Agreements on Vietnam, yet it
refuses to accept the four-point stand of the government of the Democratic
Republic of Vietnam, which is a concentrated expression of the essential
military and political provisions of the said agreements. It is harping
on the same string about unconditional discussions whose real purpose it
is to carry out the plot of conducting negotiations from the position of
strength, and attempting to force on the Vietnamese people acceptance of
U.S. terms.

3

The U.S. authorities' talks about peace are in complete contradiction
with their war schemes and acts. While making a noise about its peace
efforts, the United States is making feverish preparations to double the
U.S. military strength in South Vietnam. The third brigade of the U.S.
25th Division has just been brought in for an occupation of Pleiku. The
United States has kept on using toxic chemicals as a means of warfare
and has made public announcements to this effect. Its B-52 strategic
planes continue to bomb densely populated areas. In North Vietnam, the
United States has threatened to bomb the densely populated industrial
areas of Hanoi and Haiphong. U.S. President Johnson has also threatened
to take hard steps in Vietnam. Meanwhile, the United States has intensified its air attacks on the liberated areas in Laos and impudently
authorized U.S. troops to intrude into central and southern Laos and
into Cambodian territory, thus extending the war from South Vietnam to
these two countries.

The facts have shown that every time the U.S. authorities want to
intensify their aggressive war, they talk still more glibly about peace.
The present U.S. peace efforts are also a mere attempt to appease public
opinion at home and abroad, which is strongly opposing the U.S. policy
of aggression in Vietnam. The United States wants to turn to account
the world people's legitimate aspirations for peace in an attempt to
call black white, to pose as a peace-lover, to slander the Vietnamese
people, and thus to create a pretext for making new steps in implementation
ot its scheme to intensify and expand the war. But no matter what sophisms
the U.S. authorities may resort to in their attempt to cover up their
aggressive schemes, they can fool no one.'

The United States is thousands of miles away from Vietnam. The
Vietnamese people has never laid hands on the United States. The U.S.
Government has no right to send troops to invade South Vietnam and to
launch air arracks on the Democratic Republic of Vietnam any condition
whatsoever in exchange for stopping its air raids on North Vietnam.

U.S. imperialist aggression is the deep root and the immediate
cause of the serious situation now prevailing in Vietnam. With the
ending of this aggression peace will be immediately restored in this
country.

The Vietnamese people eagerly want peace for national construction,
but they know full well that real independence must be achieved if
genuine peace is to be secured. It is the unswerving stand of the
Government of the Democratic Republic of Vietnam to strictly respect
the 1954 Geneva Agreements on Vietnam and to correctly implement their
basic provisions as concretely expressed in the following points:

One--Reaffirmation of the basic national rights of the Vietnamese
people: peace, independence, soveriegnty, unity, and territorial
integrity. In accordance with the Geneva Agreements, the U.S.

Government must withdraw all U.S. troops, military personnel, and weapons of all kinds from South Vietnam, dismantle all U.S. military bases there, cancel its military alliance with South Vietnam. The U.S. Government must end its policy of intervention and aggression in South Vietnam. In accordance with the Geneva Agreements, the U.S. Government must stop its act of war against North Vietnam, cease all encroachments on the territory and sovereignty of the Democratic Republic of Vietnam.

Two--Pending the peaceful reunification of Vietnam, while Vietnam is still temporarily divided into two zones, the military provisions of the 1954 Geneva Agreements on Vietnam must be strictly respected: The two zones must refrain from joining any military alliance with foreign countries, and there must be no foreign military base, troops, and military personnel on their respective territory.

Three--The internal affairs of South Vietnam must be settled by the people of South Vietnam themselves, in accordance with the program of the South Vietnam National Front for Li eration without any foreign interference.

Four--The peaceful reunification of Vietnam is to be settled by the Vietnamese people in both zones, without any foreign interference.

A political settlement of the Vietnam problem can be envisaged only when the U.S. Government has accepted the four-point stand of the Government of the Democratic Republic of Vietnam, has proved this by actual deeds, has stopped unconditionally and for good its air raids and all other acts of war against the Democratic Republic of Vietnam.

The just struggle and the unswerving good will of the Vietnamese people and the Government of the Democratic Republic of Vietnam have always enjoyed the sympathy and vigorous support of the peace-loving governments and people the world over. The Vietnamese people are very grateful for this sympathy and support. The Government of the Democratic Republic of Vietnam calls on the governments and peoples of the Socialist countries, those of the Asian, African, and Latin American countries, and the peoples of the whole world, including the American people, to extend still more active support and assistance to the Vietnamese peoples' just patriotic struggle, and to oppose still more resolutely and vigorously all the U.S. imperialists' plans for intensified war as well as all their peace swindles.

So long as the U.S. imperialists still pursue the war of aggression against Vietnam, still use U.S. and satellite troops to invade South Vietnam, and launch air attacks on the Democratic Republic of Vietnam, the people in both zones of Vietnam, fearing no sacrifices, will resolutely carry the resistance war through to the end and fulfill their sacred duty of defending the sovereignty of the fatherland and the independence of the nation and contributing to the defense of world peace.

5

January 5, 1966

RANGOON 327 (to SecState), S/Nodis, Priority   , Sent 5 Jan 66; Rec'd 2:27 A.M.,
5 Jan 66 (Passed to White House 5 Jan 66, 4:15 A.M.)

Eyes Only for the Secretary

    1. . . .When I saw U Thi Han and Soe Tin as reported EmbTel 316
I asked them how fast they believed North Vietnamese communications were.
(I was interested in whether Vu Huu Binh might have been able get Hanoi's
authority to receive me.) Soe Tin said they would be quite slow unless
they used Chinese facilities.

    2. Last night Soe Tin told me Vu Huu Binh had transmitted my
message to Hanoi. He said Vu had sent two other messages to Hanoi
direct by commercial cable a few hours after I saw him. I find this
interesting and encouraging, in that this would appear to indicate Vu
communicated with Hanoi without informing Chinese Embassy here.

    . . . .

    . . . .

BYROADE

January 6, 1966

RANGOON 329 (to SecState), S/NODIS, Priority   , Sent 6 Jan 66;
Rec'd 6:45 A.M., 6 Jan 66 (Passed to White House 6 Jan 66)

Eyes Only for the Secretary

    Yugoslav Ambassador Drndic called on me at his request today and
further reinforced my belief we are still in clear as far as secrecy
of Rangoon operation is concerned.

    . . . .

    . . . .

    . . . .

    . . . .He said, "I talked with Vu Huu Binh recently and he said
he was confused because of non-receipt of instructions from Hanoi. Vu
said that he had received guidance on the party line quickly during
the last bombing pause, but that this time he hadn't had a word from
Hanoi." . . . .

    . . . .

BYROADE

6

RANGOON 336 (to SecState), S/Nodis, Priority , Rec'd 8:53 P.M.,
Jan 11, 1966 (passed White House 11 Jan 66, 10 P.M.)

Eyes Only for the Secretary

. . . .

. . . .

Tonight at a diplomatic function the French Ambassador . . .

...said that the story was being circulated that I had seen
the North Vietnamese Rep here and had given him a communication
explaining the pause in bombing. . . .

. . . .

. . . .

...I believe that this information in the hands of a not very
friendly French Ambassador, plus the fact that the White House has
announced a direct contact, will result in such speculation as to
possibly preclude the use of Rangoon as a secret contact post in
the future. . . .

BYROADE

January 20, 1966

STATE 227 (to Amembassy RANGOON), S/Nodis, Immediate, Sent 20 Jan 66

1. As part of our effort to close all circuits, you should seek
appointment with DRV Consul General, saying simply that you are doing
so under instructions.

2. Assuming he accepts, you should remind him that when you
delivered our message on December 29 you indicated that you would be
available for any response DRV might wish to make through this channel.
Since that time, USG has received no indication of any Hanoi response
either related to military action or obstacles to negotiation. Does
DRV rep have any message to convey?

3. We suspect he will be without instructions and will simply
undertake to report your call. However, if he should respond at all
on your reference to military activity, you should indicate that VC
activity in the South appears to have remained at a high level, and
we have had reliable evidence of major truck movements continuing
through Laos to South Vietnam. In circumstances, we have no alternative
but to assume that DRV is continuing to send regular units to the South
and to support high level of military activity there.

4. If he should turn conversation in direction of conditions for negotiation, you should say that our position has been made clear many times and recently summarized in fourteen points and also in Goldberg letter to UN.[3] We have had no indication of Hanoi's views on these documents, or on possibility of negotiation either without conditions or on basis of Geneva Accords.

RUSK (Drafted by W. P. Bundy)

January 21, 1966

RANGOON 365   (to SecState), S/Nodis, Immediate   , Sent Jan 21; Rec'd Jan 21, 1966, 12:46 PM. (Passed White House Jan 21, 66)

Eyes Only for the Secretary

1. Called upon DRV Consul General Vu at his residence at 8:00 P.M. tonight. . . .

2. Vu did not wait for any introductory remarks on my part but remarked as soon as we were seated that I had delivered an aide memoire to him recently which I had said I would keep confidential He said he had transmitted document to his government as he had promised. He wanted me to know however that in his own personal opinion the tone and contents of the aide memoire were such that he considered it an ultimatum.

. . . .

4. I reminded him that when I last saw him I had said I would stand by for a reply from him. So far none had been received and there was no indication of any response either related to military action or to obstacles to negotiation. I asked if he had any reply for me. He said he had had no instructions from his government to reply. He said that in the meantime his government had issued public statements which indicated its position.

. . . .

. . . .

7. Vu said he had read press reports from the White House which hinted at our direct contact. I said I was aware of this statement but Rangoon had not been singled out. He said "such news should not have been disclosed, if you sincerely wish to exchange views." I said I understood and would do all I could to preserve secrecy our contacts.

. . . .

9.

9. I made remark that I hoped I received a telephone call some day from him and was preparing to depart when he said he was ready to listen if I had anything more to say. I said I had no instructions to say more but would make one more comment. I said from Washington viewpoint it was obvious that VC initiated military activity in South Vietnam had remained at a high level. We also had reliable evidence of major truck morements continuing to South Vietnam through Laos. It seemed we had no alternative but to assume that DRV was continuing to support large scale military effort in South and send regular units there.

10. Vu said that we were now speaking informally he would comment. He said that immediately after the US made its 14 points public, 4000 US soldiers had landed in South Vietnam. He also mentioned the figure of 9000 more arrivals (but I never got period of time to which he referred). He said there are reports that 20,000 more South Koreans may come. This was ample proof that our President was not sincere.

11. I said we both had had military experience, and therefore we both knew the advance planning that had to go into major movements of military units. . . .

12. . . . Vu said out 14 points contained nothing really new. I said I hoped he would find it a useful summary of our views for study.

13. . . .

BYROADE

STATE 230 (to Amembassy RANGOON), S/NODIS, Immediate, Urtel 366, Sent 21 January 67

1. Text of U Thant's press conference Jan 20 on point you raise reads as follows:

"QUESTION: Last week when the US note was passed to the Hanoi Government in Burma, were you personally instrumental in this?"

"ANSWER: No, I was not instrumental in such a reported transaction; but of course the US very kindly kept me informed of the steps it proposed to take."

2. While you are right in assuming Thant tends by inference to substantiate reporter's assumption that contact took place in Burma, this point was not pursued in his press conference, nor was it raised with Secretary in his press conference this morning.

9

3. If we are asked, we will continue for time being to take line that US is not prepared to comment on any specific channels of communications and suggest you do same.

4. Basis of question was probably earlier New York Times story about Monday which had mentioned Burma as place of US/DRV contact. Rangoon had also been mentioned in other press reports as possible point of contact. However, Times and other references were in low key and, thus far, neither they nor U Thant remark have attracted particular press attention.

RUSK (Drafted by W. B. Buffum, P. H. Kreisberg; Approved by W.P. Bundy and Walsh)

January 24, 1966

RANGOON 370 (to SecState), S/Nodis, Immediate, Rec'd 7:36 A.M. (passed to White House 9 A.M.)

Have just received an Aide-memoire addressed to me signed by DRV Rep Vu Huu Bing. Aide memoire is confusing in that it is dated January 21. Which is the date of my second meeting with him. Text follows:

Quote :At the last meeting, you handed to me an Aide-memoire which sounds in my personal views like an ultimatum. At your request, I have, however, transmitted it to my government and kept the contact in secret.

With regard to your Aide-memoire, I have no instruction from my government to give you an answer. Still I hope you have read the statements issued recently by my government.

Lately, the press has reported news quoting White House sources which hinted the contact between you and me.

Also personally, I have some other remarks to make: Immediately after the announcement of the 14 points by the United States, some 4,000 American soldiers were introduced into South Vietnam and were stationed in Pleiku and recently, additional US troops comprising 9,000 men have landed in South Vietnam and it is now reported that South Korea is preparing to send 20,000 soldiers to South Vietnam. All these facts prove that your president is not sincere yet in settling the Vietnam question in accordance with our position.

Though I do not intend discuss things now, I should like to point out that the US 14 points contain nothing new." Unquote.

It will be noted contents above quite similar to his remarks to me as reported Embtel 365. Letter containing Aide-memoire was obviously hand carried as there were no stamps or postmarks. It sounds as if it were written prior to our second meeting but it seems if so Vu would have mentioned his reply to me. Also if hand carried why a three day delay? I can only guess that it was written after our second meeting and post dated so we cannot take position there was no reply. We will endeavor to find out about this if we can.

BYROADE

January 26, 1966

STATE 241 (to Amembassy RANGOON), S/Nodis, Immediate, Sent 26 Jan 66, 9 36 A.M.

1. Kohler saw DRV Charge in Moscow on 24th and found latter with nothing new to say. However, DRV Charge concluded conversation by saying that if USG wished any contacts they should be in Rangoon.

2. · Accordingly, you should send message to DRV Consul General saying simply that you remain available and asking whether he has any instructions. This could be in form of response to his aide memoire delivered January 24. . . .

THE SECRETARY (Drafted by W. P. Bundy)

January 27, 1966

AMEMBASSY RANGOON 374 (to SecState), S/Nodis, Immediate , Rec'd 27 Jan 66, 12:34 A.M. (Passed White House 27 Jan 66)

Ref: DepTel 241

1. At 10:32 this morning the following memorandum addressed to Vu Huu Binh was handed to a representative of DRV Consulate General here.

2. Quote I received on January 24, 1966 your Aide-memoire dated January 21, 1966 and have transmitted its contents to my government.

3. I have noted in it your statement that you have no instructions from your government to give me an answer to my Aide-memoire of December 29, 1965, and I wish to inquire whether such is still the case. In this connection I.wish to assure you again that I remain available at any time to receive any communication you may wish to address to me. Unquote.

BYROADE

January 31, 1966

RANGOON 389   (to SecState), S/Nodis, Flash   , Sent 31 Jan 66; Rec'd
3:39 A.M., 31 Jan 66 (Passed to White House 3:55 A.M., 31 Jan 66)

Am seeing DRV Consul General Vu tonight at 7:30 P.M. at his rpt
his request.

BYROADE

RANGOON 392   (to SecState), S/Nodis, Immediate   , Sent 31 Jan 66,
Rec'd 31 Jan 66, 9:02 P.M. (Passed to White House 9:45 P.M. 31 Jan 66)

Text of Aide memoire referred to in Embtel 391 as follows:
Quote I am forwarding to you the statement attached herewith made by
the spokesman of the Foreign Ministry of the Democratic Republic of
Vietnam dated January 4, 1966 regarding the so-called "Peace-efforts"
made recently by the United States.

With regards to the 14 points and the subsequent statements of
the United States Government I hold that the American authorities
still refuse to recognise the fundamental national rights of the
Vietnamese and people namely peace independence, sovereighty, unity
and territorial integrity of Vietnam as stipulated by the 1954 Geneva
agreements of Vietnam.

The United States Government states that withdrawal of its troops
from South Vietnam will be effected only under American terms, that
means the United States refuses to withdraw its troops from South
Vietnam.

The United States Government states that it seeks no military
bases in South East Asian countries but on the other hand says it has
to fulfil its commitments with the S.E.A.T.O. Bloc.

The United States Government says it respects the right to
self-determination of the South Vietnamese people on condition that
the South Vietnam National Front for Liberation lay down arms and
be granted amnesty -- that means the United States tries to maintain
a puppet regime in power countering the South Vietnamese people, does
not recognize the South Vietnam National Front for Liberation as the
sole genuine representative of the entire South Vietnamese people
and will not engage in negotiations with the Front. The United
States Government refuses to accept Point 3 of the 4-point stand
of the government of the Democratic Republic of Vietnam, that
amounts to American rejection of all the four points.

Concerning the 4-point stand of the Government of the Democratic
Republic of Vietnam. . I beg to quote the above-said statement of the
spokesman of the Foreign Ministry of the Democratic Republic of Vietnam:
"A political settlement of the Vietnam problem can be envisaged only
when the United States Government has accepted the 4-point stand of the
Government of the Democratic Republic of Vietnam, has proved this by
actual deeds, has stopped unconditionally and for good its air raids
and all other acts of war against the Democratic Republic of Vietnam.

I am ready to listen to what the Ambassador may wish to expound
on the United States position.

Rangoon dated January 31st 1966
Mr. Vu Huu Binh, Consul General of the D.R.V.   UNQUOTE

BYROADE

RANGOON 394   (to SecState), S/Nodis, Immediate   , Sent 31 Jan;
Rec'd 31 Jan 66, 9:21 P.M. (Passed to White House 10:15 P.M., 31 Jan 66)

Interpreter for DRV representative Vu called early this afternoon
to ask if I could meet with Vu at 7:30 PM tonight. I agreed and called
on him then accompanied again by Leo Reddy.

His Aide memoire was still in the typewriter and we had a rather
pleasant twenty minutes of small talk not touching on Vietnam. When
document arrived he spoke at some length about his views on Vietnam
situation. A close check with Reddy's notes indicates that he had
practically memorized contents of Aide memoire and its contents should
be accepted as accurate protrayal his remarks. He ended by asking
if I had anything to say (along lines last sentence Aide memoire).

I said I would like to revert to our previous meeting and to
his Aide memoire of January 21. The latter contained the following
sentence "All of these facts prove that your President is not sincere
yet in settling the Vietnam question in accordance with our position."
He acknowledged his rememberance of this sentence.

I said I thought it expecting just too much that our President
should be expected to be "sincere" in meeting "their" terms. They
had their four points which were called "conditions." We had
fourteen points which expressed what we believe. Was it not possible
that responsible emissaries of our two Governments could meet and
talk about all of these things together. All we asked was for unconditional talk or talks based upon the Geneva Agreements.

13

There was some confusion, based I believe on faulty interpretation, and at one point he apparently thought I had said something new as he said he would have to report to his government. On further clarification however his answer was quite clear and definite. He said there was no possibility for negotiations unless we accepted their 4 points. He said their position was the embodiment of the minimum of their national rights. If we proved our acceptance of the Geneva Agreements by actual deeds there could be a basis for a political settlement. If we rejected the Geneva Agreements, which embody their rights, there could be no negotiations. What was needed from our side was the acceptance of these points by actual deeds. There was a non-conclusive discussion as to just whom had violated the Geneva Agreements. He asked if I had anything else to say.

I said that I did because we had heard from Hanoi publicly many times that our President was not sincere, that his peace effort was a phony and that we were deceitful in the whole exercise. I wanted to raise the question as to just who was sincere and who was not. Hanoi kept repeating, even as late as yesterday, that there were no North Vietnamese regular troops or troop units in the South. Almost no one believed this. There were plenty of prisoners from these units to disprove this stand of Hanoi. Representatives of many nations in Saigon knew the facts, yet these statements continued. I could not understand this and wished his comments. Vu said he took note of my remarks and would communicate them, but would not comment otherwise.

I said that I was nothing new in the positions he had given me tonight but was glad to talk to him in at event. He said if we were not careful we could get into endless quarrels. I said that there would never be anything personal about our differences of opinion and we should keep it that way so that sometime we both could be useful to our governments. He said he would communicate at any time whatever I had to say. He showed me on the way out a back gate to his house which would be much better to use as an entrence from a security point of view.

While the above doesn't sound like it, this was our most friendly meeting to date. Vu was very cordial and hospitable and seemed in a relaxed mood. If he knew of news reports that bombing had been resumed he gave no indications of it.

BYROADE

14

February 1, 1966

RANGOON Immediate 396 (to SecState), S/Exdis, Rec'd Feb 1, 1966, 1:26 A.M.
(Passed to White House 1 Feb 66, 1:43 a.m.)

Ref: EMBTEL 394

In reviewing the bidding on last night's discussions I find
a sentence in the notes of Mr. Reddy which concerns me. This
sentence is as follows: Quote in fact, your government agreed
when the Geneva Agreements were drawn up that you would not use
force to protect them. Unquote. This remark, if it was in fact
made with use of these words, would have come chronologically at
a point near the end of para 5 in above reftel where I reported
that there was a non-conclusive discussion as to just whom had
violated the Geneva Agreements.

It should be remembered that his discussion was through an
interpreter. Our discussion at that point seemed to me at the
time to be simply an exchange of statements as to which side had
used force to violate the Geneva Agreements. On the other hand
the statement in Reddy's notes says something quite different.
It could imply that DRV in attacking South Vietnam though it
would be secure against US military action, and that we were not
playing the rules of the game as we had previously said we would
not use force in such a situation.

.   .   .   .

BYROAD

Hanoi VNA International Service in English 1737Z 1 Feb 66.

"Johnson Puts Everything in the Basket of Peace Except Peace

Text

Hanoi--Following is an article by Quang Loi in Vietnam Courier,
a Hanoi fortnightly published in English and French, playing
Johnson's deceitful search for peace campaign:

On 23 December 1965, Dean Rusk, in an interview with the
Canadian Broadcasting Company, expounded American views on a
settlement of the Vietnam problem. On 3 January 1966, the White
House issued a communique entitled "The Heart of the Vietnam
Problem." On 5 January 1966 Goldberg, U.S. Representative to

the United Nations, sent U Thant a letter in which he reaffirmed his government's desire for a negotiated solution to the Vietnam problem.

With perfect synchronization, on 24 December 1965, the Pengaton ordered a temporary suspension of the criminal bombings against the DRV.

Since then, six emissaries sent by U.S. President Johnson have traveled the length and breadth of the five continents: Goldberg to The Vatican and Western Europe; Harriman to Poland, India, Pakistan, the UAR, some Asian countries, and Australia; Williams to Africa; Humphrey to the Far East; Bundy to Canada; and Thomas Mann to Mexico....

Never has the United States engaged in a diplomatic campaign on such a scale. It has, indeed, good reasons for doing so!

The Heart of the Vietnam Problem

The existence of the Vietnam problem is an undeniable fact. The presence in South Vietnam of a 200,000-strong U.S. expeditionary corps is another undeniable fact.

A constant preoccupation of the Washington rulers is how to justify American armed intervention in Vietnam. For this would allow them to explain to public opinion why there have been re-taliations against the DRV.

This time, having found nothing better, the White House simply harked back to its old quibble: the South Vietnamese people's struggle against American interventionist troops is aggression from North Vietnam: it is this aggression from the outside which has resulted in the presence of U.S. troops. After affirming that it would be difficult to count U.S. and other countries' peace initiatives, the White House had made public U.S. contribution to the basket of peace:

1--The Geneva Agreements of 1954 and 1962 are an adequate basis for peace in Southeast Asia.

2--We would welcome a conference on Southeast Asia or on any part thereof.

3--We would welcome negotiations without preconditions, as the 17 nations put it.

4--We would welcome unconditional discussions, as President Johnson put it.

5--A cessation of hostilities could be the first order of business at a conference or could be the subject of preliminary discussions.

16

6--Hanoi's four points could be discussed along with other points which others might wish to propose.

7--We want no U.S. bases in Southeast Asia.

8--We do not desire to retain U.S. troops in South Vietnam after peace is assured.

9--We support free elections in South Vietnam to give the South Vietnamese a government of their own choice.

10--The question of reunification of Vietnam should be determined by the Vietnamese through their own free decision.

11--The countries of Southeast Asia can be nonalighed or neutral if that be their opinion.

12--We could much prefer to use our resources for the economic reconstruction of Southeast Asia than in war. If there is peace, North Vietnam could participate in a regional effort to which he would be prepared to contribute at least 1 billion dollars.

13--The President has said: The VietCong would not have difficulty being represented and having their views represented if for a moment Hanoi decides who (as received) wanted to cease aggression. I do not think that would be an insurmountable problem.

14--We have said publicly and privately that we could stop the bombing of North Vietnam as a step toward peace although there has not been the slightest hint or suggestion from the other side as to what they would do if the bombing stopped.

We have deemed it useful to reprint in full the White House's 14 points so that our readers can judge them in all objectivity.

Where Does the Heart of the Matter Lie?

If one was to believe the White House, U.S. armed intervention would be legal for the thing for the United States is to keep its commitments to South Vietnam.

But the real commitments of the United States are completely different. Everyone knows that the 1954 Geneva Agreements on Vietnam have recognized the independence, sovereignty, unity, and territorial integrity of Vietnam, and clearly stipulate that all participants in the 1954 Geneva Conference should abstain from interference in Vietnam's internal affairs. In the name of the U.S. Government, Bedell Smith, head of the American Delegation, declared at that conference that his government undertook to refrain from the threat or the use of force to disturb the execution of these Accords.[4]

From the jurisdictional and political point of view, only that solemn commitment counts. It was taken at the final session of the Geneva Conference, and the U.S. Government must fully respect it.

However, the American imperialists have completely ignored it. They have been interfering ever more seriously in South Vietnam. They have brought to power a whole series of agents in their service. Through a system of advisors and aid, they have set up a neocolonialist regime and sabotaged the reunification of Vietnam, which was scheduled for 1956. They have covered South Vietnam with a network of military bases and suppressed all aspirations to peace and national reunification with Fascist measures taken by a most tyrannical regime. Even if U.S. commitments to the pro-American puppet administration did exist, they would not be valid simply for lack of a legal basis.

It is the American imperialists' policy of intervention and aggression that is the deep cause of the serious situation in South Vietnam. The people of South Vietnam have been forced to fight in self-defense to preserve their sacred national rights and their right to live. The struggle they have been waging is just and conforms to the spirit and letter of the 1954 Geneva Agreements on Vietnam. This accounts for the growing approval and support of the world's people, including the American people, for the Vietnamese people.

On the contrary, all the efforts made by U.S. strategists to justify themselves before the American people and before history have come to grief. One remembers the White Paper issued by the State Department at the end of 1961 when the special war was launched, the Green Paper which followed it, and the second White Paper, "Why Vietnam?", published at the time when U.S. troops were being massively sent to South Vietnam.[5] One remembers the tireless declarations made by the White House, and by U.S. President Johnson himself, and the innumerable trips undertaken by U.S. emissaries to almost all countries of the world. All this has ended in utter failure; never have the U.S. rulers experienced such serious political isolation. Everywhere, peace-loving people have strongly condemned American aggression in South Vietnam and the aerial bombings against the DRV. The publication of "The Heart of the Vietnam Problem" shows that Washington's efforts, although considerable, have failed to falsify the truth and to whitewash the American aggressors.

The 14 Points--A Barefaced Lie

In its new document, the White House mentions a few things which it has so far more or less evaded: respect for the 1954 and 1962 Geneva Agreements, U.S. intention not to set up any military bases in Southeast Asia and not to maintain troops in South Vietnam, freedom for the South Vietnamese people to choose their own government and for the Vietnamese people as a whole to decide on the reunification of Vietnam, and so forth.

The Johnson Administration has made those so-called concessions to make believe that the United States has renounced its aggression in Vietnam and accepted the four-point stand of the DRV, except the third point. But this American bluff is not so shrewd as it seemed at first.

The White House affirms that the United States does not desire to retain U.S. troops in South Vietnam after peace is assured. But peace in South Vietnam has been wrecked by the sending of an American expeditionary corps for direct aggression. As long as this latter remains in South Vietnam, how can peace be restored and assured? To say that the withdrawal of American troops from South Vietnam will be effected only when peace is assured means to refuse to withdraw them until the Vietnamese people bow before American aggression.

The White House affirms that the United States wants no U.S. bases in Southeast Asia and that the countries of Southeast Asia can be nonaligned or neutral if that be their option. But in the introduction to the 14 points, it makes it clear that American commitments are based on, among other things, the SEATO Treaty. As SEATO is directed against the security of Southeast Asian countries, among them Cambodia, Laos, and South Vietnam, how can respect for the neutrality or nonalignment of Southeast Asian countries be compatible with American attachment to the objectives of SEATO? At bottom, the American imperialists remain the sworn enemy of neutral countries. It is not plain enough that they have never ceased to sabotage the neutrality of Laos and oppose the holding of an international conference guaranteeing the neutrality and territorial integrity of Cambodia? Did not Dean Rusk himself declare to the CBC on 23 December 1965 that South Vietnam's neutrality might be realized after the Viet Cong have laid down their arms and accepted the amnesty?[6] In the American conception, neutrality is but a camouflage for neocolonialism.

The White House affirms that the United States respects the South Vietnam people's freedom of self-determination and right to choose their own government through free elections. How can free elections be held when the country still remains under the control of American troops and when the United States wants, as Dean Rusk has admitted, the capitualtion of the South Vietnamese people? The American imperialists talk about the South Vietnamese people's right to self-determination: in fact, they only want to impose on them a puppet regime in the U.S. imperialists' pay.

19

The White House talks about the Vietnamese people's free
decision on the reunification of Vietnam. How can this reunification be brought about when a pro-American pupper government is
maintained in South Vietnam with the bayonets of an American
expeditionary corps? In spite of all their protestations of
good will, the American imperialists can never hide their intention
of perpetuating the division of Vietnam.

The White House drops a hint that the United States would
accept the stand of the DRV government, except its third point.
This third point says: The affairs of South Vietnam must be settled
by its own people, according to the political program of the NFLSV--
South Vietnam National Front for Liberation--without any foreign
interference.

The NFLSV, the only authentic representative of the South
Vietnamese people, controls at present four-fifths of the territory,
inhabited by 10 million people. Its program aims as realizing
independence, democracy, peace and neutrality in South Vietnam
and the eventual peaceful reunification in Vietnam. It envisages
the setting up of a democratic government of broad national union.
If it is true that the U.S. Government respects the Vietnamese
people's right to self-determination, how can it justify its
refusal to accept that third point? This refusal means simply
the negation of all other demagogic promises of the White House.
At bottom, the American imperialists stubbornly refuse to recognize
the four-point stand of the DRV government. Their own position
remains unchanged: to cling to South Vietnam, to maintain their
troops there and the Saigon puppet administration, to turn South
Vietnam into a U.S. military base and new-type colony, and to
perpetuate the division of Vietnam.

In Fact a Smokescreen.

Armed aggression in South Vietnam, aerial warfare against
the DRV, heinous crimes committed against the South Vietnamese
people--all this has aroused universal indignation against the
American imperialists. On the other hand, the just stand of the
DRV government and that of the NFLSV receive the full approval
of the whole of progressive mankind.

The noisy peace campaign and the 14 points put forward by
the White House, however skillfully concerted, nevertheless betray
the American imperialists' intention of deceiving American and
world opinion, forcing on the Vietnamese people acceptance of
their conditions, while actively preparing for the intensification
and expansion of the aggressive war in Vietnam.

20

In the first three weeks along of January 1966, the American
imperialists sent 12,000 men to South Vietnam, bringing the number
of their troops to more than 200,000. Numerous sources have revealed
their planned increase to 400,000. Massive means of extermination
are being used on a growing scale in South Vietnam, resulting in
abominable crimes.

Air reconnaissance is being continued with a view to renewed
bombings in the DRV. Several American generals have talked about
bombing raids to be conducted on the populated industrial areas of
Hanoi and Haiphong, and other criminal schemes.

The American imperialists have not only intensified their
aerial bombings in Laos and multiplied armed provocations against
Cambodia. They even talk about pursuing the Viet Cong into Laotian
and Cambodian territory, which means extending their aggressive war
to the whole of Indochina.

The American imperialists said that they have put everything
in the basket of peace. They have indeed, except peace. Let them
nurture no illusion about the effectiveness of their threats and
lies. As the spokesman of the DRV Foreign Ministry stated on
4 January 1966: The Vietnamese people eagerly want peace for
national construction, but they know full well that real independence
must be achieved if genuine peace is to be secured.

A political settlement of the Vietnam problem can be envisaged
only when the U.S. Government has accepted the four-point stand of
the DRV government, has proved this by actual deeds, and has stopped
unconditionally and for good its air raids and all other acts of war
against the DRV.

February 2, 1966

STATE 253 (to Amembassy RANGOON), S/Nodis, Immediate, Sent 2 Feb 66
8:44 P.M.

. . . .

2.   ...we wish to give some response and also to test whether
Hanoi is still willing to talk after the resumption (which your man
apparently did not know about and on which his communications might
not have permitted a cancelling message to get through on Monday).
Accordingly, you should send him a short note acknowledging his
communication, saying it is under careful study in Washington, and
that we expect to have a detailed response in a very few days.

3.   . . .

RUSK (Drafted by W. P. Bundy)
                              21

February 3, 1966

STATE Memorandum for SecState from William P. Bundy, dated Feb. 3, 1966

MEMORANDUM FOR THE SECRETARY

SUBJECT: DRV Approach in Rangoon on January 31

      It seems to me that our response to this approach will take careful thought. As a first step, since Byroade's cables are hard to read together, I have done the attached pull-together, which contains the full text of the aide memoire, and also the points made in the oral conversation. I think this gives us a much better starting point, with numerical headings, for our own reply. (Tab A).

      We may know much better, on the basis of Byroade's interim response, whether Hanoi really intended to start a dialogue after the resumption. In the meantime, the present facts appear to indicate that Hanoi may have sent the instructions prior to the resumption, but that it should have been possible to send a last-minute "recall" or "cancel" message if Hanoi had desired. Byroade reports that the DRV interpreter came to him to seek the appointment in the "early afternoon" of January 31, Rangoon time. (Rangoon time is 1 1/2 hours earlier than Saigon time.) This would suggest that the appointment was sought not earlier than 1500 Saigon time, whereas the first bombs had fallen at about 0900 Saigon time. The fact that the aide memoire was still being typed when Byroade arrived at 1930 Rangoon time would suggest that the instructions must have been freshly received and that there may even have been a preliminary instruction to seek an appointment, followed by the later trans-mission of the detailed instructions. By 1730 Rangoon time (1900 Saigon time) ten hours had elapsed after the resumption (which we assume was instantaneously reported to Hanoi). We believe that Hanoi's communications to Rangoon may go either by direct commer-cial cable or by relay through Peiping, using some cryptographic system that is presumably immune to Chicom reading. We are now checking whether NSA has any reading on message transmissions of that date, but what stands out is that it would surely have been possible for Hanoi to send a fast commercial cable that need not have said anything more than a short instruction not to carry out prior instructions. In other words, the evidence does add up to a high probability that Hanoi was prepared to go through with the contact notwithstanding the resumption. Indeed, there appears to be a substantial possibility on the timing, that Hanoi even waited till it knew of the resumption before it dispatched the instructions. Paradoxical as it may seem, Hanoi may have been unwilling to open any dialogue during the suspension, lest this appear as a sign of weakness, and fear of our bombing.

A second collateral aspect worthy of note is that Hanoi broadcast, on the evening of February 1, Saigon time, in English, a lengthy article, the so-called "Quang Loi" article, which is by far the most detailed exposition of Hanoi's reaction to the Fourteen Points. For the first time, the actual text of the Fourteen Points was published, and the article goes on to explore their meaning, with a fair amount of invective, but in general in a far more moderate and reasoned tone than the overwhelming bulk of its output during the suspension. It seems to me essential that the aide memoire received in Rangoon be read in conjunction with the Quang Loi article, which I have there-fore attached as Tab B.

Thirdly, the aide memoire itself refers to the DRV Foreign Ministry statement of January 4, and in effect incorporates this by reference. The January 4 statement, attached as Tab C, is a fairly straightforward reiteration of the Four Points, with no reference to our Fourteen Points except in highly general terms.

Because of the length of the two related Hanoi statements in Tabs B and C, I have sidelined key passages.

/s/ WPB
WILLIAM P. BUNDY

3 Encl
   1 - Tab A - Bundy Summary
   2 - Tab B - Quang Loi Article
   3 - Tab C - January 4 Hanoi Statement

THE RANGOON APPROACH OF JANUARY 31
        (From Rangoon 392-296)

        Text of Aide Memoire (See cables cited)
        (Para Numbers Added)

. . . .

Points Made in Conversation (Para Numbers Added)

8. After the reading of the aide memoire, the DRV man asked if Byroade had anything to say. Byroade reverted to the earlier Rangoon aide memoire questioning the President's sincerity, and said that it was expecting too much that the President should be expected to be "sincere" in meeting "their" terms. Hanoi had its Four Points which were called "conditions." We had Fourteen Points which expressed what we believe. Was it not possible that responsible emissaries of our two governments could meet and talk about all of these things together? All we asked was for unconditional talks or talks based upon the Geneva Agreements.

9. The DRV man was at first confused and thought Byroade had
said something new. However, on clarification, his answer was quite
clear and definite. He said there was no possibility for negotiations
unless we accepted their Four Points. He said their position was the
embodiment of the minimum of their national rights. If we proved our
acceptance of the Geneva Agreements by actual deeds there could be a
basis for a political settlement. If we rejected the Geneva Agreements,
which embody these rights, there could be no repeat no negotiations.
What was needed from our side was the acceptance of these points by
actual deeds.

10. There was then a non-conclusive discussion as to who had
violated the Geneva Accords. In the course of this discussion, the
DRV man asserted that, when the Geneva Agreements had been drawn
up, the US had agreed that it would not use force to protect them.
(Byroade's 396 thinks that this statement, in its context, conveyed
an implication that the DRV had thought that, in attacking South
Vietnam, it would be secure against US military action -- that, in
short, the DRV had been misled. The facts on this point are that
Bedell Smith said that we would not ourselves use force to disturb
the Agreements, but went on to say that we would view the use of
force by others with grave concern. In other words, the statements
by the DRV man distort the record substantially.)

11. Then, in response to the DRV man's asking whether Byroade
had anything else to say, Byroad reverted to the question of sincerity
and raised the question as to just who was sincere and who was not,
when Hanoi kept repeating, as late as January 30, that there were no
North Vietnamese regular troops or troop units in the South. Byroade
pointed out that almost no one believed this and that there were plenty
of prisoners to disprove it. Yet these statements continued. The
DRV man took note of these remarks and said he would communicate them,
but did not comment otherwise.

12. In conclusion, Byroade said that he saw nothing new in the
positions the DRV man had given him, but was glad to talk with him
in any event. He added" "He (the DRV man) said if we were not
careful we could get into endless quarrels. I said that there would
never be anything personal about our differences of opinion and we
should keep it that way so that sometime we both could be useful to
our governments. He said he would communicate at any time whatever,
I had to say. He showed me on the way out a back gate to his house
which would be much better to use as an entrance from a security
point of view."

13. Byroade's closing comment was as follows: "While the above
doesn't sound like it, this was our most friendly meeting to date.
Vu was very cordial and hospitable and seemed in a relaxed mood. If
he knew of news reports that bombing had been resumed he gave no
indications of it."

RANGOON 398 (to SecState), S/Nodis, Priority, Sent 3 Feb 66; Rec'd 3 Feb 66, 5:44 A.M.

Ref: DepTel 253

We have arranged to deliver the following memorandum ...

Text follows "I refer to our last discussion on January 31, 1966, in which you presented me with an aide-memoire which in turn enclosed a statement made by a spokesman of the foreign ministry of the Democratic Republic of Vietnam dated January 4, 1966.

I wish to inform you that these matters are under careful study in Washington, and that I think I may have a detailed response for you in a few days time."

. . .

BYROADE

February 7, 1966

RANGOON 406 (to Sec State), S/Nodis, Priority, Rec'd 7 Feb 1966, 10:42 P.M. (Passed to White House 8 Feb 66, 12:30 A.M.)

English language papers this morning frontpaged AP and UPI stories, quoting "Administration" and "informed" sources, of direct contact made by me here with DRV on Dec. 29. No mention of continuing contacts.

I have told RGUB and have passed word to Vu that I will not rpt not confirm, but will stand on no rpt no comment.

BYROADE

February 8, 1966

RANGOON 411 (to SecState), S/Nodis, Priority, Rec'd 8 Feb 66, 6:03 A.M., (Passed White House 8 Feb 66)

1. GVN Consul General Duc requested appointment see me today. . . . Responding to his expected questions re contact in Rangoon between Ambassador Byroade and DRV ConGen as reported in wire services, I took line previously agreed on with Ambassador Byroade that all embassies had strict instructions not to comment on any channels of communication with North Vietnam; that Ambassador Byroade had had similar inquiries put to him before departing for Bangkok and was not commenting. Moreover, I was in no position to speculate about contacts.

2. Duc unagressive and did not press further.

RANARD

February 16, 1966

STATE 267 (to Amembassy RANGOON), S/Nodis, Priority, Sent 16 Feb 68, 11:38 A.M.

You should seek appointment with DRV Consul General to deliver following aide-memoire:

BEGIN TEXT:

1. The USG has taken note of the Aide Memoire delivered to the American Ambassador in Rangoon on January 31, 1966.

2. The USG fully respects the basic rights of the Vietnamese people to peace, independence, sovereignty, unity and territorial integrity, as set forth in the Geneva Accords of 1954. As the USG has repeatedly said, it believes that these Accords, together with the 1962 Accords concerning Laos, are an adequate basis for peace in Southeast Asia or for negotiations looking toward a peaceful settlement.

3. The USG has repeatedly stated and hereby reaffirms that it is prepared to withdraw its forces from South Viet-Nam when peace is restored. The US has never stated that it must be the sole judge of when this condition exists. Plainly, the restoration of peace requires the adherence of all concerned to the essential provisions of the Geneva Accords dealing with the regroupment of opposing forces to their respective areas, and dealing with the obligations that the two zones shall not be utilized for the resumption of hostilities or in the service of an aggressive policy. It is the view of the USG that the DRV, in introducing armed forces, military equipment, and political cadres into South Viet-Nam, has breached the provisions of the Accords, and has thus made necessary the actions undertaken by the USG in support of the legitimate right of the Republic of Viet-Nam to self-defense. The withdrawal of US forces would be undertaken in the light of the actions taken by the DRV in this regard, and would necessarily be subject also the existence of adequate measures of verification.

The USG seeks no military bases of any kind in South Viet-Nam and has no desire whatever to retain its forces in South Viet-Nam after peace is secured.

4. With respect to the third of the DRV's four points, the US takes note that Chairman Ho Chi Minh in his letter of January 29[7] described the program of the NLF as seeking "to achieve independence, democracy, peace and neutrality in South Viet-Nam and to advance toward peaceful reunification." If this is all that is intended

when it is stated that the affairs of the South Vietnamese be settled "in accordance with the program of the NLF," the third point would not be an obstacle to negotiations.

However, it appears that in referring to the program of the NLF the DRV may contemplate that the NLF arbitrarily be accorded integral participation in a coalition government or be accepted as the "sole genuine representative of the entire South Vietnamese people" prior to, and without regard to, an election. If this is what is meant by the third point, we would consider it in contradiction of the very objectives specified above, and quite without warrant in the Geneva Accords of 1954.

It remains the essence of the USG view that the future political structure in South Viet-Nam should be determined by the South Vietnamese people themselves through truly free elections. The USG is categorically prepared to accept the results of elections held in an atmosphere free from force, intimidation or outside interference.

5. In the light of the foregoing and to make clear our understanding of a possible basis for discussions leading to a peaceful settlement, we submit for consideration of the DRV the following:

Point I - The basic rights of the Vietnamese people to peace, independence, sovereignty, unity and territorial integrity are recognized as set forth in the Geneva Accords of 1954. Obtaining compliance with the essential principles in the Accords is an appropriate subject for immediate, international discussions, or negotiations without preconditions. Such discussions or negotiations should consider, among other things, appropriate means, including agreed stages, for the withdrawal of military and quasi-military personnel and weapons introduced into South Viet-Nam or North Viet-Nam from one area to the other or into either area from any other outside source; the dismantling of any military bases in either areas, and the cancellation of any military alliances, that may contravene the Accords; and the regrouping and redeployment of indigenous forces.

Point II - Strict compliance with the military provisions of the Geneva Accords must be achieved in accordance with schedules and appripriate safeguards to be agreed upon in the said discussions or negotiations.

Point III - The internal affairs of South and North Viet-Nam must be settled respectively by the South and North Vietnamese peoples themselves in conformity with the principles of self-determination. Neither shall interfere in the affairs of the other nor shall there be any interference from any outside source.

Point IV - The issue of reunification of Viet-Nam must be decided peacefully, on the basis of free determination by the peoples of South and North Viet-Nam without outside interference. END TEXT

6.   In delivering text, you should take care not to ge beyond its terms in providing explanation to any questions asked. Naturally, we would be most interested in any comments he may care to make then or at future date.

7.   FYI: Bundy will bring to Baguio some additional material for your background in case of future contacts.[8] However, for time being, we do not wish to be drawn into extended oral discussion which might be misunderstood. END FYI.

8.   In arranging appointment, you should avoid any impression of undue urgency.

February 19, 1966

RANGOON 433 (to SecState), S/Nodis, Priority, Rec'd 19 Feb 1966, 11:33 A.M.

DRV Rep Vu received me at 7:00 P.M. . . .

Vu did not try to read document in English but listened attentively as his interpreter translated document for him.

. . . .

Vu said he would transmit our Aide-Memoire to his government. He said that if I had anything else to add that I should go ahead with it. I said that my instructions had been covered fully by the document now in his hands and that I had nothing more for the present. Vu then said that since our last meeting there had been many developments in the situation. He said that their stand on the grounds for agreement must be based on the fact that the US has resumed the bombing. He said this was a gross violation of the sovereignty and national independence of a state. American forces had been intensifying the war and following a policy of kill all, burn all, destroy all. Also there was the fact of the joint declaration of the USG and the South Vietnamese authorities.[9] He said the points made therein only served the cause of the American war.

He then said "I also wish to avail myself of the occasion of this meeting to inform you something else today. Since the US has resumed the bombing, I hold that it is inappropriate to continue our contacts."

. . . .

. . . .

...I said I wanted to be very sure I had understood correctly his statement about future contacts between us, and asked if he could amplify his remarks. He repeated verbatim his previous words except that this time he used the expression "It is imappropriate to continue our talks at your request." He said he thought he had expressed himselv clearly. He would however follow up by sending me an Aide-Memoire, as he had been speaking under instructions.

. . . .

BYROADE

February 21, 1966

RANGOON 436 (to SecState), S/Nodis, Immediate, Rec'd 21 Feb 66, 2:01 PM

Ref: EMBTEL 433

The following aide-memoire dated Feb 19 from DRV representative Vu addressed to me was hand delivered to the Embassy this evening. Quote: At this meeting held at your request, I find it necessary to make the following statements:

The resumption of the bombing of the Democratic Republic of Vietnam, the increase of American armed forces and of war aid to the South Vietnam authorities, rigged up by the United States, on order of the United States Government and the issue of a joint declaration at the Honolulu Conference by the United States and the South Vietnam authorities have exposed the true colour of the "Peace Efforts" Manoeuvred by the American government. The American government is doing its utmost to intensity and expend its aggressive war in Vietnam and Indochinese countries, bringing it to a new stage, seriously endangering peace and security of the countries in this region. The American government must bear full responsibility for the consequences resulted in by the aggressive war it wages. The bombing of the Democratic Republic of Vietnam, an independent and sovereign country, ordered by the United States Government constitutes an unpardonable aggressive act. In so doing, the American Government not only grossly violates and tramples under foot the 1954 Geneva Agreements on Vietnam which it solemnly undertakes to respect but also brazenly breaches the United Nations Charter and the most elementary norms of justice and human rights.

Conducting the destructive war in South Vietnam with every kind of American, most modern weapons including those strictly prohibited by International Law as noxious chemicals and gas, the American Expeditionary Troops and the mercenary troops have been carrying out wherever they go the scorched earth policy killing all, burning all and destroying all.[10] If the United States Government thinks that its utmost barborous and cruel aggressive policy as such can subjugate the Vietnamese people, that will be a great mistake and here day-dream.

The Honolulu Conference and the Joint Declaration signed at
that conference by the United States and South Vietnam puppet
authorities represent the entire scheme of the United States to
bring the aggressive war in South Vietnam to a new stage.   Therefore, such hypocritical terms of the said declaration a "opposition
to aggression," "fulfilment of commitments," "continuation of
peace efforts," "self-determination", "rural reconstruction program,"
etc. are in essence aimed at covering up the designs of the aggressive
war in South Vietnam.

Faced with the strength of unbreakable unity and determination
to fight and to win of the Vietnamese people who enjoy the strong
sympathy and support of the world people including the American people,
 the efforts made so far or to be made in the future by the American
Government cannot remove the more and more critical situation of the
American troops and the mercinary troops who are now falling into a
quagmire in South Vietnam but will only bring them instead even
bigger and more ignominious setbacks and eventually total defeat.
It is the Vietnamese people who decide the outcome of the war they
wage against the American invaders.   They have won and will triumph.
Such is·the truth that has been realized and admitted by the majority
of the American people and a number of persons among the American
political circle but denied by the United States Government.

If the United States Government realli wants to settle the
Vietnam question peacefully, it should accept the four-point stand
of the government of the Democratic Republic of Vietnam and prove
its acceptance by actual deeds and stop for good and unconditionally
its bombing of North Vietnam and all other war acts against the
Democratic Republic of Vietnam.   Only so can a political settlement
of the Vietnam question be envisaged.

As the United States Government has ordered the resumption of
bombing raids on the Democratic of Republic of Vietnam, I consider
it inappropriate to continue the contacts made at your request
between you and myself.   Unquote.

BYROADE

30

VI.C. 1., The Ronning Missions—March and June 1966

In early 1966, Canada tried its hand at peacemaking. Prime Minister Lester Pearson had become increasingly concerned with the way in which the war was disturbing Canadian-American relations, and he was probably also troubled by charges at home that he had identified Canada too closely with U.S. policy. He took Canada's responsibilities as a member of the ICC seriously, and he seems to have feared that further American escalation might provoke Chinese intervention, leading to a much larger and more dangerous war. He thus chose the occasion of responding to Ho Chi Minh's letter of January 24 to send a personal emissary to Hanoi to try to promote direct talks that might eventually lead to a settlement. He did not conceive Canada's role as a mediator. Rather, he merely offered its good offices to get the two combatants together. He appears also to have hoped to revive the moribund ICC by persuading the co-chairmen of the Geneva Conference, the United Kingdom and the Soviet Union, to draw up new terms of reference that would permit the commission to take the initiative in getting talks started.

Pearson chose for this delicate mission Chester A. Ronning, a retired Canadian diplomat and old Far Eastern hand. Born in China of Lutheran missionary parents, Ronning had spent his early years there before settling in the United States and then in Canada. He had returned to China as an educator in the turbulent 1920s and, once again, in 1945 as an official in the Canadian Embassy. He remained until the embassy closed in 1951, witnessing firsthand the civil war and forming acquaintances with Chou En-lai and other Chinese leaders. Subsequently, as a member of the Canadian delegation to the Geneva Conference in 1954 and as head of the delegation to the Geneva Conference on Laos in 1962, he gained some knowledge of the intricacies of the Indochina tangle and some familiarity with the North Vietnamese leaders. His linguistic skill, his knowledge of the Far East, and his sympathy for Asian revolutions made him an ideal choice from Pearson's point of view.

Ronning spent five days in Hanoi in March 1966 and, after early frustrations, felt that he had achieved a major breakthrough. "I have never worked harder or used more arguments to put the American intervention in Vietnam's civil war in the best light to persuade officials with whom I talked to try negotiations to end the war," he later recalled.[1] At first, all he got in return were ringing reaffirmations of Hanoi's determination to prevail whatever the cost. In his final conversation, with Pham Van Dong, however, his persistence appeared to be rewarded. After the usual litany of attacks on the United States,

---

1. Chester Ronning, *A Memoir of China in Revolution: From the Boxer Rebellion to the People's Republic* (New York: Pantheon, 1974), p. 259.

Pham indicated that, if the Americans stopped the bombing "for good and unconditionally, we will talk." Pham's statement seemed a significant advance beyond Hanoi's prior insistence on acceptance of the Four Points as a precondition to negotiations, and Ronning returned to Ottawa excited and full of hope.

The precise meaning of Pham's statement remains unclear. It was certainly a less equivocal reassertion of the message contained in the DRV Foreign Ministry statement of January 4, 1966, and seems, therefore, to have represented a step forward from the position taken by Hanoi the preceding year. Beyond that, however, Pham's words were carefully phrased and contained what were most probably deliberate ambiguities. The use of the word *talks* rather than *negotiations* seems to have suggested that Hanoi would be willing to engage only in preliminary contacts, not substantive negotiations, and there was no indication of any willingness to compromise on basic issues. On the other hand, Pham's forthcoming demeanor raises at least the possibility of persisting divisions within the North Vietnamese leadership as to future strategy and the search for a way out short of a military solution. A positive American response might have exacerbated the divisions in Hanoi and opened the way for a settlement that while by no means guaranteeing American goals in Vietnam might have been superior to that which was ultimately attained. At the very least, the United States might have used Ronning to probe more deeply into the ambiguous meaning of Pham's words and to explore the possibility of concessions.

As the following documents make clear, however, Washington responded quite negatively to the Ronning mission. Americans had been suspicious of the Canadian gambit from the outset, and they were particularly distrustful of Ronning, who had been openly critical of U.S. policies toward China and Vietnam. Although they had somewhat grudgingly supported the mission, they expected little from it and upon Ronning's return they were not inclined to search for hidden meanings in Pham's ambiguous language. Indeed, some saw in the North Vietnamese premier's "overture" a clever ruse. In the past, Hanoi had demanded that the United States accept its Four Points and prove its acceptance with deeds, namely, cessation of the bombing. It was argued, therefore, that acceptance of this latest offer might be interpreted as tacit agreement to the Four Points.

Even if U.S. officials had been attuned to the signals Hanoi *may* have been sending, however, the timing of the Ronning mission made a positive response unlikely. On March 10, while the Canadian was still in Hanoi, a political crisis erupted among South Vietnam's Buddhists that would last until the end of May. At several points, the uprising caused near anarchy, and eventually it had to be quelled by military force. No matter how conciliatory the message from

North Vietnam, Americans were not inclined to make concessions at a time when the situation in South Vietnam appeared so perilous.

Moreover, the Ronning mission took place against the background of another major internal debate on escalation of the war. The peace offensive of December and January having produced nothing of substance, the Joint Chiefs had intensified their pressure to expand the bombing. In April, Secretary of Defense McNamara fell into line, approving attacks on petroleum, oil, and lubrication supplies (POL) in the Hanoi-Haiphong area, as well as cement plants in Haiphong and roads, bridges, and railroads connecting the two major cities with the Chinese border. Not wanting to appear once again to be striking the North because of frustrations in the South, Johnson had deferred implementation of the plan temporarily. He was committed to the next step of escalation, however, and would have been unwilling to approve a bombing halt, the step required by North Vietnam, in the absence of some tangible and significant military or political concessions.

The United States thus flatly rejected the proposal brought back by Ronning. It delayed for more than a week responding to Canada's message, and, when it finally replied, fell back on the now standard position that North Vietnam must commit itself to reciprocal de-escalation, rather than merely promise to "talk" in return for stoppage of the bombing. Ronning pleaded for greater flexibility but got nowhere. He returned to Hanoi in June, bearing the U.S. response, he later said, with a "heavy heart."[2] During his rather perfunctory meetings with lesser North Vietnamese officials, the commitment to talk in exchange for cessation of the bombing was reconfirmed, and Hanoi made clear its interest in keeping the Canadian channel open. Predictably, however, the North Vietnamese rejected the American counterproposal, expressing, in Ronning's words, their "outright refusal even to consider such an abject, impossible condition."[3] When the word of this response reached Washington and with the political crisis in Saigon eased, the administration proceeded to escalate the bombing. Ronning later felt that he had been used, that the United States seized upon the negative response to justify escalation. Such a charge seems unduly severe, but here, as in other instances, the failure of a peace mission did mark yet another expansion of the war.—*Ed.*

2. Ibid., p. 267.
3. Ibid.

THE RONNING MISSIONS - MARCH AND JUNE 1966

Ronning Revs Up

Chester Ronning's "unofficial" trip to the Orient on behalf of peace was proposed by the Canadians in late January 1966. It evoked formal U.S. support and unvoiced U.S. trepidations. A Sinologist and retired diplomat, Ronning was known to hold a critical view of U.S. policies toward China and Vietnam. He hoped to visit Peking and Hanoi, relying for his welcome in China on a long-standing invitation from Ch'en Yi, with whom he had friendly relations, and Hanoi on his bearing Pearson's answer to Ho Chi Minh's letter of January 24.[1]

Both Washington and our Embassy in Ottawa guessed an ulterior motive for the trip: Canadian Foreign Minister Paul Martin wanted to test the wind for changes in Canadian policy on Chinese representation in the UN, possible recognition of Communist China, and, more generally, a demonstration that Canada was not a U.S. "satellite."[2] Under the circumstances (the 37 day bombing pause was still running), there seemed no proper response other than encouragement, even though the U.S. doubted the mission would produce much. (1/27/66, 2/4/66, 2/25/66)

By February 24, Peking had refused to issue Ronning a visa (2/24/66), and the reason is not difficult to guess. Ronning's itinerary and intention to visit Hanoi would have shown Peking that he hoped to play the mediator between NVN and the U.S. Chinese Communist policy insisted that the war be fought until the U.S. was defeated. Nevertheless, the DRV permitted him to come and, during his stay (March 7-11) gave him access to a number of high officials.

The March Visit: "Talks" in Exchange for a Bombing Cessation

Ronning characterized the results of his March 7-11 visit with an old Chinese saying: he had "travelled ten thousand miles to present a feather." (3/15/66) Although treated with deference,* he was unable to move the DRV leaders from their insistence on the "Four Points" as the only basis for a peaceful settlement. They felt confident of keeping up their end of the war. (They expected destruction of Hanoi and Haiphong, they said, and were evacuating women and children, dispersing factories and offices, etc.) When Ronning protested their "Four Points" as tantamount to U.S. surrender, their attitude seemed to be "that's America's problem." (3/15/66)

Toward the end of Ronning's 2-hour interview with Pham Van Dong, however, he was told that DRV willingness to enter into some form of preliminary contact hinged on a commitment by the U.S. to cease "bombing

---

* He was received by the DRV Foreign Minister Nguyen Duy Trinh, the Vice Foreign Minister, Nguyen Co Thach, Col. Ha Van Lau (NVA liaison to the ICC) and, on his last day, Pham Van Dong.

and all acts of war against North Vietnam" "unconditionally and for good." *
It was not clear whether a public declaration or something more confidential
was demanded, nor what the nature of the consequent contacts would be.
Pham Van Dong refused to be drawn out, saying only: "Our position includes
many aspects. In brief, we can say that informal talks and a cessation of
attacks against North Vietnam go together." (3/20/66)

Ronning felt that a U.S. response was desired. The importance of
secrecy was stressed to him. When earlier feelers had become public,
the DRV had been forced to deny them, he was told.

Arranging the Second Trip: Canada in the Middle

Ronning's report aroused little enthusiasm in Washington, which:

--Felt that any U.S. de-escalation should be reciprocated by
military de-escalation on the other side.

--Feared that a bombing halt would be interpreted to mean U.S.
acceptance of Hanoi's Four Points.** (4/26/66)

Martin, however, felt strongly that the channel should be kept
active and pressed Washington personally and through channels to respond.
In what may have been a veiled form of pressure, he informed Washington
that his Government "did have important information of which it was the
sole possessor." (4/22/66, 4/26/66)

By May 1, Washington had prepared a "new" message for Ronning,
restating its willingness to talk without conditions, or to de-escalate
mutually, to communicate with Hanoi directly or via intermediaries, etc.
(4/30/66)

When Ottawa approached Hanoi about a return visit by Ronning, it
was criticized by the North Vietnamese for failing to distinguish between
aggressor and victim, and of advancing proposals not conforming to the
1954 Geneva accords, etc. Toward the end of May, it obtained grudging
permission for Ronning to come along, however. (5/24/66)

---

*   Ronning was promised an Aide-Memoire on Pham's remarks, but was subsequently told that he had "misunderstood" and no such paper would be
forthcoming. In his written summary of the conversation, Ronning used
quotation marks in the manner reproduced here. Presumably, he felt
confident he was accurately repeating Pham's language.

** In his January 24, 1966, letter to heads of state, Ho had demanded that
the U.S. "accept the four-point stand of the DRV Government and prove
this by actual deeds; it must end unconditionally and for good all
bombing raids and other acts of war against the DRV."

The June Visit: No Movement by Either Side

Ronning visited Hanoi a second time, June 14-17, 1966, with even more disappointing results than in March.

He was told that Pham Van Dong was not then in Hanoi, and the highest official to receive him was Nguyen Duy Trinh, Foreign Minister and Vice Premier. Trinh expressed disappointment that the message Ronning carried was so "similar to newspaper reports with which the DRV was already familiar." Ronning, looking back a week later, felt "totally depressed following his conversation with Trinh" and did not detect "any hint on Trinh's part of a desire to put forward any new or alternative proposals." (6/21/66)

The main points made by Trinh were:

--There would be no military reciprocity for a bombing halt.

--The Canadians were abetting the U.S. "peace offensive" by appearing to mediate when they had nothing new to contribute--and doing so in a period (since March) when the U.S. was "escalating." When Ronning offered to withdraw, though, Trinh asked that the Canadian channel remain available.

--The Four Points were not mentioned per se, but their contents and the NLF Five Points were stressed as elements the U.S. would have to accept eventually.

--Neither the Four nor the Five Points were preconditions for "talks", however. If the U.S. stopped bombing completely, the DRV would talk. (6/21/66)

Although Ronning saw no promising new approach that might be offered the DRV at that time, Martin clearly wished to maintain the Canadian channel and seemed determined to find some role for Canadian peace-making efforts in the future. (6/23/66)

General Topics Raised During Ronning's Contacts

The following are topics raised with Ronning which also appear frequently during other negotiating sequences.

"Talks" vs "Negotiations"

Bundy visited Ottawa on June 21 to review Ronning's experiences with Ronning, Martin and other Canadians. As he cabled back, they concluded that "the total DRV comment appeared to add up to there being a satisfactory prior understanding, before 'negotiations' as to (1) our recognition of the status of the NLF (not spelled out); (2) return to the 1954 Agreements; (3) withdrawal of US forces (not specified whether this must take place prior to negotiations or as to the ultimate result); (4) the Four Points." In distinction to these conditions for negotiations, "the DRV reps did say categorically that acceptance of the Four Points was not a necessary condition to preliminary talks. The only condition for such preliminary talks is our unilateral cessation of bombing. However,...this appears to relate only to resumption of Rangoon-type contact, and as to any substantive negotiations the Four Points are still in the picture." (6/21/66)

"Permanent and Unconditional"

On Ronning's first visit, the North Vietnamese indicated a willingness to talk if "the bombing and all other acts of war" were unilaterally ceased "unconditionally and for good." This statement clearly contained two qualifiers: no reciprocity from Hanoi and no threat of resumption. Ronning, however, was not told that Hanoi would only "talk." The two qualifiers taken together were sufficient, but that they both were necessary was not clear. Ronning never tested this. Trinh, in January 1967, dropped the "permanent" qualifier, but at the same time, made it plain that a U.S. bombing cessation would buy only "talks."

"Peace Offensives vs. Military Offensives"

The timing of Ronning's second visit--mid-June--was awkward for the U.S., as it was planned to bomb POL facilities through the DRV, including Hanoi, at just that time.[3] Such an attack would be difficult to reconcile with our support for Ronning's mission. (5/9/66, 6/8/66, 6/15/66). An attempt to circumvent this problem was made by delaying the strikes but seeking the earliest possible report from Ronning on Hanoi's response. (6/17/66) Ronning, however, had been told to report only to Ottawa, upon his return. (6/17/66, 6/18/66) Furthermore, Martin specifically asked us not to "escalate" in the period just after Ronning's return for fear that this would "jeopardize Canadian good faith with Hanoi and make it appear the U.S. used Ronning as a means of obtaining a negative readout on negotiations which would justify escalation." (6/20/66) In effect, the Canadian initiative seemed to require that we not escalate just before, during or just after contacts with Hanoi. Moreover, Martin wished to maintain a continuing dialogue with Hanoi. The POL system was attacked toward the end of June.

Secrecy

The North Vietnamese repeatedly stressed the importance of keeping their contacts secret and repeatedly complained of leaks to the press. (6/21/66) To illustrate the gravity of the matter, the Vice Minister of Foreign Affairs told Moore (the Canadian ICC representative) that the La Pira peace feeler had been genuine, but that Hanoi had had to denounce it when it leaked.[4] (6/8/66)

4

On the other hand, an Eastern European Embassy in Hanoi
briefed Raffaelli, the AFP correspondent there, on the content of
Ronning's June exchanges with relative accuracy. The French Embassy
in Washington and Americans assumed that the information had been passed
with DRV approval, without satisfactorily resolving the question of DRV
motives in providing this leak.

Reunification

The subject of reunifying the two Vietnams was broached to
Moore on one of his routine visits to Hanoi early in June, 1966, by
Ha Van Lau. The main point stressed by Lau was that "After the fighting
stops, there should be a fairly long interval, during which the status
quo continues with the two countries divided at the 17th parallel....
After that, it would be possible to see whether there were some changed
ideas in Saigon and Hanoi." (6/8/66) When Ronning visited Hanoi, later
that month, the subject was not emphasized by the Vietnamese, but was
raised in the context of observing the 1954 Geneva Agreements. (6/21/66)

POW's

The U.S. asked Ronning to scout the possibility of exchanging
prisoners of war with the DRV or providing them with ICRC protection.
(5/15/66) Hanoi's reply was that POW's were "criminals" under DRV law
and no ICRC role would be considered. He was given no detailed information about the prisoners themselves. (6/23/66)

Another Geneva Conference?

In the event of negotiations beginning, DRV officials indicated
to Ronning that they would consider a Geneva-type conference on Vietnam
and observed that they would favor French participation. With some
prodding from an Ottawa colleague, Ronning reconstructed the following
as a possible sequence: (1) an end to the U.S. bombing on DRV terms;
(2) informal bilateral DRV-U.S. talks; (3) a multilateral Geneva-type
conference. (6/21/66)

January 27, 1966

MEMORANDUM OF CONVERSATION; Participants: H. E. Charles S. A. Ritchie, Ambassador of Canada, Mr. Chester Ronning, former Canadian Ambassador, Mr. William P. Bundy, Assistant Secretary for Far Eastern Affairs, and Mr. Paul H. Kreisberg, FE/ACA.

"....

"...Ronning said he was without illusions on the likelihood of any success from this mission but thought it was worth a try. He said the Canadian line would be to express surprise at Peking's and Hanoi's opposition to a conference in view of their participation in the Laos conference.

"....

"Ronning then inquired about the position of the NLF.

"Mr. Bundy reviewed the U.S. position on the NLF, stressing that we are prepared to have them present in some form at a conference but not in full status as a 'party' but anything short of that we would be prepared to consider. He...stressed that acknowledgment of full status for the NLF would be pre-judging the right of the NLF to participate in a future government in South Vietnam. He noted that the NLF program called for the Front to have a main role in a coalition government and said that to admit this would quite frankly lead to their ultimate victory...."

"...Ronning suggested that there might be an analogy between NLF participation in a conference and that of the Pathet Lao in the Laos conference.

"....

"Ronning said that he was convinced the DRV would continue to deny its military participation in South Vietnam but might accept something less clear-cut. He said the DRV did not want a branch of the CP in South Vietnam ever to declare its independence of North Vietnam. He suggested that bilateral U.S.-DRV talks without the GVN might offer some possibilities.

1

"Mr. Bundy said this was possible and we had offered this to the DRV during the pause. He noted that it might be necessary to arrive at some 'pre-digested' conclusion in such a forum. He observed, however, that the question of disclosure to the GVN presented a serious problem. Ronning stressed that the DRV could not sit at the conference table without the NLF since this would place all responsibility for military action in South Vietnam on itself.

"Mr. Bundy reiterated that the NLF was a really tough problem since it ran so close to the heart of the matter. It was possible to finesse other points, for example, accepting the four points implicitly by reiterating acceptance of the Geneva Accords, or simply deleting the objectionable clause in point three. Mr. Bundy said that the DRV still thought it could win the whole game but that ultimately, if it was convinced that there was no military victory possible, it might re-frame its political requirements and move for a political solution. He noted that we could without particular difficulty "de-fuse" point 13 of our 14 points by omitting the reference in that point to "aggression."[5] Mr. Bundy also noted that the DRV was concerned about the timing of U.S. withdrawal.

January 27, 1966

STATE to AmEmbassy OTTAWA 826 (SECRET-EXDIS), 27 Jan 1966:

"For Ambassador from Bundy

"1. Canadian Ambassador Ritchie and former Canadian High Commissioner ir New Delhi Ronning called on Bundy today and discussed planned visit by Amb. Ronning to Peking and Hanoi in near future. Ronning visit to be unofficial but he will travel with personal rank of Ambassador and at request of Foreign Minister Martin. Ronning has long-standing invitation from Chicom Fonmin Chen Yi to visit CPR extended when Ronning was Canadian Rep at 1962 Geneva Conference on Laos. Purpose of visit to sound out Peking and Hanoi on possible conference on Vietnam. Ronning said he without any illusions as to likelihood of success but thought visit in any event might be worthwhile.

..... "

RUSK (Drafted by P. H. Kreisberg)

2

January 28, 1966

STATE to AmEmbassy OTTAWA 830 (SECRET-EXDIS), 28 Jan 1966

"1. ...we certainly have no objection to proposed Ronning trip....

"2. It occurs to us that Ronning trip may well have ulterior motives in terms of Canadian feelers on Chicom representation in UN or even Canadian recognition...."

RUSK (Drafted by W. P. Bundy)

AmEmbassy OTTAWA to SECSTATE 974 (SECRET-EXDIS), 28 Jan 1966

"For Bundy from Butterworth

"....

"3. Ever since he became Minister for External Affairs two and a half years ago Martin has had the idea of using Chester Ronning, who was born in China and went to school with Chou En-lai, to help bring about recognition of the Chinese Communists by the UN or by Canada or both.

"....

"5. Ronning is well-known in Canada as a Sinologist and has been more often than not critical of American Far Eastern policies....

"....."

BUTTERWORTH

January 31, 1966

AmEmbassy OTTAWA to SECSTATE 981 (SECRET-EXDIS), 31 Jan 1966

"....

"2. ...Pearson confirmed Ronning mission was Martin's idea, that it entailed greater dangers than Martin had perhaps appreciated and that he had 'scared the hell out of Paul about it last night'....if anything went wrong, his government would disavow any involvement in the Ronning mission...."

BUTTERWORTH   3

AmEmbassy OTTAWA to SECSTATE 979 (SECRET-EXDIS), 31 Jan 1966

"....

"5. ...Martin volunteered that he had clearly
in mind the domestic political scene and 'Diefenbaker's
insincere support of the U.S. position in Vietnam'[6]
and that at some point he should demonstrate to the
Canadian people that Canada had not just been a U.S.
satellite but had done what it could to bring about
a solution...."

BUTTERWORTH

February 2, 1966

AmEmbassy OTTAWA to SECSTATE 996 (SECRET-EXDIS), 2 Feb 1966

"For Assistant Secretary Bundy

"...Incredible though it may seem EXTAFF official
stated Ronning's passport reads 'Special Emissary of
Canadian Government with Personal Rank of Ambassador.'
Ploy with Hanoi for obtaining visa is that Ronning
interested in discussing Ho Chi Minh letter of January 24 to Prime Minister Pearson. Text of letter
(copy being sent Dept. separately) parallels that
sent other capitals except for last two sentences as
follows: 'Your Excellency, Canada is a member of the
International Commission for Supervision and Control
for the Implementation of the 1954 Geneva Agreement
on Vietnam. In face of the extremely serious situation
brought about by the U.S.A. in Vietnam, I hope that
your Government will fulfill its obligation under
the Geneva agreements.

.....'"

BUTTERWORTH

February 4, 1966

STATE to AmConsul HONG KONG 1000, AmEmbassy SAIGON 2254,
Amembassy OTTAWA 856

".....

"2. Ronning is retired diplomat, born in China
and steeped in Sinology. He was most recently Canadian

4

High Commissioner in New Delhi and during that time
represented Canada at Geneva Conference on Laos.
We have long been exposed to his viewpoint, which
tends personally to be highly critical of U.S. policy
toward Communist China, and particularly to the advocacy of Chinese Communist admission to UN. Moreover, he apparently has long-standing personal ties
with both Chou En-lai and Chen Yi, plus fact that
his parents are buried in China, so that present
visit has some handle in an earlier Chen Yi invitation and in the idea of visiting the graves of his
parents.

"3. ...Despite our private misgivings as to his
personal views, we have naturally had to say we would
have no objection to such visit and indeed could only
welcome any constructive initiative....

.....\"

RUSK (Drafted by W. P. Bundy)

STATE to AmEmbassy OTTAWA 857 (SECRET-EXDIS), 4 Feb 1966

" You should deliver following personal letter to
Foreign Minister concerning Ronning visit:

"Dear Paul:

".....

"I must, however, express a shade of concern at
the information that we have just had from Walton
Butterworth that Ronning's passport will apparently
carry the appearance of a formal accreditation as
your special emissary with the personal rank of
Ambassador....

"I am also more seriously concerned at the possibility that Ronning may find himself engaged in discussion, especially in Peiping, of the problems relating
to Chinese representation at the UN and even, if I
understand your last conversation with Walton Butterworth
correctly, questions of recognition....

".....

"...I think we shall both have a great deal of
thinking to do on this subject in the months ahead
and I hope that in the first instance we can do it

5

on a very confidential basis between ourselves. I
have therefore welcomed the indication that you are
not discussing the Ronning trip with any other government, and I would end by repeating my hope and assumption that he will be listening only as to any matters
other than Vietnam, and that in any event we shall
have a full opportunity to talk over with you whatever he picks up in any area.

"With warm regards, Sincerely, Dean Rusk"

(Drafted by W. P. Bundy)

February 7, 1966

AmConsul HONG KONG to SECSTATE 1452 (SECRET-EXDIS), 7 Feb 1966

"We shall do what we can helpfully to influence
Ronning's thinking if opportunity presents itself.
Incidentally American in Hong Kong who will have fullest opportunity affect his thinking is NY Times correspondent Topping, who is his son-in-law."

RICE

February 24, 1966

STATE to AmEmbassy SAIGON 2512, AmConsul HONG KONG 1086; Info:
AmEmbassy OTTAWA 943, AmEmbassy MANILA 1556 (SECRET-EXDIS),
24 Feb 1966

"1. Canadian Embassy has informed Dept. Ronning
trip to Peking turned down by Chicoms but accepted by
Hanoi. Ronning now in Hong Kong and scheduled go
Saigon March 1 leaving for Hanoi March 7 and returning
Saigon March 11....

" .....

"3. ...Peking turndown of visit made through
Chen Yi message to Ronning referring to U.S. actions
in Vietnam and GOC support for these which make visit
'inopportune.' Door held open for some future visit,
however.

" ......"

RUSK (Drafted by P. H. Kreisberg)

6

MEMORANDUM to The Secretary from Samuel D. Berger, FE, Subj:
Chester Ronning Visit to Peking and Hanoi, dated 24 Feb 1966
(NODIS)

" . . . . .

"5. ...Hanoi's willingness and even enthusiasm
in agreeing to Ronning's visit results in part from
a growing feeling of isolation and in part from a
desire to project a more 'positive' foreign policy
image. The agreement by the DRV Charge in Moscow
to obtain clarification for Lord Chalfont on some points
in the DRV position and Hanoi's reversal of its decision last summer not to extend an invitation to
Nkrumah to come to North Vietnam may be other aspects
of this somewhat looser and more flexible foreign
policy. Such a policy, designed to offer a more
attractive image of Hanoi to the world at large, was
specifically urged by DRV Politburo member Le Duc
Tho earlier this month.[7] The change in policy, however, is one of form, not content thus far.

. . . . ."

February 25, 1966

AmEmbassy SAIGON to RUEHC/SECSTATE 3100 (SECRET-EXDIS),
25 Feb 1966

"1. It is true that I know that Mr. Ronning
is taking the trip, but it is quite an exaggeration
to say that I am 'fully informed of the background
of his trip.' I honestly do not feel that I am aware
of all the ins and outs and all the implications.

"2. Having in mind the British/North Vietnamese
contact in Moscow, I would appreciate knowing of whatever understanding there may be in Washington.[8]

"3. Once again we seem to be getting into direct
contacts which affect the future of Vietnam and I do
not know what to tell the Vietnamese."

LODGE

STATE to AmEmbassy SAIGON 2525 (SECRET-NODIS), 25 Feb 1966

"Eyes Only for the Ambassador from the Secretary

"Following are my own personal comments about the
Ronning visit to Hanoi:

7

"Quite frankly, the Canadians themselves seem to be of divided minds about his trip. Ronning has not been helpful on Vietnam and I have no doubt strongly favors recognition of Peiping. Mike Pearson is definitely skeptical about the whole affair but was inclined to go along with Paul Martin's guarded approval for the trip.

"I personally talked to Paul Martin about Ronning and emphasized that it was extremely important that Ronning do nothing to encourage a Hanoi miscalculation about our determination and do nothing to encourage a Hanoi miscalculation about our determination and . do nothing to undermine the publicly stated positions of the United States. Martin assured me that he would make that very clear to Ronning.

"Actually, the Ronning trip was originally designed primarily for Peiping and I suspect that the question of recognition and Peiping membership in the UN was most on Ronning's mind. However, Peiping refused to let him come since Canada's attitude toward Vietnam made his visit QTE inopportune UNQTE.

"I can assure you there is no occult understanding between Washington and Ottawa on this matter. If you need to say anything to the South Vietnamese about the Ronning trip, you can tell them that he is on no mission for us, that he has been strongly advised not to say anything or do anything which would encourage Hanoi to believe that their effort will succeed and that his visit should be considered along with such efforts as have been made by many individuals to have a go at Hanoi. Quite frankly, I attach no importance to his trip and expect nothing out of it. At the same time it would be unwise to say anything to GVN which would appear to conflict with Canadian version of trip already given GVN and reported in Deptel 2512, Para 2."

RUSK (Drafted by Rusk)

March 3, 1966

AmEmbassy OTTAWA to SECSTATE 1143 (CONF-EXDIS), 3 Mar 1966

"...Exstaff has put its ICC peace probe on ice,... it is shifting concentration of its peace efforts to Ronning visit to Hanoi next week. ...Ronning is not mediator but explorer."

SCOTT

AmEmbassy SAIGON to SECSTATE 3178 (SECRET-EXDIS), 3 Mar 1966

"1. Moore (Canadian member ICC) called to present
Ambassador Ronning who is on his way to Hanoi.

"....

"3. ...Ronning wished to find out if there was
something useful that the ICC could do other than to
implement the Geneva accords which have now been so
thoroughly violated.

"4. He explained all this to Colonel An, the
GVN liaison officer with the ICC, and was planning
to tell Tran Van Do about it. An apparently did not
object.

"5. ...Moore, who had gone to Hanoi to pave
the way for Ronning, said that Hanoi's acceptance of
the idea of Ronning's visit was 'immediate.' ...he
seemed to think they were worried about the immense
casualties which their Army was encountering and would
be encountering in South Vietnam.

".....' "

LODGE

March 15, 1966

AmConGen HONG KONG to SECSTATE 1669 (SECRET-EXDIS), 15 Mar 1966

"....

"2. Results of mission: Ronning characterized
results of his mission by quoting old Chinese saying;
he had 'travelled ten thousand miles to present a
feather.' He said he is more pessimistic about long-
range Vietnamese problem than before his trip.

"3. NVN confidence: North Vietnamese leaders
he spoke to from Pham Van Dong on down convinced they
were winning war, although they concede it will be
long struggle. In response my query how NVN expected
achieve victory (e.g., by military victory, U.S. loss
of determination, GVN collapse), Ronning said NVN
views not clear. NVN leaders told him they fully
expected stepp-up U.S. military effort, both in
South and in bombing of North, including bombing of
Hanoi, industries, etc. Explained they had few large
industries; small industries being dispersed and plans
made for evacuating government offices and populace.

9

Ronning commented to me that he did not disabuse NVN
leaders of their estimates of increased U.S. military
action. Instead, he tried to impress upon them that
U.S. could bring vastly greater military power to bear
than could the French in 1950's, and that therefore
no chance of history repeating itself (as they seemed
to believe).

   "4. Negotiations: NVN leaders were totally unwilling budge from 'four points.' His remonstrances
that strict adherence 'four points' would amount to
total American surrender and were therefore unworkable
as negotiations formula were greeted with attitude
'that's the American's problem.' Soviet Ambassador,
while expressing full support NVN, implied there was
somewhat greater possibility for negotiations by telling him that first prerequisite was permanent cessation of bombing of NVN. When Ronning asked why, if
this was the case, NVN had made no response during
recent bombing pause, Soviet Ambassador said 'they
did respond' but refused specify channel or content.
Ambassador said resumption of bombing came at just the
wrong time and gave Ronning impression resumption had
'loused up' overtures Soviets were making to Hanoi
at the time.

   "5. Sino-Soviet dispute: NVN leaders attempted
downplay importance of dispute and particularly its
impact on Vietnam situation. Told him they expected
Chicoms to attend CPSU Congress, but claimed they
did not know composition delegation.

   "6. Geneva Accords. Ronning said both GVN and
NVN leaders talked of return to Geneva Accords but
in completely different terms. GVN leaders stressed
provisions for withdrawal of NVN and VC forces, and
claimed that reunification would eventually come through
'disintegration' of communist control in north. NVN
leaders stressed elections and claimed they were confident election results would pave way to early reunification.

   "7. Ronning's treatment: Ronning found that as
a Canadian he treated better than British who support
American position fully, but made politely aware that
Canada little more than American satellite. However
Pham Van Dong appreciative of Pearson's public state-
ment of regret over resumption of bombing in north.
Ronning found his several hours of talks with Hanoi
leaders very wearing and frustrating with conversations

10

wandering down blind alleys and always returning to same
intransigent dead end. He got impression he was object
of team effort at wearing him down, as long, hard hours
of conversation with one group of officials would soon
be followed, with little rest, by another session with
fresh team. Some talks also scheduled in early morning with scarcely fifteen minutes notice, apparently
to keep him off balance. He was in constant company
of protocol cadre (with whom he could converse in
Chinese) and interpreter.

"8. Impressions of Hanoi: People adequately
clothed and fed. Ronning made special point of visiting market and found rice, fish, meat and vegetables
in seemingly good supply. Only stall with line of
people in front was selling flour. (He could not
tell whether it was Canadian or not, but noticed word
'flour' in English on bag.) Streets were practically
empty at night, and Ronning was told that many oldsters,
youth, and cadre dependents had been evacuated.

"9. Ho Chi Minh out of sight: Ho, an old acquaintance of Ronning's sent apologies explaining that
round of meetings in connection with forthcoming Soviet
Congress left no time to see him. It rumoured in Hanoi
that Ho planning attend Congress.

"10. Chinese also not in evidence: with exception
of banquet room full of Chinese cultural troupers in
Sun Yat Sen suits, Ronning saw no Chinese in Hanoi.
Chicom Embassy personnel invited to reception given
by North Vietnamese his honor did not show up.

. . . . . "

ARMSTRONG

March 20, 1966

MEMORANDUM OF CONVERSATION; Subject: Ronning Visit: Hanoi;
Participants: Canadian Ambassador Chester Ronning, Canadian Ambassador
Charles S. A. Ritchie, Embassy of Canada, Assistant Secretary for Far
Eastern Affairs William P. Bundy, Mr. Michael Shenstone, Counselor,
Embassy of Canada, Mr. Paul H. Kreisberg, OIC, Mainland China Affairs,
ACA.

"1. Ambassador Ronning passed the attached memorandum[9]
to Mr. Bundy, which summarizes his principal meetings in Hanoi.

ATTACHMENT QUOTE
Accompanied by Mr. V. C. Moore, Canadian

Emphasis was laid on the importance of absolute secrecy in any exchange that might develop from Ronning's discussions. Earlier feelers had become public and the North Vietnamese had been forced to issue a denial. ATTACHMENT END QUOTE

"2. He noted that in contrast to Saigon where he had operated completely under the ICC cloak, Hanoi was anxious that his visit there <u>not</u> be under ICC auspices. On his arrival he was escorted into the city separately from Victor Moore, the Canadian ICC representative in Hanoi.

"3. Ronning found the Vice Foreign Minister, the Foreign Minister and ICC Liaison Officer, Col. Han Van Lao all equally hard and uncompromising on negotiations. All insisted on the US acceptance of the '4 points', the role of the NLF as 'sole representative of the people of South Vietnam', etc. Col. Han Van Lao said that the DRV wanted the ICC to continue but emphasized it was important that it make the proper findings. No findings at all were preferable to bad ones.

"4. Ronning said he tried in all his conversations to argue that it was a mistake to believe the Americans were like the French and could be driven out by military means. He said that all the Vietnamese took a 'black and white' view: the Americans were wrong and the DRV was 'right'. The Foreign Minister and other subordinate officials said they expected the US to destroy Hanoi and Haiphong. They were

evacuating women, children, dispersing Government
offices and factories, and were prepared to fight to
the end. The United States, they said, could never
crush an agricultural·society like that of North Vietnam.

"6. Ronning's last substantive conversation was with
Prime Minister Pham Van Dong. Until nearly the end of
his conversation, he was as rigid as his subordinates.
In response to a question from Ronning inquiring whether
there was nothing which could be done, Pham Van Dong said
that the DRV would be prepared to have talks with the
United States if the latter declared an unconditional and
permanent halt to its bombings of North Vietnam. In
response to a request for clarification, Pham Van Dong
said he was not referring to military action in the South,
only in the North. He added at this point, however, that
this had already been included in the January 4, 1966
Foreign Ministry Statement and was not new. He agreed
in response to Ronning's request to provide Ronning with
an aide memoire on talks following a permanent halt in
bombings. Subsequently Ronning was told by an aide to
Pham Van Dong that there had been a misunderstanding and
no aide-memoire would be forthcoming. Ronning said that
at no point had an acceptance of the '4 points' been linked
to the halt in bombing by Pham Van Dong. Dong asked that
the Government of Canada convey this message to the United
States and said several times that the DRV wanted to keep
a channel open through the Canadians.

"7. Ronning said he had asked Dong why the DRV hadn't
talked to the United States during the last 'pause'. Dong
said they had (the Soviet Ambassador made this same point).
Pham Van Dong had also tossed off the Sino-Soviet conflict
as merely a 'difference of opinion' and had emphasized both
were friends of the DRV and would help defend the security
of a socialist country.

"8. Pham Van Dong concluded by observing that the
Canadians were 'men of good will' and while 'good will'
doesn't matter much, one should use it when one can.

"9. Dong accepted Prime Minister Pearson's letter
to Ho Chi Minh but expressed regret that Ho was too busy
to see Ronning. Dong said the Chinese Communists would
go to Moscow for the 23rd CPSU Congress and that Chou En-lai
would probably lead the delegation. (Ambassador Ritchie
said Ambassador Dobrynin had told him Chou would not be
going to Moscow.)

14

"10. Ronning expressed his personal opinion that the offer of talks for a complete halt to bombing was separate from the '4 points' but added that, on balance, he frankly did not himself think anything significant had emerged from his visit.

"11. Mr. Bundy observed that the Hanoi ploy was clever; since the bombing question had in the past (including Ho Chi Minh's January 24 letter) been linked publicly with the '4 points', acceptance of the DRV offer implied acceptance of the '4 points.' He said Pham Van Dong's remarks would, however, call for some careful consideration. To Mr. Bundy's question as to whether Pham Van Dong had discussed the role of the NLF in negotiations, Ronning said he had not and suggested Hanoi wanted to avoid discussing matters that pertained directly to the South."

March 31, 1966

Memorandum (SECRET/EXDIS); To: FE - Mr. Bundy; From: ACA - Harold W. Jacobson; Subject: EXDIS Response to Pham Van Dong's Remarks to Ronning.

. . . .

"2. According to Ronning's account, the only concrete proposal made to him in Hanoi was Pham Van Dong's last minute suggestion that DRV willingness to enter preliminary talks with us 'hinges' on the question of our declaration of an unconditional and permanent halt to the bombing of North Vietnam. We could hardly respond positively on this; we could, at best, only seek further information. Therefore, instead of responding directly to the Ronning message, Paul suggested, and David Dean and I concur, that the EXDIS Aide Memoire sent to the DRV through Rangoon, February 16, be resubmitted to the DRV through the Canadians in the course of their routine travels to Hanoi. At the same time we could request the Canadians to add the following oral comment: 'A representative of the US would be prepared to discuss the question of talks leading toward a peaceful settlement of the conflict in Vietnam at any time. The proposal by the North Vietnamese Premier that the US permanently and completely halt such bombings could, of course, be among the subjects for discussion in such a meeting.'"

April 22, 1966

Department of State Memorandum for the File.

"Mr. Paul Martin, Secretary of State for External Affairs, Canada, called at 9:05 AM from Ottawa, to speak to Mr. William Bundy.

. . . .

". . . . His main concern was the long interval - the Canadians had had some word from 'Asia' to the effect that they too are concerned about the length of time /since the last visit./ Mr. Martin said he felt very strongly indeed that they had to go back with something - even nothing - even something contrived.

"Mr. Bundy said that any response would not be contrived on our side; that he had reviewed a proposed message to the Canadian Government just yesterday and had mentioned previously to Ambassa- dor Ritchie that we did not feel that it would be a propitious thing to move 'while things are at white heat.'

"Mr. Martin replied that he appreciated that, but felt that what we had to do was establish with 'these people' the notion - quite genuine on the Canadian side - that we want to do something and that we are really trying. He stated that the potentiality of this matter cannot be minimized.

. . . .

"Mr. Bundy said we would couch our memorandum in such terms that it would be up to the Canadians just how our message would be conveyed."

. . . .

(Drafted by B. M. Moore)

Department of State Memorandum for the Secretary (through S/S); Subject: Pending Vietnam Matters, dated 22 April 1966.

. . . .

". . . Paul Martin is very anxious for a prompt response on the Ronning approach. We still do not see much in it but plainly our relations with Paul Martin alone would dictate as forthcoming a response as we can make. I have drafted a reply. . . ."

. . . .

William P. Bundy

16

April 26, 1966

MEMORANDUM TO THE GOVERNMENT OF CANADA

"1. The Department of State has carefully studied the
memorandum provided by Ambassador Chester Ronning following
his trip to Hanoi on March 7-11, and has further considered
Ambassador Ronning's personal report to Mr. Bundy on his visit
on March 20. . . .

"2. We agree that the Canadian channel to Hanoi that this
approach has provided should be kept open, and have refrained
from proposing a reply up to this point because of the political
crisis in Saigon.[10] To have approached Hanoi in these circumstances seemed to us unwise.

"3. As the Canadian Government is aware, a direct channel
between the United States Government and Hanoi was opened in
Rangoon during the period of the recent bombing suspension. . . .
the record stands that a direct channel has been opened, but that
Hanoi chooses for the time being not to employ it.

"4. Against this background, and in the light of repeated
North Vietnamese statements insisting upon the acceptance of
the so-called 'Four Points' before any discussions or negoti-
ations--and insisting that the US demonstrate such acceptance
by 'concrete acts' such as the unequivocal and permanent cessation
of bombing of the North--the USG is unable to evaluate the
message conveyed to Mr. Ronning as indicating any real 'give'
in Hanoi's position. We understand that Prime Minister Pham
Van Dong reiterated the DRV's 'four points,' but at the close
of the conversation suggested or hinted that Hanoi might be prepared to enter into discussions if the US would declare a
permanent cessation of bombing attacks on the North. It seems
most probable that this was still intended to be linked with
acceptance of the 'four points,' although a contrary interpretation is conceivable. In any event, it should of course be
clear that the U.S.G. could not accept a unilateral cessation
of this form of military activity without some reciprocal action
of the North Vietnamese side involving its infiltration of men
and equipment into the South and perhaps also the overall level
of military activity in the South.

"5. In the circumstances, the U.S.G. believes that a
message should be conveyed to Hanoi--either through the regular
Canadian ICC representatives, or, if desired, Ambassador Ronning--
which would explore the meaning of the North Vietnamese suggestion
as far as possible and reiterate US willingness to pursue the
matter further through the established direct channel. The
Canadian channel might continue to be used in the event of a

forthcoming response. In view of the complexity of the
issues that would be involved in any true reciprocal reduction of hostilities, it would be the US hope, however, that
if Hanoi were interested, the matter would be pursued directly
as soon as possible. Specifically, the USG suggests that an
oral message along the following lines be conveyed in Hanoi
at the appropriate level:

<u>TEXT</u>

"**A.** The Canadian Government has conveyed to the
USG the views expressed by Prime Minister Pham Van Dong
to Ambassador Chester Ronning on March 11. The reaction
of the USG indicated that it could not accept the apparent.
suggestion that the USG must agree to a permanent cessation of the bombing of North Vietnam as a unilateral
and non-reciprocated pre-condition to the holding of
discussions. The Canadian Government knows, from the
public and private statements of US representatives,
that the US is itself prepared for discussions or negotiations without any preconditions whatever, and that
it would also be prepared to consider a reciprocal
reduction in hostilities in Vietnam, which could include
the question of the bombing of North Vietnam. However,
action concerning the latter, as the Canadian Government
understands the US view, could not be undertaken unilaterally in the absence of reciprocal measures by North
Vietnam. The Canadian Government is confident the USG
would be interested in any indication the DRV was interested in such reciprocal actions, and of what sort.
Moreover, interest was expressed by the USG as to whether
the remarks of Prime Minister Pham Van Dong indicated
the possibility that mutual and reciprocal reductions
in military activity might in themselves serve to create
the possibility for holding of discussions or talks.

"**B.** The Canadian Government is assured that the
USG would be prepared at any time to discuss directly
and in fullest confidence the respective positions of
the USG and the North Vietnamese Government and the
possible means of reconciling these positions and moving
toward a peaceful settlement of the Vietnam conflict.

"**C.** The Canadian Government knows that the US would
be interested in any response, or any indication of its
position in any respect, that the Government of North
Vietnam might wish to communicate to the Government of
Canada."

<u>April 26, 1966</u>

Amembassy OTTAWA 1443 to SecState (SECRET/NODIS).

"1. I delivered the memorandum contained in reftel to Extaff Min Martin. . . .

. . . .

"3. Martin . . . said that he had been concerned that delay on our part might call into question Canada's 'credibility' and this was the reason why 'in the absence of Dean and you and Charles Ritchie' he had 'impulsively picked up the telephone' and called Bundy. He went on to say that the U.S. had been assured that nothing that was in our national interest to know would be withheld; nevertheless GOC did have important information of which it was the sole possessor. . . ."

BUTTERWORTH

<u>April 30, 1966</u>

Oral Message (Final Draft)

May 2, 1966

MEMORANDUM (SECRET/NODIS); To: Mr. Bundy; From: Paul H. Kreisberg;
Subject: Ronning II

"The draft Canadian oral message based upon our April 26th
memorandum to the GOC seems to me to be essentially satisfactory
and to accurately reflect the spirit of our original memorandum. . . ."

. . . .

May 5, 1966

Note to the Secretary (SECRET/NODIS)

"Ambassador Waller (Australia) came to see me this afternoon and asked point blank about what Chester Ronning was up
to. In the circumstances, I decided that the only thing to do
was to tell him frankly the situation. I therefore said that
Ronning had been up in Hanoi in March and had talked to Pham Van
Dong, who had reiterated the four points but then had thrown out
a teasing suggestion that they might be prepared to talk if we
agreed to stop the bombing. I said that we had sat on this
message during the recent political troubles, but were now
prepared to authorize the Canadians (I did not specify whether
it would be Ronning himself) to go back and say that we were
interested in whether Hanoi had really meant to say that it no
longer insisted on the four points and was talking only of a

cessation of bombing, and secondly that if this was the suggestion we could not accept it on a unilateral basis but would have to know what Hanoi proposed to do itself. . . ."

. . . .

William P. Bundy

May 9, 1966

Department of State, Note to the Secretary (SECRET/NODIS)

"Walt Rostow heard from the Ranch today that the President has indicated that if you wish we may give Ottawa approval of the attached revised Ronning oral message to Hanoi without checking back with him, but the President asked whether we might not have to override this political initiative with a more far-reaching one if we take the air action against NVN now being pressed by DOD.[11]

"Under these circumstances, do you wish the revised draft to be given to the Canadians at this time?"

Benjamin H. Read

May 15, 1966

STATE 1219 to Amembassy OTTAWA (SECRET/NODIS)

. . . .

"5. We would prefer that Ronning . . . make the following points:

(a) He understands that the ICRC in accordance with its traditional neutrality and independence stands ready to make its services available to prisoners on both sides of this conflict. . . .

. . . .

(c) He has reason to believe that the U.S. would be prepared to discuss arrangements for a possible release or exchange of these prisoners, either through the Red Cross, or through another intermediary, or directly. North Vietnamese receptivity to such a move would be an important step toward lessening of tension.

"6. We would not want Ronning to raise the issue of 'war

21

crimes trials', partly because there are recent indications
that Hanoi does not intend to go through with its threat to
try these men. . . ."

RUSK (Drafted by F. A. Sieverts)

<u>May 24, 1966</u>

. . . .

MOORE

June 3, 1966

OTTAWA 1635 to SecState (SECRET/NODIS)

"1.   GOC learned today that Ronning mission acceptable
to Hanoi in mid-June, so Ronning expected fly to Hanoi from
Saigon on ICC aircraft June 14 and return June 18.

. . . .

"3.   Extaff has queried whether Dept. has any comment
for it on that section of John Finney article in NY Times of
June 3 which stated that USG QUOTE has sent a new message to
Hanoi pledging willingness to cease bombing if NVN, under
some form of international verification, stops infiltrating
troops into SVN.   These diplomatic overtures have been conveyed to Peking and Hanoi in recent days through diplomatic
channels and through private, informal meetings by individuals
who were understood to know administration thinking.   END QUOTE."

BUTTERWORTH

June 6, 1966

SAIGON 5312 to SecState (SECRET/NODIS)

"1.   It would be less disturbing if Canadians were to leave
informing GVN about Ronning mission to US.   However we recognize
this might not satisfy Canadians, and that may be behind their
offer to clear their approach in advance. . . .

. . . .

"3. We, of course, will . . . . . use argument that
Canadians wished to pursue matter, we had no wish to discourage them, and while we do not expect results we will
keep GVN informed."

LODGE

June 8, 1966

BRUSSELS SECTO 87 to SecState (TOP SECRET/NODIS); Eyes Only for
Secretary McNamara from Secretary Rusk.

"Reference your telegram on Ronning, you may have seen
by telegram to the President. I am deeply disturbed by
general international revulsion, and perhaps a great deal at
home, if it becomes known that we took an action which sabotaged
the Ronning mission to which we had given our agreement.[12] I
recognize agony of this problem for all concerned. We could
make arrangements to get an immediate report from Ronning. If
he has a negative report, as we expect, that provides a firmer
base for the action we contemplate and would make a difference
to people like Wilson and Pearson. If, on the other hand, he
learns that there is any serious breakthrough toward peace, the
President would surely want to know of that before an action
which would knock such a possibility off the tracks. I strongly
recommend therefore against ninth or tenth. I regret this
because of my maximum desire to support you and your colleagues
in your tough job."

RUSK

June 8, 1966

SAIGON 5379 to SecState (SECRET/NODIS)

Section one of two.

. . . . .

"2. Moore then launched into a long talk full of miscellaneous items about what he has picked up in North Viet-Nam, as
follows:

"3. The North Vietnamese Vice Minister of Foreign Affairs
had told Moore that the La Pira peace feeler had been genuine,
but the Hanoi regime had had to denounce it when the leak came.

"4. Moore was very emphatic on the danger of leaks, and, in
fact, on the whole danger of talking a great deal and having a lot

of publicity about peace feelers. He said that Hanoi have
'played ball' as regards keeping quiet on the first Ronning
trip, and he believed they would do so this time.

"5. In particular, he deplores a U.S. statement which
he said was made by McCloskey on June 3, which gave in public
almost exactly what the substance was of what the Canadians
were planning to say in private. . . .[13]

. . . .

LODGE

Section two of two.

"12. . . . . On the matter of a public statement explaining
the reason for the Ronning trip, he said it was clear that Hanoi
did not like any talk about 'a new role for the Commission' and
that would not be used as an explanation.

"13. Moore agrees with his Polish colleague that there is
a 'will to talk' in Hanoi and cited the receptiveness to the
suggestion that Ronning could come as an illustration.[14]

"14. He talked a good deal about conversations which he
had had with Ha Van Lau, the Hanoi regime's liaison man with
the ICC, and honorary colonel and a professional French-trained
civil servant. Lau said: 'The U.S. must show its sincerity by
its deeds.' At a number of dinners and lunches, where he constantly ran into Lau, the conversation always was on Lau's part
and the other guests around him: 'How can this war be ended?'
Lau often discussed reunification, with discussions running something like this: 'After the fighting stops, there should be a
fairly long interval, during which the status quo continues with
the two countries divided at the 17th parallel, depending on
the circumstances. After that, it would be possible to see
whether there were some changed ideas in Saigon and Hanoi.'
But, Moore said, implicit in everything that Lau said was that
the NLF was the only legitimate group and would, of course, have
to be the government of South Viet-Nam."

. . . .

LODGE

June 15, 1966

STATE 3563 to Amembassy TOKYO (TOP SECRET/NODIS); Literally Eyes
Only for Ambassador from Secretary

"1. As you know from discussion at Baguio meeting,[15] we
have had under continuing consideration the possibility of
bombing key POL installations in DRV, notably Haiphong and
Hanoi installations, which are just outside city limits and
in areas where we believe civilian casualties can be kept to
extremely low figures under the prescribed operating rules of
good weather and daylight operations. Operation would involve
total of roughly seven targets and could be conducted in two good
weather days, although the likelihood of good weather and effective attack may be such as to cause it to stretch for four days
or more.

". . . . Assuming that the operation were to be conducted
between now and early July, we request your personal assessment
as to the level of Japanese reaction to be anticipated and the
attitude GOJ might take. . . .

. . . .

RUSK (Drafted by W. P. Bundy)

STATE to Amembassy VIENTIANE 802; Info: Amembassy OTTAWA 1341 and
Amembassy SAIGON 3911 (SECRET/NODIS)

. . . .

"2. . . . . your arrangement with Maclellan to see him
June 18 is exactly right. You should find occasion to re-confirm
this meeting and to make absolutely sure you see Ronning soonest as
he returns."

. . . .

RUSK (Drafted by W. P. Bundy)

Department of State Memorandum of Conversation (SECRET); Subject:
Ronning Visit; Participants: Mr. Michael Shenstone, Counselor,
Canadian Embassy; Mr. Leonard Unger, Deputy Assistant Secretary for
Far Eastern Affairs.

"1. . . . Moore recounted a conversation of Ronning
(and himself, presumably) with a senior DRV Foreign Ministry

official who said that there will be no DRV press release
on the Ronning visit this time and he hoped that the
Canadians would likewise make no public statement. The
official went on to say that his Government presumes that
Peking knows about the Ronning visit but the DRV nevertheless wished to avoid the added affront that might be given by
its being publicly announced. Moore speculated that an
added factor might be that Ho Chi Minh might still be present
in Peking. . . ."

. . . .

June 15, 1966

LONDON, JUNE 15 (REUTERS)

"Prime Minister Harold Wilson hinted today that another
peace initiative in Vietnam might be made soon.

"The Prime Minister said a mission to Hanoi last year
by junior Minister Harold Davies was greatly harmed by
premature publicity.[16]

"'I shall be careful to say nothing today,' Wilson told
a meeting of his parliamentary labor party. 'This does not
mean that there will be none.'

"Diplomatic observers in London thought Wilson may have
been referring to the mission of special Canadian Envoy
Chester Ronnings.

"Officials in Ottawa today said Ronning was now in Hanoi
on his second mission since March."

. . . .

June 17, 1966

STATE to Amembassy VIENTIANE 805; Info: Amembassy OTTAWA 1349 and
Amembassy SAIGON 3943. Eyes Only for Charge.

"In your conversation with Ronning, if he should give
negative reading, you should inquire particularly whether
he is making immediate cable report to his government in
this sense."

RUSK (Drafted by W. P. Bundy)

27

June 17, 1966

OTTAWA 1710 to SecState (SECRET/NODIS)

. . . .

"Martin said he had given Ronning instructions to be very careful, depending on what he comes out with, about what he tells our people in Vientiane. He is instructed in any case to send a full report as promptly as possible to Martin himself. . . ."

. . . .

SCOTT

June 18, 1966

SAIGON 5628 to SecState (SECRET/NODIS)

"Moore has more than clammed up. He regrets he is under strict instructions not rpt not to talk to us until he reports to Ottawa. . . . His instructions provide that Ottawa will do the talking. . . ."

LODGE

VIENTIANE 1335 to SecState; Info: Ottawa 98 and Saigon 654 (SECRET/NODIS)

"1. . . . I was unable see Ronning during his brief stopover here this morning. Maclellan apparently received two days ago categorical instructions from Ottawa that Ronning was to see no one rpt no one on his return from Hanoi. . . . "

. . . .

SWANK

June 20, 1966

OTTAWA 1722 to SecState

. . . .

"2. Martin said his primary reason for wanting to see

Kreisberg first was to emphasize his grave concern that
any escalation in military action in Vietnam by U.S. in
immediate future would jeopardize Canadian good faith with
Hanoi and make it appear U.S. used Ronning as means of
obtaining negative readout on negotiations which would
justify escalation."

. . . .

SCOTT

June 21, 1966

OTTAWA to SecState 1740 FLASH (SECRET/EXDIS); For Secretary from
Bundy.

. . . .

"2. Basically, Hanoi turned Ronning down cold on
their paying any price whatever for the cessation of
bombing. It is Ronning's impression that they understood
his message to relate to preliminary talks of the character
that we had had in Rangoon. In other words, Hanoi appeared
to Ronning to be saying that they would not even talk to us
in this fashion unless we agreed to cease bombing totally
on their terms, without any reciprocal action on their part.

"3. Ronning thinks Hanoi had hoped he was bringing
something more forthcoming than our familiar position calling
for reduction of hostilities to be reciprocal. DRV Reps
did refer specifically to our June 3 spokesman's statement
on this subject, which of course had simply repeated the
position we had stated many times, most specifically in our
reply to the British last August.[17] Martin this afternoon gave
me no hint of recrimination because of our having repeated
this position publicly, but this remains a potentially troublesome point that he may raise this evening.

"4. Having covered the question of conditions for preliminary talks, Ronning went on to have a general discussion
of the conditions under which there might be QTE a cease-fire
and negotiations UNQTE. The DRV foreign minister dealt very
generally with this subject, but the total DRV comment appeared
to add up to there being a satisfactory prior understanding,
before QTE negotiations UNQTE, as to (1) our recognition of the
status of the NLF (not spelled out); (2) return ot (sic) the
1954 Agreements; (3) withdrawal of U.S. forces (not specified
whether this must take place prior to negotiations or as to the

ultimate result); (4) the four points. Ronning did not get
into detail on these questions, but the litany sounds
familiar.

"5. The only conceivable sign of life in all the conversations is that the DRV Reps did say categorically that
acceptance of the four points was not repeat not a necessary
condition to preliminary talks. The only condition for such
preliminary talks in our unilateral cessation of bombing.
However, as I have noted above, this appears to relate only
to resumption of Rangoon-type contact, and as to any substantive negotiations the four points are still in the picture.
I conclude that the result is clearly negative and I hope
to confirm more categorically tonight that Pearson and Martin
accept this. I also expect to get into the question of what
they will be saying in their Parliament. My own thought is
that they might say that Ronning was seeking on Canadian
initiative to see whether a basis could be established for
talks among the interested parties. His conclusion was that
no such basis as yet existed. This kind of formula would
avoid Martin's saying what the positions were or whether he
agreed with the American position, which I surmise he would be
reluctant to do."

BUTTERWORTH

MEMORANDUM OF CONVERSATION (SECRET/EXDIS); Subject: Visit of
Ambassador Ronning to Hanoi, June 14-17, 1966; Participants:
Canada: The Honorable Paul Martin, Minister of External Affairs;
Ambassador Chester Ronning, Government of Canada; Mr. Ralph Collins,
Under Secretary, Ministry of External Affairs; Mr. Claus Goldschlag,
Director of Far Eastern Affairs, Ministry of External Affairs;
Mr. Thomas Delworth, Vietnam Desk Officer, Ministry of External
Affairs. United States: Mr. William P. Bundy, Assistant Secretary
for Far Eastern Affairs; Minister Joseph W. Scott, American Embassy,
Ottawa; Mr. Paul H. Kreisberg, OIC, Mainland China Affairs, FE/ACA.

"1. Ambassador Ronning said that he was met on his
arrival in Hanoi by Le Thanh, Director of the North American
Division of the DRV Foreign Ministry. He was greeted warmly
and given the best suite in the Government's guest house in
Hanoi, considerably better accommodations than he had had during
his first visit in March. The evening of the same day, June 14,
Le Thanh gave a small dinner party for Ambassador Ronning at which
he subjected Ronning to a continuous hard line presentation of the
DRV position throughout the evening. Ronning said that he had not
paid much attention to Le Thanh's remarks in view of his relatively junior status.

"2. The next day, June 15, Ronning was received by Vice
Foreign Minister Nguyen Co Thach. Ambassador Ronning conveyed

to Thach the oral message with which he had been provided
by the US Government and requested that Thach pass it on
to his superiors in the DRV Government. Thach agreed to do
so but gave his personal opinion that it was doubtful a
favorable response would be forthcoming. . . .

"3. Later in the afternoon of June 15, Ronning saw PAVN
ICC liaison officer, Col. Ha Van Lao. Ha analyzed at great
length the Vietnamese situation--both North and South--empha-
sizing that the North Vietnamese were prepared to resist
indefinitely, that no matter how much the U.S. increased its
efforts the North Vietnamese had the ability to deal with the
situation, and that the US would inevitably be defeated in
South Vietnam. He claimed the Viet Cong were winning everywhere and that recent South Vietnam political difficulties proved
the US did not have the confidence of the people.[18] He also said
criticisms of US policy in the US, specifically referring to
Senator Fulbright and Walter Lippmann, also proved that there
was a lack of American confidence in President Johnson.[19] He
said, however, that the DRV was not counting on US opinion to
win but on the strength of 'the Vietnamese people themselves.'
. . . .

. . . .

"5. On the third day, June 16, Ambassador Ronning saw
the highest official to whom he was given access on this trip,
Foreign Minister Nguyen Duy Trinh, who, however, received him
in his concomitant capacity as Vice Premier. Trinh said that the
US oral message had been considered and that the North Vietnamese
had been disappointed that Ronning had brought a reply similar to
newspaper reports with which the DRV was already familiar. He
said there was nothing in the Ronning message that the DRV had
not already considered and accused the Canadians of joining with
the US in another 'peace offensive'. He said he had considered
the Canadians to be sincere and to have had good will which was
why they had accepted the offer of good offices by the Government
of Canada. He rejected as impossible, any suggestion
that the DRV pay a price for a halt of US bombing of North Vietnam.
(Ronning's interpreter told him the next morning that part of the
reason the US proposal had been rejected was that the DRV could
not permit the US to believe it was so concerned about US bombing
that it would pay a price for its halt.) He furthermore charged
that the US had been escalating the war since Ronning's last visit
in March and asked how it was possible for Ronning to be in Vietnam 'negotiating' while this was going on. Ronning denied that
he was engaging in 'negotiations' but was simply trying to discover whether there were any mutually acceptable bases on which
movement toward a peaceful settlement of the Vietnam conflict
might be made. Ronning asked Trinh whether his remarks meant
that the March DRV proposal was now being withdrawn. Trinh said

31

it was not and that if the US was willing to accept the original DRV proposal, the DRV was prepared to 'talk'. Ronning further asked whether, if the DRV concluded that the GOC was insincere and that it lacked confidence in Canadian good will and efforts to contribute to an honorable settlement, there was any point in continuing the discussions further and in keeping the 'Canadian' channel open. Trinh again expressed regret that Ronning's presentation to Vice Foreign Minister Thach had showed 'lack of appreciation' of the DRV position but added that it was the US attitude to which the DRV objected primarily and that the North Vietnamese wished to keep the door open through the Canadians for any further developments.

"6. Ronning asked Trinh whether the DRV could put forward any new counter-proposal. He inquired, as an example, as to the possibility of an over-all settlement including a ceasefire throughout Vietnam. Trinh said 'This all depends on the US attitude'. Aside from halting its bombing of North Vietnam, which must be done before any talks could be held, the US would have to 'recognize the NLF position,' abide by the terms of the 1954 Geneva Agreements, and withdraw its forces and bases from South Vietnam.

"7. Ronning said that Trinh had referred to the NLF 'Five Points' as among those elements which would have to be accepted by the US but was ambiguous as to whether this would be part of the discussions leading toward an armistice or of a final settlement. He said that he had clarified specifically with both Thach and Trinh that acceptance of the DRV 'Four Points' and a cessation of fighting in South Vietnam were not preconditions for preliminary DRV-US talks. Ronning emphasized the DRV position was that if the US stopped bombing completely, the DRV was prepared to talk.

"8. Trinh did not himself specifically refer to the DRV 'Four Points' per se, although he mentioned individual points in the course of his presentation. (On the day of Ronning's departure, however, Le Thanh of the Foreign Ministry noted specifically to Ronning that the 'Four Points' were also 'an element', one of the problems that would have to be discussed.)

"9. Ronning asked Trinh whether, if the US clarified its position on the NLF, agreed to the withdrawal of its troops, and agreed to abide by the 1954 Geneva Agreements. The DRV would be prepared to enter into negotiations. Trinh said 'It all depended on the US reply, but the current US attitude would have to change.' Ronning emphasized that his entire presentation and all his remarks during this part of the conversation with Trinh were extremely general and that he had not attempted in any way to go into details but merely to try and feel out the general nature of the DRV position.

32

"10. On the final day of the trip, June 17, Le Thanh·
reiterated to Ronning that the DRV had confidence in Canadian
sincerity and good will and wished to keep the door open if
the Government of Canada had anything to say. Ronning added he
replied that, similarly, if the DRV had anything to say it
could contact the Canadian representative on the ICC, Moore.

"11. In response to questions asked by others present
at Ambassador Ronning's debriefing, Ronning made the following
observations which he did not attribute to specific DRV
individuals but which he said had been made during his conversations in Hanoi:

a. The North Vietnamese were confident that the
US would eventually bomb Hanoi and Haiphong and lay waste much
of North Vietnam. They expected this and were prepared for it.
He remarked that on June 15, while he was in Hanoi, there had
been an air raid alarm which had sent the population scurrying
to many shelters which had been built in the city. He thought
an observation plane might have been responsible for the alarm
and said he had seen no planes (there was a heavy cloud cover)
or heard any bombing. He noted that a US plane was said to have
been downed in the suburbs of Hanoi a few days before his
arrival and that the diplomatic corps had been taken to see
the plane and had been given fragments as souvenirs. The
Canadian ICC military representative, however, was not permitted
to make this 'excursion'.

b. DRV officials told Ronning that Premier Pham Van
Dong was not in Hanoi at the time but did not specify where he
was. In response to Ronning's own question as to Ho Chi Minh's
whereabouts, officials said Ho was not in Communist China and
labeled as 'rumors' reports that he was on such a trip. The
question of whether he had been in the CPR was not raised.

c. DRV officials on at least one occasion strongly
criticized the Government of Canada for its role on the ICC
Commission in Laos.

d. Officials had specifically told Ronning that they
would attend a Geneva-type conference on Vietnam. (This presumably came up in the context of the general conditions under which
the DRV would agree to negotiations) and observed that they
would favor French participation in such a conference.

e. No emphasis was placed in the conversations on the
subject of 'reunification' but it was raised by DRV officials
in the context of observance of the 1954 Geneva Agreements.

f. DRV officials declined to be drawn out by questions
on the relationship of the DRV with the Soviets and the Chinese,

merely reiterating that both supported North Vietnam and
were fraternal countries of the DRV.

"12. Minister of External Affairs Martin asked Ambassador
Ronning several times to make clear whether there was any ambiguity in his mind as to whether Hanoi was prepared to 'talk'
solely on the basis of an end to the US bombing. Ronning was
absolutely convinced there was no ambiguity on this point and
that he interpreted DRV reference to be to informal bilateral
talks with the US, not to formal negotiations or a Geneva-type
conference. Mr. Goldschlag summarized the DRV position as
Ronning appeared to have garnered it as a three-stage position:
(1) an end to US bombing on DRV terms; (2) informal bilateral
DRV-US talks; (3) a multilateral Geneva-type conference. Ronning
and Martin agreed this was an accurate summation as the Canadians
understood it.

"13. In a subsequent private conversation, Ronning told
Kreisberg that he had been totally depressed following his conversation with Trinh and that he had not detected any hint on
Trinh's part of a desire to put forward any new or alternative
proposals which Ronning might bring back.

"14. At the conclusion of the conversation, Mr. Bundy
observed that it was very difficult to perceive where there was
any 'handle' by which to grab hold of the views expressed by
DRV officials to Ambassador·Ronning but that the USG would carefully evaluate Ronning's observations as conveyed during the
present meeting.

"15. Comment: Ronning's manner and attitude following his
June trip to Hanoi was markedly more sober and subdued than it
was after his March trip. In March Ronning clearly felt that he may
have gotten some hint of a shift in the DRV position which posed
the possibility of further hopeful development. He was anxious at
that time for the US to consider urgently its evaluation of the
DRV line to the GOC so that some further move might be undertaken.
At no point during Ronning's remarks following his June trip to Hanoi
did he personally hint at any opening or flexibility in the DRV
position or that he had emerged from his current mission with any
information which required further consideration and might offer
the possibility for yet a third effort. Minister of External Affairs
Martin, however, repeatedly emphasized on his side that the DRV
had agreed to keep open the Canadian channel and that this was
important. Ronning did not demur from this position, and in fact
agreed that Hanoi had been willing to keep the channel open but
offered no encouragement or suggestion as to how it might be used
from here on."

June 22, 1966

Attachment to Memorandum for the Record (SECRET/NODIS); Subject:
Dinner Meeting with Paul Martin and Other Canadians, June 21, 1966.

I. - The Ronning Mission

"A. It was entirely clear at the dinner that all the
Canadian participants accepted that Ronning had found no sign
of 'give' in Hanoi's position.

. . . .

"B. While Martin attempted some recriminations in the US
handling of the mission, by the close of the discussion we
believe these had been dealt with and will not appear in any
public discussion by him.

. . . . Martin early in the dinner launched into a complaint
that our position had not been forthcoming enough. Mr. Bundy said
that we could have taken no other position on a unilateral cessation of bombing, and with this Martin wholly agreed. He then went
on to suggest that we might have said something more about the
status of the NLF, and Ronning made the suggestion that we might
indicate at some point that we were prepared to treat the NLF as
a 'belligerent group.' Mr. Bundy argued that any recognition of
the NLF as an independent party would prejudice the whole possibility of a stable political settlement in the South and simply
could not be contemplated, particularly with the existing political
weakness in the South. . . .

Secondly, Martin, and to some degree Ronning, thought that
our June 3 press statement on reciprocal reductions of hostilities
might have queered the mission. Ronning's account of his mission
(covered in Mr. Kreisberg's separate memorandum) had indicated
that the DRV representatives had referred to his press statement,
and Ronning also thought that they had expected something more
forthcoming from his mission. . . . when we had been forced to
comment on the Finney leak of June 3 about the Warsaw talks (which
Mr. Bundy noted had been forced on us by a Senatorial indiscretion)
we were bound to repeat precisely the position that we had always
taken, saying that we could consider action concerning the bombing
if Hanoi would take reciprocal action, 'for example' relating to
infiltration, military activity, and North Vietnamese military
personnel in the South. . . .[20]

Thirdly, several of the Canadians wondered what sort of
response we might have expected Hanoi to make to the agreed message.
On this, Mr. Bundy remarked that we had had one experience with
a North Vietnamese contact who had said that we should watch the
level of military activity and North Vietnamese military presence
in the South. . . .

35

. . . .

. . . . there was a long discussion of Hanoi's state of
mind. Mr. Bundy expressed the view that Hanoi had dug itself
in during December, as their handling of the pause showed, and
that the political troubles in the South would seem logically
to be encouraging to Hanoi. At the same time, we were getting
evidence that our pressures in the South were exerting an effect,
and even some third country evidence that the bombing was having
a cumulative depressing effect in the North. It was now clearly
of vital importance to get the political situation in the South
stabilized, and we hoped, established on a democratic basis through
the Constitutional elections.[21] If this could be done, Bundy thought
that Hanoi might start to show some signs of give in 3-4 months,
although he was not sanguine that Hanoi would be ready to call the
operation off by the end of the year. . . .

. . . .

II. - Points Related to Bombing Policy

"At no point did Mr. Bundy refer specifically to any forthcoming operations. However, the course of the discussion permitted
several related points to be made and discussed, as follows:

"A. Possibility of Chinese Intervention

Bundy and Ronning had a long exchange on this, in which
virtually total agreement emerged that the Chicoms would be highly
sensitive to any threat to their own territory and might well
react if they concluded that it had become our objective to destroy
North Vietnam or eliminate the Communist regime there. . . .

. . . .

"B. Mr. Bundy specifically said that we had no intention of
bombing the cities of Hanoi and Haiphong, or mining the Haiphong
harbor.

Ronning had given an interesting account of the air raid
shelters constructed in Hanoi, and Mr. Bundy said flatly that they
would not need these shelters. Ronning also expressed grave concern over any US action that tended to throw the North Vietnamese
into the arms of the Chicoms, which he thought would be disastrous
both in stiffening the North Vietnamese position and in bringing
about heavy Chicom influence and eventual control in North Vietnam.
Mr. Bundy said that we saw the same danger, and that it was a
major element in our not contemplating the mining of Haiphong.

. . . .

"C. During the above discussions, Mr. Bundy twice made clear that we might well consider actions within our present policy and within the above analysis of Chicom reactions.

These references were not picked up by the Canadians, but can hardly have gone unnoticed."

June 23, 1966

STATE 4023 to Amembassy SAIGON; Info: Amembassy OTTAWA 1382.

"1. Canadians (MinExtAff Martin and Ronning) briefed Bundy this week on Ronning's trip to Hanoi June 14-17. . . .

"2. Ronning saw PAVN ICC Liaison officer Ha Van Lao, DRV Vice FonMin Nguyen Go Thach, and FonMin and Vice Premier Nguyen Duy Trinh while he was in Hanoi. He did not rpt not see Pham Van Dong or Ho Chi Minh. DRV officials were personally cordial but demonstrated complete inflexibility on matters of policy and put forward no new positions. Hanoi reiterated its demands that the US halt the bombing of the North, withdraw its forces from SVN, 'recognize the position of the NLF' (not otherwise spelled out), and adhere to the terms of the 1954 Geneva Agreements. Communist officials maintained they were confident that the Viet Cong would win and expressed their determination to maintain their position despite US bombing of the North.

"3. Ronning expressed concern to DRV officials about US POW's in North Viet-Nam but was given standard Hanoi position that POW's were 'criminals' under DRV law and told that no ICRC protection role would be considered, and provided no detailed information about the prisoners themselves.

"4. FYI: We believe above represents basic position we should pass to GVN and that we should not refer to oral message we agreed have Ronning pass to Hanoi on reciprocal dampening down of hostilities in SVN in exchange for US move on bombing of North. You should know, however, that Hanoi absolutely rejected US message and Trinh told Ronning DRV would pay no rpt no price whatsoever for halt to bombing. Hanoi also made clear to Ronning that in exchange for total halt to bombing it prepared only to enter into informal bilateral talks of type we had in January this year.[22] Trinh and other DRV officials offered no alternative proposals to Ronning, who told us he had been profoundly depressed by Hanoi's position.

"5. Ronning said at one point in conversation in Hanoi Trinh had accused Canadians of being insincere in their good offices role and Ronning had offered leave immediately. Ronning said Trinh pulled back from his earlier position and agreed it useful

for DRV to maintain existence of 'Canadian channel' but that
even he probably now persuaded there no current prospect of
effective approach to Hanoi.

"6. Bundy took opportunity of long dinner conversation
with Martin, Ronning, and other senior ExtAff officials to review
current US position and view of future in Viet-Nam. Ronning
seemed more responsive to our approach than we had seen him before
but Martin clearly remains determined to find some role for Canada
in peace-making efforts in future. END FYI."

RUSK (Drafted by P. H. Kreisberg)

June 28, 1966

MEMORANDUM OF CONVERSATION (SECRET/EXDIS); Subject: Ronning Mission;
Participants: Mr. Roger Duzer, Counselor, Embassy of the French
Republic; Mr. Peter M. Roberts, Counselor, Embassy of Canada; Mr. Paul H.
Kreisberg, OIC, Mainland China Affairs, ACA.

"1. Mr. Duzer showed me a French telegram from Hanoi
which dealt with the Ronning mission. The telegram stated that
an unnamed Eastern European Embassy in Hanoi had briefed the AFP
correspondent in Hanoi, Raffaelli, last week on the Ronning mission.
The AFP man was told: (1) Ronning transmitted a USG message to
Hanoi offering a halt in US bombing of North Vietnam in exchange for
reciprocal reduction in Viet Cong hostilities in South Vietnam;
(2) Hanoi had categorically rejected this proposal, indicating that
they would pay no price for a halt to the 'completely unjustified'
US bombing of North Vietnam; (3) Ronning had raised the question
of US POWs and had been told emphatically that they were criminals
and that there was no question of a protecting authority being
designated; and (4) nevertheless the DRV was prepared to keep the
Canadian channel open for future contacts. The French telegram
assumed that the briefing must have been passed with DRV approval
and suggested that the story had been leaked in order to indicate
that North Vietnam, while not willing to accept the proposals
carried by Ronning, was not completely intransigent and was prepared to talk with peace emissaries.

"2. Duzer pressed me on the accuracy of the briefing described
in the telegram. I told him that this was a Canadian matter and
that any specific comment on the content of the Ronning mission
would have to come from the Government of Canada.

"3. After Duzer left, Canadian Counselor Peter Roberts, by
coincidence visited me in my office and I informed him, with
cautions as to the sensitivity of the information in terms of its
source, of the message the French had received. I told him that
I wanted it to be perfectly clear that, in the event AFP carried

a story based upon Raffaelli's information, the source was not
the USG and to note the apparent indifference of the DRV to
maintaining secrecy on the Ronning mission.   Roberts and I
agreed that the French interpretation of why Hanoi may have
leaked the gist of the Ronning mission was not completely persuasive, but we were not able to arrive at any more satisfactory
explanation."

UNITED STATES - VIETNAM RELATIONS

1945 - 1967

VI. C. 2.

VI.   SETTLEMENT OF THE CONFLICT

C.   Histories of Contacts

2.   Marigold

SANITIZED
Authority State 8-15-78 letter
By JK (ing) NARS, Date 9-6-78

VIETNAM TASK FORCE

OFFICE OF THE SECRETARY OF DEFENSE

Sec Def Cont Nr. X-

VI. C. 2.

VI.   SETTLEMENT OF THE CONFLICT

C.   Histories of Contacts

2.   Marigold

VI.C.2., MARIGOLD

Of all the peace initiatives discussed in the negotiating volumes, MARIGOLD remains in many ways the most intriguing. It appears, first, to mark the entry of the Soviet Union into the diplomacy of peacemaking. Although their role cannot be determined with any precision, the Russians may have had a hand in it and even directed it behind the scenes. At the very least, they seem to have known of it and supported it. The reasons for this apparent tactical shift in Russian policy remain unclear. The Sino-Soviet split had reached irreparable proportions by this time, and the Russians, perhaps alarmed at the continuing escalation of the Vietnam War, may have feared that China would intervene directly, forcing a Hanoi-Peking alliance. Eager to isolate China and perhaps viewing Hanoi as a means to that end, the Soviets may have sought to increase their influence with North Vietnam by helping to get the bombing stopped and by arranging a settlement on terms favorable to Hanoi. Whatever their motives, the Soviets had to keep their role low-keyed and indirect. The Chinese had frequently accused them of sabotaging the Vietnam war effort, and Soviet leaders had to avoid giving any substance to the charges. Inasmuch as they worked for peace in Vietnam, they did so primarily through other agents.

In the case of MARIGOLD, Poland was the prime mover, and its motives are equally mysterious. Warsaw may have been acting at the direction of Moscow. Or it may have been acting at least partially on its own, either in quest of international prestige—what Johnson contemptuously referred to as "Nobel Prize fever"—or as a means of fulfilling Foreign Minister Adam Rapacki's long-standing design of promoting Poland's security and economic well-being through a reduction of Cold War tensions. Although Rapacki most likely directed MARIGOLD from Warsaw, the key figure was Januscz Lewandowski, Poland's representative to the ICC, about whom there is also an air of mystery. At the time, Americans knew virtually nothing about him and frequently confused him with Bogdan Lewandowski, a Polish Foreign Office official in charge of United Nations' affairs. Janos Radvanyi, a Hungarian diplomat who defected to the West in 1967, has since identified him as a high-ranking officer in Polish intelligence and a hard-liner consistently hostile to the United States.[1]

The manner in which MARIGOLD was conducted adds to the confusion. In the early stages, it took place largely in Vietnam, with the Italian Ambassador to Saigon, Giovanni D'Orlandi, serving as intermediary between Lewan-

---

1. Janos Radvanyi, *Delusion and Reality: Gambits, Hoaxes, and Diplomatic One-Upmanship in Vietnam* (South Bend, Ind.: Regnery/Gateway, 1978), pp. 194–195.

dowski and Henry Cabot Lodge. It was handled with the utmost secrecy, Lodge frequently crouching in the back of a private car en route to the Italian Embassy to avoid detection, and, although it took place over a period of six months, it remained a closely held secret. It became widely known only after its breakdown when the Poles and Americans engaged in a heated war of leaks to justify their respective positions. Lewandowski's unorthodox approach created additional uncertainty. Shuttling back and forth between Saigon and Hanoi, he attempted to formulate from oral discussions with Lodge and North Vietnamese officials terms that might provide a basis for negotiations, rather than exchanging written statements approved by the two governments. He also concentrated on the longer-range terms of an ultimate settlement rather than the immediate and seemingly insoluble question of de-escalation. In part because of Lewandowski's peculiar approach, it was not clear at the time and remains unclear today exactly what he had accomplished.

MARIGOLD is also one of the most controversial of the numerous peace initiatives. The Poles claimed to have extracted from North Vietnam a commitment to negotiate directly with the United States on the basis of a ten-point program drafted by Lewandowski. This promising initiative, they contended, was undercut by America's subsequent insistence on "interpreting" the program that Lodge had already approved and by a series of heavy bombing raids on Hanoi on the eve of the discussions scheduled to begin in Warsaw on December 6. American critics of Johnson's policies have generally concurred with the Polish charges. They accept on faith the proposition that North Vietnam was prepared for direct talks. Some have accused the United States of deliberate sabotage. Others blame the regrettable turn of events on a woeful lack of coordination within the Johnson administration and extreme diplomatic insensitivity on the part of its top officials.[2]

Administration officials have vigorously rebutted these charges. They question whether North Vietnam was in fact prepared to negotiate and point out that there was never anything more tangible to go on than the oral assurances of Lewandowski and Rapacki. They insist that the United States had never unequivocally approved Lewandowski's Ten Points and was therefore perfectly within its rights to insist on interpretations of ambiguous items. Some have expressed regret for the ill-timed bombing, conceding that it gave the Poles and North Vietnam a convenient excuse for breaking off the talks and putting the onus on the United States.[3] Others, Johnson included, argue that, since cessation of the bombing had never been a requirement for negotiations, the bombing of Hanoi could not have been responsible for breakdown of the

2. See, for example, Porter, *A Peace Denied*, pp. 55–56, and Kraslow and Loory, *Secret Search for Peace*, pp. 51–54.

3. Bundy Oral History Interview, Johnson Library.

contact. Hanoi had never really been interested in negotiations, Johnson later claimed. MARIGOLD was not a promising channel but a "dry creek."[4]

The analysis and documents that follow trace MARIGOLD in detail from its beginnings in June 1966 through its breakdown in December and the war of leaks that came in its aftermath. They make clear the complexity of the initiative. Along with other sources, they confirm the unorthodox approaches of Lewandowski's diplomacy and the initial American skepticism that it could produce anything of substance. They also indicate that the United States was eventually forthcoming, and, if Lewandowski can be trusted, the same can be said of Hanoi, which seems to have dropped its earlier rigid insistence on a bombing halt as an essential precondition for talks. The documents seem to indicate that the United States had not given unequivocal prior approval to the Ten Points and therefore did not renege on its earlier commitments. They also suggest, however, that the bombing of Hanoi was indeed a critical factor in the breakdown of the initiative.

Many questions remain unanswered. The MARIGOLD documents shed little light on the Soviet role or on Polish motives. They leave unclear the central issue of whether Lewandowski was accurately representing the North Vietnamese position. Documents captured later indicated that in the spring of 1966 Hanoi decided the time was not ripe for negotiations. Perhaps, as Wallace Thies has suggested, the promise of a coalition government in Point 2 was sufficiently enticing to enable the North Vietnamese "doves" to win a new consensus for negotiating, and MARIGOLD may therefore have been the most promising of all the contacts.[5] There is little evidence to support this argument, however, and it is equally possible that the North Vietnamese were merely using the Poles to see what they might be able to get out of the United States or were offering vague responses simply to appear not to stand in the way of peace. If this were indeed the case, a more conciliatory American position would have immensely complicated the tasks of the policy makers in Hanoi, but the bombing got them off the hook. Even if talks had materialized, however, the adamant opposition of the United States to anything resembling a coalition government would have rendered them unproductive.

Although these questions may never be resolved satisfactorily, the documents below provide a fascinating chronicle of the secret diplomacy of the Vietnam War.—*Ed.*

4. Johnson, *The Vantage Point*, pp. 251–252.
5. Wallace Thies, *When Governments Collide: Coercion and Diplomacy in the Vietnam Conflict, 1964–1968* (Berkeley: University of California Press, 1980), pp. 337–342.

MARIGOLD

This study consists of two parts, a chronology of the principal events in the negotiating initiative known as Marigold (Part II), and an analytic discussion of some of the principal questions raised by Marigold (Part I). Part I is based on Part II, with citations to it indicated by date. While Part I can be read without reference to Part II, it may be easier going with just a few of the main dates and happenings in mind:

Late in June 1966, the Polish ICC Representative, Lewandowski, returned to Saigon from Hanoi with some ideas he felt could serve as a basis for negotiations. These were communicated to the US through the Italian government and followed up by discussions in Saigon with Lewandowski, D'Orlandi (the Italian Ambassador) and Lodge participating in various combinations. In addition, Lewandowski made several visits to Hanoi. On November 30, he presented a 10 point formulation, reflecting his understanding of the US position, which he said Hanoi would accept as a basis for direct "conversation" between US and DRV representatives in Warsaw. On December 2, Hanoi[1], which had not been bombed since mid-August, was hit by US airstrikes. On December 3, the Poles protested the attack as endangering the prospective Warsaw meeting; and the US officially accepted Lewandowski's 10 points, subject to "important differences of interpretation." On December 4, Hanoi was bombed again. During the next 10 days, the Poles and Americans argued about the pattern of US bombing and the "differences of interpretation" clause. In the interim (December 6), however, Hanoi was officially informed of the US acceptance, as qualified. On December 13 and 14, Hanoi was bombed again; and the DRV instructed the Poles to end all conversations about the proposed contact. On December 24, the US informed the Communists that it would refrain from bombing within a 10 mile radius of Hanoi's center, expressing the hope that this would permit the Warsaw meeting to take place; but the offer was not accepted.

---

[1] Strictly, the area within 5 miles of the center of Hanoi

The Role of the Polish Intermediary

The part played in Marigold by the DRV is veiled in mystery, because all US transactions in the matter passed through Polish hands. The initiative for the contact can only be traced back as far as the Poles. It begins with Lewandowski's return from Hanoi in late June 1966. Whether he acted on Hanoi's request, on Soviet urging, or his own sense of enterprise is not known. The subsequent flow of information on DRV views and reactions came almost entirely through the Polish channel, and the Poles were, intentionally, ambiguous in distinguishing between their own thoughts and Hanoi's.

Drawing conclusions from the story is a compounded problem because the Poles, by their own account, conceived of their function as quite different from neutrally passing messages:

--They acted as brokers, probing us (and perhaps Hanoi) to find elements of "give" that would narrow the gap between US and DRV positions on the terms of settlement. Their most inventive act in this role was producing a Polish formulation of the official US position as a starting point for US-DRV talks. In this way, each side had a glimpse of possible areas of negotiation, without first committing itself to specific language or firm concessions.

--They tried to steer the exchanges away from topics we preferred (especially de-escalation) toward those they said had greater chance of acceptance in Hanoi (the terms of an overall settlement).

--They acted as friends of Hanoi, not neutrals.

--Most importantly, they applied pressure on the US to participate in good faith, by the ever present threat of disclosing their version of the matter to influential world leaders or the public at large. Thus our first intimation of Marigold came via the Italian Government, which had been informed in Saigon and Rome by the Poles. We knew immediately, and were forcefully reminded at critical moments later, that US responses which might be viewed by others as reluctance in the pursuit of peace, skepticism about finding a "political" solution, or intransigence on matters of substance, might be used against us.

The only tenable working assumptions on the US side, therefore, were that the Poles pursued at least three objectives in Marigold -- and most likely a fourth as well: (1) Ending the violence in Vietnam. (2) Doing so on terms relatively favorable to the Communist side. (3) Building a case that could be used against the US, as pressure during the development of the contact or as a source of embarrassment to the US should the whole venture fail. (In addition, the Poles no doubt sought to cast themselves in a role of historical importance.)

As so often with multiple objectives, none seems to have been maximized. For example, if the Poles were concerned solely with ending the war (regardless of the terms), they should have acted with greater discretion after the contact broke down, because this would better preserve their usefulness as an intermediary in the future. On the other hand, had they been concerned solely with discomfitting the US, they could have used their ammunition to greater effect by leaking earlier and more sensationally to the press. Perhaps different individuals on the Polish side gave differing priorities to this objective or that.[1] In any case, the fact that none of the objectives was pursued to its logical maximum must mean that, in some larger Polish scheme of things, all were accorded considerable importance.

This is critical in interpreting the episode as a whole, because it implies that, with whatever degree of imprecision, the Poles were in fact trying to find areas of compromise between the DRV and US on acceptable outcomes to the war. Their effort was taken seriously enough in Hanoi to result in DRV agreement to meet with a US representative in Warsaw.[2] This in turn must mean they received some serious guidance on policy from the DRV, even though it is quite unlikely that they were privy to Hanoi's minimum bargaining positions. What they conveyed to us about promising directions for negotiations, therefore, should reflect something of Hanoi's considered judgments, but cannot of course be read as a map of firm and final DRV positions.

It was apparently not until after the Warsaw contact was canceled that the Poles were asked to specify those messages they had passed on explicit instruction from Hanoi. There were three, they said: Lewandowski's message to Lodge expressing DRV agreement to the Warsaw talks; the warning after the December 3 (sic) bombing of Hanoi that the contact was being reassessed by the DRV; and the decision to cancel the Warsaw meeting after the December 13-14 bombing of Hanoi. In addition, the Poles said they had numerous exchanges with Hanoi during the period of Gronouski's contacts with Rapacki in Warsaw (i.e., after December 5) and claimed that they were therefore able to reflect Hanoi's views accurately even when speaking on their own initiative.

---

[1]For example, the cable traffic conveys a picture of Lewandowski as more detached than Rapacki, more concerned simply with bringing the contending parties together than with exacting concessions from the US or throwing the onus for failure upon it. On the other hand, this may reflect differences between the US reporters in Saigon and Warsaw as much as actual differences between the two Poles.

[2]We do not know what the DRV expected from the Warsaw meeting nor how its prospects were represented to Hanoi by the Poles. The evidence that the DRV did in fact agree to the meeting is examined in another section.

2

How accurate and explicit they were in transmitting US views to Hanoi is not known. They seem to have made at least one major blunder (described in the next section), and may well have made others.

Did the DRV Agree?

It is at least possible that the Poles had no commitment from the
DRV at all, but on balance this seems highly improbable. By the beginning of December, they had gone far out on a limb in their contacts and
arrangements with at least the Americans, the Italians and, apparently,
the Russians. It is hard to see what could have motivated them to go
this far purely on speculation, given the consequences for them of a
revelation that the whole venture was built on air.

The evidence that the DRV did in fact agree to a meeting in Warsaw
is:

(1) Rapacki's statement to Gronouski that Lewandowski was acting
on DRV instructions in "the message he gave to Lodge . . . upon his
return from Hanoi expressing NVN positive response to the Warsaw talks"
(12/21/66);

(2) Zinchuk's statement to Bundy that "the Polish effort was
serious and that the Soviets were fully with it" and that "he had been
surprised, in discussing the Polish initiative in the Department . . .
to see that it was treated as doubtful" (12/22/66);

(3) Burchett's statement to Isham that a DRV official had actually
been en route to Warsaw for the proposed meeting when "the US resumed
bombing Hanoi" and the contact was canceled (12/6/67).

If Burchett's information is accurate, it would mean that Hanoi
had been informed by the Poles of US acceptance of the Lewandowski formulation and was satisfied with the US response. The US formally accepted
Lewandowski's 10 points on December 3, with the qualification that "several
specific points are subject to important differences of interpretation."
If the Poles accurately conveyed the US position, therefore, it would also
follow that the DRV had acquiesced in this extremely broad reservation.

Here, however, some further questions arise. Rapacki, in a meeting
with Gronouski, indicated that Lodge had "confirmed" Lewandowski's formulation on December 1, introducing the "important differences of interpretation" clause as a further condition two days later. (12/5/66)   This
would imply that Lodge accepted Lewandowski's 10 points without referring
them to Washington, which seems extremely unlikely. Apparently the Poles
informed Hanoi prematurely of US acceptance, omitting the qualification
about interpretation. (12/6/66)   But by December 6 they had conveyed
the US message in its final form. (12/7/66)   If the DRV official was
en route when the bombing of Hanoi resumed--December 13-14--the interpretation clause must have been transmitted and accepted by the North Vietnamese.

4

This would mean that the content of the interpretation clause did not in itself cause the contact to abort. However, three days (December 3-6) may have been lost while the Poles urged us to withdraw the clause and we demurred. Would the Warsaw talks actually have begun before the December 13-14 bombing if this time had been saved? Would they have been continued if the bombing occurred after the first meeting or two?

The Polish Vision of a Vietnam Solution

At four points during Marigold, Lewandowski offered sketches of
a negotiated outcome to the war. None of these is precise or complete.
None is an authoritative statement of what would be acceptable to the
DRV. They differ in content, each serving a different purpose in his
development of the contact. All, however, are consistent with each
other, suggesting they derive from a single set of concepts. They are
consistent, too, with several key planks of the revised NLF Program,[1]
released in August 1967 -- in particular, the call for new elections
with universal sufferage and the establishment of a government with
Communist participation.

His revelations have a pattern: The first was the come-on, couched
in the most attractive but vaguest terms of all. The second and third
were explorations of how much the traffic would bear, testing in turn the
reactions of the Italians (perhaps as bellwethers of "world opinion")
and of official Washington. The last was the most serious, his own
formulation of the US position, designed to provide a substantive basis
for direct talks between the US and DRV. Its language had therefore to
encompass the minimum outcomes acceptable to both sides, using ambiguity
to cloak the differences his brokerage could not eliminate.

Apparently, the best terms he hoped to obtain were eventual US
military withdrawal based on US acceptance of the NLF in a coalition
government, along with a sharp reduction in the role played in that
government by militant anti-communists. The minimum he felt acceptable
as a basis for talks is, naturally, harder to discern. It seems to have
been less a final solution to the conflict than a change in the ground
rules under which the struggle to rule SVN would continue. The principal
elements seemed to be acceptance of the Communists as legitimate contenders
for power; and the substitution of international machinery of some sort
for US armed participation in regulating the outcome. Left open is the
question of what, if anything, the Communists would give in exchange (e.g.,
NVA withdrawal, etc.)

Lewandowski's thoughts on settlement are described briefly below.
More detail is given in the chronology, for which the relevant dates are
also indicated below.

(1) The Teaser. US interest (and Italian) was first aroused
by a statement of things the DRV did not demand as part of a final
settlement. Lewandowski, just back from a trip to Hanoi in June
1966, billed this negative list as "a very specific peace offer,"
even though it lacked the positive demands that would inevitably be
in a final settlement. What Hanoi did not demand included:

6

immediate reunification; socialism in SVN; a change in SVN
relations in foreign affairs; neutralization; immediate withdrawal of US forces; DRV interference in the SVN government.
The last point, however, was modified to the extent of asking
for a government led by "someone other than Ky."

On the positive side, Hanoi's demands seemed to concern
negotiation procedures. It would enter negotiations if the NLF
could "take part" (though not as sole representative of SVN)
and if the bombing of the North were suspended. The first of
these demands, of course, is not purely procedural, since giving
the NLF a formal role in negotiations would move it toward a
position of legitimacy in SVN politics, whatever the outcome of
the negotiations.

Lewandowski, then, seemed to suggest that the war could be
brought to an end by strengthening the position of the NLF,
weakening that of Ky (and, no doubt, the anti-communist tendency
in SVN he represented), fudging all other issues over at least
the short run. (6/27/67)

(2) Ruminations. During September, Lewandowski communed
with D'Orlandi in Saigon on possible solutions. All of his
thoughts, however, returned to a single theme: coalition
government. The bulk of the ministers could be "sensible SVN
politicians," with a man or two from the right (meaning the Ky
government) and a man or two from the left (meaning the NLF) in
"unimportant ministries." Of perhaps even greater significance,
he firmly opposed any development designed to reinforce the
status quo with respect to the then existing GVN -- including,
specifically, measures for mutual de-escalation of the war.
(9/4/66-9/14/66)

Later, D'Orlandi outlined a settlement package that he
thought would get immediate, serious consideration in Hanoi.
It included US withdrawal "eventually"; internationally controlled elections "after one or two years"; leading to a
neutral, coalition government. Coalition, in his mind, was
"not a 'must.'" Whether this package reflected Lewandowski's
appraisal, or D'Orlandi's softening of the Pole's view, is not
clear. (10/16/66)

(3) Probing the US. Just before visiting Hanoi in mid-
November, Lewandowski tried to take a serious reading on US
attitudes. His questions were so phrased as to make the response
desired by the communist side apparent. They dealt with procedures that might follow a ceasefire and were no doubt an effort

to find a set of actions which, if accepted by the US, would ultimately result in a situation in SVN acceptable to the communists.

Specifically, he wanted to know if US troop withdrawal depended on GVN control over areas then governed or contested by the VC; if the US would withdraw from combat areas and not interfere in the creation of a new government in SVN; if the US would oppose progress toward peaceful reunification; if the US would accept the ICC as the machinery for bringing peace to SVN.

All but the third of these questions boil down essentially to one: to what extent would the US remove itself from the contest over who should rule in SVN? All were framed without indication of a quid pro quo. Thus they reveal nothing of DRV willingness to remove itself from the contest. (11/14/66)

(4) Speaking for the US. When Lewandowski returned from Hanoi at the end of November, he brought along his own formulation of the US position on a final settlement. The critical points on the future of SVN include: US military withdrawal after the restoration of peace; US acceptance that "the present status quo in SVN would be changed in order to take into account the interests of the parties presently opposing the policy of the US in SVN"; and US acceptance of the results of "free and democratic elections," held "with the participation of all," under "the necessary control machinery." (12/7/66)

The political complexion of the new status quo is left open, but clearly SVN communists would be entitled to contend for power. Clearly, too, the phrase "necessary control machinery" could not refer in Communist minds to the US presence or the existing GVN. On the other hand, no piece of "machinery" less forceful than these could be expected by the communists to enforce an electoral outcome regarded as unacceptable to the armed parties contending in SVN. Thus the formulation does not provide a peaceful solution to the problem of who shall rule SVN. It offers a way for the US to end its part in the war. It leaves open the question of what the communist side would do in return. This, presumably, is what the formulation left as the subject of negotiation.

8

Unilateral Concessions

Lewandowski probed for US concessions on the terms of final settlement beyond previously stated official positions, such as the Fourteen Points and the Manila Communique.[2] His method of operation was such as to conceal what reciprocity (if any) might come from the DRV. In the end, however, he got virtually no concessions of substance. As a result, it might be argued the greatest unilateral movement away from previous positions was on the DRV side, which agreed to meet with the US without a cessation of the bombing of the North. While the nature of the prospective contact remained in total obscurity -- we had no indication of what matters the DRV representative would be prepared to address -- the DRV must have hoped for something of value and was prepared to probe for it while the bombing continued. In effect, this meant tacitly accepting the bombing as an American blue chip in the bargaining process, something the DRV had sought tenaciously to avoid in the past. (See, however, the XYZ episode.)

In response to the four questions Lewandowski posed in mid-November, the US replied: the Manila formulation spoke for itself with respect to US troop withdrawal; the US supported the constitutional processes then emerging in Saigon as the route to representative government in SVN;[3] the US would accept peaceful, freely chosen reunification (as already indicated in the Fourteen Points); the machinery needed to enforce and supervise a final settlement should be decided by negotiations, taking account of problems revealed in the recent past -- i.e., with the ICC. Nothing was conceded at all. (11/14-15/66)

The US accepted Lewandowski's final 10 Point formulation as broadly reflecting its position, but qualified this by stating, "We must add that several specific points are subject to important differences of interpretation." The qualifier was not elaborated, even though the Poles urged that the specific points at issue be indicated or that the formulation be revised to eliminate the need for this sweeping reservation. The point which raised the sharpest apprehension in Washington was that indicating US acceptance that the "status quo in SVN would be changed" to take account of communist interests. Even this language, however, as State pointed out, was broad enough to mean anything from putting the NLF into the government forthwith to a simple endorsement of the electoral processes then being elaborated in Saigon. US troop withdrawal is explicitly linked to the Manila Communique, though the specific conditions of the Manila offer are not repeated. Lewandowski's fifth point, however, may have added something to the previous US stance, by calling for a GVN based on "the participation of all through free democratic elections," held under "the necessary control machinery." The US seemed to be accepting universal suffrage (no exclusion of communists and neutralists, as later specified in the RVN constitution) and supervisory machinery not controlled by the non-Communist side, though what all this could mean in practice would have emerged only through negotiations. (12/5/66, 12/7/66)

Given the suspicion with which the DRV undoubtedly views US
intentions, the Iewandowski formulation, especially when seasoned with
the "important differences" clause, is unlikely to have struck the
North Vietnamese as at all forthcoming. In spite of this, they agreed
to meet. While they may not have intended to offer much at Warsaw,
their willingness to come while the bombing continued undercut the
seriousness we would attach from then on to their declarations of
negotiating preconditions, their confidence about their military
progress, etc., etc. These factors are weighty enough to give
importance to the question: why were they willing to meet at all?
According to the reasoning above, the answer does not lie in our
responses to Lewandowski. If not, we should look for factors external
to Marigold -- the rising confusion in China,[4] perhaps, or a pessimistic
estimate of Communist military prospects in SVN, or ....   Furthermore,
if we did not lure them toward the conference table with the attractions
of our offer, the possibility arises that the other pressures pushing
them in that direction were sufficient to induce significant concessions,
had the contact occurred.

The Soviet Role in Marigold

In the materials available for this study, the first explicit discussion of Marigold between US and Soviet officials does not appear until well after the Warsaw contact had been canceled: On December 22, the Soviet Charge in Washington, Alexander Zinchuk, called on William Bundy to express Soviet support for the Polish initiative and to discourage the US from seeking a "militaristic" solution in Vietnam. Zinchuk indicated that the matter had been discussed with DRV leaders visiting Moscow in late November and again in early December. He implied that the Soviet Union had felt unable to encourage the DRV to continue with the contact because of the bombing of December 2 and 4.

The lateness of Zinchuk's approach to Bundy and the content of his message would suggest the Soviets played at most a passive role in Marigold. This would be consistent with their abandoning sponsorship of the prospective Conference on Cambodia in May 1965, their refusal to transmit the US letter to the DRV Embassy in Moscow during Mayflower (May 1965), and their frequent rebuffs thereafter of US efforts to invoke their mediation.

On the other hand, the Italians on several occasions early in Marigold indicated that they understood the Poles to be acting on Soviet instructions. D'Orlandi also quoted Lewandowski as saying that Hanoi was "tightly controlled" by the Chinese and hence preliminary talks would have to be between Washington and Moscow, with overt DRV participation only as an acceptable basis for negotiations emerged. (6/29/66, 7/9/66, 9/14/66)   There are no further references of this sort, however, after mid-September.

It is at least possible, then, that the Russians were the principal sponsors of Marigold. If so, they minimized their visibility when Marigold appeared to be succeeding, emerging to express their interest to us only after the bombing of Hanoi and the collapse of the Warsaw contact. This is followed chronologically by the unusually active Soviet role in Sunflower.[5] Given past Soviet reluctance to mediate, it is noteworthy that the Russians would come to the fore at a time when conditions seemed relatively unpropitious.

This raises at least two questions:

(1) As noted above (under "Unilateral Concessions") the DRV may have had reasons external to the Marigold exchanges for wanting direct talks with the US at just this time. Did the Russians receive encouragement from Hanoi to try further?

(2) Or was it the December bombing of Hanoi that stimulated the Russians? Zinchuk expressed apprehension both to Bundy and Harry Mac-Pherson that Hanoi might call for Soviet volunteers under the terms of the Bucharest Declaration ("if the war escalates and if help is necessary").[6] The Russians no doubt wished to avoid such "escalation," whatever Hanoi's feelings in the matter.

The Trinh formula (of January 28, 1967)[7] made these two possible motives compatible, by tying US-DRV talks to the "unconditional cessation of US bombing and all other acts of war against the DRV." At this point, the DRV attitude had hardened in one important respect, softened in another.   It officially closed the door on the possibility of talks while the bombing continued, but it implied publicly (and made explicit privately) its willingness to talk if its conditions on bombing were met. This at last gave the Russians a license to try on Hanoi's behalf, even though worsening the chances for success because of the stiff conditions demanded of the US.

Leaks and Pressures

From the beginning, Lewandowski stressed the importance of secrecy to the possible success of Marigold, the reason given being opposition by communist hardliners, especially the Chinese. In spite of this, the Poles leaked portions of their version of the episode at strategic moments during the contact in a relatively obvious effort to put pressure on the US.

The US responded in part, as the Poles wished, by cooperating with Lewandowski's initiatives. Where this proved inadequate, we took counter measures which combined the defensive leaking of the US version of portions of the episode on the one hand with incentives and exhortations intended to induce other participants to maintain the privacy of the contact on the other.

The first Polish approach to the US in Marigold was conveyed through the Italians: D'Orlandi contacted Lodge in Saigon; Fenoaltea contacted State in Washington. Meanwhile, Fanfani described the matter to U Thant. Somewhat later, Saragat took it up with Goldberg. It was immediately recognized in Washington that any indication of US reluctance to respond would quite soon be widely interpreted as lack of interest in a peaceful end to the war. We therefore undertook to develop the contact, even though skeptical about the real promise it held forth. At the same time, we protested politely to the Italians about trying to do business in this manner. (6/27-30/66, 7/6-10/66)

During the rest of the summer and fall, as Lewandowski felt he was making progress, the problem of leaks abated. Immediately following the December 13-14 bombing of Hanoi and the DRV's cancellation of the Warsaw meeting, however, pressure through leaks resumed.

On one day alone, December 15, Lewandowski revealed emotional tidbits of the episode to the Dutch Charge in Saigon, the Polish Ambassador in Rome managed to have the Pope quiz him about Vietnam, and Hanoi cabled Harrison Salisbury permission to visit the DRV. A few days later, the Polish Ambassador gave the Pope "the whole story." (12/15-19/66)

We responded first by suspending the Hanoi targets in Rolling Thunder 52, then by offering to halt all strikes within a 10 mile radius of the center of Hanoi in exchange for a similar show of restraint by the VC around Saigon, and finally putting the 10 mile Hanoi sanctuary into effect unilaterally--when the prospects of getting explicit reciprocity seemed too faint. Thus in order to revive Marigold, we offered formal assurances of restraint on our bombing that went well beyond those the Poles had urged us to accept informally after the strikes of December 2 and 4. (12/15/66, 12/21/66, 12/24/66) The US version of Marigold was explained in some detail to the Pope, U Thant, and the Canadian, Italian, Australian,

New Zealand and British Governments. The 10 mile sanctuary around Hanoi was stressed as a potential basis for reviving the contact, reflecting US goodwill and making it essential that the widening circle of those privy to the matter preserve the utmost discretion about it, secrecy being the sine qua non for success. Meanwhile a much less detailed report on the contact was given the GVN and other troop contributing countries, to forestall possible misgivings should they hear of the matter first from other sources.

By mid-January, then, Marigold was known in varying degree to a large circle of diplomats, some briefed by us, some by the Poles and most by both sides. On January 19, a brief reference to Marigold and its disruption by the mid-December bombing of Hanoi was filed in the press from Ottawa. The information was attributed to "high Canadian officials." By February 4, a much more complete version had been filed from UN Headquarters in New York. At this point, with so many possible sources for the story, there was no agreement among the Americans on the origin of the leak to the press. Goldberg thought the Poles were responsible, while Gronouski argued that it had been the Canadians. (2/1-2/67, 2/7-8/67)

The war of leaks gradually escalated during the spring. By May, the Poles were expressing concern to Gronouski over a rumor they had picked up in Washington--that the US contemplated publishing a white paper on Marigold. This would force them, they said, to retaliate in kind. Just at this time, an extremely detailed account of the episode was published by John Hightower of the AP. The most controversial point in his story was the statement that US "officials were not sure the Poles had any commitment from North Vietnam to begin talks. Some ... doubted that Mr. Rapacki was in fact ... making known Washington's readiness for talks to Hanoi." Washington felt the Hightower account was "essentially accurate and reasonably favorable." The Poles were told the US would publish no white paper. They replied that "US officials had apparently chosen another way to put out the story." However, no official Polish rebuttal was made public and the war of leaks simmered down on this acrimonious note. (5/8-9/67)

Perhaps the most interesting aspect of the war of leaks is the silence of the DRV. Although Hanoi did mount a propaganda campaign against US bombing of the DRV immediately after the collapse of the Marigold contact--e.g., through the Harrison Salisbury visit, etc.-- no mention was ever made of the prospective Warsaw contact and its cancellation after the mid-December bombing. Properly handled, this could have been made a telling point with world opinion. Presumably, secrecy about the contact was of greater value to the DRV. It is quite possible, therefore, that the Polish leaks were not appreciated in Hanoi and the Polish handling of the matter was criticized there, as in Washington. (Alternatively, however, it may be that the Polish leaks satisfied the DRV's propaganda requirements, within the constraints imposed by DRV relations with China, the maintenance of rank-and-file morale among Vietnamese communist forces, etc. In that case, Hanoi's silence would not in itself imply an adverse judgment on the Polish role.)

14

Bombing the North I: Blue Chip or Topic for Talks?

The US proposed repeatedly during Marigold that de-escalation be taken as the first topic between the two sides. What would the Communists do if the US stopped bombing?

Lewandowski with equal persistence refused to accept this question as a point of departure. The DRV would reject it, he said, because de-escalation would be viewed as strengthening the governmental status quo in SVN, whereas it was precisely a change in the SVN government that the Communist side required. Instead, therefore, he urged that this subject be left for last. Once both sides agreed on terms for the ultimate situation in SVN, finding the route there via de-escalation would be easy.

Although Lewandowski never, of course, made the argument himself, his approach meant Communist acceptance of the bombing as a blue chip in the bargaining process because the talks on settlement terms would have to take place while the bombing continued.   One inducement the Communists would have to accept terms desired by the US would be that this would end the bombing. Too, his approach saved more face for the Communist side than ours, which required that the bombing be addressed explicitly.

When, finally, the US went along with Lewandowski's approach, it upped the ante by the December bombings of Hanoi. The DRV cancellation of the contact meant, then, that it would neither accept de-escalation as a starting point for talks nor accept augmentation of the US blue chip through strikes on more sensitive targets.

The cancellation of the talks over this issue measures the failure of Lewandowski's brokerage. He had not narrowed the gulf between the two sides sufficiently. His version of possible settlement terms was not attractive enough to make the US forego upping the ante, on the one hand, or to induce the DRV to accept the higher ante, on the other.

Bombing the North II: Signals, Intended and Inadvertant

As is shown in a separate study, beginning in June 1966, there was a marked increase in the amount of ordnance expended against North Vietnam.[8] This was true for the country as a whole, for Route Package VI and for the areas within 10 miles of the center of Hanoi and 5 miles of the center of Haiphong. The general level of ordnance expenditure remained high until mid-November. During the last two weeks of November, probably on account of weather, air strikes against the North were at their lowest level since June, rising markedly again during the first and second weeks of December.

The most sensitive area of all, that within 5 miles of the center of Hanoi, was struck (with about 25 tons of ordnance) for the first time in the war during the last week of June, as part of a general attack on POL facilities. About 3 tons more were expended in this area in mid-August. It was not hit again until the first week in December (the 2nd and 4th) when almost 50 tons were expended, then hit yet again during the second week in December (the 13th and 14th) with over 100 tons. The intended targets in all of the December attacks were the Yen Vien Railroad Yard and the Van Dien Vehicle Depot, but apparently there was collateral damage in all cases. In particular, during the December 13-14 attacks, the Chinese and Rumanian Embassies seem to have been hit, along with some residential structures in central Hanoi. From the ground, then, there might appear to have been an increase in the intensity of attack, measured both in tons of ordnance expended and type of target, commencing December 2, i.e., immediately following Hanoi's assent to some form of US-DRV meeting in Warsaw.

The Poles expressed alarm about the "intensification of the bombing" on December 2, 7, 8, and 9, arguing that "such attacks could only threaten or destroy the possibility of contact in Warsaw." They expressed these views as their own, not as a message transmitted from Hanoi. However, Lewandowski told D'Orlandi (who in turn told US on December 9) that he believed Hanoi had attached significance to the fact that during the two weeks he had been in Hanoi (approximately November 16-30) the bombing had appeared to be at a reduced level. Lewandowski thought Hanoi had interpreted this as a tacit signal of US support for his mission.

In fact, the targets near Hanoi which were the object of attack in December had been authorized as part of Rolling Thunder 52, for which the execute message was sent on November 10. This was prior to Lewandowski's departure for Hanoi, though the approximate timing of his impending visit ("after the US elections") was known in Washington when the execute message was sent. (10/15-16/66) Presumably, had weather not intervened, the strikes near Hanoi might well have occurred during his visit, rather than after his return with Hanoi's "positive response." Hanoi's review of Lewandowski's proposals would have occurred in quite a different context, one reflecting more accurately, perhaps, US attitudes.

On December 10, Washington informed both the Warsaw and Saigon Embassies that it had been decided to leave the bombing pattern unchanged. Gronouski was forewarned that this might involve some targets Rapacki would insist reflected further escalation.

Apparently, the strikes of December 13-14 were so interpreted in Hanoi, which instructed the Poles on December 14 to terminate all conversations.

On December 24, the US informed the Communists that bombing within 10 miles of the center of Hanoi had been suspended as an act of goodwill in the hopes of reviving the Warsaw contact. This was a more substantial concession on the bombing than the Poles had urged after the December 2 and 4 strikes, in that it reflected an explicit, well-defined commitment, rather than the tacit, unformalized restraint suggested by the Poles. The DRV may have concluded that propaganda repercussions, actual and prospective, had forced a change in the US posture, causing Hanoi in turn to stiffen the conditions it imposed in exchange for talks. The Trinh formula of January 28, 1967, demanding an end to all bombing of the DRV, may reflect this calculation.

17

US Good Faith

Prior to the December 2 bombing of Hanoi, no conditions with respect to US military actions had been demanded by the Communists as a price for the Warsaw meeting. The only terms, as expressed by Lewandowski to Lodge on November 30, were: "I am authorized to say that if the US are really of the views which I have presented (i.e., his 10 points), it would be advisable to confirm them directly by conversation with the North Vietnamese Ambassador in Warsaw." In addition to this, he urged only speed and secrecy.

The US had several times previously suggested that mutual deescalation be undertaken by the two sides. In a major policy statement, Goldberg offered "a cessation of all bombing of North Vietnam-- the moment we are assured, privately or otherwise, that this step will be answered promptly by a corresponding and appropriate deescalation on the other side." (9/22/66)[9] But de-escalation was rejected by Lewandowski as the wrong subject with which to start. Thus the US had no commitment to avoid bombing Hanoi stemming from the agreement to meet in Warsaw, and in fact, as noted above, strikes against Hanoi had been authorized since mid-November but had not occurred, presumably for reasons of weather.

The Poles argued that there was a difference between de-escalation and non-escalation. We should have been willing to trade the latter for talks, even if not the former. Secondly, they stretched the meaning of our official position. Rapacki claimed, "you have said over and over again that you would end all bombing if there was an assurance from Hanoi that there would be a response toward peace from Hanoi; however, we did not ask that you stop bombing but only that you not intensify it." And "recalling speeches of Goldberg, the President, Secretary Rusk and others, once we received the signal we did, we would have had every right to call for a stop in the bombing." (12/19/66) Without endorsing this particular formulation, D'Orlandi indicated his general agreement with the Polish interpretation. (12/18/66) Gronouski feared it would be widely shared and that the Communists "will have no trouble convincing the leadership in every capital of the world that our stated desire for peace negotiations is insincere." (12/14/66) In their minds, the issue turned less on the precise language of previous US expressions than on a general tenor which they felt was undercut by the December bombings. Washington apparently soon came to share this view, and the 10 mile bombing sanctuary around Hanoi's center was established to underline the seriousness of US intentions.

The following chronology consists of brief
summaries and interpretative statements about
each date, followed by indented documentation.

June 27, 1966

Marigold begins with a contact between D'Orlandi, the Italian Ambassador in Saigon, and Lewandowski, the Polish Representative on the ICC, also working out of Saigon. Lewandowski, just returned from Hanoi, reported that he had a "very specific peace offer" to transmit, one that would lead to a "political compromise" settling the whole Vietnam question once and for all. The attractive features were (a) Hanoi would not ask for immediate reunification, (b) it would not demand a socialist system in SVN, (c) SVN would not have to change its relationships in the field of foreign affairs, (d) "neutralization" would not be demanded, (e) U.S. withdrawal could be scheduled along a "reasonable calendar," (f) Hanoi did not seek to interfere with the SVN government.

Hanoi's conditions for entering negotiations were that (a) the NLF "take part" and (b) there be a "suspension" of the bombing.

D'Orlandi communicated all this to Lodge in Saigon, two days later (June 29), on instructions from Fanfani, who was also transmitting it directly to Washington.

> Saigon 5840 (to SecState), TS/Nodis, 29 June 1966
> (Section 1 of 2)
> Literally Eyes Only for the President, The Secretary,
> and the Acting Secretary
>
> "1. This afternoon D'Orlandi, Italian Ambassador, telephoned to say it was urgent that I come to his office as soon as the Catholic service honoring the anniversary of the coronation of Pope Paul VI had ended. I went to his office at about 6:45, and he began as follows:
>
> "2. Two days ago, the Polish representative on the ICC, Lewandowski, came to him with a 'very specific peace offer.'
>
> "3. D'Orlandi said he had requested instructions from Fanfani, who told him (1) to submit the whole proposal to me, and (2) said that he, Fanfani, would send the whole thing to Washington for their consideration."
>
> . . . .
>
> "9. The Pole began by saying that Hanoi has been deeply disappointed by the proposals made by Ronning which, they are sure, had emanated originally from the United States and not from the Canadians. Ronning had

1

proposed that the U.S. stop the bombing if North Viet-Nam stopped the infiltration, and had talked about the exchange of prisoners' parcels and letters. This had bitterly disappointed North Vietnam. The first point, they had said, would be unconditional surrender, and they could not accept it, but they are open to a 'political compromise' settling once and for all the entire Viet-Nam question.

"10. When D'Orlandi said that he was skeptical, the Pole said that Hanoi was prepared to go 'quite a long way.' 'It is useless for me to add,' said the Pole, 'that should there not be any kind of a preliminary agreement, Hanoi will deny flatly ever having made any offer.' According to the Pole, the North Vietnamese are 'tightly controlled' by the Chinese Communists. The preliminary talks, therefore, should be between Moscow and Washington. When and if proposals should emerge which could be considered as a basis for negotiations, Hanoi would at that time and under those circumstances get into it. The Pole said that Hanoi was afraid of the Chinese Communists who have an interest in dragging on the war for many years. D'Orlandi added that the Pole was evidently 'proud of himself' for having brought these proposals about.

"11. The proposals are as follows:

        A. They insist that the so-called National Liberation Front 'take part' in the negotiations. The key word is 'take part.' According to D'Orlandi, there is 'no question of their being the representative; they are not to have any monopoly.'

        B. There must be suspension of the bombing.

"12. These are the two proposals.

"13. Then there are other points, which D'Orlandi called 'negative ones,' which are that (a) Hanoi will not ask for immediate reunification, either by elections or otherwise, of North and South Vietnam"

LODGE

(Section 2 of 2)

"(b) They will not ask for establishment of a 'socialist' system in South Viet-Nam; (c) They will not ask South Viet-Nam to change the relationships which it has in the field of foreign affairs; and (d) They will not ask for neutralization.

(e) Although they will ask for U.S. withdrawal, they
are ready to discuss a 'reasonable calendar.' (f)
Although 'we would like someone other than Ky' - to
quote the words of Hanoi - they do not want to
interfere with the South Vietnamese Government."

. . . .

"18. The Pole said that his Government would be
willing to arrange for D'Orlandi to meet with appropriate Polish spokesmen anywhere - Hong Kong or
Singapore. In response to a question by D'Orlandi as
to why they had come to him, the Pole said they wanted
'an able debater to put the case to President Johnson,
and we feel that the Italian Government has the sympathy of the United States Government.' Moreover, the
Italians have the same interest we have in agreement
between Washington and Moscow, and in shutting out
Peking.

"19. D'Orlandi's impression is that the Poles
are desperately seeking a way out on Moscow's instructions. This, he said, may need further exploration.
He had the definite impression that now Hanoi 'was
amenable to common sense' saying 'they do not want
anything that would not stop the whole war. They want
a political settlement, and are prepared to go a long
way.'"

LODGE

June 29, 1966

On the same day that D'Orlandi saw Lodge in Saigon, the Italian
Ambassador Fenoaltea brought the information to the State Department
in Washington. State saw little new in it, with two exceptions. The
Italians were therefore asked to inquire discreetly if there was real
movement on the following points:

(1) Did the condition that the NLF "take part" in negotiations
mean it need no longer be accepted as the "sole representative" of
the SVN people?

(2) Did the word "suspension" mean that a bombing "cessation"
was no longer a prerequisite to negotiations?

3

State 4108 (to Amembassy Saigon), TS/Nodis, 29 June 1966
Literally Eyes Only for Ambassador
Embtel 5840

"Italian Ambassador Fenoaltea came in today with
Faroche, Italian Ambassador-designate to Canada, who
had hand-carried message similar to that contained
reftel and who said he was under instructions to hand-
carry our reply back to Rome ...."[10]

"We told Fenoaltea that, except for use of term
'participate' with respect to NLF, which could have
implication Hanoi was not insisting NLF be "sole
representative' of SVN, and 'suspension of bombing' in
place of 'cessation of bombing,' position Hanoi indicated
to Pole was very similar to previous indications their
position. Thus in light of various translations these
words have gone through, it is not clear whether their
use has any significance. Therefore, without indicating
to Pole that message had been passed to USG, suggested
Italian Government on its own responsibility, query
Polish Rep on these two terms to determine whether formulations contained in Polish version of Hanoi's position
were used advisedly by Hanoi and indicate some shift in
position or were accidents of translation...."

    BALL

June 30, 1966

Rusk expressed skepticism about the value of the DRV proposal,
even if there were some movement on the points enumerated, because
allowing the NLF to "take part" might lead it eventually to a major --
even "fatal" -- role in SVN politics, however the negotiations came
out, and because a bombing "suspension" would produce pressures for
a "cessation." Given the risks of recrimination from Fanfani and
Rapacki, though, he felt it necessary to follow up. He also predicted,
correctly, that the POL strikes then programmed for Rolling Thunder
might stiffen the DRV position momentarily, arguing against trying
to move too fast.

Lodge, on the other hand, thought the package so forthcoming as
to arouse suspicions about the intermediary. Presumably, he was
less familiar than State with the content of previous Hanoi communications of the sort. Much of the proposal, as conveyed, was old, but
two points to which he drew attention were new: the apparent acceptance
of the existing Saigon government and of its foreign relationships.

4

Canberra 58 (to SecState), S/Nodis, 30 June 1966
Eyes Only for Acting Secretary and Ambassador
     from Secretary

     ....

     "2. I cannot from here make any full assessment of
that message. The NLF part seems vague, encouraging
only in that it abandons the 'sole representative'
position. However, this position has always seemed a
maximum opener, and we must keep in mind always that
even 'taking part' on a full basis would go very far
to give the NLF a major, and likely fatal, part in SVN
politics. On the bombing, a 'suspension' could easily
lead to heavy pressure for a 'cessation'. For the rest,
the disclaimers of any immediate 'Socialist' set-up in SVN
or of immediate reunification plans have a familiar ring
from some past noises by DRV Reps trying to make themselves sound reasonable."

     ....

     "4. All this being said, I suppose that if Fanfani
asks us to let D'Orlandi follow up, we would virtually
have to agree.... With careful instructions and
reasonable precautions, we should be able to minimize
risks. In any case refusal to follow up -- even if
message wholly phony -- would expose us to recrimination
from Fanfani and Rapacki alike...."

     "5. Moreover, there might just be something in it.
Poles and Italians may seem devious channels, but not all
that implausible if Hanoi is having any second thoughts.
If so, POL strike might stiffen them momentarily, to avoid
any appearance of weakness or effect of strike, and this
argues for not moving too fast."

     ....

RUSK

Saigon 5855 (to SecState), TS/Nodis, 30 June 1966
Literally Eyes Only for the President, the Secretary
     and the Acting Secretary

     ....

     "3. The proposals attributed to Hanoi, as a package,
go far beyond anything we have heard mentioned before.
In fact, they appear so forthcoming as to arouse

suspicion concerning the credibility of the Polish
intermediary. It seems to us that not only is the
so-called NLF being abandoned as the sole bargaining
agent, but so also is the NLF program of a 'socialist'
state, of unifying the North and South, and of
'neutralization.' Also the phrase 'reasonable calendar'
indicates a definite softening of position regarding
IGMS. Troops. The same is true of acceptance of the
Government of South Viet-Nam and its foreign relationships."

....

LODGE

July 6 & 7, 1966

Fanfani also described the contact to U Thant, who in turn passed
it on to Goldberg at UN headquarters. This increased fears of a leak
from Fanfani on the US side. In fact, the disclosure to U Thant was
considered such a leak and doubtless put pressure on the USG to protect itself by pursuing the contact, on the one hand, and by taking
defensive positions on the other.

Geneva 61 (to State), TS/Nodis, 6 July 1966
For Acting Secretary from Ambassador Goldberg

"5. Syg informed me that on recent visit to Italy
Fanfani reported to him that POL ICC Ambassador had had
conversation with Ho Chi Minh on June 27 in which Ho
presumably said that they would be prepared to engage
in serious discussions with us, notwithstanding Chinese
and Soviet objections, if bombings were suspended and
if Viet-Cong participated in talks. According to Thant,
this information relayed by POL ICC Ambassador to
Italian Ambassador in Saigon who in turn communicated
it to Fanfani. Thant further reported that Fanfani
believed message contained two new elements: (A)
that Ho was not insisting on unconditional cessation of
bombing, merely a suspension; and (B) Ho not insistent
that Viet-Cong be sole representatives of South Vietnamese people at such negotiations. Fanfani had also told
the Secretary General that he thought this message of
such importance that it warranted sending a special
Italian emissary to Washington to communicate the substance of it to United States officials. Syg said
Fanfani did this and that special emissary was asked in
Washington to remain there pending a probe through

6

Fanfani of the word, suspension, and also to inquire what
Ho meant by saying Viet-Cong would have to participate in
the talks. Fanfani swore U Thant to secrecy and the
Secretary General therefore imparted this information to
me in the strictist confidence saying he had not communicated to anyone in Secretariat. He asked in particular
that I not raise this with Fanfani, but if latter mentioned
it to me, I should disclaim knowledge of it from Syg,
except as I might receive knowledge of it from Washington."

TUBBY

State 2673 (to Amembassy Tokyo), TS/Nodis, 7 July 1966
For the Secretary from the Acting Secretary

   "As you will have already seen from TOSEC 188, Fanfani
has already begun to leak, having told U Thant of Polish
message and in turn U Thant having passed it on to Goldberg
....

   "I privately spoke to Fenoaltea today and, without
mentioning Goldberg, said that we had indirectly heard that
Fanfani had mentioned matter to U Thant. Fenoaltea said
he would drop a private note to Fanfani. Fenoaltea
expressed full understanding of problem of attempting to
do business in this manner and much skepticism as to whether
there was any real substance in approach. He said though
that, as we knew, Fanfani felt impelled to 'do something.'

   ...."

State 2619 (to US Mission Geneva), TS/Nodis, 7 July 1966
Literally Eyes Only for Ambassador Goldberg from
      Acting Secretary

   "Re paras 5 and 6 of Geneva's 61 strictly FYI, we have
received report from Italians along lines indicated by
Fanfani to U Thant...we are following up in very discreet
manner to test its authenticity...."

BALL

July 7-9, 1966

   Lodge was instructed to develop the contact further, by meeting with
D'Orlandi and Lewandowski himself in Saigon, but to tell Ky something of

a general nature in case rumors began to circulate. Lodge's inquiries
were to address procedures, but one matter of substance was raised, as
it would be again and again from the US side: What would Hanoi do to
reciprocate the suspension of bombing? He carried out these instructions two days later (July 9).

State 2626 (to Amembassy Saigon), TS/Nodis, 7 July 1966

"...we suggest that Ambassador D'Orlandi seek
discreetly to arrange a meeting between himself, Lewandowski and Ambassador Lodge in Saigon.

".... At such a meeting you should, referring to
USG's understandings of Lewandowski's statements to
D'Orlandi, and making clear that you are acting under
instructions, state as follows:

"1. State that the United States shares the
desire for an over-all political settlement.

"2. Inquire when, where and with what parties
Hanoi contemplates that negotiations would take place.

"3. Inquire what if any action Hanoi on its
part would propose to take or not take during the period
of suspension of bombing.

"4. Inquire whether Hanoi believes it realistic
to keep negotiations secret if the United States suspends
bombing with the inevitable speculation this would entail.

".... We are inclined to feel it would be desirable
for you to say something of a general nature to Ký without
disclosing specifics...."

BALL

Saigon 604 (to SecState), TS/Nodis, 9 July 1966

"1. Lewandowski, D'Orlandi and I met at D'Orlandi's
office at 4:30 July 9.

"2. After my saying it was a personal pleasure for
me to see him again, I began, pursuant to your 2626, by
referring to our understanding of Lewandowski's indication
that Hanoi was open to a 'political settlement' which
would settle the Viet-Nam question once and for all.

"3.   I added that we understood that Lewandowski had said to D'Orlandi that Hanoi in effect made two proposals:

(a)   The National Liberation Front would 'take part' in the negotiations.

(b)   There must be a suspension of the bombing in North Vietnam.

"4.   Our understanding of Amb. Lewandowski's approach to Amb. D'Orlandi was, I said, that if proposals emerged as a basis for negotiations, then Hanoi would be prepared to enter into negotiations.

"5.   I then said that acting under instructions of the United States Government, I was authorized to state the following:

"6.   And I stated the four points in your 2626."

. . . .

LODGE

July 9, 1966

Saragat gives Goldberg an account of the D'Orlandi-Lewandowski contacts in Saigon similar to that already passed by D'Orlandi to Lodge and by Fanfani to U Thant and Washington.

He adds two points to the previous versions:

i.   Lewandowski's intention is that the negotiations take place substantially between Moscow and Washington. If secrecy is preserved, this will permit Peking to be ignored.

ii. The US airstrikes against oil depots near Hanoi and Haiphong on June 28 have not, in Lewandowski's view, prejudged the effort to arrange contact.

Rome 145 (to SecState), TS/Nodis, 9 July 1966
From Goldberg and Sisco

"Amb Goldberg saw Saragat privately Friday night July 8...."

. . . .

"Following in full is text of document which Saragat gave to Amb. Goldberg.... Begin text: On June 27 the Italian Ambassador in Saigon D'Orlandi reported that the Polish representative to the ICC Ambassador Savira just back from Hanoi had told him that the North Vietnam Government were prepared to enter secret pourparlers in order to reach a political compromise with the United States at two preliminary conditions: i.e., suspension of bombing over North Vietnam and Viet Cong participation in the negotiations. As to the nature of such compromise, the Hanoi Government were willing: (1) not to ask for the immediate reunification of North and South Vietnam; (2) to relinquish their claim to imposition of U.S. socialist system in South Vietnam; (3) not to ask for changes in the existing relations between South Vietnam and the western countries; (4) to discuss the timing of the withdrawal of American troops from South Vietnam while maintaining their request for such withdrawal.

"Moreover, the Polish representative made it clear that in his own opinion negotiations were to take place substantially between Moscow and Washington. If absolute secrecy were maintained about the preliminary contacts, Hanoi, he thought, could have ignored Peking.

"On June 28 it was reported that oil depots in Hanoi and Haiphong had been bombed. The Polish Ambassador expressed some reservations as to the consequences of such initiative but later reported that the attempt to open negotiations was not in his own eyes pre-judged.

"In connection with Ambassador D'Orlandi's reports, the Italian PriMin and the Italian Minister of Foreign Affairs, who were then in Bonn, decided to send Signor Farace, Deputy Dir Gen for Political Affairs, to Washington so that he may sound, together with Ambassador Fenoaltea, the reactions of the American Govt.... Farace and Fenoaltea on July 1 met in Washington Acting Secy of State Ball (Rusk was then in Australia) and Ball's Deputy Alexis Johnson. The two American officials...suggested that D'Orlandi should request clarification from the Polish Rep on two points: (1) He should find out whether the words 'participation of the Front of Liberation to the negotiations' were meant to exclude the Govt of Saigon; (2) He should also find out whether the word 'suspension' as applied to bombing was deliberately meant as something different from 'cessation.' On July 2, 3, and 4 Ambassador D'Orlandi made clear that North Vietnam simply asked for suspension of the bombing as a preliminary condition for the beginning of negotiations aimed at reaching a political

10

compromise on the above-mentioned lines. Viet Cong
participation, furthermore, obviously did not rule out
the participation of the South Vietnam Govt. It was
only suggested that once the negotiations had begun
General Ky may be replaced with a less extremist
political personality. On July 5 Fenoaltea and Farace
in the course of a new meeting with Ball and Alexis
Johnson passed on to these two American officials the
information received from D'Orlandi. The Americans...
reserved their position because President Johnson was
away in Texas and Mr. Rusk was still abroad. According
to Ambassador Fenoaltea, further American communications
would not be forthcoming for two or three days.

"On July 7 Ambassador Fenoaltea reported that he had
again met together with Farace the two American officials.
They had expressed their opinion that Ambassador
D'Orlandi and Ambassador Cabot Lodge should get in touch
jointly and unofficially with the Polish Ambassador to
explore the possibilities of the North Vietnamese offer."

. . . .

July 10, 1966

When Lodge mentioned the matter to Ky, he expressed doubt that it
would turn out to have any real substance, but said it would be followed
up. Ky apparently went along graciously, suggesting that it might be a
good time for a US leaflet campaign in the DRV, stressing our desire for
negotiations.

Saigon 642 (to SecState), S/Nodis, 10 July 1966

"1. Pursuant your 2626, I called on Ky ostensibly
to discuss General Thi and acquisition of suitable
premises for the US consul in Danang.[11] But as I was
leaving, I remarked that 'by the way' we had been getting some rumors out of Hanoi indicating a desire to
find a way out. None of these seemed to have any real
substance, but we would follow all of them up and, if
anything important occurred, we would of course tell
him at once."

. . . .

"3. He made the following suggestion which I thought
interesting:

11

"4. The time has come for the Americans to put on
another 'good will leaflet' campaign. The message on
the leaflets should be that we (Vietnamese and Americans)
want negotiations; it is your rulers who don't."

. . . .

LODGE

July 24, 1966

When Lewandowski replied to Lodge, under instructions from Warsaw,
he could say only that there could be no results without a bombing
cessation, that the DRV's 4 points must be recognized, etc. This
seemed a step backward to all participants. The matter was left for
some weeks.

Saigon 1785 (to SecState), S/Nodis, 24 July 1966

"1. D'Orlandi, Lewandowski and I met at D'Orlandi's
office at 4:30. The meeting lasted for twenty minutes.
Lewandowski talked as follows:

"2. 'I have the following instructions from Warsaw
which I have been asked to transmit to Ambassador Lodge:

A. 'It is difficult to discuss any proposition
during the current important escalation of war activities
in the South, and of the bombing in the North.

B. 'To hold such discussions could be locked
upon as a maneuver to force the DRV to negotiate under
American conditions.

C. 'We know very well that the DRV will not
give up the fight while the United States pursues its
present policy of military pressure.

D. 'We have reasons to state that no proposition without the cessation of the bombing of the DRV will
produce results.

E. 'United States Government has no right to
bomb the DRV and no right to propose conditions for its
cessation.

F. 'If the United States desires a peaceful
solution, it must recognize the four points proposed by
the DRV and prove it in practice.

12

G.   'The United States must stop bombing and other military activity against North Viet-Nam. Only then can a political solution be expected.'"

. . . .

"16.   D'Orlandi then spoke as follows:

"17.   'This is definitely a step backward. I had thought that the first meeting was rather encouraging. Both the opening and the American questions were encouraging.   I felt something might come out and, as a matter of fact, I still feel this as a hunch. Accordingly, I hope the stiffness of your reply today is due to prevailing circumstances, and that this channel may be kept open and resumed as soon as possible. We were expecting a reply. Now we have a statement. I understood what led to this statement. It is the circumstances of the moment.'

"18.   I asked to what circumstances he was referring. He said to all of the rumors in the newspapers of peace talk." [12]

. . . .

LODGE

September 4-8, 1966

After a period of inactivity and a discouraging visit to Hanoi by Lewandowski, D'Orlandi and Lewandowski attempted to revive the contact. They saw two main problems: that their exercise not be viewed as probing for Hanoi's minimum position; and that it not be directed at reinforcing the status quo or facilitating deescalating, but rather at finding an overall settlement that would permit the war to end.

Saigon 5229 (to SecState), S/Nodis, 4 September 1966

"1.   D'Orlandi said that Lewandowski had returned from 16 days in Hanoi profoundly discouraged. His two closest contacts Pham Van Dong and General Giap were both away. His talk with Ho Chi Minh produced nothing of interest. There was absolutely no sign of a desire to stop the war."

. . . .

"4. D'Orlandi said he would be willing to work with Lewandowski to try to develop a compromise formula, which could then be submitted to Moscow or Washington.

"5. Comment: What are Department's views of this suggestion? It could be that some ideas and clarification might come out of it, and that it would not, of course, commit us to anything. I doubt whether the Pole will be authorized. End Comment."

. . . .

LODGE

State 41695 (to AmEmbassy Saigon), 6 September 1966

"... we see no objection to D'Orlandi's pursuing this with Pole if latter is so authorized..."

Saigon 5517 (to SecState), S/Nodis, 8 September 1966

"1. D'Orlandi told me that in his recent talk with Lewandowski, the problem referred to in my last telegram regarding Lewandowski and D'Orlandi working up a proposal to submit to Washington and Moscow was discussed. Lewandowski made three points:

"A. He did not want the only outcome of the procedure between D'Orlandi and himself to be to inform the United States as to 'just how far the North Vietnamese would give in.'

"B. Although Lewandowski recognizes that I had already given him ample assurances, he feels that emphasis must be given to the need of the U.S. approaching the problem so as to concern South Viet-Nam alone and not South Viet-Nam as a 'piece of a general Chinese puzzle.' Lewandowski feels that the problem could be 'simple enough' if limited to South Viet-Nam -- but not if the United States is thinking of using conversations with Lewandowski (and Lewandowski's talks in Hanoi) as a way of getting at China or Chinese questions...."

14

"C. Lewandowski said that it was only fair
to state that the 'aim of the exercise' between him and
D'Orlandi should not be to reinforce the status quo,
but to get a 'global' settlement. When he says 'global',
he obviously does not mean world-wide; he means 'over
all' as regards South Viet-Nam. This, said D'Orlandi,
quoting Lewandowski, means 'guarantees, etc.'; therefore
'not just de-escalation.'"

....

"5. Lewandowski said he was sure that something
could be done. Hanoi, he said, looks at the situation
through the distorted spectacles of the Viet Cong
through whom they get all their information about the
situation. 'My job,' said Lewandowski, 'is to explain
to Hanoi that they have a wrong view.' The last time
he had been in Hanoi neither Pham Van Dong nor General
Giap were there, and 'they are the only two in the
whole place who talk sense and understand the real
situation in the south.'"

....

LODGE

September 12, 1966

State agreed that the contact be pursued, reserved its position
on "changes in the status quo," and offered to look for a gesture of
good intent to encourage Hanoi (and D'Orlandi), such as a proposal of
mutually-timed withdrawal, or trading a bombing cessation plus a halt
in the US troop buildup for an end to infiltration.

State 44917 (to Amembassy Saigon), S/Nodis, 12 September
1966
Ref: Saigon 5517

....

"2. Lewandowski's remark that the aim of the
exercise should not be to 'reinforce the status quo'
is all right if he is talking about the present
status quo in South Viet-Nam. But we cannot buy a
discarding of the status quo ante, i.e. the 1954
and 1962 Agreements...we do not rule out consideration of revisions of the provisions of the Geneva
Agreements but we could accept no changes until we

15

had a clear picture of what was the total context
of an understanding with the Communists...."

....

"5. ... we will consider here whether there
is something that could be given to D'Orlandi for
his 'possible agreement formula' which could
demonstrate our earnest desire move forward and
smoke out Hanoi's intentions. This might lie,
for example, in realm of mutually-timed withdrawal formula, or quid pro quo on cessation of
bombing and halt in expansion US forces against
end to infiltration by Hanoi."

....

RUSK

September 14, 1966

D'Orlandi reports that Lewandowski is not interested in de-
escalation or any other sequence that will lead to preserving the
present personnel of the GVN. It is this part of the "status quo"
which must change. On the other hand, the Geneva agreements of 1954
and 1962 need not be affected.

Saigon 5965 (to SecState), S/Nodis, 14 September 1966

"1. Pursuant to your 44917 I had a long session
with D'Orlandi.

"2. He says the phrase 'status quo' refers
exclusively to the political and governmental status
quo in Saigon and has nothing whatever to do with
the 1954 and 1962 agreements....

"3. Lewandowski was definitely not referring to
the 1954 and 1962 agreements. He is not interested in
de-escalation or any kind of negotiation which would
lead to a settlement and which would at the same time
perpetuate the personnel of the present government.
Lewandowski means that those on his side are not
interested in ending military activities if, by so
doing, the political and governmental situation in
Saigon is thereby frozen."

....

16

"12. D'Orlandi would like to test how influential
Lewandowski is with Pham Van Dong and Vo Nguyen Giap,
with whom Lewandowski claims to be so close. He is
looking around for 'some little thing' which could be
interpreted as an indication. He is sure Lewandowski
speaks for Rapacki and with Moscow approval every inch
of the way. He is inclined to believe that Lewandowski
speaks for Pham Van Dong and Vo Nguyen Giap, but would
like to make sure.

"13. I ventured the guess that nothing could be
expected out of Hanoi until our November elections were
over. The time between now and then, therefore, I
suggested, could be valuable in discussing and formu-
lating proposals.

"14. D'Orlandi did not agree. He thought we
should not 'discard the possibility of discussions now'
due to the internal upheaval in China, which he
believes brought the Peking Government very close to
a breach of diplomatic relations with Moscow.[13] This,
he surmised--and not our elections--was dominating
official thinking in Hanoi...."

. . . .

LODGE

September 18, 1966

Lewandowski tells D'Orlandi that a coalition government should
be considered, the bulk of which would be "sensible SVN politicians,"
with a man or two from the right and a man or two from the NLF in
"unimportant ministries." SVN would become a "second Cambodia."
But he is discouraged about US intentions because of the incompati-
bility of "military escalation and political proposals."

Saigon 6280 (to SecState), S/Nodis, 18 September 1966

"1. D'Orlandi had a meeting with Lewandowski
Friday night. It started as a social affair on
D'Orlandi's invitation and on Lewandowski's initia-
tive became a discussion of the war. According to
Orlandi, Lewandowski said the following:

. . . .

17

"5. If the Americans ever really cared, they should especially concentrate on Pham Van Dong's fourth point concerning 'who is to speak for South Vietnam.' This does not mean that Hanoi would be trying to ram the Viet Cong down our throats. We could consider the setting up of a coalition government the bulk of which would be made up of 'sensible South Vietnamese politicians.' To preserve appearances you could have 'on the fringe' men from the 'right' in one or two 'unimportant ministries' and from on the 'left' fill one or two 'unimportant ministries with the so-called NLF.'

"6. D'Orlandi -- this is unthinkable. If this is what you want to talk about, it is better for us to stop the talks.

"7. Lewandowski asked whether D'Orlandi realized that what he meant to say was that this would be the last step not the first.

"8. D'Orlandi said: What would be the ultimate goal? If it is to have the Viet Cong in the Government of Viet Nam, I won't even submit such a proposal to Ambassador Lodge.

"9. Lewandowski said that is not at all what he meant to put to D'Orlandi. Plainly, the ultimate aim would be: 'to make of South Vietnam a second Cambodia.'

"10. D'Orlandi said that makes more sense, it is at least worth talking about.

"11. Lewandowski said: 'But I don't believe the Americans really wish to talk. They are trying to do two things at once: military escalation grouped with political proposals. You can't do both. So long as they won't make up their minds, we can't do anything. We must wait until November.'"

        ....

        LODGE

September 22, 1966

Goldberg's speech to the UN General Assembly stresses the US desire for a negotiated settlement, proposing a reduction in Communist military activities in SVN in response for a bombing cessation, and mutual withdrawal of military forces under international supervision. He reiterates President Johnson's statement that Vietcong representation in peace negotiations would not be an insurmountable problem.

18

New York Times, 23 September 1966
"Text of Goldberg's Address"
United Nations, New York, Sept. 22nd

....

"U.S. Offers 'First Step'

"...United States is willing once again to take
the first step. We are prepared to order a cessation
of all bombing of North Vietnam -- the moment we are
assured, privately or otherwise, that this step will
be answered promptly by a corresponding and appropriate
de-escalation on the other side. We therefore urge
before this Assembly that the Government in Hanoi be
asked the following question, to which we would be
prepared to receive either a private or a public response:

"Would it, in the interest of peace, and in response
to a prior cessation by the United States of the bombing
in North Vietnam, take corresponding and timely steps to
reduce or bring to an end its own military activities
against South Vietnam?

"Another obstacle is said to be North Vietnam's
conviction or fear that the United States intends to
establish a permanent military presence in Vietnam. There
is no basis for such a fear. The United States stands
ready to withdraw its forces as other withdraw theirs so
that peace can be restored in South Vietnam, and favors
international machinery -- either of the United Nations or
other machinery -- to insure effective supervision of the
withdrawal. We therefore urge that Hanoi be asked the
following question also:

"Would North Vietnam be willing to agree to a time
schedule for supervised, phased withdrawal from South
Vietnam of all external forces -- those of North Vietnam
as well as those from the United States and other countries
aiding South Vietnam?

'A further obstacle is said to be disagreement over
the place of the Vietcong in the negotiations. Some argue
that, regardless of different views on who controls the
Vietcong, it is a combatant force and, as such, should take
part in the negotiations.

19

"Some time ago our view on this matter was stated
by President Johnson, who made clear that, as far as we
are concerned, this question would not be 'an insurmountable problem.' We therefore invite the authorities
in Hanoi to consider whether this obstacle to negotiation
may not be more imaginary than real."

October 5, 1966

When D'Orlandi tells Lewandowski he plans to return to Rome shortly,
the latter protests, "You must not leave; there will be much to do after
the 15th of November."

Saigon 7712 (to SecState), S/Nodis, 5 October 1966

"1. On Tuesday, October 4, at the Apostolic Delegate's reception, D'Orlandi said to Lewandowski that
he intended to say to Fanfani that there was no longer
any reason for him to stay on in Saigon at the expense
of damage to his health when there was absolutely
nothing to do.

"2. According to D'Orlandi, Lewandowski said with
great emphasis and earnestness, 'You must not leave;
there will be much to do after the fifteenth of November.'"

. . . .

LODGE

October 14, 1966

Lewandowski probes D'Orlandi with respect to possible US-Chinese
collusion, reporting that Chinese permission for Soviet flights to Vietnam have been withdrawn. He also raises the possibility of ousting Ky,
though whether as part of the negotiating arrangements or part of their
outcome is not clear.

Saigon 8567 (to Sec State), S/Nodis, 14 October 1966

. . . .

"5. Lewandowski went on to say that he was worried
about reports about the Chinese, particularly that the

'Americans are trying to feel out the Chinese.' He
added: 'In such a case, we are out.'

"6. He said there were 'added strains' between
China and Russia and that, due to a recent Chinese
decision, there are now 'no Russian flights going
through China to Viet-Nam.'

"7. Lewandowski then, according to D'Orlandi,
asked whether he thought 'Ky could be ousted.'

"8. D'Orlandi says he replies that he absolutely
refused to 'haggle' and would not get into a situation
in which they agreed to this in exchange for our
agreeing to that. In any case, this was a matter which
would 'take care of itself' in a few months when the
new constitution goes into effect."[14]

. . . .

LODGE

October 15, 1966

State inquires if Lewandowski had a particular reason for attaching importance to the date of November 15.

        State 66655 (to AmEmbassy SAIGON), S/Nodis
              15 October 1966
        Ref: Saigon 7712

            . . . .

        "2. D'Orlandi at next suitable occasion should
    ask Lewandowski if he had particular reason to attach
    importance to the date of November 15 after which
    according to him there would be 'much to do' (Para 2,
    Saigon 7712)."

        RUSK

October 16, 1966

    D'Orlandi, on probing from Lodge, indicates that Lewandowski
reflects the views of Pham Van Dong and Vo Nguyen Giap. Neither
D'Orlandi nor Lewandowski can judge the relative influence of these

men in the Hanoi power structure. D'Orlandi refuses to pick up the lead
given by Goldberg's UN speech and help devise a bombing-infiltration
formula that might be acceptable to Hanoi. He says Lewandowski is
interested only in a total package, something "final," not de-escalation
or even a "truce to allow conversation."

To illustrate the total package he suggests: internationally controlled elections after one or two years; a neutral government; US
withdrawal "eventually"; a coalition government ("not a 'must'".)

In response to State's query, Lodge reports that Lewandowski plans
to go to Hanoi shortly after the U.S. elections.

Saigon 8583 (to SecState), S/Nodis, 16 October 1966

"1. This is in reply to your 66655.

"2. On Saturday I asked D'Orlandi this question:

Does Lewandowski's strong position against
what he calls any form of 'barter', i.e. 'We stop
doing this and you stop doing that' reflect his own
appraisal of Hanoi's position or is it based
explicitly on what he has been told by North Vietnamese?

"3. D'Orlandi's reply: This question is not
phrased so as to reflect the realities. Lewandowski's
views reflect Pham Van Dong and Vo Nguyen Giap who
are the only two North Vietnamese with whom Lewandowski
has been in contact. Are or are these not the real
power in Hanoi? Lewandowski does not know. D'Orlandi
believes you know more than we do about that.

"4. Question: Could Lewandowski envisage any
variation on Goldberg's September 22nd bombing-
infiltration formula which would be compatible both
with the principle of reasonable reciprocity and with
Hanoi's apparent determination to avoid actions which
could be interpreted as bowing to U.S. pressure?

"5. Answer: D'Orlandi says: I don't think he
would answer that question. It would be going back on
what he has said he refused to do. He wants an over-
all agreement -- not a truce which would allow conversations. He wants a 'package deal' which covers everything and which thereby avoids any chance of publicity.
Hanoi will buy something that is 'final.'

"6. When I asked D'Orlandi what would be the
elements of a package deal he said for illustration:
after one or two years, elections internationally
controlled; a Vietnamese Government which would abide
by a policy of neutrality; the United States to leave
'eventually' (this word was stressed); a coalition
government (which he said was not a 'must') which
would contain representatives of so-called 'extremists'
having nominal ministries. By 'extremists' he meant
the Ky regime on the one hand and the Viet Cong on the
other. D'Orlandi was sure there would never be an
answer to the question 'what will you do if the bombing stops?' But a 'real package deal' would get 'very
serious' consideration and it would get it 'immediately.'"

. . . .

"8. As far as the question of your paragraph 2
is concerned I think it is answered effectively by
Lewandowski's intention to go to Hanoi immediately
after the U.S. elections. Lewandowski says he 'attaches
special importance' to these elections. Even though
he says he does not understand our national politics
he knows that the fact that the elections have been
held will 'clear the air, whatever the results may be.'
It will mean that the electoral question will have been
removed and he will know that the United States 'can
deal if it wants to.'

"9. Comment: I find this interesting since it
confirms the belief which you and I have had for a long
time that they must at all costs avoid publicity and
consequent loss of face. I think long drawn out peace
talks are very dangerous for us. It appears now that
they are convinced that long drawn out peace talks are
utterly unacceptable for them. End comment."

October 25, 1966

The USG, GVN and Troop Contributing Countries propose settlement
terms at the Manila Conference.[15] These include an end to aggression;
territorial integrity for SVN; reunification by free choice, resolution
of internal differences in SVN through a program of national reconciliation; and removal of all allied military forces and installations no
later than six months after "the military and subversive forces of North
Vietnam are withdrawn, infiltration ceases, and the level of violence
thus subsides." The settlement would be assured by international
guarantees, particulars of which are open to negotiation.

The pivotal features of the proposal are that (1) the future of the insurgents is to be settled through the national reconciliation program; and (2) allied withdrawal is to come after law and order are restored. These provisions would not allow a coalition government in which the Communists or NLF participated as an organized entity.

New York Times, 26 October 1966
TEXTS OF COMMUNIQUE AND DECLARATIONS SIGNED AT
    CLOSE OF THE MANILA CONFERENCE
The Communique

••••

"27. So that their aspirations and position would be clear to their allies at Manila and friends everywhere, the Government of the Republic of Vietnam solemnly stated its views as to the essential elements of peace in Vietnam:

(i) Cessation of aggression. At issue in Vietnam is a struggle for the preservation of values which people everywhere have cherished since the dawn of history: the independence of peoples and the freedom of individuals. The people of South Vietnam ask only that the aggression that threatens their independence and the externally supported terror that threatens their freedom be halted. No self-respecting people can ask for less. No peace-loving nation should ask for more.

(ii) Preservation of the territorial integrity of South Vietnam. The people of South Vietnam are defending their own territory against those seeking to obtain by force and terror what they have been unable to accomplish by peaceful means. While sympathizing with the plight of their brothers in the North and while disdaining the regime in the North, the South Vietnamese people have no desire to threaten or harm the people of the North or invade their country.

(iii) Reunification of Vietnam. The Government and people of South Vietnam deplore the partition of Vietnam into North and South. But this partition brought about by the Geneva agreements in 1954, however unfortunate and regrettable, will be respected until, by the free choice of all Vietnamese, reunification is achieved.

24

(iv) Resolution of internal problems. The people
of South Vietnam seek to resolve their own internal differences and to this end are prepared to engage in a program
of national reconciliation. When the aggression has
stopped, the people of South Vietnam will move more rapidly
toward reconciliation of all elements in the society and
will move forward, through the democratic process, toward
human dignity, prosperity and lasting peace.

(v) Removal of allied military forces. The
people of South Vietnam will ask their allies to remove
their forces and evacuate their installations as the military and subversive forces of North Vietnam are withdrawn,
infiltration ceases, and the level of violence thus subsides.

Effective guarantees. The people of South Vietnam,
mindful of their experience since 1954, insist that any
negotiations leading to the end of hostilities incorporate
effective international guarantees. They are open-minded
as to how such guarantees can be applied and made effective.

"28. The other participating governments reviewed and
endorsed these as essential elements of peace and agreed
they would act on this basis in close consultation among
themselves in regard to settlement of the conflict.

"29. In particular, they declared that allied forces
are in the Republic of Vietnam because that country is
the object of aggression and its Government requested
support in the resistance of its people to aggression.
They shall be withdrawn, after close consultation, as the
other side withdraws its forces to the North, ceases
infiltration, and the level of violence thus subsides.
Those forces will be withdrawn as soon as possible and not
later than six months after the above conditions have been
fulfilled."

....

November 10, 1966

Rolling Thunder 52 is authorized. The targets include the Yen Vien
Railroad Yard and the Van Dien Vehicle Depot near Hanoi, the Thai Nguyen
Steel Plant, the Haiphong Cement Plant and two other targets near Haiphong.

JCS 7735 (to CINCPAC), TS/LIMDIS, 10 November 1966
Refs: (a) JCS 6008
       (b) JCS 5427

"1. (U) This is an execute message.

"2. (TS) Guidance governing ROLLING THUNDER 51
set forth in reference (a) remains in effect for ROLLING
THUNDER 52, except for added targets and additional
guidance contained in this directive.

"3. (TS) Effective upon receipt of this message,
you are authorized to conduct air strikes against the
following objectives in North Vietnam:

	TGT #	NAME	BE NUMBER
a.	18.42	Xuan Mai Hwy Br	616-0244
b.	19	Yen Vien RR Clf Yard	616-0221
c.	51.1	Ha Gia POL Stor SSW (Former Phuc Yen POL Stor)	616-0662
d.	51.18	Can Thon POL Stor (Former Kep POL Stor)	616-1340
e.	63.11	Van Dien Vehicle Dpo (Note 2)	616-0696
f.	----	Kinh No SAM Stor	616-00914
g.	----	Hanoi SAM Stor NE	616-0257
h.	----	Haiphong SAM Assembly	616-02044
i.	76	Thai Nguyen Steel Plant (Areas G, K, All Rolling Stock) (Notes 1 and 3)	616-0214
j.	76	Thai Nguyen Steel Plant (Area Q) (Notes 1 and 3)	616-0214
k.	77.1	Haiphong Cement Plant (Note 3)	616-0706
l.	80	Haiphong TPP W (Note 3)	616-0007
m.	82.12	Haiphong TPP E (Note 3)	616-0051

November 11, 1966

Rolling Thunder 52 is amended to defer strikes against the Thai Nguyen Steel Plant and the three targets near Haiphong.

JCS 7783 (to CINCPAC), TS/LIMDIS, 11 November 1966
Ref: JCS 7735

"1. (TS) Air strikes will be deferred repeat deferred (not canceled) against the following objectives in North Vietnam.

TGT #	NAME	BE NUMBER
76	Thai Nguyen Steel Plant	616-0214
77.1	Haiphong Cement Plant	616-0706
80	Haiphong TPP W	616-0007
82.12	Haiphong TPP E	616-0051

November 13, 1966 [16]

On the eve of a major visit by Lewandowski to Hanoi, State tries through Lodge to clarify Lewandowski's relationship to Hanoi and his own conception of his role. His concept of offering Hanoi a "final" settlement is challenged, on the grounds that it requires the US to modify its position before any indication of concessions from the other side. Another attempt at finding a de-escalatory formula is offered, the "Phase A-Phase B" package. (Under this concept, the US would suspend bombing as Phase A. After a while, mutual de-escalatory steps would be taken as Phase B. Thus all the reciprocity would appear to be contained in Phase B, even though the total de-escalation on each side over both phases would be matching.) This formula is offered by State as a way to save face for Hanoi while retaining reciprocity for a bombing suspension.

State 83786 (to Amembassy Saigon), TS/Nodis
13 November 1966
Ref: Saigon's 10714

. . . .

"3. These are queries to be put to Lewandowski:

a. What role does he envisage for himself? Is he, on the one hand, seeking merely to facilitate a

27

better understanding on each side of the other's
position in order to pave way toward some kind of
direct contact, and, if so, does he have reason to
believe Hanoi will agree to such contact? Or, on
the other hand, does he contemplate serving as an
intermediary, conveying a series of proposals and
counterproposals between two sides to try to
achieve agreement on specific issues?

    b. What does Hanoi consider to be his
role? Has Hanoi entrusted specific messages to
him and, if so, to whom were they to be conveyed?

    c. As we understand it, Lewandowski
wants an overall agreement and says Hanoi will buy
something that is 'final,' he doesn't want a truce
just to 'allow conversations.' How does he propose
to get from here to there? How would he envisage
overcoming our considerable reluctance to modify
our position on one point or another without having
any indication of what if any helpful response
this would evoke from Hanoi?

    d. We understand that considerations of
face inevitably play a role in Hanoi's thinking.
Does this perhaps explain, in Lewandowski's view,
why we are unable to get any meaningful response to
the question 'what would happen if the bombing of
NVN stopped?' Does Lewandowski see any way around
this? Could some package deal be worked out which
in its totality represented what both we and Hanoi
would agree to as a reasonable measure of mutual
de-escalation, but which would have two separate
phases in its execution. Phase A would be a
bombing suspension, while Phase B, which would
follow after some adequate period, would see the
execution of all the other agreed de-escalatory
actions. Hanoi's actions taken in Phase B would
appear to be in response to our actions in Phase B
rather than to the bombing suspension.

"4. Lewandowski should understand that none
of the foregoing represents a position which he is
authorized to put to Hanoi on our behalf. We will
review his replies to our questions and will then
wish to determine what we wish to propose concerning
his forthcoming visit to Hanoi."

RUSK

28

November 14-15, 1966

Lewandowski answers State's queries: His role is part broker, part interlocutor. If he can narrow differences between the two sides sufficiently, they would wish to talk directly with each other and he would step out completely. He evades as "theoretical" the difficulties in his "final" settlement concept and chooses to interpret the Phase A - Phase B proposal as a US recognition that "you can't trade the bombing suspension for something else." He expects the package deal to begin its evolution without a bombing suspension, but with an end to the bombing fitting somewhere in the evolutionary process.

He too has questions to pose:

i. Does the Manila offer mean US troop withdrawal depends on GVN control of areas not now under Saigon control?

ii. In case of a cease-fire, would the US withdraw from combat areas and not interfere in the creation of a new government in Vietnam?

iii. In case of a cease-fire, would the US not interfere in peaceful reunification, whether brought about by referendum or election?

iv. In the case of a cease-fire and negotiations, would the US publicly declare its willingness to use the Geneva machinery and ICC to bring peace to Vietnam?

State's replies are carefully worded and not fully responsive to Lewandowski's probing:

i. The Manila formulation speaks for itself. It offers a "definite withdrawal period" as a basis for negotiations which could include the mechanics of phased withdrawal.

ii. We support the presently emerging constitutional process in SVN and would abide by the results of free elections.

iii. We would accept peaceful, freely chosen reunification, a pre-requisite for which is the restoration of peace and order in SVN.

iv. The 1954 and 1962 Geneva agreements are an adequate basis for peace in SE Asia, but developments since 1954 suggest better machinery may be needed.

State reiterates that the route to a final settlement must begin with de-escalation and asks again what Hanoi would do if we stopped bombing.

The meaning of this exchange is not very clear. Lewandowski seems to be asking if we would accept procedures (troop withdrawal, international inspection, etc.) that would allow changes in the SVN government favorable to the communists. We seem to reply negatively.

Secondly, Lewandowski, by ostensibly putting the bombing question aside until more of the total package emerges, may be willing to accept our attack on the North as a pressure on Hanoi for compromising other issues. State, by attempting to address bombing as an identifiable issue, may be aggravating Hanoi's problem of face. The difficulty from State's point of view, of course, is knowing what, if any, concessions Hanoi is making on other issues as the total package is built up. Having Lewandowski, a Communist, as middleman aggravates this problem.

Saigon 10856 (to SecState), TS/Nodis, 14 November 1966

"1. I met Lewandowski at D'Orlandi's apartment at 3:00 p.m. Saigon time.

"2. ...on the eve of his visit to Hanoi.... He had four questions, as follows:

a. 'Regarding the offer at Manila concerning the withdrawal of U.S. forces from Viet-Nam on the condition that the troops of North Viet-Nam would withdraw (and, he said, North Viet-Nam, of course, doesn't admit that they are there at all), does this condition mean the United States withdrawal depends on control by the present South Vietnamese Government of territories not now under the control of Saigon?

b. 'In case of a cease-fire, would the United States be prepared to withdraw from the combat areas and not to interfere in the creation of a new government in Viet-Nam? The question of how the new government of Viet-Nam will be formed will certainly arise.

c. 'In case of a cease-fire, would the United States undertake not to interfere in peaceful progress toward unification of Viet-Nam if the people so wish, whether by referendum or by election?

d. 'In the case of a cease-fire and negotiations, would the United States be ready to use the Geneva Agreement and the machinery of the International Commission in bringing peace to Viet-Nam, and if so, would the United States pubicly declare its intention to this effect?'

"3. I said that there were questions which I would have to refer to the U.S. Government, and that I would do so and provide answers as soon as I could.

"4.   I then said I had some questions to ask, and
I asked him the four sets of questions listed in your
State 83786....

      ....

"6.   Without any prodding at all from me or D'Orlandi,
he said 'Well, some of your questions cannot be answered
now. As to your Question No. 1, my present role is in
accord with the instructions of my government who would
be prepared for me to take any role which would bring
peace nearer. The two roles set forth in your question,
that is, on the one hand, to work to facilitate a better
understanding and pave the way to contact or, on the
other, to be an intermediary, do not exclude each other.
In fact, they could be done together. If the ideas which
can be developed are not too far apart, then there can be
talks, and if the ideas then start separating, both sides
can withdraw. On the other hand, if I am successful in
bringing the two sides together and they agree on something
together, I can withdraw feeling that I have achieved
something useful.

"7.   As to the second question, Lewandowski said
'you have worked in Southeast Asia and you realize that
diplomacy in Viet-Nam is different than what it is in
Europe or the United States. Clear-cut answers are very
difficult to get, one has to be very patient and look for
indirect symptoms.' He was not, he said, an agent of the
Hanoi Government, but 'if and when they decide they want
you to know something,' he said, 'they would tell me. Of
this I am confident. Each time I go, the Prime Minister
asks me about Americans and what the Americans think.'

"8.   'On your third question, it is a frame without
a picture, it is very theoretical.'

"9.   'As to the fourth question, it recognizes that
you can't trade bombing suspension for something else.
The question of bombing suspension in the first instance
could be discussed informally. But if well founded hopes
developed for reaching some agreement, then the bombing
suspension could be brought in in the second phase.'

"10. D'Orlandi remarked that in the beginning of our
talks, Lewandowski had agreed that the bombing suspension
would not be a precondition.

31

"11. Lewandowski said, 'Yes, there must be positive
steps -- not speeches or declarations. A package deal
is not only the most practical way of going at it; it is
the only one. The A and B in your fourth question are
the beginnings of the alphabet. It might be quite useful.
We must go right through to Z, including everything that
needs to be in the package deal.'"

. . . .

LODGE

State 84238 (to Amembassy Saigon), TS/Nodis,
     14 November 1966
Ref: (a) Saigon's 10856
      (b) State 83786

. . . .

"4. ...while we remain intent on finding a path to
a reasonable and honorable settlement, we are not prepared to withdraw and find that armed subversive elements
from the North have moved in again. We are serious in
expressing our willingness to remove our troops, to dismantle our bases, and accept a non-aligned South Viet-Nam
so long as it is genuinely non-aligned. We do not regard
the genuine neutrality of South Viet-Nam as opposed to
our interests. With respect to our efforts to find an
approach toward reciprocal actions of de-escalation, we
are aware that Hanoi must assign weight to considerations
of face, and we have said that so long as we were certain
that the elements from the North were removed, we would not
insist on any acknowledgement that these forces had ever
been in the South.

"5. In addition to the foregoing, we have the following specific comments on Lewandowski's four questions:

        A. The Manila formulation on withdrawal was con-
sidered and worded with the greatest care. It was included
in the communique in the light of specific indications from
Eastern European sources that such a mention of a definite
withdrawal period would help in establishing an acceptable
basis for negotiations.[17] The mechanics of a phased withdrawal would probably have to be a matter for negotiation
although the initial de-escalatory steps might be taken by
mutual example.

32

B. We have often said that we supported free
elections in South Viet-Nam to give the South Vietnamese
people a government of their own choice. We are prepared to abide by the genuine manifestation of that free
choice. We support the emerging constitutional process
in South Viet-Nam. The orderly formation of a responsive
and representative government based on free elections will
receive our support.

C. We are on record that the question of the
reunification of Viet-Nam should be determined by the
Vietnamese of both North and South through their own
free decision, without any interference from outside.
How soon that can take place depends on a number of factors,
above all the restoration of peace and order in South
Viet-Nam so that South Viet-Nam will be in a position to
treat freely with NVN on this matter.

D. We have already declared our view that the
1954 and 1962 Geneva agreements are an adequate basis
for peace in Southeast Asia. Since 1954 there have been
many developments which have revealed sharply the need for
an effective and truly neutral mechanism of supervision
and control. We would be prepared to discuss all matters
bearing upon this complicated problem.

"6. We would also observe that what Lewandowski
terms our 'theoretical' third question of how we get from
here to there bears most directly upon his proposal for a
'package deal' including, as he put it, not only A and B
but all the other letters of the alphabet. These range
all the way from the reciprocal measures of de-escalation
to the components of a final settlement. The immediate
issue is to find out precisely and concretely even if
quite privately what steps Hanoi would take if we stopped
bombing...."

....

KATZENBACH

Saigon 10955 (to SecState), TS/Nodis, 15 November 1966

....

"2. When we three met, I read him slowly the full
text of your 84238. Then I read it a second time. Both
D'Orlandi and Lewandowski took very careful notes and
were at great pains to get everything exactly right. My
reference to Item 3.D. of your 83786 was not lost on

Lewandowski. Comment: I am beginning to wonder if this
is not becoming the crux of the matter. End Comment.

. . . .

LODGE

November 16-20, 1966

A separate attempt to elicit a response to the Phase A - Phase B
formulation is made by passing it to the Russians via George Brown
during his visit to Moscow. They indicate interest, provided that the
DRV's 4 points and the NLF's 5 points are accepted as a "basis for
discussion" in the negotiations that follow. Brown is not informed of
the Lewandowski contact, and it does not come up during his talks in
Moscow.[18]

State 86196 (to Amembassy London), S/Nodis,
        16 November 1966
Please pass following message from Secretary to
        FonSec Brown

"...Dear George: Your forthcoming visit to Moscow
is obviously of the greatest importance in sounding out
the Soviets on the possibilities of action toward peace
in Viet-nam...."

"As one way of saving Hanoi's face, you may wish
to explore on your own initiative the possibility of a
package deal which in its totality represented what
both we and Hanoi would agree to as a reasonable measure
of mutual de-escalation, but which would have two
separate phases in its execution. Phase A would be a
bombing suspension, while Phase B, which would follow,
would see the execution of all the other agreed de-
escalatory actions. Hanoi's actions taken in Phase B
might appear to them to be in response to our actions
in Phase B rather than to the bombing suspension.
Obviously, Hanoi cannot have the bombing suspension
without also accepting Phase B. We would, of course,
like to hear Moscow or Hanoi's reaction to this
admittedly general proposition before we make any
specific commitments."

RUSK

State 91787 (to Amembassy London), S/Nodis,
     20 November 1966
Eyes Only for Ambassador from Secretary

     "1.   Following text message to me from George
Brown delivered by UK Embassy here....

     "On the first day I tried hard to get Gromyko
to lay off his gramophone record and get down to
the question of the three issues (paragraph 10 of
your message).   However, he gave no ground but his
interest was sufficiently intent to encourage me to
give him an outline of the package (paragraph 14 of
your message).   This I did orally before dinner on
the first evening, giving it to him as my own proposal.   Next morning, purely for the sake of clarity,
I gave him a piece of paper.   The actual words used
are enclosed.   He was pretty suspicious but promised
to pass it on to Kosygin only.

     "It was on the basis of this piece of paper
that I talked with Kosygin this morning....   On his
side after a lot of the usual stuff, pretty muted,
about American aggression, he said that they were
prepared to make the North Vietnamese four points
and the NLF five points 'a basis for discussion.'
When I said that I had interpreted a basis of discussion as meaning that they would be flexible
neither he nor Mr. Gromyko contradicted me.   Their
package would seem to be an unconditional stopping
of the bombing, some de-escalation in the South and
then negotiations on the basis as above...."

     RUSK

November 30-December 1, 1966

     Lewandowski returns from Hanoi.   He has formulated 10 points to
reflect the US position with respect to an overall solution of the
Vietnam war.   There is sufficient interest in Hanoi, he says, that the
U.S. should, if the formulation is acceptable, confirm it directly to
the DRV Ambassador in Warsaw.   He urges speed to guard against a leak
or sabotage by those "working against a solution."   His source in
Hanoi, he says, is Pham Van Dong, who has the "Presidium behind him."

     Most of Lewandowski's 10 points reiterate familiar US positions.
His principal innovation is US acceptance that "the present status quo
in SVN must be changed in order to take into account the interests of

the parties presently opposing the policy of the U.S. in SVN." He
does not include the Phase A - Phase B formula for de-escalation, but
states that the US would stop bombing to facilitate a peaceful solution,
would "accept DRV modalities on the cessation," and would not require
the DRV to admit infiltration into SVN. Lodge believes, however, that
he did give his presentation in Hanoi in accord with the full Phase A -
Phase B formulation.

Lodge refers the 10 points to Washington, to see if they are an
acceptable representation of the US position. He points out two
difficulties himself, however: the phrase "status quo in SVN must
change" would be more acceptable if it read "status quo in SVN would
change"; and the terms for de-escalation are poorly expressed.

Saigon 12247, TS/Nodis, 30 November 1966

"Lewandowski summarized the 10 points to Lodge as
follows:

(1) The U.S. is interested in a peaceful solution through negotiations.

(2) Negotiations should not be interpreted as
a way to negotiated surrender by those opposing the
U.S. in Vietnam. A political negotiation would be
aimed at finding an acceptable solution to all the
problems, having in mind that the present status quo
in SVN must be changed in order to take into account
the interests of the parties presently opposing the
policy of the U.S. in South Vietnam.

(3) The U.S. does not desire a permanent or a
long-term military presence in SVN.

(4) The U.S. is willing to discuss all problems
with respect to the settlement.

(5) The U.S. is willing to accept the participation of 'all' in elections and the supervision of these
elections by an appropriate international body.

(6) The U.S. believes that reunification should
be settled by the Vietnamese themselves after peace
and proper representative organs are established in SVN.

(7) The U.S. is prepared to abide by a neutral
South Vietnam.

(8) The U.S. is prepared to stop bombing 'if this will facilitate such a peaceful solution.' In this regard the U.S. is prepared to accept DRV modalities on the cessation and not require the DRV to admit infiltration into SVN.

(9) The U.S. will not agree to 'reunification under military pressure.'

(10) The U.S. 'will not declare now or in the future its acceptance of North Vietnam's 4 or 5 points.'

"Lewandowski asked if these 10 points were a proper formulation of the U.S. position. Lodge said that they seemed to be in order, but that the matter was of such sensitivity and importance that he would have to refer the points back to Washington for approval. Lodge added, however, that he saw two difficulties right off. First, he suggested changing Point 2 to read 'would' instead of 'must.' Second, he questioned the phraseology in Point 8 -- 'if this would facilitate such a peaceful solution.'

"Lewandowski insisted that his statement was a serious proposition based on conversations with the 'most respectable government sources in Hanoi.' Later Lewandowski admitted that Pham Van Dong was the source and that he had the 'Presidium behind him.'

"Lewandowski stated: 'I am authorized to say that if the U.S. are really of the views which I have presented, it would be advisable to confirm them directly by conversation with the North Vietnamese Ambassador in Warsaw.'

"Lewandowski said that there was a vital need to move quickly because (1) there was a danger of a leak and that secrecy was essential for Hanoi; and (2) that delays would give those 'working against a solution' time to 'put down the clamps on talks.'"

State 94660 (to Amembassy Saigon), TS/Nodis
     1 December 1966

. . . .

"(5) Do we interpret your comment at the end of para D-8 correctly to mean that Lewandowski presented our phasing formulation fully and accurately?"

RUSK

Saigon 12323 (to SecState), TS/Nodis,
    1 December 1966
Ref: State 94660

. . . .

"5. Your para 5. Lewandowski did not repeat not
present your phasing formulation 'fully and accurately'
in his conversation with me. He merely cited 'your
Phase A and Phase B,' with clear implication that HS
(Sic) had given his presentation in Hanoi in accordance
with your formulation."

LODGE

December 2, 1966

Airstrikes are run against the Van Dien Vehicle Depot and the Ha Gia
POL Storage Facility 6.7 and 16 nautical miles, respectively, from the
center of Hanoi.

December 3, 1966

(NB. DOD files do not contain Washington-Saigon or Washington-Warsaw
traffic on Marigold for December 2-4. What follows is derived from later
cables.)

On instructions from State, Lodge meets Lewandowski again to state
that:

i. The U.S. Embassy in Warsaw will contact the DRV Embassy on
December 6 or soon thereafter;

ii. Lewandowski's 10 points broadly reflect the US position; but

iii. "Several specific points are subject to important differences
of interpretation."

Lewandowski, in turn, expresses concern about US bombing of Hanoi,
acting on instructions from Rapacki. (Saigon 12428)

December 4, 1966

Airstrikes are run against the Yen Vien Railroad Yard and the Ha Gia
POL Storage Facility, 5.5 and 16 nautical miles, respectively, from the
center of Hanoi.

December 5, 1966

Grounouski is summoned by the Foreign Minister in Warsaw and given a Polish recapitulation of Marigold.[19] According to Rapacki's account of the December 1 meeting in Saigon, Polish support for a US-DRV contact in Warsaw was extended "after Lodge confirmed Lewandowski's resume." Thus Lodge's December 3 statement about "important differences of interpretation" appears as a revision of earlier US acceptance.

Rapacki argues that the US reservations about interpretation are so broadly stated as to put the whole basis for the contact in doubt. Also, coming "after all the conversations which were held," the statement might undermine the role of Poland as intermediary. He urges instead that it be replaced by a statement defining the differences of interpretation the USG has in mind and asks Gronouski to take this up with the President.

He also refers to the "intensification of bombing near Hanoi subsequent to the Lodge-Lewandowski conversations" as likely to create doubts on the DRV side.

It is hard to know precisely what has happened in Polish-DRV communications at this point. Rapacki's account suggests that the Poles told Hanoi they had US approval of Lewandowski's 10 points after the December 1 meeting. If so, the events of December 3 (the air strikes near Hanoi and the "differences of interpretation") might well have been viewed in Hanoi as casting doubt on Polish reliability, on the sincerity of US interest in negotiations, or both. Alternatively, Rapacki may simply have been trying to extract additional concessions or statements of position from the Americans, using these developments for leverage.

> Warsaw 1363 (to SecState), 5 December 1966
> For the President and Secretary
>
>
> "1. I was called to FornMin 11:30 a.m. Dec 5 by Dirgen Michalowski who, after determining that I knew what meeting was about, took me in to see FornMin Rapacki."
>
> ....
>
> "4. Rapacki continued that on Dec 1, after return of Lewandowski from Hanoi, Lewandowski had third meeting with Lodge in which he gave a resume of USG position as he had understood it from the two previous conversations. After Lodge confirmed Lewandowski's resume, Lewandowski said contact of USG and North Vietnamese Ambassadors in Warsaw would have support of Poles.

"5. Continuing his account of prior events, Rapacki said that on the afternoon of Dec 3, at a fourth meeting between Lodge and Lewandowski, Lodge, on the basis of the President's instructions, read a statement as follows:

A. The President will instruct the U.S. Embassy in Warsaw to contact the North Vietnamese Ambassador in Warsaw on Dec 6 or as soon as possible thereafter.

B. The U.S. Embassy in Warsaw will be in a position on Dec 6 to confirm to the North Vietnamese Ambassador that the Lewandowski Dec 1 resume of the Lodge-Lewandowski conversations broadly reflects the position of the USG.

C. 'We must add that several specific points are subject to important differences of interpretation.'"

"6. Rapacki said that Lodge was unable at the Dec 3 meeting to precisely say which points were subject to differences of interpretation and what the nature of these differences of interpretation might be.

"7. Rapacki then stated that question of interpretation put in doubt whole basis on which contact with North Vietnamese Ambassador in Warsaw was to have taken place. He expressed grave concern as to how equivocation will be read by Hanoi. He added that Poles must transmit USG position to NVN Govt.; and that rather than a general reference to differences of interpretation it would be better if position transmitted contained statement defining differences of interpretation we have in mind. He said such a statement might have a significant effect on Hanoi's attitude toward both a meeting in Warsaw and the whole problem.

"8. Rapacki then asked what can be the position of Poland in its role as intermediary if after all the conversations which were held and statements made there still remains this doubt? He asked again how this reservation will be read by Hanoi, particularly with intensification of bombing near Hanoi subsequent to the Lodge-Lewandowski conversations? He said these questions had already been raised by Lewandowski during his Dec 3 conversation with Lodge."

. . . .

"12.   Rapacki asked that I transmit to the President the Poles deep concern caused by modification of USG position which has been signaled by the Dec 3 declaration of Mr. Lodge and his hope that para on differences of interpretation can be deleted on grounds that it was based on misunderstandings which have since been clarified."

....

GRONOUSKI

December 5, 1966

Gronouski is instructed to stick with the reservation as worded on the grounds that we might be charged with bad faith if we did not make clear the wide latitude for interpretation of the general language used by Lewandowski.

State 97016 (to Amembassy Warsaw), Nodis,
    5 December 1966
Ambassador Eyes Only TOSEC 14 Secretary Eyes Only
Ref: Your 1363

".... We might expose ourselves to charges of bad faith in any subsequent negotiations if we did not make clear that there is a wide latitude for interpretation of the general language used by Lewandowski.

"Lewandowski's formulation broadly reflects the position of the US Government on the issues covered and we would be prepared to accept it as the basis for direct discussions with the North Vietnamese if they are in fact interested in pursuing the matter, and if they were informed that latitude for interpretation of such general language is inevitable."

....

December 6, 1966

Gronouski carries out his instructions and is told by Rapacki that the US statement will now be transmitted to Hanoi.

Rapacki says that the DRV expects to receive at the first Warsaw meeting the precise and official position of the USG in order that it can express its position at an appropriate time. He apparently understands Lodge to have indicated that such a package proposal would be forthcoming.

Gronouski replies that he had anticipated a more limited scope for the first meeting--confirming Lewandowski's formulation, dealing with matters such as time and place, etc. He refers the matter to Washington.

Meanwhile, Lewandowski makes many of the same points to Lodge in Saigon. He adds that the "Warsaw contact was shadowed by the bombing of Hanoi" and asks the US to "avoid adding to the difficulties."

> Warsaw 1375 (to SecState), TS/Nodis,
>   6 December 1966
> Ref: State 97016
>
> "1.   Met with FonMin Rapacki 1300 hours Dec 6 and conveyed material in reftel."
>
>   ....
>
> "5.   Rapacki said that he understood Lodge to have done the following:
>
>   A.   Presented official USG position or principles for peaceful solution;
>
>   B.   Stated that a new package deal of USG proposals would be forthcoming;
>
>   C.   Expressed willingness of USG to discuss four points and any other points raised by other side. (FYI: This summary was apropos of nothing. It was simply interjected in the conversation.)
>
> "6.   After repeating his view that proposal for meeting in Warsaw was a significant NVN response, he said Poles must reserve judgment until they can study situation further to determine whether USG had actually made step forward. He expressed the opinion that what had transpired between Lodge and Lewandowski prior to latter's trip to Hanoi did represent step forward but the qualifications made by Lodge on Dec 3 cast doubt on this judgment."
>
>   ....
>
> "9.   Rapacki said that at any rate they cannot delay any longer in transmitting information to Hanoi.

He added that the original position of Lodge is known
to Hanoi, and it remains a question as to how the
qualification of Dec 3 will be interpreted by sensitive elements in the NVN Govt. Rapacki said that
information transmitted to NVN will reflect the
material presented to him today, but Poles must also
express their own doubts and misgivings over the
question of interpretation raised by Lodge.

"10. Rapacki then turned to the substance of the
first Warsaw meeting with NVN Ambassador 'in the event
it takes place.' He said it is his understanding that
during that meeting we will present to the NVN side
the position of USG in order that the NVN Govt can
express his position at an appropriate time on the
attitude of the USG and on subsequent modes of procedure. He said the NVN Govt. expects to receive at
the first Warsaw meeting the precise and official
position of the USG and he assumes (with a smile)
that it will not be different than the one presented
to Lewandowski. He said he presumed I already have
locked in my safe such a statement which will be able
to identify the specific points on which there is wide
latitude for interpretation. (FYI: Rapacki read from
a Dec 3 statement given to Lewandowski by Lodge when
making his reference to specific points.) He said he
hoped at that meeting we will be able to discuss
differences in interpretation (adding that he still
was looking for an answer to the question 'differences
with whom' inasmuch as the NVN Govt. has not yet presented their interpretation.)

"11. I said that I had presumed that the first
meeting would be more limited in scope. I expected
that the first meeting would be primarily concerned
with establishing that both sides were interested in
beginning negotiations, and deal with such matters as
time and place of negotiation session. I added that we
would also expect at the first meeting to confirm Mr.
Lewandowski's formulation of our position as broadly
reflecting the position of the USG with the qualification regarding interpretation. I added, however,
that I would inform Washington of his understanding
of the nature of the first meeting."

GRONOUSKI

43

Saigon 12601 (to SecState), TS/Nodis, 6 December 1966

"1. Lewandowski asked to meet me at D'Orlandi's today. He began by saying that he had asked for the meeting because of a communication which he had received from Mr. Rapacki in Warsaw, which asked him:

"2. 'Please turn the attention of Ambassador Lodge to the fact that the formulation of the last paragraph of the statement of December Three may be understood as raising a question about the whole position embodied in the ten paragraphs and which was to form the platform for the Warsaw Meeting.'"

. . . .

"5. Lewandowski then said, rather as an afterthought, that 'the overture of the Warsaw contact was shadowed by the bombing of Hanoi and we should, therefore, avoid adding to the difficulties.'"

December 7, 1967

Gronouski is told that the USG position was conveyed to Hanoi the previous day, that the intensification of the bombing is raising suspicions in Warsaw as well as Hanoi, and that the DRV will be keenly disappointed if the first meeting does not include a direct statement of the USG position. The DRV "is not interested in what Lewandowski said."

With respect to the bombing problem, the Poles reject the explanations that the target list cannot be suddenly altered without alerting many people that something unusual is happening and that what appears as an intensification of bombing is in fact due to improved weather conditions. Rapacki says "policy is more important than weather," and we are urged not to bomb in the vicinity of Hanoi and Haiphong.

Warsaw 1376 (to SecState), TS/Nodis, 7 December 1966
Ref: State 97016 and Warsaw 1375

. . . .

"3. Michalowski said Rapacki had conveyed USG position to Hanoi shortly after my meeting with him Dec 6...."

. . . .

"5. Michalowski said...that NVN Govt. and even some in Polish Govt. are suspicious that recently

stepped up bombing outside Hanoi is the work of some
elements in USG who are trying to undercut President's peace move. He added that when this question
was raised with Lodge the latter had replied that
such raids are planned long in advance, and that a
quick reversal would alert many people that something unusual was happening. Michalowski said that
to many people this is an unconvincing answer, and
expressed fervent hope that we can avoid future
highly sensitive bombing raids in vicinity of Hanoi
and Haiphong....

"6. Michalowski said he wanted to underscore
Rapacki's insistence that at the first meeting with
the NVN Ambassador in Warsaw we do more than confirm, with qualification, Lewandowski's resume of
Lodge's ten points. He said the NVN Govt. is not
interested in what Lewandowski said, but rather in
hearing USG position directly from us. He stressed
extreme importance of first meeting, and said the
NVN Govt. will be keenly disappointed if its expectation of receiving direct statement of USG position at first meeting is not realized...."

GRONOUSKI

Warsaw 1376 (to SecState), TS/Nodis, 7 December 1966
Ref: Warsaw 1376

"1. FonMin Rapacki called me to his office at
1800 hours Dec 7 ...."

    ....

"3. Rapacki then said that Poland could not
continue in its role unless it is convinced that we
have or will put an end to this intensified bombing.
He added that if Poland has been satisfied on this
score, and if it so happens that contact in Warsaw
between the USG and NVN Govt. will occur, then 'I
avail myself of this opportunity to state' that it
is necessary for the USG to recapitulate to the NVN
Representative its whole position as described by
Lodge with a degree of clarity so that the other side
would no longer fear that the USG position as formulated might subsequently be changed through recourse
to Lodge's 'important differences of interpretation'
clause....

"4. ...I said that if I recall correctly, there was a lull in bombing flights in late October and early November simply because of bad weather conditions, and what appears to him to be an intensification of bombing may simply be a resumption of bombing to its normal level.

"5. Rapacki responded that 'policy is more important than weather'....

"6. ...bombing against the whole of NVN was intensified and also was more directed to Hanoi. This, he added, clearly appears to be provoking."

....

GRONOUSKI

December 7, 1966

Gronouski's instructions for the first meeting are refined. He is to stick with Lewandowski's formulation, indicating its acceptability as a basis for negotiation even though subject to further elaboration and clarification as talks proceed. We do not wish to reformulate it ourselves because we would have to take harder positions than Lewandowski's if we were to be held to precise language and because any formulation attributable directly to us could be used to embarrass the GVN or our relations with them. Gronouski is therefore to avoid being drawn out on specifics, though for purposes of illustration he may point to the following:

i. In negotiating a bombing cessation (point 8), the Phase A - Phase B formula might be considered.

ii. Changes in the governmental status quo would have to be made in accordance with the desires of the people of SVN. Electoral procedures or other arrangements could be ascertained through consultations and negotiations there (points 2 and 5).

(The most contentious point, he is warned, is that calling for a change in status quo, as it could mean anything from putting the NLF into the government immediately to a simple endorsement of the election process under the Constitution then being drafted by the GVN. Gronouski is to resist discussing this altogether.)

He is to reassure the DRV that our reservation about "differences of interpretation" means only that complex matters are inevitably subject to clarification. For example, the phrase "long-term" in point 3 has been partially clarified by the 6 months provision of the Manila Communique.

46

We urge direct, secret discussion with the DRV as a matter of the highest importance and urgency. We hope that the Poles have no idea of participating and Gronouski is to avoid further substantive discussions with them if the DRV contact materializes.

State 97930 (Amembassy Warsaw), TS/Nodis,
    7 December 1966
Ref: Warsaw's 1375

"1. Your reference telegram will receive urgent consideration here tomorrow and you will receive further guidance from us then.

"2. In the meantime, you should take no further initiative with GOP.

"3. In the unlikely event that, before receiving further instructions, you should receive notice that NVN representative is ready and available for talks with us, we submit the following for your interim guidance.

"4. If such a meeting with NVN representative should occur, you should follow prior instructions. If desirable, you are then authorized to read rpt read to him Lewandowski's 10-point presentation of USG position as set forth at end of this cable, stressing that it is Lewandowski's formulation.

"5. You should then inquire whether points as presented by you are the same in all particulars as those passed on to Hanoi by Lewandowski.

"6. For your information only, one of our principal concerns about the ten points is set forth in the next following paragraph, but even if pressed you should avoid discussing the substantive problems relating to these points with the NVN representative at this stage and stress that such discussions should be the subject of actual negotiations. We would assume that NVN representative would have no authority on this first contact to do more than report your presentation to Hanoi so we would not anticipate such probing at this time. Further cable tomorrow will spell out our thinking in greater detail and may suggest initiative to be taken if you have heard nothing after additional lapse of time.

"7. Lewandowski's point two relating to change of present status quo in SVN is obviously most troublesome. This point could be interpreted variously to mean (a) NLF must be put into government of South Vietnam forthwith or (b) simple endorsement of election process under constitution now being drafted. If it is necessary to point out ambiguities in Lewandowski's statement, however, you should not refer to this point but allude to less contentious ambiguities elsewhere in statement.

"8. Lewandowski's ten point statement follows:

'1. I have insisted that the United States is interested in a peaceful solution through negotiations.

'2. Negotiations should not be interpreted as a way to negotiated surrender by those opposing the United States in Viet-Nam. A political negotiation would be aimed at finding an acceptable solution to all the problems, having in mind that the present status quo in South Viet-Nam would be changed in order to take into account the interests of the parties presently opposing the policy of the United States in South Viet-Nam, and that such a solution may be reached in an honorable and dignified way not detrimental to national pride and prestige. (FYI: Lewandowski's original presentation states status quo 'must' be changed but when Lodge questioned this point Lewandowski said he would be glad to change word from 'must' to 'would', END FYI).

'3. That the United States are not interested from a point of view of its national interests in having a permanent or long term military _____ in South Viet-Nam once a peaceful solution to the _____ reached. That is why the offer made in Manila regarding the withdrawal of U.S. troops and the liquidation of American bases should be considered in all seriousness.

'4. The United States would be ready, should other parties show a constructive interest in a negotiated settlement, to work out and to discuss with them proposals of such a settlement covering all important problems involved from a cease-fire to a final solution and withdrawal of U.S. troops.

'5. That the United States, within a general solution, would not oppose the formation of a South Vietnamese Government based on the true will of the Vietnamese people with participation of all through free democratic elections, and that the United States would

be prepared to accept the necessary control machinery
to secure the democratic and free character of such
elections and to respect the results of such elections.

'6.   The United States held the view that
unification of Viet-Nam must be decided by the Vietnamese themselves for which the restoration of peace
and the formation of proper representative organs of
the people in South Viet-Nam is a necessary condition.

'7.   The United States are ready to accept
and respect a true and complete neutrality of South
Viet-Nam.

'8.   The United States are prepared to stop
the bombing of the territory of North Viet-Nam if this
will facilitate such a peaceful solution.   In doing so,
the United States are ready to avoid any appearance
that North Viet-Nam is forced to negotiate by bombings
or that North Viet-Nam have negotiated in exchange for
cessation of bombing.   Stopping of bombings would not
involve recognition or confirmation by North Viet-Nam
that its armed forces are or were infiltrating into
South Viet-Nam.'

"At this point you should interrupt recitation of
Lewandowski's points and state as follows: QUOTE Mr.
Lewandowski clearly implied to Ambassador Lodge that
in Hanoi he had given his presentation in connection
with the point on the bombing of North Viet-Nam in
accordance with Ambassador Lodge's earlier formulation,
which was as follows: A package could be worked out
which in its totality represented what both the United
States and North Viet-Nam would agree to as a reasonable
measure of de-escalation, but which would have two
separate phases in its execution. Phase A would be a
bombing suspension, while Phase B, which would follow
after some adequate period, would see the execution of
all the other agreed de-escalatory actions. North
Viet-Nam's actions taken in Phase B would appear to be
in response to United States actions in Phase B rather
than to the bombing suspension, END QUOTE. You should
then resume the recitation of the ten points.

'9.   I have informed the proper governmental
sources that at the same time, the United States, while
not excluding the unification of Viet-Nam, would not
agree to unification under military pressure.

'10.   While the United States are seeking a
peaceful solution to the conflict, it would be unrealistic to expect that the United States will declare

now or in the future its acceptance of North Viet-Nam's four or five points.' (END OF LEWANDOWSKI'S STATEMENT)

"9. If NVN representative probes further on cessation of bombing, you should merely state that as you have already indicated Mr. Lewandowski has suggested a possible procedure for agreeing on phasing and timing which could be the subject of later discussions."

KATZENBACH

State 98754 (to Amembassy Warsaw), TS/Nodis
    7 December 1966
Ref: State 97930

"1. If a meeting with the North Vietnamese is arranged, you should proceed in accordance with instructions contained in State 96235 and State 95711 except as modified below. As regards the presentation to the North Vietnamese representative of our position, you should follow closely the following formulation:

'a. Lewandowski has informed us of his discussions with your government in Hanoi and of the position he communicated to them as that of the U.S., based on Lewandowski's prior oral discussions with Ambassador Lodge in Saigon. We assume that his discussions in Hanoi were conducted entirely orally as they were with Lodge in Saigon and that no pieces of paper have been exchanged which purport to state governmental positions. We are prepared to enter into direct discussions with your government on the basis of the position which Lewandowski has informed us he presented to your government in Hanoi.

'b. The position was stated to us by Lewandowski as follows: (Here you should read the ten points as contained in State 97930, para 8 with the additional point about bombing covered uner Point 8).

'c. We wish to emphasize that this language is that of Lewandowski and not that of the United States. Nevertheless it presents a general statement of the US position on the basis of which we would be prepared to enter into direct discussions.'

"2. FYI The North Vietnamese and perhaps the Poles
as well appear to be seeking a reformulation of our
position in order to compare it with what Lewandowski
has said. While we are entirely prepared to have Lewan-
dlowski's formulation stand as 'presenting a general
statement of the US position,' we are anxious to avoid
a restatement of our position in our own words because
(a) this would oblige us to take some harder positions
than those put forward by Lewandowski which apparently
have gone far enough to make the North Vietnamese ready
to consider talking with us and (b) any formulation
which can be attributed directly to us could be used
to embarrass the GVN or to embarrass us in our relations
with them. In other words, if we stand on Lewandowski's
formulation through the first step in discussions with
the North Vietnamese, we can always say with regard to
any specific point that we don't accept just those words
used by Lewandowski and thus maintain some room for
maneuver at least until we know the discussions are
really under way. END FYI.

"3. After reading the ten points you should point
out to the North Vietnamese that some matters, because
of their complexity and the danger of varying interpretation, would be the subject of further elaboration by us
as soon as discussions were to get under way. One of
these has to do with the package agreement containing the
so-called phases A and B with respect to bombing and a
program of de-escalation. The second relates to certain
points which directly involve matters of basic concern
to the people of South Viet-Nam (as for example points
2 and 5). Whatever detailed arrangements are made on
those matters would have to be acceptable to the South
Vietnamese people; however, this could be ascertained
through consultations and negotiations there.

"4. If the North Vietnamese refer to the earlier
point made by us that several specific points are subject to important differences of interpretation, you
should explain that this is not intended to suggest that
the statement as it stands is any less a general statement of the U.S. position but rather that it is inevitable
with matters as complex and controversial as those covered
in the ten points that they would be subject to interpretation and that their clarification would be the normal
function of the discussions which we hope we will be
embarking on. If the North Vietnamese press for an
illustration you might refer to the phrase 'long-term'
in Point 3, noting that it was specifically to clarify
this point that the Manila Communique specified a six-
month period.

"5. Otherwise you should be guided in your
discussion with the North Vietnamese by the limitation set forth in para 6 of State 97930, stressing that further discussion of substantive questions
should be the subject of the actual direct negotiations which we hope can be got under way promptly.

"6. In conclusion you should say that your
government is prepared to enter into secret discussions with the North Vietnamese Government at
any time and we regard this as a matter of the
highest importance and urgency.

"7. We understand from your latest reports
that the next step, if all goes well, will be the
opening of the direct discussions with the North
Vietnamese and if this in fact materializes you
should avoid any further substantive discussions
with the Poles. We, of course, are anxious for
direct and private discussions with the North Vietnamese and hope that the Poles have no idea of
participating therein."

....

KATZENBACH

December 8, 1966

Rusk and Katzenbach reiterate our willingness to consider a
bombing cessation or other de-escalatory measures on terms previously
indicated, but not as a precondition for talks. If Rapacki threatens
to interrupt the contact over this issue, he is to be warned the
responsibility for the breakdown will be his.

State 98924 (to Amembassy Warsaw), TS/Nodis,
    8 December 1966
For Ambassador Gronouski from Katzenbach

"1. In response to Rapacki's statements reported
in your 1394...you should remind Rapacki that the subject of bombing was one of the matters discussed in
Hanoi by Lewandowski and that we are prepared to pursue
this matter with the North Vietnamese in the same terms
which we affirmed to him. You should read reference on
package contained in paragraph 3 of Lewandowski's 10
points (State 97930) to remind him of Lewandowski's
statement to Lodge. You should underline that inherent
in this formulation is the package approach to de-
escalation.

"2. If Rapacki attempt to nail us to anything on bombing beyond our first contact with the North Vietnamese, or again threatens to break off the operation, you should inform him in no uncertain terms that if he maintains this position he will have to accept the full responsibility for the breakdown of what appears to us to be a promising possibility for peace."

KATZENBACH

Taipei 1072 (to SecState), TS/Nodis,
     8 December 1966
Ref: TOSEC 65
FOR the Acting Secretary from the Secretary

     ".... I do not believe we should be drawn into commitments about our own military operations without some indication from the other side as to what they are going to do about their military operations. Nevertheless, we should be ready to discuss this problem alongside or before a broader discussion of political matters."

     ....

McConaughy

December 8-9, 1966

Rapacki protests the "differences of interpretation" clause and the bombing of Hanoi in a strong demarche to Fanfani and, through Lewandowski, to D'Orlandi and hence Lodge in Saigon. Hanoi cannot be expected to enter discussions in the face of such "escalation." Fanfani on the one hand urges Rapacki to go ahead and arrange the contact in Warsaw, on the other instructs D'Orlandi to convey the message to Rusk (then in Saigon) and to seek a reply.

At their meeting on December 8, D'Orlandi tells Lewandowski that no contact has yet taken place because of Rapacki's apparent refusal to convey the US message to Hanoi. He is apparently unaware that the message was passed December 6.

On December 9, Rusk asks D'Orlandi to tell Lewandowski and Fanfani that we are in direct touch with Rapacki on both points. He adds that bombing can be the first topic for discussion, if this is of especial concern to Hanoi.

53

D'Orlandi gives the following as views of Lewandowski:

i. Clarifications prerequisite to the Warsaw contact should occur in Saigon, with a Lewandowski visit to Hanoi immediately possible if needed. Thus D'Orlandi surmises that Rapacki's taking over this phase may be an effort "to be clever and get the U.S. to withdraw "all reservations" before the contact is made.

ii. De-escalation is a difficult topic to start on. It is more promising to look for a final package. This might be a cabinet of 14 positions, 2 each for the Ky Group and the NLF, the remaining 10 for "neutrals or whatever." (This is the formula proposed by Lewandowski September 18.)

iii. During November 16-30, when Lewandowski was in Hanoi, bombing appeared to be at a reduced level at least in the Hanoi area. This was interpreted in Hanoi as a tacit signal of US support for Lewandowski's mission. (NB. In fact, these were the first two weeks of RT 52. Presumably, weather accounts for the lack of action against targets near Hanoi.)

Rusk stresses to D'Orlandi several times that the USG is indicating its position with no reciprocity from Hanoi or even assurance of how Lewandowski has presented the points to Hanoi. D'Orlandi urges "a little faith in Lewandowski." He himself completely credits Lewandowski's claim to have gotten Pham Van Dong to obtain Presidium agreement to the Warsaw contact.

Saigon 12953 (to SecState), TS/Nodis, 9 December 1966

"D'Orlandi asked to see Secretary and Ambassador this evening following dinner party in Secretary's honor. Conversation was a follows:

"1. Lewandowski had called urgently on D'Orlandi evening of December 8, on instructions, to express grave concern that U.S. had carried out heavy bombing attacks in Hanoi area on December 2 and December 4, directly following December 1 conversation between Lewandowski and Lodge. Lewandowski conveyed lurid reports from Polish attache Hanoi alleging that December 2 attack had included bombing and machine-gunning within city area and had caused 600 casualties. December 4 attack also described as serious and in Hanoi area. Lewandowski protested to D'Orlandi - urging him to convey message to Lodge and to Secretary if possible - that such attacks could only threaten or destroy possibility of contact in Warsaw. Lewandowski argued that Hanoi could not be expected to enter

discussions in face of such escalation. (While whole
tenor of message was extremely strong, Lewandowski
did not repeat not state that he was actually reporting Hanoi's expressions of view, but rather Warsaw
judgment.)

"2. D'Orlandi had responded to Lewandowski that
no contact had in fact taken place as yet because of
apparent refusal of Rapacki to convey firm message,
that U.S. had taken forthcoming action in declaring
itself ready for discussions and prepared to make
contact on December 6, and that it was thus not fair
to say possibility of contact destroyed by U.S. action.
D'Orlandi went on to say that his hope had been to
make contact in any event.

"3. In addition to Lewandowski message December
8, D'Orlandi had just received cable from Fanfani, on
evening December 9, reporting that Rapacki had sent
Fanfani strong demarche protesting U.S. insistence on
reservations of interpretation, and further protesting
U.S. bombing attacks. In this cable, Fanfani had
instructed D'Orlandi to convey substance of message to
Secretary, if possible, and ask for reply. Fanfani
had also included in the cable statement that he himself had replied to Rapacki urging that he go ahead
and arrange contact nonetheless.

"4. Secretary responded to D'Orlandi as follows:

A. He asked D'Orlandi to tell Lewandowski
that we were in direct touch with Rapacki on the
points raised....

B. D'Orlandi should reply to Fanfani with
same first point, adding that if Hanoi was concerned
about bombing, this could be first topic in discussions....

"5. During course of conversation, D'Orlandi provided following additional conjecture and information:

A. D'Orlandi was fairly sure that Lewandowski
had wished Warsaw contact to take place, with any points
requiring clarification to be explored through tripartite
talks in Saigon and possible Lewandowski further visit
to Hanoi (which Lewandowski had also suggested D'Orlandi
as immediate possibility). D'Orlandi therefore surmised
that Rapacki had 'tried to be clever' and get U.S. to
withdraw all reservations before contact made. (U.S.
side at no time confirmed that this was in fact exactly
what Rapacki had said in Warsaw.) Secretary suggested

that - in light of prior expressed statement that Soviets
informed - Rapacki actions might have been dictated from
Moscow. D'Orlandi expressed doubt, on basis his reading
of Lewandowski attitude and remarks by Lewandowski about
Rapacki over a period of time. Matter was dropped at
this point.

B. ...Lewandowski had particularly expounded
to him difficulties he saw in getting discussions started
on reciprocal actions in connection with bombing. Hence,
at D'Orlandi's suggestion Lewandowski had started to work
out how situation in SVN might look one or two years hence
and might be described in acceptable form to Hanoi and
Washington, so that in effect a package deal would emerge.
D'Orlandi stated that, when he asked Lewandowski just
what kind of role VC might have - would it be like Czechoslovakia, or what - Lewandowski had come up with sample
formula of 14 cabinet positions with 2 each for present
Ky Group and VC/NLF, and remaining 10 allotted to 'neutrals
or whatever.' (This is of course formula given by D'Orlandi
to Harriman, as D'Orlandi's own, in Rome conversation in
early November.)

C. In connection with Hanoi attitudes on U.S.
bombing of North, Lewandowski had told D'Orlandi that he
believed Hanoi had attached significance to fact that
during the two weeks Lewandowski had been in Hanoi (approximately November 16-30) bombing had appeared to be at
reduced level at least in Hanoi area. D'Orlandi said
Lewandowski thought Hanoi had interpreted this as tacit
signal of U.S. support for Lewandowski mission.

"6. Secretary several times pointed out that whole
episode to this point was unique in that we were acting
on Lewandowski's statement of U.S. position without any
clear indication whatever of Hanoi position, or even any
assurance Lewandowski had discussed points with Hanoi in
manner covered by statement. D'Orlandi appeared to
accept that we had indeed taken forthcoming attitude in
view of these circumstances, although he himself stressed
view that one had to have a little faith in Lewandowski,
and he appeared to credit completely Lewandowski claim
that he had finally got Pham Van Dong to obtain Presidium
agreement to Warsaw contact."

. . . .

LODGE

December 9, 1966

In Warsaw, Gronouski assures the Poles that the Lewandowski formulation is consistent with our views, that he "assumes" Phase A - Phase B de-escalation formula is the "new package deal" the Poles believe Lodge to have promised, and that the pattern of our bombing is not related to the projected US-DRV contact.

Rapacki is satisfied with respect to the interpretation clause. He rejects de-escalation as too narrow a package but blurs the issue by suggesting that "de-escalation" may be US shorthand for a deal including all outstanding issues.

On the bombing, he is adamant in his dissatisfaction. He reads what he says is a November 14 statement by Lodge, declaring USG willingness to hear suggestions on "practical measures" it might take to show its good intentions and allay the distrust the NLF and Hanoi may have of it. He feels the Pole's bombing suggestions were not received in this spirit. He implies that Lodge's statement was not conveyed to Hanoi.

As Gronouski found no threat to break off the talks, he did not issue the warning on his instructions of December 8.

Warsaw 1421 (to SecState), TS/Nodis, 9 December 1966
Section 1 of 2
Ref: State 98924

"1. Met Rapacki at my request at 1600 Dec 9. Michalowski and Janczewski present.

"2. My opening remarks, based on reftel, were as follows:

A. I have requested today's meeting as a result of consultations I have had with Washington since our meeting Wednesday afternoon.

B. I can now assure you that at the time of the first Warsaw meeting with representatives of the North Vietnamese Government, I will be prepared to confirm to the NVN Govt the position of the USG with respect to negotiations. I can also assure you that this confirmation will be consistent with the discussions Mr. Lewandowski had with them and with us.

C. With respect to the question you raised Wednesday on bombing, I can state flatly that the pattern of our bombing in NVN has nothing to do with with the current efforts of the Polish and USG's to get underway the projected US-NVN talks....

D. You will recall that the subject of bombing NVN was one of the matters discussed in Hanoi by Mr. Lewandowski. After his return from Hanoi Mr. Lewandowski clearly implied to Amb Lodge that he had discussed this matter in Hanoi in accordance with Amb Lodge's earlier formulation. Amb Lodge had suggested that a package could be worked out.... Inherent in this formulation is the package approach to de-escalation which I assume you had in mind when you referred to 'a new package deal' during our conversation last Tuesday."

....

"3. Rapacki responded...."

"4. ...with respect to my first point (presentation of USG negotiating position to NVN) he said if this is done in a way which will dispel doubt on invoking interpretation clause, then one of the difficulties has been reduced.

"5. On bombing question, he said...bombing was clearly intensified at the precise time it would create provocation....

"6. Rapacki read what he said was Nov. 14 statement by Lodge: USG understands that the Liberation Front and Hanoi have deep-seated distrust of USG; that is why USG is willing to take practical measures to show good intentions, and would be willing to hear any suggestions. Rapacki said this statement by Lodge was treated as addressed 'only to Polish ears,' adding Poles have been proved right in treating it so because in the case of their bombing suggestion they have not found such readiness to listen to suggestions as Lodge indicated.

"7. Rapacki expressed concern over my use of term 'de-escalation,' noting that Lodge said Washington was convinced that not much can be accomplished in getting talks under way with partial de-escalation. He said Lodge's accent was on the package deal which would cover all problems, including withdrawal of US troops. If my use of de-escalation represents a short-cut for a package deal including cessation of hostilities and the resolution of a variety of other outstanding problems, then his concern over my use of the term is simply a matter of semantics. He asked if my use of the term was consistent with Lodge's declaration on a package deal."

GRONOUSKI

Warsaw 1412 (to SecState), 9 December 1966
Section 2 of 2

"8.   I said I did not clearly understand what he
was driving at but referred to my opening text and
pointed out that the degree or manner of de-escalation
is not subject to unilateral determination.   I said
that this would have to be resolved in negotiating
sessions between the USG and NVN..."

. . . .

"17.   Comment: Rapacki's position was much less
intransigent today than during Dec 7 meeting.   I thought
it significant that when I stressed importance of initiating talks Michalowski, Rapacki's major adviser on
Vietnam war, nodded his head affirmatively three or four
times.   Because I found no threat to break off talks
that was implied Dec 7, I did not use para 2 of reftel."

GRONOUSKI

December 10, 1966

    Rusk and Gronouski are informed that Washington does not wish to
withdraw authorization for RT 52 at this time.[20] It is anticipated,
therefore, that some targets may be hit which Rapacki will insist reflect
further escalation.

State 100624 (to Amembassy Saigon), TS/Nodis
        10 December 1966
Ref: A.   Saigon 12953
       B.   Warsaw 1421
       C.   Warsaw 1422
For Secretary from Katzenbach

. . . .

"2.   On the bombing point, you should know that
RT-52 stands as it was at time of your departure from
Washington and targets earlier set aside remain in
suspense."

. . . .

KATZENBACH

State 10067 (to Amembassy Warsaw), TS/Nodis
    10 December 1966
Ref: A. Warsaw 1421
      B. Warsaw 1422

....

"4. FYI only (rpt. FYI only). You should be aware
that for the immediate future the bombing pattern will
remain unchanged from what it has been over the past
several weeks. This may well involve some targets which
Rapacki will insist represent further escalation, just
as in the past he took to be escalation certain variations in our bombing pattern which in fact represented
no real new departures in the pattern as a whole. With
foregoing in mind you should avoid giving Poles even
any slight indications which they might take to mean
that we are escalating or de-escalating at present.
Present bombing pattern has been authorized for some time
and we do not wish to withdraw this authorization at
this time."

....

KATZENBACH

December 13, 1966

Rapacki quotes a US Navy spokesman as saying that new targets have
recently been placed on the bombing list, adding "you can assume what
effects such statements have in Hanoi, given the fact that in recent
weeks new targets have in fact been added." He again urges restraint
in bombing, arguing that overt pressure "will be utilized by all those
who have a different vision of this peace move than we have here in
Warsaw."

Warsaw 1458 (to SecState), TS/Nodis, 13 December 1966
Section 1 of 2
Ref: Warsaw 1429

....

"8. Rapacki added that we should realize that
leadership of DRNVN does not want to and cannot yield
under pressure; every step from our side that evokes
impression that NVN is acting under pressure would be
interpreted as sign of weakness and be utilized by all
those who have a different vision of this peace move
than we have here in Warsaw. (Comment: Rapacki
repeated this point with emphasis and was, I believe,
making a clear reference to Communist China.)

"9. Rapacki said that in first position expressed
by Lodge it appeared that this truth was grasped by USG
and this is why Poles were so hopeful. However the
events of December mean, if the working hypothesis Poles
are using is sound, that US does not fully appreciate
this situation. He added that recent statements by USG
officials leave the impression that USG wants to evoke
pressure. He quoted from Reuter news story of Dec 12
US Navy spokesman's statement that US intends gradually
to increase air raids on NVN; Rapacki interjected at this
point his realization that Navy spokesman may not have
known all that was going on and this could very well be
an old idea. But he added that the Navy spokesman's subsequent reference to escalation and to new targets having
been recently placed on bombing list represented current
information. He said 'you can assume what effects such
statements have in Hanoi, given the fact that in recent
weeks new targets have in fact been added.'"

GRONOUSKI

December 13-14, 1966

The Yen Vien Railroad Yard and Van Dien Vehicle Depot are bombed.
They are both 5 nautical miles from the center of Hanoi, and have been
struck previously. Tass claims, in addition, that residential areas
in Hanoi and its suburbs were hit.

A later US official investigation shows that only these targets
were intended, but it is possible that US ordnance fell within the Hanoi
city limits by accident.

State 103586 (to Amembassy Warsaw), S/Nodis,
15 December 1966

....

"2. ... Washington approval of targets including
high level review by Defense and State is required and
takes into consideration location of targets with
respect to population centers in effort to minimize
civilian casualties. Types of targets struck have
included lines of communication, bridges, POL storage,
selected thermal power plants, military installations,
and anti-aircraft missile sites and missile facilities
that are a threat to our aircraft.

"3. Latest strikes near Hanoi were Yen Vien railroad yard and Van Dien vehicle depot, which are 5 nautical miles northeast and south of Hanoi respectively, and well outside of Hanoi city limits. Both of these targets were struck on December 13 and 14 but this was not first time in either case....

"4. Tass alleges our aircraft bombed built-up area of Hanoi at west end of Red River bridge and suburb of Dhatran to the southwest (have been unable locate Dhatran on any map). Hanoi has made similar charge. We have not received complete reports; however, nothing in reports so far to substantiate this and area alleged to have been attacked nowhere near areas targetted for attack. It is important to note that there was heavy SAM, anti-aircraft and MIG activity and our aircraft took action against SAM sites. Quite a number of SAMs were fired at our aircraft; errant SAMs or anti-aircraft shells of course could cause damage.

"5. ....

       (c) There is no basis for charging us with escalation of conflict over past few days, either in geographic terms or as to types of targets. Hanoi's POL facility three nautical miles from center of Hanoi was struck on June 29, and POL facilities on edge of Haiphong were struck June 29, July 7 and August 2. Two targets of December 14 are both five nautical miles from Hanoi's center (farther than June 29 strikes); both had been struck earlier."

       ....

       "(f) .... In comparable periods of good weather, e.g., November 22 and 23, December 2, 3, 4 and 5; and Dec 13-14 essentially same type of targets were struck, some intensity of air activity in and around Hanoi took place as has frequently been the case for at least six months...."

KATZENBACH

State 106358 (to Amembassy Warsaw), 21 December 1966

   ....

"1. Our investigation of alleged bombing in Hanoi has been thorough. The only targets were military ones more than five miles from the Hanoi city center. However we cannot rule out completely the possibility of an accident. Any US ordnance that may have fallen within the Hanoi city limits was the result of such an accident."

   ....

  RUSK

December 14, 1966

State does not interpret Rapacki's December 13 statement as a negative reply from Hanoi, closing the Marigold door. It is, however, now inclined to wonder whether the Poles ever had a commitment from the DRV for the Warsaw contact. In any case, further conversations in Warsaw are to have two objectives:

i. Keeping the door open for talks to develop.

ii. Letting the record show our persistent efforts to move forward, while refuting Polish contentions that our actions and statements blocked the opening of conversations.

Gronouski is therefore instructed to make the following points to Rapacki:

i. Military actions by both sides were taking place throughout the conversations in Saigon.

ii. As soon as the US began talking with the Poles preparatory to meeting with the DRV, new terms and conditions were put forward for opening the talks.

iii. We are now confused about what reflects the views of Hanoi, as opposed to the Polish Government. Direct contact is needed.

iv. To leave no stone unturned, we suggest taking up de-escalation along the lines of the Phase A-Phase B formula, as a manageable opening piece of the total picture.

v. If the other side prefers, though, we will start at the other end, looking first at possible terms of an agreed settlement.

vi. Rapacki is to be warned that he will bear full responsibility if Polish obstructionism prevents the contact.

While these instructions are en route, however, Gronouski is summoned by Rapacki to learn that the DRV has asked for all conversations to be terminated. The "brutal raid on the residential area in Hanoi precisely at the moment when the USG knew that the matter of a Warsaw contact with Hanoi was actively being considered" is the reason. Rapacki claims that immediately after the Poles transmitted "a direct, positive response from Hanoi about the possibility of talks in Warsaw, ...the USG reserved the possibility of modifying its attitude and, of far greater importance, entered a new stage of escalation."

Gronouski appeals to the President. If the newspaper accounts of the Hanoi raids are true, "then we are in an incredibly difficult position. I am convinced that if this represents the breakdown of the current peace initiative...the Soviets, the Poles and the North Vietnamese will have no trouble convincing the leadership in every capital of the world that our stated desire for peace negotiations is insincere .... We have no choice but to take immediate action to try to get discussions back on the track."

He proposes, therefore, to accept Rapacki's reasoning: to give no impression of bombing intensification during the negotiations about opening talks in Warsaw -- in particular, to halt bombing near Hanoi and Haiphong. "We would again express our deep desire for the initiation of talks and ask the Poles to continue their efforts."

Thus just as Gronouski is ordered to launch a pre-emptive offensive, he is himself recommending retreat.

State 162295 (to Amembassy PARIS) TS/Nodis
    14 December 1966
For the Secretary from the Acting Secretary
Ref: SECTO 62

    "I do not rpt not interpret Rapacki's statement of December 13 to Gronouski as a negative reply from Hanoi in effect closing the Marigold door. Firm instructions are being prepared for Gronouski designed to keep the dialogue going, while at the same time making a clear record of the legitimacy of our participation in the MARIGOLD effort since its inception."

    ....

State 102960 (to Amembassy Warsaw), TS/Nodis
    14 December 1966
Ref: Warsaw 1429
(Info to Amembassy Paris & Saigon: Paris for Secretary
    Eyes Only; Saigon for Ambassador Porter Only)

    "1. .... In light of Polish tactics we are now inclined to wonder whether they ever had any NVN commitment to a meeting in Warsaw or whether it is not more likely that they have been engaging in an effort to get us committed to something as close as possible to our maximum position and then see whether they could get Hanoi lined up to talk on that basis. In any event we must bear two following objectives in mind in further conversations with Poles on this subject:

(a) We mean to keep the door open as long
as there seems to be any possibility of talks developing, but at the same time sticking to our position as
generally represented by Lewandowski's 10 points, and

(b) We sincerely want to begin substantive
talks and the record should clearly show our persistent
efforts to move forward and that Polish contention that
our actions and statements have thrown roadblock in the
way of opening of conversations in Warsaw are thoroughly
refuted.

"2. Therefore you should ask for further meeting
with Rapacki and present him with following full statement of our position at present time:

(a) You should first review history of
Lodge-D'Orlandi-Lewandowski conversations starting with
November 14-15 conversations in Saigon....

(b) You should then point out to Rapacki
that before, during and after all this was taking place,
the conflict in Viet-Nam continued, including the
bombing of North Viet-Nam, the infiltration of North
Vietnamese men and supplies into South Viet-Nam, Viet
Cong terrorist bombings, assassinations, kidnappings,
etc....

(c) As soon as we began to talk with the
Polish Government in Warsaw, presumably preparatory to
our meeting directly with the North Vietnamese representatives, we found that new terms and conditions
seemed to be put forward with the opening of direct
talks contingent on our fulfilling them....

(d) But our desire is to move toward peace
and our conviction is that the best road to take is one
of direct discussion with Hanoi's representatives. We
are somewhat confused as a result of the conversations
in Warsaw as to what Hanoi has said and what represents
the views of Polish Government. Our strong impression
is that, in spite of our readiness both in Saigon with
Lewandowski and now in Warsaw to present quite fully
and frankly our position, we have not received any
communication at all from the North Vietnamese Government....

(e) Nevertheless we want to leave no stone unturned in our search for peace and would like to turn for a moment from the total picture to one sector of it in which conceivably we might begin to move. This is with respect to the possible beginning of de-escalation through a two-phased arrangement referred to in Lewandowski's eighth point.... Perhaps the coming holidays and the truces associated with them, offer an opportune occasion to take some useful steps along these lines; this in turn should make it easier for the authorities in Hanoi to proceed then to discuss other matters standing between us and a peaceful settlement.

(f) On the other hand, if they wish to proceed promptly to a total agreement representing the terms of an agreed settlement, we are prepared to move along that track including de-escalation as the final item. (FYI: In other words we will start at either end of a total agreement. END FYI)

(g) You should conclude your statement of our position with the language contained in para 2 of State 98924, leaving Rapacki in no doubt that we have done everything possible to open up the way to peaceful settlement and we are very much disturbed at our having been unable to move forward at Warsaw as we had been led to expect from the earlier conversations in Saigon."

. . . . .

KATZENBACH

Warsaw 1471 (to SecState), TS/Nodis,
     15 December 1966
For the President from Ambassador Gronouski

"1. I met with Rapacki (Michalowski and Janczewski present) at Poles' request at 1800 Dec 14. (In contrast to previous meetings, Rapacki entered the room unsmiling, and during entire meeting maintained a calm, serious and matter-of-fact attitude.)

"2. Rapacki said that first he would like to bring some precision with respect to our conversation of yesterday (Warsaw 1458). He said that this conversation took place before Poles were aware of last bombing of Hanoi. He said, 'If I had had this news then, our conversation of course would have had different character than it did.'

"3. Rapacki continued, 'Today I must state the following facts. First, that the U.S. had to be conscious of and realize the importance of establishing direct contact with Hanoi.' He added, 'You had stressed the unique possibility of a peaceful settlement that the Warsaw talks with Hanoi presented.' He continued, 'We thought so too, ever since we obtained the signal for which the USG had asked for for so long in so many official statements.' He added, 'In this instance we received more than a signal; we received a direct, positive response from Hanoi about the possibility of talks in Warsaw.'

"4. Rapacki said that immediately after this direct response was transmitted to the USG the US reserved the possibility of modifying their attitude and, of far greater importance, entered a new stage of escalation.

"5. Rapacki continued that the USG was bound to be conscious of the reaction which its conduct would evoke and of the consequences of such action. He added that the Poles have done everything in their power to dispel any illusions, noting that on six occasions in Warsaw and Saigon, 'We have warned the USG side in all seriousness and with the greatest emphasis of the consequences of their actions.'

"6. 'Yesterday,' Rapacki continued, 'The US Air Force engaged in a new and particularly brutal raid on the residential area in Hanoi precisely at the moment when the USG knew that the matter of a Warsaw contact with Hanoi was actively being considered. This,' he added, 'was the last drop that spilled over the cup. From the moment, in Hanoi and Warsaw, all doubts as to the real intentions of the USG disappeared, including doubts not only in the present case but with respect to all other instances in the past when the US has advanced positions which it has described as peaceful initiatives.'

"7. Rapacki then said, 'We understand therefore and fully share the wish of the Democratic Republic of North Vietnam, which was transmitted to us today, that we terminate all conversations begun months ago in Saigon. The Polish Govt states that the whole responsibility for losing this chance of a peaceful solution to the Vietnam

war rests on the USG.' He added, 'I would like to
express more than regrets because of the utilization
by the USG of our good will. Once again it becomes
clear how difficult it is ·to believe in your words.'
He added, 'In future only facts can be taken into
consideration.'

"8. I said that I would have no comment except
to say that I regretted this turn of events and would
immediately convey these observations to Washington.

"9. Comment: If Moscow dateline account of
latest Hanoi bombing published in Dec 14 Paris edition
of New York Times and Herald Tribune, and recounted
to me tonight by Rapacki, is true then we are in an
incredibly difficult position. I am convinced that
if this represents the breakdown of the current peace
initiative -- and it surely does unless we take decisive and immediate action -- then the Soviets, the
Poles and the North Vietnamese will have no trouble
convincing the leadership in every capital of the
world that our stated desire for peace negotiations
is insincere. If we treat this turn of events as anything less than a crisis in our world leadership role
then I believe we are making a tragic mistake.

"10. I am convinced that up till now the Poles,
accepting the genuineness of our interest in negotiation, have used whatever influence they have in Hanoi
(in all likelihood with Soviet backing) in an effort
to initiate US-NVN peace talks. I also am convinced
that Rapacki was expressing genuine concern when he
warned that the increase in bombing was destroying
what appeared to him a good chance that NVN would overcome Chinese influence and engage in Warsaw talks.

"11. We have no choice but to take immediate
action to try to get discussions back on track. For
any chance of success this would require, in my judgment, conveying to Poles that we are willing to accept
Rapacki's Dec 13 reasoning (Warsaw 1458) and are prepared now to assure the Poles that we will take care
not to create impression of bombing intensification
in NVN during the period of delicate negotiations over
the holding of Warsaw USG-NVN peace talks. We would
also assure the Poles that we do not intend to bomb in
the immediate vicinity of Hanoi and Haiphong during
this period. We would again express our deep desire
for the initiation of talks and ask the Poles to continue their efforts."

. . . .

GRONOUSKI

December 15, 1966

After consulting the President, State again instructs Gronouski to present a strong rejection of Rapacki's arguments. We doubt the accuracy of the Communists' bombing accounts and that the Poles really intend to sell their view of Marigold to world opinion.

At the same time, Rolling Thunder 52 is amended to suspend strikes against the two Hanoi targets hit December 13-14. This is not communicated, however, to the other participants in Marigold.

Meanwhile Lewandowski has begun to leak his version of Marigold by giving a few salient points to the Dutch Charge in Saigon. We do not learn of this until December 17, and know only that Lewandowski's conversation with the Dutch Charge occurred sometime between November 30 and December 15.

Harrison Salisbury of the New York Times receives a cable from Hanoi. A visa to visit the DRV, for which he had applied some months earlier, has been granted and may be picked up immediately in Paris.

The Polish Ambassador in Rome is contacted by the Pope who inquires if the former can "tell him anything with respect to Vietnam," according to a later conversation between the Polish Ambassador and Fanfani. (For source, see December 19 entry.)

> State 103342 (to Amembassy Warsaw), TS/Nodis,
>   15 December 1966
> For Ambassador Gronouski from Acting Secretary
> Ref: (a) Warsaw 1471
>   (b) State 102960
> (Info to Amembassy Paris & Saigon: Paris for Secretary
>   Eyes only; Saigon for Ambassador Eyes only)
>
> "1. Your message (reftel a) has been discussed
> with the President and he has approved the comments and
> additional instructions which are set forth below.
>
> "2. Although Rapacki's message to you reported
> ref (a) is also discouraging it does not alter our basic
> assessment as conveyed to you in State's 102960.... In
> spite of his reference in paras 6 and 7 reftel (a) to
> views and decisions of NVN, we remain doubtful about how
> much part Hanoi has played in scenario which has unfolded
> in Warsaw over past two weeks."
>
>   ....
>
> "7. Finally, and in spite of the fact that Rapacki's
> line as reported reftel (a) makes it essential that he get

the full force of our rejection of his arguments and
our indignation at the Polish Government's changing
the signals and then seeking to put the blame on us,
we feel nevertheless that you should in the course
of your presentation to Rapacki leave no doubt about
our continuing strong desire to move forward in
direct conversations with the North Vietnamese...."

"8. Your further interpretation and discussion
contained Warsaw's 1475 is very much appreciated and
I am sure you fully realize that all of us here profoundly share your concern over the turn events have
taken in the last few days. Likewise I can well
imagine that in the atmosphere of Warsaw and without
full information available, particularly concerning
the bombing of North Viet-Nam, the Polish position
may appear to be a strong one, whatever their motivation in presenting it as Rapacki has just done. We
want to assure you, however, that on the basis of the
over-all picture as we can see it from Washington,
the Polish case, except for some fairly superficial
and transitory matters, is a weak one and we wonder
whether they will try to sell it to world opinion."

. . . .

KATZENBACH

JCS 1471 (to CINCPAC), TS/LIMDIS, 15 December 1966
Ref: JCS 7735

"1. (TS) Ref authorizes air strikes against
following targets in Hanoi area.

TARGET NO.	NAME	BE NUMBER
19	Yen Vien RR Clf Yd	616-0221
63.11	Van Dien Veh Dpo	616-0696

"2. (TS) Suspend further air strikes against
these targets until further notice."

70

Saigon 13640 (to SecState), TS/Nodis
        17 December 1966

    "1. CAS Station Chief came to political counselor
Dec 17 and reported that one of his officers had been
queried by Netherlands Chargé Derksen about a statement
by Lewandowski concerning negotiations with Hanoi....

    "2. In response to request CAS submitted follow-
ing as Memorandum of conversation with Derksen:

        A. In a conversation which took place in
Saigon on an unspecified date between Nov 30 and Dec 15,
1966, Ambassador Lewandowski told Mr. Derksen that he
was recently in Hanoi for a somewhat longer period than
usual. He went on to say that 'an organization' --
later he used the word 'group' -- was negotiating with
Hanoi on the subject of peace talks. Mr. Lewandowski
did not further identify the group or organization.

        B. Mr. Lewandowski was bitter because pro-
gress in these talks was halted by the recent American
bombing of Hanoi (dates of air raids not specified). He
told Mr. Derksen he was so bitter than he planned to
write 'a paper' on the subject...."

Behind the Lines--Hanoi, by Harrison E. Salisbury
        (Bantam, July 1967), p. 8

    "Then, on the morning of December 15, Seymour
Topping, the foreign editor of The Times, walked over
to my desk and put a cablegram before me.... The visa
to Hanoi did, indeed, await me in Paris."

December 17, 1966

    State expresses alarm over the possible impact on the talks in Warsaw
and also on Ky, should Lewandowski's leak to the Dutch Charge reach him.
Lodge is told to give Ky a low key indication that a possible lead toward
peace is being investigated.

        State 104673 (to Amembassy Saigon), TS/Nodis
            17 December 1966
        Ref: Saigon 13640

    "1. Lewandowski's indiscretions are indeed most
unfortunate and potentially harmful to talks in Warsaw....

"2. This leads us to suggest you should be prepared
with line to use with Ky should outright leak occur,
should Ky raise with you on basis rumors floating around
Saigon, or should you feel rumors have reached point
where you should take initiative with Ky as preventive
measures. Our thought is that in such eventuality, you
would simply in low key take following line: As we have
told Ky before we get many apparent leads on subject of
peaceful settlement. We feel responsibility not to overlook any possible lead which might offer some promise.
Most of these leads dissipate immediately, some seem
slightly more productive and are pursued further.
Lewandowski contact with us over past few months has been
such lead. At times it has appeared to offer more
possibilities and at times less. Ky may be assured that
if any lead offers any real prospect of discussions with
Hanoi, he will be promptly consulted."

....

KATZENBACH

December 18, 1966

    D'Orlandi tends to reject our rationale for what has happened in favor
of the Polish version. He feels there is a "strong prima facie case
against us" and that we should do "something quickly in Warsaw," much the
same view expressed by Gronouski on December 14.

    Saigon 13618 (to SecState), TS/Nodis
         18 December 1966
    Ref: State 104673

        ....

    "6. D'Orlandi then said to Habib that he was himself
surprised at bombing on the 14th. He wondered 'If there
were not some people in the US who had deliberately sought
to create a problem.' This was denied in precise terms
and with an expression of surprise that D'Orlandi would
have such a thought. It was pointed out that as D'Orlandi
knew there was no connection between bombings and Lewandowski's proposals. Habib then gave D'Orlandi the rebuttal material contained in State's Circular 103849 and went
over it in detail, suggesting it be used if Lewandowski
again raises issue of bombings."

        ....

"12. Comment: Our judgment is that foregoing confirms correctness of changing venue to Warsaw. D'Orlandi is not only showing his personal pique at turn of events, but is displaying definite tendency to discard our explanations while endeavoring to induce us to do 'something quickly in Warsaw.' Instead of focusing on information provided by Habib, he launched into extended presentation of Lewandowski's latest animadversions (sic), adding his own belief that there is 'strong prima facie case against us' as well as exhortation mentioned preceding sentence."

....

PORTER .

December 19, 1966

Gronouski carries out State's instructions of December 15. In an angry exchange, Rapacki attacks both the accusations leveled against the Polish role and the US suggestion that the Warsaw contact still be attempted.

In Rome, the Pope is given the "whole story" on Marigold by the Polish Ambassador, who later reports the episode to Fanfani, adding that he had been contacted by the Pope on December 15, to ask if the Poles "could tell him anything with respect to Vietnam."

Warsaw 1513 (to State), TS/Nodis
        19 December 1966
Ref: Warsaw 1508

....

"9. .... He (Rapacki) added that Poles did not put forth new conditions but 'recalling speeches of Goldberg, the President, Secretary Rusk and others, once we received the signal we did we would have had every right to call for a stop in the bombing.' He said, 'you have said over and over again that you would end all bombing if there was an assurance from Hanoi that there would be a response toward peace from Hanoi; however, we did not ask that you stop bombing but only that you not intensify it.'"

....

"13. .... He said, 'I am astonished that at same time
you accuse us of stalling talks, you ask us to help you
get them going again.' .... Inasmuch as NVN asked Poles
to discontinue these discussions, what was new to justify
returning to NVN on this matter? ...."

GRONOUSKI

Rome 3409 (to Sec State), TS/Nodis
      28 December 1966

....

"4. Fanfani said that according to the Polish
Ambassador the Pope on December 15 sent word to the Polish
Government asking if they could tell him anything with
respect to Vietnam. On December 19 the Polish Government
responded by telling the Pope the whole story. Fanfani
indicated he did not rpt not know just what the Polish
Ambassador meant by the 'whole story' but presumably the
Polish Government had told the Pope everything they knew."

....

REINHARDT

December 21, 1966

Rapacki clarifies the Polish role in Marigold. The following were
conveyed to us on instruction from Hanoi:

i. Lewandowski's message to Lodge immediately upon his return
from Hanoi expressing a positive response to the Warsaw talks.

ii. Rapacki's warning after the December 3 bombing, that Hanoi
would have to reassess the situation.

iii. The decision to terminate discussions in Warsaw.

He added that there had been frequent exchanges between Hanoi and
Warsaw during the conversations and felt confident the Poles accurately
expressed Hanoi's views, even when acting on their own initiative.

While Gronouski is learning this in Warsaw, instructions are enroute
for him to tell the Poles that any damage from US ordnance within Hanoi
city limits was accidental. We are now prepared to state there will be no

bombing within 10 miles of the center of Hanoi for an indefinite period
if talks with the DRV can begin shortly. We "anticipate" some "appropriate reciprocal action" with respect to NLF activities within 10 miles
of the center of Saigon as "evidence of good faith."

      Warsaw 1535 (to SecState), TS/Nodis
         21 December 1966
      Ref: State 105909

     . . . .

    "2. I asked Rapacki to clarify for me the role
that Hanoi played in our discussions. Rapacki replied
that the message Lewandowski gave to Lodge (he referred
to 'three sentences') upon his return from Hanoi
expressing NVN positive response to Warsaw talks,
Rapacki's warning after the Dec 3 bombing, that Hanoi
would have to reassess the situation, and the decision
to terminate discussions in Warsaw were all decisions
by NVN which were conveyed to us by the Poles. He
said further that comments Poles made regarding danger
of creating the impression of pressure on Hanoi were
comments of the Polish Govt, but the fears that Poles
expressed in this regard were verified subsequently by
Hanoi. He also said that during process of Warsaw
discussions there were a number of other exchanges
between Warsaw and Hanoi, adding that the Poles are
confident that what they expressed on their own initiative accurately reflected Hanoi's opinion.

    "3. Rapacki then made the point, in reference to
our accusation that Poles have raised new conditions
since talks shifted to Warsaw, that interpretation clause
question was raised by Lewandowski immediately upon
hearing it expressed by Lodge on Dec 3. He said
'clearly you know that we felt this was a matter of
concern from the very beginning; it wasn't something
interjected as a new condition afterwards.' He added,
'our concern was well taken because the reaction to
interpretation clause from Hanoi turned out to be what
we predicted.'"

    . . . .

GRONOUSKI

State 106358 (to Amembassy Warsaw)
        21 December 1966

. . . .

"1. Our investigation of alleged bombing in Hanoi
has been thorough. The only targets were military ones
more than five miles from the Hanoi city center. However we cannot rule out completely the possibility of
an accident. Any US ordnance that may have fallen
within the Hanoi city limits was the result of such
an accident.

"2. Nonetheless we are prepared to state that
there will be no bombing within ten miles of Hanoi city
center measured from 21 degrees 1 minute 37 seconds
north, 105 degrees 51 minutes 21 seconds East, for an
indefinite period if talks with North Vietnamese can
be gotten underway shortly. Appropriate reciprocal
action with respect to bombs, mortar and similar
terrorist activities within ten miles of the center of
Saigon measured from 10 degrees, 46 minutes, 28 seconds
north; 106 degrees, 41 minutes, 10 seconds East, would
be anticipated by us as evidence of good faith."

. . . .

RUSK

December 22, 1966

Rapacki prefers to wait a day or two (by which time Gronouski is
to have returned to Washington for consultations) before transmitting
the new US position to Hanoi. He is afraid the suspension of bombing
near Hanoi appears to depend on reciprocal action from the NLF and a
signal that Hanoi will establish contact. Gronouski argues that we
are not asking a quid-pro-quo but simply removing the factor that had
blocked the contact and suggesting a quiet way for Hanoi and the NLF
to indicate readiness to discuss peace.

Rapacki repeats a theme expressed (less clearly) by him earlier:
"Goldberg stated that if there was some indication from Hanoi regarding
negotiations, bombing would cease throughout NVN and not simply around
a small area of Hanoi." He is presumably referring to Goldberg's
September 22 speech, though neither it nor Goldberg's December 20
letter to U Thant contain such a sweeping proposal.[21]

On the same day, Zinchuk sees Bundy in Washington to indicate
Soviet awareness of Marigold and Soviet support both for Polish actions

and the Polish interpretation of developments to date. He is appre-
hensive that the US will adopt a militaristic approach to the war. The
Soviet concern to get US-DRV talks started arises in large part the
possibility that Hanoi will call for volunteers under the Bucharest
Declaration ("if the war escalates and if help is necessary").

>   Warsaw 1537 (to SecState), TS/Nodis
>   22 December 1966
>   Ref: State 106358

    ....

    "2. Rapacki, expressing desire to understand pre-
cisely, asked for reiteration of message. In response
to his question as to whether this meant we had no
intention to bomb Hanoi proper but that it was possible
we could have inadvertently hit residential area, I
responded I did not exclude that possibility. In
response his question whether orders would be issued
to exclude from bombing area within coordinates described
for indefinite period, I responded that this my understanding reftel. After brief discussion of relationship
of cessation of terrorist activities in Saigon to cessation
bombing in Hanoi perimeter, I reread section again and
pointed out there was no direct quid-pro-quo on cessation
Saigon activities but that this was anticipated reaction
by Hanoi as measure of good faith.

    "3. I expressed again my personal conviction that
this proposal provided basis for movement in resolving
the problem of initiating negotiations....

    "4. .... Rapacki noted however that two things
intruded which might reduce the significance of this step:
(A) The text of the communication appears to make U.S.
action dependent on some signal that a contact will be
established by Hanoi; (B) There is an indirect linking --
or request -- that an appropriate step (re Saigon) will
be taken by the other side. He added that it would be
very important to avoid the appearance of forcing NVN
into negotiations.... Goldberg stated that if there was
some indication from Hanoi regarding negotiations, bombing
would cease throughout NVN and not simply around a small
area of Hanoi. Furthermore, regarding the alleged NLF
activities around Saigon, while this is admittedly
expressed in terms of an expectation, the impression is
given that you are trying to 'kill too many birds with
one stone.' This is a matter to be resolved with the NLF
and I (Rapacki) have tried to dissuade you from linking
NVN action with NLF matters...."

    ....

"8. .... I argued that Rapacki must view our
proposal not as an exercise of pressure by making
cessation of bombing dependent on Hanoi's indication
of a willingness to talk, but as a removal of what
Poles had regarded as overt pressure which Rapacki
had insisted interfered with the prospects for talks.
Cessation of action in Saigon was not a direct quid-
pro-quo but a quiet way for Hanoi and the NLF to
give an indication of readiness to discuss peace.

"9. Rapacki...concluded with statement that
he would prefer to delay day or two before transmitting our proposal but expressed willingness to
convey it now if that was what I desired.

"10. I expressed willingness to discuss matter
immediately on my arrival in Washington."

        ....

GRONOUSKI

MemCon, TS/Nodis/MARIGOLD, 22 December 1966
Participants: Alexander Zinchuk, Soviet Charge
               William P. Bundy

        ....

"2. Immediately after these exchanges, Zinchuk
launched into a discussion of MARIGOLD. After learning
that I was fully aware of the exchanges between Lewandowski and Lodge, as he put it initially, he said that
it was very hard for them to understand why we had
intensified the bombing of the North with the attacks
on December 2nd and 4th, and then again on December 13th
and 14th. He said that there was great sensitivity in
Hanoi on this subject, and strongly implied -- without
directly saying so -- that there were differing schools
of thought. Our bombing actions had left the Soviets --
and by implication, Hanoi -- in complete doubt as to
what our intentions and views really were. Speaking
more specifically for the Soviets, he said that he had
thought they pretty well understood our views, but that
this episode left them in real doubt whether there were
military forces at work and whether they simply did not
understand fully what we thought and meant to do.

"3. More specifically, he said that he himself had
been in Moscow, in late November and had gained the
impression that Hanoi (or elements in it) were seriously
interested in starting something. They had been encouraged by the apparent slackening in the pace of our bombing during this period. I at once asked whether this was
just a general impression or whether it had something
more specific behind it. He replied that it was 'more
than a general sense.' Then, following the bombings of
December 2nd and 4th, some Hanoi leaders (un-named) had
been in Moscow on their way back from Budapest, and had
met with top Soviet leaders. (I think he mentioned
Kosygin and Brezhnev specifically). In the face of our
bombings, the Soviet leaders had been unable to clarify
U.S. thinking or (by clear implication) to encourage
Hanoi to pursue the Lewandowski avenue. Then, he himself
had seen Ambassador Kohler on December 9th, intending to
convey a clear message against continued intensification
of the bombing. He thus found it particularly difficult
to understand our actions."

        . . . .

"6. I then said specifically that, while we had
made a considered decision that we should not alter the
planned bombing pattern earlier, we were definitely aware
of Hanoi's sensitivity to intensification of the bombing.
I said that therefore we had made a specific proposal
within the last 24 hours, directed to precisely this point.
I also noted that within the last 24 hours we had had a
contact that had substantially illuminated exactly what
the Polish contacts and discussions with Hanoi had been.
Finally, I reiterated that we were prepared to see really
quiet and secret talks get under way on the basis of the
approaches that had been made."

        . . . .

"8. In short, Zinchuk did not really seek to defend
Polish handling of the matter, but was most emphatically
trying to get it across that the Polish effort was serious
and that the Soviets were fully with it...."

"9. ...he said that he had been surprised, in discussing the Polish initiative in the Department at some
earlier stage in December, to see that it was treated as
doubtful...."

        . . . .

79

* * * *

. . . .

"2. He then said (as he had to Harry MacPherson
on Monday) that the Soviet concern to get something
started arose from a number of factors, but above all
the possibility that Hanoi, under the Bacharest
Declaration ('if the war escalates and if help is
necessary,' in essence) might at some point be faced
with a Hanoi request for military volunteers. He
noted the report today of North Korean pilots (which
I of course did not deny) and something unspecified
that the Cubans were doing. He said that the Soviets
would be put in a most awkward and difficult position
if Hanoi asked for volunteers, and they hoped the
issue would not arise.

"3. He then asked me about some commentator's
statement that the President saw two alternatives,
seeking a peaceful solution or escalating the war
markedly by bombing so that the American people would
become engaged in simple loyalty to their armed forces
. . . ."

. . . .

December 23, 1966

The problems of reciprocal de-escalation are illustrated by a
cable from Saigon, "assuming" that the proposed cessation of terrorist
activity in the Saigon area does not require a cessation of GVN/US
counter-VC activities.

Saigon 14089 (to SecState), TS/Nodis,
    23 December 1966
Ref: A. State 106358
      B. State 105909

"1. ...we assume department proposal on cessation
terrorist activity in Saigon area does not envisage
cessation GVN/US counter-VC activities."

. . . .

PORTER

December 24, 1966

We drop the request for reciprocal action from the DRV in maintaining the 10 mile bombing limit around Hanoi.

(NB. source needed)

December 26-27, 1966

After newspaper reports of bombing "12 miles from Hanoi," the Poles inquire if our circle about Hanoi is measured in nautical or statute miles. Gronouski expresses concern over strikes this close to the proscribed circle. He is told "not to be diverted from the main effort by niggling and haggling about whether a particular bomb fell on this side or that side of this or that circle."

> Warsaw 1567 (to SecState), TS/Nodis, 27 December 1966
> Ref: State 107911
>
> "1. ...Michalowski...asked 'for the record' whether reference in reftel to ten miles from Hanoi was in nautical or statute miles....
>
> "2. ...NY Times, AP Dispatch speaks of 'target only twelve miles from Hanoi'....
>
> "3. .... I am most concerned if we are choosing targets so close to the margin that even a slight error could put us in technical violation of our commitment...."
>
> ....
>
> GRONOUSKI

> State 108664 (to Amembassy Warsaw), TS/Nodis
>   27 December 1966
>
> "...you may inform Michalowski or Rapacki that orders have been issued to refrain from bombing within the ten nautical miles from Hanoi city center.... It is very important for you and the Poles not to be diverted from the main effort by niggling and haggling about whether a particular bomb fell on this side or that side of this or that circle. The important thing is that an area of some 314 square nautical miles will be free from bombing and that, thus far, we have not seen any readiness on the part of Hanoi to sit down

and talk business. The next move is up to them and we
cannot let them play games with a side issue in view
of the major concession we have made to clear the way
for talks...military briefers are not aware of MARIGOLD
and that some looseness in language can be anticipated."

RUSK

December 27-28, 1966

Fanfani is told by the Polish Ambassador about the latter's contact
with the Pope. We in turn tell Fanfani of the 10 mile bombing sanctuary
around Hanoi and of our continuing hopes to get talks started. We
stress the importance of secrecy, if talks are to succeed. Meanwhile
we decide to move the operation out of Saigon to the maximum extent,
for security reasons. Gronouski is instructed to take up the security
problem with Rapacki, with special reference to the leak to the Pope.
He is also apprised of doubts by Rusk that the Poles ever intended to
press Hanoi for talks without an unconditional and unreciprocated cessation of the bombing.

Rome 3409 (to SecState), TS/Nodis, 28 December 1966

"1. Points contained State 108773 were conveyed
privately to Fanfani evening Dec 28.

"2. Fanfani said he had been very severe in his
conversation with Polish Ambassador, he had emphasized
that:

A. Poles should initiate US contact with
Hanoi without further delay;

B. Lewandowski should by all means remain in
Saigon as would D'Orlandi; and

C. It was a great mistake break secrecy by
informing the Pope.

"3. Fanfani said Polish Ambassador had returned to
see him evening December 27. Polish Ambassador had said:

A. Poles cannot undertake initiate US contact
with Hanoi unless there is a cessation of bombing;

B. Lewandowski will repeat will remain in
Saigon; and

C. It was not repeat not the Polish Government
which had taken the initiative in informing the Pope but
rather it was the Pope who had approached the Polish
Government.

"4. Fanfani said that according to the Polish Ambassador the Pope on December 15 sent word to the Polish Government asking if they could tell him anything with respect to Vietnam. On December 19 the Polish Government responded by telling the Pope the whole story. Fanfani indicated he did not rpt not know just what the Polish Ambassador meant by the 'whole story' but presumably the Polish Government had told the Pope everything they knew."

....

REINHARDT

State 109639 (to Amembassy Warsaw), TS/Nodis
        28 December 1966
FOR THE AMBASSADOR FROM THE SECRETARY

".... I call your attention to the statement made by the Polish Ambassador to Fanfani on the evening of December 27 that QTE Poles cannot undertake initiate US contact with Hanoi unless there is a cessation of bombing UNQTE. This could result from Polish Ambassador Rome not being informed of our move on December 24. But it also raises the possibility that the Poles have never had any intention of pressing Hanoi for talks without an unconditional and unreciprocal cessation of bombing."

....

RUSK

State 108773 (to Amembassy Rome), TS/Nodis
        27 December 1966

"1. ....

        a. We are most grateful for prompt Fanfani report of his conversation with Polish Ambassador Rome, ...

        b. Fanfani himself should be aware that on Dec 24 we conveyed to Rapacki that we had given firm orders not repeat not to bomb within ten nautical miles of point in center of Hanoi for an indefinite period...."

c. We are most grateful to Fanfani for expressing concern that Pope has been informed. We too are concerned over this and would now appreciate Fanfani advice whether we should ourselves indicate to Pope our knowledge that he has been informed. We recognize that it may be desirable not repeat not to indicate such awareness, in order to preserve Fanfani's own sources and channels; however, we are also concerned if Pope may be receiving one-sided account.

. . . .

"2. Saigon should take no action. For security reasons alone, we are trying to get this operation out of Saigon to maximum extent possible....

"3. .... If Rapacki or Michalowski admit that Pope has been informed you should say that you must report this to Washington and have no doubt it will have disturbing effect on security grounds alone...."

RUSK

December 30, 1966

Rapacki tells Gronouski the 10 mile sanctuary has come too late and that the Poles now consider their role "at this stage as terminated."

In Washington, Dobrynin tells Thompson the Soviet Government is "frankly baffled by (US) action in Vietnam.... He said there were many, and he was one, that wondered whether some of our military were deliberately trying to frustrate a policy of moving toward negotiations."

Warsaw 1596 (to SecState), TS/Nodis, 30 December 1966 Section 1 of 2

"1. Rapacki opened by saying Poles have taken further action on my statement of Dec 24, but unfortunately this step could not make up for damage done by previous actions, particularly Air Force, during first part of December.

"2. Rapacki added that 'we have to consider our role at this stage as terminated'...."

. . . .

"7. Rapacki said, ...if that step you brought from
Washington (on 24 December) had occurred on December 4 --
admittedly after the first bombing of Hanoi -- then I
feel personally we would have had the first contact with
the DRV behind us. Moreover, I think I have sufficient
reasons for my personal feeling. Even between Dec 4
and Dec 13, the matter was again actively being re-
considered. There had been no negative reaction as yet.
We know, because we had contact with the proper quarter.
The decision regarding breaking off the talks was made
after Dec 13...."

  ....
  .

MemCon, TS/Nodis/MARIGOLD, 30 December 1966
Participants: Ambassador Dobrynin, USSR
               Ambassador Thompson

"I asked the Ambassador if he had brought back any
reply to the President's letter to Kosygin.[22] He replied
that if he could speak completely off the record he
could tell me that a reply had nearly been completed
and that it was one we would have liked but then the
bombing of Hanoi had occurred and this draft had been
torn up and another one of quite a different character
started. He said he had seen the report from their
Embassy in Hanoi and that there was no doubt in the
Soviet minds as a result of this report that our bombs
had fallen on Hanoi itself...a reply would be made in
due course."

  ....

"The Ambassador remarked that the initial stages
of this affair had given the Soviet Government considerable hope and he said rather cryptically that they
had other reasons for some optimism but that our action
in bombing Hanoi had spoiled everything. I pointed out
that our targets were selected several weeks in advance
and that it had been pure coincidence that the attacks
on the targets near Hanoi had occurred at this time.

"The Ambassador said that his Government was
frankly baffled by our actions in Viet-Nam and did not
know how to judge our policy. He said there were many,

and he was one of them, that wondered whether some of
our military were deliberately trying to frustrate a
policy of moving toward negotiations or whether our
policy really was one of military victory."

....

December 31, 1966

Porter suggests from Saigon that we switch to a more trustworthy
channel, from the Poles to the Canadians.

> Saigon 14702 (to SecState), TS/Nodis
> 31 December 1966

....

"3. With the breakdown of the Polish channel...
we suggest Department consider bringing in another party
more trustworthy as an intermediary from US point of
view...."

....

"6. We lean in favor of the Canadians. It just
so happens that the Canadian Commissioner Victor Moore
is going to Hanoi on January 6 to spend a few days making
his farewell calls at the end of his tour...."

....

PORTER

January 3, 1967

Goldberg gives the US view of Marigold to U Thant, who promises to
hold it in confidence.

As incidental intelligence, U Thant mentions that Peter, the Hungarian Foreign Minister, was visited in Budapest by Le Duan (Secretary General of the Lao Dong) early in December. Le Duan took a very hard line, much harder, Peter believes, than would Trinh, the DRV Foreign Minister. The latter had been expected, but urgent problems in Hanoi detained him and LeDuan came instead.

> USUN 3458 (to SecState), TS/Nodis, 3 January 1967
>
> "As agreed upon with the Secretary, I had an extensive discussion with U Thant this afternoon lasting almost 1-1/2 hours.
>
> "I gave him the full account of Marigold,...."
>
> ....
>
> "Syg assured me that he would keep this in confidence and I do not believe that we need be concerned about his making a public disclosure absent any additional dramatic events."
>
> ....
>
> "...he told me that when FM Peter of Hungary was at the UN, Peter had told Syg that they were expecting a visit from the North Vietnamese FM in Budapest in early December. Syg said that he had since been advised by the Hungarians -- presumably the Hungarian UN Rep -- that the North Vietnamese FM found it impossible make the visit because of urgent problems at home. In his place Hanoi dispatched the Syg of the Communist Party who visited Budapest early last month and who has since returned to Hanoi. Hungarians reported that Syg of Communist Party took a very hard line about settlement of Vietnamese conflict -- a harder line than they believe would have been taken by North Vietnamese FM. Of possible interest to US in this connection was the observation of Syg of Communist Party that it was by no means certain that the NLF would support any peace proposal which might be acceptable to Hanoi. Syg observed that this was a similar line taken by North Vietnamese Rep in Algiers in September of last year as reported to him by his Algerian sources.
>
> ....
>
> GOLDBERG

January 4, 1967

Rusk soothes George Brown's injured feelings over finding that he was not the sole intermediary for the Phase A-Phase B de-escalation proposal.

>   State 112632 (to Amembassy London), TS/Nodis
>   4 January 1967
>   PERSONAL FOR AMBASSADOR FROM SECRETARY
>
>   "Please deliver following personal message to
>   Foreign Secretary George Brown: QTE Dear George:
>   Thank you for your message. I do want to clear up
>   one point, namely, that there was nothing on which we
>   could have informed you prior to your visit to Moscow.
>   Your visit came at the time of Lewandowski's visit to
>   Hanoi but before we had any information whatever from
>   him on his visit. We understand he was in Hanoi most
>   of the last half of November, and our first report
>   upon his return to Saigon was received in a meeting
>   on December 1. In fact, we gave you for your trip
>   a major concession to the other side in the form of
>   a two-phased proposal in which we would stop the
>   bombing if they would agree that subsequently there
>   could be a de-escalation of the violence. I am
>   sorry if there has been any misunderstanding on this
>   point. With personal regards, Sincerely, Dean Rusk.
>   UNQTE."
>
>   RUSK

January 4, 1967

Gronouski takes issue with Porter, that the Canadians replace the Poles as our channel to Hanoi because they are more "trustworthy." He considers the Poles better suited to the mission because they carry more weight in Hanoi.

>   Warsaw 1631 (to SecState), TS/Nodis, 4 January 1967
>   Ref: Saigon 14702
>
>   ....
>
>   "3. .... The fact that Poles presumably acted
>   in Hanoi's interests in attempting to extract from US
>   best possible terms prior to actual negotiations is
>   no basis for concluding that Poles were not interested
>   in initiating Warsaw talks as soon as feasible.

Feasibility, however, depended on Hanoi's agreement, and I submit Poles had no reason on their own initiative to delay that agreement ten minutes....

"4. Given this analysis, I cannot conceive of Canada or any other friend of the USG being more satisfactory than Poles as intermediary (see also paras 3 and 4, Warsaw 1630); true, they would be more trustworthy from our point of view. But for this reason they would also be even less effective than Poles were in convincing Hanoi. I have no doubt that Poles had access to and exchanges with top officials of NVN, and that they delivered our messages.. I am also convinced, especially after Dec 24, that they encouraged Hanoi to meet with us in Warsaw. A trustworthy friend of USG could do no more and I suspect would be able to do much less. What we need is help of someone with more influence on Hanoi than Poles, not less. It is for this reason that I suggested we turn immediately to Soviets."

. . . .

GRONOUSKI

January 4, 1967

Goldberg gives U Thant and Ignatieff (Canadian Ambassador to the UN) a review of "the entire Marigold episode" along the lines suggested by the Department. (Source: USUN 3465, 1/4/67; TS/nodis)

January 5, 1967

Saigon reports 13 VC incidents in the Saigon-Gia Dinh area.

Saigon 14894 (to SecState), TS/Nodis, 5 January 1967

"1. We have been keeping a special watch on incidents and actions in the Saigon Gia-Dinh area ever since Christmas. As a rough approximation border of Gia-Dinh province averages about 11 miles from the center of Saigon.

"2. From Dec 28 to Jan 3 there were 13 incidents clearly initiated by VC in the area....

. . . .

"5. .... In order not to call attention to our
interest in the 10 mile radius we are using standard
statistics derived from police reports which are not
always complete or absolutely accurate."

January 5, 1967

Reinhardt gives the Pope a similar review. He stresses that the
US has been forthcoming by offering its Phase A-Phase B formula, by
affirming Lewandowski's statement of the US position with no reciprocal act from the DRV side, and by offering to meet with the DRV
to discuss all outstanding issues, and that no military preconditions
for the talks were initially asked by the other side. Even now, we
are keeping open our suspension of bombing within 10 miles of Hanoi's
center. While the DRV has given a negative response, we continue to
try to open talks. Secrecy is imperative if this effort is to succeed.
We therefore request the Pope's cooperation in maintaining complete
discretion.

State 112886 (to Amembassy Rome), S/Nodis
    5 January 1967
Eyes Only for Ambassador

"1. Ambassador should see Pope Paul soonest, ...
Since Poles, and according to their report Hanoi,
have stressed vital need for complete secrecy, USG
is deeply conscious of need to maintain rigid
security this matter. However, in view of
importance these discussions and their possible
bearing on other initiatives to which His Holiness
is a party, we now believe it essential that His
Holiness receive full and accurate account."

        ....

"7. At this stage, the US had taken two
important steps. It had put forward the possibility of a two-phase handling of the bombing
question, together with the possibility of discussing in one setting the whole range of issues
including the future situation within South Vietnam. Moreover, the USG had agreed to affirm the
statement of its position to Hanoi, subject only to
the obvious necessity of interpretation while
Hanoi itself had indicated only, as reported to
us, that it was prepared to listen to such an
affirmation. The USG at this point had not --
and still has not -- received any statement of
Hanoi's own views. Moreover, the message conveyed by Lewandowski contained no mention of any
prior condition other than secrecy, for the direct
contact in Warsaw that was proposed."

. . . .

"14. On December 22, Gronouski again saw Rapacki
to convey a new proposal on behalf of the USG. This
was that the USG was prepared to undertake that there
would be no bombing within ten miles of the center of
Hanoi for an indefinite period, if talks with the
North Vietnamese could begin shortly; in the original
proposal of December 22, this was linked with evidence
of good faith in the form of action on the other side
with respect to incidents near Saigon. However, when
Rapacki demurred to the proposed linkage and asked
reconsideration, Gronouski was authorized on December
24 to state that the US had now given firm orders not
to bomb within ten miles of the center of Hanoi for
an indefinite period. This revised US proposal stated
the understanding that, on the basis of what Rapacki
had told us, direct talks could now begin shortly.
The message also noted that, in judging the good faith
of the other side, we would be 'impressed' by similar
restraint, for example, with respect to incidents,
movement of forces (itself a violation of the Geneva
Accords) in the DMZ, or action with respect to infiltration; it was stressed that there were examples,
and the phrasing made clear that these were not preconditions. Rapacki indicated that he would convey
this message promptly to Hanoi.

"15. On December 30 Rapacki reported to Gronouski
that Hanoi had given a negative response and was flatly
not prepared for talks in Warsaw."

"Summary of Key Points

. . . .

"6. Most basically of all, the US remains entirely
prepared for secret bilateral contacts with Hanoi. Even
though Rapacki has stated that he considers the channel
now dead, the US order of December 24 remains in force
and will so remain for the present. We have in fact
reviewed this whole matter carefully with Soviet representatives, pointing out our difficulty in understanding
Polish actions at several points. Moreover, we have in
mind the continued possibility of constructive action
by the Secretary General. For all these reasons, and in
the light of our basic view that any disclosure of this
whole series of discussions could affect Hanoi's willingness to participate, we have maintained the tightest
security on the whole project, will continue to do so,
and must ask you in the strongest terms to act in same
manner."

. . . .

RUSK

January 6, 1967

Saigon is instructed to tell Ky a little more about Marigold, interpreting it primarily as a DRV peace offensive designed to get the bombing stopped and reassuring Ky about our resolution.

Rome is to tell Fanfani that we still hope to open contact with the DRV and it is, therefore, imperative to maintain the strictest security concerning what has happened in the past.

In Warsaw, the Poles tell Gronouski that the December 13-14 attacks typed the scale in favor of DRV Presidium members who felt that talking with the USG made little sense. Only a complete cessation would restore the necessary level of confidence. On the other hand, if we stopped bombing it should be possible to get negotiations going over Phase B in 3-4 weeks. Gronouski urges the Poles to try again, proposing instead a Phase B agreement between the two sides _before_ the bombing cessation and the opening of talks.

State replies by instructing Gronouski to avoid further initiatives for the time being.

> State 114277 (to Amembassy Saigon), TS/Nodis
>   6 January 1967
> EYES ONLY FOR PORTER AND HABIB
>
> "1. ...Canadians on January 2 gave us report they had obtained from U Thant on December 28, and which U Thant had received from Poles on December 23, ...
>
> "2. ...to seek to minimize leak risk, decision was taken to inform Pope, SYG, Canadians, and also British...."
>
>   ....
>
> "5. Our conclusion is that time has come when it is wise to convey word to Ky that would mitigate any MARIGOLD disclosure or any stories based on Indian or Salisbury matters. Moreover, Salisbury speculation gives us good cover for making statement to Ky now. [23]
>
> "6. Accordingly, you should see Ky if possible, and Tran Van do as well, to say that GVN may be noting wave of speculation on DRV willingness to talk. USG has been receiving a number of third country messages sometimes based on conversations with DRV representatives,

from which third nations are on occasion drawing
conclusions we do not believe warranted. We ourselves are inclined to believe that DRV, as Salisbury visit alone shows, has become much more
sophisticated in building up world opinion against
the bombing. They may well be engaged, with help
from U Thant, Soviets, and others, in a determined
effort to get us to stop the bombing or cut it
back in return for hints of DRV willingness to
talk. Moreover, DRV may be probing for any change
in our position. GVN may be assured that we have
no intention of changing our well-known position
on conditions for the cessation of bombing, or
yielding to pressures on any element of our position. As Ambassador Lodge told Ky last July
(Saigon 642 of July 10) we will of course be
following up any rumors, however unlikely, that
might indicate Hanoi was really seeking a way out.
If anything of real substance or importance happens,
we will of course be in touch with GVN at once...."

RUSK

State 114278 (to Amembassy Rome), TS/Nodis
        6 January 1967
Ref: State 112886

"1. .... You should emphasize to Fanfani that
although Warsaw phase of exercise appears to have
come to temporary conclusion we still mean to continue in whatever manner feasible to promote initiation of substantive discussions with North Vietnamese. Therefore it continued to be of prime
importance that strictest security be maintained
concerning what has occurred in past."

        ....

RUSK

Warsaw 1646 (to SecState), TS/Nodis
        6 January 1967
Section 1 of 2

        ....

"4. Michalowski opened his reply by observing
that at one point in my discussions with Rapacki I

had expressed the hope that someone was putting as much
pressure on Hanoi as Poles were placing on us to get
negotiations started. He said with some feeling that
he could assure me that Poles put heavy pressure on
Hanoi and in fact put prestige of GOP on line in getting
Hanoi to agree at outset to idea of having talks in
Warsaw. He added that he personally knew how much
pressure was brought to bear because he was engaged in
exercising some of it. He went on to say that leadership in Hanoi is by no means a monolithic group and that
from the beginning, when Poles got agreement from Hanoi
to initiate talks in Warsaw, it was a very close decision
with many of the Hanoi leadership strongly opposed. He
said they obtained such agreement after exerting strong
pressure and putting Poland's prestige on the line; but
it was a delicate matter in Hanoi, implying that agreement was by a narrow margin among the leadership. He
said at this point the Poles had been able to convince
Hanoi to have at least a small degree of confidence in
intentions of U.S. He added that bombing of Dec 3 had
given a weapon to those in Hanoi who had not wanted to
agree to negotiations in first place. He said it was
for this reason that Poles had repeatedly conveyed to
Lodge and me their fear of negative effects of a
repetition of Dec 3 bombing. But he said even after
Dec 3 when bombing was explained by Lodge as no new
departure but simply something in the military pipeline,
Poles were able to prevail in Hanoi to keep possibility
of talks open, and 'believe me we talked to them
several times a day to keep pressure on them and convince them.' But he said bombing of Dec 13-14 'undercut our whole argument, destroyed that little bit of
confidence that existed in Hanoi about intentions of
U.S., and left us wide open to charges of being completely naive.' He said with bombing of Dec 13-14
those who had initially been skeptical about negotiations
were given a powerful tool to support their case and in
fact prevailed. He added that even with Dec 3 bombing,
if we had been able to interval between Dec 3 and 13 to
come in with the message we did come in with on the 24th,
that part of leadership in Hanoi which wanted negotiations would have prevailed and he is confident that talks
would have happened. But he said by Dec 24 a whole new
condition existed; 'We were accused of being naive and
had lost our effectiveness and those who on Dec 3 had
been able to control situation and move toward negotiations were by this time discredited.' Thus he said
situation by Dec 24 in Hanoi had so changed that it was

impossible to go back to Dec 1 or the Post-Dec 3 period.
Now he said he feels that only stopping NVN bombing
completely will restore influence of those who are
interested in negotiations. He said if bombing stopped
Poles would be willing to try for a third time and that
he is quite confident that three or four weeks thereafter negotiations between U.S. and Hanoi on Phase B
could become a reality. He said, 'short of this, I am
very pessimistic of any effective role we could play,
given pressure we had exerted in Nov and Dec and the
undercutting of our position in Hanoi by events of
Dec 13-14.' He went on to say that he will never understand how this could possibly have happened but 'this
is past history, I guess.'"

GRONOUSKI

Warsaw 1646 to State
Section 2

"Conversation between Michalowski and Gronouski".

"Michalowski said that the situation had now
entirely changed. The Poles, he said, had been able
to convince Hanoi to go on with the possibility of contact after the December 3rd U.S. bombings, but that the
bombings of December 13 and 14 had made the future of
negotiations between the DRV and the U.S. very bleak.
He now maintained that only a complete cessation of U.S.
bombings will restore the necessary level of confidence
needed to get negotiations started. He added that
Hanoi's original decision to talk with the U.S. in
Warsaw had been hotly contested in the Presidium and
that the bombings had now persuaded those who wanted
to talk with the U.S. that there was little sense in
doing so.

'Gronouski noted that this now put the parties back
where they had started from. He suggested that the Poles
try to get the thing going again by proposing to the DRV
an initial Phase B agreement prior to the meeting between
the U.S. and the DRV in Moscow. This, Gronouski said,
would (1) meet Hanoi's insistence on stopping the bombing
before talks began, and (2) meet the U.S. desire for some
sort of indication that talks would occur in order to
stop the bombing.

State 114370 (to Amembassy Warsaw), TS/Nodis
    6 January 1967
Ref: Warsaw's 1648

"1. In view of complex of developments relating
to Viet-Nam problem we would like you to avoid for
the present any further initiatives along lines
section 2 reftel."

....

"3. .... It has been our conception that ...
Hanoi's actions under Phase B would be expected to
be generally equivalent to our actions in Phase B
plus repeat plus our cessation of bombing of North
Viet-Nam."

....

RUSK

January 9-10, 1967

Saigon and Rome carry out their instructions to brief the GVN,
the Pope and Fanfani. The results reported are satisfactory.

In Washington, we learn that Brown is still very hurt. Bundy
points out how complex the matter is and explains the necessity for
the US to manage its own role.

Saigon 15204 (to SecState), TS/Nodis
    9 January 1967
Ref: State 114277

"1. I sent Habib to see Tran Van do to convey
substance paragraph 6 reftel. This was done, rather
than a direct approach to Prime Minister, to keep
our dialogue with GVN in appropriate low key....

"2. .... He was pleased to note our assurance
that we have no intention of changing our position
on cessation of bombing...."

PORTER

Rome 3531 (to SecState), S/Nodis
     9 January 1967

          ....

     "2.   The Pope reiterated his deep appreciation
of being informed....   He told me that he had publicly
encouraged the Wilson-Brown initiative because they
had officially informed him of it.   He had been unable
to do the same with respect to U Thant's efforts
because he had not been officially advised of them.
He had however sent a private message to the Secretary
General to avoid any feeling on his part that the Pope
was showing preferences with respect to various
initiatives for peace."

          ....

REINHARDT

Rome 3571 (to SecState), TS/Nodis
     10 January 1967
Ref: State 114278

     "1.   I saw Fanfani last night Jan 9 and carried
out instructions in reftel.   He told me that shortly
after the New Year, Polish Ambassador had informed
him of the interruption of the procedural talks in
Warsaw and had said that it was impossible to expect
North Vietnamese to enter into discussions with the
US as long as the bombing of North Vietnam continued.
Fanfani said he had taken strong exception to this
statement and had pointed out that US proposal envisaged termination of bombing and that Poles had known
this all along...."

          ....

REINHARDT

State 118905 (to Amembassy London), S/Nodis
     10 January 1967
LITERALLY EYES ONLY FOR AMBASSADOR FROM SECRETARY

          ....

     "2.   Dean said Brown still very hurt over our
failure to tell him we were conveying new two-stage

proposal on stopping bombing through Lewandowski channel at same time that Brown was going to Moscow with it. Brown did not wish to raise direct with me, hence Bundy.

"3. Bundy made following points in reply, which we now assume will go direct to Brown and also to PM:

a. We gave proposal to Lewandowski on 13th or 14th and to Brown on 16th....

b. ...we felt that we should honor Polish insistence that L channel be kept totally secure,....

c. Brown message was the clear and solid one we were sure would get through. Moreover, Brown was armed in the rest of our letter to discuss the underlying principles in depth, as L was not. Brown could have a real exchange of views on the basis of total knowledge of our position.

d. In response to Dean remark that Soviets must have known of message to L, and that this perhaps accounted for cross-examination of Brown's authority to talk for us, Bundy said that we did not see how Brown's opportunity could have been prejudiced by this even if true...we had always regarded Soviets as much more serious and responsible, and Gromyko in October had responded to Secretary's question which Eastern Europeans were closest to Hanoi by saying pointedly: 'We are.'

"4. .... Speaking on private basis, Bundy added that we recognized absolute obligation never to put British in false position and hence to provide them with all information they needed for any contacts they had. This applied to forthcoming Kosygin visit.[24] At same time, we were playing a multiple chess game and could not be expected to cut the British in on all boards at all times....

"5. Bundy then...reminded Dean of account Secretary had given Friday night of our confidential read-out from Salisbury,[25] in which Pham Van Dong's unpublished parts of interview had spoken of Hanoi taking 'an appropriate stand' and also said 'we know what we should do' if US stopped bombing; Secretary had told Dean this was same formula used last summer to Sainteny[26] and that, since Pham Van Dong resolutely refused to elaborate, it was at most atmospherics and did not get us much further. Since Friday night report to Dean, there had been following developments:

       a. Baggs-Ashmore team had come out of Hanoi and would be giving us their report this week....[27]

       b. Sainteny had made strong pitch to go to Hanoi to pursue what would happen if bombing stopped and to get general reading. We were taking him up on this and would be arming him with the two-phase proposal ....

       c. Thompson would be talking Vietnam seriously in Moscow, probably this week...."

    ....

"7. In light of all this, I am seeking authority for you to see Wilson soonest, perhaps Monday...."

    ....

"11. For your call on Wilson, you should know that he has sent two-sentence message to President speaking of his talk with you on matter seriously affecting our relationships...."[28]

RUSK

January 18, 1967

Brown has forgiven us.

    London 5692 (to SecState), TS/Nodis
       18 January 1967
FOR SECRETARY FROM COOPER

    ....

"2. All is well. No apologies from me. No abuse from Brown. No whining from PM...."

    ....

BRUCE

January 19, 1967

Salisbury's interview with Pham Van Dong produces a number of apparently forthcoming statements couched in very general language.

We surmise they are essentially mood music, accompanying a strong attempt to get us to stop bombing without reciprocity. Gronouski is to tell the Poles, if they raise the subject, that there must be reciprocal actions.

> State 121586 (to Amembassy Warsaw), S/Nodis
> 19 January 1967

> ....

> "3. We have also received an extensive account from Harrison Salisbury of his observations in Hanoi, highlighted by Pham Van Dong's response to Salisbury's question as to what actions Hanoi would take if the US stopped bombing, namely 'we will take an appropriate stand.' He also said: (1) if the US 'stops doing harm to the North, we know what we should do'; (2) the moment the 'US puts an end to the war, we will respect each other and settle every question'; and (3) after the cessation of hostilities, there will be 'no lack of generosity on our part.' Our net judgment is that these statements are interesting mood music but do not get us very far. The first two statements are replays of earlier statements to other sources. The latter two appear to be without substance.

> "4. At the same time, while we are treating these reports seriously for action purposes, we believe we may be dealing with a strong attempt by Hanoi, perhaps aided consciously by the Poles and in any case sympathized with by the Indians, to get us to stop bombing fully without any reciprocal action except possibly some claimed willingness to talk....

> "5. ...if the Poles raise the subject, you leave them in no doubt whatever that any stopping of the bombing on our part requires a clear picture of reciprocal actions repeat actions that amount to an equitable reduction of hostilities."

> RUSK

January 19, 1967

Estabrook of the Washington Post files a story from Ottawa which apparently alludes to Marigold: "Canadian authorities blame some of the difficulty (in beginning US-DRV talks) on the accidental US bombings of Hanoi in mid-December. Private soundings then underway were disrupted, they say, and the attitude in North Vietnam appeared to harden...."

Paris Herald Tribune, 20 January 1967
Estabrook - "Ottawa Sees Hanoi Ready to Ease War" -
Ottawa, Jan 19

"Some high Canadian officials believe that North
Vietnam is now prepared to de-escalate the war in the
south if the U.S. halts bombing in the North. This
is essentially what United Nations Secretary General
U Thant and others have been saying for some time,
but there are two important distinctions: first,
Canada has a representative on the ICC who regularly
visits Hanoi and talks directly with authorities there;
second, Canada is a close friend and ally and does not
want to see the U.S. disadvantaged. The key unresolved
question authorities here assert is how soon after a
bombing halt a reciprocal move by NVN would take place.
This move could be an end to the infiltration of the
south, where U.S. sources say there are 20 identified
North Vietnamese regiments, but it probably could not
be expected immediately. These conclusions persist
despite the fact that feelers for peace discussions
have produced nothing tangible so far and are in
abeyance at the moment. Canadian authorities blame
some of the difficulty on the accidental U.S. bombings
of Hanoi in mid-December. Private soundings then
underway were disrupted they say and the attitude in
North Vietnam appeared to harden. Now they cannot be
sure whether North Vietnam wants to talk seriously
because of the propaganda success it has enjoyed
through world protests at the bombing. Nevertheless,
they would take the chance on the ground that
discussions, once started, and even with North
Vietnam's unacceptable 4-points as part of the
agenda, would inevitably broaden. They do not
believe that Hanoi has really retracted its offer to
make the 4-points a basis for discussion rather than a
mandatory outline for settlement. Although they believe
that the U.S. must be a bit more flexible, they do not
believe that a bombing halt must be unconditional. They
view as a distinct advance the U.S. offer to halt the
bombing upon some sign, public or private, that the
other side would be willing to make some comparable move.
'If I were the President,' said one high Canadian
official, 'I would simply announce that the bombing had
been stopped with no reference to conditions. If nothing
developed over a period or if NVN took advantage of the
situation the bombing of military targets could always
be resumed and the world would know that the U.S. had
tried.' Canada's own confidential initiatives on VN have

been centered in the ICC in which it shares responsibility with Poland and India. The Canadian Representative, Victor Moore, has just been summoned home
after a 10-day visit to Hanoi and will be replaced
by Norman Dier. Simultaneously, Canada is pressing
Poland to agree to a meeting of the ICC powers at
an Ambassadorial level in the hope that this will
lead to a meeting of foreign ministers. Poland last
week rejected an Indian suggestion for a conference in
New Delhi."

January 20-21, 1967

Saigon continues to check on VC incidents in Saigon-Gia Dinh area.
There may be some diminution. Permission is requested, therefore, to
inform Westmoreland about Marigold so that he may participate more
effectively in the incident watch.

State doubts that there has been a real VC slowdown and does not
wish to enlarge the circle privy to details of Marigold.

Saigon 16144 (to SecState), TS/Nodis
    20 January 1967
Ref: Saigon 14894

"1. A continuing check on VC incidents in the
Saigon-Gia Dinh area raises question of whether there
is not some diminution in number of incidents initiated by VC since January 4. This report is a sequel
to that given reftel. (underlining supplied)

"2. As best we can determine there have been
five incidents of this sort from January 4 to 20
as follows:

    A. January 4; Cholon; Body of Policeman
found. Presumed to have been victim of terrorist act.

    B. January 5; Go Vap (5 km from Saigon);
Two U.S. soldiers injured when terrorists tossed
grenade into their jeep.

    C. January 6; Thu Duc (11 km from Saigon);
Two ARVN soldiers injured when their steamroller
exploded a mine.

    D. January 13; Thu Duc (11 km from Saigon);
National Police apprehended two VC in terrorist
attempt against equipment, Inc. facility. One VC
escaped, other captured.

E.   January 18; Eastern Gia Dinh Province
(16 km northeast of Saigon); Vietcong platoon
attacked three bridge sites, slightly damaged one.
Four friendly wounded.

"3.   The question now arises 'whether we are
seeing a VC pause in the area ten miles around
Saigon as a response to our own action in the Hanoi
area. So far the answer on the surface would appear
to be negative, but the number of incidents is small
recently and some of them may not be properly counted
as either VC initiated or within the ten mile limit,
e.g., items A and E in Paragraph 2.

"4.   General Westmoreland is not aware of the
Marigold Exercise. He is, therefore, not aware of
any connection between the Hanoi bomb-free area and
our search for an equivalent VC pause in Saigon area.
I would like to be able to tell him that we have made
such a proposal to Hanoi, without revealing the
Marigold context. I think we will be able to analyze
VC actions in the Saigon area better with his help
and, more significantly, we might possibly be able
to use the knowledge to our own military advantage."

LODGE

State 123198 (to Amembassy Saigon), S/Nodis
      21 January 1967
Ref: Saigon 16017 and 16144

"1.   Reur 16144, our impression is that recent
action not far from Tan Son Nhut may have cancelled
out your impression that there may be a real slowdown
of any sort on other side.[29] Moreover, we would prefer
not to enlarge circle privy to details in this series.
Can you not create a special quiet watch on incident
rate within designated radius of Saigon on general
basis without informing Westmoreland? ...."

      ....

RUSK

January 23, 1967

In Moscow, Podgorny says that mediation by the USSR would be fruitless until the bombing stopped. With respect to Thompson's question

about what the DRV or USSR would do if we did stop bombing, Podgorny suggests we stop and see. Thompson draws attention to the agreements about Laos, which were not kept by the other side.

> Moscow 3159 (to SecState), S/Nodis
> 23 January 1967

> . . . .

> "4. .... Podgorny then asked whether end to Vietnam war was in sight.

> "5. I replied we all very much hoped war would end soon and also hoped USSR could help us in bringing this about.... Podgorny said it was difficult expect something new and stressed that since main parties to conflict were US and Vietnam one could hardly count on mediation. He then said he did not exclude possibility of Vietnam taking certain steps but pointed out pre-condition for that would be at least minimum move by US, such as, initially, cessation of bombings. Since no such move evident, hardly anyone could mediate.

> "6. I said.... It would be helpful if we knew at least when a response could be expected. Also, as Secretary had said to Dobrynin, it would be interesting to know what USSR would do if we stopped bombings and other side continued its activities.

> "7. Podgorny asserted US had always placed conditions on cessation of bombings. US had said it would stop bombings if other side gave certain guarantees....

> "8. .... As to reference to guarantees if we stopped bombing, we did not ask for guarantees but only for indication as to what would happen in response. For reason I mentioned earlier, this important to us. Podgorny interjected we could stop bombings and then we would see. I continued that in considering situation we had also to keep in mind fact that despite agreements which had been reached on Laos, Laotian territory had been used by North Vietnam to infiltrate south....

> . . . .

> THOMPSON

January 27, 1967

   Fried, the NY Daily News correspondent, tells Lodge in Saigon that
he knows of Gronouski's contact with the Poles in Warsaw.

> Saigon 16677 (to SecState), TS/Nodis
>   27 January 1967
>
>   "Joseph Fried, Viet-Nam correspondent of the
> New York Daily News, told me on Friday that he
> 'knew' that Ambassador Gronouski and the Polish
> Government had been having conversations about
> settling the war in Viet-Nam."
>
> LODGE

January 29, 1967

   Saigon continues to feel that VC incidents in the Saigon-Gia Dinh
area may have abated.

> Saigon 16785 (to SecState), S/Nodis
>   29 January 1967
> Ref: A. Saigon 16144
>   B. State 123198
>
>   "1. This is another in the series of reports
> we have been providing on VC initiated incidents
> within ten miles of Saigon. We shall send these
> reports each week.
>
>   "2. For the period January 21-27 within the
> zone there were four incidents that can be char-
> acterized as VC initiated:
>
>   A. January 22, four miles west of
> Saigon, an unknown number of enemy fired two rifle
> grenades at police station, wounded 2 VN civilians.
>
>   B. January 23, Gia Dinh City, unknown
> person threw grenade at house, no casualties.
>
>   C. January 23, 9 miles west of Saigon,
> booby trap, 2 VN killed and two wounded.
>
>   D. January 24, Saigon, unknown person
> threw grenade, wounded three VN civilians.

"3. In addition to these incidents, there were
two others in the area resulting from VN police and
ARVN making a sweep and running on to VC. These do
not meet the criteria of being VC initiated.

"4. With respect to the action not far from
Tan Son Nhut on January 20 (cited para one ref B),
we have looked into this. The record of the action
shows that elements of two ARVN battalions on a
search and destroy mission encountered a VC force
nine miles west northwest of Saigon. The ensuing
fight stemmed from that contact. There is no information as to whether VC was on the way to Tan Son
Nhut, or any other special target. No available
information as to which side fired first shot. ARVN
units, however, were definitely on the prowl. From
interrogation prisoners taken day later VC force
was sixth battalion from VC 165 Regiment which is
regularly present on fringes Gia Dinh Province.

"5. We have also examined the record of VC
initiated incidents during the area for the month
of November 1966. During that period there were 11
incidents, ranging from the shelling of Saigon on
November 1, National Day, to platoon and squad attacks
to isolated grenadings. Of the 11 incidents, seven
can be characterized as serious in the sense that
they were obviously well-planned attacks by small VC
units."

LODGE

February 1-2, 1967

Estabrook files a more complete story on Marigold from New York.
In private, he gives different versions of the story's source. He
apparently first got word of the matter from the Canadians in Ottawa
and later confirmed it with U Thant. In one conversation he indicates
that he also "had it from a high Polish source... corroborated by
'other Eastern European sources.'" In another, he denies that it
"came from the Poles." Goldberg believes the Poles to be the
original source of the story and recommends that neither they nor any
other Bloc country be used as a channel to Hanoi.

USUN 3847 (to SecState), S/Nodis, 2 February 1967

"Estabrook (Wash Post Correspondent) told
Nisoff Feb 2 that his story in Feb 2 Post about
Hanoi readiness to talk just prior to Dec 13

bombing of Hanoi was founded on several sources. He
had it from high Polish source which he would not
identify. It was corroborated by 'other Eastern
European sources.' He had been given similar impression earlier in Jan from Can FonMin Martin. He had
taken story to U Thant who stated his believ that
it was correct."

....

"(In separate brief conversation with Pedersen
Estabrook denied story came from Poles. Said it came
from Martin, while Estabrook was in Canada, and then
from U Thant. Estabrook said he had had story for
couple of weeks. In response expression of surprise
he had used word 'learned' instead of something like
'alleged', Estabrook indicated this based on evalua-
tions both of Martin and U Thant.)"

....

"My assessment is that the original source of
this story is the Poles themselves. They have quietly
been spreading this story throughout the UN; I even got
some of it from the Danish Deputy Fon Min the other day,
who attributed it to Poles."

....

".... This leads me to recommendation that we
should no longer use Poland or any other Bloc country
as channel to Hanoi. It would be far preferable in my
opinion to deal directly or through Sovs than to continue
with this type of intermediary."

GOLDBERG

State 131692 (to Amembassy Warsaw), C/Nodis
    4 February 1967
Ref: Warsaw 1895

"Test of February 4 Washington Post story by
Estabrook will reach you in form circtel. Text of
February 2 story filed from New York under February 1
dateline follows:

BEGIN TEXT:

"A Polish initiative to establish peace discussions between North Vietnam and the United States
failed because of American bombing of the Hanoi area
in mid-December, it has been learned on excellent
authority.

"Exactly how far the Poles had succeeded in
obtaining commitments from Hanoi is not clear, but
high-level outsiders who knew about it regarded
the initiative as promising before the bombing
hardened Hanoi's attitude. QUOTE The Americans
bungled it END QUOTE, one informed source stated.

"U.S. officials said that any bombing of non-
military targets was accidental, after Western
reporters observed damage to civilian areas that
the North Vietnamese claimed was caused by U.S.
bombing. Since December, U.S. planes have reportedly been ordered to stay away from the Hanoi area
unless engaged in self-defense.

"At the moment the Poles are said to have
suspended their efforts. They are represented as
extremely frustrated, not merely over the effect
of the bombing, but more particularly with the
uncooperative attitude of Hanoi.

"Recently Poland declined a suggestion of
India that representatives of the three countries
constituting the International Control Commission
in Vietnam - Poland, India and Canada - meet in
New Delhi to consider what could be done. Use of
the Commission framework to promote peace discussions is an old suggestion of Canadian External
Affairs Minister Paul Martin.

"Even after the attitude in Hanoi changed in
the wake of the bombing, the Poles kept trying.
Among other moves a top Polish diplomat, Jerzy
Michalowski, made an unreported visit to the United
States in January.

"Whether any American representative saw him
cannot be learned, but two Canadian diplomats were
sent to talk with him.

"Michalowski, a former delegate to the United
Nations and more recently in the Polish Foreign
Office, went on a special Mission to Hanoi in
January 1966, as the result of the visit to Warsaw
of roving U.S. Ambassador W. Averell Harriman.

"Apparently the Polish effort stemmed in part
from a conversation between Foreign Minister Adam
Rapacki and Martin when the Canadian Foreign Minister visited Warsaw last December.

"All this has transpired outside the United
Nations. Although he has been given a mandate by
the United States to do what he can to facilitate
peace discussions, Secretary General U Thant is said
by others to feel that nothing more can be accomplished at the moment.

"Diplomats from 11 non-aligned countries have
met here three times within the last 10 days to
discuss whether they can undertake any initiative
to advance a solution. As a result, Sudanese delegate Fakhreddime Mohamed was designated to call on
Thant to inquire whether a new initiative would be
useful. He reportedly received no encouragement.
END TEXT."

RUSK

February 3, 1967

At his press conference, the President says it would not be
helpful "to comment on any particular channel or communications
at this point." Referring to Hanoi's attitude, he adds, "I must
say that I do not interpret any action that I have observed as
being a serious effort to either go to a conference table or to
bring the war to an end."

New York Times, 3 February 1967
Transcript of the President's News Conference

"Following is a transcript of President Johnson's
news conference in Washington yesterday as recorded
by The New York Times:

. . . .

"1.   Prospects in Vietnam

Q. We've been reading and writing a good deal lately
about diplomacy aimed at a Vietnam settlement. I
wonder if you could give us your assessment of the
peace front at this time.

A. Mr. (Frank) Cormier of the Associated Press states
a question that I know is on the minds of all the
people here today and all the people in this country.
As you know, I have underlined over and over again
the very deep interest of the United States in a
prompt and peaceful settlement of all of the problems
in Southeast Asia.

      I have said many times that we are ready to go
more than half way in achieving this result. I would
remind all of you that we would welcome a conference
in Southeast Asia and this might be a Geneva conference,
it could be an all-Asian conference, or any other
generally acceptable forum.

      We would be glad to see the unconditional dis-
cussions to which I referred in my statement of
April, 1965, at Johns Hopkins. We would participate
in preliminary discussions which might open the way
for formal negotiations. We are prepared today to
talk about mutual steps of de-escalation. We would
be prepared to talk about such subjects as the
exchange of prisoners, the demilitarization or the
demilitarized zone or any other aspect which might
take even a small step in the direction of peace.

      We should be prepared to discuss any points
which the other side wishes to bring up along with
points which we and our allies very much want to
raise ourselves, or there could be preliminary
discussions to see whether there could be an agreed
set of points which could be the basis for negotiation.

      So it is against this background that we study
very carefully all of the public statements made which
appear from time to time and which bear upon Southeast
Asia and all the views which we receive from or
through other governments.

      It would not be helpful to me -- and I do not
intend to do so -- to comment on any particular
channel or communications at this point. But you may
be sure that we are diligent in our search for the
possibility of a peaceful settlement.

In all candor I must say that I am not aware of
any serious effort that the other side has made in
my judgment to bring the fighting to a stop and to
stop the war."

"2. Personal Role in Talks

Q. You've been so eloquent in the past about express--
ing your desire for peaceful negotiations. I'd like
to ask you whether or not if you thought it would
speed this war down the road to peace whether you
would be willing personally to participate in negotiations with some of your opposite numbers, such as
the leadership in Hanoi?

A. We have made clear that if the other side desires
to discuss peace at any time well we will be very
happy to have appropriate arrangements made to see
that that's carried out.

Where we would talk and who would talk and what
we would talk about are all matters that could be
worked out between the two governments involved.

We have made clear to them and to the world the
principles that we believe must govern a peace meeting
of this kind, and a settlement that we would hope
would come out of it like the honoring of the Geneva
accords of '54 and '62, the right of self-determination
of the people of South Vietnam, and to insure that they
are freed from the threat or use of force.

But we have, I must say, as of today, no indication that the other side is prepared in any way to
settle on these limited and decent terms. We hope
very much that we can have some signals in that
direction, but I, in candor, must say that as of now
we do not have."

"3. Concessions for Peace

Q. Mr. President, does your expressed willingness to
negotiate a peaceful settlement imply any willingness
to compromise on any of our stated objectives in that
part of the world?

A. I think that any peace agreement will involve
understanding on both parts and certain concession on
both parts and a certain understanding.

I don't think we can determine those before we
come together or through any press conference tech-
niques. I can only repeat what I said in the State

111

of the Union, that I wish that the conflict in Vietnam
was over and I can only repeat what I've said so many
times -- I will do anything I can on the part of this
Government to go more than halfway to bring it at an end.[30]

I must say that we face great costs, we face agony.
We do plan to carry out our efforts out there, we are
going to support our troops in the field, we are going
to work with our Vietnamese allies toward pacification
and constitutional government, but while we're doing
that, every hour of every day the spokesmen for this
Government are under instructions to explore every possibility for peace.

But I do not want to disillusion any of you and I
don't want any of you to be caught by speculation. As
of this moment I cannot report that there are any
serious indications that the other side is ready to stop
the war."

"4. Indications From Enemy

Q. You have three times now used that phrase: "no
serious efforts by the other side to bring the war to a
close." How would you characterize what has been going
on in the last couple of weeks? Do you recognize any
signs of maneuverability or fluidity in their position?

A. I see almost every day some speculation by some
individual, or some hope or desire expressed by some
Government. And I assume that different individuals
get different impressions; certainly they have different
hopes.

I can only 'speak for myself, John.' And with the
information that I have, with the knowledge that's brought
to me, I must say that I do not interpret any action that
I have observed as being a serious effort to either go to
a conference table or to bring the war to an end."

    . . . .

"Q. Would you discuss the reports that there has been a
decline in the infiltration rate to the South and say
whether you think the bombing has had any effect?

A. Well, I stated in my Baltimore speech in early '65
what we expected to come from the bombing. We felt that
it would improve the morale of the people in South Vietnam who felt that they'd almost lost the war. We felt
that it would make the North Vietnamese pay a much
heavier price for what they were doing and we felt that
it would make the infiltration more difficult.

We think it has achieved all of those expressed
purposes. We cannot speak with cold assurance on the
infiltration and the numbers each day or each week
or each month.

In some quarters of the year our indications
are that they increase. In other periods of the
year -- the next quarter -- then they go down some.
I know of nothing that I can conclude as highly
significant from the guesses and the estimates that
we have made.

Q. Sir, we have said in the past that we would be
willing to suspend the bombing of North Vietnam in
exchange for some suitable step by the other side.
Are you prepared at all to tell us what kind of other
steps the other side should take for this suspension
of bombing?

A. Just almost any step. As far as we can see, they
haven't taken any yet and we would be glad to explore
any reciprocal action that they or any of their spokesmen would care to suggest.

We have made one proposal after the other to --
we'd like to have a cease-fire; we'd be very glad to
stop our bombing as we have on two previous occasions,
if we could have any indication of reciprocal action,
but as of now they have given none and I assume they are
willing to give none until I hear further."

....

February 4, 1967

In Saigon, the VC are reported to mortar the 7th Precinct and
carry out 4 grenade attacks during the period January 28-February 3.

Meanwhile, Ky is distressed by news stories of US-DRV contacts
and asks Lodge if we still require concessions in return for a bombing
suspension and whether there are "divergences on such matters between
Washington and Saigon. Lodge is instructed to reply by giving Ky more
background on Marigold, stressing (a) our doubts about the genuineness
of the Polish contact, (b) on the other hand our obligation to follow
all potential leads, and (c) the need to avoid publicity during this
"extremely interesting and delicate" phase of diplomacy. In connection
with the latter, his attention is to be drawn to the "recent public
comments of Presidential Advisor Walt Rostow."

Saigon 17295 (to SecState), S/Nodis
    4 February 1967

"Following is the record of VC initiated incidents
within 10 miles of Saigon during the period Jan 28 to
Feb 3.

        A.   Jan 30, Saigon-grenade superficially
wounds two US servicemen.

        B.   Jan 30, Saigon-grenade injures one US
serviceman and one VN civilian.

        C.   Jan 31, 5 miles NE of Saigon-grenade
killing policemen and civilian, wounding school-
teacher.

        D.   Feb 1, Saigon-six mortar shells fired
into seventh precinct, wounding seven VN civilians.

        E.   Feb 2, Saigon-VC small arms and grenade
attack on seventh precinct outpost, one civilian
killed."

LODGE

Saigon 17317 (to SecState), S/Exdis
    4 February 1967
Readd: CINCPAC (FROM CJCS-EXCLUSIVE FOR ADM SHARP)

    "1.   During a call on Ky....

    "2.   ... he said, 'Does Washington agree that there
should be no publicity of any kind until there has been
a concrete offer from the Communist side?'

    "3.   I said that I felt sure that Washington was
very much in favor of not having publicity, since
publicity not only presented awkward problems for us
and for the Government of South Vietnam, but also made
it difficult to get any kind of a peaceful understanding
with Hanoi. He agreed that we should avoid forcing
Hanoi up against the wall by making them lose face.

    "4.   It was evident that his attention had been
attracted by the statements of Senator Robert Kennedy[31]
and the apparent leaks of the messages from Cairo and
New Delhi to a point where he wanted to be sure that
there were no 'divergencies' between Washington and
Saigon.[32] He asked whether we still believed that in

exchange for a bombing suspension we wanted some sort
of concession on their part. Did we envisage a bargaining process or were we to suspend bombing with no
quid pro quo?

"5. I called his attention to the President's
press conference and to the fact that on three separate occasions during the press conference, the President had said that so far there was nothing of substance from Hanoi...."

....

LODGE

State 131715 (to Amembassy Saigon), S/Nodis
    4 February 1967
Ref: Saigon 17317

....

"3. Believe you should also give Ky fill-in
generally.... For his information, story is, as he
may imagine, quite incomplete and misleading in a
number of respects.... We were never sure whether
the Poles were speaking for Hanoi or entirely for
themselves and we concluded ultimately that the
exercise had been primarily a fishing expedition by
the Poles in order to get us to change our position
with respect to bombing of North Viet-Nam.... Throughout this exercise we had not undertaken to make any
change in our basic position. At the same time we
had indicated a readiness to consider the possibility
of direct talks without conditions with North Viet-Nam
with the objective of bringing about a peaceful
settlement. You should add that we would naturally
be in touch with the GVN if there were really substantive developments in this field.

"4. With reference to Ky's query (para 2 of
reftel) about Washington views on publicity, suggest
you call to his attention recent public comments of
Presidential Advisor Walt Rostow. After referring to
'extremely interesting and delicate' phase of diplomatic
probes now under way Rostow noted that publicity could
destroy effectiveness of behind-the-scenes efforts to
ascertain Hanoi's intent and added 'this is a bad time
to talk about any particular stand which might turn out
to be a negotiating situation.'"

RUSK

Washington Post, 5 February 1967
U.S. Is Wary on Report of Peace Bid, by Murrey Marder

"United States attempts to launch peace talks with
North Vietnam are now in 'an extremely interesting and
delicate phase,' a White House adviser said yesterday.

"With that comment and variations upon it, the
Administration declined to confirm or deny a report
that the United States and North Vietnam had tried to
start peace talks in Warsaw in December, at American
initiative.

"Walt W. Rostow, President Johnson's special
assistant for national security affairs, said:

"'This is an extremely interesting and delicate
phase in what is or what might turn out to be a
negotiating process. Nothing has yet happened that
would justify us in saying we have a serious offer to
negotiate. This is a bad time to discuss any particular negotiating track.'

"Lack of Vigor. Rostow's comments were made
during a panel debate at a conference of college newspaper editors at the Sheraton-Park Hotel. Another
panelist, Richard N. Goodwin, who had served as an
adviser to both Presidents Kenndy and Johnson, charged
there was a lack of vigor in the present pursuit of
negotiations.

"'If Hanoi wishes to negotiate seriously,' said
Rostow, 'your government would not be embarrassed.
It would be delighted.'

"Rostow was questioned specifically by the students
about the validity of a report in The Washington Post
yesterday, by staff writer Robert H. Estabrook at the
United Nations.

"It reported that an authoritative Western source
said that U.S. Ambassador Henry Cabot Lodge, in Saigon
on Dec. 2 and 3, asked a Polish diplomat to set up
contacts with North Vietnam. On Dec. 4, the report
said, Polish Foreign Minister Adam Rapacki said Hanoi
agreed to have ambassadorial-level talks with the
United States in Warsaw. The report said that Hanoi
attached no conditions about first halting the American bombing of North Vietnam.

"<u>Withdrew in Anger</u>. According to the report Hanoi angrily withdrew its agreement after American bombing raids near Hanoi on Dec. 13-14 allegedly hit civilian areas.

"Rostow declined to get any more specific about that account except to repeat that 'this is a bad time to talk about a particular strand of what might be a negotiation.'

"Other sources sought to emphasize that the frustrated negotiating effort described in the report from the United Nations was only one of many efforts being made to launch talks.

"Some Administration sources said the point in The Washington Post account that they would challenge was that Hanoi had 'agreed' to the Warsaw talks. No official, however, would discuss whether this question of agreement was a matter of differing interpretations or not. There was no challenge by any official of the reported Lodge-initiative to arrange for talks in Warsaw.

"The State Department, in commenting Friday on earlier and considerably less-detailed versions of a similar report by The Washington Post and others said it saw 'no merit' to contentions that the bombing of North Vietnam interfered with efforts to start peace talks.

"In a new comment yesterday the State Department said:

"'As a matter of policy we do not believe it would promote the cause of peace in Vietnam to comment on accounts of any alleged private talks or events relating to them. The President fully characterized the situation at his press conference last Thursday.'

"At that press conference, President Johnson repeatedly said that 'I do not interpret any action that I have observed as being a serious effort to either go to a conference table or to bring the war to an end.' The United States, he said, was anxious 'to explore any reciprocal action' to curb or end the war.

"That comment, Administration sources said, amounted to turning down, as inadequate, a bid by North Vietnam's Foreign Minister in which he said there 'could' be talks

if there was an 'unconditional' end to the bombings
of his country.

"Administration officials emphasized that the
offer only held out the possibility, not the promise,
of talks, in any event.

"The Soviet news agency, Tass, charged yesterday
that President Johnson had spurned the 'goodwill'
gesture by North Vietnamese Foreign Minister Nguyen
Duy Trinh.[33] Tass said the minister had displayed an
'indication of willingness' by the Hanoi regime to
talk with the United States.

"The Soviet news agency added:

"'The unwillingness of U.S. ruling circles to
stop the criminal bombing of the D.R.V. (North Vietnam)
can only be regarded as a refusal to meet around the
conference table, and as a sign of their determination
to further escalate the aggressive war in Vietnam.'

"Tass's correspondent in Hanoi said President
Johnson's statements produced 'legitimate indignation'
in Hanoi.'"

February 6-7, 1967

Australia and New Zealand are briefed on Marigold in some detail.
More general accounts are given to the GVN and the Manila countries.

Ky accepts our explanation in good spirit, but points to alarm
about so-called "peace" talk among Catholic leaders, certain Buddhists
and the military in SVN. His and Thieu's strong anti-communism would
be reassuring to these elements, he believes.

> State 132347 (to Amembassy Canberra; Amembassy Wellington),
>   TS/Nodis, 6 February 1967
> Ref: DEPCIRTEL 131700
> EYES ONLY FOR AMBASSADOR
>
> "1. On February 4 Bundy separately gave Ambassador
> Waller and Charge d'Affaires Shepherd a full account of
> the discussions between USG and Poles about the possi-
> bility of direct discussions between USG and Hanoi...."

....

"27. .... While we may have erred in not informing you fully on this matter, we were guided throughout by the absolute necessity of secrecy in seeking to determine whether Hanoi was in fact prepared to sit down quietly without preconditions....

"28. This full account is being given to Australia and New Zealand, with the request for the preservation of total confidence. A more general account is being given to Saigon and to the Manila countries. We have assured Saigon, as we have repeatedly assured you, that if we should get clear evidence of a serious change in Hanoi's position we would keep them fully informed."

RUSK

Saigon 17482 (to SecState), S/Nodis
      7 February 1967
Ref: State 131715

"1. Pursuant to your 131715, I called on Prime Minister Ky Tuesday morning...."

        ....

"3. Ky seemed to accept all of the above in good spirit. He evidently thinks that the purpose of the rather careful wording is to make it possible to achieve some kind of understanding without making Hanoi lose face. In all my many talks with him, he has often voiced his belief that we should be trying to persuade Hanoi and make it easy for them to go along with us, and that we did not want to humiliate them, make them lose face, put them up against the wall.

"4. Changing the subject slightly, he then said that Catholic leaders in Viet-Nam were becoming alarmed by the so-called 'peace' talk which they feared would actually mean military advantage for Hanoi, and were taking an attitude very different from that of the Pope. He was afraid that similar divisions might occur among Buddhists and among the military. The hopeful element of the situation was that 'everyone knew' how strongly anti-Communist he, Ky, and Thieu were."

LODGE

February 7-8, 1967

   Wilson comments in Parliament about discussion with the Poles and
a definite "peace feeler" last December. Highest levels in Washington
fear this may undercut the President's February 3 remarks.

   Gronouski takes issue with Goldberg, arguing that the Canadians
were probably Estabrook's source and that the Poles remain a better
channel for communication with Hanoi.

      State 133105 (to Amembassy London), S/Nodis
         8 February 1967
      FOR AMBASSADOR AND COOPER

      "1. Highest levels are deeply disturbed by Wilson
      reference to December discussions with Poles in Parlia-
      mentary response yesterday.[34] Wilson comment is of course
      being widely reported as confirming that some definite
      'peace feeler' did exist at that time, and is therefore
      being construed to 'undercut' President's remarks of
      last week. Moreover, revelation that Wilson has 'all
      the details' is bound to have serious complicating
      effect on our relations with Saigon and with Manila
      allies, who had not repeat not received any similar
      full account...."

        ....

      RUSK

      Warsaw 1939 (to SecState), TS/Nodis
         8 February 1967
      Ref: (A) State 130580
          (B) State 131716

      "1. Based on personal knowledge of the precedents,
      I have reached quite different inferences and conclu-
      sions regarding Estabrook articles than those drawn by
      Amb. Goldberg in reftels.

      "2. With respect to Feb 2 story, while Estabrook
      referred to high Polish sources, he denied that story
      came from the Poles. Rather, he said it came from
      Canadian Fon Min Martin while Estabrook was in Canada,
      and that he had story a couple of weeks. This rings
      true, for Estabrook on Jan 19 filed from Ottawa essence
      of his Feb 2 story (which appeared in Jan 20 Paris
      Herald Tribune) saying 'Canadian authorities blame some

of the difficulty on the accidental U.S. bombing of
Hanoi in mid-December. Private soundings then under
way were disrupted, they say, and the attitude in
North Vietnam appeared to harden.' Also, note that
in his Feb 2 article Estabrook speaks of 'high level
outsiders' as source, and links Polish peace effort
to Martin-Rapacki discussions in December (which is
not true, but it does not hurt Martin's image to be
case in this role), also, note that Estabrook spoke
of Western sources in his Feb 4 story."

....

"5. What does surprise me, if we accept Estabrook's statement that story came from Martin (and I
see no a priori reason for Estabrook to implicate
Martin and U Thant and protect the Poles), is that
Feb 2 story places developments in so unfavorable a
light from standpoint of USG...."

....

"8. I am particularly concerned with recommendation in final para of reftel A, that 'we should no
longer use Poland or any other Bloc country as
channel to Hanoi.' As I noted in my analysis of
Marigold role played by Poland (Warsaw 1631), I too
had hoped that Soviets might play an intermediary
role. But to my knowledge experience has been that
Poles are only Communist country willing to take on
this chore...."

GRONOUSKI

February 10, 18, 20, 1967

Sizeable VC incidents within 10 miles of Saigon lead Lodge to
suggest that there is no further need to look for indications of reciprocity to our suspension of bombing near Hanoi. He suggests that the
10 mile limit around Hanoi be dropped.

Saigon 17759 (to SecState), S/Nodis
      10 February 1967

"Following is the record of VC initiated incidents within ten miles of Saigon during the period
February 4 to February 9."

....

"C. February 6, four miles west of Saigon -
unidentified platoon-sized unit fired submachine
bursts near police station and then withdrew."

. . . .

LODGE

Saigon 18329 (to SecState), S/Nodis
     18 February 1967

"Following is the record of VC initiated incidents within ten miles of Saigon during the period
February 10 to February 15."

. . . .

"C. February 13, Saigon - VC fired four mortar
rounds in vicinity of MACV-I (details have been
reported separately)."

. . . .

"2. With this spate of activity it is clear
that considerations behind preparing this series of
reports are no longer relevant. This will, therefore,
be the last telegraphic report of this sort."

LODGE

Saigon 18535 (to SecState), TS/Nodis
     20 February 1967

. . . .

"2. The recent mortaring in town, other terrorist incidents in the Saigon area, and the likelihood
that we will get more, prompts me to suggest we consider informing Hanoi, via the Poles, that we no
longer consider ourselves bound by the 10 miles limit."

LODGE

March 3, 1967

    Goldberg (accompanied by Lodge) sees D'Orlandi in Saigon, to hear
the latter's version of Marigold. His objective is a first-hand confirmation from an independent source of the inaccuracy of the Polish version
conveyed to U Thant. D'Orlandi's account, he finds, contains "no

discrepancies from the version we already have. In particular D'Orlandi is quite categoric in stating that the 10 points passed to Hanoi were formulated by Lewandowski, not by Lodge--as Goldberg believes the Poles told U Thant. On the other side, D'Orlandi is of the view that the December 13-14 bombing derailed the Warsaw talks. He expresses great confidence in Lewandowski's integrity.

USUN 4238 (to SecState), S/Nodis
    6 March 1967
FROM GOLDBERG

"On March 3, day before leaving Saigon, I arranged entirely private and off record meeting with D'Orlandi, with agreement of and in presence Amb Lodge. My objective was to secure first-hand confirmation from entirely independent source of inaccuracy of Polish version of late November-early December Marigold events, i.e., that it was Lodge who had formulated ten point proposal Lewandowski transmitted to Hanoi, only to take position subsequently that some of these points needed clarification. (underlining furnished)

"Without any prompting on my part, D'Orlandi really and fully recited course of events. His recital contained no discrepancies from version we already had and he was quite categoric in stating that ten points passed Hanoi by Lewandowski had been formulated by Lewandowski himself."

. . . .

"It is necessary to add, however, that D'Orlandi is of view that bombing of Dec 13-14 derailed Warsaw talks. He also expressed view that it would have furthered progress towards negotiations if Rapacki had not insisted upon transferring venue to Warsaw. D'Orlandi's view is that it would have been preferable to carry on discussions through himself and Lewandowski in Saigon, with Lewandowski commuting to Hanoi.

"D'Orlandi expressed great confidence in Lewandowski's integrity and confirmed that both Lewandowski and he will be leaving Saigon for respective home or other posts."

BUFFUM

March 14, 1967

On returning to New York, Goldberg tries to arrive at a common
version of the facts about Marigold with the Polish UN Representative,
Tomorowicz. The Polish version agrees with ours that the 10 points
were formulated by Lewandowski. Goldberg notes three points of
difference, however:

i. Their version does not mention that Lodge indicated the
need to clarify certain points at the December 1 meeting in Saigon.

ii. Their version indicates that Lodge first raised clarification at the December 3 meeting, through the "important differences of
interpretation" clause.

iii. According to their version, the Poles stressed avoiding
intensification of the bombing either before or during talks from the
December 1 meeting on.

Goldberg urges Tomorowicz to review Marigold with Warsaw so that
these factual differences can be cleared up.

> USUN 4390 (to SecState), S/Nodis
> 15 March 1967
>
> "1. I arranged meet with Polish Perm Rep Tomoro-
> wicz Mar 14 PM shortly after he had called on SYG and
> just before he was due leave for roughly ten days con-
> sultation in Warsaw."
>
> ....
>
> "3. Specifically, I noted there is one point of
> some importance re developments in early Dec on which
> there are two differing versions, namely, who formu-
> lated ten points which Lewandowski presented to Hanoi....
>
> "4. I said I had talked with D'Orlandi privately
> while in Saigon, that D'Orlandi had reviewed Marigold
> developments without any prompting from me, and that
> his review entirely confirmed our understanding of
> facts on this point. Tomorowicz said that, in princi-
> ple, facts of this point as we understood them were
> quite accurate. (underlining furnished)
>
> "5. His further comments, however, engendered
> discussion of Marigold developments throughout Dec
> which revealed three other points on which we and
> Poles have differing facts, specifically:

A) Polish version, as presented by Tomorowicz, makes no mention of fact that at Dec 1 mtg in
Saigon, when Lewandowski presented ten points to
Lodge, Lodge raised question of need to clarify some
of points, noting Points B and H in particular.
(underlining furnished)

B) According Polish version, Lodge first
mentioned need for clarification at Dec 3 mtg, when
he said there were important differences of interpretation on 'serious matters' in ten points, although
Lodge would not reply when asked to identify points
in need of clarification. (underlining furnished)

C) According Polish version, Poles placed
stress on relation between bombing and progress
toward US-NVN talks from Dec 1 mtg on: Lewandowski
allegedly told Lodge on Dec 1 that there must be no
intensification of bombing either before or during
talks; at Dec 3 mtg with Lodge, he allegedly made
strong representations re Dec 2 bombings; and, on
Dec 5, Rapacki allegedly made another strong representation re bombing to Gronouski, claiming Dec 2
and 3 bombings had not ruled out chances of direct
US-NVN talks but had certainly made progress toward
talks more difficult. (underlining furnished)

"6. As these differences came to light during
discussion, I presented our understanding of facts
and urged Tomorowicz to review Marigold developments
while in Warsaw so that we could clear up factual
differences between us...."

....

GOLDBERG

March 16-17, 1967

Fanfani writes Rusk that Lewandowski has proposed a new initiative
to D'Orlandi. Lodge is instructed to follow up, but he replies that
D'Orlandi has left Saigon for Rome. Reinhardt is therefore instructed
to contact D'Orlandi later in Rome.

Rome 4767 (to SecState), S/Nodis, 16 March 1967

....

"My Dear Secretary of State,

125

"I would feel remiss in my duty if I failed to
inform you of what Ambassador D'Orlandi has communicated to me after meeting with Lewandowski, a few
days ago, and reviewing with him the current Vietnamese situation. D'Orlandi felt he had to tell me
that, in the present circumstances, a resumption of
negotiations would require a three week long suspen-
pension of bombings and the admission, on the part
of the United States, that they are still willing
to accept the well known ten points.

"D'Orlandi adds that the duration of the suspension could be kept secret and that it should not
rpt not be difficult to secure a substantive counterpart from Hanoi, to be presented as a compensation
for some other, purely token, concession from the
United States."

....

REINHARDT

State 156826 (to Amembassy.Saigon), S/Nodis
     16 March 1967

"1. By now you will have seen...message from
FonMin Fanfani to Secretary Rusk....

"2. Points of greatest interest on which we
most want clarification are following:

        (a) When would the negotiations be
resumed, after suspension had run three weeks or
at initiation of three-week period? If the former,
should it be assumed that suspension would be
expected to continue as negotiations proceeded?

        (b) What would be the 'substantive
counterpart' from Hanoi? Presume it would not
merely be resumption of negotiations but rather
some de-escalatory action affecting infiltration,
guerrilla or terror activity in the South or the
like.

        (c) In phrase 'resumption of negotiations'
does this refer to (i) direct DRV/US talks which were
to have been undertaken in Warsaw last December 2
and which we welcomed, or (ii) resumption of arid
exchanges between Gronouski and Rapacki?

(d) What is entailed in 'accepting' the
ten points? We assume this means nothing more than
that we have in no way receded from acceptance in
terms we made known to Lewandowski and Rapacki in
November and December.

"3. Please review these matters with D'Orlandi
...."

Saigon 20590 (to SecState), S/Nodis
        16 March 1967

"1. In response to your 156826, D'Orlandi
left Saigon yesterday, Thursday, March 16...."

LODGE

State 158132 (to Amembassy Rome), S/Nodis
        17 March 1967
Ref: (a) Saigon 20590
        (b) Rome 4767
        (c) State 156826

....

"2. .... The Secretary would be most grateful
if Minister Fanfani would let Ambassador Reinhardt
know when Ambassador D'Orlandi has reached Rome so
that the two Ambassadors might discuss Lewandowski's
approach.

"3. For Reinhardt. Assuming the arrangement
outlined above works out, we would appreciate your
following up with D'Orlandi along lines sketched
out Deptel 156826...."

....

RUSK

March 19, 1967

Rapacki has told Wilson and Brown that (1) Lodge first accepted
Lewandowski's 10 points, then reneged through the "important differences of interpretation" clause, and (2) the December 13-14 bombing
had sabotaged the entire project. State cables a rebuttal: (1)
Lodge reserved the US position on the 10 points when first presented,
December 1; hence he did not renege, (2) Although Lewandowski
complained on December 3 about our bombing Hanoi, "there was no
suggestion that the prospect for DRV-US talks depended in any direct
way on such matters."

State 158246 (to Amembassy London), TS/Nodis
  19 March 1967
Ref: London's 6998 and 7172 and State's 146803

"Account in London's 6998 of Rapacki's conversations with Brown and Wilson about the events of
December provide further evidence of Rapacki's continuing vindictiveness. We assume that his feelings
will badly discolor the Polish contribution to a
'more detailed post mortem' between the British and
the Poles.

"During his London visit, Rapacki evidently
made two charges against us: (1) Lodge had reneged
after giving firm agreement to the Lewandowski Ten
Point package and (2) the December 13-14 bombing
had sabotaged the entire project.

"The cable exchanges between Lodge and the
Department in the early days of December provide
an absolutely clear record that Lodge did not repeat
not agree to Lewandowski's version of the Ten Points
and therefore did not repeat not renege. On December 1, Lewandowski told Lodge he had presented to
Hanoi his understanding of the US position based on
his conversations with Lodge on November 14 and
earlier. He then read his Ten Points, which Lodge
recorded precisely. Lodge was not, however, shown
a paper containing the Ten Points.

"At the end of his statement, Lewandowski asked
Lodge if he had correctly stated the US point of view.
Lodge responded carefully that 'obviously on a matter
of such importance, I would have to refer to my
government for a definitive reply, but I could say
off hand that much of what he cited was in keeping
with the spirit of our policy.' He then pointed out
specific difficulties with Point 2 and Points 8.
Neither in this nor in later discussions with Lodge
did Lewandowski indicate any misunderstanding of the
qualified nature of Lodge's response to his presentation of the Ten Points. For example, Lodge informed
him on December 3 that our Embassy in Warsaw would
contact the DRV representative on December 6 to confirm
that the Lewandowski formulation broadly represented
our position, although several specific points were
subject to important differences of interpretation....

".... It is also worthy of note that D'Orlandi
told the Secretary on December 9 that Rapacki had

'tried to be clever' and to get the US to withdraw
all its reservations about the Lewandowski formulation before he established a direct contact in
Warsaw between the US and DRV representatives....

".... It is true that on December 3, Lewandowski under instructions, complained to Lodge
about bombings in the vicinity of Hanoi but there
was no suggestion that the prospect for DRV-US talks
depended in any direct way on such matters.

"Subsequently, while Rapacki haggled, we were
blocked from a direct contact with the DRV at which
this and all other pertinent subjects could have
been discussed...."

KATZENBACH

April 7, 21, 1967

Reinhardt reviews prospects for resuming contact via Lewandowski
with D'Orlandi in Rome. State instructs him to arrange a three-party
meeting when Lewandowski passes through Rome in May.

Rome 5266 (to SecState), S/Nodis, 7 April 1967
State 164750 (Ref?)

"1. In lengthy private conversation today at
villa, D'Orlandi exposed his conviction that possibility to achieve something through Lewandowski was
good and should be pursued without undue delay
since Pole would be leaving Saigon in May. D'Orlandi
believed lesson of last try was that more details
should be clarified and nailed down through Lewandowski channel before actual negotiations between
principals initiated. No doubt he had discussed
these and other views in detail with Lodge. It
was clear to me that D'Orlandi considered himself
essential link to Lewandowski channel.

"2. Regarding specific questions (State 156826,
para 2), he stated:

A. Lewandowski thought that suspension
of bombing should be initiated not later than his
arrival in Hanoi to sound North Vietnamese and that
three or four weeks would be necessary to allow
sufficient time for initial exchanges, suspension
would of course be without any commitment, and whether
it continued further would presumably depend on
whether constructive developments take place.

B.   'Substantive contribution' would, he imagined, be something specific in military field which US Command considered useful.

C.   'Resumption of negotiations' he thought meant US/DRV but was not sure that Rapacki/ Gronouski stage could be completely finessed if venue were Warsaw.

D.   'Accepting ten points' he understood simply to mean reaffirmation of previous position including US reservations on interpretation and assurance that there had been no recession in US position.

"3.   D'Orlandi said Lewandowski had revealed nothing rpt nothing in his conversation which might cast light on why Hanoi published Johnson-Ho-Chi Minh exchange."[35]

. . . .

REINHARDT

State 180271 (to Amembassy Rome), TS/Nodis
      21 April 1967
Ref: Rome 5266

"1.   We appreciate having these additional comments by D'Orlandi and suggest that in order to explore Hanoi's position further, as it is understood by Lewandowski, you propose quiet meeting between the three of you next month when Lewandowski passes through Rome en route to Warsaw."

. . . .

RUSK

May 8, 1967

Hightower files a lengthy account of Marigold from Washington. The story contains enough detail to indicate that some of his sources were insiders. It is critical of the Polish role and reflects Washington's doubts the reliability of Poland as a channel to Hanoi.

New York Times, 9 May 1967
4-MONTH U.S. BID IGNORED BY HANOI, by John M.
    Hightower of the Associated Press

    . . . .

    "One of the 10 points provided that the United
States would not insist that North Vietnam acknowledge publicly the presence of its forces in South
Vietnam. The Johnson Administration decided this
should be clarified to require that if the troop
issue was to be covered up for face-saving purposes,
then the North Vietnamese forces should be withdrawn from the South.

    "Mr. Lewandowski was informed of this and other
clarification points. The others seemed mainly
matters of wording. But this one seemed to be substantial."

    . . . .

    "Mr. Rapacki's strong resistance to the clari-
fication proposal caused some concern in Washington.
Officials were not sure the Poles had any commitment
from North Vietnam to begin the talks. Some high
officials here doubted that Mr. Rapacki was in fact
relaying United States views and making known
Washington's readiness for talks to Hanoi."

    . . . .

    "Informants say an important element in the
Administration decision not to suspend the bombing
plan was an attack by Communist forces on Saigon's
main airfield and an unsuccessful attempt to blow
up a major bridge in Saigon."

    . . . .

    "United States officials publicly took issue
with this. Privately they said that while the
attack at Hanoi might have destroyed the Polish
plan, it might also have presented Hanoi or Warsaw
with a convenient pretext for not going through
with it."

    . . . .

May 9-10, 1967

    In Warsaw, Polish concern is expressed over rumors that the US
plans to publish a white paper on Marigold. This would force them,

reluctantly, to publish their own account. Gronouski recommends against publication.

Washington replies that the Hightower piece is "essentially accurate and reasonably favorable from our point of view." The Poles are to be told that we will not publish a white paper.

When so informed, the Poles respond that "US officials had apparently chosen another way to put out the story." They are especially distressed at the question raised as to whether they had actually transmitted US messages to the North Vietnamese. They state that they had delivered the messages.

> Warsaw 2700 (to SecState), S/Nodis, 9 May 1967
>
> "1. During my separate calls on Winiewicz and Michalowski this morning, both of them expressed Polish concern about news reports originating in U.S. that U.S. intends to publish within next few days a white book covering Warsaw talks of last December...."
>
> ....
>
> "5. .... Poles would be most reluctant to publish their own white book but they would be left with no alternative if U.S. published its own."
>
> ....
>
> "7. .... I would therefore recommend against publication of official dept. version of MARIGOLD events...."
>
> GRONOUSKI

> State 190899 (to Amembassy Warsaw), S/Nodis
>   9 May 1967
> Ref: Warsaw 2699 and 2700
>
> "We consider news stories filed yesterday on December peace probes to be essentially accurate and reasonably favorable from our point of view. We would prefer let matter rest there avoiding to extent feasible public exchange of interpretations with the Polish Government. When queried about story yesterday, official spokesman said he preferred not rpt not to comment on story, adding FOR BACKGROUND that he 'would have no quarrel with it.' We intend maintain this position.

"Since we have no desire exacerbate US-Polish relations over this matter, we have no present intentions publish 'White Book' on this subject. You should so inform Michalowski...."

. . . .

RUSK

Warsaw 2727 (to SecState), S/Nodis
    10 May 1967
Ref: State 190899

"1. .... When Kaiser said U.S. has no present intention of publishing white book, Michalowski responded that U.S. officials had apparently chosen another way to put out the story. He then referred to Hightower article which, he said, according to summary received by Polish FonMin, seemed to be based on high level official sources. There were disturbing distortions, errors and innuendos challenging the integrity of Rapacki and questioning whether Polish side had actually transmitted messages to North Vietnamese. He added that Poles had of course delivered messages."

. . . .

JENKINS

May 28, 1967

US Embassies in Tokyo and Seoul are given background information on Marigold.

State 203984 (to AmEmbassies: Tokyo, Seoul), S/Nodis
    28 May 1967
Ref: State 197426 to Tokyo
      State 198946 to Seoul

"We are repeating to you State's 158246 and 132347 which provide background info on Polish initiatives re Vietnam which aborted last December. Text of Lewandowski's Ten Points which were presented to Ambassador Lodge on December 1 follows:"

. . . .

RUSK

<u>June 6, 1967</u>

The three-party talks in Rome will not be possible as Lewandowski is not passing through.

> Rome 6506 (to SecState), S/Nodis
>   6 June 1967
> State 191174 and Rome 5991
>
> "D'Orlandi has informed me that Lewandowski is not repeat not coming to Rome."
>
> REINHARDT

<u>December 6, 1967</u>

Wilfred Burchett tells US officials in Paris that the DRV had an official en route to the Marigold Warsaw meeting at the time of cancellation--"when the US resumed bombing Hanoi."

> Paris 7540 (to SecState), S/Nodis,
>   6 December 1967
>
> ....
>
> "Burchett said North Vietnamese accuse us of talking peace while intensifying war. For example, North Vietnamese had agreed to talk at Warsaw last December and even had official en route when US resumed bombing Hanoi. He also mentioned North Vietnamese readiness to talk at Rangoon during 37 day pause."
>
> ....

UNITED STATES - VIETNAM RELATIONS
1945 - 1967

VIETNAM TASK FORCE

OFFICE OF THE SECRETARY OF DEFENSE

VI. C. 3.

VI.   SETTLEMENT OF THE CONFLICT

C.   Histories of Contacts

3.   Sunflower

SUNFLOWER took place in January and February 1967. It involved two separate although eventually interrelated peace moves, a direct American approach to Hanoi through the North Vietnamese Embassy in Moscow and a parallel attempt on the part of British Prime Minister Harold Wilson, working with Soviet Premier Alexei Kosygin, to bring the two belligerents to the conference table. Like MARIGOLD, SUNFLOWER was enormously complex and confusing; it provided further evidence of American diplomatic ineptitude and aroused heated controversy, this time between the United States and Great Britain. Wilson's protests to the contrary, however, it does not appear to have held out any possibility of serious peace talks. The contacts in London and Moscow quickly broke down on the issue of de-escalation, and in this sense SUNFLOWER may have represented a step backward from MARIGOLD.

The Moscow channel succeeded only to the extent that it produced the first direct contact between U.S. and North Vietnamese diplomats since the meetings in Rangoon nearly a year earlier. Immediately after the breakdown of MARIGOLD, the United States decided to try a direct approach to Hanoi through its Moscow embassy. The SUNFLOWER documents make clear that American officials were responding to some vague but enticing signals conveyed to journalist Harrison Salisbury by Pham Van Dong in early January. They acted with some assurance that Hanoi would respond, the Soviets having indicated that North Vietnam would be receptive to a proposal for direct contact. The move may have been designed to convey to North Vietnam that, despite MARIGOLD, the United States remained interested in negotiations, and Washington was certainly eager to ascertain whether, as the Poles had alleged, North Vietnam had been ready to talk in December. The North Vietnamese probably responded for much the same reason the United States had acted. Their curiosity had also been piqued by MARIGOLD, and they were probably especially interested to determine the extent to which the United States had been prepared to negotiate on the basis of Lewandowski's Ten Points.

In view of the apparent motives of the belligerents, it is not surprising that the Moscow channel led nowhere. U.S. chargé d'affaires John Guthrie met with North Vietnam's chargé Le Chang on six separate occasions and presented detailed expositions of the American bargaining position. Guthrie offered nothing that was new, however, and his restatement of earlier U.S. stands on such issues as the political future of South Vietnam may have persuaded Hanoi that nothing could be gained from negotiations at this time. Moreover, the two nations quickly reverted to the old impasse on de-escalation. Le Chang flatly rejected Guthrie's renewed offer of the Phase

A–Phase B formula originally proposed during MARIGOLD. On January 28, Foreign Minister Trinh issued with considerable fanfare what came to be known as the "Trinh formula," indicating that talks "could begin" if the United States stopped the bombing unconditionally. The tone of the statement, as well as its wording, hinted at a greater North Vietnamese willingness to negotiate and aroused widespread speculation in the press that talks might be imminent. In fact, however, the two nations were back where they had been before MARIGOLD, the United States insisting on some form of mutual de-escalation, North Vietnam demanding that the bombing be stopped without condition.

In the final stages of the Moscow contact, moreover, the American position on mutual de-escalation hardened significantly. Sometime in late January, perhaps in response to the Trinh statement, Johnson decided to address a personal appeal for peace to Ho Chi Minh. Early drafts of the proposed letter apparently contained the standard Phase A–Phase B formula, leaving a time lag between stoppage of the bombing and an end to North Vietnamese infiltration. By the time the letter to Ho was actually delivered in Moscow on February 8, however, the United States was insisting that it would terminate the bombing only after infiltration "had stopped." The SUNFLOWER documents shed little light on the precise timing or reasons for the change of policy. William Bundy later explained, however, that Washington had received "very reliable, sensitive intelligence" that North Vietnam had moved three full divisions into the area just north of the demilitarized zone. Ever suspicious of its adversary, the administration feared that Hanoi might send the troops into South Vietnam and then accept the Phase A–Phase B proposal, insisting that the United States stop the bombing and cease reinforcing its own troops in the South. "We weren't going to sit still for that," Bundy affirmed.[1]

Before the letter to Ho had been delivered, Wilson had initiated his ill-fated peace move. The Prime Minister had long regarded himself as a potential Vietnam peacemaker. Britain's role as co-chairman of the Geneva Conference gave him formal justification to intercede, London's "special relationship" with Washington appeared to give him influence with the United States, and he seems also to have cherished exaggerated notions of his influence with Moscow. Like other would-be mediators, Wilson was enticed by the prestige that could be gained from successful mediation. Perhaps more important, by early 1967 he was under considerable pressure from many members of his own Labour Party who felt he had attached Britain too closely to U.S. policy on Vietnam. According to Foreign Secretary George Brown, Wilson therefore decided to use the occasion of Kosygin's February visit to London to launch a "tremendous effort" to bring about peace talks.[2]

1. Bundy Oral History Interview, Johnson Library.
2. George Brown, *In My Way* (London: Gollancz, 1971), p. 143.

Although notably unenthusiastic about Wilson's move, the Johnson administration had little choice but to go along. Having just been burned in a third-party initiative, American officials much preferred to operate through the direct channel already opened in Moscow. They profoundly distrusted Wilson, moreover, feeling that his overeagerness might trap them into negotiations on unfavorable terms. At the same time, they could hardly appear to oppose a serious peace initiative and they hesitated to antagonize the one nation that had been consistent in its support. Reluctantly and with considerable skepticism and suspicion, they gave Wilson the go-ahead.

The recent change in the American position on mutual de-escalation hopelessly snarled the Wilson initiative. Through either sheer carelessness or bureaucratic confusion, Washington did not make clear to London the policy change written into the letter to Ho. Wilson therefore launched his peace move on the assumption that the original Phase A–Phase B formula, which he had been authorized to present to the Russians the preceding November, still represented the American position. After nearly a week of unproductive discussions, he finally persuaded a wary Kosygin to deliver to Hanoi a slightly modified version of the proposal and, before securing formal approval from the United States, actually gave the Russian a written statement purporting to be the official American stance. When a horrified Johnson administration belatedly discovered what had happened, it insisted that the earlier statement be retracted immediately and Kosygin be informed of the actual and much tougher American policy.

The misunderstanding produced Anglo-American recriminations comparable to Suez and Kennedy's cancellation of the Skybolt missile project in 1962. U.S. officials were outraged that Wilson had jumped the gun without their authorization. Only recently embarrassed in front of the Russians by American refusal to inform him of MARIGOLD, Wilson now bitterly complained of the "hell of a situation" in which he had been placed. "Never before or since has the 'hot line' between No. 10 and the White House been so hot as it was during that period," Brown later wrote.[3] Wilson's subsequent efforts to retrieve something from the imbroglio only produced additional bad feeling. The United States reluctantly approved his last-minute proposal to extend the Tet bombing truce and have Kosygin present to Hanoi yet another formula for a mutual pullback of forces and a cease-fire, but it gave him less than twenty-four hours to complete the transaction. What Wilson later described as a "historic opportunity" broke down under this "utterly unrealistic timetable."[4]

Both nations share responsibility for the SUNFLOWER debacle. Washington's failure to make clear to Wilson the change in policy stands as a classic example

3. Ibid., p. 144.
4. Harold Wilson, *The Labour Government, 1964–70: A Personal Record* (London: Michael Joseph, 1971), pp. 354–365.

of diplomatic bungling, and the Prime Minister had ample reason to assume that he was acting within his authorization. On the other hand, in his eagerness to commit Kosygin and get peace talks underway, Wilson was guilty of at least an impropriety in passing to the Russians what was presumably an American offer without first securing formal clearance from Washington.

Wilson's later claim that the United States had undermined a promising peace initiative appears a self-serving overstatement, however. After an initial period of hesitancy, Kosygin did agree to intercede with Hanoi, but the Russians were probably indulging in a delicate double game, appearing forthcoming to the West without in any way threatening Hanoi's position. Even if Kosygin was genuinely committed to using Soviet influence for peace, moreover, his leverage was quite restricted. He could not push Hanoi beyond the point it wished to go without giving substance to Chinese charges of Soviet collusion with the United States. Under these circumstances, it is difficult to see how he could have secured North Vietnam's acceptance of the Phase A–Phase B formula, which it had already rejected, or the much tougher proposal in Johnson's letter, which it would flatly turn down in Ho's response of February 15. The U.S. deadline in Wilson's second proposal was indeed unrealistic and it conveniently permitted Kosygin to get off the hook, but a more flexible timetable probably would not have made any difference. The deadlock on deescalation was firmly set. It would not be broken for another year and even then the two belligerents still adhered to irreconcilable positions on the basic issues of the war, most notably the political future of South Vietnam.

The SUNFLOWER documents provide a fascinating case study in the complexities of peacemaking and the perils of third-party intercession. Because of British involvement, they are more heavily sanitized than the other sections of the negotiating volumes. When supplemented with the memoirs of some of the key figures, however, they fill in most of the details of a complicated, confusing, and intriguing story. In the final analysis, they make clear the extent to which both North Vietnam and the United States had staked out positions that could not be reconciled by the efforts of well-meaning intermediaries and would not in fact be resolved until the stalemate on the battlefield had been broken.—*Ed.*

SUNFLOWER

This study has three parts: (1) a very brief list of the most important dates in Sunflower; (2) an analytic discussion of the major questions which arose; and (3) a detailed chronology of events and communications. Part 2 is keyed to Part 3, using dates to indicate the source material on which the discussion is based.

Part I: Principal Dates

Part I

Principal Dates During Sunflower
(January-April 1967)

Jan. 5   Embassy Warsaw is told to cease contacts on negotiations with
           the Poles; Embassy Moscow is told to attempt deliver a message
           directly to the DRV Embassy, proposing confidential US-DRV
           exchanges "about the possibilities of achieving a peaceful
           settlement" in Vietnam.

Jan. 10   The message is passed in Moscow.

Jan. 17   The DRV Embassy in Moscow seeks clarification: What is meant
           by "secure arrangements?" What is the US position on settle-
           ment terms?

Jan. 20   The US replies that its position on settlement would be the
           appropriate topic for two-way discussions, and suggests possi-
           ble subject headings for such talks. "Secure" means that no
           other parties would be informed.

Jan. 27   The DRV replies with an Aide-Memoire denouncing US aggression
           and stating that "The unconditional cessation (of US attacks
           on the North) being materialized, the DRV could then exchange
           views with US concerning the place or date for contact" as
           proposed by the US message of January 10.

Jan. 28   Burchett's interview with Trinh is broadcast by Hanoi, saying
           that "it is only after the unconditional cessation (of US
           attacks on the North) . . . that there could be talks."

Jan. 31   The US replies in writing, objecting to the broadcast of the
           "essence" of the confidential communication to it, offering
           to discuss mutual de-escalation or to hold secret talks on
           settlement terms before finding a formula for stopping the
           bombing.

Feb. 6   Kosygin arrives in London for a week's visit. He and the
           British immediately turn to the prospects for negotiations
           on Vietnam.

Feb. 8   President Johnson's letter to Ho, proposing mutual de-
           escalation, is delivered in Moscow.

Feb. 7-13 An intense round of UK-USSR talks occurs in London. The
           British work closely with US representatives on the scene.
           There are numerous communications between London and Washing-
           ton, on the one side, and between London and Moscow and
           London and Hanoi on the Communist side. The US advances
           various de-escalatory proposals, none of which is accepted.

Feb. 13   The bombing of the DRV, which had been suspended for the
          Tet truce and the balance of Kosygin's visit to London,
          is resumed immediately after his departure.

Feb. 15   Ho replies to the President, rejecting his proposal and
          re-iterating the Trinh formula about talks. The DRV
          terminates the contacts between Embassies in Moscow.

Mar. 21   The DRV broadcasts the Johnson-Ho letter exchange.

Apr. 6   Embassy Moscow delivers another note to the DRV Embassy
          proposing that contacts be resumed. It is returned the
          same day, opened but marked "unacceptable."

Part II: Discussion

I. How Sunflower Came to Focus on De-Escalation

At Polish insistence, the Marigold exchanges (roughly June-December 1966) tended to focus on possible terms for a final · settlement in Vietnam. The US had preferred, and several times proposed, mutual de-escalation as the first issue for consideration, on the grounds that this would produce a favorable atmosphere in which to discuss final settlement terms. The Poles resisted this approach, arguing that the Vietnamese Communists viewed de-escalation as preserving the SVN status quo, which they were fighting precisely to change. It would be easier to bring the DRV to the conference table, they argued, by first addressing the new status quo.

With the collapse of Marigold in December 1966, Sunflower became the primary vehicle for US negotiating efforts, as the US attempted to deal directly with the DRV. Gronouski was instructed to take no further initiative in Warsaw. (Marigold 1/6/67) Guthrie was instructed to seek direct contact with the DRV Embassy in Moscow, proposing the establishment of "completely secure arrangements for exchanging communications" between the two governments in "any capital where we both maintain posts." The proposed subject matter was extremely broad, "the possibilities of achieving a peaceful settlement of the Vietnamese dispute." Discussions could have begun with settlement terms or de-escalation. (1/5/67) This message was passed on January 10. (1/10/67)

The DRV responded first informally by asking "clarification" of the US position on terms of settlement. (1/17/67) On January 20, we replied that the DRV already had considerable information on the US position; further elaboration should now occur through the two-way discussions we were proposing. Illustrative agenda topics were suggested. (1/17/67, 1/20/67)

The DRV then replied formally on January 27 in a stiffly worded Aide-Memoire which (1) denounced the US for "intensifying the war in South Vietnam and escalating the bombing of North Vietnam"; (2) ridiculed US proposals for "conditional suspension of bombing" and "conditional withdrawal of troops" as schemes to prolong US dominance of SVN; (3) insisted that the US "recognize the 4 point stand of the DRV and the 5 point statement of the NLF" if it "really wants peace and seeks a political solution"; and (4) demanded the unconditional end of attacks on the DRV as the condition for the contacts proposed by the US note of January 10. (1/27/67)

The last point contained the obstacle to the further development of Sunflower. The operational passage reads (in Hanoi's "unofficial translation" into English): "The unconditional cessation of bombing and all other acts of war against the DRV being

1

materialized, the DRV could then exchange views with the US concerning the place or date for contact between the two parties as
the USG proposed in its message handed over on January 10, 1967."

On the following day, January 28, the DRV Foreign Minister,
Trinh, made a parallel statement in an "interview" with Burchett.
As broadcast by Hanoi in English, he said, "It is only after the
unconditional cessation of US bombing and all other acts of war
against the DRV that there could be talks between the DRV and the
US." (1/28/67)

There are several notable features of the DRV response:

--It gives nothing away with respect to terms for closing
out the war. These remain US recognition of the DRV 4 points, etc.

--It identifies a new stage in the negotiating process-"talks"
(Trinh) or the "exchange (of) views with the US concerning the place
or date for contact" (Aide-Memoire)--which is different from, and
hence undoubtedly less than, a fullfledged negotiation.

--It makes "unconditional cessation" of attacks on the DRV a
prior condition for even this level of contact.

--The language of the Aide-Memoire, a private communication,
holds forth greater promise that contact would indeed follow the
cessation of attacks on the North than does Trinh speaking publicly,
but even it is not without ambiguity. Washington is given very little
notion of what it would get in exchange for a bombing cessation.[1]

As compared with Marigold, this surely amounted to a major
hardening of the DRV position on the matter of establishing contact
with the US. At the same time, by making its position public, Hanoi
added to the considerable pressure already felt by the US to push
toward negotiations. Although the Trinh interview, the Salisbury[1]
visit to NVN, and the diplomatic campaign being waged by the Poles were
all designed to increase US embarrassment over the outcome of Marigold,
they could also be interpreted as reflecting growing DRV discomfort
under the impact of the bombing. It seemed possible, therefore, that
Hanoi was more desirous than formerly of getting the bombing stopped
and perhaps even of negotiating an acceptable end to the war.

The problem for Washington was demonstrating its responsiveness
to any opportunity to negotiate a settlement, without throwing away
its blue chip, the bombing campaign. Our solution was to ask again
for military reciprocity as well as talks in exchange for a bombing
halt.

----
[1] On February 6, Kosygin told Wilson in London that he had just been
in direct contact with Hanoi and could confirm that Hanoi would talk
if the bombing stopped. (2/6/67)

2

In one sense, then, Sunflower may have seemed a step backward from Marigold, in that it focused on conditions for starting talks to the exclusion of further consideration of settlement terms. On the other hand, it turned attention back to de-escalation, the US preferred topic.

It should be noted, however, that the U.S. alone was not responsible for turning the play back to military reciprocity and de-escalation. Hanoi's January 27 message and January 28 Trinh statement were as much, if not more, the cause of the shift. The U.S. message of January 10 was so general as to allow Hanoi to respond either with settlement terms or de-escalatory proposals. The fact that Hanoi chose the latter, probably recognizing that neither side was prepared to make further military concessions at this point, may indicate that North Vietnam was not anxious for or desirous of talks or negotiations except on its own terms in the first part of 1967.

The U.S. seemed to understand the Sunflower contacts in just this light. Referring to the Trinh statement and Sunflower, one of the U.S. principals wrote:

"Yet it may not be enough to say that Hanoi has simply been engaged in this public campaign. In order to make its own position effective, Hanoi has had to weaken and almost to eliminate its previous stress on the four points and recognition of the NLF. Its propaganda suggests that it has been somewhat pressed to explain this shift to its own people and the NLF. In short, Hanoi took some risks and perhaps, in the eyes of its people, made a significant change in its position.

"Against this background, Hanoi's rejection of our proposal, on February 14, was hardly surprising. As we knew at the time, the proposal was extremely unfavorable to them -- although also the only one we could have made in this area. Moreover, Hanoi had only five days to weigh this concrete proposal, and had to do so under what may well have been the worst possible circumstances from their standpoint -- with the high probability of our resumption hanging over them. In other words, the firm and sharp rejection was almost what we had to expect at this stage. It was not a clear indicator that Hanoi is dug in."

In short, neither side expected to enter talks at this time.

II. "Unconditional" and "Permanent"

There is, and perhaps will always remain, some confusion as to whether Hanoi's condition for talks during Sunflower was an "unconditional" or a "permanent and unconditional" cessation of the attacks on NVN.[1]   In trying to sort out this question, it is useful to distinguish four kinds of DRV demands:

(1) Demands with nothing offered in exchange. These reflect ultimate DRV objectives, no doubt, but they are non-operational, in that there is no consequence for non-compliance, no reward for compliance. As they are essentially statements of principle, they are the toughest of all.

(2) Demands posed as conditions for "establishing peace." Here, peace is the quid pro quo. It would be a large reward if earned, but it is a long way off because so many steps must be taken first. These rank second in toughness, therefore.

(3) Demands posed to provide a "basis for negotiations."

(4) Demands posed as conditions for "talks." From the Trinh interview on, these became the operational elements in the exchanges.

Sometimes more than one kind of demand is posed in the same document or statement, with the result that varying degrees of toughness are reflected in different connections.

--The DRV Aide-Memoire demanded US recognition of the DRV 4 points, etc., "if the US really wants peace" (1/27/67, para C); but it demanded the "unconditional cessation" (not "permanent and unconditional") of attacks on the DRV in exchange for talks. (1/27/67, para D.)

--The Trinh interview demanded at one point that US attacks "stop definitively and unconditionally," offering nothing in exchange (1/30/67, response to question 2); but it said at another that "only after the unconditional cessation of the bombing . . . could there be talks." (1/30/67, response to question 3) (Emphasis supplied)

--Ho Chi Minh's February 15 letter to the President contains parallel formulations: for the "restoration of peace" attacks "must stop definitively and unconditionally," the US must recognize the NLF, etc; but it is "only after unconditional cessation . . . that the DRV and the US could enter into talks." (1/15/67, para F.)

In Ho's February 13 letter to the Pope, he says the US must "end' unconditionally and definitively the bombing . . ., withdraw from SVN

---

[1] In some texts, especially DRV translations into English, the term "definitive" is used instead of "permanent." The meaning is almost certainly the same, both terms being English equivalents of the French "definitive."

4

. . ., recognize the NLFSV . . . . Only in such conditions can
real peace be restored in Vietnam." (2/13/67) Comparing this with
Trinh's statement, Mai Van Bo explained to the New York Times that
Ho's "message referred to the terms of a settlement and not to the
process of getting peace talks started. Therefore it did not constitute a change over the Vietnamese position." (2/23/67) Bo went
on to make clear that he and the Times correspondent were having a
"conversation," not an "interview." For an "interview," he would
have insisted on written questions and would have given written
answers. The point here is the emphasis laid on textual precision.
Bo complained that neither President Johnson nor Secretary Rusk had
ever quoted Trinh's statement fully or accurately, proof, he said,
of bad faith since Hanoi's real position was fully known and understood in Washington.

Bo may well have been wrong about Washington's understanding.
Unfortunately, he did not spell out the distortions he thought had
occurred. Unfortunately, too, his "conversation" added to the
ambiguity, since he is described (but not quoted) as arguing that
"any cessation of bombing that was not clearly labeled 'permanent
and unconditional' would leave the 'threat of bombing' in tact and
thus would constitute an unacceptable interference with the negotiation." Since he had not answered in writing, it is not clear if he
intentionally introduced a new formulation or if the Times synthe-
sized his views in a way he would not have done.

None of the official DRV texts examined for this study (letters
from Ho, "interviews" with DRV officials, Hanoi broadcasts, Aides-
Memoire, etc.) demand a "permanent" halt to the attacks as a condition
for talks. These materials cover the period January-April 1967. It
seems most likely, therefore, that this was not a condition during
the period in which Sunflower was active.

Inexplicably, the U.S. did not seem alive to the distinctions
being made by Hanoi. We persisted in reading the terms as demanding
both "unconditional and permanent." We also showed no awareness of
the difference between "talks," "negotiations," and "settlement"
or "peace." Whether having been alert to these distinctions would
have altered our behavior is problematical.

III. Reciprocity

Whether or not the DRV was demanding a "permanent" halt in the bombing, it is entirely clear that their demand from January 27 on was for an "unconditional" one. Hanoi was explicitly refusing the military reciprocity the US had repeatedly asked for if the bombing were to stop. At the very outset of Sunflower, then, the issue was firmly joined between the two sides on this matter.

DRV intransigence may have received some encouragement from our unilateral suspension of bombing within 10 miles of Hanoi's center on December 24, 1966. From the Communist vantage point, this may have appeared as a response to pressures on the US generated by the collapse of Marigold, the Salisbury reportage, messages from U Thant and the Pope, etc.[2] If we would give this much to keep the prospects of US-DRV contacts alive, perhaps we could be made to give much more.

On the other hand, we had indicated at the outset that our action was taken unilaterally, but in the hope of seeing a reciprocal gesture from the other side. Harriman made clear to Dobrynin on January 17 that we did not feel bound to maintain the sanctuary indefinitely in the absence of some response from Hanoi.

The response, when it came, had a little carrot, "there could be talks," and a lot of stick, "there would be no reciprocity." Our response was to probe for concealed reciprocity. Perhaps the other side would give something in exchange, if not forced to do so openly.

One point should be made clear -- the DRV has never stated that it would not reciprocate militarily at some future point. Hanoi was stating simply that it would not reciprocate prior to or in exchange for a U.S. bombing cessation. Its objective seems to have been (and still is) to remove the bombings as a "blue chip."

From our vantage point, we were working two different strategies. The first strategy was that we would not stop the bombing in exchange for talks alone; there had to be reciprocity, preferably a DRV infiltration stoppage. The second strategy was to circumvent the reciprocity issue entirely and to concentrate on getting "discussions" started without any de-escalatory act by either side. This was embodied in the statement that the U.S. was prepared for "unconditional discussions" at any time.

6

IV. Specific US Proposals for De-Escalation

When Sunflower went active, early in January, the US already had several de-escalatory proposals outstanding. During Sunflower, several more were made.

Earlier Proposals

(1) Goldberg's UN Speech. (September 22, 1966) The US offered "to order a cessation of all bombing of NVN--the moment we are assured, privately or otherwise, that this step will be answered promptly by a corresponding and appropriate de-escalation on the other side." (Marigold, 9/22/66) This proposal invited the DRV to suggest its own matching action--which would have to be accepted by, or renegotiated with, the US. Upon agreement, the US step would be taken first.

The offer was repeated in more general terms on December 31, when Goldberg wrote U Thant, "we are ready to order a prior end to all bombing of North Vietnam the moment there is an assurance, private or otherwise, that there would be a reciprocal response toward peace from North Vietnam." Goldberg specified that he was reaffirming his September offer and indicated that the NVN response should be "tangible." However, this time he did not use the terms "promptly" and "corresponding and appropriate de-escalation." (12/31/66) Carefully read, the proposal was unchanged, but an impression of greater liberality on the US side may have been given.

(2) Phase A-Phase B. This was an elaboration of the Goldberg proposal sent on a highly confidential basis to the DRV in November 1966, via the Poles and quite independently via the British (Wilson and Brown) by way of the Russians. It was intended as a face-saving package, "which in its totality represented what both we and Hanoi would agree to as a reasonable measure of mutual de-escalation, but which would have two separate phases in its execution. Phase A would be a bombing suspension, while Phase B, which would follow after some adequate period, would see the execution of all the other agreed de-escalatory actions. Hanoi's actions taken in Phase B would appear to be in response to our actions in Phase B rather than to the bombing suspension." (Marigold 11/13/66, 11/16/66) The steps to be taken by both sides in Phase B were again left open for discussion with the DRV.

(3) The Hanoi Sanctuary. On December 24, 1966, we informed the DRV via the Poles that US air strikes within 10 nautical miles of the center of Hanoi would be stopped and that the US would be impressed by some reciprocal de-escalatory step on the Communist side. (Marigold 12/24/66) We suggested the cessation of VC terrorist activity within 10 miles of Saigon's center as such a step and set up a watch in Saigon to see if the other side responded. No positive response, verbal or de-escalatory was forthcoming.

Subsequent Proposals

As Sunflower unfolded, the earlier proposals were re-iterated and some new ones advanced:

(4) Expanding on the Hanoi Sanctuary. On January 31, the US through secret channels drew DRV attention to the bombing sanctuary around Hanoi and offered "to implement additional measures to de-escalate the bombing of the North to create conditions conducive to the success of talks with the DRV. We, of course, would be impressed with similar acts of restraint on the part of the DRV," which, if forthcoming, need not be publicized. (1/31/67) This leaves it to the DRV to suggest reciprocal acts and suggests that the US would be willing to act first. (In this note, we also urged the DRV again to consider the Phase A-Phase B formula.)

(5) President Johnson's February 3 Press Conference. In response to a question asking "what kind of other steps the other side should take for this suspension of bombing," the President responded, "Just almost any step. . . . . We would be glad to explore any reciprocal action that they or any of their spokesmen would care to suggest." The language is forthcoming in tone, but makes no commitment to do more than "explore" suggestions of the other side. (Marigold 2/3/67)

(6) Baggs-Ashmore. On February 5, Harry Ashmore wrote Ho Chi Minh, conveying a message he had drafted with State's cooperation.[3] He described US officials as interested "in your suggestion to us that private talks could begin provided the US stopped bombing your country and ceased introducing additional US troops into Vietnam. They expressed the opinion that some reciprocal restraint to indicate that neither side intended to use the occasion of the talks for military advantage would provide tangible evidence of the good faith of all parties in the prospects for a negotiated settlement." The letter then asked Ho to respond to this point. (2/5/67) Thus it offered no US action until Hanoi's reciprocation was indicated, nor did it specify US willingness to stop the bombing first. The reciprocal act was to be a "tangible evidence of good faith," but one sufficient in magnitude to indicate that neither side intended to gain a military advantage.

(7) President Johnson's Letter to Wilson.[4] On February 6 or 7, the President wrote confidentially to Wilson that we planned "to inform Hanoi that if they will agree to an assured stoppage of infiltration into SVN, we will stop the bombing of NVN and stop further augmentation of US forces in SVN." This was based on the understanding that a bombing suspension was unacceptable to Hanoi and the US had to "accept an unconditional and permanent cessation of bombing." It is not really explicit about which side is to act first, though it may have read to Wilson, who had previously passed

the Phase A-Phase B proposal, as if we would stop bombing when the other side "agreed" to stop infiltration.

(8) <u>President Johnson's Letter to Ho</u>.[5] On February 8, the President sent a confidential letter to Ho in which he offered to stop bombing the DRV and stop augmenting US forces in SVN "as soon as I am assured that infiltration into SVN by land and by sea has stopped." This, for the first time, spelled out a measure of reciprocity the US would consider acceptable. As with the letter to Wilson, this proposal was based on the understanding that Hanoi required a permanent and unconditional end to attacks before talks. As compared with earlier US proposals, it clearly reversed the order of events: infiltration would stop first, then the US would stop bombing and augmenting force levels. Embassy Moscow was instructed to deliver this message on February 7, but was unable to do so until the 8th. The date of its drafting is not available in the materials used for this study.

(9.) <u>Revised 14 Points</u>. On February 9, Secretary Rusk drew attention to a newly annotated statement of the US 14 Points For Peace, of which the fourteenth included the following: "We are prepared to order a cessation of all bombing of NVN, the moment we are assured—privately or otherwise—that this step will be answered promptly by a corresponding and appropriate de-escalation of the other side. (2/9/67) Here, again, the US offers to act first and the nature of the reciprocal action is left open.

(10) <u>Goldberg's Howard University Speech</u>. On February 10, Goldberg stated, "The United States remains prepared to take the first step and order a cessation of all bombing of NVN the moment we are assured, privately or otherwise, that this step will be answered promptly by a tangible response toward peace from NVN." (2/10/67)

(11) <u>US Version of British Proposal</u>. Late on February 10, the British passed Kosygin a draft proposal, cleared by Washington. It indicated that the US would order a cessation of bombing as soon as it was assured that infiltration had stopped; within a few days, the US would stop further augmenting its force in SVN. The deal was to be communicated confidentially to Hanoi, and DRV acceptance could be kept secret as well. (2/12/67)

(12) <u>Extension of Tet Truce</u>. Late on February 12, the President wired Wilson, authorizing him to approach Kosygin with this proposal: "If you can get a North Vietnamese assurance—communicated either direct to the US or through you—before 10:00 a.m. British time tomorrow that all movement of troops and supplies into SVN will stop at that time, I will get an assurance from the US that they will not resume bombing NVN from that time. Of course the US build-up would also then stop within a matter of days." (2/12/67)

As the US had already stopped bombing for Tet, the sequence would in effect be: US bombing halt; DRV infiltration halt; US build-up halt. At British request, the time limit was later extended by six hours, to 4 p.m. British time. Even with this, the time allowed for a DRV response was short, and the problem of actually stopping the movement of men and supplies in that period would have been substantial.

TOP SECRET - NODIS

US De-Escalatory Proposals

	Proposal	Date	Parties	Channel Public or Confidential	Sequence of Steps First	Second
1.	Goldberg's UN Speech	9/22/66	Public Pronouncement		US stops bombing	Corresponding, appropriate de-escalation of other side
2.	Phase A-Phase B	mid-Nov.66	Poles	Confidential	US stops bombing	Both sides de-escalate further after adequate period
3.	Hanoi Sanctuary	12/24/66	Poles	Confidential	US had already stopped bombing near Hanoi	Some reciprocal step hoped for
4.	Expanding on Hanoi Sanctuary	1/31/67	US-DRV	Confidential	US extends bombing sanctuary	Similar act of restraint from other side
5.	President's Press Conference	2/3/67	Public Pronouncement		Sequence not specified	
6.	Baggs-Ashmore	2/5/67	Ashmore Letter to Ho	Confidential		Sequence not specified
7.	President's Letter to Wilson	2/7/67	UK	Confidential		Sequence not specified
8.	President's Letter to Ho	2/8/67	US-DRV	Confidential	DRV infiltration stops	US bombing & troop buildup stop
9.	Revised 14 points	2/9/67	Public Pronouncement		US stops bombing	Corresponding, appropriate de-escalation of other side
10.	Goldberg's Howard Speech	2/10/67	Public Pronouncement		US stops bombing	Tangible response toward peace
11.	US Version of British Proposal	2/10/67	UK-USSR	Confidential	DRV infiltration stops	US bombing & troop buildup stop
12.	Tet Truce Extension	2/12/67	UK-USSR	Confidential	US bombing was already stopped	DRV infiltration to stop, followed by stop in US troop build-up

TOP SECRET - NODIS

11

V. DRV Responses, Verbal and Military

There are indications of varying firmness that all of these
proposals were in fact conveyed to Hanoi, though it is not clear
how quickly they all arrived. The DRV Embassy in Moscow confirmed
prompt transmission of all the communications passed to it, including the President's letter of February 8. On the other hand, Ho
claimed to have received the letter only on February 10. Kosygin
indicated that he was in quick communication with DRV authorities
(a matter of hours for a message and reply) during his London visit
(see e.g., 2/6/67).[1] As the deadline for ending the Tet truce
approached on February 13, "President's Cipher" telegrams were sent
from the Soviet delegation in London to Moscow, Kosygin spoke with
Brezhnev about the proposals by telephone, and the DRV Embassy in
Moscow transmitted, then received, cipher messages from Hanoi.
(2/13/67)

In its Aide-Memoire to the US on January 27 and the Trinh interview of January 28, the DRV firmly rejected reciprocity in the matter
of de-escalation. No further direct communication with the US was
made by Hanoi until Ho's letter to President Johnson of February 15,
which repeated the Trinh formula in rejecting reciprocity. In
accompanying oral remarks, the DRV Charge also said he could no
longer meet with US representatives in Moscow.

At 3:32 p.m. British time, February 13, just 28 minutes before
the expiration of the deadline on the US proposal for using the Tet
truce to begin de-escalation, Hanoi broadcast a letter from Ho to
the Pope. Ho was sharp in tone, denouncing US aggression and demanding an unconditional and definitive cessation of all attacks on the
DRV, US withdrawal from SVN and recognition of the NLF as the conditions for "peace." He did not refer to conditions for "talks."
(2/13/67) Carefully read, therefore, the letter did not address the
question of mutual de-escalation, as a first step toward negotiations.
However, its timing and tone gave the impression of a rebuff to US
proposals.

Earlier, the DRV had positioned two divisions within or just
north of the DMZ. During the last week of January and the first
week of February, an additional division was believed to have moved
south. With the Tet truce, the movement of supplies southward
between the 19th and 17th parallels in the DRV increased sharply,
to a rate about double that of the Christmas truce and several times
that of non-truce periods. Thus throughout the first weeks of Sunflower, the Communists seemed increasingly to be positioning themselves to undertake combat operations at a substantially increased
level. (2/9/67)

---

[1]According to a forthcoming CIA study, only 2 of the 14 DRV Politburo
members were known to be in Hanoi in early February. Two had gone
to Peking. Possibly some were also in Moscow, to tighten liaison
with the Russians during Kosygin's London visit.

US sensitivity to this deployment increased as the talks in
London proceeded and the possibility that the other side might
actually accept a proposal for a bombing halt grew more vivid.
This threat was emphasized by US officials, in explaining our
sudden reluctance to agree firmly to a permanent bombing cessation which would be followed only after some interval by a halt
to infiltration. The DRV divisions might be committed during
such an interval, without technically violating the agreement.

It is not at all clear what the other side hoped to accomplish by this tactic. The deployments were occurring throughout
January and early February, and the other side was aware, through
our public statements, that we knew of them. They certainly
worked against any possibility that we would finally accede to a
truly unconditional cessation of attacks on the North. It even
made more difficult the much lesser task of inducing us to stop
bombing first on the assurance of a subsequent--probably ill-
defined--reciprocal restraint from the other side. It was well
designed, on the other hand, to produce the result which actually
followed: no agreement on de-escalation, but a sharp upsurge in
the fighting instead.

On this reading, Hanoi preferred the sword to the conference
table, except if it could get talks on its own terms. Insofar
as Hanoi believed that its terms were not buyable by the U.S.,
the Trinh interview et al seems to signal less an attempt to get
the bombing stopped and/or to talk than to find a more effective
political posture from which to continue prosecuting the war. To
put it another way, the Trinh interview may mark DRV discouragement about winning its objectives via negotiations and an increased
reliance on fighting and propaganda. Hanoi may well have been
moved toward this posture by the following factors in combination:
(1) The relatively tough stance revealed by the US during Marigold,
toward both settlement terms and the circumstances under which we
were willing to start talks; (2) The sensitivity to criticism,
leveled either against our desire for negotiations or the bombing
campaign against the North, revealed by the US after the Marigold
contact aborted and Salisbury visited the DRV; and (3) The repeated
urging of the DRV's European supporters to adopt a more forthcoming
attitude toward negotiations.

An alternative interpretation has been advanced, however, by
the Soviets. On February 17, Zinchuk told Bundy that Hanoi had
noted repeated statements by us that we had undertaken the bombing
in order to get Hanoi to talk. Hence, Hanoi had supposed that its
Burchett interview position of willingness to talk if we stopped the
bombing was a direct (and presumably acceptable) response to our own
position. This explanation does not take explicit account of the
DRV build-up around the DMZ nor conjecture as to the use that would
have been made of these forces in the event of an unconditional halt
in our bombing and US-DRV talks.

VI. The British Role

    The eagerness of the British leaders to participate with maximum
personal visibility in bringing peace to Vietnam⌟

(2/11/67,
2/12/67, 2/13/67)   At the time of Sunflower, we had direct contact
with the DRV in Moscow and needed no intermediary to make our views
known in Hanoi. On the other hand,
                                     and the importance of their support
for US policies not only in Vietnam, but elsewhere too, made the US
willing to bring the British into negotiation efforts. Furthermore,
Kosygin's visit to London in early February made British participation
inevitable. Kosygin and Wilson would discuss Vietnam and issue statements on it with or without a US input. If we stood aloof from it,
the results could be harmful to the US. And the possibility that
Kosygin could use Soviet influence in Hanoi introduced an element of
potential value, not available in direct US-DRV exchanges.

    Looking back on it, there seems little doubt that bringing the
British in was to US advantage. But there were adverse consequences
along the way:

    --Wilson made references, in Parliament and to the press, not
well veiled at all, to the transactions of Marigold and Sunflower.
(2/8/67, 2/14/67)   While these were not critical of the US, they
gave those not previously informed reason to believe that something
of substance had been afoot on the negotiations front. This was
alarming to the GVN and Troop Contributing Nations. It gave a peg
on which to hang other tendentious accounts of what "really" happened
in these episodes. And it seemed to contradict the President, who on
February 3 had said he had seen no action by the other side that he
could interpret as "a serious effort to either go to a conference table
or to bring the war to an end." (Marigold 2/3/67)

    --The battle of the tenses brought additional friction to the
US-UK relationship, including emotional personal communications between
Wilson and the President, Brown and the US Ambassador, etc., in which
the British leaders claimed to have been put in "a hell of a situation"
and questioned US intentions and consistency of policy in the search
for a negotiated settlement. This subject seems of sufficient importance to be treated separately. (See the next section.)

14

VII.   The Battle of the Tenses

By the end of January 1967, the US had outstanding at least. four de-escalatory proposals to the DRV, calling for the US to stop bombing as the first step. (See Section IV) The most detailed of these, the Phase A-Phase B proposal, actually emphasized this aspect as a face-saving device for the DRV, which would not then be forced openly to acknowledge reciprocity. This proposal had been passed via the British in mid-November 1966, and they were thoroughly familiar with it. When the President wrote to Ho, however, on February 8, he offered to stop bombing only "as soon as I am assured that infiltration into SVN by land and by sea has stopped." (Emphasis supplied.) The DRV had been assured that our contact with them would be kept entirely confidential, and no copy of the letter to Ho was given the British, nor, apparently, to the US representatives in London.

In the President's letter to Wilson (February 6 or 7) the question of which side would act first was not made explicit. Its language, therefore, was equally consistent with the Phase A- Phase B proposal or with the letter to Ho.

As soon as Kosygin arrived in London (February 6), he launched into discussions of Vietnam and China. Wilson responded by spelling out the Phase A-Phase B formula in detail. (2/6/67) When Kosygin failed to show interest, Wilson repeated the proposal on February 7 in even greater detail, giving it to Kosygin in writing and coming down repeatedly on the willingness of the US to act first. (2/7/67)

--"They (the US) recognize the need for a first and visible step. They further recognize that this step must mean the cessation of the bombing. This I believe they will do . . . ."

--"Because the USG know that the second stages will follow, they will therefore be able first to stop the bombing, ... "

So much for Phase A. Wilson structured the remainder of the President's proposal into a concrete version of Phase B.

--"The US are willing to stop the build-up of their forces in the South if they are assured that the movement of North Vietnamese forces from the North to the South will stop at the same time. Essentially therefore the two stages are kept apart."

--"But because the USG know that the second stages will follow, they will therefore be able first to stop the bombing . . . ."

The British felt encouraged by Kosygin's apparent interest and surmised that he had not understood the proposal when put to him by

15

Brown the previous November. They gave us a copy of the text
passed to Kosygin, and it was cabled that night to Washington.

Thus precisely as the President's letter to Ho was authorized for delivery in Moscow, the British were proposing a different sequence of the same actions to Kosygin in London. Their
idea was to incorporate the proposition into a joint statement by
the UK and USSR, as co-chairmen of the 1954 Geneva Conference. A
draft of such a statement was submitted to Washington, which
approved it with some revision, then passed to the Russians. In
the draft, however, the sequence of actions again became ambiguous,
as so often happens with the use of the English future tense.
(The co-chairmen were to ask assurances from the US that the bombing "will stop"; from NVN that the infiltration will stop"; and
again from the US that the troop build-up "will stop.") (2/9/67)

If the Russians demurred on the joint statement, the British
intended to push again on the Phase A-Phase B formula. As Kosygin
wanted to submit the latter to the DRV, the British gave it to him
once again in writing on the evening of February 10. At last,
however, their attention was drawn to the difference between their
sequence and the one envisioned by the US in the President's letter
to Ho. Late on the night of February 10, therefore, a revised
version was handed Kosygin, with the comment that it had been
authorized by the White House. The difference between the two
versions boiled down essentially to a change in tenses. The British
version said, "The US will stop bombing NVN as soon as they are
assured that infiltration from NVN to SVN will stop." The revised
version changed the last two words to "has stopped." (Emphasis
supplied.) (2/12/67 repeats the relevant texts.)

Wilson and Brown apparently took strong exception to the last
minute change of tenses, arguing that it undercut their credibility
as negotiators vis-a-vis the Russians and that they had based their
formulation on familiar US positions (the revised 14 points, etc.),
clearing their drafts with the US as they went along. (2/11/67)

We replied along several lines: (1) The proposal now under
discussion was different than that in the 14 points because it
offered additional US concessions: We would stop our troop build-up
as well as the bombing, in return for the DRV concession. (2) The
Russians were aware of the letter to Ho, hence they would have known
the sequence required by the US. The change in tense in the final
draft, therefore, would not surprise them or impair British credibility. (3) The NVA build-up around the DMZ posed a new military
situation, in which we simply could not risk a major assault from
the North in the interval between Phases A and B. (4) Finally,
the DRV had had the Phase A-Phase B formula for several months
without showing a "flicker of interest." It was unlikely, therefore, that the matter of sequence was critical. "Everyone seems

16

to wish to negotiate except Hanoi." (2/11/67, 2/12/67)

These answers apparently did not entirely assuage British feelings. In March, they raised the question again in a letter from Wilson to the President (3/16/67) and in conversation between Brown and Kaiser (3/21/67). They clearly hoped to continue a significant role as peacemakers and asked for reassurance on their understanding of current US positions, on avoiding similar "misunderstandings" in the future, and on the continuing US desire for negotiations.

Shortly after Kosygin's London visit, Bundy asked Zinchuk in Washington whether the problem of tenses had thrown the Soviets off; Zinchuk said that it had not significantly disturbed them. (2/17/67) However, in Moscow, about the same time, Kosygin's interpreter twitted Thompson about the episode, saying, "that was quite a switch you pulled on us in the text of your proposal." (2/17/67)

It can be argued, however, that the change in tenses was more serious. It could have been used as ammunition within the party presidium in Hanoi by those who believe the U.S. would not show "good faith" toward any agreements reached. It could still be used as part of a public propaganda exercise.

17

VIII. The Soviet Role

The British were first startled, then delighted, to find Kosygin eager to play in active role as intermediary between the US and Hanoi. Kosygin's interest was conveyed to us, of course, by the British, and we had no independent reading on his attitude. To some extent, their appraisal of his mood may have reflected their own great enthusiasm for the part. But even allowing for this, there was definitely a sharp change from previous Soviet reluctance to play the middleman, especially when subject to public exposure.[1] As already noted, Kosygin was several times in prompt, confidential communication with the DRV authorities during his stay in London. And he made a public statement expressing belief that the UK and USSR could make a "contribution to the settlement of the Vietnam issue on the basis of the Geneva agreement," by virtue of their roles as Geneva co-chairmen. (2/8/67)

What produced this change in Soviet attitudes? Were they acting on DRV behest? Or were they now willing to put pressure on Hanoi in pursuit of interests of their own?

Only a little light is shed on these questions by the materials relating to Kosygin's stay in London. He was apparently willing to transmit proposals for DRV consideration While he argued the general merits of the DRV's side of the war, he did not try to bargain or alter specifics of the proposals transmitted to him.

Yet on February 13, he was overheard (by telephone intercept) to tell Brezhnev of "a great possibility of achieving the aim, if the Vietnamese will understand the present situation that we have passed to them; they will have to decide. All they need to do is to give a confidential declaration." (2/13/67)

---

[1] In private dealings, however, the Russians apparently were not quite so aloof. This topic is treated in other studies of negotiating sequences. During Sunflower, too, there are cryptic allusions to earlier Soviet interventions. Thus Kosygin told Thompson on February 18 that

toward the proposals he was transmitting to Hanoi
suggests that he did not endorse them, but served as a more or less
neutral agent of transmission. His intermediation no doubt put the
DRV under obligation to respond seriously and with full explanations
of their decisions. This is a form of pressure, perhaps, but
not a strong one. Had he wished to invoke his full powers of per-
suasion, he should have tried for proposals he could support--or at
least for terms which, with the least possible further modification,
would seem palatable to Hanoi.

In a retrospective discussion with Thompson in Moscow, Kosygin
expressed a jaundiced view of the role of mediators, saying they
either complicated the problem or pretended they were doing something
when in fact they were not. (2/18/67) He had stepped into this
uncomfortable spot in London because "the Vietnamese had for the first
time stated they (were) ready to negotiate if the bombings were
stopped unconditionally; this was the first time they had done so and
it was a public statement." This could mean that the Trinh statement
had given him a green light that formerly was lacking. Of course,
as suggested earlier, the Trinh statement itself may have been issued
in part as a result of Soviet pressures. But the general picture,
though only faintly sketched in the materials at hand, is of considerable Soviet deference to Hanoi's views on this critical matter.:

(3/1/67)

How much the Russians had hoped in fact to accomplish during
Kosygin's London trip is impossible to know. They apparently har-
bored few expectations after his return. Kosygin complained to
Thompson about the "ultimatum" implied in the final proposal he
transmitted to Hanoi from London, saying that he knew it was hopeless
the minute he read it. He said the Soviets were not confident that
the US proposals had been serious, and that he could not venture to
propose anything constructive at that time.[1] (2/17/67)

When Bundy inquired of Zinchuk as to whether the Soviets had lost credit in Hanoi as a result of their handling of the London visit, the reply was firmly negative. Zinchuk said that "Hanoi continued to look to the Soviets to arrange a settlement that would protect their interests." (2/17/67)

To the extent that it is true, it again suggests the Russians were restrained in their advocacy vis-a-vis Hanoi.

No explanation is really satisfactory for Soviet behavior. The Kosygin-Brezhnev telephone conversation is inexplicable.

The very fact of intermediation, however, was important. No matter how much the Soviets disassociated themselves from the U.S. proposals, their willingness to transmit them was a form of pressure on the DRV. To the extent that Sunflower was a "serious" exchange, the Russians were probably playing a low cost game for the breaks.

IX.   A New Geneva Conference?

Kosygin's public reference to the UK-USSR Geneva co-chairmanship aroused British hopes that the Russians would join them in reconvening a Conference along the lines of 1954. (2/8/67) When they asked him if his remarks indicated a willingness to proceed in that direction, he replied that this was "not exactly" what he had meant to imply. "I proceeded upon the assumption that the main thing was for the UK and the Soviet Union to assist the two sides to meet together after the bombing stopped. After this has been done, there may be various proposals for moving further.
                          (2/9/67, emphasis supplied.) He emphasized that it was important to "do first things first."

Noting the bombing pause that would occur during Tet, Brown pressed him to think about asking the US not to resume and calling for a Geneva Conference to meet as soon as February 15. Kosygin said he would first want to know Hanoi's views. A Geneva Conference would be a "complicated issue."

"I could send this to Hanoi," he said, "but I am concerned about the difficulties." He decided finally to "think it over" and asked to have a proposition from the British in writing. (2/9/67) In the end, this topic was dropped, with no indication from the Russians as to what response they received from Hanoi---if indeed they ever put the issue to Hanoi at all.

21

X.   The Shadow of China

    As with Marigold, the chronicle of Sunflower is peppered with
emotional but extremely vague references to the role of the Chinese:
their antagonism toward a negotiated settlement in Vietnam, and
their baleful influence on the decision making processes in Hanoi.

(2/6/67)

    These remarks were obviously intended to put the US in a more
concessionary frame of mind. However, at the end of the interview,
Kosygin adverted to another topic, one that also arose during Marigold:

22

XI.   The End of Sunflower

·   With the resumption of bombing on February 13, after the Tet
Truce, it was relatively clear to all parties that talks were
unlikely to occur. However, events played themselves out with some
surprises.

Ho answered the President's letter with a brusque, if as yet unpublished, rejection on February 15. In handing the reply to our DCM
in Moscow, the DRV representative added several points orally: (1)
The US was "obstinate" in continuing to advance conditions for stopping
the bombing. (2) The US had used the Moscow contact to deceive public
opinion into believing that secret negotiations were going on while the
bombing continued. This may have been a reference to news leaks from
London about Sunflower, or from Washington and many other points about
Marigold. (3) The proposal for extending the Tet bombing halt was an
ultimatum. (4) The DRV wished no further contact in Moscow. (2/15/67)

The tone and substance of these communications was frosty, but
the fact that they had not been made public left the possibility that
the rejection might not be·final, as the Secretary remarked to Dobrynin
on February 23. Even this slender hope was destroyed on March 15,[6]
however, when Hanoi published the Johnson-Ho exchange of letters.

Since the President's letter referred to possible future meetings
"in Moscow, where contacts have already occurred," Hanoi's publication
of it confirmed to the world, including the Chinese and the Vietnamese
Communists, that such contacts had indeed taken place. This is
notable, in contrast with Hanoi's great insistence of secrecy in the
opening phases of the Sunflower and its complaints about publicity
when the Moscow contact was closed down.

Hanoi's decision to publish the letters was undoubtedly based on
the conviction that it would look appreciably more peace-loving than
the U.S. Never having violated the secrecy of contacts before or since,
Hanoi had to be sure of its ground and the costs in terms of future
U.S. communications and the morale of its own people. Equally, if
not more important, Hanoi could have calculated that public disclosure
of US-DRV contact could have made the GVN leaders more than uneasy.

The US tried nonetheless to keep the door to talks open and even
to resume direct contacts through another letter from the President to
Ho.[7] The message discussed the general benefits of a peaceful solution,
based on the 1954 and 1962 Geneva Accords, and urged the DRV to enter
talks toward that end. It made no specific proposals on de-escalation
or settlement terms. It was hand carried to the DRV Embassy in Moscow
on April 6, but returned by the Vietnamese to the U.S. Embassy mail box
on the same day with the original envelope having been opened, then
marked "non conforme! Retour a l'expediteur."

23

Addendum: Hindsight on Marigold

There were many allusions to Marigold during Sunflower, but only a modest amount of additional (often ambiguous) information:

--On February 17, Zinchuk told Bundy that the Soviets had gone back over Marigold with Hanoi and ascertained firmly that it had been "willing to talk, in the sense of exchanging views." The contact had been cancelled, he claimed, because of the December 13-14 bombing of Hanoi. (2/17/67)

--On February 23, Dobrynin told Rusk that the DRV Charge in Moscow came to the Soviet Foreign Ministry on December 15 to say that the DRV had instructed Rapacki to break off his talks with the US, "on the ground that the bombing just before that date meant the US thought it could pressure Hanoi to talk." (2/23/67)

--On December 23, Rapacki claimed to Brown that "after firm agreement on the original 10-point package, Lodge had consulted Washington and then reneged by raising new (unspecified) questions and points of interpretations. Before the Poles had a chance to do anything with these the December 13-14 bombings occurred, killing the entire project."

--On March 23, Dobrynin told Bundy

Dobrynin reiterated that the "bombing of December 13-14 had caused clear Hanoi rejection of the Warsaw meeting."

January 1, 1967 - New York Times

Special to The New York Times
UNITED NATIONS, N.Y., Dec. 31 - Following are the texts of a letter
yesterday by Secretary General Thant to Arthur J. Goldberg, the chief
United States delegate, and of Mr. Goldberg's reply today:

Thant's Letter

. . . .

Let me take this opportunity of reiterating my three-point program,[8]
to which I still firmly adhere:

1. The cessation of the bombing of North Vietnam;

2. The scaling down of all military activities by all sides in
   South Vietnam;

3. The willingness to enter into discussions with those who are
   actually fighting.

I strongly believe that this three-point program, of which the
cessation of the bombing of North Vietnam is the first and essential part,
is necessary to create the possibility of fruitful discussions leading
to a just and honorable settlement of the problem of Vietnam on the basis
of the Geneva Agreements of 1954.

I also wish to recall that in the course of the twenty-first session,
in the debate of the General Assembly, the majority of the delegations
have endorsed the three-point program. Many more heads of delegations
also specifically pleaded for the cessation of the bombing of North Vietnam. It seems to me that this is a very clear indication of the public
opinion of the world at large on this issue.

. . . .

Goldberg's Letter

. . . .

We have carefully reflected on your ideas, expressed in your
Dec. 30 letter and on previous occasions, about the cessation of bombing of North Vietnam. . . . I wish to assure you categorically that my
Government is prepared to take the first step toward peace: specifically,
we are ready to order a prior end to all bombing of North Vietnam the
moment there is an assurance, private or otherwise, that there would be
a reciprocal response toward peace from North Vietnam.

I am, thus reaffirming herewith an offer made before the General

Assembly-on Sept. 22 and again on Oct. 18.[9] We hope and trust that you will use every means at your disposal to determine what tangible response there would be from North Vietnam in the wake of such a prior step toward peace on our part.

. . . .

January 2, 1967

BEHIND THE LINES-HANOI, By Harrison E. Salisbury
(pp. 175-177) Chapter XVIII

. . . .

He (Pham Van Dong) then went into a discussion of the so-called "four points," the four points which Hanoi said constituted the "basis for a settlement of the Vietnam question."

There had been great controversy abroad about the significance of these four points. Were they to be considered pre-conditions for negotiation? Must the United States accept them before Hanoi would agree to sit down at a conference table?

The four points provided for (1) recognition of the peace, independence, sovereignty, unity and territorial integrity of Vietnam and the withdrawal of United States troops; (2) the noninterference of outside powers in the two zones of Vietnam; (3) settlement of South Vietnamese questions in accordance with the program of the National Liberation Front without foreign interference; and (4) peaceful reunification of Vietnam, to be settled by the people of both zones.

The attitude of the United States was that Hanoi was attempting to impose terms for a settlement before a conference, that the North Vietnamese insisted that the four points must be accepted first and that this meant talk at the conference table would be largely meaningless.

"These should not be considered 'conditions,'" Pham Van Dong now told me. "They are merely truths. The most simple thing is to recognize our sovereignty and our independence. It involves only recognizing the points in the Geneva agreements."

He said that the United States did not like to accept the four points and especially the third point about South Vietnam but, he insisted, we must come to a solution on the basis of the four points.

"Whichever way you may go around, finally you must come to the four points," he said. There were not preconditions nor conditions for talks, he said, but "conditions for a valid settlement" -- conditions necessary to reach a settlement which could be enforced.

When my dispatch reporting this discussion was published in The New York Times, it touched off a flurry of speculation, centering on the

2

thought that Pham Van Dong had modified in some way the position of the Hanoi regime on the four points.[10] This was not my understanding. I knew that on previous occasions the same interpretation had been presented by spokesmen for the North Vietnamese Government.

They had contended from the start that these were not "preconditions." However, the speculation in the West reached such intensity that the Foreign Ministry called on me and said they were going to issue a brief statement to dampen this down.[11] They were careful to note that the faulty interpretation was not mine but that of Western commentators.

When this was done, the furor gradually died away because the essence of the situation was now clear. The four conditions did not have to be accepted before we sat down at the conference table, but they would be placed on the table as the key points of the settlement which was to be negotiated. To me the whole thing seemed to be a distinction without a real difference. I did not believe that Pham Van Dong meant that the four points were to be considered an agenda in the normal understanding of the term--four points which might be modified or compromised to meet the views of the two sides. I felt that he meant--as Hanoi had from the start-- that the settlement must be constructed on this framework.

Whether there would be any give on the Hanoi side was another matter. There might well be in the end. But certainly there was no indication of it in the words he spoke to me about the four points.

He placed alongside his four points another one: that the United States halt unconditionally the bombing and all hostile activity against the North.

So far as the United States was concerned, he took the view that it was not really ready for discussions. It had not, in his view, given any sign of goodwill, and he felt this was essential if good-faith negotiations were to get under way. The pattern of American conduct, as he viewed it, was to talk peace only to mask preparations for escalation.

"Of course," he said, giving me a knowing look, "I understand this better than you because there are many things I can't tell you."

. . . .

January 3, 1967

On January 3, the British Minister, Michael Stewart, gave two cables to Assistant Secretary Bundy. The first cable, dated January 2, was from the UK Consul General Colvin in Hanoi stating that Harrison Salisbury told him the DRV had treated him as an unofficial emissary (he was not) and had given him two clear impressions at ministerial level: (a) in return for the cessation of bombing and of troop increases, Hanoi would be prepared to make military concessions and would negotiate; (b) the DRV want urgently

to discuss this with the USG on a clandestine basis but do not know how
to arrange it. Salisbury, who was seeing Pham van Dong that afternoon,
asked for advice. Colvin told him the proposed discussion could depend
on his ability to provide the USG with reliable confirmation from the
Prime Minister that concessions would include a halt to North Vietnamese
infiltration of the South. Impressions were not enough.

January 4, 1967

On the following day (Jan. 4), the UK Foreign Secretary instructed
the UK Embassy to bring this cable to the Secretary's attention and to
say that, if Salisbury is reporting faithfully, the North Vietnamese are
getting very close to the package that the Secretary authorized Brown to
put to the Soviet leaders last November in Moscow. This being so, he said,
we must take it seriously. British facilities were to be available for
any communication the US wished to make to Hanoi. Furthermore, if the US
wishes, Colvin could ask Salisbury to tell the DRV that British facilities
are available as a secure channel of communication if they wish to arrange
clandestine discussions, now or when Salisbury has left.

That evening, the Secretary gave the following message to the British
Minister, Michael Stewart, for delivery to Foreign Secretary Brown:

    a. Ask Colvin to inform Salisbury that he, Colvin, has
reported to his government--and they in turn to us--on Salisbury's
conversations "at ministerial level". Colvin should tell
Salisbury that the USG would greatly appreciate a full account
by Salisbury of any and all conversations bearing on the issues
of negotiation, cessation of bombing, or any related matters, to
be transmitted securely through Colvin's facilities.

    b. Colvin should also give Salisbury a message from us
that, if his conversations have followed the line reported to
Colvin, they could be of great importance. Hence, and having
in mind Hanoi's concern for the Chinese Communists in particular,
Colvin should emphasize to Salisbury that any such conversations
be conducted on a strictly clandestine basis. Even if nothing
develops from such conversations, it could be important to the
success of possible future clandestine contacts that Salisbury's
talks remain secure.

    c. If in fact senior members of the Hanoi government have
suggested, or should suggest, clandestine direct talks with the
US, Salisbury is authorized by us to tell the North Vietnamese that
he can convey this to us through the British secure channel, or
that we will be prepared to receive such message directly from
the North Vietnamese through direct diplomatic contacts at any
capital where we both maintain posts. Salisbury should convey to
the North Vietnamese that we place the highest priority on finding
a mutually agreeable, completely secure arrangement for exchanging
communications with them, and we will attempt to meet any suggestions
they have to offer to achieve this end.

4

d. We are most grateful for the prompt British report and for the offer of their communications facilities.

e. This message comes personally from the Secretary to George Brown. The Secretary is briefing Michael Stewart on a separate matter which may be relevant to the foregoing this

January 5, 1967

On January 5, the British Minister gave us two cables from the UK Consul General in Hanoi, dated January 4. Colvin had met with Salisbury on the afternoon of January 4 who had made the following points: (a) he will report the essence of his four hour conversation with Pham van Dong only to the Secretary; (b) the Prime Minister had treated him as an actual or potential emissary; (c) he would not use the British cipher facilities; (d) when asked if clandestine discussions had been suggested, he said this subject must be reserved for the Secretary; (e) his articles will not include reference to negotiations, etc., (f) he thought that the NVN Government "had gone further than even before, and if there were any receptivity in the US Administration there were grounds for further exploration;" (g) he said the results must not be exaggerated but he thought Colvin could be encouraged. However, he was concerned about the ability of the USG to keep the negotiations truly clandestine; and (h) he hoped to leave Hanoi on January 7, arriving in Washington on January 11.

Colvin concluded that clandestine discussions had been discussed and that Salisbury is sharply conscious of the need for clandestinity. At this point, Colvin had not been able to convey the Secretary's message (para. 3) to Salisbury.

That afternoon Scotty Reston advised the Secretary that Salisbury had an 8,000 word memcon of his talk with Pham van Dong which Reston does not know whether Salisbury will be allowed to bring out. Reston also stated that Salisbury had asked permission to stay in Hanoi another five or six days but the status of his request was unknown.

On the same day, we instructed our Ambassadors in the posts where he is most likely to be seen first (a) to offer Salisbury our private cable facilities to report to us, and (b) to caution him strongly against divulging any North Vietnamese confidences until he has reported in full to us and we can gauge whether he has received significant signals (State's 113504).

STATE 112967 (to Amembassy MOSCOW), TS/Nodis
Ref: Moscow 2887

You should seek appointment directly with departing NVN Ambassador and deliver the following message:

QUOTE: Although the USG has attempted to deliver the following message to the North Vietnamese authorities indirectly in the last few days, we would appreciate it if he would make sure that those authorities are informed directly by him upon his return to Hanoi as follows: The USG places the highest priority in finding a mutually agreeable, completely secure arrangements for exchanging communications with the government of the DRV about the possibilities of achieving a peaceful settlement of the Vietnamese dispute. If the DRV is willing to explore such possibilities with us we will attempt to meet any suggestion they have to offer regarding the time and place of such discussions and we will be prepared to receive such information directly from the North Vietnamese through direct diplomatic contacts at any capital where we both maintain posts or otherwise. END QUOTE

Slug any reply   NODIS/SUNFLOWER [12]

THE SECRETARY.

January 6, 1967

MOSCOW 2916 (to SecState), TS/Nodis, Rec'd 1341, 6 Jan 67
Ref: State 112967

1. After abortive attempt at noon, Akalovsky delivered with considerable difficulty following letter to Hoang Man'ty, First Secretary DRV Embassy, at 3 p.m. today:

A. Begin quote. Dear Mr. Ambassador: I have been instructed to deliver to you personally a confidential message from my government. I am prepared to call on you for that purpose at your earliest convenience. Please let me know when you would be available to receive me. Sincerely yours, John C. Guthrie, Charge D'Affaires Ad Interim, United States of America. End Quote.

2. Ty said he would deliver letter to Ambassador Kinh, but would not comment on mode of any reply. He did confirm Kinh leaving soon.

3. If and when Kinh receives me, I intend hand him in writing statement beginning quote the USG places . . . where we both maintain posts or otherwise end quote. And convey initial portion orally.

4. Assume Kinh will wish to touch base with Hanoi before receiving me and it therefore may be day or two before any reply received.

GUTHRIE

January 10, 1967

MOSCOW 2966 (to SecState), TS/Nodis, Rec'd 1133, 10 Jan 67
Ref: Moscow 2950

    1. ...I met with DRV Minister-Counselor Le Chang at 11 a.m. today, at DRV Embassy....

    2. ...I delivered message contained in State 112967....

    3. ...Le Chang then delivered brief tirade which struck me as pro forma, asserting that recent action by US show it continues intensify aggression in Vietnam and continues intensify its campaign of treachery and dupery regarding peace, and that it clear from everything there no good will on US part....

    5. As I was about to leave building, Le Chang came running after me and said he wanted make sure our meeting was confidential....

GUTHRIE

January 15, 1967

    The highlight of Salisbury's account to the Secretary concerned remarks by Pham Van Dong in response to his questions. Salisbury pressed him to make some response if the US were to stop bombing and Pham Van Dong made four replies:

    a. Once the US had halted its air attacks on the North, "as far as we are concerned we will take an appropriate stand."

    b. "If the US really wants a settlement, the first thing is to have good will. Of course we know what we should do if the US shows good will. If they stop the whole war, we know what we should do. If they stop doing harm to the North, we know what we should do."

    c. "The moment the US puts and end to the way, we will respect each other and settle every question."

    d. With the cessation of hostilities, "we can speak about other things. After this, there will be no lack of generosity on our part."

    Our net judgment is that these statements are interesting mood music but do not get us very far. The first two statements are replays of earlier statements to Sainteny and Petri.[13] The latter two statements appear to be without substance.

Salisbury's report contained three other interesting elements: (a) there is a deep conviction in Hanoi that our resolve will falter because of the cost of the struggle; (b) there is concern in Hanoi about the consequences of the crisis in China;[14] (c) Hanoi had two basic concerns about negotiations: (1) the Chicom pistol in their back and (2) the possibility that the morale and discipline of the Northern forces and the Viet Cong would falter. We take the latter point seriously (Memorandum to the President, January 15).

January 17, 1967

MOSCOW 3066 (to SecState), TS/Nodis, Rec'd 1015, 17 Jan 67
Ref: Moscow 3061 .

. . . .

2. Le Chang said purpose of his asking for this meeting was to seek clarification certain points in U.S. Government's message DCM delivered to him January 10. For DRV Government to be able give message serious study, following necessary:

A. Explanation of specific meaning phrase "completely secure arrangement" in message; and

B. Clarification U.S. position on settlement Vietnam problem.

3. . . . he indicated some sense of urgency by inquiring whether response could be expected soon, even this week. . . .

. . . .

THOMPSON.

STATE 120058 (to Amembassy MOSCOW), TS/Nodis, Sent 2245, 17 Jan 67

1. In conversation with Harriman last night, Dobrynin said he understood that our order concerning bombing within ten nautical miles of the center of Hanoi still stood on an indefinite basis. Harriman challenged this and said that while we were continuing the order for the present, we did not consider ourselves bound to do so indefinitely. Dobrynin asked for clarification, stating that he believed Moscow understood it in this sense, based on Bundy disclosure to Zinchuk on December 27 of proposal made in Warsaw on December 24. (This of course was prior to negative response through Polish channel on December 29.)

2. We are informing Dobrynin quietly here that negative response of December 29 in Warsaw necessarily meant that we did not feel ourselves bound to maintain the order indefinitely. At the same time, we were continuing the order for the present and watching developments closely.

3. Your instructions on Vietnam also discuss the possibility of secret talks with DRV and indicate we have had no reply. In light of latest developments, we believe you should say that we as yet have no clear indication of DRV willingness for such talks. We simply cannot guess whether DRV has informed Soviets of our message or their latest reply, and we believe it best to protect ourselves from any charge of disclosure to any party or government. If you think it wise, you might omit discussions of this point entirely while simply reiterating our willingness for direct secret talks.

RUSK (Drafted by W. P. Bundy)

STATE 120335 (to Amembassy Moscow), TS/Nodis, Sent 2430, 17 Jan 67
Ref: Moscow 3066

Literally Eyes Only for Ambassador and DCM

Following is to be held until an execute order is received:

1. Guthrie should seek appointment soonest with DRV Charge to convey message below.

2. Message is:

a. By "completely secure arrangement" USG has in mind discussions between DRV and US representatives that would not repeat not be disclosed to any other government or party whatsoever unless by mutual agreement, and that would be subject to the strictest precautions against press or public inquiry. USG is able to assure DRV that earlier message has not been disclosed to anyone.

b. We believe DRV already has considerable information by both public and private means, of US position on settlement of Viet-Nam problem, and has also received formulations from others in contact with USG. USG for its part has studied public and private statements by DRV representatives. We believe discussions should seek to establish whether common ground now exists for an acceptable settlement.

c. In discussions, USG would be prepared to consider any topic that DRV felt should be included. For illustration, topics USG would be prepared to discuss would include following:

9

(1) Arrangements for the reduction or the cessation of hostilities.

(2) Essential elements of the Geneva Accords of 1954 and 1962, including withdrawal of any forces coming from outside South Viet-Nam and now present there.

(3) Arrangements for a free determination by North Viet-Nam and South Viet-Nam on the issue of reunification.

(4) Recognition of the independence and territorial integrity of North and South Viet-Nam, or of all Viet-Nam if the people should choose reunification.

(5) The international posture of South Viet-Nam, including relationships with other nations.

(6) Appropriate provisions relating to the internal political structure of South Viet-Nam, including freedom from reprisals and free political participation.

(7) Appropriate objective means for insuring the integrity of all provisions agreed to.

d. The topics thus listed could be considered in any order, and the USG would be prepared to consider any additional topics the DRV would propose.

3. You should put these points in writing. In addition, you should note orally that while USG is prepared to conduct discussions under a completely secure arrangement at any place the DRV may wish, USG believes there are many advantages in Moscow. USG senior representatives in Moscow are fully equipped and can be supported security and without personnel moves that might attract attention. We believe physical security in Moscow can be maintained subject to appropriate safeguards.

4. As these instructions indicate, we believe our first response should be a listing of topics. However, we recognize possibility that Guthrie might be probed further about substance of USG position. He should seek to avoid going beyond this, indicating that very purpose of discussions would be to develop positions on both sides. If but only if DRV Charge should refer to MARIGOLD ten points (which you have as attachment to Dobrynin-Rusk memocon of January 5), Guthrie should be familiar with these and should respond that, as we believe has been indicated to DRV, we believe this formulation would be satisfactory basis for more detailed discussion of the points contained therein.

RUSK (Drafted by W. P. Bundy)

10

STATE 120458 (to AmEmbassy Moscow), TS/Nodis, Sent 0403, 18 Jan 67
Ref: State 120335

You may execute.

RUSK (Drafted by Mr. Read).

January 19, 1967

MOSCOW 3089 (to SecState), TS/Nodis, Rec'd 0957, 19 Jan 67
Ref: State 120453

. . . .

2. Unless instructed to contrary, DCM will touch very lightly on
Moscow as site for discussions (para. 3 State 120335).   Our movements
and telephone calls are, of course, reported to KGB by chauffers and
operators and it must be assumed that DRV Embassy is not secure from
Soviet eavesdropping. It will also be almost impossible keep repeated
calls at DRV Embassy from Western press representatives indefinitely.
From DRV viewpoint, Moscow would be doubtful choice owing predictable
ChiCom reaction.

THOMPSON

January 20, 1967

MOSCOW 3126 (to SecState), TS/Nodis, Rec'd 1713, 20 Jan 67
Ref: Moscow 3089

. . . .

4. Le Chang said would transmit our response to his government and
would meet with us again after receiving further instructions. He did
not probe further.

5. Apart from important fact that Le Chang indicated dialogue would
continue, believe his comportment during meetings may also be of significance. Except for his pro forma attack on US at initial meeting
January 10 (Moscow 2966), he has refrained from making any acrimonious
statements and his attitude at meetings, relaxed from outset, is now
bordering on friendly; he is even willing to be drawn into occasional
small talk. As department will recall, this is in marked contrast with
his attitude during one meeting he was willing have with Ambassador Kohler
year ago.[15]

THOMPSON

January 21, 1967

STATE 123196 (to Amembassy Moscow), S/Nodis
Ref: Moscow 3126

  1. We are a little disturbed at reported Guthrie statement that
we felt agenda should be clear before talks commence. This is not
repeat not our thought, as we ourselves might wish to add topics, and
above all do not wish to get into any dispute on agenda. . . .

    . . . .

RUSK (Drafted by W. P. Bundy)

January 27, 1967

MOSCOW 3218 (to SecState), TS/Nodis, Rec'd 1503, 27 Jan 67
Ref: Moscow 3194

    . . . .

  2. . . . Le Chang said he has asked for meeting to deliver, for
transmittal to US Govt, DRV Govt's Aide-Memoire containing response to
US Govt message given to him January 10.

    . . . .

    A. The United States is intensifying the war in South Vietnam
and escalating the bombing of North Vietnam. President Johnson has made
clear his scheme to go on intensifying the war of aggression against Vietnam. But the Vietnamese people are determined to fight for their fundamental national rights and the United States is doomed to dismal defeat.

    B. The United States talks peace but makes war. The conditions
which the United States demands the Vietnamese people to accept are absurd
and arrogant. "Conditional suspension of bombing", "conditional withdrawal of troops" are in fact schemes to cling to South Vietnam, to turn
South Vietnam into a new-type colony and a military base of the United
States, to prolong indefinitely the partition of Vietnam.

    C. The four-point stand of the Government of the Democratic
Republic of Vietnam embodies the fundamental principles and the main provisions of the 1954 Geneva agreements on Vietnam. It is the basis for the
most correct political solution to the Vietnam problem. The Government of
the Democratic Republic of Vietnam has declared that if the United States
really wants peace and seeks a political solution, it must recognize the
four-point stand of the Government of the Democratic Republic of Vietnam
and the five-point statement of South Vietnam National Front for Liberation,
the only genuine representative of the South Vietnamese people.

D. The Democratic Republic of Vietnam is an independent and sovereign country. The U.S. bombing of the Democratic Republic of Vietnam is a blatant act of aggression. The United States must end immediately and unconditionally the bombing and all other acts of war against the Democratic Republic of Vietnam. That is the urgent demand on the people of all countries, of all men of common sense throughout the world. The unconditional cessation of bombing and all other acts of war against the Democratic Republic of Vietnam being materialized, the Democratic Republic of Vietnam could then exchange views with the United States concerning the place or date for contact between the two parties as the Government of the United States proposed in its message handed over on January 10, 1967. End text.

5. Le Chang added that, as to US views--including several points-- conveyed to him January 20, his side would comment on them "at appropriate time." In response DCM's query if he understood correctly that Aide- Memoire is in response to January 10 message and that there no response yet to points contained January 20 paper, Le Chang said this understanding accurate and repeated that comments on latter paper would be made "at appropriate time."

6. DCM took this opportunity make point in para. 2 State 123196. Le Chang said he fully understood.

7. Le Chang then said he wished stress certain points concerning "intensification of war with us." Asserting US continuing escalate war and commit "barbarous crimes" against Vietnamese people in both parts Vietnam, cited following examples recent "most cerious escalation":

A. Destruction of Ben Xue in SVN;

B. "Barbarous murders" in Iron Triangle;

C. Bombings "densely populated" NVN areas of Viet Tri, Thai Nguyen, Ning Bing, and Thang Hoa.[16]

No signature (cable probably incomplete).

STATE 127220 (to Amembassy Moscow), TS/Nodis, Sent 2443, 27 Jan 67 Ref: Moscow 3218

Secretary would appreciate receiving your views about DRV message in reftel.

Some of the questions about the message which have been raised in our minds are as follows:

(1) Are we now, in effect, facing the start of a dialogue with the other side staking out an opening extreme position?

(2) What inference do you draw from Charge's statement that comments on January 20 paper would be made "at appropriate time": - do you read this to mean that we will hear again from him in a few days or that their further response to January 20 message will come only after cessation of bombing, etc.?

(3) What is your reading of the evident concern indicated in para. 4a and 7 of our "intensification" and "escalation"? (Incidentally, we have not been able to identify "Ben Xue" in para. 7(a))

. . . .

Do you have any indication of Soviet awareness of Guthrie/Charge talks? Is it safe to assume that Kosygin's reference to "latest (Vietnam) news not good" as reported Moscow 3213 preceded reftel discussions and was not a veiled reference to latter?

KATZENBACH (Drafted by B. H. Read: J. P. Walsh)

January 28, 1967

MOSCOW 3231 (to SecState), TS/Nodis, Rec'd 1051, 28 Jan 67
Ref: State 127220

1. DRV message strikes me as first round in oriental rug trading. Le Chang's emphasis on secrecy at each contact seems encouraging but you will note that text carefully drafted for possible publication. Suggest our reply should also be drafted with possible necessity of eventual publication in mind.

2. Believe QTE appropriate time UNQTE means after cessation of bombing but this ploy gives them the possibility of continuing the dialogue if we should break off talks or give completely negative reply their last message.

3. Concern over escalation may indicate they are hurting and also may be effort to exploit experience of Warsaw talks to hold down our bombing activity. Possibility exists that they may be concerned that further escalation will bring strong internal pressure to call for volunteers or other dangerous moves on their part. At Guthrie's request, place names were handed to him in writing. On reexamination appears to be Ben Xuc rpt Xuc.

4. Do not believe Kosygin was making veiled reference to these discussions. We can be almost certain that Soviet chauffeur would have reported Guthrie's visits to KGB. Suggest that at next meeting Guthrie might point out that fact of contacts almost certainly known to Soviets

and ask whether if queried by them we could confirm we had been in contact but not inform them of substance of talks.

5. Re future procedure following appear to be alternatives.

A. Stop bombing DRV and press for prompt meeting or alternatively state we are doing so on assumption there will be prompt meeting and mutual de-escalation.

B. State that as evidence of good faith we will confine bombing to infiltration routes in southern part of DRV and press for prompt meeting.

C. Assuming foregoing not acceptable send carefully drafted written reply which would leave us in good position if publication forced by them supplemented as necessary by oral remarks. Reply might be based on the fourteen points or Polish ten points. On bombing we might say we deplore the loss of life on both sides but point out that use of violence is not one-sided and we would welcome mutual cessation.

D. Another possibility would be simply to go back with questions about paragraph C of their reply. What do they mean by "recognize" the four and five point statements. Are they asking for our capitulation? Although we have indicated we are prepared to discuss their points we cannot agree that the NLF is QTE the only genuine representative of the South Vietnamese people UNQTE.

THOMPSON

Hanoi VNA International Service in English 0150 GMT 28 January 1967--B (FBIS, Far East, 30 January 1967)

(Text) Hanoi, 28 January--Nguyen Duy Trinh, DRV foreign minister, has granted an interview to Australian journalist Wilfred Burchett. Questions and answers follow:

1. Question: Mr. Minister, what in your view are the most signifi-cant recent developments in the Vietnam war, and what are the prospects for the immediate future?

Answer: The U.S. imperialists are waging the most barbarous war of aggression against our country, threatening more and more seriously peace in southeast Asia and the world. But they have sustained heavy defeats in South and in North Vietnam. The people of South Vietnam, fighting with great heroism, have foiled all their military plans in spite of the commitments of over 1 million U.S., puppet, and satellite troops. The people of North Vietnam have not been and will never be cowed by the barbarous bombing raids of the U.S. imperialists and have dealt them well-deserved counterblows.

All Vietnamese people are resolutely fighting against the U.S. aggressors to defend their sacred national rights and fulfill their duty to the peoples of the friendly countries now struggling for their independence and freedom. The four-point stand of the DRV Government is a stand of independence and peace, and it is the expression of the fundamental principles and the main provisions of the 1954 Geneva agreements on Vietnam. It is the basis for the most correct political solution to the Vietnam problem, a basis which fully meets the deep aspirations of the Vietnamese people, and fully conforms to the spirit of the five-point statement of the NFLSV, the only genuine representative of the people of South Vietnam.

The peoples of the world, including very large sections of the population of the United States itself, more and more strongly support our just stand and demand ever more firmly that the U.S. imperialists stop their war of aggression in Vietnam and let the Vietnamese people settle their own affairs themselves.

The U.S. imperialists talk of peace negotiations, but they still show great obduracy. President Johnson recently stated with impudence that he will go on intensifying and expanding the war of aggression in an attempt to cling to the south and to prolong the partition of Vietnam.[17] But however perfidious the maneuvers of the U.S. imperialists may be, the Vietnamese people, united as one man and fearing neither hardships nor sacrifices, are determined to carry on their resistance war to the end to safeguard the independence and freedom of the fatherland, and contribute to the maintenance of peace in southeast Asia and the world.

The Vietnamese people will win. The U.S. imperialist aggressors will be defeated.

2. Question: In the face of documentary evidence and eyewitness reports from foreign witnesses, including American journalists, Washington continues to claim that U.S. aircraft have been striking only at military targets and not at civilian targets in North Vietnam. What are your views on this subject?

Answer: The DRV is an independent and sovereign country and the U.S. imperialists have absolutely no right to violate this independence and sovereignty.

U.S. bombing of any point of its territory, whether a military or a civilian target, is a blatant act of aggression and an unpardonable crime. It is an undeniable fact that civilian targets in North Vietnam have been attacked. The peoples of the world, including large sections of the American people, are strongly protesting against the U.S. imperialists' savage acts of aggression.

The U.S. imperialists must stop definitively and unconditionally the bombing raids and all other acts of war against the DRV.

3. Question: The United States has spoken of the need for dialog or contact between itself and the DRV. Would you comment on this statement?

Answer: The United States has made such statements, but in its deeds it has shown the utmost obduracy and perfidy and continues the escalation, stepping up and expanding the aggressive war. If it really wants talks, it must first halt unconditionally the bombing raids and all other acts of war against the DRV. It is only after the unconditional cessation of U.S. bombing and all other acts of war against the DRV that there could be talks between the DRV and the United States.

The four-point stand and the correct attitude of the DRV Government enjoy, we are sure, ever stronger approval and support from all peace loving and justice-loving peoples and governments in the world. If the United States refuses to listen to reason, it will further unmask itself as an obdurate aggressor. The Vietnamese people are determined to fight until total victory to defend the north, liberate the south, achieve the peaceful reunification of the fatherland, and contribute to the maintenance of peace in this area and in the world.

January 30, 1967

STATE 128175 (to Amembassy Moscow & Saigon), S/Nodis, Sent 0318, 31 Jan 67.

For Ambassador from Secretary

1. Separate circular from FBIS will contain key parts of Burchett interview with DRV Foreign Minister published Jan 28 and Nhan Dan commentary of Jan 29.[18] We interpret these as all-out efforts to build up public pressures on us to stop bombing in return for talks. We also note that Burchett interview substantially reduces link to acceptance of four points, although Nhan Dan commentary implies such link by quoting Ho letter of January 1966.

2. Apart from these public statements, we are repeating to all addressees Cairo 4214 and New Delhi 10807. These report simultaneous DRV approaches in Cairo and New Delhi, asking them to convey message to us which both UAR. and GOI have interpreted as message that Hanoi would be prepared to talk if we stopped bombing. You will note that Indian message contains intriguing reference to absence of "publicly stated" conditions, and we will be seeking clarification through New Delhi.

3. For Moscow: We believe this background is essential for any discussions of Vietnam you may have in next few days. If DRV is going all-out to put pressure on us to stop bombing, we would expect Soviets to join in the cry on much more forceful basis than they have done in the past. You should counter by using our standard position from Goldberg speech of September and our other exchanges with the Soviets.[19] In addition, you should point to grave practical problem -- which we believe Soviets might actually

understand although not conceding it -- of situation in which we stop
bombing, Hanoi continued its actions, and we were thus under great
pressure to resume. If we stop bombing and the North Vietnamese make
no overt albeit unannounced reciprocal gesture it would be impossible to
avoid widespread speculation and indeed an assumption that talks were in
fact going on. This would jeopardize the secrecy which we and the DRV
(and we assume the Soviets as well) feel would be necessary for the success
of at least the early stages of negotiation. Aside from this, a situation
in which the North Vietnamese continue their infiltration of men and
materials southward while we are engaging in talks would produce the kind
of tensions that would make any constructive steps toward a settlement
difficult if not impossible.

4. For Saigon: You should explain privately to Do (and Ky if you
wish) that we see public statements as designed to put pressure on us and
that we have had messages in Cairo and New Delhi along same lines. You
should ask for Saigon reaction, while indicating that our position remains
as stated by Goldberg.

5. For London: This new series of moves by DRV, and our reactions
to it, should be fully in hands of Wilson and Brown before Kosygin visit.
We are considering message that would disclose Cairo and New Delhi approaches
and cover whole subject in detail, with suggestions on line British might
take with Soviets. For time being, you should confine your discussion
with British to their interpretation of Burchett interview and Nhan Dan
commentary, without at this time going into Cairo and New Delhi.

RUSK (Drafted by W. P. Bundy)

January 31, 1967

STATE 128486 (to Amembassy Moscow), TS/Nodis
Ref: Moscow's 3218 and 3231

1. Guthrie should ask to see DRV Charge soonest to deliver following
written message:

a. The USG has carefully noted the DRV message of January 27 and
the accompanying remarks by the DRV Charge. The USG has preserved the
strictly confidential nature of these exchanges, but notes that the DRV
has broadcast publicly the essence of the January 27 message and asked
other governments to inform us that the DRV is prepared to enter negotiations with the USG when bombing of North Viet-Nam stops without stated
conditions. The US has felt that it must give some response to third
nations conveying messages from the DRV, and will be conveying such responses in the near future. We believe this essential in order to protect
the existence of this strictly confidential channel. We assume the DRV
will treat third country channels in the same manner, but that strictly
confidential statements will continue to be handled through this channel.

b. The basic objective of the USG remains the holding of direct and private talks covering any elements that either side believes should be considered in reaching a peaceful solution to the Viet-Nam problem. For this purpose, the US would be prepared to include in these discussions the four-point position of the DRV or any other matter the.DRV wishes to bring up. The US would welcome DRV comments on the US message of January 20.

c. At the same time, the USG notes the concern of the DRV in discussing "intensification" or "escalation" of the bombing of North Viet-Nam as presented in the January 27 aide-memoire and the oral remarks of the DRV Chargé. We are ready to discuss this and related issues. But we remind the DRV that one step has already been taken by the USG to de-escalate the war in the North: for more than a month our planes have been ordered not to bomb within 10 nautical miles of Hanoi city center. We would like to avail ourselves of this direct private channel to inform the DRV that the USG would be prepared to implement additional measures to de-escalate the bombing of the North to create conditions conducive to the success of talks with the DRV. We, of course, would be impressed with similar acts of restraint on the part of the DRV, and we can assure the DRV that any such acts on its part need not be made public. The favorable atmosphere which would result from these mutual steps toward peace would permit the US and DRV to take additional steps toward obtaining a peaceful solution.

d. The USG is aware that the DRV is sensitive to any public link between a stopping of the bombing and reciprocal actions on Hanoi's part. In this connection, it should be observed that the cessation of bombing would lead to a world-wide assumption that talks were under way and it would become increasingly difficult to hold discussions under conditions of secrecy. For this reason, we remind the DRV of the USG suggestion that the stopping of the bombing might take place as a prior and ostensibly unilateral action. Before doing this we would want a private understanding with the DRV that additional subsequent steps would be taken that would amount in the aggregate to an equitable and reciprocal reduction of hostile action. The USG takes this opportunity to renew this suggestion as one to which the DRV may wish to give serious consideration.

e. Finally, the USG notes that the approaching TET period, during which both sides have announced cessations of military action, including the bombing of North Viet-Nam, may make the present occasion particularly appropriate for discussions along the lines suggested above. In view of the nearness of the TET period, the USG hopes that the DRV response to the foregoing will be made as soon as possible.

2. Before handing over the above written message and reading it for translation, Guthrie should note orally that the USG refutes categorically the charges about US actions and intentions concerning South Viet-Nam and the GVN contained in the DRV aide-memoire and oral remarks. However, in the interests of bringing about a constructive exchange of views, the USG will refrain from a point-by-point refutation and proceed to our formal reply to the January 27 aide-memoire.

19

3. Either at close, or at appropriate point in conversation, Guthrie should ask when DRV Charge expects new ambassador to arrive FYI: Purpose of this inquiry is to suggest possible early appointment of representative qualified for more frank and direct discussions, if DRV desires. END FYI.

RUSK (Drafted by W. P. Bundy)

February 1, 1967

SAIGON 17053 (to SecState), S/Nodis, Sent 1000, 1 Feb 67; Rec'd 1052, 1 Feb 67.

1. Pursuant to your 128175, I called Ky on Wednesday morning and cited the newspaper articles by Salisbury, Burchett, and in the Communist newspaper Nhan Dan as well as the messages in Cairo and New Delhi, all of them trying to get us to stop the bombing without any deescalation on their side. I asked Ky what he thought.

2. Ky believes that "we are getting stronger every day, and they are getting weaker every day - and they know it." They are hurt by the bombing, and by the tremendous military "meat-grinder" which devours the troops which they send into South Viet-Nam, in particular, he said, "our political progress is the worst thing for them". They know that once a constitutional government is installed in Viet-Nam, he added, they will have no more chance.[20] For that reason, Ky said, he had decided that the elections should be held three months after the promulgation of the constitution and not six months.

. . . .

5. Their difficulties were three times as great as ours, said Ky. It was important to elect a constitutional president as soon as possible for many reasons, including peace talks. Until there is an elected government in Viet-Nam, it is very important to keep all peace overtures very quiet because news of them will affect the morale of the Vietnamese....

. . . .

LODGE

STATE 129441 (to Amembassy London), TS/Nodis, Sent 2229, 1 Feb 67
Ref: Your 6167 .

Chester Cooper will be in London to brief Brown and Wilson on relevant matters prior to the Kosygin visit....[21]

Michael Stewart brought over a message to Cooper from Brown dated 30 January, the text of which follows:

UNQTE.

RUSK (Drafted by C. L. Cooper)

February 2, 1967

MOSCOW 3321 (to SecState), TS/Nodis, Sent 1515, 2 Feb 67; Rec'd 1624, 2 Feb 67.
Ref: A. State 128486;   B. Moscow 3295, para one P.

. . . . .

3. DCM began by making oral statement per para two ref State tel.
Then handed Le Chang written statement.

. . . .

9. Before parting, DCM inquired when new DRV ambassador expected to
arrive. Le Chang said "in near future."

10. During phone call this noon, Tu asked who would be coming, DCM
or Ambassador. Made no further comment when told "DCM" and subject did not
arise during meeting.

THOMPSON.

_____

USUN 3848 (to SecState), TS/Nodis, Sent 2318, 2 Feb 67, Rec'd 2414, 2 Feb 67.

For President and Secretary from Goldberg.

. . . approaches could represent either:

21

(A) A sign of serious interest on Hanoi's part in beginning process toward reaching settlement or toward mutual abatement of the conflict; or

(B) Part of an intensified propaganda effort to increase pressure of world and domestic opinion on US to end bombing.

I consider it essential that, in reacting to these approaches, we follow course which does not exclude either . . . .

With these purposes in mind, I wish to urge two additional steps to policy which has been approved for responding to Hanoi's direct approach:

First: while this approach is being explored, and until it is ascertained beyond reasonable doubt that it is not serious move on Hanoi's part, we should undertake no new or additional targeting for our bombing sorties in North Vietnam.

Second: Following the TET cease-fire, we should reduce the bombing of North Vietnam by a small but significant amount, namely: suspend those bombing sorties which are directed against targets not related to North's infiltration of men and supplies into south. As I understand from Secy McNamara's statement to Cabinet on Feb 1, this would involve suspension of approximately five percent of present sorties in North.

. . . .

The principal advantages I see to these additional steps on our part are as follows: They offer something of substance to Hanoi immediately and the prospect of something more in future; . . . . At same time, . . . On the one hand, we would be relatively free from charge that we had not responded affirmatively to Hanoi's approaches. Our public record on this score will need bolstering, for it appears the record is being rather badly clouded by Polish version of how our mid-December bombings interfered with what they conceive to be a very promising chance of talks with Hanoi. On other hand, since reduction of bombing would be relatively small and would not involve suspension of sorties directed against targets related to North Vietnamese infiltration, our action would not open us to charge of having placed in jeopardy status and security of our forces in south.

GOLDBERG.

February 3, 1967

STATE 131591 (to Amembassy Moscow), TS/Nodis, Sent 0329, 4 Feb 67.
Ref: Moscow's 3321

. . . .

5. In conversation last evening with Kohler, Dobrynin showed considerable interest in the Guthrie-Le Chang contacts. He indicated he had been informed of earlier meetings and that next move was up to us.

. . . .

RUSK (Drafted by L. Unger)   22

February 4, 1967

On February 4, the SUNFLOWER/PLUS series was established in a message to Thompson in Moscow (State 131705), informing him that consideration was being given to having Guthrie deliver to the DRV Charge at their next meeting a Presidential message to Ho Chi Minh.[22] Thompson's views were requested on the text of an attached draft which he was informed was not cleared in text or principle.

On the following day, Thompson submitted a somewhat negative view on the wisdom of the suggested action, although he did not feel strongly on the matter (Moscow's 3353). He felt (a) the draft letter merely raises the current exercise to a higher level; (b) personally addressing Ho might weaken his in-house position; (c) emphasis on TET might imply desperation on our part; (d) the letter should be held for use if an impasse is reached; and (e) if the letter is to be used, some textual revision would be in order.

STATE 131714 (to Amembassy Mowcow), TS/Nodis, Sent 2312, 4 Feb 67.

You should inform DRV rep that Estabrook story came from Polish sources.[23]

. . . .

RUSK (Drafted by L. Unger)

LONDON 6271 (to SecState), TS/Nodis, Rec'd 0544, 5 Feb 67.

For the Secretary and Harriman from Cooper

1. With Ambassador Bruce met with Foreign Secretary . . . .

. . . .

3. With respect to the forthcoming Kosygin visit, I reminded Brown of the Rusk-Gromyko conversation many weeks ago, and noted that we have not yet gotten a reply to the Secretary's query as to what the Russians would do if there were a bombing cessation. . . . .I suggested to Brown that if the opportunity permitted, the British should press the Russians on both their short-run opportunities and responsibilities to insure Hanoi against Chinese economic, political, or even military actions in the event Hanoi moved toward negotiations. In the longer term the Russians had an opportunity (and indeed they seemed to recognize this themselves) to pursue policies in Asia which would be in tandem with our own and which would be of common benefit in reducing tensions in that part of the world.

. . ; . .

23

6. I told Brown that the President and the Secretary were cognizant of the British desire to avoid a resumption of bombing while Kosygin was still here. I said that I could not give any unequivocal assurances on this, that much would depend on the behavior of the North Vietnamese during the four-day cessation. Obviously, if there were major North Vietnamese troops movements southward, we had primary responsibility to protect our own forces, ...

. . . .

8. Brown is very concerned about the low-level of the group that Kosygin is bringing with him. Indeed he is worried in the light of this whether the Russians are ready to engage in serious talks on any subject. Although he was aware of Smirnovsky's statement that the Russians were interested in a peace settlement he had not studied it (later Wilson confessed that he had not heard of it.) . . . .

. . . .

10. . . . . We had fifteen minutes alone with Brown and Wilson. I then told them of our direct contact with the North Vietnamese. I pointed out that it was at a low level, that it was still very fragile, but that we were doing everything we could to keep it going. I stressed that thus far this private exchange had revealed a less forthcoming position on the point of Hanoi than some people read into the various public statements that have been coming out of North Vietnam recently. I stressed that I could not tell them where the contact was going on, that we were unaware of the extent to which the Soviets knew about it, and that we hoped that neither Brown nor Wilson would make any reference to this in their conversations with Kosygin. I showed Wilson the seven substantive points contained in our January 20 message and indicated that if the Russians raised any of these we would be perfectly prepared to see the British discuss them. . . . .

BRUCE

LONDON 6272 (to SecState), TS/Nodis, Rec'd 0549, 5 Feb 67.

For the Secretary and Harriman from Cooper

1. I have met with Murray at the Foreign Office to go over working on the brief for Brown and Wilson. The brief stresses the need for some meaningful action the President can point to in exchange for a bombing cessation. It remind the Russians that we are conscious of Hanoi's problems about making a public commitment and our readiness to get private assurances.

. . . .

BRUCE.

February 5, 1967

"Ashmore's Letter to Hanoi Chief," The Washington Post, 18 September 1967
(Letter mailed Feb 5 by Ashmore)

Following is the text of the letter by Harry S. Ashmore to President
Ho Chi Minh:[24]

Dear Mr. President:

Mr. William Baggs and I have made a full report to appropriate officials
of the United States Government on our recent conversation with you in
Hanoi. Ambassador Luis Quintanilla has communicated his views to the U.S.
Ambassador in Mexico City.

The State Department has expressed itself as most grateful for your
thoughtful approach to the possibility of an ultimate settlement of the
hostilities between the United States and the Democratic Republic of Vietnam.

In our several discussions with senior officials of the State Department they took occasion to reiterate points we believe are already known
to you. They emphasized that the U.S. remains prepared for secret discussions at any time, without conditions, and that such discussions might
cover the whole range of topics relevant to a peaceful settlement. They
reiterated that the Geneva Accords might be the framework for a peaceful
solution.

They expressed particular interest in your suggestion to us that private
talks could begin provided the U.S. stopped bombing your country, and ceased
introducing additional U.S. troops into Vietnam. They expressed the opinion
that some reciprocal restraint to indicate that neither side intended to use
the occasion of the talks for military advantage would provide tangible
evidence of the good faith of all parties in the prospects for a negotiated
settlement.

In the light of these concerns, they expressed great interest in any
clarification of this point that you might wish to provide through a communication to us.

Speaking now wholly for ourselves, we believe the essential condition
for productive talks is an arrangement under which neither side stands to
gain military advantage during the period of negotiation. To achieve this
end it may be that preliminary secret discussions would be helpful to
determine the outline of a possible peaceful settlement.

As we see it, these are practical considerations that have nothing to
do with questions of "face." There is no doubt in our minds that the
American Government genuinely seeks peace. As private citizens, our sole
concern is in facilitating a discussion that will bring all matters at
issue to official consideration. It is in this sense that we convey these
comments, and invite any reply you may wish to make, which of course we
would report to our Government in complete discretion.

25

May I take this occasion to renew our thanks for the courteous and considerate treatment we received in Hanoi throughout our visit and for the honor of our most useful conversation with you.

If you feel that further personal conversation with Mr. Baggs and me is in order we would, of course, return to Hanoi at your convenience.

HARRY S. ASHMORE.

February 6, 1967

MOSCOW 3375 (to SecState), TS/Nodis, Sent 1500, 6 Feb 67, Rec'd 1609, 6 Feb 67.

Ref: State 131591

. . . .

5. . . . , DCM then referred to Estabrook Feb 5 Wash Post story of which he gave Le Chang brief oral summary based on STATE 131700. Said he mentioned story because he instructed tell Le Chang that story had come from Polish sources and that U.S. Govt will maintain complete silence and avoid comment on it.

6. . . . . Noting that both sides had been concerned to maintain their contact confidential and secret (Le Chang expressed full agreement with this), DCM said we concerned about certain aspects of this: (A) Soviets would know about his visits to DRV Embassy, e.g., his driver Soviet; and (B) It always possible Western correspondents might see him enter or leave DRV Embassy and ask him what he doing here. If (B) should occur, he could not deny his visit, and problem would be how to respond to questions. One possibility would be to confirm that contact had been established and refuse further comment. If we kept quiet, there might be implication that we discussing POWs. DCM said all this led him to ask if we should arrange another meeting place. Should we ask Soviets to provide us a less conspicuous place? . . . .

7. . . . . Re place of meeting, Le Chang emphatically stated his view was that we should not rpt not ask any third party to arrange for a change of venue, because of principle of confidentiality and secrecy he had mentioned. Also said he wanted reiterate that time or content of meetings should not rpt not be mentioned to anybody, including correspondents. As to how any possible press query should be answered, said he was sure that if this principle were abided by, many ways of responding could be found. In response DCM's comment correspondents would indulge in guessing, Le Chang said if they wanted to guess they could do so. . . .

THOMPSON.

LONDON 6315 (to SecState), TS/Nodis, Sent 2100, 6 Feb 67; Rec'd 2215, 6 Feb 67.

To Secretary from Cooper

. . . .

2. PM had an hour or more private session with Kosygin. Kosygin embarked immediately on discussion of China and Vietnam. According to Wilson [25]

Kosygin agreed that need to make some progress toward peace during TET "very urgent". Agreed that both USSR and UK could be "of assistance" in getting talks between "the principals" started. . . .

. . . , Wilson . . . . spelled out in detail the Phase A - Phase B formula, but got no flicker of interest . . . .

Kosygin quoted from (and subsequently referred to) Burchett interview as key to NVN readiness to negotiate. Kosygin evidenced mood of "great urgency" in plenary discussion. Referred again to TET as being "the big chance". Repeated on several occasions the point that "we can assist, but we (i.e. the USSR and the UK) cannot negotiate. The best way to do this is to get the US and the NVN together".

When Wilson asked Kosygin whether he could induce Hanoi to make unequivocal statement that they would enter negotiations if bombing stopped, Kosygin   said he and the UK would have to rely on the Foreign Minister's statement as contained in the Burchett interview. In his summary remarks he said (direct quote from interpreters notes) "our NVN friend do not rule out a negotiated solution".

The only Soviet suggestion for US-Sov action was that Kosygin and Wilson jointly endorse the NVN position as contained in Burchett interview in a private message to the President or publicly in the communique. This is "unacceptable" to the British. But British feel this is Kosygin's opening gambit and a more constructive position can be worked out.

Kosygin did not rise to Wilson suggestion re some jointly worked out arrangement to move private US-NVN agreements to an international arrangement. This could be worked on in due course. Important thing, according to Kosygin was that there should not be another Geneva conf

When Wilson was asked what suggestions UK had for immediate future, Wilson stressed need for Hanoi to "avoid provocation during TET" to which Brown added, "such as movement of troops through the DMZ". This was only point at which, according to Wilson, situation "got hairy." Kosygin made much of US troop and ship movements.

BRUCE.

LONDON 6316 (to SecState), TS/Nodis, Sent 0122, 7 Feb 67; Rec'd 0148, 7 Feb 67.

To Secretary from Cooper

    1. . . . .

    2. Kosygin then said that Wilson should send personal telegram to President. Wilson asked Kosygin if Kosygin would send a joint telegram which said: "NVN FonMin says he will negotiate in exchange for bombing cessation. I (Wilson) don't know this man, but Kosygin does and will underwrite him." Kosygin said that he would table his own draft at next session (4 PM Tues).

    3. Wilson asked if Washington could provide alternative draft for him to table - a draft acceptable to Washington and one that Sovs would hopefully sign on to. Wilson (and more particularly Brown) also feel urgent need to get "minimum reciprocal act" which US can accept. (We went through standard list re infiltration, trucks, etc.) I need whatever Wash can provide by 1300 London time.

    4. Wilson told me privately Kosygin said US was "in contact" with Hanoi.

    5. Just got a call from Pallisep to say Wilson making personal call to President.

BRUCE

February 7, 1967

    On February 7, Thompson was instructed to arrange delivery at once to the DRV Charge of a letter from the President to Ho Chi Minh (State's 132608).

LONDON 6321 (to SecState), TS/Nodis, Sent 1125, 7 Feb; Rec'd 1159 7 Feb.

For the Secretary and Harriman from Cooper

. . . .

2. . . . . I received the President's message to Wilson, and read substantial portions of it to Brown. Brown felt this would starch up Wilson and strengthen his hand in the afternoon's discussions.

3. We then went on to discuss the US-USSR communique. We explored a statement along these lines: A. Both sides (The British and the Soviets) agree that a settlement of the Vietnam war must be worked out as early as possible. B. Both sides agree to do whatever they can jointly and individually to assist such a settlement to come about. C. Both sides recognize that successful negotiations cannot take place unless bombing has stopped and mutual steps are taken toward further de-escalation (Phase A-Phase B). D. Both sides agree that they will maintain continual contact and discussion in connection with the Vietnam issue.

4. Brown thinks that he can get Wilson on board on this and that there is a good possibility that the Russians would buy something along these lines. . . .

. . . .

BRUCE

STATE 132481 (to Amembassy London), TS/Nodis, Sent 1919, 7 Feb 67

Literally Eyes Only for Ambassador and Cooper

Following message has been sent to Prime Minister from the President via White House channels:

"For the Prime Minister from the President.

"I am sending these thoughts to you on the question posed as to whether the U.S. could stop the bombing of North Viet Nam in exchange for an indication that Hanoi would enter into talks without any military acts of de-escalation on their side.

"It is important to recall that the Poles said to us in the first part of December that Hanoi would be prepared to hold discussions with us on the basis of a Polish summary of what the Poles understood our position to be. Discussion of mutual de-escalation, including a cessation of the bombing, would be a part of those talks. We promptly agreed to such talks but found that Hanoi (so the Poles told us) was unwilling to proceed with such talks because of certain bombing actions which occurred on 13-14

December. Although we had seen no real move toward talks before that date, we nevertheless removed that obstacle (if that was the obstacle) by informing Hanoi that we were refraining from bombing within a radius of 10 nautical miles of the center of Hanoi -- restrictions which have been in effect for more than a month. We took this action without conditions but did state that we would be impressed by any corresponding action by Hanoi. This was an important military move on our part. We have seen neither a corresponding military step on their side nor a use of existing channels to get on with discussions. In contacts with Hanoi since December 23 Hanoi has received messages from us but we have not had any replies from Hanoi on any points of substance. Indeed, the Burchett interview represents a step backward from Hanoi's position in December if the Poles were accurately reporting to us.

"We have recently informed Hanoi directly that we would be prepared to take additional military measures of de-escalation similar to the limitation of bombing within the Hanoi perimeter, on similar terms. We have had no reply to that suggestion.

"We are ready and willing to hold discussions with Hanoi through any feasible process -- publicly or privately, directly or indirectly. We are inclined to the view that better progress could be made if such talks were private and direct.

"If we are asked to take military action on our side, we need to know what the military consequences will be, that is, what military action will be taken by the other side. We have noted that a suspension of the bombing has been termed by the other side as unacceptable and that we must accept an unconditional and permanent cessation of bombing. That makes it all the more necessary to know what military action Hanoi would take if we in fact stopped the bombing.

"We are prepared to take up with Hanoi steps of mutual de-escalation and are prepared to have the most private preliminary conversations with them on arrangements for serious discussions of a final settlement.

"Specifically, we are prepared to and plan, through established channels, to inform Hanoi that if they will agree to an assured stoppage of infiltration into South Viet Nam, we will stop the bombing of North Viet Nam and stop further augmentation of U.S. forces in South Viet Nam.[26] We would welcome your joint advocacy of this position.

"Further, or alternatively, you should know we would recommend to the South Vietnamese military authorities that they discuss with North Vietnamese military authorities a prolongation of the Tet ceasefire.

"For your own information, you should be aware of by feeling that, in all of our various contacts with Hanoi, we have had no impression from them as to the substance of the issues which must be resolved as a part of a peaceful settlement. They have received repeated statements from us about our views. They have reiterated their four points and the

Liberation Front's five points with varying degree of vagueness as to their status, but they have not replied to our suggestions for a revision of point three of their four points or a readiness to hold preliminary discussions looking toward agreed points as a basis for negotiations.

"In sum, I would suggest that you try to separate the political processes of discussion from military action. We will participate fully in any political process including discussions of de-escalation. We are prepared to move immediately on major steps of mutual de-escalation, as indicated above. What we cannot accept is the exchange of guarantee of a safe haven for North Viet Nam merely for discussions which thus far have no form or content, during which they could continue to expand their military operations without limit.

"I doubt very much that Kosygin expected to resolve this matter on his first evening in London and it would be helpful if you could fully explore just what Kosygin is willing or able to do. If he has counter-proposals to my major suggestion of mutual military de-escalation, we will give them immediate attention.

"If Kosygin is seriously worried about China, as he told you he was, we would hope that he would exert himself to help bring peace to Viet Nam and allow North Viet Nam to participate in the peaceful development of Southeast Asia.

"Finally, I would strongly urge that the two co-chairmen not suggest a stoppage of the bombing in exchange merely for talks, but, instead, appeal to Hanoi to consider seriously the reasonable proposals we are putting before them, which would take us not merely into negotiation but a long step towards peace itself."

RUSK.

(Text received from White House).

LONDON 6360 (to SecState), TS/Nodis, Sent 2020, 7 Feb; Rec'd 2105, 7 Feb.

For the Secretary and Harriman from Cooper

. . . .

2. . . . , Kosygin did not table a draft message to the President as he said he would do. Rather, he gave a pro-forma restatement of his earlier position on importance of the Vietnamese statements to Burchett.

3. Wilson read from his prepared briefing notes. The exposition of the Phase A - Phase B formula was changed from the version contained in my para 5 London 6329. It was felt that it would be worth spelling this out

in the simplest possible terms. The final text follows:[27]

4. Kosygin showed considerable interest in this formulation. He
evidently had not understood it when Brown presented·it to him last November. He asked Wilson to repeat it and then asked Wilson to deliver the
text to him in writing this evening. This has been done. The British are
virtually certain that Kosygin is going to transmit this to Hanoi. They
hope that on Thursday afternoon when talks resume Kosygin will have a
reply from Hanoi.

. . . .

BRUCE

February 8, 1967

His Excellency
    Ho Chi Minh
        President
            Democratic Republic of Vietnam

Dear Mr. President:

I am writing to you in the hope that the conflict in Vietnam can be brought to an end. That conflict has already taken a heavy toll--in lives lost, in wounds inflicted, in property destroyed, and in simple human misery. If we fail to find a just and peaceful solution, history will judge us harshly.

Therefore, I believe that we both have a heavy obligation to seek earnestly the path to peace. It is in response to that obligation that I am writing directly to you.

We have tried over the past several years, in a variety of ways and through a number of channels, to convey to you and your colleagues our desire to achieve a peaceful settlement. For whatever reasons, these efforts have not achieved any results.

It may be that our thoughts and yours, our attitudes and yours, have been distorted or misinterpreted as they passed through these various channels. Certainly that is always a danger in indirect communication.

There is one good way to overcome this problem and to move forward in the search for a peaceful settlement. That is for us to arrange for direct talks between trusted representatives in a secure setting and away from the glare of publicity. Such talks should not be used as a propaganda exercise but should be a serious effort to find a workable and mutually acceptable solution.

In the past two weeks, I have noted public statements by representatives of your government suggesting that you would be prepared to enter into direct bilateral talks with representatives of the US Government, provided that we ceased "unconditionally" and permanently our bombing operations against your country and all military actions against it. In the last day, serious and responsible parties have assured us indirectly that this is in fact your proposal.

Let me frankly state that I see two great difficulties with this proposal. In view of your public position, such action on our part would inevitably produce worldwide speculation that discussions were under way and would impair the privacy and secrecy of those discussions. Secondly, there would inevitably be grave concern on our part whether your government would make use of such action by us to improve its military position.

With these problems in mind, I am prepared to move even further
towards an ending of hostilities than your Government has proposed in
either public statements or through private diplomatic channels. I am
prepared to order a cessation of bombing against your country and the
stopping of further augmentation of US forces in South Viet-Nam as soon
as I am assured that infiltration into South Viet-Nam by land and by sea
has stopped.[28] These acts of restraint on both sides would, I believe, make
it possible for us to conduct serious and private discussions leading
toward an early peace.

I make this proposal to you now with a specific sense of urgency
arising from the imminent New Year holidays in Viet-Nam. If you are
able to accept this proposal I see no reason why it could not take effect
at the end of the New Year, or Tet, holidays. The proposal I have made
would be greatly strengthened if your military authorities and those of
the Government of South Viet-Nam could promptly negotiate an extension
of the Tet truce.

As to the site of the bilateral discussions I propose, there are
several possibilities. We could, for example, have our representatives
meet in Moscow where contacts have already occurred. They could meet
in some other country such as Burma. You may have other arrangements or
sites in mind, and I would try to meet your suggestions.

The important thing is to end a conflict that has brought burdens
to both our peoples, and above all to the people of South Viet-Nam. If
you have any thoughts about the actions I propose, it would be most
important that I receive them as soon as possible.

Sincerely,

Lyndon B. Johnson

On February 8, Cooper had separate meetings with Brown and Wilson,
the results of which indicated that Wilson would hew to our line on
bombing cessation (London's 6321-6329). In addition, the framework of a
final communique was discussed. Further guidance on this subject was
provided in State's 132521 with particular emphasis on the British not
signing anything which calls for unilateral action by us.

On the same day, Wilson responded to a parliamentary question on
the MARIGOLD subject by stating he had "all the details" on the December
meetings which had been aborted by a "mutual understanding".

. . . .

Late that evening (Feb. 8).Ben Read telephoned Cooper and advised
him that (1) we could not draw conclusions from the single sentence on

Geneva in Kosygin's Guildhall address; (2) we would wish Wilson to probe Kosygin at the next morning's meeting; and (3) if the Soviets are serious on this issue, we would give urgent consideration to Brown's suggestion or any variant thereof.

MOSCOW 3412 (to SecState), TS/Nodis, Sent 1030, 8 Feb; Rec'd 1347, 8 Feb. Ref: Moscow 3404

. . . .

2. . . . , Le Chang . . . wished say that he could transmit message today.

3. DCM said would report Le Chang's remarks to his Govt, and also expressed pleasure at fact President's message would be transmitted today.

. . . .

THOMPSON.

London BBC Domestic Television Service in English 1510Z 8 Feb 67

(Kosygin speech at Lord Mayor's luncheon at the Guildhall in London on 8 February . . . .)

. . . .

Today the major factors of international tension are the Vietnamese events and it is the US aggression which is the real, and in effect the only, cause for the war in Vietnam. We may say that the United States was sowing the seeds of that war as far back as in 1954 when, in contrast to the Soviet Union, Britain, and several other countries, it attempted to prevent the restoration of peace in Indochina, and in the following years when it prevented universal Democratic elections as provided for by the Geneva agreements. Even then the United States began dictatorially to set up and replace, one after the other, the governments in Saigon.

. . . .

. . . . The United Kingdom is a state whose voice is heeded by many and it is precisely for this reason that the Soviet government believes that today, as in 1954, Great Britain together with the Soviet Union and other nations could make its contribution to the settlement of the Vietnam issue on the basis of the Geneva agreement, which must be implemented by the United States.

The first step in this direction should be the unconditional termination of the U.S. bombing and of all other acts of aggression against the DRV, as was recently stated by the DRV Foreign Minister. This step is essential for talks to be held between the DRV and the United States. . . .

. . . .

LONDON 6399 (to SecState), TS/Nodis, Sent 0241, 9 Feb; Rec'd 0313, 9 Feb.

For Secretary from Cooper.

2. Brown . . . impressed with Kosygin statement in Guildhall speech today that "--- the Soviet Govt considers now as in 1954, Great Britain jointly with Soviet Union and other countries, could make her contribution to the settlement of the VN question on the basis of the Geneva agreements which must be observed by USA."

3. Brown feels Sovs may be signalling a readiness to convene Geneva. . . . . Brown asked for draft written proposal. . . .

4. Gore Booth Murray and I went back to FonOff and prepared following (which they understand very clearly that this does not have any official endorsement of USG despite my participation in drafting):[29]

QUOTE:

5. If Sovs will not buy this, Brown will press them to endorse Phase A - Phase B formula as they formulated it yesterday.

BRUCE

February 9, 1967

LONDON 6406 (to SecState), TS/Nodis, Sent 1222, 9 Feb; Rec'd 1258, 9 Feb.

For Secretary and Harriman from Cooper

. . . .

3. Wilson and Brown (and also some old FonOff hands) are impressed with these aspects of conversations held thus far:

A. Kosygin's   readiness to discuss this subject without apparent inhibition.

B.   Kosygin's sense of urgency to move ahead on some formula (thus far, his own) for joint UK-Sov approach "to assist getting the US and DRV, "the two principals", to settle the war.

C. Kosygin's statements that he is in direct touch with Hanoi and his stated readiness to refer important new issues and approaches directly to Hanoi for consideration, e.g. the British version of Phase A-Phase B.

D. The low key, non-polemical tone of the talks on all issues (Gore-Booth said last night that talks on bilateral issues are moving smoothly and "not badly").

. . . .

10. . . . I have gotten a call from the FonOff to the effect that Kosygin's answer to query re significance his statement on Geneva was sufficiently forthcoming to have warranted Wilson commitment to provide Kosygin a proposition in writing "later in the day" about calling Geneva Conf presumably along lines of three-part Draft I forwarded to Wash early this morning . . . .

BRUCE

LONDON 6411 (to SecState), TS/Nodis, Sent 1439, 9 Feb; Rec'd 1523, 9 Feb. Ref: 6406

. . . .

3. . . . . Brown then asked Kosygin whether his remarks about Geneva in his speech yesterday indicated the Russians were ready to reconvene the Geneva Conference, even if the Chinese refused to attend. Kosygin replied this was "not exactly" what he meant to imply. Kosygin, according to Murray's notes, said that in his speech yesterday "I proceeded upon the assumption that the main thing was for the UK and the

Sov Union to assist the two sides to meet together after the bombing stopped.
After this has been done there may be various proposals for moving further.
The Geneva Conf could be convened

      Kosygin then went on to say that he "could not speak for Hanoi
on this point". He emphasized that it was important to "do first things
first. If we try to work out the tactics too early we might jeopardize
everything. . . . We might raise other problems such as   and Laos
(according to Murray this is the first time Laos has been mentioned in
any of the conversations)."

    . . . .

    5. Brown then said that no bombing would be going on during TET. In
light of this "thinking out loud," suppose the US should agree not to
resume bombing, and both sides agreed to take mutual and equivalent steps
would Kosygin then agree to call a Geneva Conf on 15 Feb?

    6. Kosygin said that he would first want to know Hanoi's views
before he committed himself. He reminded Brown that a Geneva Conf would
be "a complicated issue";

                         Kosygin then asked "has this
been discussed with the Americans?" Brown said that if Kosygin could
deliver his friends in Hanoi the British would try to "deliver the Americans."

    7. Kosygin responded "I could send this to Hanoi, but I am con-
cerned about the difficulties." He said he would like to "think it over,"
and asked if he could have the proposition in writing as early as possible today. Brown said he would do his best to get this to Kosygin later
in the afternoon.

    8. The next meeting will be at 1030 tomorrow morning. At this
session the British plan to point out that they have now delivered two
solid propositions to the Russians and presumably Hanoi. One of these
provides for a private series of negotiations, the other a public one,
both involve mutual and equivalent steps of de-escalation. If Hanoi is
serious about wanting to stop the war, the Russians have an obligation
to provide Hanoi's reactions, and this should be done on an urgent basis.

BRUCE

STATE 133907 (to Amembassy London), TS/Nodis, Sent 1845, 9 Feb 67.

. . . .

2. As we believe we mave made clear to you, we have major doubts whether, if Hanoi in fact accepts the deal we have proposed, they will ask to have it nailed down in public through any announcement, and might have additional misgivings about the Soviets doing so in the light of whatever degree of concern they still have about Chicom reactions. We would suppose the latter factor would also operate strongly on the Soviets, since any public announcement would carry the unmistakeable flavor that the Soviets had colluded with the US, through the UK, to put this deal across . . . . British should be left in no doubt that, while we are most grateful for their serious considered efforts, they may well have to accept results rather than overt British participation in them.

3. With this evaluation in mind, we have reviewed text in para 4 of London 6399 and note that, like the British oral formula (London 6329, para 5), it speaks only of DRV stopping "augmentation of forces" in South Vietnam. This would leave way open for DRV to continue to send equipment without restrictions and also to send forces in the guise of rotation. Moreover, there would be no restraint whatsoever on political cadre and others who could be described as not technically uniformed "forces." In light of these objections, any specific formula along these lines which the British might put forward would have to be amended along following lines:

QTE. The two cochairmen will announce immediately that they:

a. Invite the US to assure them that the bombing of North Vietnam will stop;

b. Invite the North Vietnamese to assure the cochairmen that infiltration into South Vietnam will stop, and invite the US to assure the cochairmen that it will stop further augmentation of US forces in South Vietnam. (FYI: These are the operative parts both of our own message to the British (State 132481) and of our message to Hanoi. End FYI).

c. If all the foregoing assurances are promptly received, the two cochairmen will invite members of the 1954 Geneva Conference to reconvene in Geneva on 15 February to work out a settlement of the present conflict. END QTE

. . . .

5. Seeing as we do these possibly serious difficulties with a precise formulation of the deal -- and doubting, as we do, that Hanoi will wish a really specific public announcement -- you should tell British that we ourselves would be much more inclined to have them table the more general Phase A/Phase B formula.

. . . .

RUSK (Drafted by W. P. Bundy)   39

LONDON 6429 (to SecState), TS/Nodis, Sent 2200, 9 Feb; Rec'd 2225, 9 Feb.
Ref: State 133907

   1. Met with Murray FonOff and dictated points A, B, and C para 3 which then transcribed verbatim as British proposal. This sent to Brown at Buckingham Palace dinner for handing over to Kosygin.

   2. Also passed on, orally, to Murray our preference for their Phase A - Phase B formula and he in complete agreement.

   . . . .

BRUCE

STATE 134409 (to Amembassy Saigon & London), TS/Nodis, Sent 2427, 9 Feb.

Saigon for Ambassador/London for Ambassador and Cooper

   1. Following is DoD summary of developments surrounding Tet truces, on which you should take actions indicated in succeeding paragraphs:

      a. North Vietnamese water-borne traffic along coast of North Vietnam between 19 degrees north latitude and the DMZ (17 degrees north latitude) totaled over 900 vessels of various types during the first 30 hours of the Tet truce which, ... is more than double the logistic resupply traffic during the Christmas 48-hour truce. . . .

      b. The situation described above obviously creates a hazard to our forces which we cannot overlook. Moreover, it illustrates graphically why the USG cannot cease bombing operations against North Vietnam in exchange for a promise to talk rather than a substantial military curtailment on their part.

      c. . . . : Our intelligence sources reveal that the North Vietnamese have been moving during the past two weeks an additional division from central North Vietnam southward, presumably to reinforce the two North Vietnamese divisions which are already within or just north of the DMZ. Additionally, our intelligence gives some reason to believe that the North Vietnamese units in and near the DMZ are on the alert and positioned for renewal of combat operations and infiltration, possibly soon after the Tet truce expires. The substantial resupply efforts of the North Vietnamese support this evaluation.

   2. Saigon should coordinate with MACV to make public material in para 1a above. . . .

3. Ambassador Bruce and Cooper should bring this story to the attention of highest British levels . . . . In so doing, you should not repeat not suggest that we are not still wide open to the idea of continuing the Tet bombing suspension through the 7-day period or at least until Kosygin departs London. You should emphasize, however, that we are seriously concerned about these developments and that final decision on such additional two- or three-day suspension does involve serious factors in light of this information.

4. Wireless file is carrying full account of Secretary's press conference today, at which he made more general statement about supply activity and rate of incidents.[30]

RUSK (Drafted by W. P. Bundy)

Department of State, Public Information Bulletin, February 13, 1967.

FOURTEEN POINTS FOR PEACE IN SOUTHEAST ASIA

"Secretary Rusk on January 27[*] approved the release of the following elaboration of the Fourteen Points for Peace in Southeast Asia, which were previously made public by the Department of State on January 7, 1966.

1. The Geneva Agreements of 1954 and 1962 are an adequate basis for peace in Southeast Asia.

2. We would welcome a conference on Southeast Asia or any part thereof:

-- We are ready to negotiate a settlement based on a strict observance of the 1954 and 1962 Geneva Agreements, which observance was called for in the declaration on Viet-Nam of the meeting of the Warsaw Pact countries in Bucharest on July 6, 1966. And we will support a reconvening of the Geneva Conference, or an Asian conference, or any other generally acceptable forum.

3. We would welcome "negotiations without preconditions" as called for by 17 nonalined nations in an appeal delivered to Secretary Rusk on April 1, 1965.

4. We would welcome "unconditional discussions" as called for by President Johnson on April 7, 1965:

-- If the other side will not come to a conference, we are prepared to engage in direct discussions or discussions through an intermediary.

---

* At his February 9 Press Conference, Secretary Rusk drew attention to the revised 14 points, saying , "I am today making available points we made last year under 14 different headings--annotated to reflect developments in 1966." For this study, therefore, the effective release date is taken as February 9.

5. A cessation of hostilities could be the first order of business at a conference or could be the subject of preliminary discussions:

> -- We have attempted, many times, to engage the other side in a discussion of a mutual deescalation of the level of violence, and we remain prepared to engage in such a mutual deescalation.

> -- We stand ready to cooperate fully in getting discussions which could lead to a cessation of hostilities started promptly and brought to a successful completion.

6. Hanoi's four points could be discussed along with other points which others may wish to propose:

> -- We would be prepared to accept preliminary discussions to reach agreement on a set of points as a basis for negotiations.

7. We want no U.S. bases in Southeast Asia:

> -- We are prepared to assist in the conversion of these bases for peaceful uses that will benefit the peoples of the entire area.

8. We do not desire to retain U.S. troops in South Viet-Nam after peace is assured:

> -- We seek no permanent military bases, no permanent establishment of troops, no permanent alliances, no permanent American "presence" of any kind in South Viet-Nam.

> -- We have pledged in the Manila Communique that "Allied forces are in the Republic of Vietnam because that country is the object of aggression and its government requested support in the resistance of its people to aggression. They shall be withdrawn, after close consultation, as the other side withdraws its forces to the North, ceases infiltration, and the level of violence thus subsides. Those forces will be withdrawn as soon as possible and not later than six months after the above conditions have been fulfilled."

9. We support free elections in South Viet-Nam to give the South Vietnamese a government of their own choice.

> -- We support the development of broadly based democratic institutions in South Viet-Nam.

> -- We do not seek to exclude any segment of the South Vietnamese people from peaceful participation in their country's future.

10. The question of reunification of Viet-Nam should be determined by the Vietnamese through their own free decision:

    -- It should not be decided by the use of force.

    -- We are fully prepared to support the decision of the Vietnamese people.

11. The countries of Southeast Asia can be nonalined or neutral if that be their option:

    -- We do not seek to impose a policy of alinement on South Viet-Nam.

    -- We support the neutrality policy of the Royal Government of Laos, and we support the neutrality and territorial integrity of Cambodia.

12. We would much prefer to use our resources for the economic reconstruction of Southeast Asia than in war. If there is peace, North Viet-Nam could participate in a regional effort to which we would be prepared to contribute at least one billion dollars:

    -- We support the growing efforst by the nations of the area to cooperate in the achievement of their economic and social goals.

13. The President has said "The Viet Cong would have no difficulty in being represented and having their views presented if Hanoi for a moment decides she wants to cease aggression. And I would not think that would be an insurmountable problem at all."

14. We have said publicly and privately that we could stop the bombing of North Viet-Nam as a step toward peace although there has not been the slightest hint or suggestion from the other side as to what they would do if the bombing stopped:

    -- We are prepared to order a cessation of all bombing of North Viet-Nam, the moment we are assured -- privately or otherwise -- that this step will be answered promptly by a corresponding and appropriate deescalation of the other side.

    -- We do not seek the unconditional surrender of North Viet-Nam; what we do seek is to assure for the people of South Viet-Nam the right to decide their own political destiny, free of force.

43

February 10, 1967

New York Times, 12 February 1967
Text of Goldberg's Howard University Speech[31]
Special to The New York Times
Washington, Feb. 10 - Following are excerpts from the text of an address
on "America's Peace Aims in Vietnam" delivered today at Howard University
by Arthur J. Goldberg, chief United States representative at the United
Nations:

. . . .

. . . . The United States remains prepared to take the first step
and order a cessation of all bombing of North Vietnam the moment we are
assured, privately or otherwise, that this step will be answered promptly
by a tangible response toward peace from North Vietnam.

Some analysts contend that our terms of settlement should be more
precisely defined. But it is very difficult to be more precise in advance
of negotiation, and particularly in light of the substantive ambiguities
on the other side. But whatever questions may be raised, they should and
can best be resolved in discussions between the parties who have the power
to resolve them. For our part, we stand ready to negotiate in good faith
unconditionally to resolve all outstanding questions.

. . . .

SAIGON 17769 (to SecState), TS/Nodis, Sent 0720, 10 Feb; Rec'd 0826, 10 Feb.
Ref: State 133834

1. I believe it is necessary and prudent to inform Ky of message to
Hanoi as soon as possible. . . .

. . . .

3. . . . . I will find it more difficult to explain the new element
introduced by our willingness to stop augmentation . . . . Information
giving rationale re stopping augmentation would be most useful.

. . . .

7. Do you wish me to inform General Westmoreland at the time Ky is
told?

. . . .

LODGE.

STATE 135513 (to Amembassy Saigon), TS/Nodis
Ref: State 133834; Saigon 17769

. . . .

2.   We have provided British with text of proposal.   They had
already outlined a variation of it orally to Kosygin, who expressed
interest today and asked for written text to forward at once to Hanoi.
This has been provided and reads as below.   You may convey to Ky orally
as much of digest of proposal as you deem wise in view of great necessity
for secrecy.

QTE A.   The United States will order a cessation of bombing of
North Vietnam as soon as they are assured that infiltration from North
Vietnam to South Vietnam has stopped.   This assurance can be communicated
in secret if North Vietnam so wishes. .

B.   Within a few days (with a period to be agreed with the two
sides before the bombing stops) the United States will stop further augmenting their force in South Vietnam.   The cessation of bombing of North
Vietnam is an action which will be immediately apparent.   This requires
that the stoppage of infiltration become public very quickly thereafter.
If Hanoi is unwilling to announce the stoppage of infiltration, the United
States must do so at the time it stops augmentation of US forces.   In that
case, Hanoi must not deny it.

C.   Any assurances from Hanoi can reach the United States direct,
or through Soviet channels, or through the Soviet and British Governments.
This is for North Vietnam to decide.   END QUOTE.

3.   In explaining about text, we believe British will have made clear
that our stopping "augmenting" would still permit rotation and continued
supply.   Stoppage of infiltration defined as meaning that men and arms
cannot move from DRV into South Vietnam.   You should note also that wording
of subpara A precludes any sudden last-minute reinforcements after bombing
has stopped. . . .

4. . . . . Deprived of additional men and of urgently needed equipment from the North, we believe NVA/VC forces would be significantly
weakened in concrete terms and would probably suffer serious adverse effects
on their morale.   If infiltration in fact ceases and this word can be picked
up by SVN and allied psychological warfare units, we believe there are big
chances that Chieu Hoi and reconciliation programs would produce substantially larger returns.[32] In short, we think proposal is defensible and forthcoming, if it should ever be surfaced, but at the same time clearly favorable
in terms of its effect on the military and morale situation. . . .

. . . .

45

7. Quite frankly our present judgment is that these present moves will come to nothing, but in reviewing the history of World War II and post-war crises, many other such situations have come to an end faster than we thought probable in advance and for reasons we did not fully comprehend until after the events. . . .

8. You may inform Westmoreland personally of this proposal, which is known here to General Wheeler. . . .

RUSK (Drafted by S. P. Bundy)

LONDON 6456 (to SecState), TS/Nodis, Sent 1700, 10 Feb; Rec'd 1712, 10 Feb.

Here is text of Phase A-Phase B formula which is to be sent to Kosygin at his request ASAP. Need guidance urgently.

These steps are as follows:-

(A) The United States will stop bombing North Vietnam as soon as they are assured that infiltration from North Vietnam to South Vietnam will stop. This assurance can be communicated in secret if North Vietnam so wishes.

(B) Within a few days (with the period to be agreed between the two sides before the bombing stops) the United States will stop further augmenting their forces in South Vietnam and North Vietnam will stop infiltration and movement of forces into the South.

(C) The cessation of bombing of North Vietnam and the cessation of build-up of United States forces in the South are actions which will be immediately apparent.

(D) A cessation of infiltration is more difficult for the world to observe. Nevertheless the United States will not demand any public statement from North Vietnam.

(E) Any secret assurances from Hanoi can reach the United States direct, or through Soviet channels, or through the Soviet and British governments. This is for North Vietnam to decide.

BRUCE

LONDON 6462 (to SecState), TS/Nodis, Sent 1800, 10 Feb; Rec'd 1824, 10 Feb.

For the Secretary from Cooper [33]

1. This morning's session was devoted primarily to Europe, but Wilson did take occasion to point out that he had submitted two proposals and

Soviets had not replied as yet to either. Kosygin then indicated that
he wanted to hear the Phase A - Phase B proposal once again, and having
heard it he asked Wilson to put it in a form so that he could telegraph
it as soon as possible, ...

. . . .

BRUCE.

LONDON 6481 (to SecState), TS/Nodis, Sent 0205, 11 Feb; Rec'd 0251, 11 Feb.

To Secretary from Bruce and Cooper [34]

1. White House version of message passed to Kosygin prior his departure
for Scotland with this introductory statement:

QTE. I have just received direct from the White House the
following message which they have asked me to pass to you. You may take
this now as the authentic U.S. position on the subject I discussed with
you, and on which I handed a note to you this evening. UNQTE

2. Earlier British version had been given to Kosygin by Wilson when
he saw him at Soviet reception earlier in evening.

. . . .

4. Cooper will go to Chequers (through back door) early Sunday
afternoon and will be kept informed course of discussions as they proceed.
Please provide Cooper with name of phone contact in event matters require
immediate reporting or guidance on the spot..

BRUCE

February 11, 1967

By telephone (Feb. 11) Cooper reported British concern about our
insistence that our Phase A-B formulation (para. 55) specify that infiltration "has stopped", which they noted was different than the future
tense employed in the revised Point 14 release to the press on February 9.

MOSCOW 3451 (to SecState), TS/Nodis, Sent 1035, 11 Feb; Rec'd 1111, 11 Feb.

. . . .

2. After thanking DCM for coming over, Le Chang said he wished inform him that President's message to Ho Chi Minh delivered February 8 had been transmitted to Hanoi. Ho Chi Minh had received message and reply would be forwarded later.

3. In response DCM question when message received in Hanoi, Le Chang said it had been transmitted immediately.

THOMPSON

SAIGON 17822 (to SecState), TS/Nodis, Sent 1200, 11 Feb; Rec;d 1310, 11 Feb.

1. Pursuant to your 135513, I called on Ky . . . .

. . . .

8. Our present judgment, I said, is that these moves will come to nothing, but in reviewing earlier crises, many other such situations have come to an end faster than we thought probable in advance. There may be one chance in ten that the other side is in deeper trouble than we realized.

. . . .

10. Ky listened attentively, and, after I had completed my statement, asked what kind of guarantees would there be -- meaning what kind of an inspection system.

11. I said that we were thinking of the ICC -- in the efficacy of which he expressed complete lack of confidence (as indeed do I).

12. He then said that he was afraid that if we stopped the bombing now, based on their promise and they don't keep their promise, public opinion would make it extremely difficult for us to resume the bombing . . . . .

. . . .

14. When 1 asked him whether he thought that they would accept our proposal, he first said that he did not think they would -- that there would be a loss of face for them in admitting that there ever had been a war. Then after some reflection, he said: "If I am Hanoi, I would say 'yes'. They would gain something, we would gain nothing. It is a certainty that they will not stop infiltration no matter how much they promise to do so". . . . .

15. He felt that to try a thing like this now was premature. It
was "too soon. It would be better to wait a few more months. We would
then be in a better position to see the situation more clearly. We
should not stop just as our military campaign is getting results, and
as we are making progress politically."[35]

. . ..

LODGE.

LONDON 6487 (to SecState), TS/Nodis, Sent 1227, 11 Feb; Rec'd 1250, 11 Feb.

For Secretary from Cooper

1. I have just been informed by the FonOff that the Pope sent a
private message to the PM last night asking him to urge Kosygin that
there be a joint endorsement in the communique of the Pope's recent
message to the three "warring parties."[36]

2.

BRUCE.

LONDON 6488 (to SecState), TS/Nodis, Sent 1227, 11 Feb; Rec'd 1340, 11 Feb.

For Secretary from Bruce and Cooper

. . . .

2. One of the "contingencies" which Wilson has particularly in mind
rose from what he describes as a "jocular exchange" between himself and
Kosygin at the Soviet reception last night. If the two sides did not come
to an agreement Sunday night, Kosygin and Wilson thought that next step to
consider might be sending Gromyko and Brown to Washington and for Kosygin
and Wilson to go to Hanoi. The Gromyko-Brown visit was apparently brushed
aside as a private joke, but the Kosygin-Wilson visit to Hanoi was regarded,
by Wilson if not by Kosygin, as a more serious possibility.

3. . . . . .

. . . .

BRUCE

LONDON 6493 (to SecState), TS/Nodis, Sent 1615, 11 Feb; Rec'd 1704, 11 Feb.

Eyes only for Secretary from Bruce [37]

    1.   If Secretary agrees I would appreciate this message being passed to Secretary McNamara.

    2.   I would not presume to comment on extent of the military disadvantage of our not renewing bombing in North Vietnam until Kosygin has left London. I do feel, however, absolutely compelled to express a personal opinion as to what I consider would be its adverse political effects at this time.

    3.   As I understand it, a decision by the USG for such renewal has already been taken, but would it not be possible to postpone ensuing action for the approximately thirty five hours; (reckoned in GMT) before Kosygin departs from here, and, during that period, to make no public declaration on the subject.

    4.   My reasons are:

    A.   Although there are no grounds for being more than lukewarmly optimistic over anything of substantial value emerging from the current talks, it is quite evident that Kosygin, within the limitations under which he operated, seems almost as desirous as ourselves to bring about a cessation of hostilities in Vietnam. During his stay today in Scotland, he may be disturbed, and rendered even more suspicious than usual, over what will probably appear to him the discrepancies between our last statement of conditions delivered to him last night as he was boarding a train), and certain preceding ones notably point fourteen, in our list of fourteen, which he has. I believe his concern over the disruption of other Soviet foreign policies resulting from deep involvement in Vietnam,

incline him strongly in favor of using whatever influence he may possess in Hanoi to bring about negotiations between Ho and ourselves.

    B.   Since renunciation of bombing of the North with reciprocal response from Hanoi has become almost everywhere a symbol of US seriousness in desiring a peaceful settlement, bombing as a term has taken on a political connotation independent of its military significance.

    C.   I would expect Kosygin, who has been acting in concert with Brezhnev, will not disclose his full hand until the meeting at Chequers tomorrow evening. But if at that time it is evident that he does not have sufficient prestige to postpone even for the short time he will still be on British soil a resumption of the type of operation he has steadily inveighed against, I would guess that he will prove definitively intransigent, and henceforth far more difficult to seek cooperation from. Then, too, his opinion of Wilson's credibility, already shaken by last night's imbroglio, may lead his Russian suspiciousness into dark imaginings.

50

D.   It seems to me by refraining still for a matter of hours from punishing the North Vietnamese for a flagrant breach of the truce, we might, though we would have no assurance of it, succeed in not alienating the great potential usefulness of our until recently improbable ally.

BRUCE.

STATE 135627 (to Amembassy London), TS/Nodis, Sent 1908, 11 Feb.

1.   This responds to your telecons relaying message from Wilson about resumption of bombing.

2.   As you know, we did not want to make any commitments to extend the TET bombing stand-down. You also know that our basic position remains not to stop bombing in return for mere willingness to talk.

3.   However, we have great respect for your opinion and accept your recommendation not to conduct military actions against the North until Kosygin leaves. It must be absolutely clear to Wilson that we would then go ahead and that we will not consider a further deferral.

4.   Wilson should not refer to resumption of bombing on his own initiative. If Kosygin asks about it, we suggest that Wilson relay that he is not familiar with details of allied military plans but that US attitude on this point has been made clear.

5.   Wilson should be left in no doubt that we cannot prolong suspension of bombing in absence of firm word on infiltration. He should also know that when we say "stop infiltration" we mean "stop infiltration." We cannot trade a horse for a rabbit and will react to bad faith on this point. We are losing lives today because such commitments in Laos Accords of 1962 were treated with contempt by Hanoi and Co-Chairmen and ICC could do nothing about it.

6.   About Wilson trip to Hanoi, we see little point in it. We thought two Co-Chairmen had concluded that best prospects lie in bilateral contact between US and Hanoi. Further, we could not become involved in a visit which would raise problem of another unrequited suspension of bombing.

7.   Wilson is of course already aware that the South Vietnamese and we are resuming operations in the South tomorrow (112300 Zulu) and that we have been carrying on bombing operations in Laos throughout.

8.   Septel will contain our comments on the question of tenses in our proposal.

RUSK (Drafted by W. P. Bundy)

51

STATE 135662 (to Amembassy London), TS/Nodis, Sent 2145, 11 Feb.

For Ambassador and Cooper Only

1. This responds to your report of British concern about our insistence that draft specify that infiltration "has stopped." We gather they are pointing to apparent inconsistency between this position and the future tense employed in the revised point 14 released here Thursday.

2. You should give them the following:.

a. As previous message made clear, we face immediate specific problem of possible three divisions poised just north of DMZ. We must be in position to insist that these cannot be moved into SVN just before their undertaking takes effect.

b. We recognize that revised point 14 spoke in future tense, but that formulation related to a different proposal, i.e., bombing cessation alone on our side, not bombing cessation plus troop augmentation which of course are two major commitments on our part.

c. British should be aware (as we realize State 133834 did not make clear) that message conveyed to Hanoi was in same terms as final corrected draft, i.e., that we must be assured that infiltration has stopped. In the last 24 hours, we have information that Soviets are aware of contents of this message, presumably through their Hanoi contacts, so that change in tense in final draft given to Soviets did not repeat not come as surprise to Soviets or Hanoi and cannot have impaired British credibility.

d. In any event, our position on this point remains firm because of the special problem posed by the divisions north of the DMZ. We very much doubt whether Soviets or Hanoi will reject proposal for this reason. If they should come back on it, we would of course wish to be informed.

RUSK (Drafted by W. P. Bundy)

STATE 135675 (to Amembassy Saigon), TS/Nodis, Sent 2215, 11 Feb.

Literally Eyes Only for Ambassador

1. We are sending you separate instruction to inform Ky that we have decided that we should refrain from bombing the North until Kosygin leaves London. In conveying this to Ky, you should make clear that this decision was dictated solely by extreme British concern and vital importance of British support, ...

. . . .

RUSK (Drafted by W. P. Bundy)

STATE 135676 (to Amembassy Saigon), S/Nodis, Sent 2215, 11 Feb.

Eyes only Ambassadors

1. Saigon, Bangkok and Vientiane are receiving military message directing that bombing and naval operations against North Viet-Nam not repeat not be resumed until after Kosygin leaves London. This decision . . . . constitutes a one-shot exception to our standing policy, ... Our policy on not repeat not stopping bombing in return for talks remains unchanged.

2. Saigon should inform GVN of this decision. We leave it to Bangkok and Vientiane whether they think some notification would be desirable. . . .

. . . .

4. Canberra, Wellington, Seoul and Manila may in their discretion arrange unobtrusive contacts . . . .

(Not signed - Drafted by W. P. Bundy)

February 12, 1967

Late on February 11, Bruce and Cooper reported that they had had a stormy session with Wilson and Brown (London's 6495),[38] who were relieved that the bombing stand-down would continue while Kosygin was in London but concerned that the bombing would begin immediately after his departure. A greater problem, however, was the change in tenses in respect to the stoppage of bombing. Their formulation of the paragraph was based on an earlier message passed to Kosygin on February 7. This formulation was based on the last of the 14 Points. Since Washington raised no objection to this formulation earlier in the week, they assumed they were on safe ground. They now feel the ground has shifted under them. Furthermore, if we had passed the message directly to Hanoi on February 7, in terms of the past tense, why did we not inform them of this?

In the early morning hours of February 12, Wilson sent two messages[39] by private wire to the President, outlining in the first the "hell of a situation" he is in for his last day of talks with Kosygin and emphasizing his need to reestablish trust because not only will Kosygin have doubts about Wilson's credibility but, in addition, Kosygin will have lost credibility in Hanoi and possibly among his colleagues. Wilson said he planned to tell Kosygin that the present situation arises from deep US concern about the intensive North Vietnamese movements during the TET period. He felt he had to get Kosygin into as relaxed as possible posture and to tell him that the USSR-UK position must be not to concern themselves with military activities but to concentrate on the longer term political situation.

Wilson expressed considerable anguish about the shift in tense. He said he now realized Kosygin had bit on February 10 because he realized

Wilson had given him a softer version than the message passed directly to
Hanoi. Under the circumstances, Wilson felt he must stand by his version.
If Kosygin accepted, he would have to press his line on the President. If
it is impossible for the President to accept, Wilson felt he and the President would have to reason together about the situation which would then
arise. More generally, he hoped to get Kosygin into a position where he and
Wilson accepted joint responsibility for trying to assist the parties concerned in the fighting to reach agreement. This, he recognized, would be
difficult particularly when the bombing restarts. He hoped to nail Kosygin
to a continuing acceptance of a joint role of lawyers representing respective
clients who must try to get a settlement out of court, ad referendum to the
two clients. In view of the "clear breakdown" in communications and understanding during this week; Wilson felt he should meet with the President
very soon.

In his second message, Wilson described in detail the misunderstanding
that had arisen about the tense used in the infiltration paragraph.

At 0336, February 12, a direct response was sent by the President
to Wilson (repeated to London as State's 135718), pointing out that the
matter does not hang on the tense of verbs. Moscow had the Phase A-B
formulation in November from George Brown. Hanoi had it from the Poles.
Meanwhile, their build-up of forces has continued through three periods of
no bombing (Christmas, New Year's and TET). We have heard nothing from
Hanoi, although many intermediaries have attempted to negotiate with us.
We cannot stop the bombing while three or more divisions dash south from
the DMZ before Hanoi's promise to stop infiltration takes effect. We do
not agree that our statement to Wilson on February 7 is inconsistent with
either our message to Hanoi or our formula for Wilson and Kosygin on
February 10. We asked on February 7 for an "assured stoppage" of infiltration. In Wilson's version of the A-B formula it was transmuted into
an assurance that infiltration "will stop". This is a quite different
matter. We promptly recognized this and informed Burke Trend by telephone
that we would transmit our response shortly. The President emphasized
that no formula can be satisfactory to us--and perhaps to Hanoi--unless
there is clarity about two matters:

    a. the timing of a cessation of bombing, cessation of infil-
tration, and no further augmentation of forces; and

    b. how assurance in this matter of infiltration will be established.

Wilson was also informed that Hanoi had received our message and has
told us that a direct response would be forthcoming. The President emphasized the importance of the US and UK staying together and not permitting
the other side to play one position off against another.

The President concluded with a statement of deep appreciation for Wilson's efforts, an affirmation of intent to express publicly our thanks, and a disavowal of the possibility of giving him a power of attorney.

Wilson promptly responded by private wire, expressing full agreement about the grave danger of a PAVN rush southward if there is an interval of even two or three days between the stoppage of bombing and the stoppage of infiltration. He said he had been considering an alternative way of securing the required guarantee, namely that the prior two-way assurance should contain a time-table if possible underwritten by or communicated through the Russians. What might be provided is that the US would agree in advance to stop the bombing in return for Hanoi's prior assurance that they would stop the infiltration, say six hours or less afterwards. He said he would try it as his idea on Kosygin if the atmosphere were right. Finally, the Prime Minister noted that there had been a misunderstanding as a result of his reference to a "power of attorney".[40] Clearly, he said, that would be out of the question. The key words, he added, were "ad referendum" (repeated to London as State's 135731).

STATE 135718 (to Amembassy London), TS/Nodis, Sent 0948, 12 Feb 67

Literally Eyes Only for Amb Bruce and Cooper from Walt Rostow

The following message was transmitted at 3:36 a.m. 12 Feb to Downing Street.

I have carefully read and considered your two messages bearing on your talks later today with Kosygin.

I would wish to leave these thoughts with you on the present position.

I really do not believe that the matter hangs on the tense of verbs. Moscow had from George Brown in November the Phase A - Phase B formulation. Hanoi also had it from the Poles. Hanoi has shown no flicker of interest for more than two months. Meanwhile their build-up continues and they have used 3 periods of no bombing (Christmas, New Year's and TET) for large scale movement and preparation of their forces for further military action.

I want to emphasize that we have had nothing yet from Hanoi. They receive our messages - but thus far it has been a one-way conversation. Many intermediaries have attempted, from time to time, to negotiate with us. Everyone seems to wish to negotiate except Hanoi. I wish someone would produce a real live North Vietnamese prepared to talk.

Understandably your present preoccupation is Kosygin's attitude. But thus far, Kosygin has not transmitted one word from Hanoi except to endorse their Foreign Minister's interview with Burchett in his own press conference.

From an operational point of view, we cannot stop the bombing while three (possibly four) divisions dash south from the DMZ before - underline word their rpt their - promise is to take effect. I hope you will see the importance of this for the men out there who are doing the fighting.

We do not accept the view that our statement to you of our position on February 7 is inconsistent with either our message to Hanoi or our formula for you and Kosygin of February 10. We asked on February 7 for an "assured stoppage" of infiltration. In your version of an A-B formula it was transmuted to an assurance that infiltration "will stop". This, in our view, is a quite different matter. We so recognized promptly on receipt of your formula and telephoned Burke Trend that we were drafting and would transmit our response shortly.

The problem of substance is that no formula can be satisfactory to us - and perhaps to Hanoi - unless there is clarity about two matters:

- The timing of a cessation of bombing, cessation of infiltration, and no further augmentation of forces.

- How assurance in the matter of infiltration will be established, you have correctly pointed out that the cessation of bombing and the stoppage of augmentation by us will necessarily be public.

I would not expect Kosygin to come in at Chequers with anything firm and definitive by way of a positive response. In that case we can take stock and see where we go from here on the diplomatic tract. If he does respond positively and constructively, we can then proceed to the clarifications that both sides will surely require.

Hanoi has received our messages and has just today informed us that a direct response to us from Hanoi will be forthcoming. We suppose that we shall not hear from them until your talks are concluded. There is importance, then, in our staying together. We must not let them play one position off against another.

Let me add that I much appreciate your dedicated effort during this week - and will, of course, express publicly our thanks. I'm always glad to know that you are in my corner but I would have some difficulty, in view of my responsibilities and problems here, in giving anyone a power of attorney. I hope for peace more than you can possibly know and will be much interested in what happens at Chequers.

(Text received from White House)

STATE 135734 (to Amembassy Moscow), TS/Nodis, Sent 1815, 12 Feb 67.

For Monday morning delivery to Ambassador unless instructed otherwise
by SEPTEL.

. . . .

3. State of play in London is that British on Feb. 7 gave Kosygin
as their own draft a summary of the proposal contained in the President's
letter to Ho. However, unlike that letter, the British draft of that
date clearly separated the stopping of the bombing from the actual stopping of infiltration, although it required assurance of the latter before
the former would be done. This differs from the President's letter to Ho,
which of course spoke of assurance that infiltration had stopped already.

4. This difference has since caused difficulty with the British. On
Feb. 10, Wilson repeated the substance of the British Feb. 7 version to
Kosygin, who expressed real interest . . . . -- we corrected the British
draft so that it insisted that we have assurance that the infiltration had
stopped. . . . the British. . . . caught Kosygin just as he took his train
that evening, but it is possible, indeed probable, that the earlier "will
stop" version was transmitted by the Soviets to Hanoi.

. . . .

6. From your standpoint, the important thing is whether the Soviets
may have been misled at any stage. From a direct Dobrynin reference with
the Secretary on Friday evening, we now know that the Soviets are familiar
with the contents of the President's letter to Ho, and this direct statement means that you can assume this in any conversations with the Soviets.
In short, they knew our position very shortly after the President's letter
was delivered, and again had it in clear form when we cleared the authorized
version for transmission to Kosygin on the evening of the 10th. At most,
they may have been very briefly misled on the afternoon of the 10th . . . .

. . . .

RUSK (Drafted by W. P. Bundy)

STATE 135735 (to Amembassy Moscow), TS/Nodis, Sent 1816, 12 Feb 67.

For Monday morning delivery to Ambassador unless instructed otherwise
by SEPTEL.

Relevant texts to go with our septel on dealings with the British
are as follows:[41]

1. Oral text used by Wilson on Feb. 7:

QTE.

END QTE.

2. Original British written text of Feb. 10, given the Soviets at the reception that eventing:

QTE.

END QTE.

3. Final version cleared by us and given to Kosygin late on the evening of Feb. 10:

END QTE.

RUSK (Drafted by W. P. Bundy)

STATE 135744 (to Amembassy Saigon), S/Nodis, Sent 2439, 12 Feb.

Eyes Only for Ambassador

1. Situation in London is that at his suggestion we have just author-ized Wilson to tell Kosygin that if Hanoi accepts our proposal by 10 a.m. tomorrow London time we would continue bombing suspension.[42] Requirement remains that Hanoi assure us that infiltration has ten stopped, with our cessation of augmentation to follow in a few days.

2. Military orders have now gone out for operations to be planned for execution at 2400 February 13 your time, subject to final execute message to be sent at 2030 your time. . . .

. . . .

RUSK (Drafted by W. P. Bundy)

STATE 135748 (to Amembassy London), ~~TS/Nodis~~, Sent 0205, 13 Feb 67.

The following message from the President was sent this afternoon by private wire to the Prime Minister:

BEGIN TEXT

As I pointed out early this morning, the A-B offer has been outstanding now for about three months. I gather from Cooper that as of the time you went into dinner tonight, you had no reply from Kosygin. We have had no reply from Hanoi.

Nevertheless, you have worked nobly this week to bring about what all humanity wants: A decisive move towards peace. It is an effort that will be long remembered. I feel a responsibility to give you this further chance to make that effort bear fruit. We will go more than half way. I am prepared to go the last mile in this week's particular effort; although none of us can regard a failure tonight as the end of the road.

I must, of course, also bear in mind my responsibility to our men who are fighting there, to our allies, to the people of South Viet-Nam who are counting on us to bring about an honorable peace consistent with our commitments to them.

Therefore I agree with you that you should go forward and try once again with Kosygin saying to him:

BEGIN QUOTE

If you can get a North Vietnamese assurance--communicated either direct to the United States or through you--before 10:00 a.m. British time tomorrow that all movement of troops and supplies into South Viet-Nam will stop at that time, I will get an assurance from the US that they will not resume bombing of North Viet-Nam from that time. Of course the US build up would also then stop within a matter of days.

This would then give you and me the opportunity to try to consolidate and build on what has been achieved by bringing the parties together and promoting further balanced measures of deescalation. END QUOTE

With this deal consummated, we would, of course, be prepared to move promptly to a neutral spot to engage in unconditional negotiations designed to bring peace to the area.

Herewith some further observations.

It is significant that Kosygin reflects no further word from Hanoi. Our own private line with Hanoi remains silent. Actually, Kosygin may prefer that any final deal come bilaterally after he leaves London

Presumably two co-chairmen would continue to be in touch with each other. It would be helpful if communique could express support of two co-chairmen for 1954 and 1962 accords and agreement that any differences arising out of these accords should be settled by peaceful means.

END TEXT

RUSK (Text from White House).

STATE 135751 (to Amembassy London), S/Nodis, Sent 0210, 13 Feb 67.

We plan announcement tomorrow about noon EST as follows:

BEGIN QUOTE

As you know, the South Vietnamese Government announced on the 11th that its forces and those of other nations assisting South Viet-Nam would resume normal operations during the day on February 12. This resumption was in accordance with the truce period announced by the South Vietnamese Government some weeks ago. As the South Vietnamese Government had made clear in early January and again last week, it was prepared to discuss extension of the truce period at any time. There was no response to this offer.

During the Tet period, bombing and other military operations against North Viet-Nam were also suspended. This suspension was continued for short additional period in order to avoid any possibility that earlier resumption would be misconstrued in relation to Mr. Kosygin's visit to London. Operations have now been resumed. END QUOTE

Press here is already printing large number of speculative stories that continued suspension is due to Kosygin visit. We assume press will eventually reach correct conclusion that we did not wish to make any announcement of added suspension in order to avoid implication of putting pressure on London decisions.

RUSK (Drafted by J. P. Walsh)

February 13, 1967

On February 13, Cooper reported that at C955 London-time Wilson and Brown had queried Kosygin as to whether he had received an answer from Hanoi. Kosygin replied in the negative but said he was still trying (London's 6498).

On the same day, Cooper reported that he had been told in the Foreign Office that: (a) between 3:00 a.m. and 3:47 a.m. London-time (13 February), three priority "President's Cipher" telegrams were sent from the Soviet delegation in London to Moscow; (b) at 9:30 a.m. today according to a telephone intercept Kosygin called Breshnev and said "a great possibility of achieving the aim, if the Vietnamese will understand the present situation that we have passed to them, they will have to decide. All they need to do is to give a confidential declaration"; (c) Breshnev confirmed that Kosygin's telegram to the Vietnamese had been sent (London's 6500). NSA also reported that the North Vietnamese transmitted a 201-group message from Hanoi to Moscow at 1609Z (1109 EST); also a 500-group message was transmitted to Hanoi from Moscow at 0820Z (0320) EST). Thompson was informed of these developments (State's 135853).

STATE 135758 (to Amembassy London), TS/Nodis, Sent 0707, 13 Feb 67

Literally Eyes Only for Amb Bruce from Walt Rostow

The following was transmitted to 10 Downing Street at 130120 A.M. EST.

We have considered the case for further delay to receive a message from Hanoi beyond 10:00 a.m. British time, which you suggested.

I have gone into this with my senior advisers and, after carefully considering your suggestion, the problems you presented, and the problem here -- including the morale of our uniformed men -- we are extending the time by 6 hours. This is as long as we believe is advisable.

I am sure you would want to know that our Joint Chiefs, CINCPAC, and General Westmoreland have unanimously opposed the Tet and other truces and extensions thereto -- not only on the grounds of troop morale but because of the cost in human lives. We will wait, then, for information that may be forthcoming until 11:00 a.m. Washington time -- 4:30 p.m. your time. Military operations against the North will be permitted to resume between 11:00 a.m. and noon our time.

In making this decision I bore in mind Moscow's and Hanoi's problems of transmittal two ways. But I also was conscious of the fact that they have had the possibility of responding to essentially this message for the 3 months since we gave it to the Poles and you gave it to the Russians; and the 5 days since it was transmitted direct to Hanoi and also given by you to Kosygin.

If there is any interest in some such A-B proposition, there has -- and still is - been ample time for them either to agree or to come back with a counter-proposal.

Your gallant last minute effort -- which I consented to -- is one on which they must move. On receiving it they must be either ready to

make a response or not. A few hours either way cannot be significant.
Bear in mind that the offer for a reciprocal de-escalation has not been
withdrawn. It can be accepted any moment they may desire to do so, even
though operations are in effect. They could be suspended momentarily.
The channels for discussions on these or other lines will remain open.

Right now supplies and weapons are moving down from the North at a
high rate. While bearing in mind the safety of more than a half million
of our men, I feel I should, nevertheless, go as far as possible to meet
your suggestion and, therefore, am stretching the beginning of military
operations by another 6 hours.

Considering all the time and conversation that has gone on before,
this allows added time for talk if they are really serious.

I hope you have a good chance to catch up on sleep after this arduous
and interesting week which, I am inclined to believe, will prove in the
end to have been most constructive.

KATZENBACH

(Text received from White House)

SAIGON 17875 (to SecState), TS/Nodis, Sent 1100, 13 Feb, Rec'd 1202, 13 Feb.

1. Pursuant to your 135744, I flew to Dalat Monday afternoon and
saw Ky.

. . . .

7. I said that many speculative press stories were now appearing,
adding that General Westmoreland and I had made (and would make) no comment whatsoever about the matter before this statement is issued in
Washington. I repeated that secrecy on this matter is of the highest
importance.

8. Finally I recalled his expression of concern Saturday regarding
the effectiveness of the International Control Commission in verifying
possible infiltration from the North. I said I would like to add to what
I said then that in the unlikely event that Hanoi should take up the proposal we would expect ourselves to conduct extensive reconnaissance. Our
reconnaissance capabilities together with other intelligence operations
in Laos should, I said, give us a virtual certainty of detecting any substantial North Vietnamese violations of an undertaking to stop infiltration.

. . . .

LODGE

63

STATE 135799 (to Amembassy London & Moscow), TS/Nodis, Sent 1700, 13 Feb 67.

. . . .

3. For Moscow background, Wilson last night requested an additional 24 hours of suspension, and we replied that we would extend only until 1600 British time, which is of course 1100 our time. Time period was specifically conveyed to Kosygin by British this morning in London prior to Kosygin departure. Neither last night nor this morning, apparently, did Kosygin himself urge a longer period or object to the clearly implied time limit as in any sense an ultimatum. . . .

4. . . . . . British must realize that Soviets went out on a very long limb, and that any exposure of serious discussions in fact carried on could do serious and indeed irreparable harm to future Soviet role.

XGDS-3

. . . . It goes without saying that British silence is imperative whatever they think of positions we put forward or timing of our resumption.

. . . . .

KATZENBACH (Drafted by W. P. Bundy)

LONDON 6516 (to SecState), TS/Nodis, Sent 1735, 13 Feb; Rec'd 1909, 13 Feb.

Eyes Only for Secretary and Rostow from Cooper

1. Although some of the events of the past 24 hours have been over-taken, and some other strain credulity, it might be well to try to recon-struct them for the record.

2. As I indicated over the telephone to the Secretariat Duty Officer Sunday morning, the message from the President to the Prime Minister that had been just received in London seemed, on the basis of preliminary re-actions, to have cleared the air. (This was confirmed later in the day.)

3. In the early afternoon, I met Palliser at Downing Street (back door), and was then hustled out to Chequers (tradesmen's entrance). I was installed in the garret "prison room" (graced by Lady Mary Grey in 1565).[43]

. . . . .

7. After about an hour, Murray (FonOff) emerged with a draft com-munique on Vietnam which the Sovs proposed as an alternative to the British draft. Murray and I reworded the Sov submission and with one or two miniscule modifications, the Sovs bought the revised version -- an anodyne and not very nourishing document.

8. Murray left a copy of the message the PM had sent to Washington earlier in the day (I had not seen it until then). Hedging against the possibility of being queried later in the evening for a reaction to this, I called Washington (Read) and was informed that the first para (which acknowledged the danger to American Forces of the buildup North of the DMZ) had met with a favorable reception. Read was non-committal on the second para (i.e., Wilson's proposal for a telescoped time period between Phase A-Phase B), and I did not press him. However, I did suggest that the PM might, one last time, warn Kosygin about the implications of the buildup North of the DMZ and see if he could get Kosygin to pass his own warning on to Hanoi. Read indicated this would do no harm.

9. . . . . Kosygin expressed concern regarding British press reports (Henry Brandon in the Sunday Times was a good example) that the "Hawks" in Washington were in the ascendancy.

10. . . . . I suggested to Wilson that he might try to get Kosygin to press Hanoi to stand fast north of the DMZ. Wilson thought this would be worth a try. We then worked out a somewhat broader formula which Trend, Palliser and I was later spelled out in writing and checked with Wilson, I then transmitted this by telephone to Read and by teletape to Rostow. Wilson said he would not submit this proposition until he had the President's okay.

11. Wilson obviously felt that even if Kosygin rejected the formula, he would be better off in the House of Commons for this last minute attempt.

. . . .

14. Wilson, Brown, Burke, Trend, Palliser, Murray, Amb Bruce, and I assembled at Downing Street shortly after midnight. Wilson was delighted with the message he received from Washington, and dashed out to Claridges with Brown and the interpreter at his heels.

15. He returned at about 0215 to report that Kosygin had evidenced great interest in the proposal. Kosygin said he would transmit it to Hanoi but expressed concern about the brief time available before an answer was expected. Wilson reported that Kosygin was in fact writing a message as he talked. (We have had later confirmation of this.)

. . . .

KAISER

STATE 135973 (to Amembassy Buenos Aires ToSec), TS/Nodis, Sent 2141, 13 Feb.

Amb. Dean delivered following personal message from Foreign Secretary Brown to Secretary Rusk to the Acting Secretary at noon today.   BEGIN TEXT of Message dated February 13:

END TEXT

KATZENBACH (Drafted by B. H. Read)

STATE 138142 (to Amembassy Saigon), TS/Nodis, Sent 2258, 13 Feb 67.

. . . .

3.   For disclosure to Ky at your discretion and timing, fact is that we have not repeat not had any response whatever from Hanoi.   We interpret Hanoi broadcast reply to the Pope, carried Hanoi Radio 1532Z on Feb 13, as a typical Hanoi method of signing off.   This broadcast was made just a half-hour before the expiration of the time limit for response that we had given to Kosygin through the British.   (FYI.   Our plans had always run toward noon our time, but we formally extended the deadline to 1100 our time at British request on Sunday night.   End FYI). . . .

KATZENBACH (Drafted by W. P. Bundy)

Hanoi VNA International Service in English 1642 GMT 13 Feb 67--B (FBIS, Far East, 14 February 1967).

(Text) Hanoi, 13 February--Pope Paul VI recently sent a message to President Ho Chi Minh, expressing the wish to see an early peaceful solution to the Vietnam problem.

President Ho Chi Minh today sent a message of reply to the Pope.   Full text of the reply message reads:

I wish to thank Your Holiness for his message of 8 February 1967.   In his message, Your Holiness expressed the wish to see an early peaceful solution to the Vietnam question.

Our people sincerely love peace in order to build our country in independence an freedom. However, the U.S. imperialists have sent to South Vietnam half a million U.S. and satellite troops and used more than 600,000 puppet troops to wage a war against our people. They have committed monstrous crimes. They have used the most barbarous arms, such as napalm, products, and toxic gases, to massacre our compatriots and burn down our villages, pagodas, churches, hospitals, schools . . . . Their acts of aggression have grossly violated the 1954 Gnneva agreements on Vietnam and seriously menaced peace in Asia and the world. To defend their independence and peace, the Vietnamese people are resolutely fighting against the aggressors. They are confident that justice will triumph. The U.S. imperialists must put an end to their aggression in Vietnam, end unconditionally and definitively the bombing and all other acts of war against the Democratic Republic of Vietnam, withdraw from South Vietnam all American and satellite troops, recognize the South Vietnam National Front for Liberation, and let the Vietnamese people settle themselves their own affairs. Only in such conditions can real peace be restored in Vietnam.

It is my hope that Your Holiness, in the name of humanity and justice, will use his high influence to urge that the U.S. Government respect the national rights of the Vietnamese people, namely peace, independence, sovereignty, unity, and territorial integrity as recognized by the 1954 Geneva Agreements on Vietnam.

With my high regards, Ho Chi Minh.

February 14, 1967

SAIGON 17949 (to SecState), TS/Nodis, Sent 1050, 14 Feb; Rec'd 1302, 14 Feb.

. . . .

2. I wonder . . . whether it might not be of greater value to equate the cessation of bombing and non-augmentation of forces not only with infiltration but also with the ending of the assassination, torture, and kidnapping of village and other local officials.

. . . .

9. D'Orlandi told me (septel) that he considers cessation of assassination of local officials "much more feasible" than cessation of infiltration.

LODGE

LONDON 6543 (to SecState), TS/Nodis, Sent 1053, 14 Feb; Rec'd 1259, 14 Feb.

For Acting Secretary and Rostow from Kaiser and Cooper

. . . .

2. The mood of Wilson and the others was friendly, understanding, and cheerful. . . .

. . . .

4. Wilson recognizes that he will have some difficult moments with his Party in Commons (indeed 100 Labor MPs have already signed a petition against resumption of bombing) but he seems confident that in the light of everything that has taken place this past week he can deal with it.

5. Wilson said he had given a background press conference to the lobby correspondents following his appearance in the House. He pointed out to them that Hanoi could have peace if they had shown any readiness to respond to the efforts that had been exerted to reach a settlement. This morning's London papers have taken this line and have given the US, the UK and the Russians very high marks for their efforts. Hanoi is universally regarded as the villain in the piece. . . .

KAISER

BUENOS AIRES 3082 (to SecState), S/Nodis, Sent 1624, 14 Feb; Rec'd 1821, 14 Feb.

For Acting Secretary from Secretary

Please pass to Pat Dean following for George Brown from me: QTE Many thanks for your good message and, more particularly, for your extraordinary labors during the past week. I hope that the long and late hours invested in these probes may stir some response from Hanoi even though Ho's message to the Pope is not encouraging. I was much interested in seeing that Kosygin at least seems to take their co-chairman role seriously and reflected a desire to bring this war to a conclusion. My own guess is that the Russian position has in fact moved somewhat but they and we face the same difficulty in getting Hanoi to move, but we will do our best over here, both in the battle and on the diplomatic front. Again my warm thanks. UNQTE.

RUSK

STATE 136999 (to Amembassy London), TS/Nodis, Sent 2415, 14 Feb 67.

1. You should know that both Michael Stewart, at our request, and later Walt Rostow have called Palliser to express our grave misgivings about extent of Wilson disclosure in House and particularly his statement that agreement appeared "very near," that there was some secret plan, etc.[44]

2. . . . , they have put us on the spot, since we had disclosed the whole proposal only to Ky personally, and had not told even such key allies repeat allies as the Australians and Koreans. . . .

3. . . . . . this has just got to stop repeat stop.

KATZENBACH (Drafted by W. P. Bundy)

February 15, 1967

Letter to President Johnson from Ho Chi Minh.

To His Excellency Mr. Lyndon B. Johnson,
President,
United States of America,

Your Excellency:

On February 10, 1967, I received your message. This is my reply.

Vietnam is thousands of miles away from the United States. The Vietnamese people have never done any harm to the United States. But contrary to the pledges made by its representative at the 1954 Geneva conference, the U.S. Government has ceaselessly intervened in Vietnam, it has unleashed and intensified the war of aggression in South Vietnam with a view to prolonging the partition of Vietnam and turning South Vietnam into a neo-colony and a military base of the United States. For over two years now, the U.S. Government has, with its air and naval forces, carried the war to the Democratic Republic of (North) Vietnam, an independent and sovereign country.

The U.S. Government has committed war crimes, crimes against peace and against mankind. In South Vietnam, half a million U.S. and satellite troops have resorted to the most inhuman weapons and the most barbarous methods of warfare, such as napalm, toxic chemicals and gasses, to massacre our compatriots, destroy crops, and raze villages to the ground. In North Vietnam, thousands of U.S. aircraft have dropped hundreds of thousands of tons of bombs, destroying towns, villages, factories, schools. In your message, you apparently deplore the sufferings and destruction in Vietnam. May I ask you: Who has perpetrated these monstrous crimes? It is the United States and satellite troops. The U.S. Government is entirely responsible for the extremely serious situation in Vietnam.

The U.S. war of aggression against the Vietnamese people constitutes a challenge to the countries of the socialist camp, a threat to the national independence movement, and a serious danger to peace in Asia and the world.

The Vietnamese people deeply love independence, freedom and peace. But in the face of the U.S. aggression, they have risen up, united as one man, fearless of sacrifices and hardships. They are determined to carry on their resistance until they have won genuine independence and freedom and true peace. Our just cause enjoys strong sympathy and support from the peoples of the whole world, including broad sections of the American people.

The U.S. Government has unleashed the war of aggression in Vietnam. It must cease this aggression. That is the only way to the restoration of peace. The U.S. Government must stop definitively and unconditionally its bombing raids and all other acts of war against the Democratic Republic of Vietnam, withdraw from South Vietnam all U.S. and satellite troops, recognize the South Vietnam National Front for Liberation, and let the Vietnamese people settle themselves their own affairs. Such is the basis (sic) content of the five-point stand of the government of the Democratic Republic of Vietnam, which embodies the essential principles and provisions of the 1954 Geneva agreements on Vietnam, it is the basic (sic) of a correct political solution to the Vietnam problem.

In your message, you suggested direct talks between the Democratic Republic of Vietnam and the United States. If the U.S. Government really wants these talks, it must first of all stop unconditionally its bombing raids and all other acts of war against the Democratic Republic of Vietnam. It is only after the unconditional cessation of the U.S. bombing raids and all other acts of war against the Democratic Republic of Vietnam that the Democratic Republic of Vietnam and the United States could enter into talks and discuss questions concerning the two sides.

The Vietnamese people will never submit to force, they will never accept talks under the threat of bombs.

Our cause is absolutely just. It is to be hoped that the U.S. Government will act in accordance with reason.

Sincerely,

Ho Chi Minh

MOSCOW 3501 (to SecState), TS/Nodis, Sent 1043, 15 Feb; Rec'd 1131, 15 Feb.

Le Chang handed DCM at 1:00 p.m. Ho Chi Minh's reply to President's letter. Reply completely unyielding and in subsequent oral remarks, Le Chang said he could no longer meet with US representatives in Moscow. Text and full report follow.

THOMPSON

SAIGON 18022 (to SecState), TS/Nodis, Sent 1130, 15 Feb; Rec'd 1359, 15 Feb.

1. The decision authorizing me to tell Ky about the episode involving Wilson and Kosygin was unquestionably wise.

2. I also believe that it will save us a great deal of trouble in the end if we make it a practice to tell the GVN what we are planning to do ahead of time whenever it is likely that they will find out about it anyway. . . .

. . . . .

4. There is a strong streak of fatalism in these people and if they feel they are left out of decisions which vitally affect them, they are quite capable of desperate action which would be contrary to our interests. Also this capacity for desperate action is what under other circumstances makes them valuable as allies.

LODGE

MOSCOW 3503 (to SecState), TS/Nodis, Sent 1150, 15 Feb; Rec'd 1257, 15 Feb.

Ref: Moscow 3501

. . . .

2. Le Chang handed DCM Ho Chi Minh's reply to President's message delivered February 8, requesting that it be transmitted to President (septel). Le Chang then made following additional oral statement:

A. Position and attitude of DRV Govt. are very correct and serious, and enjoy strong support of world public opinion, including American people. US, however, always obstinate and perfidious, and it continues advance conditions for cessation of bombings.

B. US had made use of DRV representative's receiving US representative in Moscow to deceive public opinion that secret negotiations going on while bombings continue.

C. Lately, US extended so-called suspension of bombings during Tet. Less than two days later, bombings were resumed on pretext that there had been no response from Hanoi. This constitutes insolent ultimatum to compel Vietnamese people to accept unacceptable conditions.

D. In such circumstances, DRV representative does not consider it possible receive US representative in Moscow on US proposal. Responsibility for this rests completely with us.

3. After making sure he understood Le Chang's final statement correctly, DCM called his attention to President's February 13 statement and cited sentence stating that door to peace is and will remain open and US prepared go more than half way to meet any equitable overture from other side.

4. In response, Le Chang quoted final portion Ho's message, beginning with sentence stipulating cessation of bombings and all other acts of war against DRV as precondition if US really desires conversations.

THOMPSON.

STATE 137496 (to Amembassy Buenos Aires), TS/Nodis, Sent 1818, 15 Feb.

We are sending to you by separate cables in this series following immediately after this one Ho Chi Minh's reply to the President and the report of the latest Guthrie conversation on February 15.

Paragraph f of the Ho letter is clearly a combination of the formulations used by the DRV in Ho's February 13 reply to the Pope and the Trinh January 28 interview with Burchett. We find it interesting that in this post resumption period DRV is adhering to the exact formula in the Trinh interview, i.e. "It is only after the unconditional halting of the American bombing and all other acts of war against the DRV that the DRV and the US could begin talks and discuss questions affecting the two parties."

The President is anxious to have a "stocktaking" with you on where we go from here, and I think he would like to be assured that you will be back in time for luncheon next Tuesday. . . .

. . . .

KATZENBACH (Drafted by B. H. Read).

February 16, 1967

STATE 138755 (to Amembassy Moscow & Buenos Aires), TS/Nodis

Ref: Moscow 3525

. . . .

2. . . . . . Here, we are evaluating the situation tomorrow and
would much appreciate your over-all assessment of possible impact of
last week's events. To us it appears tentatively that the Soviets went
quite far in even offering to present our proposal and the variant introduced by the British with the highly specific time limit factor. (We
were very struck at absence of any indication of Kosygin referring to its
ultimatum flavor.) Moreover, if Soviets in fact urged acceptance of this
proposition, they went even further. Thus, unless they had some indication
from Hanoi of possible give, we are inclined to wonder whether they may
not have strained their credit very heavily indeed in Hanoi and caused
Hanoi (or at least Chinese-oriented elements in it) to consider them a
solid but compromise-minded friend. In these circumstances, our minds
run to the thought that Hanoi may now be assessing its position in the
most basic manner against this reading of Soviet policy, and might even
be making a somewhat desperate appeal to the Chinese Communists to pull
themselves together and give the kind of full support the Soviets are
clearly not now inclined to give. In short, we believe possibilities of
last week's developments could be very far reaching indeed.

. . . .

KATZENBACH (Drafted by W. P. Bundy)

February 17, 1967

MOSCOW 3533 (to SecState), TS/Nodis, Sent 0833, 17 Feb; Rec's 0909, 17 Feb.

Ref: State 138755.

. . . .

2. At film showing at Embassy last night Sukhodrev, Kosygin's interpreter, who was present at all important conversations in London, remarked
to me QTE that was quite a switch you pulled on us in the text of your
proposal UNQTE obviously referring to the change in tenses. . . .

. . . .

4. Possibility open to Soviets to use excuse of Chaos in China to
slow down deliveries to North Vietnam but I doubt that they will do this.[45]

THOMPSON

LONDON 6680 (to SecState), TS/Nodis, Sent 1730, 17 Feb; Rec'd 2009, 17 Feb.

Ref: State 136999

    1. I saw Michael Palliser today and conveyed the full substance of reftel. I emphasized the fact that Prime Minister's suggestion that there was "secret plan" and that peace was very near had put us on the spot with our allies and was causing us considerable embarrassment at home. . . .

      . . . .

    3. Palliser stated . . . . It would have been difficult for the PM to make so effective a case for the US and British positions without saying the things he did in public. Palliser also recalled that the excellent British press on Tuesday, from the US point of view, was due largely to the Prime Minister's backgrounder the evening before. . . .

    6. Comment. While Palliser was obviously genuine in expressing his understanding of the nature of our problems, he also made it clear that the PM was more bullish about the significance of last week than we were. Palliser stressed on several occasions the "dramatic" change in Kosygin's attitude in contrast to last July when the PM visited Moscow and even as late as November when Brown was there . . . . It is also the firm conviction of the British that Kosygin did transmit our last proposal to Hanoi and very possibly with the recommendation that "they give it serious considera-tion."

     . . . .

KAISER

STATE 139631 (to Amembassy Moscow & Buenos Aires), TS/Nodis, Sent 2333, 17 Feb.

    1. Bundy saw Zinchuk for private lunch today. Conversation made clear that Soviets were fully informed on Ho reply to us and on all our direct exchanges in Moscow, apparently in full detail. . . .

    . . . .

    3. Bundy then reviewed position we have taken on conditions for cessa-tion of bombing, starting with Goldberg speech of September and followed by presentation of Phase A/Phase B formula through Brown to Soviets and simul-taneously through Lewandowski to Hanoi. He added that in January we had noted Ho conversation with Baggs and Ashmore in which Ho had referred to cessation of US reinforcement, in addition to bombing, while of course insisting that Hanoi could not reciprocate . . . .[46] Thus, Hanoi had had a general proposal along these lines for three months and this specific ver-sion on February 7 or 8.

    . . . .

6.   Zinchuk then said that the Soviets were "disappointed" and "uneasy" at our resumption of bombing. He did not repeat not charge us with any breach of any undertaking in so doing, but did say that the combination of our December 13-14 bombings, causing Hanoi to reject the Warsaw proposal for quiet talks without condition, and our present action, bringing to an end for the time being any chance of a favorable Hanoi reply on the London proposal, had caused Moscow to wonder whether it had become the basic US view that the military situation was steadily improving from our standpoint and that we therefore did not really want negotiations at the present time in the belief that the situation had become steadily more favorable to us.

7.   There was then a long specific discussion of the December events, in which Bundy noted that the original message from the Poles has been exceedingly vague and had never made clear to us what Zinchuk was now asserting--that Hanoi was definitely willing to talk in the sense of exchanging views. Zinchuk responded that they had gone back over this with Hanoi and had ascertained firmly that this was the Hanoi position at that time. Secondly, Bundy noted that Rapacki's behavior between December 4 and December 10 had been and remained inexplicable to us; we had thought our position in mentioning the necessity for interpretation was entirely reasonable and simply could not understand why Rapacki had not gone ahead in that period but had on the contrary conveyed a negative Hanoi view to us as late as December 10. In short, Bundy argued that we had simply had a clear misunderstanding as to what Zinchuk now described as Hanoi's intent at that time.

8.   As to the London outcome, Zinchuk argued that Hanoi had noted repeated statements by us that we had undertaken the bombing in order to get Hanoi to talk. Hence, Hanoi had supposed that its Burchett interview position of willingness to talk if we stopped the bombing was in direct response to our own position. Bundy noted that all our statements on the purposes of the bombing had stressed its necessity in order to counter and impede infiltration above all, and had placed its relevance to negotiation in a much broader context than Zinchuk's summary of Hanoi's view would suggest. . . .

. . . .

12.   As between these two approaches, Bundy said we saw some advantage in the latter. He pointed out that to take a dramatic series of actions envisaged in the London proposal would inevitably create a glare of publicity that might be unfavorable for subsequent talks. Was it not then wiser to talk quietly so that we knew the outlines of where we might come out before dramatic and visible actions were taken.

13.   Zinchuk noted both these avenues, but went on to say that within the last 2-3 days the Soviets had had a firm communication from Hanoi to the effect that they simply could not talk in any fashion as long as the bombing

was not stopped. Zinchuk argued--in the only faintly coluratura passage of the whole exchange--that Hanoi felt very strongly that it was inherently unequal for two competent nations to talk while one was hitting the other's territory but the other, by force of circumstances, was not hitting the first. Hanoi felt that to talk in these circumstances had the flavor of capitulation. . . .

14. Bundy then asked whether Hanoi's message to the Soviets had conveyed any suggestion that Hanoi was displeased with the Soviet handling in London. In blunt terms, had the Soviets lost credit in Hanoi? Zinchuk promptly and apparently frankly replied that this had not repeat not been the case--that on the contrary Hanoi continued to look to the Soviets to arrange a settlement that would protect their interests, and the Soviet standing had progressively increased in Hanoi over the past several months. He cited the fact that Hanoi had kept the Soviets fully informed on the direct US channel, and said that this showed Hanoi's desire to deal with and through the Soviets.

15. Bundy then asked whether the change of tenses between the British version of our proposal and our own final version had in any way thrown the Soviets off: he noted that our letter to Ho had used the "has stopped" language, so that we did not repeat not suppose Hanoi had been misled. He explained that our reason for this language was our belief that two or three DRV divisions were poised just north of the DMZ and might have been moved into South Viet-Nam before the cessation of infiltration went into force. Zinchuk expressed no surprise at this explanation, and said frankly that the change of tenses had not significantly disturbed the Soviets . . . .

. . . .

17. Bundy then said that it seemed to us barely conceivable that Hanoi would conclude that we now had in mind some sharp change in our military operations or even some change in our objective vis-a-vis North Viet-Nam. While making clear that he could not exclude some additional actions on our part, Bundy said that he hoped Hanoi had no such view, since the US continued to have no intention of destroying North Viet-Nam or changing its path of action in any drastic fashion. . . .

18. . . . .

. . . .

21. . . . .

KATZENBACH (Drafted by W. P. Bundy)

STATE 140121 (to Amembassy Mowcow), TS/Nodis, 17 Feb 67.

Buenos Aires for Secretary only repeat only

Ref: State 139631

1. In your conversation with Kosygin tomorrow, you should raise the subject of Vietnam.

2. For your own information, you should know that the situation will be reviewed here next week in an effort to assess where we are and what actions, political and military, seem most desirable. We will be considering a wide range of proposals, including significant additional actions against North Vietnam.[47] These could include new targets for aerial bombardment such as power stations, cement plant, etc., and mining of inland waterways and Haiphong harbor. Some targets could be within 10-mile radius of Hanoi. Accordingly, nothing that you say to Kosygin should be open to interpretation which would foreclose any of these options.

. . . .

4. . . . . Since there was no response from Hanoi to 10-mile radius, we have not for some time regarded our prior statements in this connection as limitation on our freedom of action, although we have not in fact bombed within the radius. . . . .

5. . . . . you will note para 15 reftel dealing with change of tenses, and same para dealing with position of 2 - 3 DRV divisions . . . .

. . . .

KATZENBACH (Drafted by W. P. Bundy)

February 18, 1967

MOSCOW 3562 (to SecState), TS/Nodis, Sent 1737, 18 Feb; Rec'd 2108, 18 Feb.

1. I broached Vietnam by saying . . . . we had had a very direct and negative reply to what we believed was reasonable proposal. We did not know if other side had been serious in starting discussions in first place . . . . In any event, people in Washington were pleased to see indication that USSR also wanted to see problem settled. I said I did not know where we should go from here . . . .

2. I then pointed out that during 4 or 5 day Tet holiday and estimated 25,000 tons of supplies had been sent southward, i.e., as many supplies had been shipped in 4 or 5 days as normally had been sent in a month. Thus we wondered what the purpose of this exercise was . . . .

3. Kosygin said he wished make it clear he not authorized negotiate for North Vietnam and therefore could not say his remarks would represent Vietnamese point of view. He did not wish to mislead us. However, he could state his own views. His estimate of latest events was as follows: Vietnamese had for first time stated they ready negotiate if bombings were stopped unconditionally; this was first time they had done so and it was a public statement. When he came to England, he supported this proposal publicly. He did it because he had good reason for taking such a step. Although he believed that mediators in this situation either complicated the problem or merely pretended they doing something, he took that step because he had seen a basis for US-Vietnamese talks. Wilson had been in touch with Washington but not on his, Kosygin's initiative. However, Wilson kept him informed and he was in touch with Hanoi. Then came latest message, which had nature of ultimatum. It said that if by such and such time, i.e., ten o'clock, Hanoi failed to do certain things, bombings would resume. Time given to Hanoi was very short--just a few hours--and situation was even more complicated because of time difference between London and Hanoi. Thus there was no opportunity for Hanoi to consider message and conduct necessary consultations. In fact, US received Ho Chi Minh's reply after bombings had already resumed. Kosygin continued that in his view US had made basic mistake. First, nothing would have happened if US had delayed bombings another three or four days. Second, US had couched its message in terms of an ultimatum. Third, US talked about 25,000 tons going to South--nature of which he did not know-- but US said nothing about its own reinforcements. During that period US had sent additional troops, had moved its naval vessels to North Vietnamese shores, and had increased number its aircraft carriers in area from three to five. US accusing other side of having sent 25,000 tons but US itself probably sent as much as 100,000 tons. In other words, US seems believe its infiltration is all right but infiltration by other side is not. Thus other side has no confidence in US intentions.

                                                        This was another proof of his step having been a deliberate and responsible one. Yet what he received from US was message that bombings would be resumed if something wasn't done by 10 o'clock.

4. After reiterating that he not authorized represent Vietnamese views and that his remarks reflected only Soviet views, Kosygin said Soviets not confident US proposal had been very serious. Confidence was most important in this situation.

Another example of this need for confi-
dence was fact that despite fact US and USSR had reached understanding
to reduce their military expenditures US raised its budget without informing
USSR. As for USSR, it kept its word; in any event, if it had deemed
necessary to take certain steps it would have informed other side.

5. . . . .

Thus problem was
now to find way toward unconditional cessation of bombings so as to start
negotiations. He wished to stress, however, that question was only of
direct US-North Vietnam contact, for North Vietnam's prestige was involved
here.
much more impor-
tant thing was a stake here, i.e., search for peaceful settlement. As
to how to proceed further, he did not know. Road he had conceived of had
been disrupted by US ultimatum

Kosygin said he could not venture to propose
anything constructive now. He had no basis for doing so and he did not wish
to make unrealistic propositions. He had spoken very frankly with me--
as he would have not spoken with anyone else--because he knew that I would
transmit his views only to President.

5.(sic). After thanking Kosygin for his comments, I said I wished to
make a few remarks of my own. I said I did not believe it justified compare other side's infiltration with sending of our own reinforcements.
For one thing, we were in South Vietnam at request SVN Govt. Moreover, our
bombings were for purpose of impeding North Vietnamese supplies to South,
whereas North Vietnamese could not stop our own supplies. Thus stopping
of our bombings gave advantage to North Vietnamese.

6. Kosygin interjected that this interesting reasoning, after all,
NLF--which certainly more solid organization than US puppets in Saigon and
which controlled three fourths of SVN territory--also asking North Vietnam
for support.

7. I continued we had told North Vietnam that if they stopped infiltration we would stop our reinforcements. Important point here was that
North Vietnam should not gain any advantage.

8. Kosygin again interrupted by asserting US was talking from position of strength.

. . . .

11. I said . . . . if in face certain US steps, such as restriction

of bombings around Hanoi, other side continued killing people, including Americans, in South, US would feel free take any action necessary to stop infiltration . . . .

12. . . . Kosygin said US must realize its bombings, defoliation, operations, etc., not successful. Thus US must look for constructive steps.

He continued that he knew that objectively we would agree there was no Saigon Govt even though we would of course never admit that. Saigon regime was sitting on island surrounded by sea of civil war. Its situation could be compared to that of Kolchak or Denikin during Russian civil war. . . . Of course, there was internal dissent in US over this problem. There were Goldwaters and Nixons in US, but he was confident that they would not be supported by US people if a settlement were reached.[48] He said he wished repeat that what should be looked for were constructive steps, certainly not ultimata: US should not send messages stating that something should be done by ten o'clock for it would receive reply that would make it necessary start all over again . . . .

. . . .

14. . . .

He emphasized, however, that this statement was strictly private and not for publication. . . . Referring again to message he had transmitted to Hanoi from London, he said he knew it was hopeless the minute he had read it.

15. As Kosygin indicated he wished break off discussion on Vietnam, I raised another subject, leased line for our Embassy.

16. Discussion then turned to leased line (septel).

THOMPSON

February 19, 1967

MOSCOW 3568 (to SecState), TS/Nodis, Sent 1330, 19 Feb; Rec'd 1334, 19 Feb.

Ref: State 140121

. . . .

2. So far as our bombing is concerned, ... I hope that following will be taken into consideration. Kosygin made quite a point of the shift in the Soviet position which he had publicly made clear in London. British Ambassador thinks Kosygin probably went considerably beyond anything that had been agreed upon before he left Moscow and he is concerned that Kosygin may be in some trouble with his colleagues. Any early escalation of our bombing pattern will make more difficult his getting support within the Soviet regime as well as any pressure Soviets may be willing to bring on Hanoi to work for a political settlement.

. . . .

4. Mining of Haiphong Harbor would provoke a strong reaction here and

. . . .

8.

THOMPSON

———————————

STATE 140351 (to Amembassy Moscow), TS/Nodis, Sent 2002, 19 Feb.

. . . .

3. . . . , you should know that Soviet people here and in New York have been nosing around quite a bit about our attitude
    and at lower levels have expressed to private contacts suspicion (though possibly for bait) that we were dealing covertly with Peking.[49] Bundy mentioned this to Zinchuk in lunch talk Friday, and said in casual fashion that Soviets could hardly think we had capacity for such dealing even if we wanted them. However, this falls short of clear negativity you now suggest, which we shall consider further for possible additional talk by you with Kosygin.

4. . . . . .

he went out on a limb even with his colleagues.

KATZENBACH (Drafted by W. P. Bundy).

February 20, 1967

MOSCOW 3570 (to SecState), TS/Nodis, Sent 0920, 20 Feb; Rec'd 1009, 20 Feb.

Ref: State 140351

. . . .

2. My guess is that for the moment Soviets will do nothing except perhaps to express their disappointment to Hanoi and possibly take their time in sending by sea any Soviet supplies that Chinese may have delayed or prevented from going to rail or failed to supply themselves . . . .

. . . .

THOMPSON

February 22, 1967

New York Times, 23, 24 February

In a conversation with New York Times' reporters on February 22, MAI VAN BO said the recent Trinh statement on the possibility of negoti- ations was an important gesture of good will toward the United States. He repeated over and over again that the halt of US bombing had to be "permanent and unconditional" because any cessation which was not clearly labeled "permanent and unconditional" would leave the "threat of bombing" intact and thus would constitute an unacceptable interference with the negotiations. Asked how a distinction could be made between a temporary and a permanent halt to bombing, he replied the US would have to declare at the outset that the halt was "permanent and unconditional." Bo said the Trinh offer constituted a basic change in DRV policy and added that the US demonstrated bad faith in its response. He said the four points were "the most correct" solution to the Vietnam problem, and that the DRV regarded the NFLSV as the only "authentic representative" of the South Vietnamese people; thus peace could only come about if the US settled South Vietnamese problems with the Front. In a speech on February 24, Cambodia's Prince SIHANOUK stated Mai Van Bo had asked him to clarify that "the only condition the DRV poses for eventual conversations between North Vietnam and the United States is a definitive and unconditional cessation of bombing of North Vietnam, because the North Vietnamese will not talk under duress. As for the American demand for reciprocity in de-escalation, Mai Van Bo gave me the following explanation: 'it would be impossible for the Government of Hanoi to stop helping and aiding its brothers in the South who must liberate themselves from invasion and American occupation.'"

During a television interview on February 22, AMBASSADOR HARRIMAN said "there's some indication that they're (Hanoi) coming around to a point where they may be willing to talk, and it looks at the moment as if it's more apt to be private discussions rather than something that would be public." Asked whether the US would be prepared to accept the Front as an equal in negotiations, he replied that should there be a formal public peace conference, "we will not, of course, accept them as a government" but "they could come with Hanoi."[50]

In late February, Hanoi protested to the ICC about US artillery bombardment across the DMZ (called a "new and extremely serious step of war escalation");[51] on 1 March, Nhan Dan termed the Viet Cong attacks on Danang and movements of (North Vietnamese) guns south of the DMZ as "reasonable reciprocity" for the new escalation steps taken by the U.S. The NLFSV representative to the DRV (28 February) called the "Johnson clique's" talk of pecce a "mere hoax" and said the real US aim was to "cling to South Vietnam at any cost and perpetually partition Vietnam."

The New York Times, Thursday, February 23, 1967

HANOI OFFERS ANEW TO JOIN U.S. IN TALKS IF BOMBING IS ENDED, by Henry Tanner (Special to The New York Times)

PARIS, Feb. 22 - A spokesman for Hanoi reaffirmed today its offer to enter into talks with the United States if American bombing attacks against North Vietnam were unconditionally and permanently halted.

Mai Van Bo, the North Vietnamese representative in Paris, indicated that his Government's position on this point had not changed in spite of the resumption of American bombing Feb. 14 following a six-day suspension.

. . . .

Before his state.. .., there had been widespread speculation for several days that the North Vietnamese position had hardened after the resumption of the bombings and the failure of the mediation attempted in London by Prime Minister Wilson and the Soviet Premier, Aleksei N. Kosygin.

The principal reason for this speculation was a message from President Ho Chi Minh to Pope Paul VI on Feb. 13 restating Hanoi's four-point demands, including withdrawal of American forces from Vietnam.

. . . .

President Ho Chi Minh, in his message to the Pope, phrased the demands as follows:

"The U.S. imperialists must put an end to their aggression in Vietnam, end unconditionally and definitively the bombing and all other acts of war against the Democratic Republic of Vietnam, withdraw from South Vietnam all American and satellite troops, recognize the South Vietnam National Liberation Front and let the Vietnamese people themselves settle their own affairs."

Mr. Bo said today that the President's message had referred to the terms of a settlement and not to the process of getting peace talks started. Therefore, he added, it did not constitute a change in the Vietnamese position.

Mr. Bo repeated over and over that the halt of American bombing had to be "permanent and unconditional."

He said the North Vietnamese would not talk "under bombs" or "the threat of bombs." He said that any cessation of bombing that was not clearly labeled "permanent and unconditional" would leave the "threat of bombing" intact and thus would constitute an unacceptable interference with the negotiation.

Asked how a distinction could be made between a temporary and a permanent halt to bombing, he answered that the United States would have to declare at the outset that the halt was "permanent and unconditional."

Mr. Bo said that Nguyen Duy Trinh, the North Vietnamese Foreign Minister, made an important gesture of goodwill toward the United States in late January when he told Wilfred Burchett, an Australian correspondent, that talks between Washington and Hanoi would be possible if the bombing stopped.

The North Vietnamese representative said that that had constituted a basic change in Hanoi's position. Earlier, he said his government's stand was that if the United States stopped bombing unconditionally, this new fact would be studied and that, if Washington then proposed to negotiate, this proposal also would be studied.

. . . .

He asserted that neither President Johnson nor Secretary of State Dean Rusk had ever quoted Mr. Trinh's statement fully or accurately.

This, he added, was proof of bad faith since Hanoi's real position was fully known and understood in Washington.

. . . .

He made it clear that this was a "conversation" and not an "interview." He said that for an interview he would have insisted on written questions and would have given written answers. He asked that his remarks be reported fairly and correctly.

Mr. Bo indicated, but did not specifically say, that the four point program of Hanoi was subject to negotiation once United States-North Vietnamese talks had started.

When asked whether the four points constituted absolute terms for a settlement or whether a compromise might be possible, he answered that he could not say what would happen in any talks since no talks were now taking place.

Mr. Bo called the four points "the most correct" solution. Asked whether this could be translated into English as "the best" solution, he said "no."

It is "the most correct" solution, he declared, because it would assure the North Vietnamese people the full exercise of their national rights, real independence and lasting peace.

Mr. Bo was asked about the third of the four points, which calls for the settlement of the affairs of South Vietnam according to the program of the National Liberation Front.

He said that the North Vietnamese Government regarded the National Liberation Front as the only "authentic representative" of the South Vietnamese people.

He said the program of the front was to give South Vietnam independence, democracy, peace and neutrality. He added that Hanoi supported this program and regarded all the problems of South Vietnam as the sole concern of the front.

Therefore, he stated, there could be peace only if the United States settled South Vietnamese problems with the front.

. . . .

February 23, 1967

JCS 6957 (to CINCPAC; info COMUSMACV), TS/LIMDIS.

Subj: Employment of Artillery Fire

1. You are authorized to conduct artillery fire from positions in SVN against valid military targets in Laos, in the DMZ both north and south of demarcation line, and in NVN north of DMZ.

2. State concurs.

C. M. Gettys, Brig. Gen., USA
(Drafted by VAdm Mustin, USN, Dir, J-3)

MOSCOW 3622 (to SecState), TS/Nodis, Sent 1520, 23 Feb; Rec'd 1735, 23 Feb.

Ref: Moscow 3568

1. At no point did Kosygin mention necessity of US withdrawal.
This may not be particularly significant in view my having mentioned
our public declaration of willingness withdraw under certain conditions,

2. Kosygin's statement that we disagreed on whether there were one
or two Vietnams appears a step backward.

3.

. . . .

THOMPSON

February 24, 1967

STATE 143101 (to Amembassy Moscow), TS/Nodis, Sent 1530, 24 Feb 67.

Secretary saw Dobrynin February 23 to discuss Viet-Nam.

4. . . . . . Hanoi had our 14 points, the Lewandowski 10-point draft,
and at an earlier time we had proposed a possible revision of Hanoi's
third point along the lines of paragraph 5 of the Lewandowski draft. With
such formulations, we could either start by stages of action, or could "go
to the end and work back." For example, the Secretary noted that Kosygin
in London had expressed concern about the fate of the men fighting in the
South if our London proposal had been accepted (calling for an end to infiltration of supplies as well as men). To deal with this problem, it might
be possible to work out amnesty arrangements for the southerners fighting
in the South and safe conduct for the northerners to return home, although
we recognized that Hanoi might not wish to admit the presence of the latter.

5. . . . . The Secretary wondered whether there might be some significance in the fact that Ho did not make his reply to the President public; did this mean that Hanoi's rejection of continued talks might not be final? Dobrynin said he saw no connection. . . .

6. . . . . The DRV Charge had given the Soviets the message that Hanoi felt that our resumption of bombing meant we were not repeat not interested in talks. Therefore, Hanoi was breaking off the Moscow channel . . . .

7. The Secretary then said that it was out of the question for us to stop bombing and see a completely new military situation develop without knowing at all what talks would produce. Dobrynin responded that we could try and asked what would we lose. . . .

. . . .

9. The Secretary reiterated that there were very important military considerations behind our position, and noted the massive re-supply that Hanoi had made during the TET period. Dobrynin objected that the US too had re-supplied its forces. He said that this really could not be the major point behind the US position, and that there must be something more (this presumably implying that the US was really resolved to get a military solution). The Secretary quickly rejoined that we drew a distinction between our activity in support of South Viet-Nam and North Viet-Nam activity against South Viet-Nam. Dobrynin said that the Soviets likewise made a distinction, but not the same one we did. He added that our disagreement on this had been fully discussed and further discussion would not lead anywhere.

. . . .

12. . . . . Dobrynin responded that Hanoi's objection to talking unless the bombing stopped was a major difficulty and a real one. He then recounted that on the 15th (apparently of December) the DRV Charge had come to the Soviet Foreign Ministry to tell the Soviets that they had told Rapacki to break off his talks with us, on the ground that the US bombing just before that date meant the US thought it could pressure Hanoi to talk, and this they would not do.

13. Dobrynin then went on that Hanoi (and by implication the Soviets as well) took an unfavorable view of our refusal to accept the 7-day TET truce period proposed by Hanoi. The Secretary said that we were bound to be influenced by how they would have used the longer period. Dobrynin argued that nonetheless the impression was left that the US wished a military solution and not talks. He noted that Hanoi was angry on this point as well . . . .

. . . .

15.. The Secretary then noted that Hanoi would not even tell us what the three divisions just north of the DMZ would do if the bombing stopped. Dobrynin queried whether the divisions were not fully north of the DMZ, and the Secretary responded that some elements were south of the DMZ, some were in the DMZ and some to the north.

. . . .

17. The Secretary then asked whether the appointment of a new DRV Ambassador in Moscow might make a difference to Hanoi's willingness to talk in some fashion. Dobrynin said that of course an Ambassador would have more authority than a Charge, but the decisions would still be made in Hanoi and an Ambassador would be acting under instructions. . . .

18. The Secretary then noted that Ho's message to the Pope really asked for capitulation and US withdrawal. Similarly, Mai Van Bo appeared to be referring again to our recognizing the NLF as the sole legitimate representative of the South. . . .

. . . .

21. The Secretary concluded that we continue to wish to stay closely in touch with the Soviets. He noted that there had once been a time when it had seemed clear that the Soviets did not wish to discuss the problem with us, referring to his talk with Kosygin in New Delhi. Dobrynin agreed. Now, it seemed clear that the Soviets were prepared to discuss the matter with us, and perhaps it would have helped if we had been in touch with them on one or two specific occasions. The Secretary emphasized that we really did wish to see the conflict finished, and noted that a general feeling of impatience was our real problem, not the views expressed by such people as Senator Fulbright. If the other side kept up and increased its military activities, as it appeared to be doing, it was inevitable that we ourselves would take action.

RUSK (Drafted by W. P. Bundy)

February 25, 1967

LONDON 6893 (to SecState), S/Nodis, Sent 1348, 25 Feb; Rec'd 1539, 25 Feb.

. . . .

2. . . . . Rostow read substance of STATE 143029 and explained background which led to Presidential decision to undertake this new series of actions.[52] Brown took news calmly and left room to call Prime Minister so that he would not hear about artillery bombardment across DMZ over radio. Brown observed that since Kosygin departure, Vietnam issue had quieted down

in UK, but he thought this new action would be interpreted as "escalation" and could stir people up again -- not just left wingers, but also "soft" groups and elements in the center of Labor's political spectrum.

. . . .

4. Rostow also stated that the Russians now feel that negotiations will not come about through intercession of a mediator, but rather through direct contact between Hanoi and Washington. Rostow reminded Brown that the American Government and the American people were very conscious of the Korean experience when negotiations were carried on for two years while the fighting continued. During the two-year period, American casualties more than doubled. We were determined to prevent that from happening again in Viet-Nam. Brown said in reply to this point that the important thing about Korea was that negotiations were going on. "Fighting while negotiations were taking place was preferable to fighting without negotiations."
. . . .

. . . .

KAISER

March 1, 1967

LONDON 6998 (to SecState), TS/Nodis, Sent 1656, 1 Mar; Rec'd 1830, 1 Mar.

1. Viet Nam was subject of two conversations with Rapacki during London visit. On first day (22nd) . . . . Thomson got strong impression Rapacki felt he had taken a personal risk in December project, had gotten burned, ...

2. Rapacki version to Brown of December events was that after firm agreement on original 10-point package, Lodge had consulted Washington and then reneged by raising new (unspecified) questions and points of interpretations. Before the Poles had chance to do anything with these the December 13-14 bombings occurred, killing entire project.

3. Rapacki's general attitude was illustrated by two minor exchanges.

XGDS-3

4. In luncheon conversation between PM and Rapacki on 23rd Wilson opened with question of how the quote misunderstanding unquote of November-December arose, observing that Lewandowski in Hanoi must have gone beyond what Lodge had said. Rapacki replied vehemently that no misunderstanding was possible. Lewandowski had gotten Lodge's approval of his written version

of what Lodge had said. Only problem was bombing of Hanoi just before
Warsaw talks of two principals scheduled to begin. In response to Wilson's
question as to why things went wrong, Rapacki quote hinted unquote that
sabotage by quote Saigon hawks unquote was responsible, referring again to
December 13-14 bombings. When Wilson suggested failure of quote human
communication unquote Rapacki again insisted there had been no misunderstanding or inaccuracy in transmission of messages.

5. On Wilson's suggestion, Rapacki agreed a more detailed post mortem
between British and Poles on the December affair would be useful. The
British Embassy Warsaw had subsequently been informed Poles will give
them a more detailed account of their version, though how specific and
whether in writing is not clear. UK Ambassador Brimelow, who not well
informed on Viet Nam issue, has been instructed only to listen and not talk.

6. When Wilson referred to Harriman talks in Warsaw a year ago re
possibility of misunderstanding Rapacki was equally categoric in insisting
there had been no misunderstanding or garble of Harriman suggestions
declaring he had personally initialed written record of Harriman talks.[53]

7.

XGDS-3

Unquote. While taking usual hard line that cessation of bombing is essential
pre-condition for any progress, Rapacki gave no hint of what might happen
if bombing stopped. But he declared that if bombing continues, scale of
hostilities will grow, and US will find itself involved in Laos, possibility
also in Cambodia, Thailand and directly in North Viet Nam.

XGDS-3

KAISER

March 4, 1967

MOSCOW 3756 (to SecState), TS/Nodis, Sent 0930, 4 Mar; Rec'd 1204, 4 Mar.

. . . .

2. Yesterday when discussing China with Kuznetsov he jokingly stated
we should be well informed in view of our several hundred secret talks
with Chicoms. A number of my diplomatic colleagues have mentioned Soviet
suspicions of our relations with Chinese.

THOMPSON

STATE 149089 (to Amembassy Moscow), TS/Nodis, 4 Mar 67.

You are hereby authorized at your discretion to deny flatly that we had any approach from the Chicoms on negotiations with North Vietnam.

RUSK (Drafted by J. P. Walsh)

March 11, 1967

STATE 153528 (to Amembassy Moscow), TS/Nodis, Sent 0123, 12 March.

Ref: Moscow's 3501

1. We have transmitted to you USUN's 4318 in which Kulebiakin expressed view to Buffum and Finger that now is good time for talks between US and North Vietnam and that these could take place without stoppage of bombing. Moreover, fact that new DRV Ambassador Nguyen Tho Chan, has presented his credentials provides opportunity to try to establish the direct line of communications between Ambassadors to which we had hoped the Guthrie-LeChang talks would lead. We realize that Le Chang's February 15 statement appears to close door on further conversations and Ho's message seems adamant on ruling out talks while bombing continues. Nevertheless, in earlier Guthrie-Le Chang conversations it seemed implicit that they were going through exercise which might be regarded as preparatory to direct contacts at Ambassadorial level when DRV Ambassador arrived on scene and Kulebiakin in NY has specifically suggested level of talks in Moscow should be raised. Therefore, request you seek meeting with Chan and make following points:

2. Basic message we would like to convey to Hanoi via Ambassador Chan is that we continue to favor prompt peaceful settlement and we remain persuaded that the shortest road is through direct talks between our representatives. Would not appear from record that we and DRV disagree on this point but rather that we have been unable to find way of moving toward talks.

3. You should point out that in the President's press conference of March 9 the President said in answer to a question with respect to Quote reciprocal action Unquote that he would be ready to entertain Quote just almost any reciprocal action on the part of North Vietnam . . . We are prepared to discuss anything they are willing to discuss. Unquote.[54]

4. FYI We recognize that the new DRV Ambassador is probably under instructions not to establish contact with you at this time. Thus even if he provides an opportunity for a brief call, he is likely to reiterate the stand the Charge made to Guthrie at their last meeting. We recognize that we have to give the DRV Ambassador enough ammunition to warrant his requesting a change in instructions. For this reason you should emphasize that we are ready now, without preliminaries, to get down to serious substantive and entirely secret discussions on all questions involved in a peaceful settlement itself, in order to bring this matter to a prompt

conclusion. We will provide further instructions along this line if your
initial talk indicates the possibility of establishing a dialogue.

RUSK (Drafted by Unger)

March 13, 1967

MOSCOW 3880 (to SecState), TS/Nodis, Sent 0930, 13 Mar, Rec'd 1047, 13 Mar.

Ref: State 153528

. . . .

    2. In view our recent escalation bombing, this strikes me as a
singularly inappropriate time make this approach.[55] It will almost certainly be rebuffed by DRV who will not wish to give appearance of sub-
mitting to increased military pressure. More importantly believe our
approach at this time will be interpreted by Soviets as cynically timed
to insure refusal and merely build up our record of peace efforts. (I am
inclined by skeptical Kulebiakin). Moreover, failure arrange discussion
now will make more difficult approach at more opportune time. Nevertheless,
will endeavor carry our instructions unless cancelled by department.

THOMPSON

STATE 154303 (to Amembassy Moscow), TS/Nodis, 13 Mar 67.

For the Ambassador from the Secretary

    Despite your 3880 I believe that you should suggest to the DRV Ambassa-
dor that a private talk might be constructive.

    As far as recent bombings are concerned, there is very little prospect
that we will let up in bombing unless we see some response through private
contacts. We have been maintaining the ten nautical mile radius around
Hanoi but cannot guarantee to do so indefinitely.

    We, too, are inclined to be skeptical about Kulebiakin. The fact that
he was accompanied on his second talk by another Russian and his greater
detail of suggestion about procedure indicates the possibility that he was
in fact acting under instructions.

    The immediate result might well be a preemptory refusal by the DRV
Ambassador to talk but if he attributes his refusal to our bombing, we
might as well follow through and tell him that we are prepared to discuss
that problem. Given the potentialities which lie ahead, we are not indif-
ferent to establishing a record if that is all that Hanoi will permit.

I fully understand the considerations underlying your 3880 but believe you should know that we do not see a better time, so far as bombing is concerned, coming up in the near future unless we see some indication that the other side is prepared to do business.

RUSK (Drafted by D. Rusk)

March 16, 1967

On March 16, Prime Minister Wilson sent a communication to President Johnson (State's 158462, March 20), recalling that he had been worried during the Kosygin visit about a misunderstanding with the USG which had risen. He asked if Pat Dean could see the President around April 1 to discuss this problem and to make sure that there is no question of a similar situation arising in the future. He also asked for confirmation that the message which the President had sent him to hand to Kosygin on the night of February 21 still represents the US position.[56]

MOSCOW 3947 (to SecState), TS/Nodis, Sent 1350, 16 Mar; Rec'd 1558, 16 Mar.

Ref: State 154303

1. . . . Akalovsky reached Hoang Manh Tu by phone today at 11:45 and conveyed my request for meeting with DRV Ambassador . . . .

2. Tu said would check and asked Akalovsky call him again . . . .

3. Tu . . . was in his office at 14:45. Said his Ambassador not available "for the moment" and therefore he could give no answer at this time. When asked if this meant answer could be expected later in day, Tu said Ambassador might not be available until Saturday, and suggested Akalovsky call him Saturday morning (March 18).

4. It clear Ambassador Chan asked Hanoi for instructions. Noteworthy is fact that, contrary to his past practice of calling back himself, Tu now unwilling do so and asking Akalovsky call him.

THOMPSON

March 17, 1967

STATE 157597 (to Amembassy Moscow), TS/Nodis, Sent 2258, 17 Mar.

Ref: Moscow 3963

. . . , we now see some advantage in delaying your session with the

93

DRV Ambassador for several days while developments in connection with the U Thant initiative mature to the point where we know the nature of our own response and perhaps that of Hanoi.[57] Nonetheless, if Akalovsky gets a call on Saturday, March 18, and you have an appointment, the Secretary General's proposal might provide a useful opening gambit. We would suggest that you simply mention that we have gotten the proposal from the Secretary General and you have been informed that Washington is studying it carefully.

FYI. We have strong indications from Saigon that if anything more formal than the kind of talks you might be engaged in in Moscow were to take place the GVN would want to participate.

RUSK (Drafted by C. L. Cooper)

March 21, 1967

MOSCOW 4020 (to SecState), TS/Nodis, Sent 1134, 21 Mar; Rec'd 1251, 21 Mar.

Ref: State 157597

1. Having delayed contact with DRV Embassy for several days per reftel, I had Akalovsky phone Hoang Manh today . . . . , latter said he had been authorized give following response . . . .

2. At present, US carrying out every day new steps of grave escalation of aggressive war against people of NVN. At same time, US is mounting a game of contacts with DRV reps in order to deceive world public opinion and to cover its criminal acts of war. In view of this, DRV Ambassador in Moscow cannot receive US Ambassador.

3. . . . . .

THOMPSON

LONDON 7602 (to SecState), S/Nodis, Rec'd 1020, 21 Mar.

For Walsh to hold for Secy return or relay as desired

Ref: State 158462

. . . .

2. . . . in my private talk with Brown last night . . . he made clear that what is still bothering Wilson and him is the change of tenses in the message we gave them on Friday, as compared to the A/B formula and the draft that they had made and of course actually gave the Russians on Friday without our authority.

3. I told Brown flatly that I was absolutely sure this change
of tenses had nothing whatsoever to do with the outcome. . . .

. . . .

5. . . . , Brown asked earnestly whether the President's attitude
remained as he had stated it to Brown in October, that he was ready to
seize even a 40 percent chance for peace. I did not try to gloss this
remark, but did assure him categorically that the President was absolutely
determined to follow any road that could lead to peace and that there had
been no change whatever in this attitude. I noted that the Bunker appointment placed in Saigon our most experienced field negotiator, and that this
was simply another evidence of our position.[58] I do not think this got across,
but it is apparent that Wilson and Brown do a lot of churning over the
Kosygin visit and may still have some scars from our having given the
Phase A/Phase B formula to the Poles in November without telling Brown.

KAISER

March 23, 1967

MOSCOW 4069 (to SecState), TS/Nodis, Sent 1530, 23 Mar; Rec'd 1811, 23 Mar.

Ref: State 149089

During my call on Gromyko today, I . . . said that my inquiry with
Department confirms my response to Kosygin, i.e., that there had been no
such suggestions.

THOMPSON

March 24, 1967

STATE 162643 (to Amembassy Moscow), TS/Nodis, Sent 2302, 24 Mar.

Ref: State 143101

In Bundy/Dobrynin conversation on evening March 23, following . . .
were highlights:

1. Dobrynin stuck throughout to same basic line as in reftel, that
Hanoi simply would not repeat not talk unless we stop the bombing. He
repeated argumentation that Hanoi could not possibly accept our insistence
on reciprocal action without accepting whole US view of nature of conflict.
. . . .

2. Conversation then got onto U Thant proposal, as to which Dobrynin had already indicated that Hanoi response would be negative. . . .

3. Bundy then said that Hanoi revelation of letters continued to puzzle us very much, as we had formed clear impression that if Hanoi ever wished to move seriously it would do so in some secret and private manner.[59] Hence we were genuinely distressed that Hanoi had damaged, if not destroyed, privacy of Moscow channel. Dobrynin did not respond directly, and did not take possible occasion to indicate any hope Moscow channel could be resumed. . . .

4. . . . . Bundy noted that Hanoi had never responded to our January 20 message, and that this had been one of major negative factors, together with lack of any response to President's letter, that had led us to go ahead with resumption on February 13. He stressed that discussion of January 20 topics need not be described as "talks" but could simply be exploratory "non-conversations." If we were able to arrive at a clear picture of an agreed final settlement, question of more formal talks and even of stopping the bombing might take on different hue. Dobrynin obviously understood the point, but did not respond in any hopeful way.

5. Bundy then remarked that if Hanoi were so insistent that we stop the bombing before any talks could take place, it was hard to suppose that there could have been any substance to what the Poles told us in December about a willingness to meet in Warsaw.

Bundy merely said Soviets knew facts as we clearly understood them. In this exchange, Dobrynin returned to theme that our bombing on December 2 and 4 and thrown Rapacki off, and that bombing of December 13-14 had caused clear Hanoi rejection of Warsaw meeting. . . .

6. In commenting on our February 13 resumption, Dobrynin did complain that we had not given additional time for Hanoi response . . . . our resumption had given impression in Moscow that USG or some elements in it, were impatient and anxious to press forward with military pressures.

7. Dobrynin expressed hope that there would not be "dramatic developments" in USG actions against NVN. . . .

8. . . . . .

. . . .

RUSK (Drafted by W. P. Bundy)

April 5, 1967

On April 5, Thompson was instructed to arrange delivery to the
DRV mission by the means he deemed best suited to maximize the chances
of early transmission to Hanoi of a letter dated April 6 from President
Johnson to President Ho Chi Minh (State's 169339).[60] The following points
were made in the letter: (1) the President was disappointed that Ho did
not feel able to respond positively to his letter of February 8; (2) we
remain prepared to talk quietly with Ho's representatives to establish
the terms of a peaceful settlement and then bring the fighting to a stop;
or we are prepared to undertake steps of mutual deescalation which might
make it easier for discussions of a peaceful settlement to take place.
Talks could take place in Moscow, Rangoon, or elsewhere; (3) it is clear
that we must one day agree to reestablish and make effective the Geneva
Accords of 1954 and 1962; let the people of SVN determine in peace the
kind of government they want; let the peoples of North and South Viet-Nam
determine peacefully whether and how they should unite; and permit the
peoples of SEA to turn all their energies to their economic and social
development; (4) the President and Ho will be judged in history by whether
they worked to bring about this result sooner rather than later; (5) Ho's
views were invited on these matters.

April 6, 1967

MOSCOW 4284 (to SecState), TS/Nodis, Sent 1353, 6 Apr; Rec'd 1521, 6 Apr.

Ref: State 169339

1. I had Akalovsky deliver President's message to DRV Embassy today.
. . . .

. . . .

3. While there is good chance letter will be returned, hopefully DRV
Embassy will make copy before doing so.

THOMPSON.

MOSCOW 4294 (to SecState), TS/Nodis, Sent 1645, 6 Apr; Rec'd 1808, 6 Apr.

Ref: Moscow's 4284

President's message returned by DRV Embassy. Original envelope which
had been opened, found in Embassy mail box at 1745 and bore following in
French: "Non conforme! Retour a l'expediteur."

THOMPSON

April 10, 1967

STATE 172325 (to Amembassy Moscow), TS/Nodis, 10 Apr.
Info: USDEL PUNTA DEL ESTE
PUNTA: Eyes only for Secretary Rusk
MOSCOW: For Ambassador Thompson Only

Request you seek early appointment with Gromyko to make following points:

. . . .

5. A few weeks ago Mr, Kulebiakin of USSR Mission in New York mentioned to a representative of our UN Mission that Mr'. Pham Van Dong would soon be in Moscow and suggested that we might wish to contact him there. My Government is ready to establish such a contact . . . .

6. . . . , you would appreciate Gromyko's reaction to this proposal and most especially any assistance that he could render to facilitate confidential discussions with Mr. Pham Van Dong or members of his party.

. . . .

KATZENBACH (Drafted by C. L. Cooper)

April 12, 1967

Dept of State Memorandum of Conversation, 1815 12 Apr 67
Place: Soviet Embassy, Washington, D.C.
Participants: Soviet Ambassador Anatoliy F. Dobrynin
               Deputy Under Secretary Foy D. Kohler

During my long luncheon conversation with Ambassador Dobrynin . . . . I asked him about the reports of a new agreement between Moscow and Peking to facilitate the transit of Soviet arms aid to North Viet-Nam.[61]

. . . . I said that some of the present interpretations speculated that the new arrangement was a precursor to a considerable increase in the quantity and quality of Soviet arms aid to North Viet-Nam. I hoped that this was not the case because escalation on their side could only add to the pressures for further escalation on our side. He replied that in fact pressures on them to increase their aid resulted from our escalation. He knew that Moscow wanted to avoid any direct conflict with us in Viet-Nam and was sure that care would be exercised. On the other hand, he could not say categorically the Vietnamese were not even now asking for new quantities and forms of arms and that Moscow did not feel under considerable pressure to provide them.

. . . . I was sure the President . . . . did not want war to spread or any direct conflict to develop. However, he certainly could not feel

himself bound to any previous restraints so long as all his attempt to
find a way to reduce the intensity of the battle or bring it to a peaceful
conclusion had been rejected.

. . . .

(Initialed by Kohler)

April 13, 1967

MOSCOW 4378 (to SecState), TS/Nodis, Sent 1300, 13 Apr; Rec'd 1713, 13 Apr.

Ref: State 172325

1.   I met with Gromyko ten a.m. today and made presentation along
lines reftel.

2.   Gromyko said Sovs "of course" could not assume role of intermediary between US and DRV and NLFSV, for reasons explained to US Govt on
number of occasions. US should address itself to Vietnamese re any matter
it may wish discuss. . . .

3. . . . , Gromyko continued, there are ways of establishing US-DRV
contact, and first prerequisite for this is unconditional cessation of
bombings. . . .

. . . .

6.   I pointed out that we prepared have military actions and bombings
as priority item for discussion with DRV, and that we also prepared have
de-escalation even without any agreement. Yet whenever we had suspended
bombings in part, other side had sought to use pause to increase its strength
in south. All we want is assurance--not necessarily public--that this would
not happen again. . . .

7.   Gromyko pointed out . . . . US had begun contact with DRV in
Warsaw and elsewhere, but they had been stopped by US actions. . . .

. . . .

THOMPSON

April 20, 1967

The exchange of views with Brown and his approaching visit to Moscow
prompted Thompson to express his views on our negotiation posture (Moscow's
4491). He suggested that we should consider whether in present circumstances

our continuing campaign of peace moves really serves to further the possibility of peace negotiations. He doubted that further initiatives, insofar as US public opinion is concerned, could be helpful. Insofar as the Soviets are concerned, initiatives that have little chance of success are positively harmful, particularly if we are trying to involve them. In respect to the DRV and NLF our continued peace moves must be counter-productive by suggesting to them that we will not stay the course. On the other hand, Thompson did not think an escalation of bombing was the answer to the problem. He suggested that consideration be given to a Presidential statement listing all our recent moves combined with a resolute declaration that, while we will always be prepared to move to the conference table, we have no course open to us but to step up our operations in SVN and to con-tinue to use our bombers to hold down infiltration from the north. Against this background, Thompson suggested that Brown should convey to the Soviets a sense of our determination to see this affair through rather than making peace noises when he visits Moscow.

April 25, 1967

MOSCOW 4590 (to SecState), S/Nodis, Sent 1030, 25 Apr; Rec'd 1218, 25 Apr.

. . . .

2. Dobrynin remarked that he had known that his government felt strongly about Vietnam but had not realized how strongly until his consul-tations here.

THOMPSON

BONN 12782 (to SecState), S/Nodis, Sent 2123, 25 Apr; Rec'd 2259, 25 Apr.

For the Acting Secretary from the Secretary

Referring to the last sentence of Moscow's 4590, you might wish to prepare a telegram for Thompson, asking him to have a further talk with Dobrynin to clarify the elementary situation on Viet-Nam. If the Soviet Union is concerned about the fact that a fellow Socialist country is being bombed by the US, there is no quarrel between Washington and Moscow on that point. This bombing could be stopped immediately, as far as we are concerned. If, however, the Soviets are determined to support North Viet-Nam in a seizure of South Viet-Nam by force, we have a major issue with the Soviet Union. As we see it, the Soviet Union does not have sufficient influence in Hanoi to cause Hanoi to take the steps which would result in a complete cessation of US bombing of North Viet-Nam. Perhaps we should try to break through this fundamental policy point with the Soviets so that at least we and they can fully understand exactly where we are.

McGHEE

May 15, 1967

STATE 194946 (to Amembassy London), TS/Nodis, Sent 0200, 16 May.

For the Ambassador from the Secretary

Please pass the following message from me to Foreign Secretary Brown.

1. QUOTE. Dear George: We welcome your trip to Moscow and wish you well. I would like to pass along some views and a suggestion or two which might be of some use. . . .

. . . .

5. There is one central point which, if clearly accepted by the USSR, could move us a long way toward peace. We are prepared to recognize the interest of the Soviet Union in the safety of a Communist regime in North Viet-Nam. They must recognize our interest, confirmed by treaty, in the safety of South Viet-Nam and the ability of the South Vietnamese to have their own government. Surely, if we and the Soviets recognize each other's important interests here, we ought to find a way to pull North and South Viet-Nam apart militarily.

6. We recognize that our military actions against North Viet-Nam present many problems for the Soviet Government. We are prepared to cease such military actions at any time, but cannot do so without some serious military response on the part of the North Vietnamese . . . .

7. Perhaps you could press the Soviets as to what Hanoi's reaction would be under any of the following alternatives:

(a) A combination of our stopping the bombing of North Viet-Nam, their stopping their infiltration and our stopping augmentation of forces. If the Russians have any variant or counterproposal on this formula, we would be glad to take a look at it.

(b) Pulling apart our opposing forces at the DMZ. This would be following up on our offer of April 19 which has been rejected, but which might lead to some countersuggestion on the Russian side.[62]

(c) A partial suspension of bombing such as the 4-month stand-down in over 300 square miles around the center of Hanoi in exchange for some serious gesture of de-escalation in the South. We were disappointed that Hanoi showed no interest in this act of restraint, and no reciprocity, because we are prepared to use this device on an expanding scale as a means of de-escalation.

8. On the military side, we just cannot accept a permanent uncondi-tional cessation of bombing in the North while they continue unabated with their armed assault on the South. The large North Vietnamese forces

in and on both sides of the DMZ are at this moment heavily engaging our Marines in the border provinces of South Viet-Nam. They are firing artillery from well across the Seventeenth Parallel. We expect a major attack in the Central Highlands from forces now in refuge in Cambodia.
. . . .

    9. Another issue that may well arise in your conversations is the matter of Laos. . . . I have long felt that reconvening the 1962 Laos Conference might offer some opportunities for dealing with the problem of South Viet-Nam as well as Laos.

    . . . .

    12. . . . . Good Luck. Dean UNQUOTE

RUSK (Drafted by C. L. Cooper)

May 17, 1967

STATE 196078 (to Amembassy London), TS/Nodis, Sent 2053, 17 May.

Info: Amembassy Moscow

    Following message from Foreign Secretary Brown received by Secretary Rusk today transmitted for your information:

    QTE

UNQTE

RUSK (Drafted by B. H. Read)

<u>May 18, 1967</u>

STATE 196827 (to Amembassy London), TS/Nodis, Sent 1614, 18 May.

Info: Amembassy Moscow

Please deliver following message from Secretary Rusk to Foreign Secretary Brown:

QUOTE: Dear George:

I find it difficult to reply precisely to the questions put in your message of May 16. What we really need is some indication that Hanoi is prepared to talk business.

. . . .

. . . no one has been able to tell us of any military move which North Viet-Nam is prepared to make if we take steps on your side to de-escalate. . . .

. . . .

Is it not really better for you, with a briefcase full of interesting proposals on our side, to explore the situation with the Soviets to find out if there are any points anywhere on which some · progress might be made? This you can do on your own responsibility as Co-Chairman.

I hope I do not appear to be unresponsive but I rather feel that until we get some word from the North Vietnamese we are talking in a vacuum - a vacuum created by Hanoi.

. With warmest regards, Sincerely, Dean. UNQUOTE.

RUSK (Drafted by D. Rusk)

103

September 18, 1967

"Chronology of Viet Peace Efforts," by Chalmers M. Roberts, The Washington Post, 18 September 1967.[63]

The record indicates that the Ashmore-Baggs peace effort ran afoul of a change in American policy which occurred at the moment they were involved in Vietnam diplomacy.

This is the record, as far as it is now known, of the pertinent events:

December 4, 1966 - Poland reported to the United States that North Vietnam was prepared to send a man to Warsaw to meet an American representative and to do so without demanding as a pre-condition an end to the American bombing of the North.

American officials subsequently contended that independent checks showed this to be a Polish view, not that of North Vietnam.

December 13-14, 1966 - American planes raid near Hanoi. Poland later privately blamed the raids for ending chances for a meeting. After the raids Hanoi began to stress the demand that bombing must cease unconditionally before there could be talks.

December 26   January 6, 1967 - Harrison Salisbury of the New York Times created a furor over dispatches from Hanoi picturing civilian destruction from the American raids. Officials here said Hanoi had let Salisbury in as part of a campaign to force an end to the bombing. Ashmore and Baggs arrived in Hanoi the day Salisbury left.

January 12, 1967 - Ashmore and Baggs met Ho Chi Minh who stressed an end to the bombing Ashmore now writes that "we had not brought back" from this interview "any hard proposal" from Ho "beyond the reiteration of his unqualified commitment to enter into negotiations" if the U.S. halted the bombing.

Ashmore reported to State Department officials that he and Baggs felt that "Ho seemed prepared to consider a specific proposal based on a formula of mutual de-escalation" of the fighting.

Early January to early February -- The United States secretly sent four memoranda to Hanoi describing, officials say, possible methods of deescalation. These messages, yet to be made public were handed by an American embassy official in Moscow to a North Vietnamese representative.

January 27, 1967 - Hanoi's man in Moscow gave a reply to the American official. Later the State Department described the reply as "a diatribe against the United States."

January 28, 1967 - North Vietnamese Foreign Minister Nguyen Duy Trinh in an interview with Australian Communist journalist Wilfred Burchett said that "it is only after the unconditional cessation of U.S. bombing and all other acts of war against the DRV (North Vietnam) that there could be talks between the DRV and the U.S."

February 2, 1967 - President Johnson prepared a letter to Ho in which he took up the Burchett interview points. Mr. Johnson said he would "order a cessation of bombing" and also halt "further augmentation of U.S. forces in South Vietnam as soon as I am assured that infiltration into South Vietnam by land and sea has stopped." These "acts of restraint," he said, "would make possible serious private discussions." This letter, however, was not turned over to Hanoi's man in Moscow until Feb. 8 and the delay has never been explained.

February 4, 1967 - Ashmore and Baggs met at the State Department with Undersecretary Nicholas deB. Katzenbach and other top officials but not including Secretary Dean Rusk.

A letter from Ashmore to Ho was drafted with Assistant Secretary William P. Bundy, whose area includes Vietnam, as the chief department draftsman.

The key sentence in the letter stated that "senior officials" at State "expressed opinion that some reciprocal restraint" was necessary along with a halt to the bombing and an end to the influx of American troops if talks were to take place.

February 5, 1967 - The draft letter was delivered to Ashmore at Fulbright's house. Ashmore mailed it that afternoon. The letter did not specify the "reciprocal restraint" although the President's letter of three days earlier had specified an end to North Vietnamese infiltration into the South.

In addition, on the day (Feb.2) the Administration said the Presidential letter was drafted, Mr. Johnson told a press conference that "just almost any step" would be a suitable response from Hanoi. He also had said that "we would be glad to explore any reciprocal action." Sometime between Feb. 2 and 9 the official American terms were hardened.

February 8, 1967 - Soviet Premier Alexei Kosygin, who was in London Feb. 6-12, said at a press conference that the Trinh interview with Burchett "boils down" to saying that if the U.S. unconditionally stopped the bombing, "then it would be possible" to open talks. Kosygin thus publicly changed Trinh's crucial word "could" into "would." He was never contradicted by Hanoi on this. Furthermore, Kosygin passed the word to Washington, which had inquired as to when talks would begin, that they could start in three or four weeks.

105

February 9, 1967 - Secretary Rusk at a press conference which had been announced by the White House, said that "for some time now there has been evident a systematic campaign by the Communist side to bring about an unconditional and permanent cessation of the bombing of North Vietnam without any corresponding military action on their side, in exchange for the possibility of talks -- talks which are thus far formless and without content."

· Rusk also distinguished between a "pause in the bombing"(here he seemed to indicate he would agree to a pause in exchange for talks) and a "permanent cessation." For the latter to take place, he said, "we must know the military consequences." The U.S., he said, cannot stop the bombing without reciprocity for that would be "closing off one-half of the war while the rest of it goes on full force."

In short, Rusk was surfacing the central point of the President's letter to Ho, the contents of which were not made public until Hanoi broadcast it March 21.

February 10, 1967 - Ho said he received the Johnson letter on this day. Ashmore assumes it arrived before his own letter with the less specific request on the point of reciprocity.

During this period, February 8-14, there was a pause in the bombing over the Tet holiday in Vietnam, including a Presidentially ordered short extension.

February 13, 1967 - Ho in a letter to Pope Paul VI assailed the U.S. He coupled an unconditional end to the bombing with the withdrawal of American forces and the recogntion of the National Liberation Front, the political arm of the Vietcong. In Washington this was taken as a reply to the President. Resumption of the bombing was ordered.

February 15, 1967 - Ho replied to the President in words similar to the Pope. "A little later," writes Ashmore, he and Baggs received a reply to the Ashmore letter saying there did not seem to be any point to their making a second visit to Hanoi.

September 18, 1967

"Text of State Department Comment on Peace Feeler," The New York Times, Sept. 18, 1967.[64]

WASHINGTON, Sept. 18 - Following is the text of a statement issued by the State Department today regarding a report that President Johnson had undermined a peace approach to North Vietnam:

We have had a number of inquiries concerning news stories published today, based on an article by Mr. Harry Ashmore in a publication of the Center for the Study of Democratic Institutions (C.S.D.I.).

The facts concerning the department's contacts with Messrs. Ashmore and Baggs /William C. Baggs, editor of The Miami News/ are as follows:

(1) During the summer of 1966, Mr. William Baggs told the department that C.S.D.I. was planning a major conference in May of 1967 in Geneva, to follow up on the first Pacem in Terris meeting held in New York in February of 1965. Mr. Baggs disclosed to us efforts that the center was making to invite North Vietnam to attend, and the department responded sympathetically to the idea of the conference and to these efforts. These initial contacts were with Mr. George Ball and Mr. William Bundy. The President and Secretary Rusk were informed, and Mr. Ball was elected to handle contacts with Mr. Baggs on behalf of the United States Government.

(2) In mid-November and again in early December, Mr. Baggs was joined by Mr. Ashmore in calls at the department. In these calls, the progress of the conference plans was reviewed, and the two visitors indicated that they had a tentative invitation to go to Hanoi, with Mr. Luis Quintanilla of Mexico. Messrs. Baggs and Ashmore also suggested that, if they were able to conduct useful explorations of North Vietnamese views wards peace (sic). Mr. George Ball having then left the department, the primary responsibility for these conversations passed to his successor, Mr. Katzenbach, who kept the President and the Secretary of State informed as a matter of course.

In these conversations, department representatives accepted the Baggs-Ashmore suggestions and undertook to cooperate fully. Accordingly, the position of the United States Government on key issues relating to peace was discussed at some length, so that Baggs and Ashmore could represent it accurately in Hanoi.

(3) On Dec. 23, Baggs visited the department just prior to the departure of the three-man group on Dec. 28. At that meeting, the basic understanding of the United States Government position was reaffirmed, and it was further agreed that Baggs and Ashmore would report confidentially what they were able to pick up in Hanoi.

(4) Messrs. Baggs and Ashmore visited Hanoi from Jan. 6 to Jan. 14. They then returned to the U.S. and on Jan. 18 dictated for the department a full and confiden- ticular (sic) a conversation with President Ho on Jan. 12. In this conversation, Ho had insisted that there could be no talks between the U.S. and Hanoi unless the bombing were stopped, and unless also the U.S. stopped all reinforcements during the period of the talks. Ho was reported to be adamant against any reciprocal military restraint by North Vietnam. The record does not show that he solicited any U.S. Government response to these remarks.

(5) Concurrently, prior to Jan. 18 on U.S. initiative and without any connection to the Baggs-Ashmore actions, U.S. Government representatives had established a direct channel for communication with North Vietnamese representatives in Moscow. With the apparent agreement of both sides,

this channel was being kept wholly confidential, and was therefore not revealed to Messrs. Baggs and Ashmore in their discussions at the department.

It is, of course, fundamental to the U.S. Government dealings with Messrs. Baggs and Ashmore that there existed at the time this direct and secret channel. Exchanges through this direct channel continued through January and early February and culminated in President Johnson's letter to President Ho of Feb. 8 (mistakenly stated by Mr. Ashmore as Feb. 2). As has been stated by representatives of the department, a wide variety of proposals was put before Hanoi in these Moscow contacts, without at any time producing any useful response.

(6) Toward the end of January, Messrs. Baggs and Ashmore returned to Washington and expressed to the department the strong hope that they could be given a message for transmission to Hanoi. The department decided that, while the direct channel in Moscow was crucial and must at all costs be preserved, it would be useful to send a more general message through Messrs. Baggs and Ashmore, which would be consistent with the important messages being exchanged in Moscow. In view of this channel (of which Baggs-Ashmore were unaware) there was some question as to the further utility of detailed informal communications.

It seemed clear from the account given by Messrs. Baggs and Ashmore that their channel of communication had been established with the primary purpose of exchanges concerning North Vietnamese attendance at the May conference. Nevertheless, Baggs and Ashmore said they could send any messages for Hanoi through the regular mail to a North Vietnamese representative in Pnompenh, who in turn would relay it to a North Vietnamese official who had been the principal contact of Messrs. Baggs and Ashmore in Hanoi. Accordingly, the letter now published by Mr. Ashmore worked out with the representatives of the department, and authorized to be sent on Feb. 5. We were subsequently informed by Mr. Ashmore that this letter reached Pnompenh on Feb. 15.

(7) No useful purpose could be served by giving further details on what took place in the Moscow channel. We can say, however, that on Feb. 7, while that channel was still open and in operation, separate discussions were initiated in London between Prime Minister Wilson and Premier Kosygin of the U.S.S.R.

The combined reading of the Moscow channel and of these discussions led to the dispatch on Feb. 8 of President Johnson's letter to President Ho. This letter was of course published unilaterally by Hanoi on March 21, and is a matter of public record. It rested on, and was of course read by Hanoi in relation to, the various proposals that had been conveyed in the Moscow channel. There was no change of basic position whatever between Feb. 3 and Feb. 8, but President Johnson's letter did include a specific action proposal that speaks for itself, as does the tone of his communication.

(8) As already noted, Hanoi had not responded in any useful way to the variety of suggestions conveyed in the Moscow channel. Its sole and apparently final response was reflected on Feb. 13, in a letter by President Ho to Pope Paul VI. This letter, in the words of one press account today, "coupled an unconditional end to the bombing with the withdrawal of American forces and the recognition of the National Liberation Front." On Feb. 15, President Ho replied formally to the President in similar terms. At the same time, Hanoi broke off the Moscow channel.

(9) Hanoi's attitude remained negative throughout. The Baggs-Ashmore efforts were necessarily handled by the department with an eye to the direct and then-confidential channel that existed concurrently to Hanoi. The latter appeared to be by far the more reliable and secure method of ascertaining Hanoi's views.

(10) Finally, we note with regret that Mr. Ashmore is apparently ignorant of the subsequently published reports of the Moscow contacts, and of their confirmation by department representatives. We noted with still greater regret that at no time since has he consulted with the department in order to attempt to understand the interrelationship that necessarily obtained between the Moscow channel and his own efforts. As this case shows, the Administration has been prepared at all times to cooperate with private individuals who may be in contact with Hanoi in any way, and who are prepared to act responsibly and discreetly. This policy continues, although it seems clear that the present disclosure will not reassure Hanoi that such private contacts will be kept secret.

UNITED STATES - VIETNAM RELATIONS

1945 - 1967

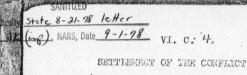

VI. C. 4.

SETTLEMENT OF THE CONFLICT

Negotiations, 1967 - 1968

HISTORY OF CONTACTS

VIETNAM TASK FORCE

OFFICE OF THE SECRETARY OF DEFENSE

Sec Def Cont Nr. X-

VI. C. 4.

SETTLEMENT OF THE CONFLICT

Negotiations, 1967 - 1968

HISTORY OF CONTACTS

VI.C.4., Settlement of the Conflict, Negotiations, 1967–1968

The six contacts discussed in this volume took place during the year between the end of SUNFLOWER and the Communist Tet Offensive of February 1968. As with those that preceded them, they produced little of substance. The two sides modified their bargaining positions only slightly, and the April 1968 agreement for talks in Paris resulted primarily from the shock caused by the climactic events of Tet and appears to have been influenced only slightly, if at all, by the intensive diplomatic maneuvering of the preceding year.

The 1967–1968 contacts occurred against a backdrop of deepening escalation and persisting military stalemate. Since 1965, the United States had steadily expanded the bombing of North Vietnam without appreciable effect on the rate of infiltration into the South or Hanoi's willingness to negotiate. By early 1967, American forces in Vietnam had increased to nearly 400,000 men. North Vietnam had matched each American escalation, however, and although its regular units and those of the Vietcong had suffered heavy losses they remained intact. The impasse on the battlefield was clearly reflected in the diplomacy of the belligerents. They had each repeatedly professed their willingness to negotiate, but as long as they retained hope of securing their objectives by military means they refused to make the concessions necessary to get negotiations underway.

The enormous costs imposed by the war did force each side to re-evaluate its policies in 1967. In the United States, opposition to the war increased dramatically, and within the government a debate on strategy raged throughout the year. To break the stalemate, the Joint Chiefs of Staff and the military command in Saigon pressed Johnson for an unrestricted bombing campaign against North Vietnam and the mining of Haiphong harbor, expansion of the force level by an additional 200,000 men, and the invasion of North Vietnamese sanctuaries in Laos and Cambodia and across the demilitarized zone. Increasingly certain on the other hand that the United States could not achieve its aims at acceptable costs, Secretary of Defense McNamara and his civilian advisers in the Pentagon began to advocate efforts to extricate the nation as gracefully as possible from a situation they felt had become untenable. McNamara proposed placing a ceiling on the number of ground troops to be committed to Vietnam and shifting from Westmoreland's aggressive search-and-destroy strategy to a defensive "population control" strategy. He advocated reducing the bombing to the area below the twentieth parallel or terminating it altogether, combined with determined attempts to secure a negotiated settlement even if this required modifying the long-standing objective of preserving an independent, non-Communist South Vietnam.

Torn between the conflicting advice of his aides, a frustrated and uncertain Johnson made concessions to each without opting for either of their alternative approaches. Fearful of the consequences of an expanded war, he approved only a modest increase in the force level, rejected the military's proposals for a major expansion of the ground war, and refused to authorize a "knockout blow" from the air. To pacify "doves" in the cabinet and country, he backed away from the rigid negotiating position set forth in the February 8 letter to Ho Chi Minh. Unwilling to concede defeat in any form, however, he refused to modify American objectives or alter American strategy, and he permitted major escalations of the bombing in the spring and again in the summer. Despite growing public restlessness with the war, U.S. policy continued throughout 1967 on the familiar path of slow but steady escalation in search of that elusive breaking point at which Hanoi would be forced to negotiate on American terms. The major initiative undertaken by the administration at the end of the year was a massive and modestly successful public relations campaign designed to reassure an anxious nation that progress was in fact being made in Vietnam.

The strains of war appear also to have provoked heated internal debate in North Vietnam. Massive American intervention had set back Hanoi's timetable for victory and had imposed enormous demands on its manpower and resources, reopening by 1967 the old debate between those who had preferred a protracted, low-level guerrilla war in the South, perhaps combined with negotiations, and those who advocated a large-scale war fought and directed by North Vietnam. The growing intensity of the Sino-Soviet split exacerbated Hanoi's problems, raising fears that indefinite prolongation of the military stalemate might result in Chinese or Soviet intervention, forcing North Vietnam into a position of dependence on one or the other of its major allies, neither of whom placed its interest foremost.

In contrast to the Americans, the North Vietnamese seem to have altered their strategy in 1967 in an effort to resolve their most pressing difficulties. Sometime in the spring, the leadership apparently shifted from the essentially defensive strategy pursued since 1965 to a more aggressive strategy of "fighting while negotiating," the centerpiece of which was a projected three-phase offensive in South Vietnam. The first phase, launched in late 1967, consisted of a series of probes designed to tie down large numbers of U.S. troops in the isolated Central Highlands and along the demilitarized zone. The second phase, the Tet Offensive of February 1968, called for a massive, large-scale assault against the cities and towns of South Vietnam, the purpose of which was to increase political pressures for American withdrawal, undercut the South Vietnamese army and government, and perhaps even provoke a general uprising among the South Vietnamese people. A third and final stage, apparently set for the summer of 1968, projected a decisive, set-piece battle that would deliver the final blow to an already beleaguered South Vietnam and its American ally.

The precise role to be played by negotiations in the strategy remains unclear. The North Vietnamese were determined to get the bombing stopped, and they may have been prepared to negotiate as soon as they could extract this vital concession from the United States. It seems more likely, however, that they preferred to time the opening of negotiations to coincide with the Tet Offensive, reasoning that the shock of the campaign against the cities would force the United States into negotiations on their terms and give them a favorable position from which to secure a settlement. In either case, North Vietnam viewed negotiations as a means of heightening domestic pressures for withdrawal in the United States and of bringing out into the open the latent differences between the United States and South Vietnam. Whatever their strategy, the North Vietnamese did not modify their position on negotiations until late December 1967 when Foreign Minister Trinh changed the verb in his January 1967 formula to indicate that talks "will begin" when the bombing was stopped unconditionally.

In view of the strategies being pursued by each side, the peace contacts of 1967 necessarily represented little more than diplomatic shadowboxing. During the spring and summer, the Swedes and Norwegians took the lead in initiatives code-named respectively ASPEN and OHIO. Like British Prime Minister Wilson and other would-be peacemakers, the leaders of Sweden and Norway were undoubtedly enticed by the prestige that would accrue to anyone able to help end an immensely destructive international conflict. As in Britain, Vietnam had become a divisive issue in Sweden and Norway, threatening internal harmony and political stability. The governments of both countries therefore arranged contacts with North Vietnam through their ambassadors in Peking in an effort to bring about negotiations. In each case, the North Vietnamese sent out the familiarly vague signal that if the United States stopped the bombing they would "know what to do." Skeptical of the signals and the conveyors of them, especially the Swedes, the United States repeatedly and unsuccessfully sought clarification of the meaning of Hanoi's statements and insisted on some form of mutual de-escalation. The Swedish contact played out in 1967. OHIO lasted into 1968, but it was overshadowed much earlier by channels regarded as more reliable and potentially more productive.

Of all the contacts discussed in VI.C.4., PENNSYLVANIA, which took place in Paris between August and October 1967, has attracted the most attention. It marked the debut in global shuttle diplomacy of future National Security Adviser and Secretary of State Henry A. Kissinger. Then a professor of government at Harvard University, Kissinger was drawn into peacemaking by two

French acquaintances, Raymond Aubrac and Herbert Marcovich, the former a long-time friend of Ho Chi Minh. With the blessings of the U.S. government, Aubrac and Marcovich visited Hanoi in late July and discussed the possibilities of negotiations with Ho and Pham Van Dong. The contact continued through mid-October in Paris, with Aubrac and Marcovich serving as intermediaries between Kissinger and Mai Van Bo and attempting, without success, to arrange direct talks between the two.

PENNSYLVANIA also brought forth a modification of the American position on mutual de-escalation. At his Glassboro, New Jersey, summit meeting with Kosygin in June, Johnson had retreated from his earlier insistence that the bombing would be stopped only after infiltration had stopped, affirming that he would terminate it upon assurances that the North Vietnamese units then north of the demilitarized zone would not be moved south. In an effort to demonstrate his commitment to negotiations, he went a step further in August, indicating through Kissinger that he would stop the bombing if given private assurances that this would lead "promptly to productive discussions" and "on the assumption" that North Vietnam would not take "military advantage" of the halt. Kissinger later explained the no-advantage statement to mean that North Vietnam would not *increase* the flow of men and supplies south, and on September 29, 1967, in a speech at San Antonio, Johnson publicly elaborated what would henceforth be known as the San Antonio formula.

Although the North Vietnamese kept the Paris contact alive for several months, they never displayed any real inclination to accept the proposal. Major escalations of the American bombing in August and again in September gave them a convenient pretext for refusing to make concessions and eventually closing the Paris channel. In any event, it seems likely that at this time, with the first phase of their offensive just underway, they were not prepared to negotiate for anything less than an unconditional bombing halt, and they may have preferred to delay negotiations until the Tet Offensive gave them the anticipated advantage. Johnson's observation that in PENNSYLVANIA North Vietnam demonstrated "no interest in serious talk about peace except, as always, on its own stiff terms," may in fact understate Hanoi's position during the fall of 1967.[1]

Just weeks after the demise of PENNSYLVANIA, the United States began energetically pursuing another contact, this one through Rumania. The Rumanians had been actively involved in peacemaking for more than a year, and Washington regarded them as reliable intermediaries. When they indicated in November that they had been in direct contact with Hanoi, Johnson immediately dispatched Averell Harriman to Bucharest. The Rumanians' report suggested no change in Hanoi's position, but Harriman seized the occasion to

---

1. Johnson, *Vantage Point*, p. 268.

present a detailed explanation of the no-advantage statement of the San Antonio formula. North Vietnam's subsequent response, delivered privately through the Rumanians and later publicly in Trinh's December 29 statement, seems to have raised American hopes as high as at any time since the onset of the war. For a brief period, Washington regarded the Rumanian contact as the most promising yet undertaken, "slugging" it PACKERS (for Green Bay Packers) because, as the State Department's executive secretary, Benjamin Read, commented, it looked like a "winner."[2] The United States responded with a formal, written statement of the no-advantage formula and requested clarification of Trinh's statement in terms of the likely time lapse between the end of the bombing and the beginning of talks. To underscore its seriousness, it reduced the bombing around Hanoi and Haiphong during the period of the Rumanians' return visit.

What the United States viewed as the most promising peace initiative may well have been the least. The intent of North Vietnam's policy at this stage remains quite unclear. Hanoi may have been using the Rumanian contact, as it had used previous channels, to probe for American concessions, most notably the unconditional bombing halt it had sought from the start. It is also possible, however, that the North Vietnamese were using the Rumanian contact and the Trinh statement as an exercise in deception designed to lull the United States into a false sense of military security and to increase domestic and international pressures for negotiations on the eve of the military blow to be delivered at Tet. In any event, the response through Rumania did not arrive in Washington until mid-February, two weeks after the Tet Offensive had begun. The Americans viewed it as a "very, very flat turndown," and along with Tet it momentarily hardened attitudes against negotiations.[3]

In the meantime, the Tet Offensive was significantly altering the military and political context in which both Hanoi and Washington operated. On January 30, 1968, North Vietnamese and Vietcong units unleashed a staggering blow, simultaneously attacking thirty-six provincial capitals, five of South Vietnam's major cities, including Saigon and Hue, sixty-four district capitals, and fifty hamlets. Taking advantage of the element of surprise, they scored major early gains, carrying the war to the U.S. Embassy, Tan Son Nhut airport, and the presidential palace in Saigon and seizing control of much of the city of Hue. The United States and South Vietnam quickly recovered, however, driving the attackers from most of the positions they had gained in the early hours of the offensive and inflicting huge losses.

Although Tet seems merely to have reinforced the stalemate that had prevailed since 1965, it also produced pressures for changes in policy on both

2. Benjamin Read Oral History Interview, Johnson Library.
3. Ibid.

sides. Despite the U.S. military's claims of victory and its urgent appeals to Washington for additional troops and authority to escalate the war to take advantage of an unexpected opportunity, the Tet Offensive had a devastating psychological impact in the United States. Coming in the immediate aftermath of the administration's bullish public relations campaign of late 1967, it widened an already large credibility gap and raised serious questions in and out of government whether success could be attained at acceptable cost. The strategic debate of 1967 resumed with a new intensity, this time resulting in major changes of policy. In Hanoi, too, Tet seems to have compelled fundamental reassessments. The general uprising that had been hoped for if not necessarily counted upon did not materialize, and the heavy losses suffered may have made it impossible to launch the third phase of the offensive. The "hawks" who had forced the shift in strategy in 1967 appear to have been discredited by the failure of Tet, and Hanoi, sometime in the spring of 1968, seems to have shifted to a defensive, protracted war strategy to be combined with negotiations that presumably would increase the already significant political pressures in the United States.

While these reappraisals were taking place in both capitals, another peace contact was developing in Rome. Sometime in January, North Vietnam's Ambassador in Prague informed Italian Foreign Minister Amintore Fanfani that the idea of negotiations had general approval in Hanoi, and, shortly after, Hanoi Radio broadcast the message that talks would begin as soon as the bombing stopped, an apparent answer to the basic questions raised by the United States during the Rumanian contact. The United States dutifully and with obvious lack of enthusiasm responded to the contact (code-named KILLY), and Fanfani subsequently held separate meetings with the North Vietnamese ambassador and U.S. representatives. As in MARIGOLD, Fanfani attempted to get around the troublesome question of mutual de-escalation and focus on the framework of a political settlement. The major result of the meetings, however, appears to have been at least a vague North Vietnamese commitment to a variation of the no-advantage formula first offered by Kissinger six months earlier.

Ironically, although it may have been one of the more serious North Vietnamese overtures of the war, KILLY seems to have played no more than a peripheral role in the April 1968 agreement to initiate talks in Paris. After nearly two months of frequently heated internal debate, Johnson on March 31, 1968, announced a series of dramatic decisions. He ordered a partial bombing halt and affirmed that the bombing would be stopped entirely if North Vietnam demonstrated similar military restraint. He reiterated American willingness to negotiate, named Harriman his personal representative should talks materialize, and most drastically, to underscore the seriousness of his commitment to peace, announced his withdrawal from the presidential race. Johnson seems to have acted primarily in response to domestic pressures and in the certainty that the military situation in South Vietnam was well in hand and even favorable to the United States. Although he does not specifically mention KILLY, he does suggest in his memoirs that various signals received from Hanoi influenced his decisions.[4] The administration did not pursue the Italian contact vigorously after early March, however, and the President adamantly refused to order the total and unconditional bombing halt that was assumed in KILLY. Most important, the administration seems to have acted on March 31 on the assumption that Hanoi, as before, would reject its proposals.

The significance of the Italian contact from the standpoint of North Vietnam remains quite unclear. The original overtures to Fanfani may have been timed to coincide with the opening of the Tet Offensive and in anticipation of military success, the obvious purpose being to exploit the anticipated political backlash in the United States and to open negotiations under favorable military conditions. By the time the contact actually took form, Hanoi may already have shifted its strategy in response to the failure of Tet, and the positive signals given Fanfani may have been designed to secure an end to the bombing and get negotiations underway. In any event, it is clear that North Vietnam had altered its policy by the time of Johnson's speech. Hanoi responded quickly and positively, and, although it attempted to save face by indicating that it was agreeing to talks merely to get the bombing stopped, its willingness to talk on the basis of a partial bombing halt suggests that long-standing conditions had been significantly modified in the aftermath of the failure of Tet.

The no-advantage formula that was an intergral part of the peace contacts of 1967–1968 did provide the basis for an understanding worked out in late 1968 to bring about substantive negotiations. At the outset of the Paris talks, the two sides had reverted to their established positions, North Vietnam insisting on a total and unconditional end of the bombing, the United States demanding assurances that Hanoi would not take military advantage of such a move. After months of deadlock, Harriman finally worked out an informal arrangement by which the United States would stop the bombing with the expectation that serious talks would follow and on the assumption that North Vietnam would not continue its rocket attacks on Saigon and other cities and that it would restrict infiltration across the demilitarized zone. He combined this with an ingenious formula that got around the old and equally sticky issue of Vietcong and South Vietnamese participation by setting up a two-sided negotiation and permitting each side to determine the composition of its delegation without prejudice to the position of the other parties. This arrangement, in theory at

4. Johnson, *Vantage Point*, p. 369.

least, set the groundwork for the substantive negotiations that had been the professed goal of each nation from the outset.

The agreement to negotiate represented more a change in tactics than a change in goals, however. Its time in office running out, the Johnson administration was determined to hold on, and, even though the South Vietnamese blocked negotiations awaiting the outcome of the presidential election and the coming of a new and presumably more sympathetic Republican administration, there is no evidence to suggest that the President ever seriously considered abandoning the objective of maintaining an independent, non-Communist South Vietnam. His successor, Richard M. Nixon, embraced that goal as his own and clung to it stubbornly to the end. Their forces decimated by the Tet Offensive, the North Vietnamese reverted to a defensive military strategy and attempted to use the Paris negotiations to increase pressures on the United States for a settlement while holding tight to their fundamental goal of a unified Vietnam under their control. It would thus require four more years of fighting while negotiating before a settlement was arranged, and that settlement merely provided for American withdrawal without in any way resolving what had always been the basic issue of the war—the political future of South Vietnam.—*Ed*.

L.H. Gelb/R.H. Moorsteen
May 8, 1968

VIETNAM NEGOTIATIONS, 1967-1968

This book contains statements and messages exchanged between the U.S. and the DRV on negotiations, primarily in the form of closely held private communications. It is in three parts:

--The Setting: A description of the intermediaries and the attitude of the DRV.

--Conditions for "Talks": Conditions for meeting laid down by the two sides.

--Settlement Terms: Proposals made by the two sides on a final settlement of the war.

    1. Troop Withdrawals

    2. Free Elections

    3. Who Represents SVN in the Government and in Negotiations

    4. Reunification

    5. International Guarantees and Inspection

    6. Cease-Fire

The last two sections each contain a summary, followed by the references cited in chronological order.

THE SETTING

I.   INTRODUCTION

Since mid-1964, there was a halting but gradual diplomatic movement by both NVN and the U.S. toward a negotiated settlement. Hanoi
had been insisting previously on U.S. withdrawal from SVN, acceptance
of the Four Points as the only correct solution, the NLF as the sole
legitimate representative of the South Vietnamese people, and a permanent as well as unconditional cessation of U.S. action against NVN,
prior to beginning either talks or negotiations. In other words, Hanoi
was demanding that the U.S. make all the requisite concessions before
the two sides even sat down at the table. By mid-1967, it seemed clear
that the only condition for talks was the cessation of U.S. bombardment
and all other acts of war against NVN. While the U.S. repeatedly maintained the position of either "unconditional discussions" at any time,
or de-escalation, or both, it too gradually modified its stand. By the
end of 1967, the U.S. no longer pressed for a virtually immediate withdrawal of North Vietnamese forces or for "assurances that infiltration
has stopped." The San Antonio formula was a recognition that the war
in the South might continue at about the present rate, even if negotiations were in process.

Diplomatic differences were narrowed to the point where though
there will be real disputes at the bargaining table, initial contacts
leading to negotiations could readily begin. All these diplomatic moves
served as a quiet backdrop to the war in Vietnam itself. The fighting
in South Vietnam stepped up as both sides increased their force levels
and ambitions. The U.S. bombardment of North Vietnam escalated as new
targets were struck throughout 1967.

II.   THE INTERMEDIARIES

From the close of SUNFLOWER in September 1967 until President
Johnson's dramatic speech of March 31, 1968, diplomatic activity to
bring the opposing sides to the conference table was carried on essentially through five different and sometimes overlapping channels.[1]

First, there was the Rumanian track (to become "PACKERS" in
December 1967) which extended from October 1966 through February 1968.[2]
Periods of intensity in this track were January 1967, October and

1

November 1967, and December 1967 through January 1968. Private exchanges in this track were being confirmed by public statements on both sides.

Second, the Government of Sweden ("ASPEN") played a continuing though minor role from November 1966 through February 1968. Swedish-DRV contacts were intense in November of 1966, February 1967, with contacts occurring throughout the whole 1967-68 timeframe.

Third, there were infrequent and low-key contacts between the Norwegians and the DRV ("OHIO") which lasted from June 1967 through to March of 1968. There was not much activity in OHIO, since we preferred to use other channels, but the key messages in this channel were passed in June 1967 and March 1968.

Fourth, there was a contact in Paris ("PENNSYLVANIA"), with great intensity and frequency of exchanges in September and October of 1967. Private exchanges in this track were being confirmed by public statements.

Fifth, the Italian-DRV track ("KILLY") was seemingly being considered a prime channel by both sides in February and the beginning of March 1968.[3] This was the last contact prior to President Johnson's speech of March 31, 1968.

The difference in the quality of reporting and intermediation in these tracks is, in retrospect, quite pronounced. Since very few written messages were exchanged, we were continually relying on the ear, predilections and prejudices of the intermediary. Since all the intermediaries, in one way or another, had a definite interest in the success of their role as well as in bringing the opposing sides to the conference table, all transmissions from them have to be viewed with some skepticism. All of their efforts seem to focus on one issue--the cessation of U.S. bombing. It must be assumed that in addition to good offices and good will, all of these intermediaries wanted us to stop the bombing. Since Hanoi was apparently representing to them that nothing else could occur unless the bombings were stopped, they tended to take this declaration as a given. All were, in one way or another, wary of the spread of the war, international tensions, and especially of the impact of the war on their domestic policies.

The Rumanians constantly pressured us on the bombing issue. At one time, they were claiming they had received the "signal" from Hanoi in response to Goldberg's UN speech in the fall of 1966. (Goldberg had stated that Hanoi only needed to give "an indication as to what /it/ would do in response to a prior cessation of bombing by the U.S.") Later, they admitted that they had received no specific "signal." The

Rumanians were quite frank about admitting that they were only interested in the stopping of the U.S. bombing. They accepted that the two sides were now far apart, but argued that once they sat down at the table "then the other nations desirous of seeing an end to conflict would try to push the two sides together." Terms of final settlement, they believed, should not be discussed before the bombings stopped since it would only drive the parties further apart. The Rumanians were also saying that they did not blame either party for the Vietnam situation, and that they were only interested in a peaceful settlement.

The whole Swedish role was very much dominated by their domestic politics: there were frequent press leaks on GOS-DRV contacts; Vietnam policy was frequently and vituperatively discussed in the Swedish Parliament; the Russell War Crimes Tribunal began to hold its hearings in July 1967;[4] and the GOS kept hinting about establishing consular relations with Hanoi. Swedish GVN relations began to strain, and in the spring and summer of 1967, Sweden reduced the level of its diplomatic representation in Saigon. Finally, on November 4, 1967, the GOS publicly denounced U.S.-Vietnam policy.

The U.S., because of the above, never put much stock in the Swedish messages, and this track never became an important one.

The Norwegian role was not treated with great importance by Washington, and the track was never a very active one. Nevertheless, in retrospect, the exchanges between the DRV Ambassador and Peking (Loan) and

3

the Norwegian Ambassador in Peking (Algard) were probably the most reliable of all. Algard seems to have been a careful note-taker, and his messages look like he was using Hanoi turns of phrases. Many of the points made by Algard were subsequently borne out by other contacts and by public DRV statements.

Because Norway, unlike Sweden, was not visibly more friendly to the DRV than to the U.S., Hanoi did not seem really comfortable in activating this channel into a major one. On November 2, 1967, Loan hinted to Algard that Norway's role was "not neutral" and that Norway was "indirectly involved." Norwegian domestic politics were, like those in Sweden, vehemently anti-American on the Vietnam issue, but this never seemed to get in the way of objective Norwegian Government reporting.   Unlike the Swedes, the Norwegians did not press us hard on the bombing issue.

The exchanges among the PENNSYLVANIA participants (two unofficial Frenchmen, Mai Van Bo and Henry Kissinger) seemed to have been handled with great care and accuracy. While the two Frenchmen, Marcovich and Aubrac, were clearly committed to getting the U.S. to stop the bombing, there is no evidence that their reporting, or message carrying, was adversely affected. Kissinger for the U.S. handled the play with consummate skill, clarifying points and making interpretations that could lead to a continuing dialogue. Both Hanoi and Washington treated this channel as a major one, and yet little was accomplished except the clarification of the U.S. "no advantage" formula. This clarification was to be lost in subsequent reformulations of the U.S. position on "no advantage."

The Italians were old hands at playing the role of intermediary. Their role in MARIGOLD had been respected by both sides. They were not pushy about interposing themselves between Hanoi and Washington and always stood ready to break off contacts if the U.S. so desired. It is important to remember that in Killy the North Vietnamese sought out d'Orlandi (according to d'Orlandi) and not the reverse. The Killy contacts were between d'Orlandi and the DRV Ambassador in Prague, Suu. It is also important to remember that d'Orlandi had a very special view about the role of intermediation. Unlike all the other go-betweens who were interested almost solely in a cessation of U.S. bombing, d'Orlandi's approach was to focus on terms of final settlement. Only when the future of South Vietnam could be foreseen, d'Orlandi argued, would the two sides sit down and genuinely and seriously negotiate.

III. NORTH VIETNAMESE STRATEGY

It has always been clear that insofar as Hanoi is interested in negotiations, it is only as another way of achieving its objectives. Since the earliest months of 1966, party leaders in Hanoi have been preparing their people for a "fight and negotiate policy." Captured documents have reaffirmed the prevalence of this policy.

Hanoi frames its strategy in terms of two stages: "decisive victory" and "final victory." "Decisive victory" is defined in terms of breaking the U.S. will to persist -- namely, when the course of war in the South reaches a "deadlock." The U.S. recognition of this "deadlock" and its willingness to negotiate on Hanoi's terms then would be tested at the bargaining table. Moreover, when negotiations are in process, Hanoi says that it would create "another front" with which to "disintegrate" South Vietnamese armed forces and exacerbate "contradictions" within the Saigon Government and between U.S. and Saigon. "Final victory" could come when all Vietnam was effectively under Hanoi's control.

Seen in this light, Hanoi's failure to assure military reciprocity for a bombing cessation in advance of talks could be (a) a matter of principle, as they assert, or (b) a question of strategy -- that is, a test of U.S. will to persist, or (c) simply a tactic, a way of concealing their willingness to retreat until convinced that the U.S. has made its best offer.

Hanoi's designing of the three stages of bargaining (talks, negotiations, settlement) can be viewed as part of this same fabric. Each stage is so constructed that it depends on the successful completion of the preceding stage. Hanoi recognizes its own morale problem and does not want to risk creating expectations of a settlement until it is pretty sure that the settlement will accord with its objectives.

5

THE U.S. AND DRV CONDITIONS FOR "TALKS" CONVERGE

As of SUNFLOWER (February, 1967), the DRV position on conditions for "talks" with the U.S. had been conveyed as follows:

(1) Publicly, Trinh had said, "It is only after the unconditional cessation of US bombing and all other acts of war against the DRV that there could be talks between the DRV and the US." (Trinh interview with Burchett of 1/28/67, as broadcast in English by Radio Hanoi.)

(2) Privately, in writing, the DRV said, "The unconditional cessation of bombing and all other acts of war against the DRV being materialized, the DRV could then exchange views with the US concerning the place or date for contact between the two parties as the USG proposed in its message handed over on January 10, 1967." (DRV Aide-Memoire given us in Moscow, 1/27/67, in Hanoi's "unofficial translation" into English. This replied to our Aide-Memoire suggesting exchanges on "the possibilities of achieving a peaceful settlement of the Vietnamese dispute.")

(3) Kosygin privately told the British (they said) on 2/6/67, that he had been in direct contact with Hanoi and could confirm that Hanoi would talk if the bombing stopped. He repeated this in essence to Thompson in Moscow on 2/18/67. (See London 6316, 2/7/67, and Moscow 3562, 2/18/67.)

Our position was that we would enter talks without conditions, or we would stop the bombing in return for some reciprocal act of military restraint but that we would not stop bombing simply in exchange for talks.

After SUNFLOWER, the two sides bounced varying formulations back and forth eventually inching toward each other. The U.S. position remained essentially unchanged until August 25, 1967, when the San Antonio formulation was privately passed to the DRV.[5] The meaning of this proposal seems to have been obscure to Hanoi. Several later messages passed in clarification varied among themselves, and the DRV persisted in seeing "conditions" attached to the San Antonio formula, making it unacceptable by Hanoi's lights. The U.S. was probing to see if Hanoi understood our "assumption"; and this probing was apparently interpreted by the DRV as asking advance assurance that the "no advantage" would in fact be taken, a condition. By the end of KILLY (3/1/68), however, when d'Orlandi (as he reported) warned that "if bombing stopped and talks began, assaulting Khe Sanh,[6] invading or trying to detach the two northern provinces of SVN, launching a second wave of attacks against one or more cities or creating a sensation with something else like an assault on Camp Carrol,[7] would sink the whole thing," DRV Ambassador Su gave his "personal" view: "From the moment the two sides meet, it was obvious no such thing could happen." (Rome 4590, 3/4/68.)

At this point Hanoi probably felt it had replied affirmatively and officially to the "prompt" and "productive" conditions. (In public statements, the DRV had indicated that talks could begin "as soon as" the bombing and all other acts of war stopped, and that the subject of the talks would be "questions related to a settlement of the Vietnam problem on the basis of the 1954 Geneva agreements on Vietnam....also questions which could be raised by either side.") Assuming Su was accurately reported, it had also gone part of the way on "no advantage," though not so far as to acknowledge it had troops in the South or to give us an official pledge against which we could allege violations, resume bombing or break off talks.

In early April, Hanoi indicated its representative at the contact would have ambassadorial rank and would be empowered to agree on a date, place and level for "formal talks" after the bombing cessation. In the event, the DRV representative Xuan Thuy, has ministerial rank and his proposed contact with us in Paris has been described by Hanoi (in English) as "formal talks."

What follow are the major statements, public and private, made by the two sides since SUNFLOWER.

1a

<u>CHRONOLOGY</u>

<u>DRV (6/14/67)</u>. The DRV Ambassador to Peking, Ngo, told the Norwegian Ambassador there that the cessation of U.S. bombing is the only condition for their coming to the conference table.

OSLO 4531 to SecState (SECRET-EXDIS), 14 June 1967:

"2. Following is my informal rendition Algard's report, transposed from first to third person:

<u>U.S. (6/20/67)</u>. The U.S. repeated that it required "at least some private assurance of appropriate reciprocal action by North Vietnam.".

State 213389 to Oslo (SECRET-EXDIS), 20 June 1967:

"2.c. Expressed concern that U.S. intends to stay perma- nently in Vietnam is of interest. We assume GON is fully aware

of our repeated statements of intent to withdraw and most specifically the precise wording used in the Manila Communique,[8] which
your should furnish them.

"d. Discussion of cessation of bombing of only condition
for talks fits with other private readings as well as Trinh-
Burchett interview [9] and appears to us highly plausible.

"c. USG accepts that 'cessation' of the bombing of the
North and military action against the North is only NVN condition for holding talks. NVN has referred to cessation being
on 'unconditional' basis: What is meant by this? (Purpose
here is to clarify whether there may be any distinction between
usual NVN statements that bombing must be stopped 'indefinitively
and unconditionally' --which we have construed to mean permanently -- and occasional other statements that stoppage of bombing must merely be 'unconditional.' We ourselves have assumed
that no difference is intended between these two formulations,
but direct inquiry could be useful in nailing this down.)

"d. Assuming that NVN condition calls for, in effect,
permanent cessation of bombing, USG position remains as it has
been stated throughout and particularly by Ambassador Goldberg
in September 1966 at UN and by Secretary Rusk in January.[10] U.S.
view is that cessation of bombing, without at least some private
assurance of appropriate reciprocal military action by NVN,
would create situation of major military advantage to NVN and
would not be conducive to fruitful talks. USG has put forward
several general suggestions for timing and nature of NVN reciprocal actions, and President's letter to Ho contained one specific
proposal that added the element of stopping of reinforcement
by USG in the South.[11] Canadian proposal of April called for link
between cessation of bombing and restoring demilitarized status
of DMZ under effective supervision, but Hanoi rejected this.[12]
What is present Hanoi view on these proposals, or do they have
any other suggestion to make?

DRV (7/27/67). Pham Van Dong told Aubrac and Marcovich (PENNSYLVANIA)
that the DRV would settle for a de facto stoppage, though it preferred a
public statement.

"Now I shall talk to you about negotiations and
solutions. We have been fighting for our independence
for four thousand years. We have defeated the Mongols
three times.[13] The United States Army, strong as it is,
is not as terrifying as Genghis Khan. We fight to have
peace at home; we have no wider aims. We have made

clear our position in our four points and in the interview
of January 28, 1967.[14] /Pham Van Dong did not explain
what this interview was; Aubrac and Marcovich did not
know, nor do I./ We are ready to talk at any time
provided that actions against the North are unconditionally
ended. I want to repeat what I said yesterday: we are
willing to settle for a defacto stoppage." Marcovich
interrupted to ask whether he correctly understood that
no public acknowledgment of an end of bombing was needed.
Pham Van Dong replied that he would prefer a public
statement, but would settle for a de facto cessation.
/There was disagreement between Aubrac and Marcovich
about the meaning of de facto cessation. Aubrac thought
that a bombing pause could be followed within a few days
by an invitation to negotiate; Marcovich was of the view
that Hanoi might want a more formal--though secret--
assurance./

U.S. (8/25/67). The "no advantage" formulation was passed to the
DRV via Kissinger and Mai Van Bo in Paris. (PENNSYLVANIA)

Messrs A and M met with Bo in Paris to inquire
why their visas had not been received. Bo
told them it was too dangerous to visit Hanoi
due to the bombing. M and A then informed Bo
they had assurances in that respect, without
identifying the nature of the assurances, which
would be effective until September 4.

Messrs M and A then presented the US message
as set forth below to Bo for the first time.
He read it with interest and observed that it
was "clearly significant". Bo queried them
about the significance of para. 2 of the message.
He was _nformed that it expressed US doubt that
the existence of US/DRV discussions could be
kept secret if bombing ended, and Bo recognized
that this would be a problem. Bo was impressed
and was told that the message was authorized by
top levels of the USG. M and A gave Bo a
written description of their contacts with
Kissinger. Bo agreed to cable the message to
Hanoi and to report their desires to visit Hanoi

to discuss the message. Bo believed a reply
should be available by August 29.

The English text of the message given to Bo
in both French and English is as follows:

"The United States is willing to stop the aerial and naval bombardment of North Viet-Nam with the understanding that this will lead
promptly to productive discussions between representatives of the United States and the Democratic Republic of Viet-Nam looking toward a
resolution of the issues between them. While discussions proceed
either with public knowledge or secretly, the United States
would assume that the Democratic Republic of Viet-Nam would not
take advantage of the bombing cessation. Any such move on the
part of the Democratic Republic of Viet-Nam would obviously be
inconsistent with the movement toward resolution of the issues
between the United States and the Democratic Republic of Viet-Nam
which the discussions are intended to achieve.

   The United States is prepared to enter into discussions
either openly or secretly. It would seem, however, that a
total cessation of the bombing is inconsistent with keeping
secret the fact that discussions are taking place. Accordingly,
the Democratic Republic of Viet-Nam may prefer to consider the
alternative of a cutback in the magnitude or scope of the bombing
while secret discussions are in progress.

   The United States is ready to have immediate private contact
with the Democratic Republic of Viet-Nam to explore the above
approach or any suggestions the Democratic Republic of Viet-Nam
might wish to propose in the same direction."

DRV (9/11/67). A number of new, sensitive DRV targets were struck
on August 21-22, 1967, but restrikes and strikes near Hanoi were suspended on August 24 as a gesture of goodwill.[15] The DRV reacted negatively,
however, to both the gesture and the "no advantage" proposal, terming
them threatening, conditional, etc., in line with the general DRV objective of removing the bombing as a bargaining blue chip for the U.S.
(PENNSYLVANIA)

   In response to a phone request from Bo at
   6:00 p.m. (Paris time), Sunday, September 10,
   Marcovich called on Bo at 9:30 a.m. After

an exchange of pleasantries Bo handed to M the
following text of Hanoi's official reply to the
August 25 message:

"The essence of the American propositions.
is the stopping of the bombing under conditions.
The American bombing of the Democratic Republic
of Viet-Nam is illegal. The United States   any
should put an end to the bombing and cannot pose/
conditions.

"The American message has been communicated
after an escalation of the attacks against Hanoi
and under the threat (menance) of continuation
of the attacks against Hanoi. It is clear
that this constitutes an ultimatum to the
Vietnamese people.

"The Government of the Democratic
Republic of Viet-Nam energetically rejects
the American propositions.

"The position of the Government of the
Democratic Republic of Viet-Nam is that the
United States should cease definitely and
without conditions the bombing and all
other acts of war against the Democratic
Republic of Viet-Nam. It should withdraw
American troops and satellites from South
Viet-Nam, recognize the National Liberation
Front of South Viet-Nam and let the
Vietnamese people themselves regulate their
internal affairs. It is only after the unconditional stopping by the United States of
the bombing and all other acts of war against
the Democratic Republic of Viet-Nam, that it
would be possible to engage in conversations."

(unofficial translation)

Bo told M to give the text to Kissinger and
added that "as soon as there is a reply" M
should communicate with Bo at any time of day
or night. When M urged Bo to meet Kissinger,

6

Bo said "give the message to Kissinger and
when the reply is here we shall see about
meeting". In commenting on the text of the
DRV message Bo made the following statement:

"The bombing of Hanoi at the same time as the
sending of the (August 21) message constitutes
a pressure. Stopping of the bombing along with
the threat of a renewal has the character of an
ultimatum." (Paris 3097).

U.S. (9/16/67). We protested that the DRV must have misunderstood
the 8/25/67 message, as it contained neither conditions nor threats. We
merely wished to confirm that a bombing cessation would lead promptly to
productive discussions leading to peace. We did not ask the DRV to reply
to the "no advantage" assumption. (PENNSYLVANIA)

M and A met with Bo for over an hour, starting
at noon. A, who did most of the talking at the
meeting with Bo and kept the notes, reported
on the meeting. Bo greeted A and M affably and
offered them drinks. Bo said Ho had charged
him with inquiring about the health of A's
family. A then handed to Bo in a sealed
envelope French and English texts of the
following US message:

September 13, 1967

"The USG believes that the September 11
message from the DRV may be based on a misunderstanding of the American proposal of
August 25. The American proposal contained
neither conditions nor threats and should
not be rejected on these grounds.

7

"It has been the understanding of the
USG that the DRV would be willing promptly
to engage in productive discussions leading to
peace when there was a cessation of aerial and
naval bombardment. The USG sought to confirm
this fact in its proposal which the DRV has in
front of it.

"As a demonstration of its good faith and
in order to create the best atmosphere for
the consideration of its proposal the US
voluntarily undertook not to bomb Hanoi from
August 25 onward - the day on which its proposal
was submitted to Hanoi. This restraint has been
maintained without time limit even though
activities by opposing forces in the south have
in fact been stepped up since August 25.

"The August 25 proposal of the USG remains
open." (END OF MESSAGE)

A told Bo he did not know the content of the
message but described it as "conciliatory",
a word which Bo made him write down. Bo did
not open the envelope in M and A's presence.

A asked Bo about the significance of the AFP
September 14 Hanoi story (State 38031), quoting
"reliable sources" as indicating that talks would
start three or four weeks after a bombing
cessation, and A showed Bo Paris press stories
based on the AFP report. Bo replied that the
three-to four-week interval between the end
of bombing and the beginning of negotiations
was "an invention of journalists". He noted
that Pham Van Dong's statement had given no
ground for the time period mentioned in the
newspapers.

8

· · U.S. (9/25/67). We ask Hanoi to confirm our understanding of U.S./
DRV differences: We are willing to stop bombing if Hanoi confirms that
this will lead promptly to productive negotiations; Hanoi has implied, ·
but not confirmed, that this would be the result.   (PENNSYLVANIA)

M called on Bo at 8:30 a.m. and read to Bo the
following five point message from Kissinger:

"(1) I will transmit to the appropriate
Washington officials later today the message ·
· you (Bo) gave M yesterday. (2) I see no point
in trading charges and countercharges about
past activities. In fact Washington has offered
to stop bombing based on the assumption it
would lead to prompt, productive talks. That
offer remains open. It was made sincerely.
If accepted, there will be no need to discuss
escalation or bombing problems. (3) The
exchange indicates that Washington and Hanoi
have great difficulty understanding each
other's thought processes. This makes direct
· US/DRV contact essential. Intermediaries, no
matter how trustworthy, are not satisfactory
substitutes. (4) American military actions
during the past month reflect in part the
extreme secrecy with which Washington has
handled this exchange. The USG has considered
it unwise to change decisions made prior to the
report of M and A's trip to Hanoi, except in
regard to bombing Hanoi itself, because it
wanted to keep the circle of awareness of this
exchange as small as possible to avoid premature
public debate. (5) The difference in the positions of the two governments could be summarized
as follows: Washington has indicated its ·
readiness to stop bombing and has only asked
to confirm its understanding of Hanoi's
view that this would lead promptly to productive negotiations. Hanoi has implied that
an end of bombing would in fact have this result
If this is indeed the view of both governments,
the remaining obstacles to direct talks can be

9

··· overcome. I am certain that the above correctly
reflects US views. Could Bo confirm that it
also reflects the view of Hanoi.".   ·ᴸ

M said Bo's response to the foregoing message
was favorable. M then questioned Bo about

U.S. (9/29/67). The President speaks at San Antonio, publicly
confirming the "no advantage" formulation and noting that it had been
given repeatedly to Hanoi.

"As we have told Hanoi time and time again, the heart of
the matter is this: The United States is willing to stop all
aerial and naval bombardment of North Vietnam when this will
lead promptly to productive discussions. We, of course,
assume that while discussions proceed, North Vietnam would
not take advantage of the bombing cessation or limitation."
(President's remarks in San Antonio before the National
Legislative Conference.)

DRV (10/2/67). Marcovich, after taking careful notes on Mai Van Bo's
comments, described Trinh's 1/28/67 statement as a "solemn engagement to
talk after the unconditional end of the bombing." Two days later, Bo
denied using the term "solemn engagement"," to which Marcovich took strong
exception. (PENNSYLVANIA)

··· M following the meeting and after a flight
to Rome where he discussed the message in
detail with A from Rome ··· mailed it by
special delivery air-post to Kissinger in
Boston late on October 2. The text of the
note received by Kissinger follows:

"The position of the RDVN remains always
the same. If the United States really
wished to talk, let them stop first without
conditions the bombardment of the territory
of the RDVN.

:"Starting from that position there are
several eventualities: —·

(a) A public declaration by the Government
of the United States about the cessation.
This declaration could take place either
before or after the cessation.

(b) An official declaration but non-public
preceding the cessation of the bombardment.
This declaration could be communicated by
the channel K/A-M (officieusement)-not
quite officially, and after this indication
it can be transmitted officially by an
accredited person.

(c) An end of bombardment without preceding
official declaration followed by an official
but not public communication of the Government of the United States.

"Eventuality (a) would represent a public
declaration replying to that made on the 28th
of January by M. Trinh, Minister of Foreign
Affairs of the RDVN, which constitutes a
solemn engagement to talk after the unconditional end of bombing. This public declaration would be followed by the transmission of
an official text by an accredited person.

U.S. (10/8/67). We offered to set a date for stopping the bombing
and a date and place for beginning discussions if the DRV indicated it
would enter promptly into productive discussions on U.S./DRV issues.

M and A called on Bo at 9:00 a.m. Paris
time and spent 1½ hours with him. As in
the past Bo was cordial to his visitors
throughout the meeting.

M and A handed the written portion of the
message from Kissinger to Bo, which Bo read
closely. M and A then read to Bo Kissinger's
four "oral points," and Bo wrote them down
carefully in his own notes. (M and A did
not leave with Bo the "oral" part of the
message.) The written message and oral points
are as follows:

11

"M should tell B that K would be authorized
to deliver to B in writing the following message
whenever B is prepared to meet with him
officially or unofficially:

'The United States Government understands the position of the Democratic
Republic of Vietnam to be as follows:
That upon the cessation by the United
States of all forms of bombardment of
the Democratic Republic of Vietnam,
without expression of condition, the
Democratic Republic of Vietnam would enter
promptly into productive discussions with
the United States. The purpose of these
discussions would be to resolve the issues
between the United States and the Democratic
Republic of Vietnam.

'Assuming the correctness of this
understanding of the position of the
Democratic Republic of Vietnam, the
United States Government is prepared,
in accordance with its proposal of
August 25, to transmit in advance to
the Democratic Republic of Vietnam the
precise date upon which bombardment of
the Democratic Republic of Vietnam would
cease and to suggest a date and a place
for the commencement of discussions.'

"In addition M should convey to B the
following oral points from K:

"1. K believes that this understanding
is consistent with B's statements of
October 4, as reported by M, and with the
proposal of the United States Government
of August 25.

"2. When B meets with K, K would also
be prepared to state the precise date on
which the cessation of bombardment would occur

12

and to give the suggestions of the United States
with respect to the date and site of the discussions following the cessation of bombardment,
and K would be authorized to receive the views
of the Democratic Republic of Vietnam with respect
to these and other modalities.

"3. K noted that the Democratic Republic
of Vietnam had not commented on observations by
the United States Government on August 25 with
respect to secrecy of the fact of discussions
between the Democratic Republic of Vietnam and
the United States Government.

"4. K observed that officials of the United
States Government had taken note of a reduction
of military activities in the vicinity of the
demilitarized zone. Undoubtedly, the Democratic
Republic of Vietnam had noted the absence in
recent weeks of aerial bombardment in the
immediate vicinity of Hanoi."

Bo told M to tell Kissinger how much Bo
appreciated K's personal efforts. Bo then
dictated to M and A the following short
message of acknowledgment to K:

"M and A have passed the note from K to
B. In case B will have a reply to make,
he will make it through this channel."

U.S. (10/12/67). The San Antonio formula was explained to the
Swedes. "No advantage" was not a "condition" but a "self-evident description" of what would constitute good faith. They were asked to find out
if Hanoi would agree to a degree of restraint that would compromise a no
advantage situation in return for stopping the bombing.

STATE 54361 to Amembassy Stockholm (SECRET, NODIS, ASPEN),
12 October 1967.

"4. During this conversation the Secretary made a
number of observations on the main points raised by the
Foreign Minister's paper. We would have nothing to add
to his comments at this time beyond reaffirming the importance of eliciting any additional details on Foreign
Minister Trinh's remark to Ambassador Petri in June that

Hanoi 'understood' the importance the United States
attaches to reciprocal action on the part of North Vietnamese in connection with a halt in the bombing.[16] We
note Ambassador Petri's view that some concrete act of
reciprocity can be expected after the cessation of the
bombing, even if Foreign Minister Trinh gave no precise
indication that Hanoi was considering taking such a step, and
we would of course always be keenly interested in any new
evidence which Ambassador Petri might obtain from North
Vietnamese officials which would bear out his view.

"5. Since the Secretary's conversation with Foreign
Minister Nilsson, President Johnson in his speech of
September 29 has set forth our willingness immediately to
stop aerial and naval bombardment of North Viet-Nam when this
will lead promptly to productive discussions.[17] As the Foreign
Minister will have seen from this speech, as well as from
Ambassador Goldberg's September 21 speech at the United
Nations, we are interested in two points -- whether there
would be productive discussions, and whether we could
reasonably assume that Hanoi would not take advantage of a
bombing stoppage.[18] The latter point has not been posed as
a 'condition,' but rather as a self-evident description of
a state of affairs that would evidence good faith on both
sides. Foreign Minister Nilsson may note that the desired
'no advantage' situation would require restraint from Hanoi,
but this might fall short of total cessation of arms dispatch
and infiltration to South Viet-Nam. If Hanoi were prepared
to consider such a cessation, a balanced arrangement, not only

stopping the bombing but also cessation of reinforcement
by United States and others, would be possible. But
there remains the possibility that Hanoi might be prepared to agree to some lesser restraint, in return for
stopping the bombing only, that could comprise an
effective 'no disadvantage' situation.

"6. If Ambassador Petri could elicit any precise
information on Hanoi's position concerning these points
during his forthcoming visit to Hanoi, this could be of
the greatest importance. As the Secretary remarked at the
conclusion of the conversation, we would hope that we could
be informed in advance of the timing of Ambassador Petri's
next visit to Hanoi so that we might consider whether we could
submit any additional points to make during his discussions
with North Vietnamese officials."

RUSK (drafted by Isham)

DRV (10/17/67). Through the PENNSYLVANIA channel, Bo gave us a written message changing the verb "could" (Trinh's 1/28/67 interview) to "can." He also indicated the DRV took "productive" to mean that the U.S. insisted on discussing SVN in U.S./DRV exchanges.

"M" saw Bo, expressed hope to keep the channel open, and handed "M" the following message:

"Actually the U.S. has been following a policy of escalation of an extremely serious nature. In these conditions the U.S. proposals of peace are double-faced. At a time when the U.S. is pursuing a policy of escalation we cannot receive Kissinger, nor comment on the American proposals transmitted through this channel.

"The position of the Government of the DRV is perfectly clear: it is only when the U.S. has ended without condition the bombardment that discussions can take place."

"M and Bo discussed what 'the conditions' were in the U.S. proposal. M said he thought that the U.S. meant that we wanted a guarantee of serious discussions when we used the word 'productive.' Bo said the DRV thought that by use of the word 'productive' we meant that we wanted to talk about objectives in the South also, since discussions could not be fully productive without this subject being considered.

DRV (10/20/67). Burchett reported the DRV would offer nothing "except talks" for a cessation of the bombardment. He stressed the distinction between "talks" and "negotiations," without making clear what the difference would be. He quoted Trinh as saying the talks would be "meaningful," but whether they would be "fruitful" or "productive" would depend on the U.S.

The following article by Wilfred Burchett was read in Washington on this date:

"Hanoi, North Vietnam AP - There is no possibility of any talks or even contacts between Hanoi and the U.S. government unless the bombardment and other acts of war against North Vietnam are definitively halted.

15

"This is the position stated to me during conversations
in the last few days with Premier Pham Van Dong, Nguyen Duy
Trinh, foreign minister and deputy premier, and other high-
ranking government and party leaders.

"Hanoi is in no mood for concessions or bargaining
and there is an absolute refusal to offer anything --
except talks -- for a cessation of the bombardment. The
word stressed is 'talks,' not negotiations.

"During an informal talk, however, Trinh repeated
that his statement to this correspondent last January 28 --
that talks could start if the bombing was halted -- still
held good. He said there could be 'meaningful' talks.
Whether they would be 'fruitful' or 'productive' depended
on the United States.

U.S. (11/3/67). The Russians were told that we would stop the
bombing if they could tell us that the DRV would stop its infiltration.

MemCon, dated Nov 3, 1967   (approved in S: 11/8/67) (SECRET/NODIS)

Part II of IV

Subject: Vietnam

Participants: U.S.
                         The Secretary
                         Foy D. Kohler, Deputy Undersecretary
                         John M. Leddy, Assistant Secretary for EUR
                         Malcolm Toon, Country Director, SOV

                         USSR
                         V. V. Kuznetsov, First Deputy Foreign Minister
                         Anatoliy F. Dobrynin, Soviet Ambassador
                         Yuri N. Chernyakov, Minister-Counselor, Soviet Embassy
                         Igor D. Bubnov, Counselor, Soviet Embassy

. . . .

"THE SECRETARY said we had no problem with this at all. The Soviets,
however, must be perfectly clear on one fundamental point. We will continue to oppose the spread of world revolution by force. With regard to
Vietnam the Secretary saw no need for a conflict of interest between the
United States and the Soviet Union. It was important that the Soviets
recognize that we have a vital interest in what happens in South Vietnam,
just as we recognize that the Soviets have an interest as to what happens
in North Vietnam. We are prepared to stop the bombing now if the Soviet
Union can tell us that the North Vietnamese will stop its infiltration."

·U.S.· (11/23/67). The Swedes were given illustrations of DRV actions that would run counter to the "no advantage" assumption. They were asked to seek clarification from the DRV.

"7. The third point relates to the understanding of a 'no advantage' situation, as described in the President's San Antonio speech and in my October 6 message to you in connection with a bombing cessation and the start of talks. One way to clarify this is in terms of questions that I emphasize are illustrative of examples only. What would happen with respect to the flow of supplies and men into South Viet-Nam and to positions directly threatening South Viet-Nam? For example, if following a cessation or limitation of bombing, there was a marked increase in the flow of trucks southward; if a new North Vietnamese regiment were to appear; or if we saw a massive increase in the flow of supplies just to the north of the DMZ, we would be negatively impressed. Similarly, to take another example, we would want to know what would happen with respect to the three North Vietnamese Divisions now in the area of the Demilitarized Zone which have been employed as part of offensive operations against our forces south of the DMZ. Would artillery located north of the demarcation line be employed against our forces? And, if so, would we be expected not to bomb these artillery positions?

"8. These questions are, of course, not easy ones to answer. Nevertheless, we believe they are central to an accurate understanding of what is involved on both sides. We would be grateful for any clarification that you might be able to obtain through your contacts with North Vietnamese repre-, sentatives on these matters."

U.S. (12/27/67). The Russians gave their understanding of San Antonio as requiring Hanoi to agree in advance to a de-escalation of the conflict before the bombing would stop. Harriman corrected them, drawing attention to the DMZ as a special problem, however.

MemCon; Dated December 27, 1967   (SECRET/NODIS)

TIME: 12:45 to 3:45

PLACE: 3038 N Street

Participants: Soviet Ambassador Dobrynin
               Ambassador at Large W. Averell Harriman

17

" . . . . (3) I stated that the San Antonio formula was certainly a reasonable one and went as far as the US Government could be expected .to go. I asked whether his Government could inform us why it had been rejected by Hanoi and also whether the Soviet Union had a practical alternative suggestion. He asked some detailed questions regarding the San Antonio formula. I repeated what I had told him in my last conversation. 'Productive discussions' did not, as Hanoi had interpreted it, mean a guarantee of favorable conclusion, but considering our Korean experience, we wanted assurance that talks would be serious and in good faith and in an attempt to find an agreement. He told me that his Government had gained the impression that the President's statement 'we would, of course, assume that while discussions proceed North Viet-Nam would not take advantage of the bombing cessation or limitation' meant that Hanoi would have to agree in advance to a de-escalation of the conflict. I stated that this was not true. 'Taking advantage' meant what it said, namely, that Hanoi would not use the advantage of no bombing to send more supplies and reinforcements to the South than were now getting through. I also referred to the DMZ as a special problem. They were using artillery, and our bombing of the gun positions and other bases just north of the DMZ was a tactical operation which would have to continue unless there was mutual restraint in that area which we thought would be the best solution.

"Dobrynin said that he would inform his Government, but underlined that both his Government and Hanoi believed that Hanoi had interpreted the San Antonio formula, taken in connection with other statements, to mean that Hanoi would have to agree in advance to some sort of de-escalation of its operations if we were to stop the bombing."

. . . .

DRV (12/29/67). Trinh, speaking publicly, changes the verb from "could" to "will" talk.

. On December 29, Trinh spoke at a Mongolian reception. The substance of his talk was broadcast by Hanoi VNA in English on January 1. He stated in part:

"The stand of the Vietnamese people is quite clear. That is the four-point stand of the DRV Government and the political program of the NFLSV. That is the basis for the settlement of the Vietnam question.

"The U.S. Government has unceasingly claimed that it wants to talk with Hanoi but has received no response. If the U.S. Government truly wants to talk, it must, as was made clear in our statement on 28 January 1967, first of all stop unconditionally the bombing and all other acts of war against the DRV. After the United States has ended unconditionally the bombing and all other acts of war against the DRV, the DRV will hold talks with the United States on questions concerned."

DRV (1/4/68). The Swedes were told of DRV concern that "no advantage" would "leave our brothers in the South unprotected."

STOCKHOLM 662 to SecState (SECRET, NODIS, ASPEN), January 4, 1968. Ref: Stockholm 649.

"3. Oberg saw Charge Vu Bach Mai (Oberg's spelling) Dec 21 and handed over paper described Para 2A. Paper had been translated into French; illustrative examples Para 7 State 73693 were also given in English.

"4. NVN Charge raised three points which Oberg on instructions refused to discuss saying that Swedes had this paper from US aide and that Swedes not competent go beyond what was in paper.

"5. Three points NVN Charge raised were:

A. Did Swedes have any suggestions on how to describe bombing pause?

B. On question of flow of material in no-advantage situation Charge said 'we cannot leave our brothers in the South unprotected.' It was not clear to Oberg whether he was referring to NLF in South Vietnam or to supplies to NVN troops north of DMZ. (Oberg commented that in his contacts NVN representatives never referred presence NVN troops in South Vietnam.) C. On question seriousness of negotiations Charge said this was unclear to him. In any negotiation both sides started from positions widely apart and with quite different aims. In such cases there would be different interpretation of 'serious or productive.'"

DRV (1/5/68). The Rumanians reported that Trinh made clear to them that the condition for talks was an "unconditional" but not "permanent" bombing cessation. They also claimed that the DRV would not insist on U.S. acceptance of the 4 Points as the basis for negotiations; each side would come with its own views.

"Material in quotation marks was read slowly and carefully by Macovescu.

"Here is the answer to the question that you asked Mr. Harriman. From this point on there is a passage which in the text is in quotation marks.

'We affirm the following. If the USG really wants
discussions with the Government of the DRV it should first
unconditionally cease bombing and any other act of war
against the DRV. After the unconditional cessation of all
bombing and of any other U.S. act of war against the DRV and
at the end of an appropriate period of time the government
of the DRV will enter into serious discussions with the USG.'

"While he was reading this paragraph I stopped him and told him
comrade Minister when I mentioned cessation I said final and unconditional. Trinh looked at me and reread the sentence. I said I
mentioned 'final and unconditional cessation.' He reread the
sentence again. I interrupted for the third time. May I understand you are no longer speaking of final cessation. His answer
was that publicly we may continue to mention it but with a view
to negotiations. What I have said is our position.

"I asked him whether the Government of Romania is authorized
to pass this communication to the USG. He said yes. He repeated
it but he said to retain spirit of the message."

Harriman said that the Trinh public statement was much the same as
the M & I message, but that the M & I statement placed more emphasis on
the acceptance of the four points as a basis of negotiations.[19] M said that
he did not establish any connection between his visit to Washington,
unknown to Hanoi, and the Trinh public statement. Harriman argued that

"there must be some connection." M responded that he did not believe
there was a contradiction between the two messages:

"In the public statement it says the basis for negotiations
is the four points, but in private conversation they say we will
come with this basis but the U.S. side, we expect, will come
with its own point of view. They especially said this."

Harriman then questioned whether it was the DRV view that discussions
will be fruitful only if we accept their four points. M responded:

"That is not the impression I gained from my discussions.
They will come with their claims but would have to negotiate on
what the U.S. puts forth. They said this specifically."

With respect to the timing of discussions, M said that Trinh stated
there could be no contacts "as long as U.S. acts of war continue,...
but as soon as bombing and other acts of aggression against North Vietnamese cease, we are prepared to receive anybody...." Trinh added: "We
shall consider these contacts as normal diplomatic activities. The
American representative will be received by our diplomats at their suggestion.

Harriman questioned further on the timing, specifically as to the meaning of "after a suitable length of time." Here, M retreated to the DRV text--"the appropriate and necessary period of time." M explained this as a period in which

"they will try to test (I don't know by what means) the sincerity of your intentions--your wish to have discussions. I could not deduce the period, but I do not think it will be too long. If an understanding is reached that you stop, at a certain established period, discussions, not negotiations, will take place."

* * *

M then read from a document:

"As long as the US acts of war go on we cannot have any contacts with them. As soon as they cease the bombings and discontinue the acts of aggression we shall be prepared to receive any person, even a representative of the United States, who may wish to make known to us the American point of view or to get informed on our viewpoint. We shall regard these future contacts as normal diplomatic activity. The American representatives will be received by our representatives at the former's suggestion."

* * *

"1. The Democratic Republic of Vietnam has communicated to the United States Government this statement of the Democratic Republic of Vietnam position:

'If the United States Government really wants discussions with the Government of the Democratic Republic of Vietnam it should first unconditionally cease bombing and any other acts of war against the Democratic Republic of Vietnam. After the unconditional cessation of all bombing and of any other United States act of war against the Democratic Republic of Vietnam and at the end of an appropriate period of time the Government of the Democratic Republic of Vietnam will enter into serious discussions with the United States Government.'

* * *

21

DRV (1/16/68).   Bo says that talks would begin "after a suitable time following" the halt of attacks, and that the two parties would then meet to agree on the level and scope of their talks.

QUES 2: THE HALTING OF THE BOMBING IS CLEAR. BUT WHAT DOES "THE CESSATION OF ALL OTHER ACTS OF WAR AGAINST THE DEMOCRATIC REPUBLIC OF VIET NAME" MEAN TO YOU?

ANS: [THE CESSATION] OF ANY MILITARY ACTION THAT VIOLATES THE SOVEREIGNTY AND THE TERRITORY OF THE DEMOCRACTIC REPUBLIC OF VIET NAM.

QUES 3: IN WHAT WAY MUST THE AMERICAN GOVE ANNOUNCE THE END OF THE BOMBING?

ANS: THE US GOVT MAY ANNOUNCE THIS UNCONDITIONAL HALTING OF THE BOMBING AND OF ALL OTHER ACTS OF WAR THROUGH A DECLARATION OR IT MAY MAKE USE OF ANY OTHER PROCEDURE CAPABLE OF ESTABLISHING ITS REALITY.

QUES 4: HOW MUCH TIME WILL ELAPSE BETWEEN THE END OF THE BOMBING AND THE OPENING OF THE NEGOTIATIONS?

ANS: THE TALKS WILL BEGIN AFTER A SUITABLE TIME FOLLOWING THE UNCONDITIONAL HALTING OF THE BOMBING AND OF ALL OTHER ACTS OF WAR AGAINST THE DRVN.

QUES 5: AT WHAT LEVEL IN YOUR OPINION, ARE THESE NEGOTIATIONS TO BE HELD AND WITH WHAT QUESTIONS ARE THEY TO DEAL?

ANS: FOLL THE UNCONDITINAL CESSATION OF BOMBING AND OF ALL OTHER ACTS OF WAR AGAINST THE DRVN, THE TWO PARTIES WILL MEET IN ORDER TO REACH AGREEMENT ON SUCH QUESTIONS.

(Emphasis Added)

U.S. (1/25/68).   Clifford defined the "no advantage" assumption to the Senate Armed Services Committee as assuming the enemy "will continue to transport the normal amount of goods, munitions, men, to SVN."[20]

"SENATOR (STROM) THURMOND: When you spoke of negotiating, in that case you would be willing to have a cessation of bombing. I presume that that would contemplate that they would stop their military activities, too, if we would be expected to have a cessation of bombing.

"A. No, that is not what I said. I do not expect them to stop their military activities. I would expect to follow the language of the President when he said that if they would agree to start negotiations promptly and not take advantage of the pause in the bombing.

"Q. What do you mean by taking advantage if they continue their military activities?

"A. Their military activity will continue in South Vietnam, I assume, until there is a cease fire agreed upon. I assume that they will continue to transport the normal amount of goods, munitions, men, to South Vietnam. I assume that we will continue to maintain our forces during that period. So what I am suggesting is, in the language of the President, that he would insist that they not take advantage of the suspension of the bombing.

"Q. How would you keep them from taking advantage if we had a cessation of bombing?

"A. There is no way to keep them from taking advantage. If they state they are going to refrain from taking advantage, and then refuse to do so, then they have not met their agreement, and the conditions for the negotiations have failed.

"Q. And then, if they did violate that, you would favor then resuming bombing, I would presume.

"A. I would assume we would have no alternative. If they did not meet their obligations or we do not meet our obligations, then I assume there is absolutely no sense in negotiating. It would be a useless task. To negotiate there has to be good faith if any result is to be achieved and if, during the negotiations, bad faith is evidenced then there is no need to negotiate."

DRV (2/8/68). Trinh defined the questions to be raised in "talks" as "questions related to a settlement of the Vietnam problem on the basis of the 1954 Geneva agreements on Vietnam. They are also other questions which could be raised by either side." This blurred, possibly erased, the distinction that may have existed earlier between "talks" and "negotiations." He also said talks would begin "as soon as" the U.S. "proved" it had stopped attacks.

"Question: In your 29 December 1967 speech, you stated in part: After the unconditional cessation of the bombings and all other acts of war against the DRV, the DRV will hold talks with the United States on relevant problems. What do you mean by relevant problems?

"Answer: They are questions related to a settlement of the Vietnam problem on the basis of the 1954 Geneva agreements on Vietnam. They are also other questions which could be raised by either side.

"Question: It has been subsequently clarified that the talks can begin after an appropriate time following the unconditional cessation of the bombings and all other acts of war against the DRV. Could you clarify further the meaning of appropriate time?

"Answer: The talks will begin as soon as the United States has proved that it has really stopped unconditionally the bombings and all other acts of war against the Democratic Republic of Vietnam."

U.S. (2/17/68). The Swedes were asked to explain the San Antonio formula to the DRV. "Productive" was defined as "serious exchanges" in which either side could raise "any matter." Attention was called to the Tet offensive, as casting doubt on Hanoi's intentions, but it was not labeled a breach of "no advantage."

"The U.S., consistent with President Johnson's statement of April 7, 1965, remains willing to enter into talks without preconditions at any time.

"The U.S. position on the cessation of the bombardment of North Viet-Nam is set forth in President Johnson's September 29, 1967 speech in San Antonio. As the President said:

'The U.S. is willing to stop all aerial and naval bombardment of North Viet-Nam when this will lead promptly to productive discussions. We, of course, assume that while discussions proceed, North Viet-Nam would not take advantage of the bombing cessation or limitation.'

"The U.S. is not assuming that North Viet-Nam will cease its support to its forces in the South. On the contrary, as Secretary of Defense designate Clark Clifford testified before the Senate Foreign Relations Committee, we assume that until a cease fire is agreed on, Hanoi 'will continue to transport the normal amount of goods, men and munitions.'

"In setting forth its assumption, the U.S. is not setting a
condition but attempting to make clear to North Viet-Nam that
any cessation of U.S. bombing followed by actions by Hanoi taking
advantage of the cessation (such as an increase by Hanoi of its
infiltration of men and supplies or attacks in the area of the
DMZ) would constitute such bad faith on Hanoi's part as to make
continued U.S. forebearance impossible. If Hanoi, by taking
advantage, forces the U.S. to resume bombing the possibilities of
a negotiated solution would drastically recede. Under such
circumstances calls for intensified U.S. military action would
increase and the possibility of another halt in the bombing would
be low. The U.S. is trying to ascertain whether Hanoi appreciates
this vital fact and fully understands the importance the U.S.
attaches to the no-advantage assumption.

"At San Antonio the President, in addition to setting forth
his assumption, stated his readiness to stop the bombing when such
action would lead 'promptly to productive discussions.' 'Productive
discussions' are serious exchanges in which either side will be
able to put forward for full consideration in good faith its position on any matter. 'Prompt' of course refers to a willingness by
Hanoi to begin discussions with the U.S. immediately after cessation
of bombing.

"It is worth noting that Hanoi is unwilling to give a clear
response to questions as to the length of time between a U.S.
bombing cessation and the beginning of talks. If Hanoi were
serious in desiring talks then surely its response would have
been one of unequivocal readiness to begin immediately.

"The U.S. evaluation of Hanoi's current position takes into
account Hanoi's actions as well as its words. The unprecedented
offensive against most of South Viet-Nam's urban centers, which
Hanoi treacherously launched in the midst of the traditional Tet
holidays, causing widespread civilian casualties and suffering,
was made notwithstanding the fact that we were still exploring with
Hanoi its position through diplomatic channels, and that we had
exercised restraint in bombing targets in the immediate vicinity
of Hanoi and Haiphong. In this context, we cannot but weigh
Hanoi's words with great skepticism and caution. These actions
carry a harsh political message.

"The U.S. favors every effort to obtain clarification of Hanoi's
position. We shall continue to evaluate all information and to
pursue every possible avenue which promises to bring us closer to
the resolution of this conflict through serious negotiations."

(State 117383)

U.S. (2/20/68). The Norwegians were asked to convey the same message as the Swedes.

"The US, consistent with President Johnson's statement of April 7, 1965, remains willing to enter into talks with/out - amended State 118719/ preconditions at any time.

"The US position on the cessation of the bombardment of North Viet-Nam was set forth in President Johnson's September 29, 1967 speech in San Antonio. As the President said:

'The US is willing to stop all aerial and naval bombardment of North Viet-Nam when this will lead promptly to productive discussions. We, of course, assume that while discussions proceed, North Viet-Nam would not take advantage of the bombing cessation or limitation.'

"The US is not assuming that North Viet-Nam will cease its support to its forces in the South. On the contrary, as Secretary of Defense designate Clark Clifford testified before the Senate Foreign Relations Committee, we assume that until a cease-fire is agreed on, Hanoi 'will continue to transport the normal amount of goods, men and munitions.'

"In setting forth its assumption, the US is not setting a condition but attempting to make clear to North Viet-Nam that any cessation of US bombing followed by actions by Hanoi taking advantage of the cessation (such as an increase by Hanoi of its infiltration of men and supplies or attacks in the area of the DMZ) would constitute such bad faith on Hanoi's part as to make continued US forebearance impossible. If Hanoi, by taking advantage, forces the US to resume bombing, the possibilities of a negotiated solution would drastically recede. Under such circumstances, calls for intensified US military action would increase and the possibility of another halt in the bombing would be low. The US is trying to ascertain whether Hanoi appreciates this vital fact and fully understands the importance the US attaches to the no-advantage assumption.

"At San Antonio the President, in addition to setting forth his assumption, stated his readiness to stop the bombing when such action would lead 'promptly to productive discussions.' 'Productive discussions' are serious exchanges in which either side will be able to put forward for full consideration in good

faith its position on any matter.   'Prompt' of course refers
to a willingness by Hanoi to begin discussions with the US
immediately after cessation of bombing.

"It is worth noting that Hanoi is unwilling to give a
clear response to questions as to the length of time between
a US bombing cessation and the beginning of talks.   If Hanoi
were serious in desiring talks then surely its response would
have been one of unequivocal readiness to begin immediately.

"The US evaluation of Hanoi's current position takes into
account Hanoi's actions as well as its words.   The unprecedented
offensive against most of South Viet-Nam's urban centers, which
Hanoi treacherously launched in the midst of the traditional
Tet holidays, causing widespread civilian casualties and
suffering, was made notwithstanding the fact that we were
still exploring with Hanoi its position through diplomatic
channels, and that we had exercised restraint in bombing
targets in the immediate vicinity of Hanoi and Haiphong.   In
this context, we cannot but weigh Hanoi's words with great
skepticism and caution.   These actions carry a harsh political
message.

"The US favors every effort to obtain clarification of
Hanoi's position.   We shall continue to evaluate all information
and to pursue every possible avenue which promises to bring us
closer to the resolution of this conflict through serious
negotiations."

(State 118092)

DRV (2/24/68).   "All other acts of war" was defined to mean that
"no airplanes were permitted to fly over DRV territory."

27

(STOCKHOLM 901)

DRV (3/1/68).   DRV Ambassador Su told d'Orlandi that his "personal view" was there would be no assault on Khe Sanh, etc., etc., once the two sides had begun to talk.

D'Orlandi met with Meloy and Davidson to report on his March 1 meeting in Prague with Ambassador Su. D'Orlandi asked Su if he were ready to answer the question concerning the period of delay between the stopping of the bombing and the first U.S.-Hanoi meetings? Su responded rather lamely that he thought this contact had come to an end and, therefore, he was not able to supply a precise answer. "He could state that the matter of a date would be no problem. The real problem was San Antonio."

D'Orlandi said that he had dictated to Su the first portion of the Davidson MemCon of the February 28 meeting to the North Vietnamese, but the North Vietnamese did not comment on this.

The most important point that Su made in these talks was with respect to "no advantage." Although he said he was speaking personally, it is highly doubtful that he would have said the following without specific instructions:

"....D'Orlandi then told Su that if bombing stopped and talks began, assaulting Khe Sanh, invading or trying to detach the two northern provinces of South Viet-Nam, launching a second wave of attacks against one or more cities or creating a sensation with something else like an assault on Camp Carrol, would sink the whole thing. Su replied that, speaking personally and not on instructions, such thing would be out, that from the moment the two sides meet it was obvious no such thing could happen. (I questioned d'Orlandi about this remark of Su's and d'Orlandi replied that while he took no notes he is certain this is the sense of what Su said.) D'Orlandi told Su that whatever he or Su thought of the effect of bombing, it is a fact that the US Government and US public opinion considers bombing of the North a most important weapon and that no President could give away such a weapon while something terrible was happening either in the DMZ or the South. Su did not respond to this comment. D'Orlandi also remarked that it might be necessary for him to go to Hanoi to receive assurances directly from the top and again Su did not reply."

28

DRV (3/10/68). Trinh gave Norwegian Ambassador Algard to understand that the DRV did not require the U.S. to accept its 4 Points "beforehand" (apparently before negotiations) though the DRV would insist on them as the "foundation for a political resolution of the conflict" at the talks.

OSLO 3570 - Summary of Ambassador Algard's visit to Hanoi, March 3-10:

. . . .

DRV. (4/8/68). Trinh, in his interview with Collingwood, repeated DRV attacks on reciprocal restraint as the condition for a complete bombing halt.[21] He specified that the DRV representative at the contact to complete the bombing halt would have Ambassadorial rank and would be prepared to reach agreement on "the date, place and level of the formal talks" between the DRV and U.S.

"Question: President Johnson said that 'even this limited bombing of the north could come to an early end if our restraint is matched by restraint in Hanoi.' Would your government be willing to make such a move?

"Answer: The Democratic Republic of Vietnam is an independent and sovereign country some 10,000 miles away from the United States, and has done no harm whatsoever to it. The unwarranted U.S. bombing of the Democratic Republic of Vietnam is an impudent act of aggression. The United States must bring it to an end.

"To ask for 'reciprocity' as a condition, or 'restraint' as a price, is nothing but a trick to blur the distinction between the aggressor and the victim of aggression. The United States has shown no 'restraint' in using its huge war machine against a small country, and still demands that we should show 'restraint' and should not exercise our sacred rights to defend our fatherland. This is pure nonsense."

. . . .

"Question: In its 3 April statement, your government declared 'its readiness to appoint its representative to contact a U.S. representative with a view to determining with the American side the unconditional cessation of the U.S. bombing raids and all other acts of war against the Democratic Republic of Vietnam so that the talks may start.'[22] Mr. Minister, what will be the rank of your representative? When and where will he make contact with the U.S. representative? When and where will the formal talks between the Democratic Republic of Vietnam and the United States start, and at what level?

Answer: A representative with ambassadorial rank of the Government of the Democratic Republic of Vietnam is ready to make contact with a representative of the U.S. Government in Phnom Penh or in another place to be mutually agreed upon. In the course of this contact, the American side will specify the date when the unconditional cessation of the U.S. bombing raids and all other acts of war against the Democratic Republic of Vietnam will become effective; then the two sides will reach agreement on the date, place, and level of the formal talks between the Democratic Republic of Vietnam and the United States."

. . . .

DRV (5/3/68). The DRV appointed Xuan Thuy as its representative to enter "formal talks" with the US in Paris.

" ... the DRV Government is of the view that the formal talks between Hanoi and Washington should be held immediately. The DRV Government has decided to appoint Minister Xuan Thuy as its representative to enter into formal talks with the U.S. Government's representative, to determine with the U.S. side the unconditional cessation of the U.S. bombing raids and all other acts of war against the DRV, and then hold talks on other problems of concern to the two sides."

30

SETTLEMENT TERMS

1. Mutual Withdrawal

Summary

The U.S. position on withdrawal of forces is clear and, yet, leaves us with a great deal of flexibility. We have said in the 14 Points (1/3/66) that "we want no U.S. bases in Southeast Asia," and that "we do not desire to retain U.S. troops in South Vietnam after peace is assured." In other words, the U.S. is on record as being committed against keeping its forces in South Vietnam when peace is restored. The U.S. record is also clear in insisting on mutual withdrawal of forces. In the 4 Points which were passed to the DRV in Rangoon (PINTA 2/16/66), we stated that discussions should consider "appropriate means, including agreed stages, for the withdrawal of military and quasi-military personnel and weapons introduced into South Vietnam or North Vietnam from one area to the other or into either area from any other outside source...and the regrouping and redeployment of indigenous forces." U.S. flexibility on withdrawal is built into its "until peace" qualification. In the Manila Declaration (10/25/66), we stated that allied forces "shall be withdrawn, after close consultation, if the other side withdraws its forces to the north, ceases infiltration, and the level of violence thus subsides. Those forces will be withdrawn as soon as possible and not later than six months after the above conditions have been fulfilled."

The DRV has always given the principle of U.S. withdrawal top billing. Pham Van Dong directly told us (PENNSYLVANIA 7/25/67) that the end of the war means "a withdrawal of U.S. forces." In the 4 Points, for example, Hanoi states: "The US Government must withdraw from South Vietnam US troops, military personnel, and weapons of all kinds, dismantle all US military bases there, and cancel its military alliance with South Vietnam." Hanoi has, however, displayed increasing flexibility on the timing of U.S. withdrawal. Recent statements indicate that they would be prepared for us to stay until a political settlement in the south had been achieved. Hanoi's hooker on this issue is similar to those other matters on which it has evinced flexibility (reunification and free elections), namely, that this is an issue of secondary importance compared to the crunch point on who governs in the south. Tactically, then, Hanoi is likely to present an initial hard front on this matter and then "give in" in order to gain concessions on the central issue of power in the south.

NVA presence in South Vietnam

Hanoi has repeatedly denied the presence of regular PAVN forces or even North Vietnamese volunteers in South Vietnam. These public denials are important to Hanoi for several reasons: the denials reaffirm their propaganda about the war being essentially a South Vietnamese affair fought by the South Vietnamese themselves, that is a civil war. The denials may also have been tied to their anti-U.S. bombing campaign, allowing them to maintain that the U.S. was committing aggression against the north without the north committing aggression against the south. Also, at this time, Hanoi has an interest in not making itself out to be a liar for all these years. As far as we know, they have even been telling the Russians that they do not have regular forces in the south. In other words, this fiction has assumed propaganda and leverage value which Hanoi will not give up easily.

While Hanoi's public record on this issue has been consistent, there have been two private slips in which they were on the verge of admission. The first occasion was in the XYZ contacts when Bo did not deny DRV troop presence in South Vietnam (8/18/65) or even that the 325th NVA division was in South Vietnam--although he claimed that "it was not then engaged in military operations" (9/3/65). After the XYZ contacts had ended, Bo said there were no regular troops in Saigon, but northern volunteers might have joined the Viet Cong (11/27/65). The second occasion of near truth telling came during the MARIGOLD contacts. Lewandowski asked us (11/14/66), regarding the offer at Manila concerning the withdrawal of U.S. forces from Vietnam on the condition that the troops of North Vietnam would withdraw, and, he said, "North Vietnam, of course, doesn't admit that they are there at all...." Later in the 10-Point MARIGOLD formulation (11/30/66), the 8th Point read: "In this regard the US is prepared to accept DRV modalities on the cessation /of bombing/ and not require the DRV to admit infiltration into South Vietnam."

Would the DRV withdraw?

When played off against the public statements of denial, these private statements provide a hint as to how the DRV might handle this issue. The fiction of no presence will be maintained, but it will not be allowed to stand in the way of actual North Vietnamese troop withdrawals should the conditions be appropriate. In all likelihood, however, these withdrawals will be de facto, unannounced, unilaterally made -- and not necessarily back into North Vietnam itself. The more likely stopping place on their way home from South Vietnam would be the Laotian Panhandle. The furthest Hanoi ever went on dealing with this issue was again in the XYZ contacts. Because Bo did not deny NVA troop presence in South Vietnam, he was able to agree with the principle that troop withdrawals would have to be mutual, balanced and phased (8/15/65). Bo reaffirmed his agreement to this principle (8/18/65), but then denied any such agreements (9/3/65).

What emerges is the link between North Vietnamese troop withdrawals and their control of the south. When Lewandowski asked us about the Manila withdrawal formula (11/14/66), the tie was clear: "...does this condition mean the U.S. withdrawal depends on control by the present South Vietnamese government of territories not now under the control of Saigon?" Hanoi will ask us this question again, and depending upon our answer will decide to withdraw or not.

2

Timing -- the DRV view on the timing of U.S. withdrawal.

As the DRV began to play out its diplomatic hand over the last two years, it has become increasingly flexible on when it would like the U.S. to leave. Bo told us that U.S. withdrawal was a "technical problem" (11/16/65). Lewandowski said that they could take place according to a "reasonable guarantee" (6/27/66). Loan told Algard (OHIO, 8/16/67) that the timing "was not a decisive question." In this connection, Lewandowski pointed out the agreement on withdrawal of French troops as an example. He added that the Americans "would have to accept the political situation in South Vietnam as it is, as De Gaulle did in Algeria." All this does not mean that Hanoi will leave the issue open to principle. One of Lewandowski's 10 Points (MARIGOLD, 11/30/66) stated: "The U.S. does not desire permanent or long-term military presence in South Vietnam." The most forthcoming of all DRV statements on this issue was the one made by Pham Van Dong (PENNSYLVANIA, 7/25/67): "Some US troops would have to stay /in South Vietnam/ until the end of political settlement." This probably means that the U.S. forces would be allowed to linger on as long as they did not interfere with the process of political settlement. Indeed, the continued presence of U.S. troops in South Vietnam during this period could add legitimacy to the new government.

Non-Intervention

. The DRV also wants to get some guarantee in principle that the U.S. will refrain from intervening in Vietnam after a political settlement has taken place. In the 4 Points, Hanoi states that the U.S. "must end its policy of intervention and aggression in South Vietnam," and that during the period pending reunification, the two zones must refrain from entering into any military alliances with foreign countries and there must be no foreign military bases, troops, or foreign military personnel in their respective territory.

2. Self-Determination for SVN: Free Elections?

Summary

The main parties to the war agreed early on the principle of self-determination for the people of SVN. It is endorsed, inter alia, in the first NLF program (2/11/61),[23] President Johnson's Johns-Hopkins speech (4/7/65), the DRV's 4 Points (4/8/65) and the GVN's 4 Points (6/22/65).[24] The Vietnam Alliance of National, Democratic and Peace Forces (ANDPF) is for it, too (4/26/68).[25] But the different sides have different ideas about how the people of SVN should express their will. The U.S. and the GVN prefer the electoral processes of the current Constitution, whereas the DRV and NLF want to scrap that Constitution and set up a new electoral authority. The ANDPF has not stated a formal position on the Constitution, but is clearly opposed to the GVN as the country's electoral authority. Everyone no doubt suspects that the outcome of elections will be determined by who runs them. Thus to a large extent, the war is now being fought over who shall run future elections, making the apparent agreement on "self-determination" illusory. In addition, while both sides have expressed themselves favorably about elections, neither is irrevocably committed to elections as the only means of self-determination.

*   *   *

The 4 Points (4/8/65) call only for self-determination "in accordance with the program of the NLF without any foreign interference." When these Points were first published, the NLF program (issued 2/11/61) called for overthrowing Diem and substituting a coalition government as one phase, apparently the first, in bringing about "progressive democracy," including a new constitution and elections.

Later in 1965, Mai Van Bo stressed self-determination as the "one basic premise" that would permit all other problems to be solved (XYZ, 7/16/65), but he subsequently amended this to say that self-determination through elections would only be possible after U.S. military withdrawal (XYZ, 1/27/66). As he explained, "How can elections be held in a country over which no authority is exercised?" (XYZ, 5/6/66) He was probably not worried about the mechanics of holding elections. More likely, he felt the electoral authority would determine the outcome.

These stands were repeated by Trinh (to the Swedes), who said he wanted a coalition government and general elections (ASPEN, 11/11/66).

When Lewandowski was probing us on settlement terms (MARIGOLD, 11/14/66), he asked, "In case of a cease-fire, would the US be prepared to withdraw from the combat areas and not interfere in the creation of a new government in Vietnam?" He also wanted to know if the Manila withdrawal provisions depended on GVN control of areas not then under its control and whether we would declare our willingness to accept the Geneva and ICC machinery in "bringing peace to Vietnam," perhaps including inspection of an election.

He was no doubt searching for a formula under which NLF authority could be exercised prior to U.S. withdrawal. When he formulated his 10 Points (MARIGOLD, 11/30/66), he indicated our willingness to "accept the participation of 'all' in elections and the supervision of these elections by an appropriate international body." If, as the Poles and Russians claimed, the DRV was willing to enter discussions on this basis, they may have been willing to see elections of this sort before U.S. withdrawal. Who would run the elections, and how, would be subject to negotiation--as, therefore, in DRV eyes would be the probable outcome.

When the new NLF Program was issued, just after the election of Thieu, Ky and the lower house, it lists first the goal of abolishing the "puppet administration," the "puppet national assembly," and their constitution.[26] It called for "free general elections," for a new national assembly that would work out a new constitution, and for the establishment of a "national union democratic government." While it does not specify the order in which things are supposed to happen, it is clear enough that abolishing the GVN and its constitution would have to come before new elections, etc. In the list of objectives, new elections and the new constitution also come before establishing the coalition government. Perhaps this hints that the issue is negotiable (9/5/67).

However, at the end of February 1968, the DRV position expressed to Fanfani by Ambassador Su was: Hanoi wanted "absolutely free general elections. To insure liberty of vote, it was necessary to constitute a government with very broadly based participation" (KILLY, 2/23/68).

The ANDPF Program attacks the GVN as a "lackey administration," calls for setting up a coalition government and speaks of the future political regime in SVN as a "republic" with "just and honest elections." Again the sequence is not crisply specified, but the program seems to call for setting up the coalition government as a condition necessary to "winning back national sovereignty." This would make it a condition for ending the war--something to be negotiated or won on the battlefield, rather than the outcome of an electoral process (4/25/68).

3. The Legitimate Representative of SVN: GVN or NLF?

Summary

As noted in the previous section, elections as an impartial way of deciding who shall govern SVN may not solve the problem. The composition of the government may have to be negotiated or decided in battle. A prime war aim of the communists is establishing legitimacy for the NLF, while undercutting that of the GVN. The GVN is fighting to bolster its authority, while destroying that of the NLF. Thus "who shall govern SVN" is what the war is all about, and "who shall represent SVN" in negotiations is one round in the battle.

As opposed to the principle of "self-determination," the issue of who shall represent SVN--at the conference or in Saigon--is one on which almost no agreement has been reached between the U.S. and DRV. Essentially, each side has insisted on the legitimacy of its party in SVN, denied the legitimacy of the other's, but offered a way for individuals from the other's party to enter political life by "reconciling" themselves. The communists are probably prepared to go beyond this, accepting three "political tendencies" (right, neutral and left) as theoretically co-equal, in exchange for our agreeing that a new government be formed by the "tendencies"--after the model of the 1962 Agreements on Laos.[27]

*   *   *

The DRV and NLF.

From the outset, the communists' carrot has been their willingness to see "non-communists" included in the government or at the conference table. The unpalatable part has been their insistence on a role for the NLF and no role for the GVN as an institution.

In June 1964, Pham Van Dong insisted to Seaborn, "The Laos pattern of 1962 should serve as a guide for SVN." There should be a coalition, including the NLF. When Seaborn said the NLF might dominate, Dong said only, "There is no reason to have such fears."

In his statement embodying the 4 Points, Pham Van Dong said the NLF was "more and more recognized by...world opinion as the sole genuine representative of the SVN people" (4/8/65). The following January, Ho Chi Minh said, "If the US really wants peace it must recognize the NLF as the sole genuine representative..." (1/24/66). This public stance was softened in various private communications passed subsequently, but never to the extent of conceding legitimacy to the GVN.

6

The DRV rebutted the U.S. 14 Points (Rangoon, 1/31/66) by rejecting the legitimacy of the GVN: asking the NLF to "lay down its arms and ask amnesty" amounted to maintaining a "puppet regime" in Saigon.

In Lewandowski's first overtures (MARIGOLD, 6/29/66), he represented the communists as asking only that the NLF "take part" in negotiations--"they are not to have any monopoly"--and said that Hanoi did "not want to interfere with the SVN Government," though "we would like someone other than Ky." Later he suggested a coalition government made up mainly of "sensible SVN politicians" with men "on the fringe" from the "right" and the left, "the so-called NLF," in one or two "unimportant ministries" each" (MARIGOLD 9/18/66). This too is after the Laos pattern. (Souvanna's neutralists with 11 ministries, Boun Oum with 4 and Souphanóvong with 4.)

Much the same proposition came to us through the Swedes (ASPEN, 11/11/66).

Burchett, claiming to reflect the views of senior DRV and NLF officials, reported that Ky and Thieu would not be acceptable in a coalition, but "some members of their cabinet or...previous Saigon governments" might be. The communists considered "negotiations between Hanoi and the Ky government" as "an impossibility." Ky and his top supporters were expected to emigrate (2/10/67).

In July 1967, Pham Van Dong repeated that the coalition could be "broad" and could include members "du gouvernement fantoche et cadres d'armee fantoche." He said the NLF need not participate in negotiations-- as long as the issues do not concern SVN (PENNSYLVANIA, 7/25/67).

The latter point was repeated through the Norwegians in August (OHIO, 8/16/67). But in the end, the Americans would "have to accept the political situation in SVN as it is, as de Gaulle did in Algeria." "The question of representation was of great importance" (OHIO, 8/16/67). Later, the Norwegians were asked to find out if the U.S. was "willing to accept the liberation front as a political factor" (OHIO, 8/21/67). The Norwegians took this to mean as a "factor in preliminary talks, actual negotiations (and) in a post-settlement situation." They also conveyed to us the DRV's desire for a "non-communist" coalition government in SVN. (The DRV indicated to them that it considered the NLF "non-communist" too.) Their interlocutor's "tone gave the impression" that members of the GVN would be acceptable, although this was not made explicit; the North Vietnamese did concede that the GVN "was a political factor in SVN (9/8/67). This too is in the pattern of the Laos settlement, in which representation at the conference finally devolved upon three political "tendencies" (right, neutral and left), which ultimately became the three elements of a coalition government.

Last February, DRV Ambassador Su told the Italians that there should be a "very broadly based" government, "excluding only 'war criminals' (undefined)"(KILLY, 2/23/68).

As late as March, the Norwegians were told again that a political solution for SVN "was a question which must be discussed with the NLF and Hanoi cannot speak on behalf of SVN."

The ANDPF Program denounces the GVN as a "lackey administration" and says the NLF "cannot be excluded from the settlement of all problems in SVN. We advocate contacts with the NLF...." But it offers, apparently acting alone, "to discuss these problems with the US government" (4/25/68). This is possibly intended as a face saving way for the U.S. to begin negotiations with the communists without according status to the NLF. The ANDPF may also offer the "neutralist" political tendency from which a solution after the Laos pattern could be fashioned: NLF members on the left; ANDPF in the middle; selected GVN members on the right.

The GVN

Throughout, the GVN has insisted upon its sole right to speak for SVN. Its 4 Points state, "the Hanoi Communist regime must dissolve all the puppet organizations it has formed in SVN under the names of 'Front for the Liberation of the South,' 'Liberation Radio' and the 'Peoples Revolutionary Party' (6/22/65). Thieu's current position is that the GVN and Hanoi are the parties to the war. If there are to be negotiations, they should be the protagonists with no role for the NLF. His prime objective is clearly to win recognition for his government from Hanoi, without our according any further status to the NLF. Although the present GVN constitution excludes communists and "pro-communist neutralists" from the electoral process, Thieu has accepted the principle of "one man-one vote," and agreed to meet with individuals who leave the NLF, but he would not accept the NLF itself as a "political entity" (Bunker's Meet the Press interview, 11/19/67).[28]

The U.S.

Our position has been consistently that the NLF had no role "as of right" in SVN and that we would not guarantee a role for it before elections, because to do so would be contrary to free determination. Individual members of the NLF, however, could participate in the political process in SVN (XYZ, 9/8/65; Rangoon, 2/16/66). Should the DRV decide to negotiate, "the Viet Cong would not have difficulty being represented and having their views presented" (U.S. 14 Points, 1/3/66; Goldberg, 2/10/67). We drew attention to the internationally recognized status of the GVN and argued that the GVN's National Reconcilation Program offered a route by which individual members of the NLF could participate in the "normal political processes of SVN" under GVN auspices (Manila Communique, 10/25/66; Goldberg, 2/10/67).[29]

8

Several episodes may have suggested to the DRV some elements of "give" in our position: Gullion's instructions stated, "At most, the future of the NLF should be a matter for discussion, not something settled in principle before negotiations begin" (XYZ, 8/15/65). Lewandowski's 10 Points, accepted by us "subject to important differences of interpretation" said, "the present status quo in SVN would be changed in order to take into account the interests of the parties presently opposing the policy of the US in SVN" (MARIGOLD, 11/30/66). Goldberg (11/2/67) told the Senate Foreign Relations Committee that the U.S. "would not stand in the way of groups, including the NLF," being invited to appear before the UN Security Council.[30] The U.S. privately indicated to the UN Secretariat that visas would be issued for such a group if certain clarifications were obtained; the latter, however, were apparently not forthcoming and no visas were actually issued. In his March 31 speech, President Johnson said, "there may come a time when South Vietnamese-- on both sides--are able to work out a way to settle their own differences by free political choice rather than by war."[31]

4. Reunification

Summary

The U.S. position on reunification of Vietnam can be separated
into what we have been saying publicly and what we really want. Publicly, the U.S. 14 Points (1/3/66) state:

"10. The question of reunification of Vietnam should be
determined by the Vietnamese through their own free decision;

"11. The countries of Southeast Asia can be nonaligned
or neutral if that be their option;"

The U.S. position is perhaps more accurately stated in the Manila
Communique (10/25/66):

"The Government and people of South Vietnam deplore
the partition of Vietnam into North and South. But this
partition brought about by the Geneva Agreements of 1954,
however unfortunate and regrettable, will be respected
until, by the free choice of all Vietnamese, reunification
is achieved."

President Johnson has gone even further (4/7/65) when he said that "our
objective is the independence of South Vietnam and its freedom from
attack." Our preference is clearly for the continued separate existence
of South Vietnam, but the impression of our public statements has been
that we favor reunification through free Vietnam-wide elections after
aggression has ceased.

The North Vietnamese position appears forthcoming and appears similar
to the impressions of our own public statements. They have indicated that
they would not press for reunification, that reunification could be determined well in the future by free decision of all the Vietnamese people,
and that the interim state in South Vietnam would be non-socialist and
neutral. Hanoi can afford to make their reunification position look
appealing because it is really a secondary issue. Their position is and
they will press for a political solution in South Vietnam favorable to
them, and then let the issue of reunification take care of itself -- in
a time period when U.S. interests will not be humiliated.

What is the DRV position?

There are several statements in the 4 Points which bear on this
issue: (a) "The USG must...dismantle all U.S. military bases /in SVN/,
and cancel its military alliance with SVN"; (b) "Pending the peaceful
reunification of Vietnam, while Vietnam is still temporarily divided

10

into two zones...."; and (c) "The peaceful reunification of Vietnam is to be settled by the Vietnamese people in both zones, without any foreign interference."

In June 1964, Pham Van Dong told Blair Seaborn that reunification is a "drame national, fondamental." He added, somewhat inconsistently, that neutrality for SVN, and by implication reunification, would be something for the people of SVN to decide; he did not "prejudge" the outcome. More recently (PENNSYLVANIA 7/25/67), Pham Van Dong said that Hanoi goals for South Vietnam were "independence, democracy, peace, and neutrality."

What do these general statements add up to in operational terms? When?

On the timing of reunification, the DRV has given a range of statements including, "no hurry" (XYZ 7/16/65), "indefinite postponement" (OHIO 8/16/67), "until South Vietnam is ready," "10 or 20 years" (Burchett 2/11/67). But, as the Swedes informed us (ASPEN 11/11/66), Trinh said to them that it is necessary to create such conditions as will permit a move in the direction of reunification. In other words, reunification, according to the DRV need not occur at any specific or early time, but that it will happen at some future point must be assured by present decisions. These decisions basically seem to revolve around a political settlement in South Vietnam. As Loan told Algard (OHIO 3/3/67), "first there must be a political solution in South Vietnam." At first glance, Hanoi's position on reunification looks like a compromise. Indeed, Hanoi has been playing it up as a compromise, indicating that postponement of reunification is at variance with the 1954 Geneva Accords which called for reunification within two years of settlement, i.e., 1956. The hooker, of course, is that the realization of reunification in the future is merely a corollary of other points, mainly control of the government in the south, and need not be fought for in its own terms.

How and by Whom?

Lewandowski (MARIGOLD 11/14/66) spoke of reunification by free determination, adding that this could take the form of either a referendum or an election. While he did not spell out this issue, apparently a referendum would be a Vietnam-wide single issue vote on reunification. By elections, he could have meant that reunification would be decided on a government to government basis (the DRV with the new South Vietnam government), each government having been chosen by "free elections." In support of the latter method, Pham Van Dong stated (PENNSYLVANIA 7/25/67): "Once the war in the South is settled, we shall discuss with the South and find the best means." Additionally, and to confuse the issue further, virtually all the DRV statements on this issue stress that reunification is to come through free determination "by the people in both zones" (the 4 Points). This is the wording of the 1954 Geneva Accords, and it means that the people of South Vietnam alone will not decide the matter, that the people in the north must have their say as well. By this country-wide vote formula, it is likely that even a solid majority vote in SVN against reunification would be overtaken by the near unanimous vote for reunification in North Vietnam.

A final and related qualifier is that the free decision on reunification must be without foreign interference. Presumably, this is to convey the DRV belief that no outsiders can or should be present in Vietnam when the decision on reunification is being made.

Nature of interim state in South Vietnam?

The DRV has used three elements to define what the Government of South Vietnam would look like pending reunification. First, Hanoi has described it as neutral in the "Cambodian manner" (MARIGOLD 9/18/66). This implies independence, but more reliance on Asian and particularly Asian communist influences. Cambodian neutrality is not noted for being sympathetic to the U.S., nor is it noted for knuckling under to China or North Vietnam. Cambodia has also renounced SEATO protection. Hanoi has also described this government as being "non-socialist." After talking with the DRV leadership, Burchett (2/11/67) said that Hanoi thought of itself as a "socialist country and a member of the socialist world but without military alliances or foreign military bases, militarily but not politically neutral," and thought of the south as "non-socialist and neutral militarily, politically, and diplomatically." In a very revealing statement (PENNSYLVANIA 7/25/67), Pham Van Dong said: "Some people think we want to impose socialism on the south. We are convinced that the NLF will not make such an error." It is important to recall, however, that the communists consider the NLF to be "non-communist," a front of diverse political groupings. The third element has been the implication that there need be no change in the foreign affairs of the interim South Vietnam government (MARIGOLD 6/27/66). Such a statement would imply that South Vietnam could continue under western alliance protection and that the government would be able to receive aid from all countries. This element, reported only in the first MARIGOLD contact, is in contradiction with the first element emphasizing neutrality. Except, perhaps, for the aid provision, it is probably nothing more than a come-on.

What do these statements add up to?

They seem to mean that Hanoi understands that the U.S. has a definite stake in South Vietnam, and that even in the future would not take happily to the appearance (or the reality?) of South Vietnam being absorbed into the communist bloc. When Pham Van Dong said that "the NLF will not make such an error," he probably meant that they understood the importance in U.S. eyes of appearances. The DRV must get its way, but it is saying that it will not do so in a way that will threaten western interests.

Relation of interim South Vietnam government to DRV?

Burchett (2/11/67) even gives us a glimpse of how Hanoi views relations between the two interim zones or governments. He says: "For regulating north-south relations, there would be a type of general assembly, presumably nominated by the respective parliaments to handle questions important to both zones, such as, trade, post and telegraph, inter-zonal travel, including sports and cultural exchanges. The assembly, in fact, would have some resemblance to the inter-German council, an idea being tried out by the West German social democratics as a means to handle current practical problems between East and West Germany. This idea goes back as far as 1955, when the DRV introduced the proposal for the Fatherland Front.[32]

5. INTERNATIONAL GUARANTEES AND INSPECTION

This has always been a very real and important issue to the U.S. and the GVN on the one hand, and kind of a non-issue to Hanoi on the other hand. In the four points which we handed to the DRV in Rangoon (PINTA 2/16/66), we stated: "Strict compliance with the military provisions of the Geneva Accords must be achieved in accordance with schedules and appropriate safeguards to be agreed upon in the said discussions or negotiations." Later, in the Manila Communique (10/25/66), it was stated that: "The people of South Vietnam, mindful of their experience since 1954, insist that any negotiations leading to the end of hostilities incorporate effective international guarantees. They are open-minded as such guarantees c n be applied and made effective."

There are four DRV statements on this subject:

First, Pham Van Dong has stated (SEABORNE 6/18/64) that "as far as the ICC is concerned, we are very glad to have you here. But don't put too many items on the agenda, don't give yourself too much work to do."

Second, Lewandowski asked us (MARIGOLD 11/14/66): "In the case of a cease-fire and negotiations, would the U.S. be ready to use the Geneva Agreement and the machinery of the International Commission in bringing peace to Vietnam, and if so, would the U.S. publicly declare its intention to this effect?"

Third, in Lewandowski's ten points (MARIGOLD 11/30/66), the fifth point states: "The U.S. is willing to accept the participation of 'all' elections and the supervision of these elections by an appropriate international body."

Fourth, Su told d'Orlandi (KEELY 2/23/68): "Both parties felt that problem of guaranteeing an agreement was increasing to decisive importance." According to d'Orlandi, Su seemed to categorically exclude the UN as a guaranteeing agency and Fanfani and Su agreed that the ICC was not in a position to guarantee anything.

These statements do not add up to much, but they are suggestive of the DRV's willingness to compromise on a point that they know is important to the U.S. -- as in the case of many other issues, so long as it does not detract from the central issue of who controls the government in the South. Hanoi's opposition to the UN is wellknown and of long standing, and they would probably object to UN supervision. The problem of North Vietnam and Communist China not being members of the UN would seem to preclude the UN's playing a role. Similarly, the DRV has evinced no affection for the ICC. However, the DRV has over

the years continued to report violations of the Geneva Accords to
the ICC, and because of the importance which the DRV attaches to the
Geneva Accords, would not likely take a stand against a future ICC
role.   In all probability, nevertheless, Hanoi would not itself propose
the ICC.   It is also doubtful that they would accept an enlarged and
strengthened ICC proposed by us.   The possibility remains of an all- ·
Asian supervisory body established on an ad hoc basis to deal with
Vietnam, but we have no evidence that Hanoi would be receptive to this.

    As long as the DRV feels assured that their control in the South
is becoming a reality or is a reality, they are not likely to quarrel
seriously over inspection and guarantee machinery.

6. CEASE-FIRE

Although Hanoi has repeatedly stated, and we have assumed all along, that the DRV will adopt a fighting-while-negotiating strategy, there is some chance that they will take the initiative in proposing a cease-fire once negotiations are underway.

We have had two hints on this possibility. The first came from Lewandowski (MARIGOLD 11/14/66), when he asked the following questions:

"In case of a cease-fire, would the United States be prepared to withdraw from the combat areas and not to interfere in the creation of a new government in Viet-Nam? The question of how the new government of Viet-Nam will be formed will certainly arise.

"In case of a cease-fire, would the United States undertake not to interfere in peaceful progress toward unification of Viet-Nam if the people so wish, whether by referendum or by election?

"In the case of a cease-fire and negotiations, would the United States be ready to use the Geneva Agreement and the machinery of the International Commission in bringing peace to Viet-Nam, and if so, would the United States publicly declare its intention to this effect?"

The second indication came from the very reliable Algard Loan exchanges (OHIO 2/10/68). Loan said that "Hanoi presupposed (assumed) that the military operations be stopped while negotiations are being conducted . . . ."

Hanoi's interest in a cease-fire does not mean that they would be interested in a genuine cease-fire. More likely, as in the case of Laos, they will pursue a strategy of negotiate-cease fire-fight-cease fire-fight, breaking the ground rules whenever they believe it appropriate.

Hanoi's possible interest in a cease-fire has a readily determinable purpose. If agreed to by us, it would give the NLF unchallenged authority in the areas it now controls. Such civil administration arrangements as may be made (as in the period following the 1954 Geneva Accords) would allow the NLF to develop local coalition governments.

The U.S. is on record publicly as favoring a cease-fire. The U.S. Fourteen Points, for example, state: "A cessation of hostilities could be the first order of business at a conference or could be the subject of preliminary discussions."

President Johnson has made repeated and unqualified statements about our willingness to accept a cease-fire.

SEABORN MISSION TO HANOI, JUNE 18, 1964

(EXCERPTS)

Seaborn Report on Initial Visit to Hanoi:
Call on PM Pham Van Dong

SEABORN MISSION TO HANOI, JUNE 18, 1964

(EXCERPTS)

Remarks of Prime Minister Pham Van Dong
to J.B. Seaborn, Hanoi, June 18, 1964

. . . .

"President Ho Chi Minh has explained what we mean by a just
solution. First it requires an American withdrawal from Indochina.
Secondly it means that the affairs of the South must be arranged
by the people of the South. It must provide for the participation
of the Liberation Front. No other group represents the broad wishes
of the people. The programme of the Front is the best one possible.
There must be peace and neutrality for South Vietnam, neutrality in
the Cambodian manner. Thirdly, a just solution means re-unification
of the country. This is a 'drame, national, fondamental'. But we
want peaceful reunification, without military pressures. We want negotiation 'round a table. There must be sincere satisfaction with
the arrangement for it to be viable. We are in no hurry. We are
willing to talk but we shall wait till SVN is ready. We are a
divided people, without even personal links across the dividing line.

"The United States must show good will, but it is not easy for
the USA to do so. Meanwhile the war intensifies. USA aid may increase
in all areas, not only for the SVN army but in terms of USA army personnel as well. I suffer to see the war go on, develop, intensify. Yet
our people are determined to struggle. It is impossible, quite impossible (excuse me for saying this) for you Westerners to understand the
force of the people's will to resist and to continue. The struggle of
the people exceeds the imagination. It has astonished us too.

"Since the fall of the Ngo brothers, it has been a 'cascade'.
The prospect for the USA and its friends in SVN is 'sans issu'. Rein-
forcing the Khanh army doesn't count. The people have had enough.
The SVN mercenaries have sacrificed themselves without honour. The
Americans are not loves, for they commit atrocities. How can the
people suffer such exactions and terror?"

. . . .

"Let me stress, insofar as the internal situation in SVN is
concerned, the realistic nature of the Liberation Front's programme.
It is impossible to have a representative government which excludes

3

the Front. The idea of a government of national coalition 'fait
boule de niege' in the South. The Laos pattern of 1962 should serve
as a guide for SVN.

"To return to Vietnam, it is a question of a 'guerre a outrance',
which the USA won't win in any event, or neutrality. He had not (as
I had suggested) referred to neutrality as a first step only. Whether
SVN would continue neutral would depend upon the people of SVN. He
did not prejudge the issue.

"The DRVN realize that the 'loss' of SVN for the Americans would
set off (what was the atomic expression?) a chain reaction which would
extend much further. The USA is in a difficult position, because
Khanh's troops will no longer fight. If the war gets worse, we shall
suffer greatly but we shall win. If we win in the South, the people
of the world will turn against the USA. Our people will therefore
accept the sacrifice, whatever they may be. But the DRVN will not enter
the war.

"If the war were pushed to the North, 'nous sommes un pays socialiste, vous savez et le peuple se dressera'. But we shall not force
the USA, we shall not provoke the USA.

"As far as the ICC is concerned, we are very glad to have you
here. But don't put too many items on the agenda, don't give yourself
too much work to do."

PRESIDENT JOHNSON, "PATTERN FOR PEACE IN SOUTHEAST ASIA,"
April 7, 1965

(EXCERPTS)

. . . .

"Our objective is the independence of South Viet-Nam and its
freedom from attack. We want nothing for ourselves--only that the
people of South Viet-Nam be allowed to guide their own country in
their own way. We will do everything necessary to reach that objective, and we will do only what is absolutely necessary."

. . . .

"These are the essentials of any final settlement.

"We will never be second in the search for such a peaceful
settlement in Viet-Nam.

"There may be many ways to this kind of peace: in discussion
or negotiation with the governments concerned; in large groups or
in small ones; in the reaffirmation of old agreements or their
strengthening with new ones.

"We have stated this position over and over again 50 times and
more to friend and foe alike. And we remain ready with this purpose
for unconditional discussions.

"And until that bright and necessary day of peace we will try
to keep conflict from spreading. We have no desire to see thousands
die in battle--Asians or Americans. We have no desire to devastate that
which the people of North Viet-Nam have built with toil and sacrifice.
We will use our power with restraint and with all the wisdom that we
can command. . .

"But we will use it."

. . . . .

"The first step is for the countries of Southeast Asia to associate themselves in a greatly expanded cooperative effort for development.
We would hope that North Viet-Nam would take its place in the common
effort just as soon as peaceful cooperation is possible."

. . . .

"For our part I will ask the Congress to join in a billion-dollar
American investment in this effort as soon as it is underway. And I
would hope that all other industrialized countries, including the Soviet
Union, will join in this effort to replace despair with hope and terror
with progress."

5

EXTRACT FROM PHAM VAN DONG SPEECH
April 8, 1965

DRV FOUR POINTS

. . . .

"...The unswerving policy of the DRV Government is to respect strictly
the 1954 Geneva agreements on Vietnam and to implement correctly their
basic provisions as embodied in the following points:

"1.   Recognition of the basic national rights of the Vietnamese people--
peace, independence, sovereignty, unity, and territorial integrity.   According to the Geneva agreements, the U.S. Government must withdraw from South
Vietnam U.S. troops, military personnel, and weapons of all kinds, dismantle
all U.S. military bases there, and cancel its military alliance with South
Vietnam.   It must end its policy of intervention and aggression in South
Vietnam.   According to the Geneva agreements, the U.S. Government must stop
its acts of war against North Vietnam and completely cease all encroachments
on the territory and sovereignty of the DRV.

"2.   Pending the peaceful reunification of Vietnam, while Vietnam is
still temporarily divided into two zones the military provisions of the 1954
Geneva agreements on Vietnam must be strictly respected.   The two zones
must refrain from entering into any military alliance with foreign countries
and there must be no foreign military bases, troops, or military personnel
in their respective territory.

"3.   The internal affairs of South Vietnam must be settled by the South
Vietnamese people themselves in accordance with the program of the NFLSV
without any foreign interference.

"4.   The peaceful reunification of Vietnam is to be settled by the
Vietnamese people in both zones, without any foreign interference.

"This stand of the DRV Government unquestionably enjoys the approval
and support of all peace and justice-loving governments and peoples in the
world.   The government of the DRV is of the view that the stand expounded here
is the basis for the soundest political settlement of the Vietnam problem.

"If this basis is recognized, favorable conditions will be created for
the peaceful settlement of the Vietnam people, and it will be possible to
consider the reconvening of an international conference along the pattern
of the 1954 Geneva conference on Vietnam."

. . . .

"The NFLSV, the mobilizer and organizer of the patriotic forces in South
Vietnam, the leader which has taken the people to ever greater victories, is
now controlling three-fourths of the territory and two-thirds of the population of South Vietnam.   It has ever higher international prestige and position, and is being more and more recognized by foreign countries and world
public opinion as the sole genuine representative of the South Vietnamese
people."

. . . ..

6

EXTRACT OF SPEECH BY SOUTH VIETNAM
FOREIGN MINISTER TRAN VAN DO
June 22, 1965

TRAN VAN DO'S FOUR POINTS

1. Since the present war in Viet-Nam was provoked
by Communist aggression and subversion, first of all,
it is important that subversive and military activities
undertaken, directed and supported by outside forces
against the independence and liberty of the people of
South Viet-Nam must cease. The principle of non-
interference in the internal affairs of the two parts--
principles declared in the Geneva Accords of 1954 as
well as by international morality -- must be respected.
Consequently, the Hanoi Communist regime must dissolve
all the puppet organizations it has formed in South Viet-
Nam under the names of "Front for the Liberation of the
South," "Liberation Radio" and the "People's Revolutionary Party." Also it must withdraw from South Viet-
Nam troops, political and military cadres it had illegally
introduced into South Viet-Nam.

2. South Viet-Nam must be left alone, to choose and
shape for itself its own destiny in accordance with
established democratic processes without any intervention
of whatever form and whatever source. Obviously these
could be realized only when the aggression initiated by
the Hanoi regime is ended and its intimidation campaign
against the South Vietnamese people decisively suppressed.

3. Only when aggression has ceased, and only then, it
will be possible for the Government of the Republic of
Vietnam and for nations which provide it with assistance,
to withhold defensive military measures on the territory of
South Viet-Nam and outside its borders. Such measures are
presently necessary for defending the territory of South
Viet-Nam against Communist aggression. Besides, the
Government of the Republic of Viet-Nam is ready to ask
these friendly countries to withdraw their military forces
from South-Vietnam. However, it shall reserve its right
to take all measures to restore order and law on the entire
territory of South-Viet-Nam and to assure security for the
people of South Viet-Nam as well as the right to call again
for foreign assistance in case of renewed aggression or
renewed threat of aggression.

4. Finally, the independence and liberty of the Vietnamese people must be effectively guaranteed.

7

PRESIDENT JOHNSON, "PRESS CONFERENCE,"
July 28, 1965

(EXCERPTS)

. . . .

"What are our goals in that war-stained land?

"First, we intend to convince the Communists that we cannot be defeated by force of arms or by superior power. They are not easily convinced...."

. . . .

"Second, once the Communists know, as we know, that a violent solution is impossible, then a peaceful solution is inevitable.

"We are ready now, as we have always been, to move from the battlefield to the conference table. I have stated publicly and many times, again and again, America's willingness to begin unconditional discussions with any government at any place at any time...."

. . . .

"...we do not seek the destruction of any government, nor do we covet a foot of any territory, but we insist and we will always insist that the people of South Vietnam shall have the right of choice, the right to shape their own destiny in free elections in the south, or throughout all Vietnam under international supervision, and they shall not have any government imposed upon them by force and terror so long as we can prevent it."

. . . .

U.S.-DRV CONTACTS ("XYZ" FOUR POINTS),
August 6, 1965

The following was given to Mai Van Bo on August 6, 1965:

"Point I - The basic rights of the Vietnamese people to peace, independence, sovereignty, unity and territorial integrity are recognized as set forth in the Geneva Accords of 1954. Obtaining compliance with the essential principles in the Accords is an appropriate subject for immediate, international discussions without preconditions and subsequent negotiations. Such discussions and negotiations should consider, among other things, appropriate means, including agreed stages, for the withdrawal of foreign military and quasi-military personnel and weapons from South and North Viet-Nam; the dismantling of foreign military bases in both areas; the cancellation of military alliances in contravention of the Accords; and the regrouping and redeployment of indigenous forces.

"Point II - Strict compliance with the military provisions of the Geneva Accords must be achieved in accordance with schedules and appropriate safeguards to be agreed upon in the said discussions and subsequent negotiations.

"Point III - The internal affairs of South and North Viet-Nam must be settled by the South and North Vietnamese peoples themselves in conformity with the principles of self-determination without any foreign interference.

"Point IV - The issue of reunification of Viet-Nam must be decided peacefully, on the basis of free determination by the peoples of South and North Viet-Nam without foreign interference."

9

U.S.-DRV CONTACTS ("XYZ" FOUR POINTS)

Mai Van Bo Statements During "XYZ" Contacts

During these contacts, Bo did not deny DRV troop presence in SVN (8/18/65), or even that the 325th NVA Division was in SVN, but claimed it was not then engaged in military operations (9/3/65). After the XYZ contact had ended, Bo said there were no regular northern troops in SVN but that northern volunteers might have joined the Viet Cong (1/27/66).

Because Bo did not deny NVA troop presence in SVN, he was able to agree with the principle that troop withdrawal would have to be mutual, balanced, and phased (8/18/65). Bo reaffirmed his agreement to this principle on 8/18/65, but then denied any such agreements on 9/3/65.

On the timing of U.S. troop withdrawals, Bo, at first, said that this would be a "technical problem, as easily solved as with the French in 1954," and that "it could take place over 2 or 3 years" (7/16/65). Bo also said that the final settlement should see troop withdrawals completed (8/18/65). At the end of these contacts, Bo was insisting that U.S. troops must leave before elections were held (9/3/65).

After the contacts were over, Bo told a French journalist: "It contemplates three stages--in the first stage, the U.S. would agree on the principle of their departure before the South Vietnamese settled by themselves their problems, which cannot be resolved so long as a foreign army is on their national territory. The second stage is that of negotiation. The third is departure." (5/6/66)

With respect to self-determination, Bo had said to Duntov that this was "the one basic premise" needed for a solution to the Vietnam problem (7/16/65). Later, Bo seemed to be arguing that the Vietnamese will be left to solve their problems through elections only after the Americans have left (1/27/65). Much later, Bo told a French journalist (5/6/66): "How can elections be held in a country over which no authority is exercised?" Did he mean the exercise of authority is decisive in the electoral process? No doubt. In which case, the question of who should organize the elections--the NLF with DRV help, or the GVN with U.S. help--would be the real issue.

The U.S. position throughout the contacts was that the NLF had no role "as of right" in South Vietnam (9/8/65) and would not guarantee a role for it before elections because to do so would be contrary to "free determination." Individual members of the NLF could participate in the political process. At most, the future of the NLF should be a matter for discussion, not something settled in principle before negotiations began (8/15/65). In the event of a cease-fire, it was the U.S. intention to insist on the GVN's right to operate throughout SVN (9/1/65).

With respect to reunification, both the U.S. and Bo agreed (8/6/65) that it come about "on the basis of free determination." Bo said that the DRV was in a hurry to see reunification accomplished (7/16/65).

UNITED STATES FOURTEEN POINTS

January 3, 1966

1. The Geneva Agreements of 1954 and 1962 are an adequate basis for peace in Southeast Asia;

2. We would welcome a conference on Southeast Asia or any part thereof;

3. We would welcome "negotiations without pre-conditions" as the 17 nations put it;

4. We would welcome unconditional discussions as President Johnson put it;

5. A cessation of hostilities could be the first order of business at a conference or could be the subject of preliminary discussions;

6. Hanoi's four points could be discussed along with other points which others might wish to propose;

7. We want no U.S. bases in Southeast Asia;

8. We do not desire to retain U.S. troops in South Vietnam after peace is assured;

9. We support free elections in South Viet-Nam to give the South Vietnamese a government of their own choice;

10. The question of reunification of Vietnam should be determined by the Vietnamese through their own free decision;

11. The countries of Southeast Asia can be non-aligned or neutral if that be their option;

12. We would much prefer to use our resources for the economic reconstruction of Southeast Asia than in war. If there is peace, North Viet-Nam could participate in a regional effort to which we would be prepared to contribute at least one billion dollars;

13. The President has said "The Viet Cong would not have difficulty being represented and having their views represented if for a moment Hanoi decided she wanted to cease aggression. I don't think that would be an insurmountable problem."

14. We have said publicly and privately that we could stop the bombing of North Vietnam as a step toward peace although there has not been the slightest hint or suggestion from the other side as to what they would do if the bombing stopped.

12

DRV AIDE MEMOIRE, "PINTA-RANGOON,"
January 31, 1966

RANGOON 392

"Text of Aide memoire referred to in Embtel 391 as follows: Quote
I am forwarding to you the statement attached herewith made by the spokesman of the Foreign Ministry of the Democratic Republic of Vietnam dated
January 4, 1966 regarding the so-called 'Peace-efforts' made recently by
the United States.

"With regards to the 14 points and the subsequent statements of the
United States Government I hold that the American authorities still refuse
to recognise the fundamental national rights of the Vietnamese and people
namely peace independence, sovereignty, unity and territorial integrity
of Vietnam as stipulated by the 1954 Geneva agreements of Vietnam.

"The United States Government states that withdrawal of its troops
from South Vietnam will be effected only under American terms, that means
the United States refuses to withdraw its troops from South Vietnam.

"The United States Government states that it seeks no military bases
in South East Asian countries but on the other hand says it has to fulfil
its commitments with the S.E.A.T.O. Bloc.

"The United States Government says it respects the right to self-
determination of the South Vietnamese people on condition that the South
Vietnam National Front for Liberation lay down arms and be granted amnesty --
that means the United States tries to maintain a puppet regime in power
countering the South Vietnamese people, does not recognize the South
Vietnam National Front for Liberation as the sole genuine representative
of the entire South Vietnamese people and will not engage in negotiations
with the Front. The United States Government refuses to accept Point 3
of the 4-point stand of the government of the Democratic Republic of Vietnam,
that amounts to American rejection of all the four points.

"Concerning the 4-point stand of the Government of the Democratic
Republic of Vietnam. . I beg to quote the above-said statement of the
spokesman of the Foreign Ministry of the Democratic Republic of Vietnam:
'A political settlement of the Vietnam problem can be envisaged only
when the United States Government has accepted the 4-point stand of the
Government of the Democratic Republic of Vietnam, has proved this by
actual deeds, has stopped unconditionally and for good its air raids
and all other acts of war against the Democratic Republic of Vietnam.

"I am ready to listen to what the Ambassador may wish to expound
on the United States position."

. . . . .

13

<u>MARIGOLD TEN POINTS AND RELATED CABLES,</u>
<u>September–December, 1966</u>

Saigon 6280 (to SecState), S/Nodis, 18 September 1966

"1. D'Orlandi had a meeting with Lewandowski Friday night.
It started as a social affair on D'Orlandi's invitation and on
Lewandowski's initiative became a discussion of the war. According
to Orlandi, Lewandowski said the following:

. . . .

"5. If the Americans ever really cared, they should especially
concentrate on Pham Van Dong's fourth point concerning 'who is to
speak for South Vietnam.' This does not mean that Hanoi would be
trying to ram the Viet Cong down our throats. We could consider
the setting up of a coalition government the bulk of which would be
made up of 'sensible South Vietnamese politicians.' To preserve
appearances you could have 'on the fringe' men from the 'right' in
one or two 'unimportant ministries' and from on the 'left' fill one
or two 'unimportant ministries with the so-called NLF.'

"6. D'Orlandi -- this is unthinkable. If this is what you
want to talk about, it is better for us to stop the talks.

"7. Lewandowski asked whether D'Orlandi realized that what he
meant to say was that this would be the last step not the first.

"8. D'Orlandi said: What would be the ultimate goal? If it
is to have the Viet Cong in the Government of Viet Nam, I won't even
submit such a proposal to Ambassador Lodge.

"9. Lewandowski said that is not at all what he meant to put to
D'Orlandi. Plainly, the ultimate aim would be: 'to make of South Vietnam
a second Cambodia.'

"10. D'Orlandi said that makes more sense, it is at least worth
talking about.

"11. Lewandowski said: 'But I don't believe the Americans really
wish to talk. They are trying to do two things at once: military
escalation grouped with political proposals. You can't do both. So
long as they won't make up their minds, we can't do anything. We must
wait until November.'"

. . . .

LODGE

TEXT OF THE JOINT COMMUNIQUE ISSUED AT THE MA-
NILA SUMMIT CONFERENCE, MANILA, THE PHILIPPINES[1]

INTRODUCTION

1.   In response to an invitation from the President of the Republic
of the Philippines, after consultations with the President of the Republic of Korea and the Prime Ministers of Thailand and the Republic of
Vietnam, the leaders of seven nations in the Asian and Pacific region
held a summit conference in Manila on October 24 and 25, 1966, to
consider the conflict in South Vietnam and to review their wider purposes in Asia and the Pacific. The participants were Prime Minister
Harold Holt of Australia, President Park Chung Hee of the Republic
of Korea, Prime Minister Keith Holyoake of New Zealand, President
Ferdinand E. Marcos of the Philippines, Prime Minister Thanom
Kittikachorn of Thailand, President Lyndon B. Johnson of the United
States of America, and Chairman Nguyen Van Thieu and Prime
Minister Nguyen Cao Ky of the Republic of Vietnam.

BASIC POLICY

2.   The nations represented at this conference are united in their
determination that the freedom of South Vietnam be secured, in their
resolve for peace, and in their deep concern for the future of Asia and
the Pacific. Some of us are now close to the actual danger, while others
have learned to know its significance through bitter past experience.
This conference symbolizes our common purposes and high hopes.
3.   We are united in our determination that the South Vietnamese
people shall not be conquered by aggressive force and shall enjoy the
inherent right to choose their own way of life and their own form of
government. We shall continue our military and all other efforts, as
firmly and as long as may be necessary, in close consultation among
ourselves until the aggression is ended.
4.   At the same time our united purpose is peace--peace in South
Vietnam and in the rest of Asia and the Pacific. Our common commitment is to the defense of the South Vietnamese people. Our sole demand on the leaders of North Vietnam is that they abandon their
aggression. We are prepared to pursue any avenue which could lead
to a secure and just peace, whether through discussion and negotiation
or through reciprocal actions by both sides to reduce the violence.
5.   We are united in looking to a peaceful and prosperous future for
all of Asia and the Pacific. We have therefore set forth in a separate
declaration a statement of the principles that guide for common
actions in this wider sphere.
6.   Actions taken in pursuance of the policies herein stated shall be
in accordance with our respective constitutional processes.

PROGRESS AND PROGRAMS IN SOUTH VIETNAM, THE MILITARY EFFORT

7.   The Government of Vietnam described the significant military
progress being made against aggression. It noted with particular
gratitude the substantial contribution being made by free world forces.

[1] White House press release dated Oct. 25, 1966.

8. Nonetheless, the leaders noted that the movement of forces from North Vietnam continues at a high rate and that firm military action and free world support continue to be required to meet the threat. The necessity for such military action and support must depend for its size and 'duration on the intensity and duration of the Communist aggression itself.

9. In their discussion, the leaders reviewed the problem of prisoners of war. The participants observed that Hanoi has consistently refused to cooperate with the International Committee of the Red Cross in the application of the Geneva Conventions, and called on Hanoi to do so. They reaffirmed their determination to comply fully w :h the Geneva Conventions of 1949 for the Protection of War Victims, and welcomed the resolution adopted by the Executive Committee of the League of Red Cross Societies on October 8, 1966, calling for complicanc with the Geneva Conventions in the Vietnam cc iflict, full support for the International Committee of the Red Cross, and immediate action to repatriate seriously sick and wounded prisoners of war. They agreed to work toward the fulfillment of this resolution, in cooperation with the International Committee of the Red Cross, and indicated their willingness to meet under the auspices of the ICRC or in any appropriate forum to discuss the immediate exchange of prisoners.

PACIFICATION AND REVOLUTION DEVELOPMENT

10. The participating governments concentrated particular attention on the accelerating efforts of the Governments of Vietnam to forge a social revolution of hope and progress. Even as the conflict continues, the effort goes forward to overcome the tyranny of poverty, disease, illiteracy and social injustice.

11. The Vietnamese leaders stated their intent to train and assign a substantial share of the armed forces to clear-and-hold actions in order to provide a shield behind which a new society can be built.

12. In the field of Revolutionary Development, measures along the lines developed in the past year and a halt will be expanded and intensified.[33] The training of Revolutionary Development cadres will be improved. More electricity and good water will be provided. More and better schoold will be built and staffed. Refugees will be taught new skills. Health and medical facilities will be expanded.

13. The Vietnamese Government declared that it is working out a series of measures to modernize agriculture and to assure the cultivator the fruits of his labors. Land reform and tenure provisions will be granted top priority. Agricultural credit will be expanded. Crops will be improved and diversified.

14. The Vietnamese leaders emphasized that underlying these measures to build confidence and cooperation among the people there must be popular conviction that honesty, efficiency and social justice form solid cornerstones of the Vietnamese Government's programs.

15. This is a program each of the conferring governments has reason to applaud recognizing that it opens a brighter hope for the people of Vietnam. Each pledged its continuing assistance according to its means, whether in funds or skilled technicians or equipment. They noted also the help in non-military fields being given by other countries and expressed the hope that his help will be substantially increased.

16

ECONOMIC STABILITY AND PROGRESS

16. The Conference was told of the success of the Government of Vietnam in controlling the inflation which, if unchecked, could undercut all efforts to bring a more fulfilling life to the Vietnamese people. However, the Vietnamese leaders reaffirmed that only by constant effort could inflation be kept under control. They described their intention to enforce a vigorous stabilization program, to control spending, increase revenues, and seek to promote savings in order to hold the 1967 inflationary gap to the minimum practicable level. They also plan to take further measures to insure maximum utilization of the Port of Saigon, so that imports urgently needed to fuel the military effort and buttress the civil economy can flow rapidly into Vietnam.

17. Looking to the long-term future of their richly endowed country, the Vietnamese representatives described their views and plans for the building of an expanded postwar economy.

18. Military installations where appropriate will be converted to this purpose, and plans for this will be included.

19. The conferring nations reaffirmed their continuing support for Vietnamese efforts to achieve economic stability and progress. Thailand specifically noted its readiness to extend substantial new credit assistance for the purchase of rice and the other nations present reported a number of plans for the supply of food or other actions related to the economic situation. At the same time the participants agreed to appeal to other nations and to international organizations committed to the full and free development of every nation, for further assistance to the Republic of Vietnam.

20. The representatives of Vietnam noted that, even as the Conference met, steps were being taken to establish a new constitutional system for the Republic of Vietnam through the work of the Constituent Assembly, chosen by so large a proportion of the electorate last month.

21. The Vietnamese representatives stated their expectation that work on the Constitution would go forward rapidly and could be completed before the deadline of March 1967. The Constitution will then be promulgated and elections will be held within six months to select a representative government.

22. The Vietnamese Government believes that the democratic process must be strengthened at the local as well as the national level. The Government of Vietnam announced that to this end it will begin holding village and hamlet elections at the beginning of 1967.

23. The Government of Vietnam announced that it is preparing a program of National Reconciliation. It declared its determination to open all doors to those Vietnamese who have been misled or coerced into casting their lot with the Viet Cong. The Government seeks to bring them back to participate as free men in national life under amnesty and other measures. Former enemies are asked only to lay down their weapons and bring their skills to the service of the South Vietnamese people.

17

24. The other participating nations welcomed the stated expectation
of the Vietnamese representatives that work on the Constitution
will proceed on schedule, and concurred in the conviction of the Government of the Republic of Vietnam that building representative,
constitutional government and opening the way for national reconciliation are indispensable to the future of a free Vietnam.

THE SEARCH FOR PEACE

25. The participants devoted a major share of their deliberations to
peace objectives and the search for a peaceful settlement in South
Vietnam. They reviewed in detail the many efforts for peace that have
been undertaken, by themselves and other nations, and the actions of
the United Nations and of His Holiness the Pope. It was clearly
understood that the settlement of the war in Vietnam depends on
the readiness and willingness of the parties concerned to explore and
work out together a just and reasonable solution. They noted that
Hanoi still showed no sign of taking any step toward peace, either
by action or by entering into discussions or negotiations. Nevertheless,
the participants agreed that the search for peace must continue.

26. The Government of the Republic of Vietnam declared that the
Vietnamese people, having suffered the ravages of war for more than
two decades, were second to none in their desire for peace. It welcomes
any initiative that will lead to an end to hostilities, preserves the
independence of South Vietnam and protects the right to choose their
own way of life.

27. So that their aspirations and position would be clear to their
allies at Manila and friends everywhere, the Government of the
Republic of Vietnam solemnly stated its views as to the essential
elements of peace in Vietnam:

(1) Cessation of aggression.--At issue in Vietnam is a struggle
for the preservation of values which people everywhere have
cherished since the dawn of history: the independence of peoples
and the freedom of individuals. The people of South Vietnam
ask only that the aggression that threatens their independence
and the externally supported terror that threatens their freedom
be halted. No self-respecting people can ask for less. No peace-
loving nation should ask for more.

(2) Preservation of the territorial integrity of South Vietnam.--
The people of South Vietnam are defending their own territory
against those seeking to obtain by force and terror what they have
been unable to accomplish by peaceful means. While sympathizing with the plight of their brothers in the North and while
disdaining the regime in the North, the South Vietnamese people
have no desire to threaten or harm the people of the North or
invade their country.

(3) Reunification of Vietnam.--The Government and people of
South Vietnam deplore the partition of Vietnam into North and
South. But this partition brought about by the Geneva Agreements of 1954 however unfortunate and regrettable, will be
respected until by the free choice of all Vietnamese, reunification is achieved.

18

(4) Resolution of internal problems.--The people of South Vietnam seek to resolve their own internal differences and to this end are prepared to engage in a program of national reconciliation. When the aggression has stopped, the people of South Vietnam will move more rapidly toward reconciliation of all elements in the society and will move forward, through the democratic process, toward human dignity, prosperity and lasting peace.

(5) Removal of allied military forces.--The people of South Vietnam will ask their allies to remove their forces and evacuate their installations as the military and subversive forces of North Vietnam are withdrawn, infiltration ceases, and the level of violence thus subsides.

(6) Effective guarantees.--The people of South Vietnam, mindful of their experience since 1954 insist that any negotiations leading to the end of hostilities incorporate effective international guarantees. They are openminded as such guarantees can be applied and made effective.

28. The other participating governments reviewed and endorsed these as essential elements of peace and agreed they would act on this basis in close consultation among themselves in regard to settlement of the conflict.

29. In particular, they declared that Allied forces are in the Republic of Vietnam because that country is the object of aggression and its government requested support in the resistance of its people to aggression. They shll be withdrawn, after close consultation, as the other side withdraws its forces to the North, ceases infiltration, and the level of violence thus subsides. Those forces will be withdrawn as soon as possible and not later than six months after the above conditions have been fulfilled.

CONTINUING CONSULTATION AMONG THE PARTICIPATING NATIONS

30. All the participants agreed that the value of a meeting among the seven nations had been abundantly demonstrated by the candid and thorough discussions held. It was further agreed that, in addition to the close consultation already maintained through diplomatic channels, there should be regular meetings among their Ambassadors in Saigon in association with the Government of the Republic of Vietnam. Meetings of their Foreign Ministers and Heads of Government will also be held as required.

31. At the close of the meeting, all the visiting participants expressed their deep gratitude to President Marcos and to the Government of the Republic of the Philippines for offering Manila as the conference site, and expressed their appreciation for the highly efficient arrangements.

SWEDISH-DRV CONTACTS (ASPEN)

(Excerpts from Rusk-Nilsson MemCon, November 11, 1966)

. . . .

MARIGOLD TEN POINTS AND RELATED CABLES,
September-December, 1966

Saigon 10856 (to SecState), TS/Nodis, 14 November 1966

"1.   I met Lewandowski at D'Orlandi's apartment at 3:00 p.m.
aigon time.

"2.   ...on the eve of his visit to Hanoi.... He had four questions,
as follows:

a.   'Regarding the offer at Manila concerning the withdrawal
of U.S. forces from Viet-Nam on the condition that the troops of North
Viet-Nam would withdraw (and, he said, North Viet-Nam, of course,
doesn't admit that they are there at all), does this condition mean
the United States withdrawal depends on control by the present South
Vietnamese Government of territories not now under the control of Saigon?'

b.   'In case of a cease-fire, would the United States be prepared to withdraw from the combat areas and not to interfere in the
creation of a new government in Viet-Nam? The question of how
the new government of Viet-Nam will be formed will certainly arise.'

c.   'In case of a cease-fire, would the United States undertake not to interfere in peaceful progress toward unification of
Viet-Nam if the people so wish, whether by referendum or by election?'

d.   'In the case of a cease-fire and negotiations, would the
United States be ready to use the Geneva Agreement and the machinery
of the International Commission in bringing peace to Viet-Nam, and if
so, would the United States publicly declare its intention to this effect?'

"3.   I said that there were questions which I would have to refer
to the U.S. Government, and that I would do so and provide answers as
soon as I could."

. . . .

LODGE

MARIGOLD TEN POINTS AND RELATED CABLES,
September-December, 1966

Saigon 12247, TS/Nodis, 30 November 1966

"Lewandowski summarized the 10 points to Lodge as follows:

"(1) The U.S. is interested in a peaceful solution through negotiations.

"(2) Negotiations should not be interpreted as a way to negotiated surrender by those opposing the U.S. in Vietnam. A political negotiation would be aimed at finding an acceptable solution to all the problems, having in mind that the present status quo in SVN must be changed in order to take into account the interests of the parties presently opposing the policy of the U.S. in South Vietnam.

"(3) The U.S. does not desire a permanent or a long-term military presence in SVN.

"(4) The U.S. is willing to discuss all problems with respect to the settlement.

"(5) The U.S. is willing to accept the participation of 'all' in elections and the supervision of these elections by an appropriate international body.

"(6) The U.S. believes that reunification should be settled by the Vietnamese themselves after peace and proper representative organs are established in SVN.

"(7) The U.S. is prepared to abide by a neutral South Vietnam.

"(8) The U.S. is prepared to stop bombing 'if this will facilitate such a peaceful solution.' In this regard the U.S. is prepared to accept DRV modalities on the cessation and not require the DRV to admit infiltration into SVN.

"(9) The U.S. will not agree to 'reunification under military pressure.'

"(10) The U.S. 'will not declare now or in the future its acceptance of North Vietnam's 4 or 5 points.'

"Lewandowski asked if these 10 points were a proper formulation of the U.S. position. Lodge said that they seemed to be in order, but that the matter was of such sensitivity and importance that he would have to refer the points back to Washington for approval. Lodge added, however, that he saw two difficulties right off. First, he suggested changing Point 2 to read 'would' instead of 'must.' Second, he questioned the phraseology in Point 8 -- 'if this would facilitate such a peaceful solution.'

"Lewandowski insisted that his statement was a serious proposition based on conversations with the 'most respectable government sources in Hanoi.' Later Lewandowski admitted that Pham Van Dong was the source and that he had the 'Presidium behind him.'

"Lewandowski stated: 'I am authorized to say that if the U.S. are really of the views which I have presented, it would be advisable to confirm them directly by conversation with the North Vietnamese Ambassador in Warsaw.'

"Lewandowski said that there was a vital need to move quickly because (1) there was a danger of a leak and that secrecy was essential for Hanoi; and (2) that delays would give those 'working against a solution' time to 'put down the clamps on talks.'"

23

ADDRESS BY AMBASSADOR ARTHUR J. GOLDBERG, UNITED
STATES REPRESENTATIVE TO THE UNITED NATIONS,
AT A SPECIAL CONVOCATION AT HOWARD UNIVERSITY,   1
WASHINGTON, D.C., FRIDAY, FEBRUARY 10, 1967 /Excerpts/

Our effort to open the door to peace in Vietnam has been continuous. In recent weeks public attention has been focused on this
effort by an unusual number of statements, reports and events:
pronouncements by the governments involved, appeals by world
leaders including Pope Paul and Secretary General Thant, new stories
ε d interviews with various personalities--and the perplexing events
in Mainland China. Right now we are in the midst of another pause
in the fighting, the Lunar New Year Truce. Thus this may be a good
moment to assess the present status of our efforts for peace.
      In such an assessment, a responsible official, must in all that he says
in public, avoid damaging the hopes for progress through private
diplomacy. But in a free society he must also accept the inescapable
responsibility to keep the public adequately informed. It is difficult
to deal on both levels at once but it is essential to do so as well as
we can.
      Let me begin, then, by recalling the basic American peace aims in
Vietnam. These aims have been stated many times by President
Johnson and other responsible spokesmen of the United States.
They have been stated over a span of two years, but the ebb and flow
of the military situation during that time has not made them any less
valid as guidelines for peace negotiations. We do not subscribe to the
false notion that a strong military position obviates the desirability
of seeking peace through negotiations. Today, therefore, I wish to
review the essence of these American aims.
      The United States seeks a political solution in Vietnam. We do not
seek the unconditional surrender of our adversaries. We seek a settlement whose terms will result not from dictation, but from genuine
negotiations--a settlement whose terms will not sacrifice the vital
interest of any party. In the words of the Manila Communique:
"The settlement of the war in Vietnam depends on the readiness and
willingness of the parties concerned to explore and work out together
a just and reasonable solution." As President Johnson said a week

---

1 U.S. mission to the United Nations press release No. 13, dated Feb. 10, 1967.

ago here in Washington: Such a solution "will involve . . . concessions on both parts."   .   ·

We are not engaged in a "holy war" against communism. We do
not seek an American sphere of influence in Asia; nor a permanent
American "presence" oa ny kind--military or otherwise--in Vietnam; nor the imposition of a military alliance on South Vietnam.

We do not seek to do any injury to Mainland China nor to threaten
any of its legitimate interests.

We seek to assure to the people of South Vietnam the affirmative
exercise of the right of self-determination--the right to decide their
own political destiny free of external interference and force and
through democratic processes. In keeping with the announced South
Vietnamese Government's policy of national reconciliation, we do
not seek to exclude any segment of the South Vietnamese people
from peaceful participation in their country's future. We are prepared to accept the results of that decision whatever it may be. We
support the early consummation of a democratic constituti nal
system in South Vietnam, and welcome the progress being made to
this end.

As regards North Vietnam, we have no designs on its territory,
and we do not seek to overthrow its government whatever its ideology.
We are prepared fully to respect its sovereignty and territorial integrity and to enter into specific undertakings to that end.

We believe the reunification of Vietnam should be decided upon
through a free choice by the peoples of both the North and the South
without any outside interference; and the results of that choice also
will have our full support.

Finally, when peace is restored we are willing to make a major
commitment of money, talent and resources to a multilateral cooperative effort to bring to all of Southeast Asia, including North Vietnam,
the benefits of economic and social reconstruction and development
which that area so sorely needs.

These, then, are the peace aims of the United States. They parallel
the objectives stated by the South Vietnamese Government at Manila.
Our aims are strictly limited and we sincerely believe they contain
nothing inconsistent with the interests of any party. Our public
pronouncements of them--both in Washington and at the United
Nations--are solemn commitments by the United States.

Our adversaries--have also placed their aims and objectives on
the public record over the past two years. The major statement of
these aims is the well-known four points of Hanoi, which I will summarize without departing too much from their own terminology.

The first point calls for recognition of the basic national rights of
the Vietnamese people: peace, independence, sovereignty, unity and
territorial integrity. It also calls for the cessation of all acts of war
against the North; the ending of United States intervention in the
South; the withdrawal of all United States troops, military personnel
and weapons of all kinds, the dismantling of American bases and the
cancellation of what they term the United States "Military Alliance"
with South Vietnam.

The United States would not find any essential difficulty with a
reasonable interpretation of any of the terms included in this point.
Our chief concern is what it does not include: namely, that North
Vietnam also cease its intervention in the South, end all of its acts
of war against the South, and withdraw its forces from the South.

Such a requirement is obviously essential to the "peace" to which this first point refers.

The second point relates to the military clauses of the Geneva agreements. It provides that, pending the peaceful reunification of Vietnam, both the North and the South must refrain from joining any military alliance; and that there should be no foreign bases, troops of military personnel in their respective territories.

Here again, the only real difficulty is the omission of any obligation on the North to withdraw its military forces from the South--although the Geneva Accords which established the demarcation line in Vietnam forbids military interference of any sort by one side in the affairs of the other, and even goes so far as to forbid civilians to cross the demilitarized zone.

The third point calls for the settlement of the South's internal affairs "in accordance with the program of the National Liberation Front for South Vietnam." This point, of course, was not a part of the Geneva Accords at all. It introduces a new element which I shall discuss later in this analysis.

The fourth point calls for the peaceful reunification of Vietnam, to be settled by the people of both zones without any foreign interference. We have no difficulty with this point as was indicated in my speech to the General Assembly on September 22.

There has apparently been added a fifth point--put forward and repeatedly endorsed by both Hanoi and the National Liberation Front since the enunciation of the four points in April 1965. This fifth point was stated by Ho Chi Minh in January 1966 when he said that if the United States really wants peace, it must recognize the National Liberation Front as the "sole genuine representative" of the people of South Vietnam, and engage in negotiation with it. This, like the third of the "Four Points," introduces a new element which was not part of the Geneva Accords.

Now, from this brief summation of our aims and those declared by Hanoi, it is clear that there are areas of agreement and areas of disagreement. Recent public statements by Hanoi have been helpful in certain aspects, but how great the disagreements are is still uncertain because the stated aims of Hanoi still contain a number of ambiguities. I would like to discuss some of these ambiguities because they relate to very consequential matters.

There is ambiguity, for example, on the role of the National Liberation Front in peace negotiations. I have already noted the statement of Ho Chi Minh and other spokesmen for our adversaries who have said that we must recognize the Front as "the sole genuine representative of the South Vietnamese people, and negotiate with it." If this means that we are asked to cease our recognition of the Government in Saigon and deal only with the Front, insistence on this point would imperil the search for peace. For the Front has not been chosen by any democratic process to represent the people of South Vietnam. Nor has the Front been recognized by the world community. It is pertinent to recall that more than 60 nations recognize the Government of the Republic of Vietnam in Saigon, whereas none recognizes the National Liberation Front as a government.

On the other hand, some public statements seem to call for the National Liberation Front to be given a place or voice at the negotiating table. If this were the position of our adversaries, the prospects would be brighter; for President Johnson, as long ago as July 1965, said that "the Viet Cong would not have difficulty in being represented and in having their views presented if Hanoi for a moment decides that·it wants to cease aggression." He added that this did not seem to him to be "an insurmountable problem," and that "I think that could be worked out."

A further ambiguity relates to the role of the National Liberation Front in the future political life of South Vietnam. Hanoi asks that the affairs of South Vietnam be settled "in accordance with the program of the National Liberation Front." · Our adversaries, in their various comments on this point, take no notice of the internationally recognized Government of South Vietnam or of the steps which the South Vietnamese leaders have taken, and have currently under way, and the institutions they are now creating, for the purpose of providing their country with a constitutional and representative government.

Nor would their statements seem to leave any place for the South Vietnamese who have participated in and promoted such steps. Such an interpretation would pose serious obstacles to a settlement.

However, some claim that what the National Liberation Front really seeks is no more than the opportunity to advance its program peacefully along with other elements and groupings in the South in a free political environment.

We have already made it clear that we do not wish to exclude any segment of the South Vietnamese people from peaceful participation in their country's future and that we support a policy of national reconciliation endorsed by the South Vietnamese Government in the Manila Communique. Indeed, as Secretary Rusk said in an interview last week, if the Viet Cong were to lay down their arms, ways could be found to permit them to take part in the normal political processes in South Vietnam.

Further ambiguities arise concerning the question of foreign troops in South Vietnam. What does Hanoi mean by "foreign troops?" They clearly include in this term the forces of the United States and other countries aiding the South, but they have never admitted the presence of their own forces in the South. Of course, a one-sided withdrawal by our side would not lead to an acceptable peace. All external forces must withdraw, those of Hanoi as well as ours, if peace is to be achieved.

There is ambiguity also in Hanoi's position on the timing of the withdrawal of external forces. Do our adversaries consider withdrawal of forces as a precondition to negotiations, as some of their statements imply? If so, this again would raise a serious obstacle to progress. But if they look on withdrawal of forces as a provision to be incorporated in a settlement this clearly could be worked out. The United States and its allies are already on record in the Manila Communique that their forces "will be withdrawn . . . as the other side withdraws its forces to the North, ceases infiltration, and the level of violence thus subsides. Those forces will be withdrawn as soon as possible and not later than six months after the above conditions have been fulfilled." Further, we have indicated our willingness to join in a phased and supervised withdrawal of forces by both sides.

Next, there is ambiguity in Hanoi's position on the cessation of bombing of North Vietnam. At times their public statements have demanded that the bombing be ended unconditionally, without any

reference to a possible response from their side. On the other hand
quite recently a spokesman of Hanoi said that "if, after the definitive
and unconditional cessation of the bombardments, the American
Government proposes to enter into contact with the /North Viet-
namese/ Government. . . . this proposal will be examined and
studied." And just this week we have seen a further statement, in an
interview by the North Vietnamese Foreign Minister, that cessation
of the bombings "could lead to talks between North Vietnam and the
U.S." Many of their statements, insisting that the bombing cease
have also contained other expressions, such as that the American
military presence in South Vietnam be completely withdrawn and
that the "Four Points" of Hanoi must be recognized and accepted as
"the" basis--or possibly as "a" basis--for settlement of the conflict.
This creates an additional ambiguity as to whether Hanoi means to
add still other prenegotiating conditions.

The position of the United States on this bombing question has
been stated by a number of Administration spokesmen, including me
at the United Nations. The United States remains prepared to take
the first step and order a cessation of all bombing of North Vietnam
the moment we are assured, privately or otherwise, that this step
will be answered promptly by a tangible response toward peace from
North Vietnam. In his letter of February 8 to His Holiness, Pope Paul,
President Johnson said: [34]

. . . I know you would not expect us to reduce military action unless the
other side is willing to do likewise. We are prepared to discuss the
balanced reduction in military activity, the cessation of hostilities or
any practical arrangements which could lead to these results. We shall
continue our efforts for a peaceful and honorable settlement until they
are crowned with success.

Some analysts contend that our terms of settlement should be more
precisely defined. But it is very difficult to be more precise in advance
of negotiation and particularly in light of the substantive ambiguities
on the other side. But whatever questions may be raised, they should
and can best be resolved in discussions between the parties who have
the power to resolve them. For our part, we stand ready to negotiate
in good faith unconditionally to resolve all outstanding questions.

The United States approach to negotiations is flexible. We and our
applies do not ask our adversaries to accept, as a pre-condition to discussions or negotiations, any point of ours to which they may have
objections. Nor do we rule out the discussion of any points of theirs,
however difficult they might appear to us. We are willing to discuss
and negotiate not only our own points but Hanoi's four points and
points emanating from any other sources, including the Secretary
General of the United Nations.

It remains to be seen whether our adversaries share this concept of
negotiations. As I have already pointed out, their various public
declarations of peace aims have often been coupled with statements
that the goals they put forward must, for example, be "accepted" or
"recognized" as the "sole basis" or "the most correct basis" or "the
only sound basis" or "the basis for the most correct political solution."

Such statements contain still further ambiguity--in one sense the most fundamental of all, since it relates to the concept of negotiation itself. Do these statements mean that Hanoi is willing to enter negotiations only if there is an assurance in advance that the outcome will be on their terms and will, in effect, simply ratify the goals they have already stated? Such an attitude would not be conducive to peace and would make the outlook for a settlement bleak indeed.

If, on the other hand, North Vietnam were to say that their points are not pre-conditions to discussions or negotiations, then the prospects should be more promising.

Our negotiating approach would permit each side to seek clarification of the other side's position. It does not require the acceptance in advance of any points, least of all those whose meaning may be in need of clarification. We do not ask that of Hanoi--and progress toward a settlement will be facilitated if Hanoi does not ask it of us.

In this situation, how can we best move toward a settlement?

One essential early step is to analyze the positions of all parties in order to ascertain whether there is some element or some kernel common to all. Many students of the subject have pointed to one fact which may prove to be such a kernel--namely, the fact that both sides have pointed to the Geneva Agreements of 1954 and 1962 as an acceptable basis for a peaceful settlement.

But I must add quickly that this does not necessarily indicate a real meeting of the minds, because of doubts that all sides interpret the Geneva Agreements in the same light. Hanoi has said that the essence of the Geneva Agreements is contained in its "four points." But the fourt points would not put Hanoi under any restraint or obligations in its hostile activities against the South, which the Geneva Accords explicitly prohibit. Besides, as I already pointed out, these points insist that the South's future be regulated in accordance with the program of a group which was not referred to in the Geneva Accords and did not even exist when they were written, and in any case, if the Geneva Accords were to serve as a basis for settlement, it would obviously be necessary to revitalize the international machinery which they provided for supervision--which is presently operating under severe limitations; to incorporate effective international guarantees; and to update other provisions of the Accords which on their face are clearly out of date.

Despite these problems of interpretation, it can be said that if the meaning of the Geneva Agreements were accepted as a matter for genuine negotiations, then the constant reference to these agreements by both sides would be more than a verbal similarity; it would be a significant and hopeful sign of the prospects for settlement.

From all this analysis, there emerges one basic and practical question, and it is this: How are all these apparent obstacles to a settlement to be overcome?

The first and essential pre-requisite is the will to resolve them-- not by unconditional surrender or by the dictation of terms, but through a process of mutual accommodation whereby nobody's vital interests are injured, which would be a political solution. Speaking for the United States Government, I affirm without reservation the willingness of the United States to seek and find a political solution.

29

The next question, then, is by what procedures such a political
settlement can be reached.   One well-tested and time-proven way is
the conference table.   President Johnson has repeatedly stated our
readiness to join in a conference in Geneva, in Asia, or in any other
suitable place.   We remain prepared today to go to the conference
table as soon as, and wherever, our adversaries are prepared to join
us.

There is also a second procedure by which to pursue a political
settlement: namely, private negotiations--either by direct contact
or through an intermediary.   There is much to be said for this private
method, for ain a situation as grave as this, with its complex historical
background and its present political cross currents, it would be exceedingly difficult to negotiate in a goldfish bowl.

I therefore affirm that the United States Government stands ready
to take this route also toward a political settlement.   And we give our
assurance that the secrecy and security of such private explorations
would be safeguarded on our side.   Of course we do not and should
not ask that freedom of expression be curtailed in the slightest degree.
Nevertheless--as that conspicuous champion of free expression, Dr.
Erwin D. Canham, recently reminded us--no one's credibility ought
to suffer because of what is better left unsaid under such circumstances.

Let me quickly add that at this juncture I do not want to raise
any false hopes by this remark.   I am simply stating a principle which
is inherent in the concept of the secrecy and security of private
explorations.

Such then is my analysis of the problems involved and the methods
to be employed in seeking a negotiated solution of the Vietnamese
conflict.   Nor should we overlook the possibility that negotiations
private or public, might be preceded or facilitated by the process of
mutual de-escalation or a scaling down of the conflict without a
formally negotiated ceasefire.   This, of course, would be welcome on
our part.

It is altogether possible, too, that there will be no negotiations
culminating in a formal agreement; that our adversaries will sooner
or later find the burden of the war too exhausting and that the conflict
will gradually come to an end.

Perhaps this will indeed prove to be the outcome.   But our most
respected military authorities have cautioned us not to expect that
this will happen quickly, and that we must face the possibility of a
long struggle.   Surely, if there is any contribution that diplomacy can
make to hastening a just and honorable end of this struggle, we cannot
in all conscience spare any effort or any labor, day or night, to make
that contribution--no matter how difficult and frustrating the effort
may be, or how many false starts and failures and new beginnings it
may entail.

As students of history know, one obstacle to a negotiated end of
any war can be psychological.   The frame of mind appropriate to
fighting and the frame of mind appropriate to peacemaking are by
nature very different.   And yet a stage inevitably comes when both
these seemingly contradictory efforts must go on side by side.

30

Many citizens, viewing this complex dual process, are likely to be
confused and distressed by what seems like an inconsistency in their
leaders' policies. Some complain that the talk of peace suggests a
weakening of our resolve and of our will to win. Simultaneously others
complain that the continued military effort suggests an attempt to
bring the adversary to his knees, to break his will--and thus casts
doubt on the sincerity of our will to peace.

The great difficulty of achieving peace should serve to remind us
that there are substantial conflicting interests at stake which stubbornly resist solution; that peace cannot be bought at any price, nor
can real conflicts of purpose be waved away with a magic wand. By
the same token, the ferocity of war should not be an incitement to
hatred but rather a stern discipline--a reminder of the imperative
duty to define responsibly the limited interests for which our soldiers
fight and which a peace settlement must protect.

The effort to make such a responsible definition, and to carry it
through the process of peace negotiations, is "piled high with difficulty." A genuine meeting of the minds may never be wholly achieved.
It is unlikely that terms of settlement for this stubborn conflict can.
be found which would be wholly pleasing to either side. But it is in
our highest national interest that an acceptable, livable solution
should be found.

Lt no one suppose that patriotism, which is so inspiringly displayed
on the battlefield, is not also present at the negotiating table. All our
recent Presidents have testified to our country's dedication to negotiation as a means of peacefully bridging difference.

President Eisenhower said in 1955, on the eve of the first Summit
Conference with the Soviet leadership:

We shall work with all others so that peaceful and reasonable negotiations
may replace the clash of the battlefield.

President Kennedy, in his Inaugural Address, said:

Let us never negotiate out of fear. But let us never fear to
negotiate.

An President Johnson has summed up the true value of negotiation
as follows:

To negotiate is not to admit failure. It is to show good sense. We
believe that collective gargaining is working as long as parties stay in
negotiation. Only when bargaining breaks off do we speak of failure. And
so also in foreign policy. There, too, the rule of law and the resort to
the bargaining table are the hallmarks of success.

An to these words the President added specifically:

This rule applies without qualification to Vietnam. We shll count it
a mark of success when all the parties to that dispute are around a conference
table. We Americans are experienced in bargaining; we have nothing to fear
from negotiation. And we Americans know the nature of a fair bargain; none
need fear negotiating with us.

31

I am sure all three of these Presidents would agree today that the effort to discover through negotiation, the common ground on which to build a just and honorable peace, is worthy of our most sincere and dedicated efforts.

WRITER GIVES PLANS OF HANOI AND VIETCONG FOR
FUTURE VIETNAM [1]

The Associated Press asked Wilfred Burchett, an Australian Communist writer, to report the strategy of Hanoi and
the Vietcong as he had been able to discern it in his trips
to Vietnam. Burchett has often been a Communist spokesman
in Korea, Vietnam and Germany.

Phnom Penh, Cambodia, Feb. 10 (AP)--How Hanoi and the Vietcong view a future Vietnam which might emerge out of any negotiated
settlement was revealed in a series of talks I recently had with top
Vietnamese leaders of North Vietnam plus Liberation Front (Vietcong)
representatives in Hanoi and talks last August with the Front's
president, Nguyen Huu Tho, whom I met for the fourth time in his
jungle headquarters in South Vietnam.

The general idea is that Vietnam as such must be an independent
country without any foreign presence. Reunification is a long-range
project realizable only in the far distant future, which Vietnamese
leaders in the North and Liberation Front leaders in the South
privately agree may be 10 to 20 years away.

Meantime, the North would remain a Socialist country and a member of the Socialist world but without military alliances or foreign
military bases, militarily but not politically neutral. The South
would be non-Socialist and neutral militarily, politically and diplomatically.

The seeds for all this are provided for in North Vietnam's four-point
plan enunciated by Premier Pham Van Dong in April, 1965, and
acceptance of which until very recently had been thought in Washington to be a precondition for talks.

But in Foreign Minister Nguyen Duy Trinh's replies to my questions,
in which he said talks could start if bombings stopped, it was made
clear that acceptance of the four points was not posed as a precondition,
and far less was withdrawal of U.S. troops from South Vietnam made
a prior condition, as seems to have been though over a long period
in Washington.

The formula used by Foreign Minister Trinh was that the "four-
point stand and correct attitude the government of the Democratic
Republic of Vietnam enjoy were sure of even stronger approval and
support from all peace--and justice--loving peoples and governments
the world."

That this is not being posed as a precondition is one of the most
important of the clarifications in the Foreign Minister's statement.

But if Washington took a long, hard look at the four points one
top Vietnamese official said, it would find they entail important
concessions compared to the Geneva agreements.

The latter provided reunification by 1956, with the assumption that
the pro-Communist Vietminh would rule over the whole country.

---

[1] From the Washington Post, by Wilfred Burchett, Feb. 11, 1967.

The four points, which neatly dovetail into the five-point plan of the
National Liberation Front, were specifically formulated, according
to the same official, to facilitate American disengagement. While the
plan contains nothing contrary to the Geneva agreements, it makes
an important concession the indefinite postponement of reunification,
halts the spread of communism south of the 17th Parallel, and accepts
certain restrictions on the sovereignty of the North.

/The Geneva agreements of July 21, 1954, which partitioned Vietnam along the 17th Parallel, provided for unification elections by
July 20, 1956. However, the Ngo Dinh Diem regime in South Vietnam
spurned any such vote.

/Pham Van Dong's four points of April, 1965, included: (1) Withdrawal of all U.S. military forces from South Vietnam and an end
to all acts of war against the North; (2) No foreign military alliances
for either North or South; (3) Settlements of South Vietnam's internal
affairs in accordance with the program of the National Liberation
Front; (4) peaceful reunification without foreign interference./

What type of regime could the North and the Liberation Front
accept in the South? The Liberation Front considers it is in a strong
enought position militarily and politically to have a "decisive place
and voice" in any settlement of the Southern half of the problem.

In fact, as the Front's President Nguyen Huu Tho told me last
August, he envisages that a "broad coalition government of national
union" could be formed which, while excluding personalities like
Generals Nguyen Cao Ky and Nguyen Van Thieu, the present
Premier and President respectively, would not exclude some members
of their cabinet or others who served in previous Saigon governments
far back, even including that of Diem.

Such a government must be irrevocably committed to an autonomous South Vietnam independent and neutral. But explicit in the
Liberation Front and the North's five and four points is that independence means withdrawal of all U.S. forces and the dismantling
of bases.

/U.S. officials in Washington examined with interest the Communist
viewpoint as reported by Burchett, John Hightower of the Associated
Press reported.

/The officials said Communist acceptance of the idea of a long-term
non-Communist regime in the South was an interesting indication of
flexibility, Hightower reported.

/The plan for a coalition government in the South was also viewed
with interest, but the United States was pictured as being unwilling
to accept any such coalition that included "a decisive place and voice"
for the National Liberation Front. The U.S. view is said to be that
participation in South Vietnamese political life by individual Vietcong
leaders who would be loyal to an independent government would be
acceptable, but not participation by the NLF as an organization./

The Front's leaders, including those of the Marxist Revolutionary
Party, insist that although they would carry out the distribution of
land--this has already been done in areas administered by the Front--
they do not intend the collectivation of land or the socialization of
industry and commerce. They would accept aid from the West and
East, protect existing foreign interests, and would accept foreign

33

investments to help rebuild and develop the country when this did not infringe national sovereignty.

In this connection it is interesting to note that Nhan Dan (The People)--which is North Vietnam's Pravada--commenting on the Foreign Minister's statement on the possibilities of talks, seven times mentioned the term "peace and independence" as defining the Vietnamese main aims, but not a single mention of socialism. This fact is noted by foreign diplomats in Hanoi. This certainly does not imply any intention of abandoning socialism in the North, but does mean that the emphasis is on national aims, which do not foresee a Socialist regime for the South. And "socialism for the north, Democracy in the South" was the title of speech by Le Duan, secretary of the North's Communist Party, early in January.

A few months ago a bureau of the National Liberation Front was established in Hanoi--housed in the repainted, refurnished former American consulate.

Unlike other diplomatic missions it is not accredited to the government of the Democratic Republic of Vietnam, but in careful political distinctions is called the "representation of the National front for the liberation of South Vietnam in North Vietnam."

The desired implication of this, as carefully explained by gray-haired NLF central committee member Nguyen Van Tien, who has the "representation," is that it is a "concrete image of reunification" with the clear implication of South and North enjoying equal status.

When I asked if there was not a contradiction between the North's stated aims of "defending the North, liberating the South and reunifying the country," the Front's program of independence and neutrality, and his own statement that reunification is nearing, he said "no" and then gave the clearest exposition of how the North and South--as represented by the Liberation Front--viewed the future of North and South relations if the war ended and the Front was the dominant element of a government in the South.

His views are summed up as follows:

North and South Vietnam remain autonomous in internal and foreign affairs. The North would remain Socialist and a member of the Socialist bloc. The South would be neutral, unallied to any blocs. Each would have its own foreign ministries and own diplomatic representatives abroad. The Front already has over a dozen de facto embassies abroad.

For regulating North-South relations, there would be a type of general assembly, presumably nominated by the respective parliaments to handle questions important to both zones such as trade, post and telegraphs, interzonal travel, including sports and cultural exchanges. The assembly in fact would have some resemblance to the inter-German council, an idea being toyed with by the West German Social Democrats as a means to handle current practical problems between East and West Germany.

The question of negotiations between Hanoi and the Ky government in Saigon is seen as an impossibility. The latter is considered as representing no national interests or any section of the population and would die a natural death the moment serious negotiations started.

It is assumed Ky and a handful of his top supporters would make suitable dispositions, as so many of their predecessors did, for a comfortable exile. But it is also considered that national reconciliation is entirely possible with personalities and groups less engaged, if they

are prepared to take a clear stand on the question of complete national
independence. On that belief everyone is adamant. Ho Chi Minh
told a group, including myself, "the United States is offering us the
choice of colonial slavery or victory. Obviously we fight till the end."

Another personality, in replying to a question whether North Vietnam is prepared to offer anything in exchange for an American withdrawal, shrugged his shoulders, laughed and said:

"What do they want?

"Do they want us to invite into the North 400,000 Chinese, 40,000
North Koreans and a few thousand Cubans and then propose their
withdrawal as a counterpart for withdrawal of the United States
and her Allies from the South? Is that what they are after?"

NORWEGIAN-DRV CONTACTS (OHIO)

OSLO 4531 to SecState (SECRET-EXDIS),14 June 1967:

KISSINGER-BO CONTACTS (PENNSYLVANIA)

July – October 1967

Second Meeting with Pham Van Dong. July 25, 1967. Present: Aubrac, Marcovich, Pham Van Dong, Tach, note-taker.

. · . . . .

"Pham Van Dong resumed. 'Ending the war for us has two meanings: 1) An end of bombing which is permanent and unconditional; 2) A withdrawal of United States forces. We like the formula of President de Gaulle.'[35] Marcovich interrupted to say that it was not realistic. Pham Van Dong agreed and said that he realized that some U.S. troops would have to stay until the end of the process of political settlement. He added: 'We do not want to humiliate the U.S. Lenin did not like war but fought when necessary. As Lenin we are Communists.'

"'Now let me speak of U.S. policy and the NLF. We should have had unification in 1956. The period 1956-59 was a political fight. It saw the mutual assistance pact between the U.S. and Saigon and the introduction of U.S. staffs. This led to the formation of the NLF. The second period, 1960-64, saw a disintegration of the U.S. position to which the U.S. responded by 'special' war. /I suppose he meant 'special forces' war./ In 1965, the United States started a 'limited' war which lasts until today. At the same time the NLF has expanded its activities from the country into the cities and from inside Vietnam to the outside. Our position is: North Vietnam is socialist and wants to remain so. As for the South, our goals are national independence, democracy, peace and neutrality. Some people think we want to impose Socialism on the South. We are convinced that the NLF will not make such an error. The NLF envisages a broad coalition government, including all significant groups and religions without consideration of past activities including members du gouvernement fantoche et cadres d'armée fantoche. /He repeated the underlined words./ The essential thing is to forget the past. ·

"'As for unification, we recognize that the important first step is a political settlement of the South. We agree not to push things toward unification. Once the war in the South is settled, we shall discuss with the South and find the best means. Our people are magnificent.

"'Peace would have been easy for the U.S. three years ago. But with every year the political situation worsens. We do not like secret negotiations, but we recognize their necessity in this situation. As long as the issues do not concern South Vietnam, the NLF need not participate. However, we do not believe that the United States is ready for a settlement.' Then turning to Aubrac he asked: 'Que veulent les Americains?'"

These statements were confirmed by Bo on October 9, 1967--after persistent requests by the U.S. through M & A for confirmation. Bo said: "He who does not say 'no' agrees."

37

NORWEGIAN-DRV CONTACTS (OHIO)

OSLO 664 to SecState (SECRET-EXDIS), 16 August 1967

NORWEGIAN-DRV CONTACTS (OHIO)

OSLO 722 to SecState (SECRET-EXDIS), 21 August 1967:

NORWEGIAN-DRV CONTACTS (OHIO)

OSLO 1063 - Meeting on Friday, September 8.

. . . .

"5. _[Cooper]_ sought clarification of Loan's comments on the role
f the NLF, specifically whether 'political factor' meant as a factor in
preliminary talks, actual negotiations, or in a post-settlement situation.
Algard said his impression was that Loan meant all three stages. I then
laborated on the extent to which we recognized the NLF as a political
.actor in a post-settlement situation and/or the ways they might participate in negotiations. We cannot recognize them as a government or as .the
sole representative for the people of Vietnam. In the last analysis, we
believe the NLF question should be resolved in South Vietnam by the various
elements there. We will be prepared to accept anything which the Government of South Vietnam is ready to accept. It will be troublesome if in
the preliminary negotiations the NLF must participate in every stage.
We need clarification on this point. Algard said he was not quite sure,
but he had the impression that the North Vietnamese divided the problem
into questions affecting relations between Hanoi and the U.S. on the one
hand, and South Vietnamese problems on the other. Loan had stressed that
Hanoi could not speak for the NLF on matters affecting South Vietnam.
Algard said Loan had not been more specific on this point."

"7. On the question of 'non-communist South Vietnam,' I said that,
if indeed Loan had said they would accept a non-communist South Vietnam
and had said so under instructions, this was probably the first time this
formula had been used. Algard said Loan had stressed that Hanoi was
willing to accept a non-communist government which was a neutral government, and which would have relations with both East and West and received
aid•from both sides. Subsequently, at a reception on the day before
Algard left, Loan had said that Hanoi recognized the fact that they had
to live for some years to come in a Vietnam which would have two different
social and political situations.

"8. Loan had not explained what he meant by a 'coalition government'
and, in fact, used the terms 'coalition government' and 'non-communist
government'. almost interchangeably without giving an indication as to the
possible structure of the government, political grouping, etc.. He had
not stated that they would accept representatives of the present South
Vietnamese Government, but his tone gave the impression that they would.
In fact, Loan had said he deeply disliked the South Vietnamese Government
but, nevertheless, it was 'a political factor' in South Vietnam. (Algard
cautioned that in considering the term 'non-communist government' Loan
has indicated from time to time he does not consider the NLF communist.)
Loan told Algard he envisages a government with communist participation

but which is not communist-controlled. Loan had repeated his remarks
about a non-communist government directly to Algard in French at a
subsequent casual meeting, again using the phrase 'non-communist.'

  "9. I raised the question concerning Loan's comment that the
matter of the U.S. withdrawal was not decisive. Algard said Loan had
referred to the Geneva Agreement in this context using the example
of the withdrawal of French troops which, he said, had been no problem."

<u>RUMANIAN-DRV CONTACTS (PACKERS)</u>,
<u>December 16, 1967</u>

January 5, 1968 - Harriman-Macovescu Memorandum of Conversation:

The following statements were made by Trinh:

"'The basis for settlement of the Vietnamese issue is provided by the four points of April 8, 1965; the Ministry of Foreign Affairs subsequently issued its January 28, 1967 statement.[36] This is our position of principles on which no concession is possible.'"

. . . .

"'We are not against discussions but any discussions should take place according to principle. As soon as discussion engaged in, our attitude will be serious and responsible but it depends on attitude of the U.S. whether such discussions are fruitful.'"

<u>NORWEGIAN-DRV CONTACTS (OHIO)</u>

OSLO 3275 to SecState (SECRET-NODIS), 10 February 1968:

. . . .

"2. ..../Loan/ said that Hanoi presupposed (assumed) that the military operations be stopped while negotiations are being conducted...."

. . . .

ITALIAN-DRV CONTACTS (KILLY)

February-March, 1968.

<u>February 23, 1968</u> - Excerpts from Meeting of D'Orlandi-Su.

"....Both parties felt that problem of guaranteeing an agreement was increasing to decisive importance. Su seemed to categorically exclude the UN as a guaranteeing agency and Fanfani and Su agreed that the ICC was not in position to guarantee anything."

. . . .

"(J) Su stated that declared and also real aim of Hanoi was to have absolutely free general elections. To insure liberty of vote, it was necessary to constitute a government with very broadly based participation excluding only 'war criminals' (undefined). There was discussion of various South Vietnamese personalities as possible members of a Government. Su would raise a name and d'Orlandi would comment. Su generally did not reveal his opinion but Ky was obviously unacceptable to him."

. . . .

OSLO 3570 - Summary of Ambassador Algard's visit to Hanoi, March 3-10:

. . . .

OHIO

<u>NORWEGIAN-NORTH VIETNAMESE CONTACTS, JUNE 1967 - FEBRUARY 1968</u>

June 1-15, 1967   -   Meeting No. 1

OHIO began, in effect, with a transmission by Ambassador Tibbetts of a conversation in Peking on 1 June between Ambassador Ole Algard, Norwegian Ambassador to Peking, and the North Vietnamese Ambassador to Peking, Ngo Loan. Norwegian Foreign Minister Lyng gave the substance of the Algard-Loan conversation to Tibbetts. Despite some very interesting and important statements made by Loan, this cable and subsequent cables for several months were EXDIS and were not given a code name.

Loan stressed four points to Algard: (1) NVN fear that the U.S. intended to stay permanently in Vietnam; (2) that Hanoi had only one condition for negotiations (sic), namely the cessation of U.S. bombing; (3) that when Hanoi came to the conference table, it "would be very flexible," and is "ready for very far-reaching compromises to get an end to the war"; and (4) that Hanoi felt it was able to cope with almost any U.S. military activity with its own resources -- except for direct occupation of all North Vietnam.

Algard expressed concern about North Vietnamese treatment of U.S. prisoners. Loan said that formal recognition of these men as anything but "war criminals" would "legalize American participation in the war."

OSLO 4531 to SecState (SECRET-EXDIS), 14 June 1967:

"2. Following is my informal rendition Algard's report, transposed from first to third person:

TIBBETTS.

June 20, 1967

•State responded with an expression of interest and a desire to have
the Norwegians continue the contact. Noting the four major points in the
first Algard-Loan conversation, and admitting that Loan's statement that
bombing was the only condition for talks, was "highly plausible," State
suggested Algard react as follows: (1) ascertain the authority with which
Loan spoke; (2) stress the Manila Communique in general terms in response
to Loan's fear of the U.S. intending to stay permanently in Vietnam; (3)
ascertain whether North Vietnam was insisting on a permanent bombing cessation; (4) stress the U.S. view that the bombing cessation must be accompanied by "at least some private assurance of appropriate reciprocal
action by North Vietnam"; (5) indicate that the Geneva Accords of 1954
could be a basis for settlement and try to probe Loan on the compromises
envisaged by NVN.

State 213389 to Oslo (SECRET-EXDIS), 20 June 1967:

"2.c. Expressed concern that U.S. intends to stay permanently in Vietnam is of interest. We assume GON is fully aware
of our repeated statements of intent to withdraw and most specifically the precise wording used in the Manila Communique, which
you should furnish them.

"d. Discussion of cessation of bombing as only condition
for talks fits with other private readings as well as Trinh-
Burchett interview and appears to us highly plausible.

2

"e. Key passage appears to us to be reference to NVN
position being 'very flexible' and NVN being 'ready for very
far-reaching compromises.'

"f. Statements on NVN view of U Thant likewise seem
plausible, although GON may be interested that we had strong
indications NVN was displeased with U Thant's latest initiative
being launched after NVN had apparently given negative reaction
in Rangoon meeting.[1]

"g. References to NVN reluctance to seek Chinese help
are highly interesting. We are not repeat not ourselves sanguine
that NVN would not call for Chinese help in event of U.S. invasion, but report of Loan position remains extremel·· interesting as indicating depth of NVN reluctance.

"h. We are particularly appreciative of Algard remarks
on U.S. prisoners in NVN, which we believe hit exactly right
note.

"3. On basis of this evaluation, we believe it would be
extremely useful for Algard to have further conversation with
Loan. This could be through special meeting or chance encounter, and we would see no problem with special meeting, since
we surmise Loan remarks were intended to elicit some reaction
and that NVN would have assumed that we would be informed.

"4. Points we suggest Algard make would be as follows:

"a. Earlier conversation reported to USG, and GON has
reviewed U.S. views on matters stated. Both GON and U.S. assume
that Loan was speaking with authority. (This could be so put
as to elicit any contrary indication.)

"b. From conversations with USG, GON is clear that USG
fully understands NVN concern as to whether USG intends to stay
permanently in Vietnam. From discussions with USG over long
period, GON is convinced that USG is totally sincere in repeated
statements that it would seek no permanent military presence
or bases in Vietnam once settlement is reached, and that USG
and other nations assisting SVN meant just what they said in
Manila Communique. (We would prefer that this portion of
message be left in this general form. It is possible that Loan
would pick up elements of Manila statement, such as requirement
of withdrawal of both 'military and subversive' forces. If
this question should arise, Algard might say that it is GON
understanding that U.S. is referring to regular NVN military
forces but also to personnel originally from South who accepted
move to NVN in 1954 and were thereafter sent back to South.
Algard might say that he would be glad to get further clarification on this point if desired.)

"c. USG accepts that· 'cessation' of the bombing of the North and military action against the North is only NVN condition for holding talks. NVN has referred to cessation being on 'unconditional' basis: What is meant by this? (Purpose here is to clarify whether there may be any distinction between usual NVN statements that bombing must be stopped 'indefinitively and unconditionally' -- which we have construed to mean permanently -- and occasional other statements that stoppage of bombing must merely be 'unconditional.' We ourselves have assumed that no difference is intended between these two formulations, but direct inquiry could be useful in nailing this down.)

"d. Assuming that NVN condition calls for, in effect, permanent cessation of bombing, USG position remains as it has been stated throughout and particularly by Ambassador Goldberg in September 1966 at UN and by Secretary Rusk in January.[2] U.S. view is that cessation of bombing, without at least some private assurance of appropriate reciprocal military action by NVN, would create situation of major military advantage to NVN and would not be conducive to fruitful talks. USG has put forward several general suggestions for timing and nature of NVN reciprocal actions, and President's letter to Ho contained one specific proposal that added the element of stopping of reinforcement by USG in the South. Canadian proposal of April called for link between cessation of bombing and restoring demilitarized status of DMZ under effective supervision, but Hanoi rejected this.[3] What is present Hanoi view on these proposals, or do they have any other suggestion to make?

"e. USG naturally particularly interested in Loan remark that NVN would be flexible and prepared for compromises. Basic USG position is that settlement could be based on Geneva Accords of 1954, and USG would be prepared an any time to talk directly or indirectly about all the elements of such a settlement, including any aspects NVN wished to discuss. If Loan could at least indicate areas in which NVN envisages 'compromises,' this might be helpful in furthering better understanding of positions. Would the areas of possible compromise include the timing and sequence of actions related to withdrawal of forces on both sides, for example? Would they relate to position of NLF in the South? USG has consistently taken position that NLF cannot possibly be regarded as 'sole legitimate representative' of SVN and has also made clear that it cannot accept third of Hanoi four points, for which it finds no warrant in Geneva Accords of 1954? Is Hanoi suggesting its position on these points is now flexible? (Purpose of this inquiry is of course to feel out the key question of what Loan had in mind. If we knew the area Loan was referring to, a most fruitful exchange of views might then become possible, and we would of course be

4

prepared to discuss these issues in depth with GON.) In this connection, USG has made it clear to GON that it too is prepared to discuss realistic compromises, viewing the matter of an ultimate settlement from the standpoint of the Geneva Accords of 1954. USG has repeatedly noted NVN statements likewise expressing approval of Geneva Accords of 1954, and areas of common ground of compromise might well be found within this framework.

"f. We would leave it to Algard whether to raise the subject of prisoners again. We would have nothing to add to his excellent presentation, and it may be that he should merely say that his previous remarks reflected GON view, and that he would be interested in anything Loan might have to say to him on this subject. (We think representations on prisoners can be more effective coming, as they did in first conversation, from viewpoint of GON itself, and that USG support might if anything be less helpful in explicit form.)

"g. We would not repeat not suggest Algard try to reflect any USG views on conditions of NVN calling for Chinese help. If this topic should come up, Algard might express clear GON understanding that USG has repeatedly said it does not threaten NVN territory or regime and has no objective other than permitting SVN to determine its own future without external interference." KATZENBACH (Drafted by W.P. Bundy)

June 29, 1967

Tibbetts reported that after his first conversation with Algard, Loan had left for Hanoi, and that he was not expected to return to Peking until August. Algard was going back to Oslo for further instructions.

August 5-16, 1967   -   Meeting No. 2

The second meeting between Algard and Loan carried both dialogue and substance forward. Algard made it plain that he was informed of U.S. views, and Loan said that he would report to Hanoi. Loan did add, however, that he was prepared to comment "from a personal nature." This may indicate that Loan's standing in party circles is quite high and secure.

After reiterating the two main points of the first meeting (bombing pause is the only condition for talks and flexibility and compromise once talks begin), Loan made several interesting observations. He said that every time NVN "had previously shown willingness to negotiate, it had been misunderstood in the U.S. and seen as a weakness. The consequence...each time /being/ a new escalation on the American side." In this respect, he noted that world opinion was against the U.S. and that negro riots in the U.S. were part of this overall picture.

Loan emphasized a very new element in Hanoi's thinking. He said that "unsuccessful negotiations would be worse than no repeat no negotiations at all...It therefore appeared desirable to assure, prior to the starting of negotiations, that they would yield results." As a sign of Hanoi's flexibility in this regard, Loan gave examples of compromise: (1) reunification could be "postponed to an indefinite point of time in the future"; (2) "NVN is today ready to accept a separate South Vietnamese state which is neutral and based on a coalition government"; and (3) that the timing of the withdrawal of U.S. troops is not a decisive issue.

There was some question as to whether Loan used the phrase "non-communist" when describing this South Vietnamese state. It subsequently turned out that he had.

Loan expressed a desire to maintain the contact.

OSLO 664 to SecState (SECRET-EXDIS), 16 August 1967 (Section 1 of 2):

<u>August 18, 1967</u>

State responded matter-of-factly to the second meeting between Algard and Loan. While there seemed to be many provocative statements made by Loan, State's analysis said that except for the point about talking in advance of negotiations in order to assure that the negotiations are successful, everything else was old hat. Further explanation on this talks-negotiations point was needed.

State also began to grapple with the thorny problem of North Vietnamese reciprocity for U.S. bombing pause. The cable said that the U.S. was "flexible as to the form and nature of some corresponding restraint." In other words, Hanoi need not make a formal declaration of reciprocity. A bone was thrown in to the effect that we would discuss at a very early stage recognition of North Vietnamese sovereignty.

State 23083 to Oslo (SECRET-EXDIS), 18 August 1967

"1. We have read with greatest interest Ambassador Algard's full report of his August 5 conversation with North Vietnamese Ambassador Loan. For most part, views expressed by Loan do not represent substantive change from known Hanoi positions, e.g. seeming flexibility on such matters as timing of U.S. withdrawal and reunification coupled with unbudging insistence that U.S. accept NLF-type coalition and apparently recognize and negotiate with NLF on Algerian parallel. This of course goes to heart of matter, whether NLF is to be permitted dominant role in south, and Loan's comments add nothing to what we already know on this score.

"2. Nevertheless, one passage of report we find of considerable interest, namely, Loan's conclusion that if 'negotiations' were begun and broke down, this might lead to consequences which would be difficult to foresee, and that it would therefore appear desirable to assure in advance that negotiations would yield results. Loan's subsequent statement that 'the possibilities for a favorable result would thus have to be clarified to a certain degree in advance' represents perhaps clearest indication that we have had thus far that Hanoi might be interested in preliminary secret, private discussions in order to explore outline of possible settlement.

"3. We think it important to clarify this point without waiting for response from Hanoi to Loan's report of August 5 conversation. (We note Loan's expression of doubt on August 15 that he would receive any reaction.) We would therefore propose that Algard be instructed to contact Loan right away and take following line:

8

(A) Norwegian government has noted Loan's observation that unsuccessful negotiations would be worse than no negotiations at all and that it is desirable to explore in advance all possibilities to that negotiations could yield results. The Norwegian government has reason to believe that the USG is prepared to consider practical means to avoid this difficulty, if in fact it arises, and to explore all possibilities that exist for favorable outcome of negotiations. Norwegian government would be interested in learning Ambassador Loan's views on this.

(B) In this connection, with respect to Ambassador Loan's comment that cessation of bombing was question involving sovereignty of North Vietnam, and that if North Vietnam agreed to responsive action it would have to admit existence of a state of war with U.S. Norwegian government believes that this issue does not in view of USG represent insuperable obstacle. USG has never sought any formal declaration by North Vietnamese government as to what it might do in response to bombing cessation and has always made clear that it was flexible as to form and nature of some corresponding restraint. On this point also Norwegian government believes USG could furnish assurances as to recognition of North Vietnam sovereignty and that this question should be subject for preliminary secret discussions mentioned above."

RUSK (Drafted by E. Isham)

In Oslo 693, Tibbetts clarified Loan's "non-communist" statement. Tibbetts reported: "Algard said Loan had spoken of a separate South Vietnamese state which would be neutral in foreign affairs and of which coalition govt would be non-communist and that Loan clearly assumed such govt would not repeat not be communist dominated, even though it would have Viet Cong participation."

State responded on the same day in 23631, saying that "We have heard the same noise before," but would be interested in seeing if Algard could elicit "specifics on safeguards against eventual communist domination."

August 21, 1967 - Meeting No. 3

Loan invited Algard to come to Hanoi for further discussions. The Norwegians recommended Algard's accepting the invitation. Loan also showed interest in what the U.S. meant by being "flexible" on "some corresponding restraint."

OSLO 722 to SecState (SECRET-EXDIS), 21 August 1967:

9

TIBBETTS.

August 22 - September 15, 1967

Ambassador Algard returned to Oslo from Peking, and on September 8 and 13 met with Chester Cooper to receive further instructions. In this meeting the Norwegians stressed that they "would not in any sense serve as a mediator." Cooper queried Algard on a number of points. First, Algard said that it was his impression that Loan intended the NLF role as a "political factor" in all stages of negotiations. Cooper said that it would be troublesome to have the NLF represented at the preliminary negotiations. Algard said that he had the impression that NVN divided the negotiations into questions "affecting relations between Hanoi and the U.S. on the one hand and South Vietnamese problems on the other." Secondly, on the "non-communist issue," Algard said that Loan stressed Hanoi's recognition of the need to live with two different social and political situations "for some years to come." Third, Loan said that the present GVN was "a political factor" in SVN, implying that there would have to be dealings with it.

Cooper indicated to Algard that we would be "prepared to indicate near the beginning of negotiations and in detail our conception of the final settlement."

There was much discussion about obtaining a visa to Hanoi for Algard, and general acceptance that some considerable delay would be entailed.

State Memorandum from S/AH - Chester L. Cooper for S/S - Benjamin H. Read, dated September 15, 1967, Subject: Report on Conversations in Oslo with Mr. Jacobsen of the Norwegian Foreign Office and Ambassador Algard, Norwegian Ambassador to Peking:

"A. Meeting on Friday, September 8 (sent as Oslo 1063)

"5. I sought clarification of Loan's comments on the role of the NLF, specifically whether 'political factor' meant

10

as a factor in preliminary talks, actual negotiations, or in
a post-settlement situation. Algard said his impression was that
Loan meant all three stages. I then elaborated on the extent
to which we recognized the NLF as a political factor in a post-
settlement situation and/or the ways they might participate in
negotiations. We cannot recognize them as a government or as the
sole representative for the people of Vietnam. In the last analysis, we believe the NLF question should be resolved in South
Vietnam by the various elements there. We will be prepared to
accept anything which the Government of South Vietnam is ready
to accept. It will be troublesome if in the preliminary negotiations the NLF must participate in every stage. We need clarification on this point. Algard said he was not quite sure, but
he had the impression that the North Vietnamese divided the problem
into questions affecting relations between Hanoi and the U.S.
on the one hand, and South Vietnamese problems on the other.
Loan had stressed that Hanoi could not speak for the NLF on
matters affecting South Vietnam. Algard said Loan had not been
more specific on this point.

"7.   On the question of 'non-communist South Vietnam,'
I said that, if indeed Loan had said they would accept a non-
communist South Vietnam and had said so under instructions, this
was probably the first time this formula had been used. Algard
said Loan had stressed that Hanoi was willing to accept a non-
communist government which was a neutral government, and which
would have relations with both East and West and received aid
from both sides. Subsequently, at a reception on the day before
Algard left, Loan had said that Hanoi recognized the fact that
they had to live for some years to come in a Vietnam which would
have two different social and political situations.

"8.   Loan had not explained what he meant by a 'coalition government' and, in fact, used the terms 'coalition government' and 'non-communist government' almost interchangeably
without giving an indication as to the possible structure of the
government, political grouping, etc. He had not stated that
they would accept representatives of the present South Vietnamese
Government, but his tone gave the impression that they would.
In fact, Loan had said he deeply disliked the South Vietnamese
Government but, nevertheless, it was 'a political factor' in
South Vietnam. (Algard cautioned that in considering the term
'non-communist government' Loan has indicated from time to time
he does not consider the NLF communist.) Loan told Algard he
envisages a government with communist participation but which is
not communist-controlled. Loan had repeated his remarks about a
non-communist government directly to Algard in French at a subsequent casual meeting, again using the phrase 'non-communist.'

11

"9. I raised the question concerning Loan's comment that the matter of the U.S. withdrawal was not decisive. Algard said Loan had referred to the Geneva Agreement in this context using the example of the withdrawal of French troops which, he said, had been no problem.

"10. I asked about the statement Loan had made to the effect that if negotiations failed it would be worse than no negotiations at all. Algard said this had been a rather sudden statement by Loan who had not elaborated further.

"11. I said we had thought it might be useful to have a type of pre-negotiation negotiation which would create the setting and mood and clear away some of the problems, Jacobsen said this would give them no trouble. Algard said it would depend on where the preliminaries ended.

"14. In response to questions, I dealt at some length on our recognition of the problem of 'face' for North Vietnam. I said we can go fairly far, but there are North Vietnamese troops in South Vietnam (we have North Vietnamese prisoners as well as documentary evidence); they must get out and their departure must be monitored. This would be a matter for the negotiations phase rather than for Algard to deal with. We are very flexible as to how the negotiations should proceed, whether in secret or public view, and also flexible as to level and, within limits of security and communications, place. The problem of withdrawing military forces is extremely complicated and will present great difficulties for the North Vietnamese if they refuse to acknowledge their presence in South Vietnam. But so long as they get out and we are sure they get out, Hanoi can deal with its 'face' problem.

"15. Algard said it seemed that we were thinking of two phases, the first to establish the conditions of negotiations, the second the negotiations themselves; his mission would be in the first phase. I said that we are prepared to indicate near the beginning of negotiations and in detail our conception of the final settlement. In effect, we are prepared to settle first and negotiate later. Hanoi knows pretty much already from our public statements what we will agree to, including our willingness to accept self-determination within South Vietnam and for Vietnam as a whole. We are ready to have the people of South Vietnam decide the extent to which the NLF participates in its government.

"B. Meeting on Wednesday, September 13 (sent as Oslo 1087)

"7. Algard said his Swedish colleague in Peking is convinced that there is a marked divergence between Hanoi and the NLF,

to which I replied that there may, of course, be natural
differences of view between North and South and long-time combatants
as opposed to more recent reinforcements, but this did not change
the basic factor of North Vietnamese control.

State 35015 sent on 9 September indicated that further study was required of the Norwegian conversations. State also indicated some concern
about Cooper's remarks to Algard with respect to his impending trip being
"construed as an insurance related to our bombing of Hanoi." Tibbetts
responded in Oslo 1079 of 11 September that the insurances given Algard
were vague and that there was no problem with respect to commitments on
U.S. bombing while Algard would be in Hanoi.

State responded to both Oslo conversations with instructions to hold
off on the "immediate pursuit of OHIO channel" since USG was now in "indirect
channel of communication to Hanoi." Responding to Cooper's suggestion on
rejecting the MARIGOLD ten points, State suggested, instead, confining
Algard's future comments to the North Vietnamese to points previously made
by Loan and to the reciprocity issue.

> STATE 36328 to AmEmbassy Oslo (SECRET-NODIS), 12 September 1967,
> Ref: State 35015; Oslo 1063, 1087:
>
> "1. As you can surmise, developments in another area[4]
> have caused us to hold off in giving you instructions on
> message that Algard might take. Weighing delay and possi-
> ble GON feeling that we have lost interest, we now believe
> you should inform them in utmost confidence that indirect
> channel of communication to Hanoi opened up following
> Algard's last contact, and that we are now pursuing cer-
> tain inquiries through that channel. Response is so far
> negative, but we are continuing to probe; and therefore
> frankly feel immediate pursuit of Ohio channel could be
> embarrassing to Algard and ourselves. Please request
> Algard to notify us as soon as he has heard from his post
> in Peking re travel permit to Hanoi, and advise him that
> we will then give him most meaningful, timely message
> we can then devise in light of all developments up to
> point of his departure.
>
> "2. In conveying this message, you might add that,
> since Hanoi is of course aware of the indirect channel
> currently in use, it would be our best guess that they
> will hold off in giving Algard his visa. In short, they
> will probably be playing a waiting game just as we are.

13

"3. You should make clear that this reflects no decline whatever in our interest in developing the Algard channel. As sophisticated diplomats, they must realize that this kind of duplication of channels can arise in a situation of this sort, and that it then becomes unwise to attempt duplicate channel.. At same time, other channel is tenuous and may break down, and this among other factors prevents us from describing to GON what exactly is being discussed.

"4. FYI. Provisionally we are negative on inject- ing the Polish Ten Points, which Hanoi has never taken up in any way. We are more inclined to think that any use- ful message through Algard will confine itself to the subjects, other than reciprocal action for bombing, on which he has had faintly interesting comments from Loan. But we are holding our fire completely until we see how the next few days develop. End FYI."

Tibbetts responded in Oslo 1132 of 13 September, saying that the Nor- wegians understood the sensitivity and would wait for further instructions from Washington.

Oslo 1366 of 28 September and Oslo 1407 of 30 September dealt with the problem of Algard's returning to his post in Peking. It was learned that Ambassador Loan had departed Peking for Hanoi on 7 September and had returned to Peking probably around 29 September. Loan had not as yet given any indication regarding the authorization of Algard's visit to Hanoi, nor did he give any sign of interest on substantive matters. In the meantime, a Norwegian journalist indicated that he suspected Algard's return to Peking might have something to do with North Vietnamese contacts and a Vietnam peace settlement.

3 - 17 October 1967

State (47603) responded to Oslo 1366 and 1407 on 3 October. The gist of the message was that USG desired that Algard stay on in Norway until at least the end of that week, giving "further time both to see whether Hanoi follows up in providing visa, and to permit us to weigh other indi- cations of Hanoi's attitude that might emerge following President's speech of September 29 and other developments.[5]

Bovey replied in Oslo 1457 on 3 October that there would be no diffi- culty in Algard remaining at least to the end of the week. Some problems were also raised with respect to communications between Oslo and Peking. It was decided that communications were not adequate for rapidity or security.

On 5 October, Bovey sent Oslo 1503 which repeated that there were no
further developments on the Algard trip to Hanoi, and that Algard felt
he should not delay his return to Peking. Algard's intention was to
leave Oslo on 19 October unless he hears otherwise regarding authorization to visit Hanoi. In this same cable, Bovey reported that the Norwegian Charge in Peking passed the following message: "During absence
Loan in September NVN Embassy Peking had stated that Hanoi still interested in contact and Algard did not RPT not think this was merely casual
remark." Algard explained Hanoi's inaction regarding his visit in terms
of increased U.S. bombing in NVN.[6]

On 9 October in Oslo 1567, Bovey reported the following message
from Norwegian Charge in Peking:

"2. Begin text

Algard, therefore, decided to depart for his post on 12 October.

On 10 October, State 51536 reported that U.S. still regarded an Algard
trip to Hanoi as constructive, and that "we are interested in obtaining
elaboration of mention by Loan of possible contact Hanoi-Washington via
Soviets as well as other aspects of Loan's remarks to Charge." Bovey
responded in Oslo 1597 on 11 October that State 51536 had been received
and executed.

October 18, 1967

On 16 October, Algard transmitted further details on conversation
between Norwegian Charge and Loan.

OSLO 1739 to SecState (SECRET-NODIS), 18 October 1967,
Ref: Oslo 1567 and 1597

"2. Begin Msg

November 2, 1967

The Norwegians handed Bovey a further elaboration of recent despatches from Peking. One point that emerged clearly was Loan's questioning of Norway's role as a middleman in negotiations, implying that the Norwegians were really bartering for the Americans. Loan also gave the Norwegians to understand that Hanoi would not negotiate under present circumstances, especially the U.S. bombings. Loan added that Peking was an "insecure" place for contacts, and that Moscow would be more desirable.

OSLO 1903 to SecState (SECRET-NODIS), 2 November 1967,
Ref: Oslo 1739

"1. FonOff (SecGen Boye and Desk Sandegren) handed me evening Nov one translation of (A) despatch dated Oct 10 from Amb Algard in Peking and (B) enclosure thereto which is Norwegian Charge's fuller report of his talk with Loan Oct 10, mentioned reftel.

November 14, 1967

In Oslo 2033, Tibbetts reported that Norwegian politics might complicate and compromise the OHIO track. It seemed that in a recent visit of Prime Minister Lyng to Poland, he and Rapacki exchanged information about negotiations contacts. Lyng claimed that Rapacki had told him "in great detail about the Polish effort 'on U.S. behalf' to open contact in December 1966." In reply, Lyng said that the Norwegians had also unsuccessfully tried to open contact. Jacobsen brought to Lyng's attention, in the meantime, that "Algard channel not RPT not so dead as FonMin seemed to believe, since on November 9, the day Lyng left for Poland, a message had been received from Algard stating that Loan had expressed interest in continuing discreet contacts with Algard (as well as telling Algard he had been satisfied with Mr. Lyng's speech in the UN)."[7] Tibbetts feared that Lyng might be tempted to use the Norwegian contact as "a possible easy way out of domestic difficulty over foreign policy."[8] Tibbetts asked State authorization to tell Lyng that "we consider this channel too important to create prejudice against it." On 14 November in State 69391, State concurred in Tibbett's request. On 16 November in Oslo 2120, Tibbetts said: "Estimates are that government will survive debate with narrow margin despite pigheadedness of some liberals. So maybe Lyng will relax for time being."

December 14, 1967

Loan sought out Algard on two occasions in early November. Loan's message was simple -- American escalation meant that there was no purpose in Hanoi negotiating at this time.

> OSLO 2501 to SecState (SECRET-NODIS), 14 December 1967, Ref: Oslo 2083:
>
> "1. There follows text fuller report received by FonOff by pouch from Amb Algard Peking re further contacts with NVN Amb Loan (Ngo). This report, which is dated Nov 10, expands info already given by under Secy Jacobsen (para four reftel) to Amb Tibbetts Nov 14.

UNQUOTE

"2. In conveying this report Desk Officer Sandegren called my attention to phrasing which indicates
that Loan appears to have taken initiative on both
occasions and that on second he seems to have sought
Algard out.

"3. Norwegian FonOff regards second Loan apprach
Nov 7 and implications of last sentence, however de-
viously conveyed, as hopeful indication NVN desire
not RPT not to close down circuit entirely. Sandegren
said expression QUOTE days after this one UNQUOTE
implies in Norwegian that better days may lie ahead."

BOVEY

January 4, 1968

OSLO 2727 to SecState (SECRET-NODIS), 4 January 1968,
Ref: Oslo 2501:

"1. Ansteensen called me on January 4 to give me
the following translation of a cable sent by GON Amb
to Peking January 3, 1968.

TIBBETTS

January 9, 1968

OSLO 2789 to SecState (SECRET-NODIS), 9 January 1968,
Ref: Oslo 2727:

"2. Second text is the translation of a cable received by Foreign Office from Ambassador Algard in Peking dated January 3:

February 10, 1968

Loan once again invited Algard to come to Hanoi, and he also indicated a desire to send an NVN representative to Norway. Loan also introduced a very new element into the play: "that Hanoi presupposed (assumed) that

20

the military operations be stopped while negotiations are being conducted."

OSLO 3275 to SecState (SECRET-NODIS), 10 February 1968,
Ref: Oslo 2930:

"1. Boye and Ansteensen called me in morning
February 10 and passed me following message from
Algard in Peking received late February 9 in Oslo:

UNQUOTE

"3. Boye said with respect to foregoing that if
US Govt feels Norwegian Foreign Service can be of any
help in establishing contacts with Hanoi, they are
prepared to do so but, of course, GON does not RPT
not want to mess up anything which may be in progress.
If USG considers it desirable, GON prepared to ask
Algard to come to Oslo for consultations with a US
rep either from Embassy or from Washington in middle
of February. Algard could then be asked to proceed
to Hanoi as soon as possible although GON will have
to think hard as to what would be appropriate cover
story for such visit at this time. As regards proposal for arranging a journey to Oslo for some North
Vietnamese rep, further info will be passed on to
USG as soon as received from Norwegian Embassy Peking
as indicated Algard's tel, but in meantime GON would
appreciate any views and comments USG might have on
this subject. Norwegians standing by for earliest
possible reply from Washington."

TIBBETTS

21

February 19, 1968

The Norwegians informed Tibbetts that the North Vietnamese Ambassador in Moscow might be planning a trip to Norway as well. (OSLO 3394)

February 20, 1968

In the event of the North Vietnamese Ambassador's visit to Oslo, State sent the following explanation of "no advantage" for use by the Norwegians. The explanation of "no advantage" stressed our desire "to ascertain whether Hanoi appreciates /the consequences of taking advantage/ and understands the importance the U.S. attaches to the 'no advantage' assumption."

"The US, consistent with President Johnson's statement of April 7, 1965, remains willing to enter into talks with/out - amended State 118719/ preconditions at any time.

"The US position on the cessation of the bombardment of North Viet-Nam was set forth in President Johnson's September 29, 1967 speech in San Antonio. As the President said:

'The US is willing to stop all aerial and naval bombardment of North Viet-Nam when this will lead promptly to productive discussions. We, of course, assume that while discussions proceed, North Viet-Nam would not take advantage of the bombing cessation or limitation.'

"The US is not assuming that North Viet-Nam will cease its support to its forces in the South. On the contrary, as Secretary of Defense designate Clark Clifford testified before the Senate Foreign Relations Committee, we assume that until a cease-fire is agreed on, Hanoi 'will continue to transport the normal amount of goods, men and munitions.'

"In setting forth its assumption, the US is not setting a condition but attempting to make clear to North Viet-Nam that any cessation of US bombing followed by actions by Hanoi taking advantage of the cessation (such as an increase by Hanoi of its infiltration of men and supplies or attacks in the area of the DMZ) would constitute such bad faith on Hanoi's part as to make continued US forebearance impossible. If Hanoi, by taking advantage, forces the US to resume bombing, the possibilities of a negotiated solution would drastically recede. Under such circumstances, calls for intensified US military action would increase and the possibility of another halt in the bombing would be low. The US is trying to ascertain whether Hanoi appreciates this vital fact and fully understands the importance the US attaches to the no-advantage assumption.

22

"At San Antonio the President, in addition to setting forth his assumption, stated his readiness to stop the bombing when such action would lead 'promptly to productive discussions.' 'Productive discussions' are serious exchanges in which either side will be able to put forward for full consideration in good faith its position on any matter. 'Prompt' of course refers to a willingness by Hanoi to begin discussions with the US immediately after cessation of bombing.

"It is worth noting that Hanoi is unwilling to give a clear response to questions as to the length of time between a US bombing cessation and the beginning of talks. If Hanoi were serious in desiring talks then surely its response would have been one of unequivocal readiness to begin immediately.

"The US evaluation of Hanoi's current position takes into account Hanoi's actions as well as its words. The unprecedented offensive against most of South Viet-Nam's urban centers, which Hanoi treacherously launched in the midst of the traditional Tet holidays, causing widespread civilian casualties and suffering, was made notwithstanding the fact that we were still exploring with Hanoi its position through diplomatic channels, and that we had exercised restraint in bombing targets in the immediate vicinity of Hanoi and Haiphong.[9] In this context, we cannot but weigh Hanoi's words with great skepticism and caution. These actions carry a harsh political message.

"The US favors every effort to obtain clarification of Hanoi's position. We shall continue to evaluate all information and to pursue every possible avenue which promises to bring us closer to the resolution of this conflict through serious negotiations."

(State 118092)

February 23, 1968

The Norwegians reported that they had heard nothing further about the North Vietnamese Ambassador's visit to Oslo. A Swedish radio report said that he was returning to Moscow from Stockholm. (OSLO 3446)

February 24, 1968

Boye and Ansteensen informed Tibbetts that on February 23 Loan again approached Algard concerning the latter's visit to Hanoi and suggested the date of February 29. (OSLO 3464)

March 1, 1968

Jacobsen informed Tibbets that Algard had left for Hanoi by plane on February 29. The U.S. had not been consulted prior to Algard's departure. Jacobsen offered domestic politics as the explanation of the need for the Algard trip. (OSLO 3570)

April 5, 1968

Following is a summary of Ambassador Algard's visit to Hanoi, March 3-10:

(OSLO 4120, Sections 1 & 2 of 2)

April 5, 1968

Algard sent a second report on his visit to Hanoi. This one discussed the leadership in North Vietnam.

April 5, 1968

Algard met with Loan in Peking.

(OSLO 4133)

SWEDISH - NORTH VIETNAMESE CONTACTS, OCTOBER, 1966 - 1968

November 11, 1966

The first exchange in the Aspen track came on 11 November in a meeting between Secretary Rusk and Swedish Minister of Foreign Affairs Nilsson. Nilsson informed Rusk of Swedish contacts with the DRV in Warsaw and in Hanoi. Both contacts with the DRV dealt with "creating a climate favorable to negotiations." The DRV contact in Warsaw called for: (1) "an unconditional and unlimited stop of the bombing of Vietnamese territory, North as well as South Vietnam;" (2) "the FNL must be regarded as a legitimate party to negotiations." He added that "no military actions should be undertaken in the DMZ" and a "process of evacuation of allied forces should be begun." The Hanoi contact, also talking about a climate for negotiations, listed two conditions that appeared a little softer than the Warsaw counterpart: (1) "the bombing of North Vietnam must be put to an end, without any conditions and definitely;" (2) "recognition of the FNL, 'as one of the spokesmen for' the South Vietnamese people;" in addition, the Hanoi contact, Mr. Trinh, described additional matters for "a final settlement": coalition government, general elections, and eventual steps toward reunification.

In response, Secretary Rusk indicated that "we could not impose a coalition government on the south." He also said that: DRV insistence on a permanent end to the bombing represented "an increased demand on their part and we must have something in exchange for a permanent cessation." As a way out of the reciprocity dilemma, Secretary Rusk suggested a process of deescalation by mutual example rather than final agreement. Rusk also recognized the difficulty of proceeding with bargaining at initial stages because "Hanoi was hesitant about discussing the first step until they saw how the negotiations would end."

> Department of State Memorandum of Conversation (TOP SECRET, NODIS, ASPEN), dated November 11, 1966, Subject: Swedish Diplomatic contacts with North Viet-Nam. Participants - United States: Secretary Rusk; Leonard Unger (Dep Asst Secy); David McKillop (EUR/SCAN); Heyward Isham (EA/VN). Sweden: Minister of Foreign Affairs Torsten Nilsson; R. Hichens-Bergstrom (Dir of Political Affairs, Foreign Ministry); Hubert de Besche (Ambassador to United States); J. C. S. Oberg (First Secretary, Pol. Div., Ministry of For. Affairs).

> "After preliminary exchange of greetings, Foreign Minister Nilsson read a report of two recent conversations between Swedish diplomats and representatives of North Viet-Nam which took place in Warsaw and Hanoi (The text of this paper is attached).

(END TEXT)

Having read the paper, the Foreign Minister summarized the
salient points of what DRV Foreign Minister Trinh had told
Ambassador Petri in Hanoi: North Viet-Nam preferred a political
to a military solution and was interested in a climate favoring

a political settlement provided certain conditions were fulfilled; withdrawal was not specifically mentioned; the National
Liberation Front was described as <u>one</u> of the spokesmen for the
South Viet-Nam people although the most valid one. Regarding
the possibility of reaching a final settlement, the NLF and
Hanoi supported the formation of a National Coalition Government
in South Viet-Nam founded on a broad basis including all political
and religious groupings as well as all social classes generally
desiring to achieve national independence. Moreover, conditions
should be created permitting moving in the direction of future
re-unification....

"....The Secretary went on to note that there were one
or two positive and one or two negative elements in what had been
told to the Swedish representatives. On the positive side,
Hanoi's interest in a political rather than a military solution
represented a small step forward.

"....After all this, Trinh had sent him an invitation to
come see him; Petri had not asked to be received by Trinh. While
there was no discussion of conveying Trinh's remarks to the United
States, neither did Trinh say Petri could not do so and he emphasized the importance of maintaining secrecy. The Swedes interpreted Trinh's attitude as a tacit indication that his remarks
could be conveyed to the United States.

"The Secretary, continuing his commentary on Trinh's remarks
said the missing element was what Hanoi would in fact do on the
military side. At least 19 regular North Vietnamese regiments
were in the South and three North Vietnamese divisions were in
the DMZ and north of it. They could attack our Marines at any
moment. If we committed ourselves to stop bombing permanently,
we must know what would happen on the ground militarily. We
could not possibly make a commitment on the ground unless we knew
what Hanoi would do with those 19 regiments. Trinh had used the
phrase, 'We know what we will have to do' in the event their
conditions were accepted. The Secretary said we would want to
know what that phrase means.'

"....Ambassador Petri had observed to Trinh that if the two
conditions were fulfilled, the North should follow suit. Bergstrom
did not indicate whether there had been any comment to his remark.

"The Secretary said that Hanoi had denied, even to the
Soviets, that they had troops in the South. However, we must
have corresponding action on the ground; we could not be children
in this matter. As to the role of the Front, we knew who their
leaders were including North Vietnamese Generals in the South
using a variety of names. The Liberation Front is Hanoi. Some

southern individuals with other associations were included
in the Front, but they had no influence. When Trinh said
the Front was the most valid spokesman for the South Vietnamese people and that the situation must be consistent with
moving toward reunification, he was expressing Hanoi's political
objective of permanently unifying the country on a Communist
basis. We were prepared to have South Viet-Nam decide on a
solution through elections but so far Hanoi was not prepared
to do so. The Secretary said we could not impose a coalition
government on the South; we could not turn our men around and
start them shooting in the other direction to impose a coalition
government. If the South Vietnamese people were to decide on
this it was up to them and we would abide by the result, but a
coalition would not be imposed by our arms and our power....

   "....The Secretary added that the other side had made
clear we must end the bombing permanently, since they insisted
that a suspension would imply an ultimatum. This represented an
increased demand on their part and we must have something in
exchange for a permanent cessation.

   "The Swedish Foreign Minister noted that they had contacts
with the Front or Hanoi in Algiers, Warsaw, Moscow and Hanoi
as well as Peking. The Secretary noted that the only serious
interlocutor was Hanoi - not the Front. The Secretary said that
we did not discount the importance of any third party channels.
In past crises, we never knew which channel would be important.
In this case, we did not know whether Hanoi would say something
important through the Swedes rather than through someone else....

   "The Secretary went on to say that the Eastern European
countries would probably be interested in settling for the status
quo ante at the 17th Parallel but on account of Peking, were unable to move forward. We are prepared, he said, to accept the
Communist world's interest in North Viet-Nam if they are prepared
to accept our interest in the South. Until Hanoi abandoned its
objective of seizing South Viet-Nam, there could be no peace. It
was as simple as that....The Secretary continued that two things
were vital: (1) Hanoi must abandon its attempt to seize South
Viet-Nam by force, and (2) the people of South Viet-Nam must
have a chance to decide what government they want and to express
their views on reunification without being subjected to force by
the North....We had suspended bombing in the DMZ to see if there
would be any response, but there was none and the ICC had been
denied access to the area under the North. Nevertheless the
Trinh statement could be important if we had more precision.

   "Ambassador Unger called attention to the reference by the
North Vietnamese in Warsaw to 'no military action being undertaken
in the demilitarized zone'. He suggested, and the Secretary agreed,
that this was also a point on which the Swedes might make further

5

soundings in Hanoi. We were certainly ready to see the zone
truly demilitarized and would welcome an end to violations of it
by North Viet-Nam.

"The Foreign Minister mentioned possible differences of
opinion between the Front and Hanoi and pointed out that all
elements of the Front were not Communists. The Secretary
responded there was no problem about contact with the Front;
the South Vietnamese were able to communicate with its representatives. South Viet-Nam could take care of the indigenous
problem through reconciliation and bringing the dissidents back
into the body politic. United States troops had only entered
when North Viet-Nam regulars had come down. If the Swedes were
in the same position, they would not accept a coalition government thus imposed on them.

"....The Secretary noted three channels to Hanoi: the
direct one through which little was said because of Hanoi's fear
of Peking; the channel through Moscow to which we attach importance because of Moscow's attitudes and influence -- but here
again Hanoi was probably afraid of Peking; and finally a channel
through a third party, which could be Sweden. But, he continued,
this represented perhaps 50% of the question; the other 50% was
the possibility of resolving the problem by defacto action on
the ground in the pattern of the Greek insurrection and the
Quemoy-Matsu crisis.[1] Ho Chi Minh might prefer to pull back
troops rather than enter negotiations, calculating that Americans
might go home and could not come back, although, the Secretary
said, we can get back faster than they can. We would be prepared to try this route. There need be no confessions that they
have 19 regiments in the South.

"In response to an analysis by the Foreign Minister of
Hanoi's problem, the Secretary noted that we had reports from
Eastern European sources that confirmed this precisely: Hanoi
feared the effect of negotiations on the morale of the Viet Cong
and Hanoi's present leaders feared that they could not survive
a failure to achieve their objectives. However, the Secretary
said on this we cannot help them; they are in places they have
no right to be.

"Further, on the point of gradual de-escalation, the Secretary said that since January we had made clear our interest in
responding to actions on the ground -- what we call a process
of 'mutual example' -- without evoking thus far any interest
on Hanoi's part. If Trinh's phrase pointed in the direction of
positive Hanoi response, this could be important.

"As to Trinh's own alignment in the regime as between hawks
and doves, Mr. Bergstrom commented that the French considered

6

"The Foreign Minister asked whether it would be necessary to specify how long we would halt the bombing. The Secretary said that under our system the press and Congress would force us to answer this question. A permanent bombing halt would require a very important reciprocal action. Ambassador Unger commented that Trinh's remarks implied some readiness to discuss now not only conditions for negotiation but also the terms of an eventual settlement. The Secretary agreed that Hanoi was hesitant about discussing the first step until they saw how the negotiations would end. He indicated that another reason for keeping further inquiries on the basis of a Swedish-DRV dialogue was to avoid having to bring Saigon into the picture, which we were disinclined to do at this stage.

"The Secretary suggested as a technical point it might not be wise to pursue the dialogue with Hanoi through other capitals. In order to protect Trinh's position if there are divisions within the leadership it was important not to have communications from abroad available to too wide a group in Hanoi. Foreign Minister Nilsson agreed with this suggestion. The Secretary emphasized the importance of examining very carefully all indications bearing on Hanoi's position but as he had told the press on another occasion, we could only negotiate with those who could stop the fighting. If we entered into too great detail on our conditions for settlement, the other side would just put that in their pockets and then propose to split the difference. We were not worried about real southern insurgents -- 16,000 of them had defected this year -- but the Northern Generals must go home. We would even be prepared to give them a villa on the Riviera!....

"....Responding to a final question from the Foreign Minister about Hanoi's difficulty of believing that the United States could abandon such expensive United States bases, the Secretary pointed out that the United States' capacity in this regard should not be underestimated. We had built roads in India, over the hump, and Alaska during the war which we had never used, and we had demobilized 100 divisions after World War II.[2] In the last five years we had closed 600 bases. As the President had said, we had no intention of leaving our soldiers in South Viet-Nam as tourists.

"Following the general conversation, Ambassador Unger privately mentioned to Minister Nilsson and Mr. Bergstrom our concern over reports that Ambassador Petri had spoken rather openly about his contacts in Hanoi.

7

November 18, 1966

As a result of the Rusk-Nilsson meeting, State cabled Stockholm on "points for clarification."

STATE 88128 to Amembassy STOCKHOLM (TOP SECRET, NODIS, ASPEN), 18 November 1966.

"1. . . . .

"2. . . . .

'1. What does the North Vietnamese Foreign Minister intend that his government would do when he says 'We know what we will have to do' /i.e., if US stops bombing of NVN/? Mr. Trinh named two conditions which the United States must fulfill to bring about a climate for negotiations. It is understood of course that if those conditions were fulfilled, negotiations could promptly be undertaken, but since the fulfillment of those conditions would represent significant steps for the United States, what would be the reciprocal actions by North Viet-Nam? It is encouraging to know that the North Vietnamese apparently recognize this reciprocity but it is essential, if their position is to be accurately evaluated, to know what it is that they recognize they 'will have to do!.

'2. What is the significance of the FNL being characterized, as Mr. Trinh puts it, as 'the most valid' spokesman for the South Vietnamese people? What is this intended to convey concerning the status of the FNL vis-a-vis other spokesmen?

'3. With reference to the question of reunification, Mr. Trinh referred to the necessity of creating conditions in South Viet-Nam 'to permit a move in the direction of a future reunification'. The conditions in South Viet-Nam as Mr. Trinh himself implied would grow out of general elections held in an atmosphere of freedom and democracy. Would Mr. Trinh not envisage that the question of unification would be resolved at that time in accordance with the mandate given a new government by the people through those general elections?

'4. If Mr. Trinh should mention the point raised by the North Vietnamese representative in Warsaw, namely that no military actions should be taken in the demilitarized zone', Mr. Trinh might be asked whether this is intended to be in effect a proposal for the strict observance of the Geneva Accords in the demilitarized zone north and south of the demarcation line with the full functioning of the ICC throughout the zone.'"

"6. There was some substantive discussion of the issues which might arise in Petri's next conversations in Hanoi, it being understood that this exchange was between the Swedes and ourselves

and not for discussion in Hanoi. Unger mentioned Goldberg
formula's reference to private and other assurances about a
response to bombing cessation and illustrated the kinds of
de-escalatory actions by Hanoi which we would take to be appropriate responses, such as a cessation of infiltration, a reduction of the level of military activity and/or terror in South
Viet-Nam or some troop withdrawal from South to North. In
response to further Swedish probing as to what would come next
after these first steps toward de-escalation and their mention
of a possible ceasefire, Unger said it was not possible without
knowing more of Hanoi's views, to carry the process farther.
We would hope that once a beginning has been made it would
be possible to establish some mode of communication with Hanoi
to arrive at some understanding of the next phases of de-escalation,
although it was not to be ruled out that this might proceed by
mutual example. He also made clear our recognition of the problem of face for Hanoi and our readiness to consider ways to meet
with problem. With reference to the fourth point in the "Points
for Clarification" Unger emphasized that we were suggesting this
be raised only if the North Vietnamese themselves refer to the
DMZ problem. He added that it would always have to be understood
that any arrangements that might conceivably be worked out for
the DMZ would have to provide for a reasonably reliable means of
detecting and dealing with violations; we could not agree to
putting American and Vietnamese forces in jeopardy exposed to
surprise action by the North Vietnamese or Viet Cong."
RUSK (Drafted by Unger)

November 28 thru December 21, 1966

On 28 November, Parsons cabled State, in Stockholm 641, saying that
"Swedes will not repeat not be ready talk with me before mid-week at
earliest."

On 29 November, responding to State 88128 with Stockholm 652, Parsons
said that in amplifying aide memoire "there was no doubt at all in Petri's
mind that Trinh meant and expected what he had said would be passed on to
US." Petri also wanted to qualify that when Trinh used the phrase "most
valid spokesman" with respect to NLF, that these were not Trinh's precise
words, but the meaning. Petri also emphasized that he could not draw Trinh
out on meaning of his "we know what we will have to do" statement. Also,
on 29 November, in Stockholm 653, Petri confirmed the contents of the memo
transmitted to Secretary Rusk on 11 November. The intention was that Petri
return to Hanoi by way of Peking about 10 December.

On 30 November, in Stockholm 659, Parsons added a piece to the
previous conversation with Petri in Stockholm 652. This was that: "also,
Petri had not repeat not put in his reports, Trinh had shown 'good deal
of understanding' that problem of face existed also for US."

On 3 December, State (STATE 96326) queried about cryptographic facilities for Petri, and worried about public speculation on Petri's "frequent visits to Hanoi." State added: "This will also bear on question of when we bring GVN into picture, something we do not contemplate for present."

On 5 December Bergstrom and Parsons met once again.

> STOCKHOLM 681 to SecState (TOP SECRET, NODIS, ASPEN), December 6, 1966. Ref: State 96236.
>
> "3. As Swedes feel there is no denying they have been in touch with us at Fon Minister level, formula arrived at in Petri's instructions is for him to describe what he tells Trinh as 'impressions', perhaps 'general impressions' formed by Nilsson in Washington. Precise formulation has to be left to Petri's discretion. However, he is enjoined to be most careful not to say he is speaking at our request or conveying message from us. Bergstrom says Petri will also take 'great care not to affect any American interest in a negative way.'
>
> "4. On substance, primary point of interest for Petri to emphasize is that Nilsson felt we were interested in finding road to political solution and that this road not closed. Petri is not to volunteer any suggestions or attribute any to us. However, he will try hard to ascertain what response there would be from Hanoi's side if US should--as mentioned in first of our points--stop bombing North Viet-Nam. Here again exact formulation will depend on Petri's judgment in light circumstances of talk, but I was assured he will try to cover points on which we need more information.
>
> "5. If Petri concludes Trinh does not want to react at time, he is not to press but merely say that he would be at Trinh's disposal at any time."

PARSONS

On 9 December, in Stockholm 702, Parsons reported that Oberg, Foreign Ministry Officer in Charge of Asian Affairs, indicated that
On 10 December, in Stockholm 707, Parsons reported that Trinh was at a Communist Party meeting in Budapest and was not expected in Hanoi until the 19th. It was agreed that Petri should wait for Trinh to return to Hanoi rather than intercepting him en route. On 10 December, in State 100645, State agreed on holding the line against   and on waiting for the Trinh return to Hanoi. On 21 December, in Stockholm 739, Parsons reported that Bergstrom had informed him that Petri had not yet been granted an entrance visa to Hanoi. Petri could not explain the delay.

January 11, 1967

On 11 January, in State 116773, State wanted Bergstrom to query Petri on the latter's assessment of recent Hanoi efforts to increase pressures for unilateral bombing halt. State also wanted to know if Petri felt there was any connection in the delay in obtaining his visa and recent U.S. bombings.

January 13, 1967

Word had been received from Petri that Hanoi wanted him to come to North Vietnam as soon as possible. Because of the delay, the GOS had decided on its own to reactivate its Warsaw channel.

Bergstrom questioned Parsons on whether a declaration on Hanoi's part to negotiate would lead to a U.S. bombing stop.

> STOCKHOLM 822 to SecState (TOP SECRET, NODIS, ASPEN), January 13, 1967. Ref: State 116773.
>
> "4. Late on 12th word came from Petri that North Vietnamese wanted him come to Hanoi by January 16. He had replied in accord his instructions on giving Stockholm adequate lead-time that he could not make it before 19th. This response has today been approved here.
>
> "5. In meantime, not having heard from Hanoi, GOS decided reactivate Warsaw channel which they had earlier avoided so as not to cross wires.. (Response to my query why was so vague as to lead me believe second and third rationales paragraph 3 above weighed more with Swedes than Bergstrom admitted.) Bergstrom said Oberg of Ministry had this week been sent Warsaw renew his contact with North Vietnamese representative there. (This is first disclosure to us of this previously tightly held channel to DRV and it is interesting to note Swede is regular FonMinistry official.)
>
> "6. Oberg's instructions signed out by Nilsson were to pave way for Bergstrom himself proceed Warsaw about 16th to explore situation. Now that Petri has his visa, Ministry today has hastily instructed Oberg not to make contact in Warsaw, but it is not yet known whether he had already done so. In any event Bergstrom will not now go there next week."
>
> "8. One question which Bergstrom put to me for referral Washington was whether a firm, or at any rate more precise, declaration on Hanoi's part of its willingness to negotiate could lead to a bombing stop. On this point, I described

Department's impressions of Dong's prepared statement to
Salisbury.[3] Bergstrom is of course thoroughly familiar with
Hanoi's obvious tactics in seeking obtain unilateral cessation
of bombing but there is lingering disposition to hope Dong
statement is significant."

PARSONS

January 17, 1967

Bergstrom reported on an Oberg contact in Warsaw. The North Vietnamese contact told Oberg: (1) "'A final and unconditional cessation
of the bombing was an absolute and indispensable prerequisite in order
to pave the way for negotiations. As soon as the bombings had ceased,
the North Vietnamese GOVT was prepared to take all peace offers from
the American Government under consideration;'" (2) The four points
were not a precondition for negotiations but only a foundation for negotiations; (3) the NLF problem could be disposed of "through recognition on
the part of the Americans of the right of the Front to take place at
the negotiation table;" (4) Reunification was an internal matter to be
settled "after the restoration of the peace."

STOCKHOLM 831 (CC) to SecState (TOP SECRET, NODIS, ASPEN),
January 17, 1967. Ref: State 118951

"3. Oberg (knowledge of his identity as source should
not rpt not be revealed) has reported from Warsaw (para 5
Stockholm 822). His visit there required no special rationale
as North Vietnamese reps had agreed he would take contact from
time to time. As this visit was pre-arranged, Hanoi rep had
had time to inform his principals and in Oberg's opinion had been
carefully briefed by them. At outset Oberg's contact, who was
second-ranking man in Hanoi representation, said door was always
open to Oberg and then proceeded to give following as Hanoi's
position. Text in sub-paragraph below is Bergstrom's translation
from Oberg's Swedish message except where Oberg incorporated
Hanoi reps exact words in French:

"4. Although Hanoi rep in Warsaw was aware of Nilsson's
visit to U.S. in November, he did not rpt not ask Oberg about
any talks with U.S. officials and latter did not rpt not refer
to Nilsson's talks with Secretary and Vice Pres in any way.

"5. Oberg also explained to DRV man that when he had proposed Bergstrom also visit Warsaw to meet Hanoi reps, GOS had
not rpt not known that Petri was about to visit Hanoi. Now
that this visit was to take place (which was obviously already
known to Warsaw Hanoi rep), there seemed no need for Bergstrom
visit Warsaw now....

"6. Oberg's report has been repeated to Petri in Peking,
with comment that GOS will be interested to learn if Trinh
parallels exactly Warsaw Hanoi reps statement to Oberg."

PARSONS

January 20, 1967

In Stockholm 847, Parsons reported that "Oberg found FNL rep /in
Warsaw/ both knowledgeable and intelligent. There was 'mutual briefing'
on previous Swedish contacts with FNL reps at Algiers and Moscow...."
State queried on the same day (State 122506) on more information about
Swedish-NLF contacts in Algiers and Moscow.

January 26, 1967

In Stockholm 868, Parsons reported that a Social Democratic afternoon
tabloid had revealed from authoritative sources that: "Ambassador Petri
during his talks with the Hanoi Government and the FNL 'is naturally also
seeking to send sentiments and views' concerning the proposals for peace
negotiations."

January 27, 1967

In Stockholm 870, Parsons cabled that Petri had returned to his post in Peking and had only sent a brief telegram on his Hanoi talks. In the meantime, Parsons noted press publicity continued and was probably designed "to serve democratic political needs of social democrats."

February 2, 1967

In Stockholm 907, Parsons indicated that the Swedes seem to be getting "a bit nervous about their Aspen role now." Bergstrom did not want to wind up "looking foolish." Bergstrom also indicated that Petri's report was not sufficiently precise and that the Foreign Ministry was waiting for a full written report before passing it on to the U.S. Bergstrom did say that the brief telegram from Petri contained "nothing spectacular." Bergstrom added, however, that 'there were one or two possible signs.'

Bergstrom avoided answering questions about Swedish contacts with the NLF. Bergstrom's remarks, however, indicated some sympathy for the NLF. Along this same line, Bergstrom threw out the thought that Sweden might be interested in establishing consular relations with Hanoi, but then back tracked when pressed on this point.

> "4. When I asked Bergstrom substance and timing of Swedish-NLF contacts in Algiers and in Moscow, he replied that his memory not sure enough to attempt answer without having records available. He agreed without much enthusiasm to revert to this later. In the meantime all he could recall was that contact in Algiers began about August 1965, at time when many people looked toward NLF as perhaps authoritative source for bringing war to end. (Under circumstances I did not challenge this to me strange statement.) Now however it was more apparent that Hanoi was focal point and so there was less interest in NLF contacts. Wachtmeister, new Ambassador in Algiers, had seen NLF representative, but not with any prescribed mission.

> "5. Given frequent de facto contacts in Hanoi and need for channel to handle Swedish medical and other relief assistance to North Viet-Nam, Bergstrom 'would be tempted' to recommend establishment consular relations were it not for 'German problem'.[4] I said if this happened, he might also have an 'American problem' on his hands. He then backtracked, saying that he had no thought of recommending this to Minister...."

PARSONS

February 7, 1967

Still not having passed on the substance of exchanges in Hanoi and
Warsaw, the Swedes suddenly asked "if appropriate American could be
available at Stockholm or possibly Warsaw in utmost secrecy to talk with
Hanoi representative during TET talks while bombing suspended.".

STOCKHOLM 926 to SecState (TOP SECRET, NODIS, ASPEN),
February 7, 1967. Ref: Stockholm 910.

"1. After having met with Foreign Minister Nilsson on
reports from Petri in Peking and Oberg again in Warsaw Belfrage
and Bergstrom sent for me ten p.m. Stockholm time Seventh.
While emphasizing their information was difficult to evaluate
perhaps insubstantial, they inclined to believe Hanoi had moved
quite a bit towards real desire for 'contact' (as distinct from
negotiations) with American official qualified to talk.

"2. As possibility of 'contact' apparently linked to TET
truce which limited, so they understood, to four days beginning
February 8, it was of utmost urgency to know if appropriate
American could be available Stockholm or possibly Warsaw in utmost
secrecy to talk with Hanoi representative during TET truce while
bombing suspended. Bergstrom is proceeding Warsaw Thursday the
ninth to explore situation further and also so as to be in position relay any American reaction to information which he and
Belfrage gave me tonight and which I am reporting in message
to follow this one.

"3. I can not evaluate how seriously we should take this
but there is no doubt Swedes privy to Petri and Oberg reports
think Hanoi may be in earnest provided there is face saving
formula. Whether Hanoi is in earnest about (1) seeking peace,
(2) prolonging TET bomb pause or (3) searching for basis on
which to negotiate, Swedes could not say. However, they prepared send Bergstrom to Warsaw anyway and first point on which
they hope to have immediate answer is whether we can get someone here or to Warsaw during TET truce. If so they think they
will be in position to find out if Hanoi could and would also
authorize someone (probably their Warsaw Ambassador) to be
available for contact during truce.. . ."

PARSONS

That same evening, the Swedes finally passed on Petri's report and
the report of Oberg's recent and unreported crash mission to Warsaw.

While admitting that the Petri-Trinh talks "did not yield much," the
Swedes felt there were some encouraging signs. Most important in their

minds was the indication from the Warsaw contact that the North Vietnamese "was apparently willing to have a direct contact with U.S. even without knowing how long bombing was suspended (so long as this not announced)." The Swedes apparently felt that this position in Hanoi was a sufficient response to the President's policy of talking "whenever we can get other side to do so."

Petri's contacts with Trinh in Hanoi did not yield much by way of clarifying the four State queries (the four queries in State 88128 of 18 November 1966). Trinh talked about the FNL being "a spokesman" or "the spokesman."

> STOCKHOLM 927 to SecState (TOP SECRET, NODIS, ASPEN),
> February 7, 1967. Ref: Stockholm 926.
>
> "2. In Hanoi, Petri-Trinh talks 'did not yield much.'
> Trinh was bitter about alleged intensification of war since
> October and emphasized unconditional bomb stop was prerequisite
> to anything else.[5] There could be no preconditions to bombstop.
> This was closest Petri got to answer to point 1 set forth in
> State 88128 for clarification of meaning Trinh's cryptic remark
> 'we know what we will have to do.'
>
> "3. Trinh encouraged Petri to think Swedish effort for peace
> was laudable. He did so with apparent but not explicit recog-
> nition Swedes had been in touch with Washington. On Point 2
> Trinh said merely FNL could be 'a spokesman' or 'the spokesman'
> for South Vietnamese people. Petri did not raise Point 3 on
> reunification. He thought answer to query in final sentence
> was 'yes' but that it would have been useless to press Trinh
> on this. Point 4 on DMZ which contingent on mention by Trinh
> did not come up.
>
> "4. After Petri returned to Peking about January 25th Hanoi
> charge there sought him out and drew his attention to Trinh's
> statement to Australian journalist Burchett that talks could take
> place as soon as bombing stopped. Petri told Charge's US wanted
> some indication first that Vietnamese willing deescalate war.
> Hanoi Charge replied such request from Americans would appear to
> make bomb stop conditional and would therefore be unacceptable.
>
> "5. When this word reached Ministry some days ago Foreign
> Minister decided send Oberg back to Warsaw. On taking contact
> Oberg was received not by subordinate as before but by North
> Vietnamese Ambassador, a change which Swedes though significant.
> Oberg told his superiors on returning to Stockholm this evening
> that it was clear Warsaw Ambassador was fully briefed on Petri's
> recent visit to Hanoi as he had been on earlier one. He said he
> told Ambassador that since he had been received at higher level
> his principals would be willing to send Bergstrom to Warsaw.
> Ambassador replied in French this would be 'suitable.' Accordingly
> Foreign Minister has told Bergstrom proceed (as reported Stockholm
> 926).

"6. Crux of Oberg's talk in Warsaw was possibility that TET stand down in military operations might provide opportunity for contacts between Hanoi and USA organized by and in presence of Swedes. Place not mentioned but Swedes assumed Warsaw, Stockholm, even third capital possible. Oberg got impression that if bombing was in suspense even for an unspecified period, Hanoi would want to have contact with us. However, if we announced bombing would stop for four days only, Hanoi would not agree to contact. (Thus possibility if any may be foreclosed). It was clear to Oberg that it was intended that this message should reach us.

"7. In thinking foregoing over Swedes said they impressed that (1) Hanoi has moved Warsaw contact to a higher level and (2) Hanoi Warsaw Ambassador evidently interested in American contact if face can be saved all around. When I remarked it did not appear Hanoi had met our view that some signal must first be given as to what Hanoi would do if we stopped bombing Swedes replied that was true but on other hand Hanoi was apparently willing to have a direct contact with us even without knowing how long bombing was suspended (so long as this not announced). Maybe, Swedes conceded, Hanoi only maneuvering to get bombing stopped by diplomatic maneuver but they thought Hanoi's situation might have become such, especially given China situation, that their desire for contact with us was genuine. This is what led Swedes to ask if when Bergstrom met Hanoi Ambassador in Warsaw he could say US was also prepared to send representative to make contact in utmost secrecy.

"8. In this context Belfrage cautiously observed Hanoi has never told Swedes it would be willing to talk with us if bomb stop not explicitly unconditional; it has merely shown some signs of interest in talking if we did not put an explicit date on resumption of bombing. Belfrage concluded that he understood President had said that our policy was to talk whenever we could get other side to do so. I reminded him of distinction between 'unconditional discussions' on one hand and some prior private or public indication of what Hanoi would do if we stopped bombing on other hand (State 130520 Circular)."

PARSONS

February 8, 1967

State wanted clarification on statement from Warsaw contact suggesting a desire for preliminary contact during TET and the statement to Petri that unconditional bombing was a prerequisite to anything else. State also wished Bergstrom to explore military reciprocity. On the point of the readiness of the U.S. representative, State said that the U.S. would be prepared to respond to "talks without conditions."

STATE 133671 to Amembassy STOCKHOLM (TOP SECRET, NODIS, ASPEN), February 8, 1967. Ref: Stockholm 926, 927.

"1.   It is not clear on the basis of information reported
reftels precisely what DRV Ambassador in Warsaw told Swedes which
gave them impression that Hanoi might have real desire for
contact with American official qualified to talk during Tet truce
period. As reported by Swedes, Hanoi would not agree to contact
if we announced bombing would stop for four days only, and we have
already announced (and presume Hanoi aware of it) that duration of
Tet truce would be for 96 hours, with implication bombing could
resume thereafter. Nevertheless we certainly wish to leave no
possibility unexplored and,
                                                    we accept as
you do their good faith in passing this information along. We
therefore suggest you convey following to Foreign Ministry, bearing
in mind we are not sanguine anything can in fact e worked out in
connection Tet truce and we do not wish to seem to be urging
Warsaw trip on Bergstrom:

a.   We are most grateful for these recent reports of
Swedish conversations with DRV representatives in Hanoi and
Warsaw. We think Bergstrom visit and talk with DRV Ambassador
could be useful in clarifying DRV position. Among points on which
he could seek further precision are relationship between DRV
Ambassador's statements to Oberg suggesting desire for preliminary
contact with US representatives during four-day Tet truce and DRV
Foreign Minister's statement to Ambassador Petri that unconditional
bombing halt was prerequisite to anything else. Bergstrom could
emphasize his conviction that US remains prepared for secret
discussions at any time, without conditions, and such discussions
might cover whole range to topics relevant to peaceful settlement.

b.   In connection with finding mutually acceptable
basis for initiating preliminary talks, Bergstrom could express
opinion that some reciprocal restraint to indicate that neither
side intended to use the occasion of the talks for military
advantage would provide tangible evidence of good faith of all
parties in prospects for negotiated settlement.

c.   As to Swede's specific question whether appropriate American official could be available Stockholm or possibly
Warsaw in utmost secrecy to talk with Hanoi representative during
Tet truce, US would be prepared to respond immediately and positively to any serious indication of Hanoi interest in having
talks without conditions.

d.   Bergstrom should know that decision on duration of
Tet truce and arrangements for carrying it out were made some
time ago. If press stories refer to 96 hour period because of
information given out earlier pursuant to these decisions and
arrangements, Hanoi would have no basis for charging that US
had disregarded suggestion made February 8 to Swedes in Warsaw.
That suggestion was known in Washington well after our position

18

on duration truce had been made public in Saigon. We trust
Bergstrom will bear this fully in mind in case DRV Ambassador
takes that line."

RUSK

February 9, 1967

The Swedes indicated that although they had nothing tangible to go
on they wished to pursue the contacts. They were pegging what optimism
they had on the DRV statement to the effect that Hanoi will talk if the
bombing stopped unconditionally.

STOCKHOLM 934 to SecState (TOP SECRET, NODIS, ASPEN),
February 9, 1967. Ref: State 133671.

"2. Bergstrom had time only to say that Swedish impression
based on admittedly tenuous evidence but, as described 927,
sufficiently impressive to lead them to actions which they have
taken, namely, report to me and sending Oberg back to Warsaw
eight to make appointment for Bergstrom there ninth (which is
to be at 9 P.M. Feb 9), Warsaw time, presumably to allow
Ambassador time obtain further instructions from Hanoi).

"3. Belfrage in accordance his usual caution began by saying
that only formal statement DRV Reps have made to Swedes on talks
is to stress their willingness if unconditional bomb stop. He
too said evidence tenuous, but they were encouraged by progression
from Trinh's opening attitude in Hanoi Jan 23 which was harsh
and terse to point reached in Warsaw sixth when Amb 'jumped at'
proposal meet with Bergstrom. Belfrage said initially on 23rd
Trinh said in effect 'since our Oct talk whatever you said to
Americans led them to intensify bombing and war'. Later he was
somewhat mollified and in end Petri was launched by Vice Minister
and urged to come back again. Then came North Vietnamese Charge's
unsolicited approach to Petri in Peking which struck Swedes
as possibly more a sign of interest in talks than in propagandizing
them with Burchett article. Finally, as Petri's contacts inconclusive, the decided send Oberg to Warsaw where higher level and
interest in pursuing subject brought Swedes to present position.

"4. Belfrage asked if Bergstrom definitely could say American
could come during Tet truce or after and I referred him text para C
REFTEL adding that trouble to get talks was not repeat not with US
but Hanoi. I also reiterated per para B Bergstrom could emphasize
his conviction U.S. prepared for secret discussion at anytime without conditions. We then had some discussion of mechanics and agreed
that if Bergstrom receives impression tonight that leads him to take
responsibility of urging an American should come at once, Bergstrom

should via Ministry send me flash report to this effect. I
added that if he were to to urge without firm assurance that
a DRV Rep would duly be made available to talk, I personally
thought Washington would, if willing at all, have to opt for
Stockholm where American visitors presence could probably be
kept secret...."

PARSONS

Belfrage indicated that we should be prepared for sudden contact.

STOCKHOLM 935 to SecState (TOP SECRET, NODIS, ASPEN),
February 9, 1967. Ref: Stockholm 934.

"1. Belfrage telephoned me in guarded terms message
received six P.M. local time Feb. 9 from Warsaw where
Bergstrom has already had meeting with DRV representative.

"2. He said message said DRV showed interest and
expected give reaction February 10. Oberg will remain to
receive reply while Bergstrom returns here morning of 10th.
It obvious DRV rep is consulting Hanoi.

"3. Impression gained was that if reply is affirmative,
Warsaw is likely be favored over Stockholm as locale. However, this, like nature of reply itself, 'very doubtful' and
Belfrage cautioned against optimism. However, he thought we
would be well-advised have 'someone on starting line' as idea
had been certainly not repeat not turned down."

PARSONS.

February 11, 1967

Bergstrom returned from Warsaw, leaving Oberg in case a follow-up was
needed. Parsons got the impression that Bergstrom had not fully communicated
the U.S. position.

STOCKHOLM 940 to SecState (TOP SECRET, NODIS, ASPEN),
February 11, 1967. Ref: Stockholm 935; State 133671.

"2. Bergstrom confirmed DRV ambassador took his
approach seriously and said he would communicate at once
to Hanoi. Ambassador had Deputy with him who intervened
from time to time with usual Hanoi line but Ambassador
himself did not indulge in arguments and was matter-of-fact.

"3. Bergstrom said he stressed point set forth in
Para C State reftel and also closely related point in last
sentence Para A. Thus he believes it entirely clear to
Hanoi reps that US would respond positively at once if

there were Hanoi desire for 'contact.' Bergstrom said he stressed idea of 'contact' rather than negotiation...."

"5. Bergstrom said that while he had well in mind substance Para D State reftel, question of charge of bad faith did not come up and so this never seemed germane to his discussion with DRV Ambassador. As Bergstrom also remarked that he did not emphasize all the other points in reference message, I suspect he touched only lightly on substance Para B State reftel on reciprocal restraints during truce which must have been over 40 hours old, by time of his talk...."

PARSONS

February 12, 1967

STOCKHOLM 941 to SecState (TOP SECRET, NODIS, ASPEN), February 12, 1967. Ref: Stockholm 940.

"1. Oberg called Bergstrom from Warsaw February 12 to report that when he went to say goodbye at DRV embassy he was urged to stay although apparently with no promise of an answer. Bergstrom on own authority authorized Oberg remain Warsaw until February 13.

"2. Bergstrom also authorized Oberg to tell DRV Embassy that Americans had asked 'if there was any news.' Bergstrom had cleared this gambit with Nilsson but not repeat not with me.

"3. Bergstrom aware risks in international phone call from Warsaw but he believes caution plus pre-arranged signals have masked game."

PARSONS

February 13, 1967

STOCKHOLM 944 to SecState (TOP SECRET, NODIS, ASPEN), February 13, 1967. Ref: Stockholm 941.

"1. About noon 13th Bergstrom told me Oberg in Warsaw has had no reply yet from DRV.

"2. GOS has authorized Oberg remain over Tuesday.

"3. FonMinister has also authorized him to tell DRV Ambassador that should latter wish to see Bergstrom again, Minister would be willing to make him available."

PARSONS

STOCKHOLM 948 to SecState (TOP SECRET, NODIS, ASPEN),
February 13, 1967. Ref: Stockholm 944; State 133671.

"1. In talks with Bergstrom over week end and again
today we went over several points connected with his Warsaw
visit reported Stockholm 940.

A. He showed me his record of briefing he had
received from me before leaving for Warsaw early 9th (Stockholm 934) which was based on State reftel. From this I am
satisfied there could have been no misunderstanding of US
position by Swedes on this first occasion when, as Bergstrom
pointed out, Swedes could acknowledge they were authorized
transmit our views.

B. Bergstrom thought it best in Warsaw not to
emphasize 96 hour Tet truce period in connection Para C
State reftel.

C. Contrary to my earlier understanding he did,
however, remind DRV ambassador in accordance Para D that
sequence of events was such that press references to already
settled 96 hour period could provide no basis for any Hanoi
charges of bad faith in regard to February 6 suggestions to
Swedes in Warsaw. I am quite sure he did this on his own
initiative rather than because DRV Ambassador took any such
line.

D. As I suspected, Bergstrom did not discuss Para B
State Reftel (reciprocal military restraint during any preliminary US-DRV talks) because he felt it would merely touch
off standard DRV recriminations."

....

PARSONS

February 15, 1967

STOCKHOLM 961 to SecState (TOP SECRET, NODIS, ASPEN),
February 15, 1967. Ref: Stockholm 948.

"1. Belfrage and Bergstrom remained behind when FonMin
Nilsson left after lunch at residence Feb 15 to discuss possible
future contacts between Swedes and DRV Embassy Warsaw.

"2. Swedish position is now that Oberg instructed remain
Warsaw until morning Feb 17 when he is to tell DRV Embassy he
must return Stockholm for personal reasons but that Bergstrom
or he available return Warsaw on short notice should DRV ask.

"3.   After probing without success for any information
from us on Kosygin-Wilson activity re Viet-Nam, Bergstrom then
outlined Swedes' estimate present situation:

A)   Swedish contacts with DRV apparently independent
of other channels US may have available;

B)   Because Bergstrom did not repeat not mention
'bomb stop' or 'bomb pause' at any time in his talks with DJH,
Swedes do not consider that either end Tet cease-fire or
resumption US bombing DRV has estopped their channel from
further possible use;

C)   Swedes therefore feel free make offer availability
set forth para 2 above;

D)   In addition, Swedes would want feel free at some
time in future to return to DRV in Warsaw saying that Swedish
appreciation US position such that Swedes on own initiative (not
on our behalf) would ask if DRV has anything to say, and

E)   Swedes would at that time ask if DRV still interested
preliminary contact with us on general lines originally set forth
Stockholm 926.

"4.   I replied that 3 D and 3 E went beyond my current
instructions in so far as availability US official is concerned.

"5.   In giving detailed account atmospherics of his talk
with DRV Ambassador, Bergstrom raised point of whether or not
DRV were under necessity checking with FNL before replying to
Swedes. Questioning of Bergstrom elicited that Swedes see
problem that DRV may be interested in US-DRV contact without
prejudice to FNL political position or FNL political and military
activity South Viet-Nam. Belfrage at this point offered that
he would think such contact would be 'of interest' to us.

"6.   I replied that Secretary's statements seemed clear that
we want to talk to Hanoi and added we considered FNL not independent Hanoi.

"7.   Only other operational problem arose earlier in lunch
when Nilsson pointed out that he must face foreign affairs council
Feb 16 when he expects to be asked specifically what GOS has done
to get peace in Viet-Nam and when question may well be put in
terms of what Petri has done in Hanoi.

XGDS-1

I reiterated our position that strict secrecy
has been and continues essential in order not damage any possible
prospective channel for peace."

. . . .

PARSONS

February 16, 1967

State indicated no objection to the Swedes renewing their offer of availability to return to Warsaw on short notice should the DRV ask. State, however, had a number of problems on substance.

> STATE 138786 to Amembassy STOCKHOLM (TOP SECRET, NODIS, ASPEN), February 16, 1967. Ref: Stockholm 961.
>
> "....In connection with question raised paragraph 1. b. State reftel (reciprocal restraint during preliminary talks as tangible evidence of good faith), you should explain to Bergstrom that this observation was not restricted to effort to arrange talks during Tet truce, but has general applicability as means of creating favorable atmosphere for holding of talks. On the other hand agreement on reciprocal restraints is not intended by us to be a precondition to talks.
>
> "(c) We wish to avoid linking any US/DRV contacts with explicit or implicit understanding, as suggested by Swedes, that DRV would be speaking for itself, not for NLF. As you correctly pointed out, it is our position that Hanoi is ultimate center of power and decision-making relative to settlement; should Hanoi decide to have unconditional bilateral talks with US, including discussions of matters which nominally fall within purview of Front, this would be problem for Hanoi to handle. It should be noted that Hanoi in its campaign to exchange permanent bombing halt for indication of vague bilateral talks has itself not mentioned participation or role of Front. We see no reason to introduce this subject gratuitously.
>
> "(d) We remain interested in keeping Swedish channel open and are grateful for efforts of Swedes thus far in probing Hanoi's intentions. Continued secrecy is of course mandatory if this channel is to have continued usefulness. We trust Swedes will not jeopardize their potential role as mediators by any considerations of temporary political advantage."
>
> KATZENBACH

February 18, 1967

> STOCKHOLM 970 to SecState (TOP SECRET, NODIS, ASPEN), February 18, 1967. Ref: State 138786.
>
> "1. At Noon 17th I briefed Bergstrom on contents reftel.
>
> "2. On Para C, Bergstrom seemed at first to interpret this as indicating we would not object to Swedes volunteering to DRV Ambassador that NLF could come independently to talks with us.

I said that from final two sentences of Para C, it was quite clear Swedes should not do so on our behalf. He then asked if we would object in event Hanoi Amb should take initiative in seeking to bring FNL rep with him to any talks which it might be possible to arrange. I replied that in my opinion we would not object should DRV in effect sponsor FNL rep as participant."

....

PARSONS

February 22 thru March 8, 1967

State (STATE 142081) approved the line the American Embassy was taking in Stockholm on clarifying NLF participation and on discouraging another Swedish effort to communicate with the DRV in Warsaw. State believed that the DRV was stalling. On February 23, in Stockholm 994, Parsons reported that on leaving Warsaw on the 17th Oberg had already made a firm appointment for himself for March 1. If the DRV representative at the March 1 meeting raised the subject of a Bergstrom visit, Oberg was to be non-committal. On March 8, in Stockholm 1045, Parsons reported that Oberg was returning from Warsaw and that "nothing important transpired" in the contact.

March 11, 1967

STOCKHOLM 1069 to SecState (TOP SECRET, NODIS, ASPEN), March 11, 1967. Ref: Stockholm 1045.

"1. Late Tenth Bergstrom reported:

A. Oberg's trip Warsaw March 1-3 had been undertaken despite some doubts as to wisdom of going at all and with strict instructions to listen and not exert any Swedish pressure at all.

B. Oberg gained impression Hanoi Rep under similar wraps. In any event no real dialogue developed.

C. Hanoi rep asked if Bergstrom was in Warsaw.

D. Both Hanoi rep and Oberg were reluctant to refer to contacts during Tet truce.

E. Hanoi rep asked for briefing on Swedish internal political situation on which he showed himself knowledgeable. He also asked especially about Riksdag discussion on possible recognition of DRV.[6] (Nilsson discouraged this).

....

25

G. Hanoi rep extremely bitter in word and manner at resumption US bombing plus mining coastal waters, naval and trans DMZ shelling.[7] He said this prime example us bad faith just when Trinh through Burchett had paved way for entering on talks with US.

H. It was agreed keep channel open for future and Hanoi rep professed great gratitude for Swedish efforts.

. . . .

"4. Bergstrom commented bit ruefully on report Italian Foreign Minister had publicly claimed he had had private channel to Hanoi too.   X G DS- 1

He wondered if Italians had had valid channel. I said I didn't know."

. . . .

PARSONS

March 18, 1967

STATE 158220 to Amembassy STOCKHOLM (TOP SECRET, NODIS, ASPEN), March 18, 1967. Ref: Stockholm 1069).

"1. At next appropriate occasion you should express our appreciation for latest word on Swedes Warsaw talks, noting continuing importance of keeping contact secret notwithstanding sterility of latest phase since one can never foretell when this channel might usefully be reactivated....".

RUSK (drafted by Isham).

April 13, 1967

STOCKHOLM 1187 to SecState (TOP SECRET, NODIS, ASPEN), April 13, 1967.

"1. During call on SecGen Belfrage 13th, I asked if there had been any ASPEN developments. He said no, but he has accepted invitation Polish Vice Minister Winiewicz to visit Warsaw May 8-13. Ministry now considering whether Belfrage should attempt contact Hanoi ambassador just to see if latter has anything to say and how he says it.

"2.   Later FonMin Nilsson volunteered that if US has any proposal to make through Swedish channel, GOS remains ready to pass   it along to Hanoi representative."

. . . .

PARSONS

April 14, 1967

STOCKHOLM 1199 to SecState (TOP SECRET, NODIS, ASPEN), April 14, 1967. Ref: Stockholm 1187.

. . . .

"2.   Bergstrom said that it now probably that Belfrage would be asked to contact Hanoi representative in Warsaw next month and, if so, it would be useful to have 'something tangible in his baggage'....

"3.   Bergstrom said GOS would probably send Petri to Hanoi again in May or June to learn what he could.

"4.   Continuing in speculative vein, Bergstrom said that Nilsson thought there was only one card left for Swedes to play. On own responsibility they might say privately to Hanoi they were convinced from their contacts with Americans that 'if Hanoi would do thus and so, Swedes confident such and such would happen on American side'. GOS, however, could not come up with any specifics on 'thus and so' and 'such and such'. They therefore uncertain if or how they could proceed, but they did feel Hanoi had some confidence their good faith. Minister himself might find it possible to seek meeting with Trinh. Bergstrom then said it would be useful to know if we saw any possible opening or had any ideas on such a give-and-take process for which Swedes would in effect be guarantors of genuineness of proposals."

. . . .

PARSONS

April 18, 1967

STOCKHOLM 1219 to SecState (TOP SECRET, NODIS, ASPEN), April 18, 1967. Ref: Stockholm 1199.

"1.   During discussion at residence April 16 about Foreign Minister's announced intention reduce level Swedish

27

diplomatic representation in Saigon, Bergstrom commented

"2. In follow-up talk April 17, Bergstrom speculated
that one possible effect of Swedish action might be to
increase Hanoi's receptivity to Swedish efforts promote
peace negotiations, Bergstrom commented that now 'Hanoi may
listen to us more' (Stockholm 1207). In this connection,
Foreign Minister quoted in Svenska Dagbladet April 18 as
saying in reply question: 'We have not offered to appear
as mediator but rather to negotiate contacts which could
lead to mediation.'"

. . . .

CAMERON.

April 22, 1967

With some Swedish pressure for a new U.S. move on negotiations,
State responded to the effect that the U.S. stands on the President's letter
to Ho,[8] the President's Nashville speech and Secretary Rusk's 9 February
press conference.

State also showed dismay at the fact that the GOS could not renew
accreditation of its ambassador to the GVN.

STATE 180598 to Amembassy STOCKHOLM (TOP SECRET, NODIS, ASPEN),
April 22, 1967. Ref: Stockholm 1187, 1199.

"1. We are not sanguine about possibility of giving
Belfrage something 'tangible in his baggage' for his visit
to Warsaw next month. Hanoi does not now seem interested
in discussing tangibles, as witness its treatment of offer
contained in President's February 8 letter to Ho, and seems
unwilling to consider any offer short of US acceptance of
the Trinh-Burchett formula. Swedes are of course familiar
with our position on that formula (President's Nashville
speech, Rusk February 9 press conference).

. . . .

"3. In meantime, we cannot refrain from expressing
our disappointment over apparent GOS decision not to renew
accreditation to GVN of Swedish Ambassador Thailand after

present incumbent departs. Our views on this development
are contained in separate message but in your discretion may
be drawn upon in this channel. In particular, considering
Stockholm's 1219 just received, you should convey our skepticism
over Bergstrom's remark that now 'Hanoi may listen to us more.'
Any increased Hanoi receptivity to Swedes as a result of this
action in our judgment is likely to be marginal. In fact, if
Swedes should appear over-eager to sell GVN short, Hanoi's
most likely reaction would be to toughen its position regarding
Swedish mediatory efforts, not to moderate it."

Excerpts from RUSK NEWS CONFERENCE on Vietnam, February 9,
1967, as recorded by The New York Times.

"There's been a good deal of discussion in recent days
about the prospects for peace in Vietnam.

"President Johnson has pressed for peace in Southeast
Asia in capitals all over the world, over and over again.

"We've made it clear that we want no bases in Southeast
Asia, and do not wish to retain United States troops in Vietnam after peace is assured.

"We have affirmed our full support for free elections in
South Vietnam, to give the South Vietnamese a government of
their own choice, and have stated that the question of reunification should be determined by the Vietnamese through their
own free decision. .

"We have emphasized that we would much prefer to use
our resources for the economic reconstruction of Southeast
Asia rather than war and that peace could permit North Vietnam to participate in a regional effort to which we would
be prepared to contribute at least one billion dollars.

"On the military side, we have on two occasions stopped
the bombing of North Vietnam.

"In May, 1965, a pause was limited to five and a half
days, because it was rejected by the principal Communist
capitals during the first three days.

"At the beginning of 1966, there was a cessation for
37 days--a period much longer than had been indicated might
produce some constructive results.

"It elicited no response other than the continuation
of the movement of men and arms into the south, and an
assertion that Vietnam must be settled on Communist terms.

"We must know the military consequences of such a military
action on our part. They must not expect us to stop our military action by bombing while they continue their military
action by invasion. No one has been able or willing to give
us any information on this subject.

"We've been trying in every way known to us to invite
and to engage in such talks.

"Unfortunately, I cannot report to you today any tangible
forward movement in this direction.

"But all channels remain open and are being utilized.

"Our objective in Vietnam is and always has been a
limited one. A South Vietnam able to determine its own
future without external interference. I need hardly repeat
that this and this alone is our objective, but for the
benefit of members of the press who may not be fully familiar
with all our statements, I am today making available points
we made last year under 14 different headings annotated to
reflect developments in 1966.

"These are, and remain, not in any sense preconditions
for discussions but rather statements of the elements which
we believe could produce peace in Vietnam.

"Let me say quietly and sincerely to all capitals on the
other side, let good sense take charge for all of us in
this situation. Recognize the necessity for elementary
reciprocity."

QUESTIONS

"Q. Mr. Secretary, you mentioned the 14 points that were
put out a year ago. Would you say that the atmosphere or the
climate for peace negotiations has improved in any way since
that time, particularly since the conflict in China has become
so intense?

"A. It's hard to judge atmosphere, because what we really
must count upon is specific, tangible indications of a readiness to move toward peace.

"So what the atmosphere really will amount to turns upon
whether we can in fact engage the other side at points where

we and they, together, can move this matter toward the conference table or toward a peaceful settlement.

"Q. Mr. Secretary, you have talked about the need to recognize the principle of elementary reciprocity. Since so much of the current discussion seems to hang on this, sir, could you give us some idea of whether by this you mean a specific promise to negotiate if we stop the bombing or specific military action?

"A. Well, I have pointed out in my statement that we cannot stop our military actions involving the bombing while they continue their military actions of invasion.

"I think some elementary reciprocity is required and common fairness would require that if there is an interest toward peace that both sides help move toward it because you can't stop this war simply by stopping a half of it.

"Q. Here's another question, Mr. Secretary. Are there any contacts or discussions of any kind going on to extend that four-day cease-fire in the seven-day cease-fire they say they're going to honor?

"A. Well, Prime Minister Ky has indicated some time ago that he would be prepared to discuss with the North Vietnam authorities the question of that cease-fire.

"This is something which can be discussed, which can be looked into, but I could not give you any details today as to whether or not there are discussions pointing in that direction. There are some difficult operational questions about that.

"Q. Mr. Secretary, a year ago, you recall, we offered to maintain our bombing pause if the other side would only come to talk. In fact we sent convoys around the world looking for some signal from Hanoi of a willingness to talk. Why is it that now we are unwilling to make such an offer during the current pause?

"A. Well let me point out that the other side is not talking about a pause. The other side is demanding an unconditional and permanent cessation of the bombing.

"Now that is a very significant military step for us to take; and unless it is accompanied by military action on their part, it would create a situation in which they would be safe and secure and comfortable while sitting there

sending their men and their arms down the Ho Chi Minh Trail
and across the 17th parallel to attack South Vietnam.

"Q. Is it the shift in position on Hanoi's side in the
terms for the bombing cessation that has caused the shift in
our position?

"A. Well, there's no shift in our position. In the sense
that we are prepared to take up political questions through
political channels. We are prepared to deal with military
matters as military matters. And we are prepared to discuss
with the other side what action each side might take of a
military character that would move this matter toward peace."

. . . .

Secretary Rusk said that the Communist side is waging a "systematic
campaign" to bring about a permanent cessation of U.S. bombing "without
any corresponding military action on their side."   He rejected the
January 28 Trinh formulation that stopping the bombing could lead to
talks. The U.S., he declared, is not prepared to end the bombing in
exchange for some "formless" possibility of talks. Before the U.S. will
take such a step, he emphasized, "we must know the military consequences."

March 15, 1967

President Johnson's Nashville Speech.

The central element of this speech was the President's statement
that "reciprocity must be the fundamental principle of any reduction in
hostilities."

"Our Position Today," by Lyndon B. Johnson, President
of the United States, Delivered before the Tennessee
Legislature, Nashville, Tennessee, March 15, 1967.

. . . .

."Now this brings me to final point: the peaceful and just
world that we all seek.

"We have just lived through another flurry of rumors of
'peace feelers.' Our years of dealing with this problem have
taught us that peace will not come easily.

"The problem is a very simple one: It takes two to negotiate at a peace table, and Hanoi has just simply refused to
consider coming to a peace table.

"I don't believe that our own position on peace negotiations can be stated any more clearly than I have stated it
many times in the past--or that the distinguished Secretary
of State, Mr. Rusk, or Ambassador Goldberg, or any number
of other officials have stated it in every forum that we could
find. But I do want to repeat to you this afternoon and
through you to the people of America the essentials now lest
there be any doubts:

"The United States representatives are ready at any time
for discussions of the Vietnam problem or any related matter,
with any government or governments, if there is any reason
to believe that these discussions will in any way seriously
advance the cause of peace.

"We are prepared to go more than halfway and to use any
avenue possible to encourage such discussions, and we have done
that at every opportunity.

"We believe that the Geneva accords of 1954 and 1962
could serve as the central elements of a peaceful settlement.
These accords provide in essence that both South and North
Vietnam should be free from external interference, while at
the same time they would be free independently to determine
their positions on the question of reunification.

"We also stand ready to advance toward a reduction of
hostilities without prior agreement. The road to peace
could go from deeds to discussions, or it could start with
discussions and go to deeds.

"We are ready to take either route. We are ready to move
on both of them.

"But reciprocity must be the fundamental principle of any
reduction in hostilities. The United States cannot and will
not reduce its activities unless and until there is some reduction on the other side. To follow any other rule would be to
violate the trust that we undertake when we ask a man to risk
his life for his country.

"We will negotiate a reduction of the bombing whenever the
Government of North Vietnam is ready, and there are almost
innumerable avenues of communication by which the Government
of North Vietnam can make their readiness known.

"To this date and this hour there has been no sign of
that readiness. Yet we must and we will keep on trying.

"As I speak to you today, Secretary Rusk and our representatives throughout the world are on a constant alert.
Hundreds and hundreds of quiet diplomatic conversations free
from the glare of front-page headlines, of the klieg lights--
these conversations are being held and they will be held on
the possibilities of bringing peace to Vietnam.

"Governor Averell Harriman, with 25 years of experience
in trouble-shooting on the most difficult international problems that America has ever had, is carrying out my instructions
that every possible lead, however slight it may first appear, from
any source, public or private, shall be followed up.

"So let me conclude by saying this: I so much wish that
it were within my power to assure that all those in Hanoi
could hear one simple message--America is committed to the
defense of South Vietnam until an honorable peace can be
negotiated."

. . . .

April 25-26, 1967

In Stockholm 1266, Cameron cabled that he had given Bergstrom
the text of the Secretary's press conference and the President's Nashville
speech. On April 26, Cameron cabled (Stockholm 1273) that Bergstrom
and Oberg "seem more inclined than earlier to accept possibility that
Swedish action on its representation in Saigon now followed by lack of
effective action on 'Russell tribunal' would cause Hanoi toughen its
position and make their efforts establish useful contacts more difficult."[9]
The Swedes, nevertheless, placed increased importance on Belfrage's May
visit to Warsaw and said that "it now even more essential for Sweden to
make every effort explore possibilities 'on other side.'"

May 9, 1967

Nilsson-Quang Thu (NVN Ambassador, Bucharest) Conversation.

Nothing new in this contact. Thu merely reemphasized the January 28
Trinh position and Ho's letter to the President. The Swedes, however,
showed a strong disposition, as they have done before, to playing very
active role in bringing the two sides together.

STOCKHOLM 1358 (CC) to SecState (TOP SECRET, NODIS, ASPEN),
May 9, 1967.

34

. . . .

"3. Thu said he had read encouraging reports of Russell
Tribunal meeting Stockholm and that he appreciated GOS attitude toward Viet-Nam issue. This attitude not only expressed
in press but had been shown by Petri talk in Hanoi with Trinh
and Bergstrom's talks in Warsaw.

"4. Nilsson explained Swedish desire explore if in some
way Sweden could help produce contact between warring parties.

"5. Thu stated NVN position is based on Trinh-Burchett
four points and Ho Chi Minh correspondence with President.
It would be, he said, simple to organize a contact if US
would without conditions finally and definitely stop its
bombing of North Viet-Nam. US would gain prestige in eyes of
world. (At this point, Bergstrom said his notes were not
clear, but he believed Thu said
In any event, Thu concluded that West must understand that after
centuries of fighting invaders,
Vietnamese people will in the end win however big military
effort US makes.

"6. Nilsson said he did not believe in military solution
but in a political solution which must start somewhere. Thu
said it must start with bombing stop. Nilsson said he understood this, but asked was a contact or a dialogue in present
situation at all 'thinkable' if North Viet-Nam did not give any
sign, even the smallest, which US could seize upon? If Sweden
could be of any use, Nilsson concluded, it would be at disposal
both parties.

"7. Nilsson then explained that theoretically speaking he
could conceive of situation under certain circumstances where
Sweden might even take responsibility for a position which it
felt convinced about. For instance, if Sweden were convinced
of it, GOS might say that if the South would do one thing, the
North would do another.

"8. Thu concluded that he appreciated Nilsson good will
and he would carefully and immediately report talk.

"9. Bergstrom also told us that Belfrage trip Warsaw
put off for another ten days or so."

CAMERON

May 10 thru May 18, 1967

On 10 May, in Stockholm 1372, Cameron cabled that there may be a serious
problem of maintaining the secrecy of the Swedish contacts in Warsaw. Swedes

public position on this was to be that the "GOS wanted to be informed of Hanoi's position on war in Vietnam." The North Vietnamese Embassy in Warsaw was evincing some alarm about publicity. The reporter who had the story was told that publication "would severely limit possibility for Sweden to be helpful in contributing to peace....

As an interest aside, Bergstrom asked Cameron, without pressing it, what he could tell him about the Lewandowski affair. The Hightower story had recently broken.[10]

On 12 May (Stockholm 1382), Cameron reported that Swedes had been successful in at least temporarily halting the publication of the story.

On 17 May, in Stockholm 1405, Oberg reported that the only matter of substance raised in his talk with his North Vietnam contact on May 9-11 was with respect to the 20 April U.S. bombing of Haiphong.[11] The North Vietnamese contact said this represented a "new stage in war." According to Oberg, Belfrage planned to follow up his Bucharest talk when he arrived in Warsaw. On 18 May, State responded (STATE 197584) that the Swedes should continue these contacts, divorced from domestic political considerations, and that they should continue to explore and clarify Hanoi's attitudes.

May 27, 1967

Belfrage-North Vietnam Ambassador, Warsaw Conversation, May 18, 1967.

Nothing new emerged from this contact. The North Vietnamese Ambassador resisted any thought of reciprocal action from Hanoi. The Swedes warned of an intensification of the war.

STOCKHOLM 1463 to SecState (TOP SECRET, NODIS, ASPEN), May 27, 1967.

"1. Foreign Ministry Secretary General Belfrage asked DCM to come see him late afternoon May 26. Bergstrom also present most of talk.

"2. Belfrage said he wanted give us run-down on his talk with NVN Ambassador in Warsaw May 18 which Belfrage said had taken place in friendly, quiet atmosphere. Because nothing new had come out of this conversation he had not called us earlier.

"3. Belfrage said he told NVN Ambassador that he came with no message. He explained that GOS appreciated opportunity maintain contacts with Hanoi through NVN Ambassador.

"4. According Belfrage, NVN Ambassador had repeated well known Hanoi position. NVN Ambassador said U.S. bombing in north must cease before there could be 'contacts, talks or negotiations.' NVN Ambassador commented that U.S. talks peace but intensifies the war. He alleged U.S. not sincere about negotiations and cited President's letter to Ho as evidence. NVN Ambassador asserted it not reasonable for U.S. to ask reciprocal action from Hanoi; aggressor and victim could not be treated alike. He told Belfrage NVN would resist all aggression.

"5. Belfrage said NVN Ambassador seemed particularly interested in possible effect of increasingly critical international opinion on U.S. policy in Viet-Nam.[12] Belfrage acknowledged to him that perhaps international opinion was becoming more critical of U.S. Viet-Nam policy. However, he said it was Swedish assessment that effect of this development on U.S. policy determination should not be overemphasized. Belfrage said he made this point several times. He told NVN Ambassador Swedes thought that very large U.S. majority was behind President Johnson's policy. He also told NVN Ambassador that since there seemed to be a deadlock in U.S. and NVN positions on negotiations, it was Swedish impression that intensification of the war could be expected."

. . . .

"10. Belfrage said he had also discussed the Viet-Nam war with Rapacki and Winiewicz. Poles emphasized necessity for U.S. to stop bombing in North before talks could take place.

HEATH.

June 20, 1967

STOCKHOLM 1518 to SecState (TOP SECRET, NODIS, ASPEN), June 20, 1967. Ref: Stockholm 1463

"1. Oberg (Far East Desk FonMinistry) informed us June 20 that Petri departing Peking for Hanoi June 21 or 22. He will remain Hanoi until June 27, probably then returning directly to Peking prior to home leave in Sweden from early July until September.

"2. Petri had originally requested NVN visa May 29, explaining he wanted be able bring back latest information

to Stockholm. He was told June 15 that he could not
be received until 'late July.' On June 19 he was told
by NVN Embassy Peking that he was 'welcome at any time,
in fact right now.'

    "3. FonMinistry instructed Petri June 20 that there
was nothing new to say to NVN after Warsaw and Bucharest
conversations, but Petri was to listen to anything NVN
wished to say or to have him report. These instructions
in accord Petri's own estimate that present time not ripe
for any initiative, according Oberg."

    . . . .

    HEATH

June 23, 1967

    STATE 215754 to Amembassy STOCKHOLM (TOP SECRET, NODIS, ASPEN),
June 23, 1967. Ref: Stockholm 1518.

    "2. FYI. NVN Ambassador in Peking recently approached
Norwegian Ambassador stressing Hanoi's readiness for 'compromises' if negotiations began on basis bombing halt. NVN
Ambassador said he would be making similar approach to
Swedish and Danish colleagues. Without revealing source you
might have opportunity to ascertain whether Petri was in
fact approached along these lines."

    KATZENBACH

July 6, 1967

    PARIS 244 to SecState (SECRET, NODIS, MARIA THREE),
July 6, 1967.

    "3. /Petri/ met the Soviet Ambassador to Hanoi, Mr.
Tcherbakov, with whom he has some personal ties. He said

BOHLEN

July 12, 1967

STOCKHOLM 063 to SecState (TOP SECRET, NODIS, ASPEN),
July 12, 1967. Ref: State 215754

"1. Oberg (Far Eastern Desk FonMinistry and currently
aide to FonMinister) gave Plocoung run-down on four Petri
dispatches from Peking on evening July 11 at meeting set
by Oberg. Despatches dated between June 28 and July 1 and
received in Stockholm morning July 10....

"2. First despatch covered visit to Hanoi which ended
June 27. Petri met DRV FonMinister Trinh and Deputy Huang
Van Lo (phonetic). At separate interviews both told Petri
that January statement to Burchett remained DRV position
on negotiations, i.e., bombing of North and 'other acts of
war' must be stopped before talks could begin. Trinh added
that Ho letter to President remained 'road to peace.'

"3. Trinh expressed appreciation of Bucharest talks
(Stockholm 1358) and of Belfrage's 'good' talk in Warsaw
(Stockholm 1463). Trinh also said Russell proceedings in
Stockholm were 'appreciated' by DRV; Petri reported he made
no comment on this last.

"4. Petri told Trinh that he understood that January
statement to Burchett was still valid, and Petri added
that when bombing stopped, it was important that DRV take
some 'practical step' which could be 'noticed in Washington.'
Trinh did not comment but said he 'understood this way of

thinking.' Trinh concluded that DRV interested in keeping
open channel to Swedes. Petri who was under instructions
to 'keep a formal line' reciprocated GOS interest in conversations with DRV.

"5. Petri's evaluation of foregoing is 'there is no change.'"

. . . .

HEATH

July 13, 1967

STATE 6375 to Amembassy STOCKHOLM (CONFIDENTIAL, LIMDIS),
July 13, 1967. Ref: Stockholm 065.

"1. Would appreciate your clarifying as soon as possi-
ble with Oberg following points on his conversation with
North Vietnamese representatives at Stockholm Viet-Nam
Conference: [13]

a. Did Nguyen Minh Vy employ term bombing
'pause' rather than 'cessation', and if so was his use of
this term consistent throughout conversation? If he blurred
distinction between temporary pause and permanent unconditional cessation as stipulated by DRV Foreign Minister
Trinh January 28, does Oberg think this was by accident
or design?

b. In saying that unconditional bombing stop
is not necessary and all that was needed was 'proof of good
faith', did Vy in Oberg's judgment mean to imply that proof
of good faith could take forms other than unconditional
bombing stop?

c. What was date of Oberg's conversations, and
did he see two reps separately or together? Why did he
discount significance of their comments?

d. Does Oberg know whether DRV or Front delegates
took similar line with other foreign contacts in Stockholm
inasmuch as our reports indicate uniformly hard line characterized their statements?

e. Does Oberg have any confirmation of reports he
cited that conference had been threatened with a split between
NLF and DRV reps on conditions for negotiations?"

. . . .

RUSK

July 14, 1967

>STATE 7393 to Amembassy STOCKHOLM (TOP SECRET, NODIS, ASPEN),
>July 14, 1967. Ref: Stockholm 063.

>"1. We note that Petri makes no particular mention
>in his recent dispatches of having had conversations with
>North Vietnamese Ambassador Loan. From other sources
>we understand Loan was anxious to talk with all Scandinavian
>representatives in Peking....Knowing Petri's reputation for
>thorough and meticulous reporting and his good contacts with
>many Communist representatives in Peking, we are somewhat
>surprised that by now we have not had some reports from him
>on Loan."

>RUSK (drafted by Isham)

July 15, 1967

Oberg-Vy Conversation.

Oberg clarified Vy's remark to the effect that the word "pause"
was used intentionally throughout the conversation. The North Vietnamese
also told Oberg that negotiations could begin "very soon after a bombing
pause" and that the duration of the pause need not be announced by the
U.S. in advance. Oberg also reported that rumors of differences between
the NLF and the DRV were being bandied about town.

>STOCKHOLM 071 to SecState (SECRET, EXDIS), July 15, 1967.
>Ref: State 6375.

>"1. Oberg gave us July 14 following clarification his
>July 11 remarks:

>A) Vy began by quoting Trinh-Burchett January 28
>conversation using term 'permanent unconditional cessation'.
>Then Vy switched to term 'pause' and used latter term through-
>out conversation. Oberg thinks term 'pause' intentional.
>Oanh said negotiations could begin 'very soon after
>bombing pause' and duration of pause need not be announced in
>advance.

>B) Oberg has no indication that say 'US act of
>good faith' other then bombing stop would be acceptable to DRV.

>C) Date of interview July 11. Vy and Oanh were
>together. Oberg feels that their comments were not expressing
>a change in policy but in 'nuance' (his word) which might be
>more personal than official. He does not take their statements

to be a signal.

D) Oberg knows of no similar conversation with other foreign contacts.

E) Oberg has no confirmation of split but heard around town of disagreement between NLF and DVN over preconditions for negotiations with FNL taking harder line."

. . . .

"3. Vy and Oanh expressed fear US will bomb Red River Delta dams during rainy season causing 1 to 1.5 million dead plus additional 500 thousand refugees. Bombing would be blamed on mistake but would really be by design because US has run out of military targets in NVN. Even such losses would not weaken NVN resolve. Oberg said he had spoken to General 'Big' Minh a few years ago who had cited same figures. Oberg passed Vy-Oanh prediction to Swedish Foreign Minister Nilsson who made no comment."

HEATH

July 18, 1967

STOCKHOLM 083 to SecState (TOP SECRET, NODIS, ASPEN), July 18, 1967. Ref: State 7393.

"Oberg told Embassy officer July 18 that he was not aware any recent conversations between DRV Ambassador Loan and Swedish Ambassador Petri. In next few days Oberg will have opportunity check this point with Petri who is in Sweden on leave. Oberg will then get in touch with us."

HEATH

July 20, 1967

STOCKHOLM 094 to SecState (TOP SECRET, NODIS, ASPEN), July 20, 1967. Ref: Stockholm 083.

"Oberg told us July 19 that DRV Ambassador Loan made a courtesy call on Petri on June 1, but according Petri nothing repeat nothing of interest was discussed. Petri told Oberg that Loan called upon Norwegian and Danish Ambassadors about the same time."

HEATH.

August 1, 1967

The Swedes began to push two lines of thought: (1) that the DRV had softened its position on talks and was not now demanding a public U.S. statement that the bombing cessation be unconditional; (2) that Hanoi was no longer using intractible language on the issue of reciprocity, but was stating that they "understand" the U.S. position.

STOCKHOLM 116 to SecState (TOP SECRET, NODIS, ASPEN), August 1, 1967. Ref: Stockholm 094.

"1. In a call August 1 on Oberg at Foreign Ministry about another matter, Oberg raised subject of Viet-Nam. He said that in recent talks with Petri (who is in Sweden on leave) an attempt had been made to assess significance Petri's last talks in Hanoi. Oberg said Swedes think they have detected that North Vietnamese may have shifted their position somewhat concerning preconditions for 'talks' which might lead to negotiations. Oberg was imprecise in explaining this shift and he turned aside repeated efforts to clarify his language.

"2. Oberg said that Swedes do not believe that DRV demands public statement by U.S. that a bombing stop is unconditional for such a stop to lead to 'talks.' The U.S. could let Hanoi know this privately.

"3. In respect to U.S. demand for DRV reciprocity for bombing stop, the DRV position has softened somewhat, he said. Whenever Swedes explained U.S. demand for reciprocity from DRV in the past, Hanoi answered 'why should we reciprocate, we are not bombing Washington.' In recent talks, however, North Vietnamese told Petri they 'understand' U.S. position on reciprocity. Oberg said Swedes interpret this to mean that DRV might be prepared take reciprocal action in a way U.S. would understand but not in a way which would cause DRV lose face publicly."

. . . .

HEATH

September 27, 1967

Rusk-Nilsson Conversation. Memorandum of Conversation (Sent
USUN 1046), Subject: The Secretary and Swedish Foreign Minister
Nilsson's Discussion Regarding Vietnam, Wednesday, September 27,
1967, 3:30 P.M. USUN. Participants: U.S.: The Secretary,
Mr. Glitman (notetaker), Mr. Clement (Interpreter); Foreign:
Foreign Minister Nilsson, Ambassador deBesche, Mr. Bergstrom
(Director General for Political Affairs, MFA), Mr. Oberg
(Chef de Cabinet)

"Mr. Nilsson called at his request. He said he preferred
to open the conversation by reading the attached paper concerning recent Swedish contacts with Hanoi, because the subject was important and required precision.

ATTACHMENT QUOTE.

ATTACHMENT END QUOTE

"Following Nilsson's presentation the Secretary said
he had been particularly interested in the sentence which
stated that North VietNamese Foreign Minister Trinh had
told Swedish Ambassador Petri that Hanoi understood the
importance the U.S. attaches to reciprocal action on the
part of North VietNam in connection with a halt in the
bombing. He asked whether Mr. Nilsson could provide any
further details on this point.

"Mr. Nilsson said he had already asked Ambassador Petri
for more details but Petri had replied he did not believe
he could obtain specific details. However, Petri said he
was absolutely convinced Hanoi would take reciprocal steps
if the US stopped the bombing.

"The Secretary said the US also has contacts with Hanoi
and it is the U.S. impression that reciprocal action would
not follow upon a cessation of the bombing. Indeed, the
U.S. has never succeeded in obtaining a specific statement
regarding what steps Hanoi would take if the U.S. stopped
the bombing. Moreover, captured North VietNamese documents
talk of a fighting/negotiating strategy. The U.S. could
not accept an arrangement under which it stopped the bombing
and negotiated while North VietNam negotiated and continued
fighting.

"The question of reciprocity is vital. The U.S. had
said it would take the first step but it could not accept
a permanent and unconditional cessation of the bombing
without knowing what steps Hanoi would take. Hanoi, he
added, in response to Mr. Nilsson's question, had indicated a halt in the bombing must be accompanied by a clear
statement that it was permanent.

"No one, the Secretary said, has been able to tell
us what Hanoi would do if we stopped bombing. Indeed,
the U.S. has not found anyone who can even tell us if
their view would change should we take this step. Would
Sweden, he asked support us if we stopped bombing and
Hanoi continued the war?

"Sweden is a small country Mr. Nilsson replied. However, Sweden would ask Hanoi to begin negotiations and to

take reciprocal action of the U.S. stopped bombing. Sweden
wants to see the war ended because it is disturbed that the
U.S. has suffered a loss of good will in Scandanavia and
because it is concerned over the deterioration in relations
between the U.S. and the USSR caused by the war.

"No one wants peace more than President Johnson the
Secretary replied, but the U.S. cannot purchase a temporary
improvement in relations by abandoning its commitments.
The issue involves more than VietNam for it also embraces
Australia, New Zealand, Thailand and Korea. The fundamental
point in the matter, he continued is that the U.S. maintains
the same standard of fidelity in the Pacific as it does in
NATO. We have no master race theory which permits us to
be loyal in Europe and disloyal in Asia.

"The alternative to the maintenance of our commitment,
the Secretary said, is isolationism. The same senators who
oppose U.S. involvement in VietNam also oppose U.S. presence
in Europe and interest in the Middle East.

"The Secretary said he appreciated Sweden's interest
in attempting to bring an end to the VietNam war. The
Swedish paper merited a considered written reply. His
comment during the discussion regarding the points raised
in the paper should not, therefore, be taken as definitive
and repeated to Hanoi. The Secretary said he would have to
consult with the President but he hoped he could respond
before Mr. Nilsson returned to Sweden on October 7.

"The Secretary also suggested the Swedish Government
provide the U.S. with three or four days advance notification of Ambassador Petri's next trip to Hanoi, since the
U.S. might be able to provide the Ambassador with some
useful information. Mr. Nilsson said Ambassador Petri's
next visit to Hanoi would probably take place in October
or November. The Swedish Government would give the exact
date to the U.S. Embassy in Stockholm. Mr. Nilsson noted
that Hanoi had shown an interest in using the Swedish
channel for communicating with the U.S. and said he hoped
Sweden could continue to play a useful role in this regard.

"The conversation ended on the same note of cordiality
which had marked its entire course."

October 12, 1967

On 6 October, Secretary Rusk approved a response to the conversation
in the form of a written message delivered to Nilsson before his departure
on 7 October. The key element in this written message was an elaboration

and explanation of the meaning of the San Antonio formula. The message
made clear that "no advantage" has "not been posed as a 'condition,' but
rather as a self-evident description of the state of affairs that would
evidence good faith in both sides." "No advantage...would require
restraint from Hanoi, but this might fall short of total cessation of
arms dispatch and infiltration into South Vietnam." It should be noted
that this interpretation of "no advantage" was not the same as the one
given to the Rumanians on 1 November. This latter transmission talked
a` out "not increasing," and added the no "attack /or/ forces from north
o₁ the DMZ." The "no advantage" message to the Swedes was one in a series
of many different explanations of the San Antonio speech.

STATE 54361 to Amembassy Stockholm (SECRET, NODIS, ASPEN),
12 October 1967.

"4.   During this conversation the Secretary made a
number of observations on the main points raised by the
Foreign Minister's paper. We would have nothing to add
to his comments at this time beyond reaffirming the importance of eliciting any additional details on Foreign
Minister Trinh's remark to Ambassador Petri in June that
Hanoi 'understood' the importance the United States
attaches to reciprocal action on the part of North Vietnamese in connection with a halt in the bombing. We
note Ambassador Petri's view that some concrete act of
reciprocity can be expected after the cessation of the
bombing, even if Foreign Minister Trinh gave no precise
indication that Hanoi was considering taking such a step, and
we would of course always be keenly interested in any new
evidence which Ambassador Petri might obtain from North
Vietnamese officials which would bear out his view.

"5.   Since the Secretary's conversation with Foreign
Minister Nilsson, President Johnson in his speech of
September 29 has set forth our willingness immediately to
stop aerial and naval bombardment of North Viet-Nam when this
will lead promptly to productive discussions. As the Foreign
Minister will have seen from this speech, as well as from
Ambassador Goldberg's September 21 speech at the United
Nations, we are interested in two points -- whether there
would be productive discussions, and whether we could
reasonably assume that Hanoi would not take advantage of a
bombing stoppage. The latter point has not been posed as
a 'condition,' but rather as a self-evident description of
a state of affairs that would evidence good faith on both
sides. Foreign Minister Nilsson may note that the desired
'no advantage' situation would require restraint from Hanoi,
but this might fall short of total cessation of arms dispatch
and infiltration to South Viet-Nam. If Hanoi were prepared
to consider such a cessation, a balanced arrangement, not only

stopping the bombing but also cessation of reinforcement
by United States and others, would be possible. But
there remains the possibility that Hanoi might be prepared to agree to some lesser restraint, in return for
stopping the bombing only, that could comprise an
effective 'no disadvantage' situation.

"6. If Ambassador Petri could elicit any precise
information on Hanoi's position concerning these points
during his forthcoming visit to Hanoi, this could be of
the greatest importance. As the Secretary remarked at the
conclusion of the conversation, we would hope that we could
be informed in advance of the timing of Ambassador Petri's
next visit to Hanoi so that we might consider whether we could
submit any additional points to make during his discussions
with North Vietnamese officials."

RUSK (drafted by Isham)

October 26, 1967

STOCKHOLM 423 to SecState (SECRET, NODIS, ASPEN),
October 26, 1967. Ref: State 54361.

"1. At lunch at my residence October 26 Nilsson
and Bergstrom told me that latter had returned from
Warsaw October 23. In Warsaw Bergstrom had seen North
Vietnamese Ambassador and had conveyed to him summary of
Swedish presentation to Secretary Rusk (State 54361) and
summary substantive points of Secretary's reply (State
54184). In addition Bergstrom gave summary Swedish
impressions US attitudes.

"2. Bergstrom said dominant impression he got from
North Vietnamese in Warsaw was that they wanted to find
face saving formula which will allow them to come to
negotiating table.

"3. Bergstrom said North Vietnamese Ambassador
showed definite interest in clarification of 'no disadvantage' situation. In one and a half hour conversation North
Vietnamese Ambassador returned continually to this point.
Bergstrom said he felt diffident about attempting an
explication of this point and therefore did not go very far."

"6. Nilsson said Petri would probably be going to
Hanoi this fall. Foreign Minister promised let us know
in advance."

HEATH

November 4, 1967

A Bergstrom-Heath conversation on three successive days did much to cloud the Swedish role. Bergstrom tried to argue that recent Swedish government denunciations of US policy in Vietnam did not impair the Swedish negotiating role, but, in fact, strengthened it.[14] He tried to explain recent GOS actions as Sweden's way of extricating sinking U.S. prestige in the world over Vietnam and avoiding further U.S. escalation along the Chinese border. He added that his government "are convinced NVN interested in negotiations or at least talks preliminary to negotiations." On instructions, Bergstrom pressed very hard for a Nilsson interview with President Johnson. He warded this effort off strongly.

STOCKHOLM 456 to SecState (SECRET, NODIS, ASPEN), 3 Sections, November 3, 1967 (rec'd 0332 4 Nov 67). Ref: Stockholm 423.

Section 1

"3. Bergstrom then repeated his impression of keen North Vietnamese interest in clarification 'no disadvantage' situation as evidenced NVN Ambassador in Warsaw (Stockholm 423). Bergstrom said FonMin Nilsson would therefore like to discuss clarification with Secretary.

"4. Nilsson was thinking in terms of going back to UN soon for week or ten days, ostensibly for UN reasons but really to go from there to Washington, if appointment could be arranged with Secretary...."

"6. At November 1 meeting....Bergstrom then said that he, FonMin and PriMin had reviewed November 1 history of their contacts with NVN (i.e. Aspen history) and agreed latest Warsaw conversation most hopeful. They are convinced NVN interested in negotiations or at least talks preliminary to negotiations. Therefore Nilsson was requesting appointment with Secretary (through de Besche) and he repeatedly said PriMin would like me to personally arrange for Nilsson an appointment with President for two reasons: ..

A) This would convince North Vietnamese that they were receiving latest US position from highest authority;

B) The President might make a more liberal clarification of US conditions than Secretary Rusk.

"7. Upon inquiry as to timing of proposed visit, he insisted it must be prior to their Poland and Moscow visits. I replied I must be frank--while the decision obviously was not mine, I personally felt that for President Johnson so soon after PriMin, FonMin and party's bitter denunciations

of USA and PriMin's public association of Swedish Government with North Viet-Nam (NLF) seemed to me incompatible
and possibly could be used either for their political
advantage and our resulting disadvantage in their 'balancing
act' of on the one hand catering to our enemies by abusing
us and immediately thereafter proving to our friends in
Sweden and the world that they must be all right after all
because their FonMin had been received by our President
at White House...."

Section 2

"11. Next morning November 2 Bergstrom called and said
he had just reported our latest conversation and they decided
not to rush things but would now have de Besche see if Secretary were available in 'next several weeks' for discussion
with Nilsson. On other matter (i.e., Presidential appointment)
they thought I should wait and they would call me when they
had appointment with Secretary. He indicated concern Secretary not think 'they were trying to go round State to
President.'

"12. This morning, Nov 3, Bergstrom telephoned again
and said 'they' had talked with de Besche again last night,
that Secretary Rusk had kindly agreed to see FonMin Nilsson
on date not yet determined probably around Nov 13 or 14, that
Bergstrom and Nilsson were leaving for UN Tuesday, Nov 7,
returning in time for the Polish and Moscow trips, that upon
reflection they had concluded it best for FonMin to request
directly of Secretary Rusk that he arrange appointment with
President Johnson, and that therefore my further helpfulness
in that regard would not be needed...."

Section 3

"13. Comment: A) I have strong doubts about meaningful
response from North Vietnamese through Ambassador in Warsaw.
(B) I am also aware that while Swedes profess to want to keep
(1) their criticism of us on Viet-Nam and (2) their negotiation efforts in separate watertight compartments, this would
not be possible in case of high level Washington visits....
(C) I am also somewhat concerned over vagueness of exact NVN
'interest' in these 'clarifications.'"

"16. However, I assume Department does not want to
allow any possibility for peace in Viet-Nam to go unexplored
and therefore I recommend that if possible the Secretary agree
to see Nilsson and offer him such clarifications as may be
possible....

"17. I think we should not seek to involve the President
in this exercise at this time...."

HEATH

November 7, 1967

STATE 66424 to Amembassy Stockholm (SECRET, NODIS, ASPEN), November 7, 1967. Ref: Stockholm 423, 456.

"1. We think that you took exactly right line in speaking frankly to Bergstrom....

Appointment will not rpt not be made. However, Secretary will receive Minister at 12:15, November 15."

RUSK (drafted by Isham)

November 21, 1967

STOCKHOLM 511 to SecState (SECRET, NODIS, ASPEN), November 21, 1967.

"1.   Oberg reports he is going to Warsaw November 24, as Bergstrom apparently told Assistant Secretary Bundy November 18.

"2. Oberg, Bergstrom and Nilsson due in Moscow November 26."

HEATH

November 23, 1967

FonMin Nilsson met with Secretary Rusk on 16 November. He recapitulated recent contacts in Warsaw, adding that the North Vietnam Ambassador had remarked that a "new element" may have been introduced if the President's "no advantage" formula indicated that the U.S. was dropping its demand for reciprocity.

In this cable, which is a response to the Nilsson memorandum, U.S. set out three basic elements for getting talks started: (1) "any contact at any time without any conditions"; (2) "contacts accompanied only by a modest and unpublicized reduction in the level of areas of bombing"; (3) the San Antonio formula

In this message, State also inquired into three general areas of Hanoi's position: (1) the public description of a bombing cessation; (2) the nature of the talks that would follow; (3) Hanoi's understanding of "no advantage." Illustrative examples of "no advantage" were given, and special emphasis was addressed to the DMZ situation. It seemed clear that State was asking two things: (1) Did Hanoi understand what the U.S. meant by "no advantage?" and (2) What would Hanoi do to demonstrate that understanding?

STATE 73693 to Amembassy Stockholm (SECRET, NODIS, ASPEN), November 23, 1967.

"1.   During November 16 meeting with Secretary, Nilsson presented memorandum recapitulating what Swedes had already told you about October 22 discussions in Warsaw between Bergstrom and North Vietnamese Ambassador. Nilsson added no new details except for North Vietnamese Ambassador's remark that 'new element' might have been introduced if formulation on 'no advantage' indicated elimination of reciprocity. In addition, Nilsson passed on subsequent comment by North Vietnamese Embassy Warsaw official on October 28 who said intensification of bombing in Hanoi area had affected general atmosphere in negative way, while at same time stating that what was said during October 22 conversation 'continued to be relevant.'"

"3.   Please convey following message to Nilsson from Secretary: BEGIN TEXT....The observations which follow will summarize what Mr. Bundy, with my approval, told Ambassador Bergstrom on November 18.

"4.   There are three basic elements in our position with respect to getting talks started. Consistent with the President's statement of April 7, 1965, we are prepared to have any contact at any time without any conditions. Second, we are prepared to consider at any time possible contacts accompanied only by a modest and unpublicized reduction in the level or areas of bombing. We would be impressed by some corresponding action on the other side, but this is not to be understood as imposing a condition. Third, there is the President's San Antonio proposal to which I referred in my message of October 6. In addition, there are three points which call for clarification.

"5.   First, how is a cessation of bombing to be described publicly, and what is to be the private understanding of this term? On the basis of Hanoi's position as formulated in the January 28, 1967 interview of Foreign Minister Trinh with Wilfred Burchett, we are bound to interpret Hanoi's terms as requiring that the cessation be permanent and be characterized as permanent. It would be useful to know whether this is what Hanoi means or whether there is some other condition attached.

"6. The second point turns on the nature of any talks
that might take place following such a cessation, however defined.
What degree of assurance would there be that talks would actually take place? How soon would they take place following a
bombing cessation? How serious or productive would they be?
Our own viewpoint on these questions is clear: We would expect
our representatives to sit down somewhere for hard discussions
of the main issues covering all points the other side wished
to discuss.

"7. The third point relates to the understanding of a
'no advantage' situation, as described in the President's San
Antonio speech and in my October 6 message to you in connection
with a bombing cessation and the start of talk.. One way to
clarify this is in terms of questions that I emphasize are
illustrative of examples only. What would happen with respect
to the flow of supplies and men into South Viet-Nam and to
positions directly threatening South Viet-Nam? For example,
if following a cessation or limitation of bombing, there was
a marked increase in the flow of trucks southward; if a new
North Vietnamese regiment were to appear; or if we saw a
massive increase in the flow of supplies just to the north of
the DMZ, we would be negatively impressed. Similarly, to take
another example, we would want to know what would happen with
respect to the three North Vietnamese Divisions now in the area
of the Demilitarized Zone which have been employed as part of
offensive operations against our forces south of the DMZ.
Would artillery located north of the demarcation line be employed
against our forces? And, if so, would we be expected not to
bomb these artillery positions?

"8. These questions are, of course, not easy ones to
answer. Nevertheless, we believe they are central to an
accurate understanding of what is involved on both sides. We
would be grateful for any clarification that you might be able
to obtain through your contacts with North Vietnamese representatives on these matters."

(Drafted by Isham)

December 9, 1967

Oberg indicated to Cameron that the "Swedes would probably back us
if Hanoi failed respond bombing halt, although Oberg talked in terms 6-8
weeks grace period for Hanoi response." Oberg told us this, and that he
would be going to Warsaw to meet the DRV Ambassador in a week's time.

STOCKHOLM 585 to SecState (SECRET, NODIS, ASPEN),
December 9, 1967.

"1. Oberg (FonMin's aide) told EmbOff Dec. 8 he leaving
for Paris Dec. 10 Council Europe Ministerial Meeting and from
there going Warsaw Dec. 15 or 16 to meet DRV Ambassador who is
now in Hanoi.

"2. Oberg plans give DRV Ambassador verbatim examples
no-advantage situations outlined Secretary's reply to
Nilsson paper (State 73693).

"3. Oberg summed up Swedish view DRV attitudes:
. A) DRV expects levelling Hanoi, Haiphong; bombing
dikes and invasion NVN; plans made for movement government
from Hanoi.
       B) DRV really has no expectations US elections will
change anything;
       C) Swedes still see split between DRV and NFL, with
specific point being absence reunification plank in NFL's new
programs first phase.[15]

"4. In Moscow (reported Stockholm 580 and being amplified
in follow-up telegram) Soviets were persistent in stressing
Hanoi's independence.

"5. Oberg repeated point made para 2 D) Stockholm 580 that
Swedes would publicly back us if Hanoi failed respond bombing
halt, although Oberg talked in terms of 6-8 weeks grace period
for Hanoi response.

"6. Petri not rpt not planning go Hanoi in immediate
future unless something worthwhile develops...."

CAMERON

December 11, 1967

STOCKHOLM 590 to SecState (SECRET, NODIS, ASPEN),
Ref: Stockholm 511.

"To complete record, Oberg (FonMin's aide) told EmbOff
Dec 8 that his meeting with DRV Ambassador in Warsaw Nov 24
was 'routine contact.' DRV Ambassador did re-state his
interest in 'no advantage situation.' Oberg did not have
Secretary's reply to Nilsson's paper (State 73693) giving
examples of 'no advantage situation' at that time."

CAMERON

January 3, 1968

Bundy-de Besche Conversation.

De Besche indicated to Bundy that the North Vietnamese Chargé said he would promptly pass the illustrative examples of "no advantage" to Hanoi. He also asked for Bundy's interpretation of the 29 December 1967 Trinh statement.[16] Bundy indicated there was in fact a change from "could" to "will," that there might be a change in talking about the bombing pause as unconditional rather than permanent, but that this was not clear, and that Trinh was still silent on "no advantage," and Trinh's emphasis on the 4 points and the NLF program still indicated hard line.

STATE 93140 to Amembassy Stockholm (SECRET, NODIS, ASPEN), January 3, 1967.

"2. ....Nilsson has instructed Oberg to travel to Warsaw (probably January 4) to obtain exact text of statement from North Vietnamese. Foreign Office queried whether US desired to transmit any questions at this time or otherwise seek clarification of Trinh statement.

"3. In reply Bundy said that while we were obviously interested in obtaining any clarification of what might underly Trinh statement, choice of available channels and timing of their use required greatest possible care and precision in order to avoid creating confusion. Moreover, it would in any event be difficult to frame careful and precise questions in short time remaining before Oberg's departure for Warsaw. At this juncture, Bundy said, we would not therefore there be inclined to ask GOS to put any specific questions to North Vietnamese which could be construed as coming from us. Bundy said he would check this with Secretary and be in touch with de Besche; this position was later confirmed and de Besche informed. Bundy noted that the Swedish Government could of course seek any clarification on its own behalf. De Besche accepted this and promised to keep us informed.

"4. In response to de Besche's request for interpretation of latest Trinh statement, Bundy commented:

(a) use of verb 'will' in context of talks was plainly a change from previous Trinh formulation of 'could';

(b) use of term 'unconditionally' rather than 'permanently' or 'definitively' could be construed as a more gentle formulation, although it was not yet possible to draw any clear conclusions on this point, particularly because of the reference in the latest statement to the January 28, 1967 Trinh interview which with accompanying Hanoi commentary posed condition of permanent cessation;

(c) Trinh remained silent on issue of mutual restraint or 'no advantage', although Bundy noted one would not necessarily expect this to be covered by public statement; and

(d) Hanoi's basic hard line reflected in Trinh's emphasis on Hanoi's Four Points and NLF political program as the basis for Viet-Nam solution.

"5. In short, Bundy commented that questions contained in Secretary's memorandum to Nilsson remained highly relevant.

"6. Foregoing drafted before receipt of Stockholm 662. Oberg's detailed report of conversation with North Vietnamese Charge is most useful and it appears clear that Foreign Office is not yet providing de Besche with as much detail as Oberg is conveying directly to us in Stockholm.

"7. We would in any event prefer that Oberg or his superiors be authoritative source of such reporting."

RUSK (drafted by Isham)

January 4, 1968

Report on Oberg-Warsaw Talk of December 21-22, 1967.

Before describing his conversation in Warsaw, Oberg said that verbatim examples of "no advantage" situations as outlined in State 73693 have been given to the DRV Ambassador without comment. Oberg also noted that during Nilsson's recent visit to Moscow, the Soviets were no longer urging the Swedes to play an intermediary role. The Swedes inferred from this that the Soviets were pessimistic about chances for peace.

In response to illustrative examples of "no advantage" the DRV Charge made three points. (1) How would the bombing pause be described? (2) "We cannot leave our brothers in the South unprotected;" (3) What would productivity and seriousness of negotiations mean? His second point indicated that either he had not understood the "no advantage" formula or that he was referring to the NLF rather than NVN troops.

STOCKHOLM 662 to SecState (SECRET, NODIS, ASPEN), January 4, 1968. Ref: Stockholm 649.

"3. Oberg saw Charge Vu Bach Mai (Oberg's spelling) Dec 21 and handed over paper described Para 2A. Paper had been translated into French; illustrative examples Para 7 State 73693 were also given in English.

"4. NVN Charge raised three points which Oberg on
instructions refused to discuss saying that Swedes had
this paper from US aide and that Swedes not competent
go beyond what was in paper.

"5. Three points NVN Charge raised were:

A. Did Swedes have any suggestions on how to
describe bombing pause?

B. On question of flow of material in no-advantage
situation Charge said 'we cannot leave our brothers in the South
unprotected.' It was not clear to Oberg whether he was referring
to NLF in South Vietnam or to supplies to NVN troops north of
DMZ. (Oberg commented that in his contacts NVN representatives
never referred presence NVN troops in South Vietnam.)
C. On question seriousness of negotiations Charge
said this was unclear to him. In any negotiation both sides
started from positions widely apart and with quite different
aims. In such cases there would be different interpretation
of 'serious or productive.'"

"7. Oberg's general impression aside from fact that paper
had been well received was that

"8. In Jan 2 conversation Oberg did not mention any
further Swedish move at this time presumably because Foreign
Ministry thinks NVN may comment on paper. However, Oberg
called Jan 3 to say he was returning to Warsaw Jan 4 on Foreign
Minister's instructions to attempt to get clarification and
text Trinh statement on Hanoi radio. De Besche being instructed
inform Department of this and to say that Swedes do not consider
it connected to Aspen operation."

CAMERON.

February 16, 1968

The Swedes informed Heath that they were expecting a visit from the North Vietnamese Ambassador in Moscow. The North Vietnamese Ambassador was scheduled to arrive in Stockholm on February 20. (STOCKHOLM 877)

February 17, 1968

The Swedes were given the same private statement of the U.S. position as had been given to the Norwegians to use in their talks with the North Vietnamese Ambassador to Moscow.

"The U.S., consistent with President Johnson's statement of April 7, 1965, remains willing to enter into talks without preconditions at any time.

"The U.S. position on the cessation of the bombardment of North Viet-Nam is set forth in President Johnson's September 29, 1967 speech in San Antonio. As the President said:

'The U.S. is willing to stop all aerial and naval bombardment of North Viet-Nam when this will lead promptly to productive discussions. We, of course, assume that while discussions proceed, North Viet-Nam would not take advantage of the bombing cessation or limitation.'

"The U.S. is not assuming that North Viet-Nam will cease its support to its forces in the South. On the contrary, as Secretary of Defense designate Clark Clifford testified before the Senate Foreign Relations Committee, we assume that until a cease fire is agreed on, Hanoi 'will continue to transport the normal amount of goods, men and munitions.'

"In setting forth its assumption, the U.S. is not setting a condition but attempting to make clear to North Viet-Nam that any cessation of U.S. bombing followed by actions by Hanoi taking advantage of the cessation (such as an increase by Hanoi of its infiltration of men and supplies or attacks in the area of the DMZ) would constitute such bad faith on Hanoi's part as to make continued U.S. forebearance impossible. If Hanoi, by taking advantage, forces the U.S. to resume bombing the possibilities of a negotiated solution would drastically recede. Under such circumstances calls for intensified U.S. military action would increase and the possibility of another halt in the bombing would be low. The U.S. is trying to ascertain whether Hanoi appreciates this vital fact and fully understands the importance the U.S. attaches to the no-advantage assumption.

"At San Antonio the President, in addition to setting forth his assumption, stated his readiness to stop the bombing when such action would lead 'promptly to productive discussions.' 'Productive discussions' are serious exchanges in which either side will be able to put forward for full consideration in good faith its position on any matter. 'Prompt' of course refers to a willingness by Hanoi to begin discussions with the U.S. immediately after cessation of bombing.

"It is worth noting that Hanoi is unwilling to give a clear response to questions as to the length of time between a U.S. bombing cessation and the beginning of talks. If Hanoi were serious in desiring talks then surely its response would have been one of unequivocal readiness to begin immediately.

"The U.S. evaluation of Hanoi's current position takes into account Hanoi's actions as well as its words. The unprecedented offensive against most of South Viet-Nam's urban centers, which Hanoi treacherously launched in the midst of the traditional Tet holidays, causing widespread civilian casualties and suffering, was made notwithstanding the fact that we were still exploring with Hanoi its position through diplomatic channels, and that we had exercised restraint in bombing targets in the immediate vicinity of Hanoi and Haiphong. In this context, we cannot but weigh Hanoi's words with great skepticism and caution. These actions carry a harsh political message.

"The U.S. favors every effort to obtain clarification of Hanoi's position. We shall continue to evaluate all information and to pursue every possible avenue which promises to bring us closer to the resolution of this conflict through serious negotiations."

(State 117383)

February 20, 1968

Petri suggested that he visit Hanoi on February 22 and his Foreign Ministry had given approval. The Swedes said there was nothing special about the date or the visit, merely that "it was time for him to go to Hanoi again." Cameron suggested that the Swedes defer the Petri/Oberg trip to Hanoi until after the North Vietnamese Stockholm visit. (STOCKHOLM 883).

February 23, 1968

Foreign Office Political Director Wachtmeister told Heath that he believed the North Vietnamese Ambassador's "main purpose for Stockholm visit was to impress Swedes with North Vietnam's 'self-confidence' in its position." (STOCKHOLM 896)

February 24, 1968

Foreign Minister Nilsson sent Heath a "short account" of his talks with the North Vietnamese Ambassador. The Ambassador, Mr. Chan , elaborated on the Trinh statement of December 29.

(STOCKHOLM 901)

PENNSYLVANIA

DEPARTMENT OF STATE
Office of
AMBASSADOR AT LARGE

August 2, 1967

MEMORANDUM FOR THE NEGOTIATIONS COMMITTEE

EYES ONLY PARTICIPANTS

FROM: S/AH - Chester L. Cooper

SUBJECT: Visit to Hanoi by Two Unofficial
             French Representatives

   Early in June a small group of Pugwash participants[1]
met in Paris to discuss the situation in the Middle East and
Vietnam. Representatives of the group came from the Soviet
Union, the UK, France and the US. The American participants
were Kissinger, Doty (Harvard), and Feld (MIT). As an
outgrowth of this discussion, one of the French participants,
Marcovich of the Pasteur Institute, and Kissinger (with the
knowledge and endorsement of the Soviet participant) agreed
that it would be useful for Marcovich to proceed to Hanoi for
the purpose of sounding out the North Vietnamese on their
views toward negotiations, and to present unofficially the
Phase A - Phase B formula which had been discussed in general
terms at the Pugwash session. Marcovich was to be joined by
a M. Aubrac, an official of FAO who knew Ho Chi Minh
personally (Ho had stayed in Aubrac's home during the 1946
negotiations with the French). De Gaulle was made aware of
the trip and interposed no objection on the condition that
the two Frenchmen were acting "unofficially".

   Marcovich and Aubrac arrived in Hanoi by way of Phnom
Penh on July 21. They left Hanoi on July 26 and returned to
Paris via Phnom Penh. Kissinger saw them "within hours of
their return to Paris".

   During their stay in Hanoi Marcovich and Aubrac had
two conversations with Pham Van Dong and one with Ho Chi Minh.
They were also shown a hospital, some damaged dikes and other
evidence of American "aggression". They were given a bamboo
surgical kit (which they said was developed to meet the

shortage of steel surgical instruments), a propaganda film
on American bombing and some pellets from "anit-personnel
bombs". (Arrangements are being made to get these to us.)

Attached are Kissinger's notes describing the sessions
between the two Frenchmen and the Vietnamese officials.
The material preceding the notes of the conversations (pages
1 - 11 of Kissinger's notes) is a lengthy background discussion and a chronology of the trip.

Several interesting points emerge from the conversation
with Pham Van Dong.

1.   Dong's reiteration of the offer to negotiate soon
after a bombing cessation and, in particular, his statement
that the cessation need only be a "de facto" one. (pp 12 and 15)

2.   Dong's statement to the effect that they would be
prepared to negotiate secretly with the U.S. on matters directly
affecting North Vietnam and that the NLF need not be present.
(p 17). In subsequent sessions in which the political
problems of South Vietnam were to be discussed the NLF would
have to be present. (p.13).

3.   Dong's recognition that, "some U.S. forces would have
to stay until the end of the process of political settlement".
(p. 16).

4.   Dong's statement that the NLF envisaged a "broad
coalition government" which would include members of the
present GVN. (p. 17)

5.   Dong's statement that Hanoi would not"push things
toward unification" until after there was a political settlement. (p. 17)

6.   Dong's sense of optimism about the eventual outcome. (p.15)

The conversation with Ho is more interesting in terms of
color and mood than in terms of substance.

****

2

An analysis of these conversations and some possible follow-up actions will be the principal matter for discussion on Thursday,. August 3, in Governor Harriman's office.   It *:* hoped that participants will have an opportunity to read the attached before the meeting.

Chester L. Cooper

ATTACHMENT: As stated

cc: Mr. Rostow
      Gov. Harriman
      Mr. Sisco
      Mr. Warnke
      Mr. Habib
      Mr. Read

III.   CONVERSATIONS WITH PHAM VAN DONG AND HO

   A.   Meeting with Pham Van Dong, July 24, 9 a.m.
   B.   Meeting with President Ho, Afternoon, July 24.
   C.   Second Meeting with Pham Van Dong.

NOTE: These conversations are drawn from reports by
Aubrac and Marcovich within hours of their return to
Paris. Quotations are direct quotes as they appeared
in Aubrac's notes made during the meeting. The conversations are reported in the order in which they occurred.

A.   Meeting with Pham Van Dong, July 24, 9 a.m.   Present
     Aubrac, Marcovich, Pham Van Dong, Tach (Minister of
     Health), note-taker.

     Pham Van Dong opened the meeting by saying that
he was happy to see Aubrac and Marcovich. The visas
had been given on the basis of Aubrac's reputation,
therefore, it was up to Aubrac to present his ideas.
Aubrac then described the background of the trip to
Hanoi as sketched in Part I. He said that he would
report to me and I would report to the U.S. government.
Marcovich continued by outlining as a private idea the
two-part proposal: 1) an end to U.S. bombing, 2) coupled
with an assurance by North Vietnam that "le taux des
approvisionment ne serait pas accru a la faveur de cette
arrête." Aubrac interrupted to say that the control
problem would have to be solved and Hanoi should make
proposals. Pham Van Dong replied that he had been
wondering when that issue would be raised. Marcovich
said that part of the control might be through overflights
for reconnaissance purposes. Pham Van Dong said: "This
is our country. We cannot discuss the problem in this
manner." Pham Van Dong added: "We want an unconditional
end of bombing and if that happens, there will be no
further obstacle to negotiations." Aubrac asked what he
meant by unconditional. Pham Van Dong replied that
North Vietnam could not negotiate while being bombed.
Aubrac asked whether Pham Van Dong wanted an official
déclaration that the bombing had stopped, or would he
be satisfied with a de facto end of bombing. Pham Van
Dong replied that a de facto cessation would be acceptable.
Aubrac asked whether there should be some delay between
the end of bombing and the beginning of negotiations.

Pham Van Dong replied: "This is not a problem."
Aubrac asked what channels should be used. Pham Van
Dong replied: "This is not a problem but it should be
someone authorized by both parties." He then went on
to say initial negotiations could be on those matters
affecting the U.S. and North Vietnam as principals.
When issues affecting South Vietnam were raised, the NLF
would have to be present. /Aubrac and Marcovich had the
impression that the scenario envisaged by Pham Van Dong
involved an end of U.S. bombing to be followed within
a matter of days by the opening of negotiations under
acceptable auspices./

Pham Van Dong then said that he thought that the
next escalatory step would be a bombing of the dikes.
All preparations had been made to mitigate the consequences,
but the human suffering would be severe. He asked Marcovich
and Aubrac to help influence world opinion against
such a step. Aubrac replied that their usefulness depended
on not joining any propaganda effort. However, they
might talk to the papal mission in Paris about the
problem.

Pham Van Dong then closed the meeting with a
little speech: "You see, dear friends, that the problem
is very complicated. You may think your travels are
useless. In fact you have given us much to think about.
I will see you again and we will talk again."

Aubrac and Marcovich were struck by Pham Van
Dong's insistence on the complexity of the problem, as
well as by the fact that in neither conversation did he
mention Communist China.

Tach remained behind. He joined Aubrac and Marcovich
at lunch and told them that the two-step bombing proposal
should be discussed officially rather than informally.

B. Meeting with President Ho, Afternoon, July 24.
    Present: Ho, Aubrac, Pham Van Dong, Tach and note-
    taker.

Aubrac said that what struck him immediately was
how old Ho had become. He was dressed in a Chinese gown
and walked with the aid of a cane. However, his
intelligence was unimpaired; his eyes still had their

old sparkle. He seemed to enjoy playing the role of a
grandfather-figure, not concerned with details. Aubrac
had brought as a gift a little colored stone egg. Ho
gave three presents in return: silk for Aubrac's daughter,
some books and a ring made of metal from the 2000th
 .S. plane claimed to have been shot down over Vietnam.
He remembered the first names of all of Aubrac's three
children. After speaking about Aubrac's family for about
15 minutes, Aubrac said: "Mr. President do you know
 hy I have come?" Ho answered "Yes." Aubrac asked
whether he had any comments. Ho replied by saying that
he did not like the phrase "peace in Vietnam." It gave
an impression of moral equivalence between the United
States and North Vietnam; in fact the U.S. is the aggressor
and must be condemned. Ho praised De Gaulle for understanding this distinction. Moreover the details of
negotiations were in the hands of Pham Van Dong. Ho
then added: "Remember, many people have tried to fool
me and have failed. I know you don't want to fool me."
He then turned the conversation back to family matters.
He expressed regret that Aubrac had sold the house
where he had stayed twenty-one years ago. "Where shall
I live when I next come to Paris?" He then asked whether
he would be welcome in Paris, but avoided the question
of whether he wanted an invitation.

He terminated the conversation after fifty minutes
and was escorted from the room by Tach. Pham Van Dong
walked with Aubrac to his car. He said that "we try to
spare President Ho as many details as we can. He is an
old man; we want him to live to see his country unified."
He told Aubrac that he was thinking about their conversation
of the morning. He moved up the next day's appointment
by an hour to allow more time before Aubrac's and
Marcovich's departure in the evening.

C.   Second Meeting with Pham Van Dong. Present: Aubrac,
      Marcovich, Pham Van Dong, Tach, note-taker.

The meeting consisted of a talk by Pham Van Dong
speaking from notes. Aubrac reported that the talk went
something like this: "Dear friends. Our conversation
yesterday was very useful. If you want to understand
the problem in Vietnam, I advise you to read the book
by Morris West called The Ambassador.[2] /Neither Aubrac

nor Marcovich knew of the existence of this book./ We
are facing a problem which is at the same time very
simple, very complex and of great importance for the
world. It is simple because it concerns the freedom
of a people. It is complex because many considerations
are involved. It is of great importance because it has
involved so many peoples. We have come to the opinion
that the U.S. government is trying to solve the problem
within its present limits. /Aubrac and Marcovich took
this to mean that Pham Van Dong was convinced that the
U.S. was not in Vietnam as a prelude to an attack on
China./ We also think that the U.S. government is trying
to get a clear picture of the present position. Our
view is this: U.S. power is enormous and the U.S.
government wants to win the war. President Johnson is
suffering from a pain and this pain is called South
Vietnam. We agree that the situation on the battlefield
is decisive; the game is being played in South Vietnam.
From the newspapers we see that some people want to confine
the war to the South. However, the White House and
Pentagon seem determined to continue the war against the
North. Therefore we think that attacks on the North are
likely to increase. We have made provisions for attacks
on our dikes; we are ready to accept war on our soil.
Our military potential is growing because of aid from
the USSR and other Socialist countries. /Aubrac and
Marcovich pointed out that this was the only time a
Communist country was mentioned by name in the two
conversations extending over five hours. Aubrac and
Marcovich also felt that Pham Van Dong was eager to
give the impression that the situation was under control./

As for the situation on the battlefield, it is
improving all the time. The dry season was good and the
wet season will be better. The Marines are in difficulty.[3]
The United States is forced to replace its well-trained
troops by ever-younger soldiers. We fight only when we
choose; we economize on our resources; we fight only for
political purposes.

For example, news from Saigon suggests that Ky
is considering moving his capital because it is no longer
safe. This is true. We could easily step up our actions
inside the city. But we take only those actions which
have political meaning and which economize human lives.

"Now I shall talk to you about negotiations and solutions. We have been fighting for our independence for four thousand years. We have defeated the Mongols three times. The United States Army, strong as it is, is not as terrifying as Genghis Khan. We fight to have peace at home; we have no wider aims. We have made clear our position in our four points and in the interview of January 28, 1967.[4] /Pham Van Dong did not explain what this interview was; Aubrac and Marcovich did not know, nor do I./ We are ready to talk at any time provided that actions against the North are unconditionally ended. I want to repeat what I said yesterday: we are willing to settle for a de facto stoppage." Marcovich interrupted to ask whether he correctly understood that no public acknowledgment of an end of bombing was needed. Pham Van Dong replied that he would prefer a public statement, but would settle for a de facto cessation. /There was disagreement between Aubrac and Marcovich about the meaning of de facto cessation. Aubrac thought that a bombing pause could be followed within a few days by an invitation to negotiate; Marcovich was of the view that Hanoi might want a more formal--though secret-- assurance./

Pham Van Dong resumed. "Ending the war for us has two meanings: 1) An end of bombing which is permanent and unconditional; 2) A withdrawal of United States forces. We like the formula of President de Gaulle."[5] Marcovich interrupted to say that it was not realistic. Pham Van Dong agreed and said that he realized that some U.S. troops would have to stay until the end of the process of political settlement. He added: "We do not want to humiliate the U.S. Lenin did not like war but fought when necessary. As Lenin we are Communists."

"Now let me speak of U.S. policy and the NLF. We should have had unification in 1956. The period 1956-59 was a political fight. It saw the mutual assistance pact between the U.S. and Saigon and the introduction of U.S. staffs. This led to the formation of the NLF. The second period, 1960-64, saw a disintegration of the U.S. position to which the U.S. responded by 'special' war. /I suppose he meant "special forces" war./ In 1965, the United States started a 'limited' war which lasts until today. At the same time the NLF has expanded its activities from the country into the cities and from inside Vietnam to the outside. Our position is: North

Vietnam is socialist and wants to remain so. As for the
South, our goals are national independence, democracy,
peace and neutrality. Some people think we want to
impose Socialism on the South. ⌐We are convinced that the
NLF will not make such an error.⌐ The NLF envisages a
broad coalition government, including all significant
groups and religions without consideration of past activities
including members du gouvernement fantoche et cadres
d'armée fantoche. ⌐He repeated the underlined words.⌐
The essential thing is to forget the past.

"As for unification, we recognize that the important
first step is a political settlement of the South. We
agree not to push things toward unification. Once the
war in the South is settled, we shall discuss with the
South and find the best means. Our people are magnificent.

"Peace would have been easy for the U.S. three
years ago. But with every year the political situation
worsens. ⌐We do not like secret negotiations, but we
recognize their necessity in this situation.⌐ As long as
the issues do not concern South Vietnam, the NLF need
not participate. However, we do not believe that the
United States is ready for a settlement." Then turning
to Aubrac he asked: "Que veulent les Americains?"

Aubrac answered that he had been convinced by me
that the U.S. wanted an honorable settlement and that
an end to bombing could be envisaged provided it was
not used as a breathing space to step up the war in the
South. ⌐This led to a discussion of the meaning of the
term reinforcement.⌐ Pham Van Dong again stressed that
an end of bombing would lead to negotiations. Marcovich
said that if negotiations go on any length of time, the
problem of reinforcement is serious. Pham Van Dong replied:
"If the Americans stop bombing and we understand that
they are willing to talk there is no question of delay."

Pham Van Dong then told Aubrac and Marcovich that
they could communicate with him through Bo or Sung in
Paris. Aubrac and Marcovich said that they would inform
him of the U.S. reaction.

9

On August 11, 1967, the President approved the following message and asked that Dr. Henry Kissinger use M and A to convey it to Pham Van Dong:

"The United States is willing to stop the aerial and naval bombardment of North Vietnam if this will lead promptly to productive discussions between representatives of the U.S. and the DRV looking toward a resolution of the issues between them. We would assume that, while discussions proceed either with public knowledge or secretly, the DRV would not take advantage of the bombing cessation or limitation. Any such move on their part would obviously be inconsistent with the movement toward resolution of the issues between the U.S. and the DRV which the negotiations are intended to achieve."

Dr. Kissinger was given the following additional instructions:

"You should say further to Messrs. Marcovich and Aubrac that the United States is prepared to negotiate either openly or secretly. It would seem, however, that a total cessation of the bombing is inconsistent with keeping secret the fact that negotiations are taking place. Accordingly, the DRV may prefer to consider the alternative of a cutback in the magnitude or scope of the bombing while secret negotiations are in progress.

"The U.S. is ready to have immediate private contact with the DRV to explore the above approach or any suggestions the DRV might wish to propose in the same direction."

10

Revised and supplemented after
review by Kissinger September 8,
1967.

August 17, 1967 - Pursuant to USG instructions, Henry Kissinger
met for 5 hours with Messrs. Aubrac and Marcovich
(hereinafter A and M) in Paris at the latter's
house. Kissinger repeated Washington's understanding of M and A's conversations in Hanoi
on July 24 and 25, and M and A confirmed these
interpretations with the already reported difference
between them that A thought that an end to bombing
would be enough to start US/DRV talks, while M
thought some secret communications between
US and DRV might be necessary before talks
started. Mr. Kissinger followed his instructions
and handed A and M the message which he requested
them to take to Hanoi. In answer to a question
Kissinger stated that the message reflected the
views of the Secretaries of State and Defense
and had been approved by President Johnson.
During the discussion Kissinger made the
following points:

(1) The phrase "take advantage" refers to "any
increase in the movement of men and supplies
into the south";

(2) The phrase "productive" discussions indicated
the determination to avoid extended Korean-type
negotiations during unabated military operations;

(3) The bombing pause might make it impossible
to keep the fact of negotiations secret for
more than three weeks at the outside, though
we could of course guarantee secrecy as to
their substance. Therefore it might be desirable
to conduct preliminary talks while tonnage,
geographic or sorty limitations or reductions
in the bombing occurred, with a complete end
of the bombing when final negotiations took
place. But the choice of secret or open
talks was up to Hanoi; and

(4) The decision to add new targets was made[6]
before information of A and M's Hanoi discussions
had reached Washington and in the absence of

meaningful negotiations the intensity of
violence was likely to continue to rise.
Debate of specific escalation was futile since
the offer included stopping bombing all together.

A and M suggested substituting another phrase
for the word "if" in the first sentence of
the message. They said that they were persuaded
that a trip to Hanoi would be useful and proceeded
to discuss mechanics of travel. At the end
of the conversation A and M asked whether some
restriction would be placed on the bombing of
Hanoi for reasons of personal safety and to
show good faith. See Kissinger memcon.

August 17, 1967   -   Kissinger cabled the Department suggesting
elimination of the word "if" in the first
paragraph of the message and its replacement
by "with the understanding that" and this
authority was granted Paris 1997, 2017 and
2034, 2074; State 2312 and 22969. Other minor
changes in French text were agreed to in the
same messages.

August 17, 1967   -   M and A requested an appointment with DRV Rep
Sung, which was granted on 20 minutes notice.
Sung was cordial and said he had been instructed
to transmit messages from A and M to Hanoi.
When M and A requested visas for Hanoi, however,
Sung said he had no instructions concerning
visas and would refer the requests to Hanoi.

August 18, 1967   -   Mr. Kissinger met with M and A at M's house in
the morning, and the latter reported on their
meeting with Sung on the evening of August 17.
Kissinger told A and M that Washington accepted
their language change and a further minor
modification was suggested. The rest of
the conversation concerned technical problems of
visas, travel costs and A's scheduled two-weeks
leave. A code was agreed to between Mr. Kissinger
and A and M to cover certain likely requests
for clarification or debriefing. A and M. stated
they had not talked to the Elyses or to

12

anyone else and Mr. Kissinger urged continuing secrecy.

August 18, 1967   -   Mr. Kissinger met with M and A in the afternoon to introduce Mr. Chester Cooper in case he should have to pick up the contact in the future and to give a greater formality to the message. See Kissinger memcon.

August 18, 1967   -   M and A sent their first message to Hanoi requesting visas to travel to the DRV during the week of August 20.

August 19, 1967   -   Mr. Kissinger met Messrs M and A for the fourth time the morning of August 19 at the Pont Royal Hotel. Mr. Cooper was present part of the time. As instructed by Secretary McNamara Mr. Kissinger told M and A "that effective August 24 there would be a noticeable change in the bombing pattern in the vicinity of Hanoi to guarantee their personal safety and as a token of our good will."[7] There was no mention of exact distances. Mr. Kissinger said these orders were "generally good for 10 days." When M and A asked whether this was an ultimatum, Kissinger replied that we would hardly talk of an ultimatum when we had offered to end bombing altogether.

August 19, 1967   -   During the early evening of August 19 Mr. Kissinger met again with Messrs. M and A at the Pont Royal Hotel. After further discussion between Mr. Kissinger and Secretary McNamara, Mr. Kissinger said that he wished to make clear that the restrictions on bombing in the immediate vicinity of Hanoi would end September 4.. M and A indicated that they were well impressed with US seriousness and considered the US offer very meaningful. They stated they thought it essential to take the text of the message to Hanoi themselves and present it with background information. They reviewed a cable which they had prepared to send to Hanoi through the DRV Mission in Paris if Hanoi rejected their visa applications or if no answer had been received by August 22.

August 21, 1967 - M phoned Kissinger in Paris on the evening of August 21 to tell him of Hanoi's refusal of their visa application. Mr. Kissinger told them to pass the message which he had discussed with them on August 19 to Hanoi through the Paris DRV Mission if the answer to their first telegram remains negative. See Kissinger mem con.

August 21, 1967 - Messrs. M and A gave the DRV Mission the second message urgently requesting visas to travel to Hanoi with an important message. See Kissinger phon conversations with Messrs M and A.

August 22, 1967 - Mr. Cooper informed the Department that A and M got a turn down on their initial visa request and had sent an urgent appeal by telegram.

August 25, 1967 - Messrs A and M met with Bo in Paris to inquire why their visas had not been received. Bo told them it was too dangerous to visit Hanoi due to the bombing. M and A then informed Bo they had assurances in that respect, without identifying the nature of the assurances, which would be effective until September 4.

Messrs M and A then presented the US message as set forth below to Bo for the first time. He read it with interest and observed that it was "clearly significant". Bo queried them about the significance of para. 2 of the message. He was informed that it expressed US doubt that the existence of US/DRV discussions could be kept secret if bombing ended, and Bo recognized that this would be a problem. Bo was impressed and was told that the message was authorized by top levels of the USG. M and A gave Bo a written description of their contacts with Kissinger. Bo agreed to cable the message to Hanoi and to report their desires to visit Hanoi to discuss the message. Bo believed a reply should be available by August 29.

The English text of the message given to Bo in both French and English is as follows:

--14

"The United States is willing to stop the aerial and naval bombardment of North Viet-Nam with the understanding that this will lead promptly to productive discussions between representatives of the United States and the Democratic Republic of Viet-Nam looking toward a resolution of the issues between them. While discussions proceed either with public knowledge or secretly, the United States would assume that the Democratic Republic of Viet-Nam would not take advantage of the bombing cessation. Any such move on the part of the Democratic Republic of Viet-Nam would obviously be inconsistent with the movement toward resolution of the issues beween the United States and the Democratic Republic of Viet-Nam which the discussions are intended to achieve.

The United States is prepared to enter into discussions either openly or secretly. It would seem, however, that a total cessation of the bombing is inconsistent with keeping secret the fact that discussions are taking place. Accordingly, the Democratic Republic of Viet-Nam may prefer to consider the alternative of a cutback in the magnitude or scope of the bombing while secret discussions are in progress.

The United States is ready to have immediate private contact with the Democratic Republic of Viet-Nam to explore the above approach or any suggestions the Democratic Republic of Viet-Nam might wish to propose in the same direction."

According to M and A, Bo's cable to Hanoi, after transmitting the above message in English and French texts, noted that texts were confirmed by Cooper and that both Kissinger and Cooper had stated they were prepared at a very high level of the USG and approved by the President. A message sent to Hanoi also included the following points which had been made by Kissinger according to M and A:

(a) The US is handling this problem confidentially and requests Hanoi to do likewise;

(b) The US is particularly interested in the possibility that the DRV envisages direct secret discussions;

(c) The attacks on the dikes were accidental;[8]

(d) The US requested message to be brought to the attention of Pham Van Dong as soon as possible;

15

(e) The US is ready to submit the information in the message directly and secretly by special representative. Vientiane, Moscow or Paris were suggested as possible sites; and

.(f) The US would continue to utilize the Kissinger-A/M channel if Hanoi wished.

In addition, M and A said that the August 25 message stated that "for personal assurances of safety and to establish authenticity, bombing attacks in the immediate vicinity of Hanoi" would stop for ten days, beginning August 24. Finally, M and A urged that they be permitted to come to Hanoi as requested by Kissinger, to provide additional information.

August 29, 1967 - Bo told Messrs. M and A that he had not
received a response but expected a reply
on August 30.

August 30, 1967 - Bo told M and A that there had been a "technical
break in communications with Hanoi" but Bo
expected a reply by COB August 30 and he
assured M and A that their message was being
taken very seriously.

August 31, 1967 - Aubrac visited Bo, who told him that he still
had no answer to the August 25 message, but he
had heard from Hanoi rejecting M and A's August 21
appeal of the turn down of their visa applications.
Bo stated that his government noted unfavorably
that the receipt of the August 21 message coincided
with the escalation of bombing of the North with
Hanoi as its objective.[9] Under these conditions
it is impossible for the DRV to grant visas to
permit M and A to carry the August 25 message to
Hanoi. When Aubrac told Bo of his intent to
return to Rome on September 2, Bo asked him to
stay in Paris until September 5, particularly
since M was out of town for a short while.

September 1, 1967- M returned to Paris.

September 2, 1967- M and A visited Bo who repeated his comments
of August 31. A indicated that M's return
should permit A to leave for Rome on September 3
but Bo asked him to stay until September 5 since
a message from Hanoi could arrive at any time.
Bo asked M to make sure that nothing "happened
to Hanoi in the next few days.". Bo said he
would talk to M and A again on September 4.

17

September 3, 1967 - M and A saw Bo after receiving information
from Mr. Kissinger that the bombing pattern
around Hanoi would remain in effect three
days longer. They told Bo that the bombing
pattern around Hanoi was extended for another
72 hours through September 7. Bo received
this information "icily", but asked M and
A again not to leave town because Bo still
had not received an answer.

September 4, 1967 - Bo told M and A that he still had no answer
from Hanoi. Bo indicated that an answer would
have been simple if it hadn't been for US
bombing actions on August 21, 22 and 23. Bo
told M and A to come back on September 6. A
told Bo that he planned to go to Rome and Bo
raised no objections.

September 5, 1967 - Aubrac returned to Rome.

September 6, 1967 - Bo told M he still had no answer and again
referred to the fact that M and A's second
cable urgently requesting visas arrived in
Hanoi on a day when the city was hit particularly
hard.

September 7, 1967 - After conversations with Mr. Kissinger and A
and a phone call from A with Bo, M called on
Bo after receiving an appointment 15 minutes
after it was requested. M told Bo the USG
was "standing by - waiting for an answer".
M said the atmosphere during the conversation
was friendly and relaxed and Bo said several
times that he hoped M and A's efforts would
work out better than past efforts by others.
When Bo was informed (incorrectly) that
Kissinger would be in Paris on the weekend
of September 16, Bo said on his own initiative
that he would ask the DRV immediately for
authority to see Kissinger. When M said he
did not know whether Kissinger would be authorized
to see Bo and suggested that Bo might want to see
someone less close to the USG, such as Bernie
Feld, Bo rejected the suggestion and said he

<u>September 7, 1967</u>
(cont'd)

wanted to have authority to see Kissinger
so that a direct conversation between Bo
and Kissinger would be possible. Bo said
he still had no answer from the DRV to the
USG message: Bo again cautioned "strictest
secrecy" regarding the contact and M gave him
this assurance.

When M told Kissinger of the preceding
conversation, Kissinger asked M to call
Bo to inform him that Kissinger would be
in Paris on September 9 to correct the
information he had given him earlier. M
reported back that he had called Bo later
on the afternoon of September 7 to correct
the dates of Kissinger's Paris visit.

<u>September 7-8, 1967</u> - Kissinger came to Washington to discuss
his meeting with M this coming weekend at
Paris and possible meetings with Bo.
Mr. Kissinger left Boston on evening flight
for Paris on September 8.

At 11:00 a.m. EDT on September 8, Kissinger
phoned A in Rome from Washington to ask A to
return to Paris while K was there.

<u>September 8, 1967</u> - M visited Bo and told Bo of Kissinger's request
today that A return to Paris. M told Bo that
A and M vouched for K, but if Bo wanted
additional reassurances Millienshikov (Vice
Chairman of the Soviet Academy of Science and
President of the Supreme Soviet of the
Russian Soviet Republic) could come to Paris
to verify the origin of the mission. Bo
rejected this proposal and said the existing
M/A-K channel was satisfactory. Bo cautioned
about the great need for secrecy. In response
to Bo's question, M said K planned to be in
Paris for about 10 days. Bo said if there were

September 8, 1967   - no bombing of Hanoi "something could well
(Cont'd)   happen" during that period (Paris 3070).

September 9, 1967 - Kissinger arrived in Paris in the morning,
                     just before Aubrac who returned from Rome
                     at K's request. After a conversation between
                     K, M and A (Paris 3070) A called Bo to
                     arrange an appointment for A and M, which was
                     set for 4:00 p.m. Paris time. At the meeting
                     with Bo, the latter told A and M he had been
                     instructed by Hanoi to keep in close touch
                     with A and M, and Bo was available to A and
                     M at any time. M told Bo that Kissinger had
                     been in touch with senior USG officials,
                     later identified as the President, Secretary
                     Rusk and Secretary McNamara, who were "growing
                     impatient with the absence of any response from
                     Hanoi". Bo asked if Walt Rostow had cleared
                     the message and A and M had not heard his
                     name mentioned by Kissinger. M reported that
                     Washington did not know whether the (August 25)
                     message had ever been received in Hanoi. To
                     this, Bo replied that his government accepted
                     the message as "absolutely authentic" and "it
                     was being studied now in the light of developing
                     conditions". Bo added that A and M must
                     recognize the DRV situation is quite complex.
                     M urged Bo to meet Kissinger and Bo replied
                     that he had not yet received authorization to
                     talk to Kissinger, but that he was in effect
                     talking to Kissinger now through A and M. In
                     response to a question, A told Bo that Kissinger
                     had indicated a desire to discuss some matters
                     with Bo privately without the presence of A
                     and M, and A recommended a private meeting,
                     although M urged that M and A be present. Bo

20.

September 9, 1967 - was noncommittal but said if a meeting
   (Cont'd)   with Kissinger was arranged through any
                      other channel he would let M and A know.
                      Bo then said "what I really want to know
                      is whether the (August 25) message is still
                      valid". A and M assured him that it was but
                      repeated Kissinger's statement about US
                      restiveness with respect to the long delay
                      in Hanoi's response. M and A told Bo
                      they were personally convinced by Kissinger
                      that the August 21-23 bombings were un-
                      related to the August 25 message. Bo asked
                      about the "McNamara line" (barrier) and said
                      Hanoi viewed it as "political action to make
                      the separation of brothers permanent".[10] M viewed
                      it as "an alternative to bombing". Bo hoped
                      A would not return to Rome and again stressed
                      secrecy. (After checking with K, A re-
                      turned to Rome to be on call.)

September 11, 1967 - In response to a phone request from Bo at
                      6:00 p.m. (Paris time), Sunday, September 10,
                      Marcovich called on Bo at 9:30 a.m. After
                      an exchange of pleasantries Bo handed to M the
                      following text of Hanoi's official reply to the
                      August 25 message:

                      "The essence of the American propositions
                      is the stopping of the bombing under conditions.
                      The American bombing of the Democratic Republic
                      of Viet-Nam is illegal. The United States   any
                      should put an end to the bombing and cannot pose
                      conditions.

                      "The American message has been communicated
                      after an escalation of the attacks against Hanoi
                      and under the threat (menace) of continuation
                      of the attacks against Hanoi. It is clear
                      that this constitutes an ultimatum to the
                      Vietnamese people.

eptember 11, 1967 -   "The Government of the Democratic
  (Cont'd)   Republic of Viet-Nam energetically rejects
                        the American propositions.

                        "The position of the Government of the
                        Democratic Republic of Viet-Nam is that the
                        United States should cease definitely and
                        without conditions the bombing and all
                        other acts of war against the Democratic
                        Republic of Viet-Nam. It should withdraw
                        American troops and satellites from South
                        Viet-Nam, recognize the National Liberation
                        Front of South Viet-Nam and let the
                        Vietnamese people themselves regulate their
                        internal affairs. It is only after the un-
                        conditional stopping by the United States of
                        the bombing and all other acts of war against
                        the Democratic Republic of Viet-Nam, that it
                        would be possible to engage in conversations."

                         (unofficial translation)

                        Bo told M to give the text to Kissinger and
                        added that "as soon as there is a reply" M
                        should communicate with Bo at any time of day
                        or night. When M urged Bo to meet Kissinger,
                        Bo said "give the message to Kissinger and
                        when the reply is here we shall see about
                        meeting". In commenting on the text of the
                        DRV message Bo made the following statement:

                        "The bombing of Hanoi at the same time as the
                        sending of the (August 21) message constitutes
                        a pressure. Stopping of the bombing along with
                        the threat of a renewal has the character of an
                        ultimatum." (Paris 3097).

September 13, 1967 - M met for 35 minutes with Bo on short
notice at noon. Pursuant to revised
Departmental instructions to Kissinger ·
(State 35967 and 36554) which K discussed
with M in part at breakfast on September 13
(Paris 3242), M handed Bo the following
message from K in a sealed envelope:

"I have a reply from the USG to the
Hanoi message which was received on Monday
(September 11). I have also been given
a commentary on this message. Because of
the importance of the United States reply and
because   the commentary refers to other
discussions with Hanoi which we have promised
not to reveal I have been instructed to deliver
it personally. I am available for a meeting at
any time and any place which is convenient
to Mr. Mai Van Bo."

Bo asked M whether he had seen the message
from K. M said he had not, and Bo did not
show the message to M. In response to M's
urging that Bo see K, Bo said "because of
the continued threat of bombing Hanoi which
has the character of an ultimatum, a direct
meeting with Kissinger cannot take place."
M asked what assurances Hanoi wanted. Bo
replied that this was a US problem. M asked
whether contacts through the M/A channel
should continue and Bo replied "definitely
yes. We consider that we wish to continue
talking through this channel." Bo said he
would accept any communication open or
sealed through this channel, specifically
including any such message from Kissinger.
Bo   reiterated "We
want to keep this channel open". In reply to
a question Bo said that as long as M was in
Paris he saw no need for A to return from Rome.

23

Bo then turned to the (September 11) bombing
of Haiphong.[11] He said that bombing within
one kilometer of the center of town in effect
meant attacking populated areas. He did not
establish any relationship between the bombing
of Haiphong and the sending of any message in
the M/A channel. Bo emphasized to M Pham Van
Dong's view that the DRV would continue
fighting no matter how badly it was bombed --
even if Hanoi was totally destroyed. He
referred M to the Schoenbrun September 10
television program as evidence of Hanoi's
determination to continue fighting (Paris 3288
and 3257).[12]

September 14, 1967 - M saw Bo at noon. In accordance with instructions to Kissinger (State 36927 approving
Paris 3257) which Kissinger discussed with him
on the morning of September 14 (Paris 3329), M
handed Bo the following message from K in a
sealed envelope:

"Hanoi's attitude with respect to the
kind of restraint we have employed in this
channel is baffling. If we bomb near Hanoi
we are accused of bringing pressure. If we
voluntarily and without any suggestion from
Hanoi impose a restraint on our actions and
keep this up without time limit we are accused
of an ultimatum. In fact, the American proposal
contained neither threats nor conditions and
should not be rejected on these grounds".

Bo did not open it but said he would study it
later. He asked whether it contained the
principal message, and M said K had asked for
instructions about whether the principal
message could be transmitted through A and M.
Bo asked whether M was sure there was a message
and Bo said he was certain there was and that
K would receive instructions soon. M then read
to Bo from his handwritten notes containing
the following official explanation:

"The enclosed paper contains Washington's
view about the significance of the restraint
in the Hanoi area and the unconditional
nature of our message of August 25."

M then gave Bo Kissinger's "personal"
explanation as follows:

"The enclosed declaration in my judgment
erases the possibility of any charge that we
are proceeding by ultimatum."

Then as arranged with Kissinger (Paris 3329),
M gave Bo the following "official" comment
from Kissinger:

"Washington does not consider the attacks
of September 11 as escalation. The attacks
closest to the center of Haiphong were in an
area which had been attacked three times
previously, most recently on June 26.
Mr. Kissinger is prepared to give more detailed
clarifications".

M then added Kissinger's "personal" comment:

"(A) Bo should remember that the number
of officials aware of the current exchange of
views is very small. This makes it very
difficult to reverse decisions taken prior
repeat prior to the decision to send the
message of August 25 and maintain secrecy.
(B) It seems more useful to seek a solution
to the present situation than to debate about
how we got there. Hanoi should remember that
the U.S. message of August 25 offered to end
the bombing and all other acts of war against the
DRV in circumstances which the United States
Government considers not to involve conditions
but which rather repeat statements made by Hanoi.
If Bo wants clarification, I stand ready to
give it."

25

M also gave Bo Kissinger's concluding
"personal" comment:

"The present exchanges can be useful if
they enable both sides to gain a clearer
understanding of the issues before them. I
must point out, however, the concern expressed
to me by high officials in Washington that too
often these communications are one-way streets."

M agreed to Bo's request that he leave his
notes containing the above comments for Bo
to study and Bo would return them on the
morning of September 15.

M mentioned that at some point the Elysee would
have to be informed but Bo replied "The fewer
people know about this the better." M again
said he hoped Bo and Kissinger would be in
direct contact soon (Paris 3383; 3329; and
(French text) - 3415).

September 16, 1967 - Kissinger met for about two hours with M and A,
immediately after A's return from Rome on the
morning of September 16. K told M and A he was
authorized to give them the sealed message from
Washington for delivery later in the day to Bo
and turned over the message to them. K
cautioned M and A not to tie the continuation
of their channel to K's presence in Paris but
suggested that they ask Bo about Bo's views on
how to continue the channel thereafter. K
reminded M and A that the US is prepared to talk
on an official level at any mutually convenient
place. M and A indicated their willingness to
continue on the present basis and reluctantly
agreed to hand sealed envelopes for delivery to

Kissinger to an Embassy officer (later
specified as Wallner) after K left Paris,
although they indicated a preference for
communicating with K by ordinary mail or
telephone.

K urged M and A not to permit Bo to gain
any misimpression that he had a future
assurance from the USG against bombing in
the Hanoi area and M and A promised to leave
no ambiguity on this point. .Kissinger asked
M and A to make the points with Bo that (a) the
US has consistently attempted to phrase its
proposals in conciliatory and realistic
language, but the replies from Hanoi have
not been responsive and have not addressed
key elements of the US proposals; and (b) the
failure of Hanoi to deal with US proposals
and the interjection of outside elements, such
as specific military actions, have raised
doubts in the minds of US officials about the
willingness of Hanoi to enter into productive
discussions (Paris 3492).

September 16, 1967 - M and A met with Bo for over an hour, starting
at noon.   A, who did most of the talking at the
meeting with Bo and kept the notes, reported
on the meeting. Bo greeted A and M affably and
offered them drinks. Bo said Ho had charged
him with inquiring about the health of A's
family. A then handed to Bo in a sealed
envelope French and English texts of the
following US message:

September 13, 1967

"The USG believes that the September 11
message from the DRV may be based on a misunderstanding of the American proposal of

27

August 25. The American proposal contained
neither conditions nor threats and should
not be rejected on these grounds.

"It has been the understanding of the
USG that the DRV would be willing promptly
to engage in productive discussions leading to
peace when there was a cessation of aerial and
naval bombardment. The USG sought to confirm
this fact in its proposal which the DRV has in
front of it.

"As a demonstration of its good faith and
in order to create the best atmosphere for
the consideration of its proposal the US
voluntarily undertook not to bomb Hanoi from
August 25 onward - the day on which its proposal
was submitted to Hanoi. This restraint has been
maintained without time limit even though
activities by opposing forces in the south have
in fact been stepped up since August 25.[13]

"The August 25 proposal of the USG remains
open." (END OF MESSAGE)

A told Bo he did not know the content of the
message but described it as "conciliatory",
a word which Bo made him write down. Bo did
not open the envelope in M and A's presence.

A asked Bo about the significance of the AFP
September 14 Hanoi story (State 38031), quoting
"reliable sources" as indicating that talks would
start three or four weeks after a bombing
cessation, and A showed Bo Paris press stories
based on the AFP report.[14] Bo replied that the
three-to four-week interval between the end
of bombing and the beginning of negotiations
was "an invention of journalists". He noted
that Pham Van Dong's statement had given no
ground for the time period mentioned in the
newspapers.

28

A asked Bo whether there was any utility
in the continuation of the M and A channel
and wondered whether they should now
withdraw. Bo replied that M and A had been
received as friends and they were "not at
the end of the tether" because of the
continued validity of the channel. Bo
said: "We trust you and you trust Kissinger.
What you have been doing is useful ... You
see you have produced results. There was a
message to us from the USG which we
accepted. We replied, to be sure, negatively.
This week we have had two brief communications
and today a formal message, so you are being
useful." Bo again referred back to the fact
that their visa request had been turned down
because it had been made concurrent with the
bombardment of Hanoi and to have let them come
to Hanoi at that time "would have discredited
us and ultimately you".

M again urged Bo to see K, and Bo asked a
number of questions about K's plans for the
coming week. When M suggested he could
arrange coffee for K and Bo at a private
residence, Bo said "Let me think about how
best to arrange a meeting and I will let you
know. I will call you as I called you last
week." '

When M mentioned reporting to the Elysee if
the present effort failed, Bo said again that
the M and A channel is "not at the end of its
usefulness. I see no need to bring anyone
else in. Complicated matters may take some
time to mature and become more complicated if
too many people intervene."

When M asked whether Dzu, runner-up in the
SVN Presidential campaign, would be acceptable
to the NLF in a more broadly based government,
Bo said that Dzu was a "heel", however, and
there were many reasonable people in the south,

including high-ranking military officers."
When A asked about Thieu, Bo replied that he
did not understand a man who got himself
elected "on the basis of inviting foreigners
to bomb his compatriats", but A was struck
by the relative mildness of his comment.

When asked about the political situation in
the US, M and A said that the main lines of
American foreign policy would not change no
matter who won in 1968, unless it was Reagan [15]
in which case "there would be a greater
possibility of escalation than of peace
overtures." Bo seemed surprised.

Bo returned M's handwritten notes of a meeting
of September 14 and said they had been useful
but he had studied them sufficiently.
(Paris 3501)

30

September 18, 1967 - Aubrac called on Bo for five minutes
on the way to the airport on the
morning of September 18. (A is leaving
for Rome and will be back on September 20.)
At K's request, A told Bo that Hanoi's
response need not be confined to any one
particular channel. A suggested the
following possibilities: (a) a personal
meeting between Bo and K; (b) a message
in a sealed envelope via A and M to K;
(c) an open message via A and M,as Hanoi's
note of September 11; (d) a message to be
given to a US official in Paris or elsewhere;
(e) any other channel that seemed appropriate
to Hanoi. Bo replied: "There will be (sic)
answer. Things may seem to move slowly.
In fact, they are moving at their 'normal'
speed for exchanges of this kind". (Paris
3536)

September 20, 1967 - George Brown received message dated September 19
from Secretary Rusk informing him of the texts
of the US messages of August 25 and September 13
and the DRV message of September 11. Brown will
pass on information to Prime Minister Wilson
only. (State 39656; London 2126)

September 20, 1967 - A returned to Paris from Rome and phoned Bo
to suggest jokingly that Bo have dinner with
K. Bo laughed and said he was still without
instructions. (Paris 3765)

September 21, 1967 - A and M met with Bo for an hour-and-a-half
starting at noon. M read to Bo the following
message from K, which he left with Bo at Bo's
request:

"I am leaving Friday evening to give
a speech in Hannover Sunday. I plan
to return to the US on Sunday. If before
Saturday evening you know that there will
be a reply from Hanoi either Sunday or

31

Monday, please inform M and I shall
return via Paris.

"Washington is still standing by
for an answer to its message of
September 13.

"We have noted your interest in the
A & M channel and we are ready to
continue it.

"I remain available at Cambridge
to receive message either directly
or through A & M. If desirable, I
could come to Paris to receive messages
directly or through A & M either in
sealed envelope or openly.

"Alternatively, Washington is ready
to send an official to receive any
message either directly or through
A & M in a sealed envelope or not."

In response to a question M told Bo that
the text of the message had been agreed
by K. Bo replied, according to A's notes:
"This channel is very convenient for us.
If I have a reply before Saturday evening
(9/21) I shall call you (M). I shall also
be in touch with you afterwards as soon as
I hear something but you should be aware of
the mood Hanoi has expressed in our Foreign
Ministry statement of September 19". (Ed.:
the DRV ForMin statement was a detailed
complaint about US bombing in the area
immediately above the 17th parallel.) Bo
also mentioned the bombardment of Haiphong,
but briefly and without conviction according
to A.

32

When M urged Bo to see K, Bo replied that
he could see private Americans at his
discretion, but he could not see any
American who spoke for the USG or reported
directly to the USG without Hanoi authorization, which he had not received.
Bo added that Hanoi is reluctant to talk
under duress with any officially connected
American. Bo said "the Americans are playing a
double game—on the one hand they are offering
us peace; on the other they increase their
bombing." At the same time Bo repeated his
desire to keep the Pennsylvania channel open
and said "he will accept a communication at
any time. He will be in touch as soon as
he has anything to say...we want you (A and M)
and Kissinger to continue."

M showed Bo the text of the draft report
(Paris 3804) he intended to give the Elysee
if the channel failed or was publicized and
told Bo of K's desire to delete the text of
the US and DRV messages; a point which Bo
agreed upon. Bo said if the report was given
to the Elysee, it should be made clear that
it was not done at Bo's request or instigation.
(Paris 3803; Paris 3765)

September 22, 1967   ▾ M saw Bo and gave him the following message:

"Washington is still waiting for an
answer to its message of September 13.
The offer of August 25 as further explained
in the message of September 13, remains
open. At present Washington has nothing
further to say." (Paris 3908)

When M delivered this note, Bo saw him only
briefly because he was tied up with Columnist
Joe Kraft. Bo said that he still had no
instructions and if he had something he would
get back in touch with M. (Kissinger/Read
9/24 telecon)

33

ptember 23, 1967   –   Bo called M at 1300 and asked M to come over.
M met with Bo for more than an hour starting
at 1800. Bo read the following message to
M, which M took down in his own notes and
read back to Bo to check for accuracy:

"1. The whole world knows that the US has
pursued a constant policy of escalation
against North Vietnam.

"2. After Hanoi was bombed, US planes hit
Campha and Haiphong. As regards
Haiphong, US planes have bombed it
several times in a row and very violently
attacked the DMZ and Vinh Linh Province.[16]

"3. As a result every one agrees that
the bombing has been intensified in recent
weeks.

"4. Washington's explanation about the
bombing of Haiphong cannot be received.

"5. These are the circumstances under
which you have suggested contacts with
Kissinger. I accept your expression
of confidence in Kissinger, but at the
moment when US is increasing its escalation, it was not possible for me
to see him.

"6. Turning to more general topics,
I have spoken to you of the two-faced
policy of the US.

"7. What has happened has confirmed me
in that opinion, for the attitude of the
US exhibits all kinds of contradictions.
It is possible to highlight this by a
few examples:

(a) Together with the message of
August 25, Kissinger has let me

know through you as intermediaries
that the US has stopped bombing of
Hanoi for 10 days; then for 72 hours,
and now the US tells us that the
bombing of Hanoi is suspended without
time limit. What do you think of
the assertion that the USG of its own
free will has suspended the bombing
without setting a time limit?

(b) In fact what has happened is the
stopping of bombing of Hanoi but the
intensification of bombing elsewhere
as in Campha, Haiphong and Vinh Linh
Province, where the bombing has the
character of extermination and systematic
destruction.

(c) To say that by stopping of bombing
of Hanoi the US has wanted to create
better atmosphere is not true.

"8. With respect to the August 25 message, the
essence of the US position is to offer to
stop bombing with conditions.   In a message
delivered by sealed envelope the US has
replied that the offer is without conditions
while asserting that the message of
August 25 is still valid.

"9. As far as you and A are concerned, I
have received you any time you have requested.
I listen to you. I accept messages from you.
I transmit them. I report fully to Hanoi.
I call you when I have something to say.
I believe that this demonstrates our good will
sufficiently.   However, as I have pointed
out earlier, we have no illusions about
American policy. What do you think of all
this?" (end of message)

35

When Bo asked M for his reactions, M said that:

(a) M would state his own personal view that each US message had been accompanied by deescalation. With respect to Haiphong, M said he knew only what K had told him, which was confirmed by the press reports--that US attacks had concentrated on communication links, not on systematic destruction of the town itself. Nevertheless, M agreed that American actions had made discussions more complicated.

(b) M thought that the US suspension of bombing of Hanoi, first for ten days, then 72 hours, then without time limit, reflected contradictions in American approach to the channel.

(c) M asked whether a reversion by the US to the "level of bombing in early August" would permit initiation of discussions. On the last point Bo replied that his Prime Minister had "already answered that question".

Finally, M asked Bo to ascertain from Hanoi whether M and A had correctly understood Pham Van Dong's remark to M and A in July, which M read to Bo from A's notes. (The portion of the exchange is found on pages 12-13 and 16 of the Kissinger memorandum of August 1, 1967   in which Dong is reported to have indicated that delay following a de facto cessation would not be a problem and that talks should be conducted by persons authorized by both sides.) Bo said that Dong's reported statements to A and M differed from the public position of his government, and Bo would send the exchange to Hanoi to ask if it were a true representation of Dong's position.

Bo again enjoined them to use greatest secrecy.
(Source: Kissinger/Read 9/24 telecon)

September 25, 1967 - M called on Bo at 8:30 a.m. and read to Bo the
following five point message from Kissinger:

"(1) I will transmit to the appropriate
Washington officials later today the message
you (Bo) gave M yesterday. (2) I see no point
in trading charges and countercharges about
past activities. In fact Washington has offered
to stop bombing based on the assumption it
would lead to prompt, productive talks. That
offer remains open. It was made sincerely.
If accepted, there will be no need to discuss
escalation or bombing problems. (3) The
exchange indicates that Washington and Hanoi
have great difficulty understanding each
other's thought processes. This makes direct
US/DRV contact essential. Intermediaries, no
matter how trustworthy, are not satisfactory
substitutes. (4) American military actions
during the past month reflect in part the
extreme secrecy with which Washington has
handled this exchange. The USG has considered
it unwise to change decisions made prior to the
report of M and A's trip to Hanoi, except in
regard to bombing Hanoi itself, because it
wanted to keep the circle of awareness of this
exchange as small as possible to avoid premature
public debate. (5) The difference in the positions of the two governments could be summarized
as follows: Washington has indicated its
readiness to stop bombing and has only asked
to confirm its understanding of Hanoi's
view that this would lead promptly to productive negotiations. Hanoi has implied that
an end of bombing would in fact have this result
If this is indeed the view of both governments,
the remaining obstacles to direct talks can be
overcome. I am certain that the above correctly
reflects US views. Could Bo confirm that it
also reflects the view of Hanoi."

M said Bo's response to the foregoing message
was favorable. M then questioned Bo about

what Bo had meant in their conversation of
September 23 when Bo had said that his Prime
Minister had already answered M's question
about whether US/DRV talks would be possible
if the US cut back to the level of bombing
of early August. Bo replied that the DRV
Prime Minister had made clear publicly that
there could be no formal discussions between
the US and the DRV as long as any level of
bombing continued in the North. Bo added,
however, that preliminary discussions between
Bo and Kissinger might not fall under such
prohibition, and Bo said that he would let
M know in a few days whether such preliminary
discussions would be possible.
(Source: Kissinger/Read 9/25 telecon)

September 30, 1967 - M and A called on Bo at 9:00 a.m. on September 30
and spent two hours with him. The atmosphere
was friendly and cordial throughout and Bo gave
them tea.

M and A told Bo that they had been in touch with
K, and K had had further discussions with his
Washington friends. M and A noted that K and the
USG had put a proposal and questions to the DRV
through the Bo channel to which there had been
no substantive responses. The US August 25th
offer without conditions remained open. M and
A noted that K's Washington friends were
interested in learning whether Bo had received
an answer to the point Bo had raised on September 25
about the possibility of "preliminary discussions."

Bo replied that he had an answer to the latter
point. Bo said that he could not talk directly
to a US validated individual even in a preliminary
way because "too much had happened since July."
(M and A got the impression from Bo that he
feared that "preliminary discussions" would simply
be a ruse on our part to get into substantive talks
with the DRV while the bombing continued.)

38

When Bo referred again to the "conditions"
contained in the US position, M and A asked
him to point out what conditions he was
referring to. Bo said in the first paragraph
of the US August 25 proposal the words "with
the understanding that" really amounted to a
condition on our part, as did the words
"productive" and "prompt". He indicated there
were other complications with the proposal.

M and A referred to the forthcoming sentences
in President Johnson's September 29 speech which
repeated US willingness to stop the bombing
"when this will lead promptly to productive
discussions" on the assumption that the DRV would
"not take advantage of the bombing cessation
or limitation" during the discussions. Bo said
he had not had a chance to study the President's
speech, but he was glad that they had brought this
portion of the speech to his attention, because
the French press headlines made the US position
sound conditional.

They discussed the Viet-Nam statements in the
U.N. debate to date, and Bo said the DRV was
highly displeased with George Brown's speech
but pleased with the French and Canadian statements
in New York. Bo added jocularly that he
"claimed some credit" for the French position.
Since M and A did not know the content of the
French or Canadian positions and Bo did not
elaborate, there was no discussion about what
features of the GOC or GOF positions Bo was
referring to.[17]

Bo expressed the thought that the "present political
trend" in the US was favorable to the DRV.[18]

At one stage of the discussion M and A found the
opportunity to underscore the point that the US
had made no commitments regarding its future
actions.

39

A asked whether Bo had received an answer to the
September 23 inquiry regarding the accuracy of
A's notes of his discussion in Hanoi with Pham
Van Dong on the point that there would be "no
question of a delay" between the end of bombing
and talks both sides "knew how to meet each
other." A again vouched for the care and accuracy
of the notes of his conversation with Dong. Bo
said he had not had an answer to this inquiry
which he had made on September 23, but he
expected an answer early next week. Bo did say
that if there was a halt in the bombing "Kissinger
should put on his hat and come to Paris immediately." When A and M asked for clarification of the
conflicting reports of the DRV position regarding
the delay between a bombing halt and talks as
reflected in September 26 AFP column and a
September 28 Le Monde article, Bo said he hoped
that the answer he would get from Hanoi to the
question regarding the Dong/M and A July exchange
would clarify this issue.[19]

M and Bo arranged to meet again on Wednesday,
October 4. Bo repeated the point he had made
before: he was available at any time to M and A
to talk to them, meet with them, discuss matters
with them, and report to Hanoi on their discussions. He said he would advise them as soon
as he had received anything from his government.

October 2, 1967 -   On his own initiative M went to see Bo on the
afternoon of October 2 and spent an hour and a
half with him. M said that he had sought the
appointment to pass on information received
from K that morning that indicated growing
impatience in Washington and the feeling on the
part of K's Washington colleagues that they had
received almost nothing from Hanoi through the
M and A channel. It was decided that a message
should be sent to Kissinger, and M stated that
he took elaborate notes on which to base the
message, which was put together in final form

by M following the meeting and after a flight
to Rome where he discussed the message in
detail with A from Rome they mailed it by
special delivery air-post to Kissinger in
Boston late on October 2. The text of the
note received by Kissinger follows:

"The position of the RDVN remains always
the same. If the United States really
wished to talk, let them stop first without
conditions the bombardment of the territory
of the RDVN.

"Starting from that position there are
several eventualities:

(a) A public declaration by the Government
of the United States about the cessation.
This declaration could take place either
before or after the cessation.

(b) An official declaration but non-public
preceding the cessation of the bombardment.
This declaration could be communicated by
the channel K/A-M (officieusement)-not
quite officially, and after this indication
it can be transmitted officially by an
accredited person.

(c) An end of bombardment without preceding
official declaration followed by an official
but not public communication of the Government of the United States.

"Eventuality (a) would represent a public
declaration replying to that made on the 28th
of January by M. Trinh, Minister of Foreign
Affairs of the RDVN, which constitutes a
solemn engagement to talk after the unconditional end of bombing. This public declaration would be followed by the transmission of
an official text by an accredited person.

41

"Eventualities (b) and (c) reflect the
propositions of M and A as they result from
their understanding of their conversation
in July in Hanoi with the Prime Minister.
A confirmation is expected soon." (End of
message)

As explained by letter from M, point (a) in the
above message was written entirely by Bo as well
as the preamble. Points (b) and (c) were written
on M's suggestion but practically controlled and
re-read phrase by phrase by Bo. The point about
the non-public declaration was also discussed
at length. M and Bo also discussed the word
"officieuse" and agreed that it was a term
applying to a person mandated by the Government
of the United States. According to M , Bo
said "on several occasions" that Trinh's
February 28 speech constituted a "solemn engagement" by the DRV before world opinion, and a public
declaration by the US would be a reply having the
same character of commitment.[20]

Bo told M to be sure to report to Bo immediately
by phone what Kissinger's reactions to the message were. (Sources: M's October 2 letter to
K; Kissinger/Read 10/4, 1 p.m.; telecon.)

October 4, 1967 (p.m.) - At K's request M took the "message" received in
the mail by Kissinger to Bo on the afternoon
of October 4 to seek confirmation of paragraph
(b). Bo read the document and then said that
he had still not received word from Hanoi about
the accuracy of M and A's understanding of his
July talk with Pham Van Dong, so Bo could not
comment at this time on the formulation of
eventualities (b) and (c).

42

Bo did confirm the accuracy of the opening
paragraph of the communication, the formulation
of eventuality   (a) and the paragraph of
description of eventuality (a), except Bo said
he had not used the words "solemn engagement".
M took strong exception with Bo, saying that
M's own notes and clear recollection of their
October 3 conversation on this point were very
clear. M said to Bo that if he (M) was capable
of such misunderstanding M's usefulness was at
an end. Bo energetically denied that M's utility
was at an end and expressed the view that the
channel was of definite continuing utility. Bo
and M discussed what phrase should be used in
place of "solemn engagement" without reaching
a firm conclusion. (Source: Kissinger/Read 10/4,
1:00 p.m. telecon)

ber 4, 1967 (later — After a full discussion with K, M called Bo
       p.m.)   to say that K's reaction to the last M/Bo
conversation was that Bo's backing away from
the phrase "solemn engagement" would be viewed
in Washington as a serious substantive change.
He also passed on K's view that it would have
been better to receive no communication then
one in which a key point had been retracted.
Bo instructed M to come over and see Do
immediately. (Source: Kissinger/Read 10/4,
4:00 p.m., telecon)

4, 1967 (late —
   evening)   M visited Bo and spent an hour and a half with
him at approximately 2230-2400 Paris time. M
told Bo of K's views of the serious reactions
in Washington to the change of the text which
K had received this morning, and he asked Bo
to review that text again with him. Again
Bo confirmed the accuracy of the opening
paragraph of the earlier text and the accuracy
of the statement of the first eventuality ("A
public declaration by the Government of the
United States about the cessation. This
declaration could take place either before
or after the cessation.") Bo said since he
had not heard from Hanoi about the M and A
conversation there in July, he could not
comment on the other two eventualities which
were mentioned in the message K received this

43

morning. Bo would not discuss further
his renegging on the words "solemn
engagement" or the paragraph in which
those words appear.

Bo then said that he wanted M to send a
message to K which would come as close as
possible to eventuality (b) in the communication K received in the mail. M wrote out
the text in French and read it through with
Bo three times to assure its accuracy. M
also did an English translation for Bo.

Message from M to K:

"After having discussed with Bo and
after having obtained confirmation of his
country's position regarding the eventuality
of talks you should know that if the US
really wants to talk it is necessary first
to stop without conditions the bombing and all
other acts of war against the DRV. I have come
to the conclusion, recalling also a previous
conversation in the presence of A, that the
scenario could be the following: The Government
of the United States would send a first message
through our channel (K/M-A) announcing
unequivocally the unconditional cessation of
bombing. Once this has been effectively
realized, a second message still through our
channel might suggest the opening of the
dialogue at a date and site proposed by you.
If you and your friends agree on such a
scenario, let Bo know this agreement through
a written message which I will then transmit
to Bo. I do not know if what I say is appropriate
you know this better than I."

M said the last sentence of the message was
added when Bo told M to end with something
"friendly and conciliatory". Bo told M he would
stand by to get K's reaction (Source: Kissinger/
Read 10/4, 8:30 p.m. telecon)

44

DISPATCHED

<u>October 8, 1967</u> - M and A called on Bo at 9:00 a.m. Paris time and spent 1½ hours with him. As in the past Bo was cordial to his visitors throughout the meeting.

1967 OCT 10 18 53

OFFICE OF THE
SECRETARY OF DEFENSE

M and A handed the written portion of the message from Kissinger to Bo, which Bo read closely. M and A then read to Bo Kissinger's four "oral points", and Bo wrote them down carefully in his own notes. (M and A did not leave with Bo the "oral" part of the message.) The written message and oral points are as follows:

"M should tell B that K would be authorized to deliver to B in writing the following message whenever B is prepared to meet with him officially or unofficially:

'The United States Government understands the position of the Democratic Republic of Vietnam to be as follows: That upon the cessation by the United States of all forms of bombardment of the Democratic Republic of Vietnam, without expression of condition, the Democratic Republic of Vietnam would enter promptly into productive discussions with the United States. The purpose of these discussions would be to resolve the issues between the United States and the Democratic Republic of Vietnam.

'Assuming the correctness of this understanding of the position of the Democratic Republic of Vietnam, the United States Government is prepared, in accordance with its proposal of August 25, to transmit in advance to the Democratic Republic of Vietnam the precise date upon which bombardment of the Democratic Republic of Vietnam would cease and to suggest a date and a place for the commencement of discussions.'

45

"In addition M should convey to B the following oral points from K:

"1.   K believes that this understanding is consistent with B's statements of October 4, as reported by M, and with the proposal of the United States Government of August 25.

"2.   When B meets with K, K would also be prepared to state the precise date on which the cessation of bombardment would occur and to give the suggestions of the United States with respect to the date and site of the discussions following the cessation of bombardment, and K would be authorized to receive the views of the Democratic Republic of Vietnam with respect to these and other modalities.

"3.   K noted that the Democratic Republic of Vietnam had not commented on observations by the United States Government on August 25 with respect to secrecy of the fact of discussions between the Democratic Republic of Vietnam and the United States Government.

"4.   K observed that officials of the United States Government had taken note of a reduction of military activities in the vicinity of the demilitarized zone.   Undoubtedly, the Democratic Republic of Vietnam had noted the absence in recent weeks of aerial bombardment in the immediate vicinity of Hanoi."

Bo told M to tell Kissinger how much Bo appreciated K's personal efforts. Bo then dictated to M and A the following short message of acknowledgment to K:

"M and A have passed the note from K to B. In case B will have a reply to make, he will make it through this channel." .

M suggested that Bo add a sentence saying that

46

Bo was studying the message but Bo refused.

Bo then said on first reading of the written
note from K, it seemed to him that all that
appeared after the opening phrase stating
US willingness to stop the bombing without
conditions did in fact constitute conditions.
In particular B characterized as "conditions"
the words "prompt", "productive" and "in
accordance with the proposal of August 25."

M and A said that the latter phrase really
meant that neither side should take advantage
of a standdown of bombing while US/DRV discussions were in process, as stated in the
August 25 proposal and the President's San
Antonio speech. In this regard M and A
mentioned specifically that serious hostilities
in the DMZ would make productive talks impossible.
(M and A noted that Bo made no

rejoinder to the point about the DMZ
in the oral message from K or when they referred to the DMZ at this place in the
conversation.)

M asked what Bo's response would be if the
words "prompt" and "productive" were taken
out. Bo replied that if this happened he
would have to refer back to his government
before answering.

Bo read the third oral point in K's message
as referring back to the portion of the
August 25 message which referred to the
possibility of partial limitations of actions
against the DRV because of the difficulty
of keeping discussions secret after bombing
stopped altogether. Bo said this was
"clearly unacceptable".

Bo also referred to the "usual American
double game"---that on September 29 or 30,
US planes hit a school in Haiphong, killing
30 children.

M and A underscored to B the new features
in the Kissinger message. (Sources: State
49772 and Kissinger/Read 10/8 telecon)

October 9, 1967 - On his own initiative M called on Bo for an
hour early on the afternoon of October 9,
1967. M told Bo that K had made three
principal points in his phone discussions
with M and A following the latter's October 8
meeting with Bo:

(1) The message given to Bo from K
on October 8 had been prepared with great
care. It represented an important and
detailed suggestion about bringing about
discussions to resolve US/DRV differences
following a cessation of bombing.

(2) As K's Washington colleagues continued to note, there had been a virtual

absence of considered responses from
Hanoi to US proposals in this channel
to date.

(3) K is holding open the possibility
of coming to Paris next weekend (as A and
M had urged him to do) but K's decision on
making the trip will be influenced by what
we get back through this channel during
this week.

Bo professed surprise that K or M and A saw
anything new in the October 8 message, and M
pointed out to Bo that for the first time
in the October 8 message the US was offering
to provide a specific date for the
cessation of bombing.

M pressed Bo for an answer to the inquiry
Bo had informed M and A earlier he was
sending to Hanoi regarding confirmation of
the July conversations with Pham Van Dong
regarding the delay between a stopping of
the bombing and talks. Bo replied with a
French idiom which translates as follows:
"Who does not say 'no', agrees".

Bo mentioned unidentified French reports
charging new US air attacks on Hanoi and
other reports about the concern on the part
of the diplomatic community in Hanoi of
possible strikes against dikes.

Bo took careful notes of the points made by
M and said that if K came to Paris next
weekend he (Bo) would be available all day
Saturday and Sunday to see M and A. (Source:
Kissinger/Read 10/9 telecon)

October 10-11, 1967

Kissinger received a phone call from "M" who pleaded with "K" to come to Paris this weekend. "K" advised against his returning to Paris at this time in order to continue to maximize pressures on Bo to get something back through the channel. (Kissinger/Read telecon.)

"K" phoned "M" on 11 October to say that he would return to Paris as soon as it becomes clear that Hanoi will not respond to the channel. "K" made three points to "M": (1) that he would not come to Paris this weekend; (2) that the past U.S. messages to Bo are clear and speak for themselves; and (3) Washington has nothing further to say. (Kissinger/Read telecon, 11 October).

October 17, 1967

"M" saw Bo, expressed hope to keep the channel open, and handed "M" the following message:

"Actually the U.S. has been following a policy of escalation of an extremely serious nature. In these conditions the U.S. proposals of peace are double-faced. At a time when the U.S. is pursuing a policy of escalation we cannot receive Kissinger, nor comment on the American proposals transmitted through this channel.

"The position of the Government of the DRV is perfectly clear: it is only when the U.S. has ended without condition the bombardment that discussions can take place."

"M and Bo discussed what 'the conditions' were in the U.S. proposal. M said he thought that the U.S. meant that we wanted a guarantee of serious discussions when we used the word 'productive.' Bo said the DRV thought that by use of the word 'productive' we meant that we wanted to talk about objectives in the South also, since discussions could not be fully productive without this subject being considered.

"Bo asked M if K was coming to Paris this weekend, and when M informed him that K and A would both be in Paris, Bo said that these were 'positive factors' and indicated satisfaction."

(Kissinger/Read Telecon, October 17, 1967).

October 19, 1967

"K" was given guidance for his discussion with "M" and "A". These were viewed as talking points exclusively for use with "M" and "A".

"1. From the time of your opening discussions with M. tonight, you should make it entirely clear to him that Washington considers that the DRV has rejected the forthcoming USG proposals to bring about an end to the bombing and prompt and productive US/DRV discussions with no advantage being taken by the DRV on the ground. You should indicate that we base this conclusion not only on the negative DRV message of Oct. 17 but also upon Hanoi's negative public statements, and, most importantly, upon renewed DRV hostile actions in the vicinity of the DMZ....but it should be your objective from the start to indicate that the patience of your Washington friends is running out and that they feel that Hanoi has been unwilling to respond on any significant point."[21]

"2....

"g. You should emphasize that when the DRV messages in this channel of September 11, September 23 and October 17 are analyzed they show that the DRV has been unwilling at any time (1) to indicate in this channel or otherwise that for its part it will engage in discussions with the US even if the bombing had stopped in accordance with US proposals; or (2) to make any substantive counter proposal on how to proceed to discussions leading to peaceful settlement of differences.

"h. Note that on this date, October 19, a Reuters dispatch from Hong Kong indicates that 'North Vietnam today rejected the American offer for a conditional bombing pause in return for peace talks' as offered by President Johnson on September 29 and repeated by Secretary Rusk at his October 12 press conference...."

"3. In reviewing this channel with M. and A. you are authorized to show to them the text of the September 13 USG message and other messages which you sent during your last visit in Paris which they have not yet seen.

"4. Without requesting M. and A. to see Bo, which we assume they will promptly do to report your mood of discouragement and concern, you should indicate interest in learning

what essential differences Bo (not M. and A.) could find,
if any, with the main points in your review of the channel.

"5. If pressed, you are authorized to state that the
US proposals do remain open at this time but that you are
not empowered to speak about future US views or actions."

(State 56516 to Amembassy Paris, 19 Oct 67).

October 20, 1967

"K" had the following conversations with M. & A on this date.
They added up to a stalemate in the channel.

"M. met me at the airport in a state of advanced
euphoria. According to him, the last message from Bo
made all the frustrations worthwhile. When I asked
him for the cause of his optimism, he called attention to
the distinction between escalation and bombing and the
change of tense in the last sentence. I quickly disillusioned him. I said that the issue was really quite simple.
If Hanoi wanted to negotiate it should be able to find some
way of expressing this fact by means other than subtle
changes in tense and elliptical references full of double
meanings." (Amembassy Paris 5472 to State.)

"A. replied that he did not think it was quite fair
to charge Hanoi with failing to respond completely. They
had given up the demand for a public declaration that
bombing would stop. Their last message was much soberer
than the first and said nothing about the withdrawal of
American forces from SVN. Nevertheless he thought it
urgent that he and M see Bo as soon as possible. I said
that the decision was up to him as long as it was clear
that the USG had nothing to say. If they met Bo they
should understand that four points were of particular
concern to Washington: (A) that a bombing stop be followed by prompt negotiations, (B) that these negotiations
not be indefinitely delayed, (C) that no advantage would
be taken on the ground, (D) the special situation along the
DMZ." (Amembassy Paris 5507 to State.)

"....A then wrote down the following phrases and asked
me about my reaction: 'The bombardment and other acts of
war against the territory of the DRV are the sole obstacle
to meaningful negotiations. As soon as the bombing ceases,
negotiations can begin.' A. said that he was prepared to
put his personal position with Ho behind these phrases.
I replied that while I could not speak for the US Government

these phrases would be a big step forward. The DMZ problem would still have to be dealt with. (I had not seen the Burchett interview reported in your 57498 then).

"I left M's house at 2030 and returned to my hotel to await word about the appointment with Bo. At 2130 A. called in great distress that Bo had refused to see them. We agreed to meet at 2230. The following is their report of the conversation. A did the talking and M. listened on the extension and took notes.

"A: We would like to see you urgently.

"Bo: There is nothing new to say. The situation is worsening. There is no reason to talk again.

"A: There is repeat is something new and very important.

"Bo: Repeated word for word the same phrase as before.

"A: There is something very important - perhaps the most important juncture of our exchanges.

"Bo: Repeated word for word the same phrase but then added: What is the important matter.

"A: It has to do with the meaning of the last sentence of your last message and the sequence with which steps have to be taken.

"Bo: Our position is perfectly clear. We stand on the Trinh interview with Burchett of January 28. Bo then repeated word for word the original phrase."

(Amembassy Paris 5545 to State.)

October 20, 1967

The following article by Wilfred Burchett was read in Washington on this date:

"Hanoi, North Vietnam AP - There is no possibility of any talks or even contacts between Hanoi and the U.S. government unless the bombardment and other acts of war against North Vietnam are definitively halted.

"This is the position stated to me during conversations in the last few days with Premier Pham Van Dong, Nguyen Duy Trinh, foreign minister and deputy premier, and other high-ranking government and party leaders.

"Hanoi is in no mood for concessions or bargaining
and there is an absolute refusal to offer anything --
except talks -- for a cessation of the bombardment. The
word stressed is 'talks,' not negotiations.

"During an informal talk, however, Trinh repeated
that his statement to this correspondent last January 28 --
that talks could start if the bombing was halted -- still
held good. He said there could be 'meaningful' talks.
Whether they would be 'fruitful' or 'productive' depended
on the United States.

"The mood of Hanoi is one of toughness and confidence.
Although leaders expect Hanoi and Haiphong will probably
be destroyed and that the war may last many more years,
they feel the worst is behind them, that the daily bombings
are absorbed into the country's organism.

"Despite the air assault on Haiphong and intensified
attacks on bridges along the rail link with China, traffic
continues to move out of Haiphong almost normally over
pontoon bridges, and the rail link with China is still
functioning, although occasionally halted for a day or two.
Many tens of thousands of Chinese are working along this
line and elsewhere, keeping rail and road communications
open and repairing bridges."

    . . . .

"It is repeated at every level that total independence
with complete American withdrawal from South Vietnam is the
unalterable aim of the Hanoi government and the Liberation
Front for South Vietnam. They are prepared to fight 10 or
20 years to achieve this, and life is being reorganized on
this basis.

"Hanoi denies that this means export of communism to the
South and insists it agrees with the Liberation Front that the
South should remain a separate entity with a neutral, non-
Socialist regime as advocated in the recently published new
political program of the front, having its independent entity,
with reunification a very long-range, step by step process."

October 22, 1967

Bunker was informed by Bundy that the PENNSYLVANIA track "came
to a negative conclusion on Friday, with opposing party refusing even
to accept further contact with intermediaties. We ourselves read
this, in conjunction with concurrent publication of Burchett article

from Hanoi (sent to you septel) as clear indication that Hanoi rejects the San Antonio/UN formula and appears to be thoroughly dug in at least for the time being."   (State 58070 to Amembassy Saigon.)

October 23, 1967

Ambassador Bohlen reviewed PENNSYLVANIA and made the following suggestion:

"....For example to the communist mind for us to insist that talks must be 'productive' means that we would already have determined how the talks should come out and would amount to the acceptance of an American solution to the talks before they have even begun. Since no one can possibly tell whether the talks would be productive, I would recommend that this and any other qualification be dropped. A simple statement to the effect that as soon as a date and place have been agreed upon for a meeting we would cease all aerial and naval bombardment of North Vietnam should be sufficient."

ROMANIAN-NORTH VIETNAMESE CONTACTS, OCTOBER 1966 - NOVEMBER 1967

October 22, 1966

Ambassador Goldberg had a series of conversations with Romanian Foreign Minister Manescu in late October. The thrust of Manescu's remarks was that a U.S. bombing cessation was necessary to create a "better climate" for negotiations. Goldberg responded with a new bombing formula to the effect that Hanoi only needed to give "an indication as to what /it/ would do in response to a prior cessation of bombing by the U.S." Goldberg emphasized the importance of the words "indication" and "prior."

USUN New York 1777 to SecState (SECRET-NODIS), 22 October 1966, Refs: USUN's 1764 and Deptel 69440:

"4. Said (reftel) 'We would welcome from Hanoi through your good offices -- if that is their desire, as it is ours -- or, if not, through any other channel of their choosing, an indication as to what North Vietnam would do in response to a prior cessation of bombing by the US.' Goldberg then repeated this statement. Manescu then inquired what Goldberg considered new in this statement compared to past positions. Goldberg said words chosen carefully, that he did not want to assert anything was new but that he presumed most important word is 'indication.' Manescu, stating he needed to understand precise meaning, then inquired 'are you ready, then, to cease bombing in return for an indication?' Goldberg replied that significance was that we not asking for advance agreement but rather a statement through a trusted intermediary as to what North Vietnam would do if US following suggestions by Manescu and others to cease bombing. Manescu remarked 'this means that QUOTE indication UNQUOTE has to have a certain content.' Goldberg replied 'we do not believe we can specify the contents in advance, as that would suggest we imposing conditions. We merely say we willing consider suspending bombing if we receive encouraging indication. Of course, if nothing is going to follow, and the war is continued by North Vietnam as now, US will not suspend bombing.' Manescu then stated: 'Vietnam question very important, very sensitive. Smallest misunderstanding in this regard could have consequences no one desires. War in Vietnam does not cause victims only in Vietnam. No misunderstanding or misplaced words can be allowed. It may not be possible to have another mtg prior to my departure since I am leaving Oct 26 or 27, so this may be final talk. When I said that cessation of bombing can create better climate for solution, I

did not put that forward as a personal opinion. The
answer I am taking to Bucharest is the following.
QUOTE On the basis of an indication by North Vietnam,
you would consider cessation bombing. In answer my
question as to what indication should consist of you
said if they go on with war, you would not cease
bombing UNQUOTE.' Goldberg clarified this by emphasizing: 'If they go on with the war as they are going
on with it now.' He added 'an indication of value to
US would have to demonstrate a desire to move toward
peaceful settement. I cannot define it further. I
would rather say QUOTE We are willing to take a step
toward peace if they are willing to take a step toward
peace UNQUOTE. We understand you think cessation
bombing by US would create better climate. We want
to know what step by them would create better climate.
We do not say what this step should be because we
feel this would be badly received. Steps can be
later discussed.' Manescu observed that when Romanians discuss problem of Vietnam among themselves, they
realize US has its honor and prestige to consider in
approaching a solution. 'Please take into account
that other party has same consideration.' Goldberg
replied that we had chosen words to take that into
account. He emphasized the word 'prior' stating we
were not asking for 'prior' move by Hanoi, such as
removing its 19 regiments from South Vietnam prior to
US suspension of bombing. We had deliberately indicated US would make 'prior' move if we got indication as to what would follow from North Vietnam
after prior suspension of bombing. Manescu
then concluded by making special appeal for discretion and agreeing that any inquiries about meeting
would be met with statement that discussion concerned
matters on agenda of UN of common concern to both
parties. Goldberg assured Manescu that as far as
US concerned he would share contents of discussion
only with Secretary and President..."

GOLDBERG

On the same day, Acting Secretary Katzenbach saw Italian Ambassador
Fenoaltea at the latter's request. The Ambassador repeated the Romanian
message. It should be noted that Katzenbach's explanation of the response
which the U.S. desired from Hanoi differed from the Goldberg explanation.
Katzenbach said that the U.S. would want to know "in specific terms,
publicly or privately, what response would be forthcoming."

STATE 71460 to AmEmbassy Manila, Manila TOSEC 52,
22 October 1967:

"1.   ...Romanian Ambassador had informed Italians
that, after careful analysis of Vietnam situation and
on basis of their various contacts, Romanian govt had
concluded that if US were to suspend bombing of NVN
without any time limit or conditions 'appropriate
and positive reaction would not be lacking.'....

"2.   Acting Secretary said that US position
on bombing cessation is as stated by Goldberg. Acting Secretary noted that it was difficult to know
who was speaking for Hanoi, if they were actually
able to speak for Hanoi, and furthermore what specific response to bombing cessation would be. Acting
Secretary expressed some skepticism regarding Romanian
approach and suggested that Italian Foreign Minister
might push Romanian Ambassador hard on what specific
response US bombing suspension likely to be. Acting
Secretary pointed out that USG could not turn bombing of NVN on and off lightly and that we had to
know in specific terms, publicly or privately, what
response would be forthcoming. ..."

KATZENBACH (Drafted by R.H. Miller, FE/VN)

January 23, 1967

Returning by train from the "annual hunt," Ambassador Davis was called
in for a late night conversation by the Romanian President, Council of
State, Chivu Stoica, and Foreign Minister Manescu. They told Davis that
they were now giving him the "signal" which the Americans had long awaited
from Hanoi. Davis requested permission to follow up this conversation.

BUCHAREST 892 to SecState (SECRET-NODIS),
23 January 1967:

"5.   Discussion then turned to Vietnam and we
went over familiar ground with difference this time,
which may be important that Manescu (Stoica let Manescu
conduct almost all conversation on Vietnam). In context of referring to necessity of cessation bombing
North Vietnam in order that peace talks could begin
said 'you always say you must have signal as to what
would happen. What I tell you is the signal.' I
probed as deeply as I could asking specifically whether
this was based on recent contact with North Vietnamese.
Manescu refused to be drawn out insisting that Romanians
had continuous contact with them and that Romanians
convinced information or 'signal' he had given me
was accurate. He specifically requested I convey

3

this information to Washington. At one point during
this dialogue Stoica intervened to emphasize that
I should note Romania did not seek to blame either
party for Vietnam situation; they were interested only
in peaceful settlement of problem. Romanians realized
US prestige involved but Vietnamese had problem with
'face' too. At another point both Stoica and Manescu
responded in negative to my question whether import
of what they telling me meant Romania offering to
mediate...."
DAVIS

January 25, 1967

State gave Davis authorization to follow up his conversation.
Davis' instructions stressed the need for "concrete" reciprocity
from Hanoi. Examples of reciprocity were also given: infiltration and reduction of incidents in South Vietnam. Goldberg's UN
speech of 22 September was stressed as authoritative.

> STATE 125269 to AmEmbassy Bucharest (SECRET-NODIS),
> 25 January 1967, Ref: Bucharest 892:
>
> "3. However, it must be made clear to the Romani-
> ans that the United States could in no event stop the
> bombing in return for mere agreement to talk since the
> stopping of our bombing would improve Hanoi's military
> position and expose our troops to the dangers of in-
> creased DRV infiltration and military action. The
> Secretary's conversation with Manescu on October 5,
> 1966 emphasized this lack of reciprocity in an exchange
> of no bombing for talks. Therefore, the reciprocal
> response required from Hanoi must be concrete and one
> that gave promise of setting in motion a true process
> of de-escalation. Actions relating to infiltration
> appear to be those which would have greatest promise.
> A significant reduction in the number of Viet Cong
> attacks and incidents of terror while important and
> to be considered, would be somewhat less satisfactory
> since such actions could be resumed easily whereas
> reduction or stoppage of infiltration automatically
> reduces Viet Cong capability.
>
> "4. You should also state that the US is not
> thinking in terms of a written and categorical state-
> ment by Hanoi of what it will do if we stop bombing.
> We appreciate the difficulty Hanoi might find in ad-
> mitting openly or even in an indirect message to us
> what they are doing. But, particularly after the
> failure of last January's bombing pause, we cannot

4

accept simple statements that 'something' would happen.
We must have some substantial information from a reliable source of Hanoi's position. We would want to have,
in advance, a reasonably accurate picture of what Hanoi's
meaningful, discernable, responsive action would be.

"5. You should also point out the possibility
raised in Ambassador Goldberg's UN speech of September 22 [1]
of a stopping of bombing 'prior' to the other side's taking 'timely' responsive action providing we had received
assurances, private or otherwise, that the other side
will take such action. That speech remains an authoritative statement of the US position.

"6. You should assure the Romanians of the seriousness of the US undertaking, spelled out in the Manila
Communique, to withdraw its troops from SVN within six
months after the fulfillment of the stated conditions.[2]

"7. You should try to find out whether the 'signal'
relates to Hanoi's willingness to begin negotiations if
the bombing stops, or whether it relates to responsive
reciprocal actions as described above. You should also
continue your efforts to determine the extent to which
the 'signal' comes from Hanoi as well as the precise
details of the 'signal.'

"8. If the Romanians are at all forthcoming, you
should ask them to tell Hanoi that the US is prepared
at any time to hold direct and discreet talks with Hanoi."

RUSK (Drafted by D.I. Davidson, EA)

January 28, 1967

Davis met with Manescu to emphasize Washington's feelings on reciprocity
and to inquire further about the "signal." Manescu admitted that he had
no specific knowledge for this signal.

BUCHAREST 913 to SecState (SECRET-NODIS), 28 January 1967,
Ref: State 125269:

"2. ...I wanted to mention two important points:
(A) United States could in no event stop bombing in
return for a mere agreement to talk. Secretary Rusk
emphasized in his conversation with the FonMin on
October 5 the lack of reciprocity in an exchange of
no bombing for talks; (B) the reciprocal response
requested from Hanoi must be concrete and one that

gave promise of setting in motion true process of
de-escalation. I then asked if Manescu's statement
concerning the 'signal' related only to Hanoi's
willingness to talk if bombing stops or whether it
related to some responsive reciprocal actions by
Hanoi.

"4. I then asked if Manescu could tell me whether
his statement to me on train had been based on any new
information or recent contact with Hanoi, i.e., something new, say in the period between his October talk
with the Secretary and now. Correctly speaking, he
replied, no, but it was based on all information and
developments which Romanian government had noted."

DAVIS

January 31, 1967

Davis met with Deputy Foreign Minister Macovescu and Secretary General
Ceausescu. Ceausescu said he was not clear on what guarantees U.S. wanted.
The DRV, he said, "wants /U.S. bombing cessation/ as a deliberate decision
of U.S. itself." Cessation of bombing, Ceausescu concluded, had to be
the first step. The second step, according to Ceausescu, was recognition
of the NLF, for "it not possible for DRV to speak on behalf of NLF." In
an important addition, Ceausescu said that "leaders of DRV do not wish to
have intermediaries but would like to talk directly with you."

BUCHAREST 925 to SecState (SECRET-NODIS), 31 January 1967,
Ref: Bucharest's 913:

"5. I then went beyond these points made with
Manescu on January 28 and in accordance with State
125269 said US not thinking in terms of written and
categorical statement by Hanoi but we must have some
substantial information from reliable source of Hanoi's
position and reasonable accurate picture of what
Hanoi's responsive action would be to cessation bombing.

"8. Ceausescu said US referred to wanting guarantees or assurances but he was not clear what guarantees US wanted. DRV does not require cessation
of bombing as something forced on US but wants this
as deliberate decision of US itself. This would in
no way affect prestige of US but on contrary strengthen
that prestige. Must also think of Hanoi's prestige.
If US looking for honorable solution why not give
other side opportunity for honorable way out. In

6

summary, Ceausescu concluded, his view was first step must be unconditional cessation of bombing.

"9.   Second was problem recognition of NLF. Negotiations with Hanoi not alone sufficient and it not possible for DRV to speak on behalf on NLF. Romania believed political solution must be found...

"11.   Ceausescu replied he could not foresee but under present circumstances 'I cannot obtain' assurances which US seeks.   He not do so but it was his firm belief that cessation bombing would smooth way to negotiations...At this point he made only remark which I would consider of possibly new significance. Ceausescu said 'insofar as I know, leaders of DRV do not wish to have intermediaries but would like to talk directly with you.   Intermediaries tend to get things mixed up and DRV does not like intermediaries.'

"12.   ...In accordance with paragraph 8 State Tel 125269 I said US is prepared at any time to hold direct and discreet talks with Hanoi and if Romanian government felt it possible we would appreciate their telling Hanoi this...They would tell Hanoi this..."
DAVIS

February 1, 1967

Davis summarized the current status of the Romanian track.

BUCHAREST 932 to SecState (SECRET-NODIS), 1 February 1967, Ref: Bucharest's 925:

"2.   We neither expected nor received any hint of change in Romanian position, i.e., first step toward peaceful settlement should be unconditional cessation of bombing of North.   But it is perhaps noteworthy that his references to recognition and negotiations with NLF and withdrawal of US troops were not as categorical as expressed in Warsaw Pact declaration on Vietnam of last July to which Romania had affixed its signature.[3]   Moreover, though declining in any respect to act as intermediary, he did tell us on his own initiative Hanoi preferred to talk directly to US and he assented to convey to Hanoi that US prepared to have direct and discreet talks."
DAVIS

7

October 25, 1967

On no notice and several weeks after his return from Hanoi, Prime Minister Maurer called in Davis for a Vietnam discussion. Maurer began by recalling his conversations with Secretary Rusk and President Johnson during the time of the extraordinary General Assembly session. He stressed the President's central point -- the South Vietnamese being able to decide their own destiny, i.e., "if they want to adopt communism, let them or vice versa; if they wish to unify with NV, let them or vice versa." The thrust of Maurer's position was contained in a two-point proposal: (1) "US must stop, immediately, unconditionally, and once for all bombing NVN; and (2) "NVN must declare its agreement to start negotiations...." Maurer assumed that "talks would start with armed action in SVN continuing." He added that "military actions can cease only when both sides find satisfactory political solution." Maurer explained that Hanoi's willingness to start negotiations was tied to President Johnson's acceptance of the Geneva Agreements of 1954 as a "real basis for discussions." Davis asked Maurer whether Hanoi accepted the principle of the South Vietnamese deciding their own destiny, and Maurer responed in the affirmative.

Ambassador Davis asked Maurer whether the President's San Antonio speech made any impact on his discussion in Hanoi, and Maurer replied that the speech was available but that the official text was not received by Hanoi at that time. Arguing that NVN did not really have many troops in the South, as the whole US approach to NVN infiltration asserted, Maurer said that the President's no advantage formula is "not based on reality and cannot be followed by NVN." Not fully understanding the formula, Maurer said that Hanoi could not stop supporting whatever troops it had in the South.

Maurer stressed that this was, indeed, a propitious time to get negotiations started, that the Soviet Union and Hanoi were in agreement with the information he had just passed on to Davis. Maurer concluded with a very interesting approach to the problem, saying that the two sides were indeed far apart, but once both sides were at the table, "then the other nations desirous of seeing an end to conflict would try to push two sides together."

> BUCHAREST 604 to SecState (SECRET-EXDIS), 25 October, 1967
>
> "3. .... He summarized these views, which he presented to Hanoi, as follows: world wants to see end of VN war, not only public opinion but governments. There was unity in USG on Vietnam question. Witness his separate conversations with President and Secretary Rusk, and he described to North Vietnamese USG position as outlined by them. Romanians believed that under present circumstances prospects were opening up for discussions with possibility discussions leading to

peaceful solution. Certainly solution would not come
immediately after sitting down at negotiating table.
But if talks conducted in constructive and realistic
fashion with aim to provide Vietnamese people right
to decide their own destiny: to take into account dignity and prestige of each state and to create conditions
for establishment of normal relations and stability
between VN and US, then possibility solution existed....

"4. Maurer then said that after this exposition
to Hanoi leaders, they discussed possibilities of
starting negotiations. Maurer had explained Romanian
position as follows: US must stop immediately, unconditionally, and once for all bombing NVN; NVN must
declare its agreement to start negotiations with US
on elimination of conflict. Certainly at this time
armed action in SVN would not cease. It is one thing
to mobilize and demobilize a force such as US has in
SVN. US could leave within three days and come back
again within three days. But if popular forces in
SVN demobilized, then remobilization would require
much more time. So talks would start with armed action
in SVN continuing. Aim of negotiations would be to
put an end to these armed actions. They would cease
effectively when discussion would lead to mutually
acceptable decisions and details could be discussed
further.

"5. At this point, I broke in to ask whether
Maurer was saying that initial discussions would
center on cessation of military actions to be followed
by political discussions.

"6. PrimeMin replied he did not separate these
questions then or now. Military actions can cease
only when both sides find satisfactory political
solution. As long as no guarantees existed that
SVN could decide its own destiny, there was no reason
for them to put aside weapons. So, Maurer continued,
he had requested North Vietnamese friends to declare
categorically that, in case bombardment ceased unconditionally and forever, they would be willing to
start negotiations because US position as explained
to him by President Johnson and Rusk for a solution
within framework Geneva Agreements of 1954 provided
real basis for discussions.

"7. According to Maurer, Vietnamese replied
in a sense which essentially agreed with Romanians,
i.e., if bombardment ceased, they would be prepared
to enter negotiations. To my question whether Vietnamese
would state readiness to negotiate before or after

9

bombardment ceased, Maurer replied he did not discuss details: it was possible Vietnamese could make
this statement before or after; this was up to them.

"8. Maurer commented that his discussions with
North Vietnamese had covered many aspects, but he
would emphasize only those of interest for US to
know.

"A. They had reviewed capacity of North
Vietnamese resistance in case war goes on. From
all points of view, military economic, political and
social, 'I can tell you NVN can carry on long-term
struggle.' This affirmative NVN assertion well known
throughout world.

"B. North Vietnamese leaders are aware they
cannot and could not try to humiliate US. Discussions
should be conducted in such way so that actual recognition of South Vietnamese people to decide on destiny
should have agreement and support of US. Besides,
North Vietnamese do not look upon settlement of SVN
problem as necessarily leading to immediate reunification. It would depend upon what SVN would decide.

"D. In sum, Maurer asserted that he found
in NVN 'position much more rational than we found
year ago in talks of much same content.' He asserted
this position was not determined by diminuition NVN
military capacity; it was no secret fighting capacity
of NVN growing and would continue to grow because of
more important aid from socialist countries.

"9. Maurer then said he would like to add some
other aspects as he saw them in conjunction his desire
to put at disposal of US the most complete information
possible to help USG with its judgment.

"12. At this point, I asked whether NVN had
accepted this principle of full liberty SVN people decide
own destiny. Maurer replied 'yes -- absolutely yes.'
He asserted that from their common discussions there
emerged quite clearly acceptance principle SVN should
decide own destiny and indeed there emerged possibility of diplomatic relations and special ties between US and SVN state as result of talks ending
conflict.

10

"13. This shows NVN leaders do not see aim of solution as reunification....

"15. At this point, I asked whether President's San Antonio speech on Vietnam had been available to him during course his discussion in Hanoi. Maurer replied in affirmative, saying it had come over radio during course their discussions last day. I then had interpreter read President's two sentences in regard cessation bombardment NVN as quoted in Secretary Rusk's opening statement his news conference October 12 and asked whether North Vietnamese had reacted to this to PrimeMin. Maurer replied negatively, saying President's statement came by radio on eve his departure and North Vietnamese had no definitive text.

"16. Maurer then said that he wished to make clear his view on a central problem which in his opinion is looked upon in an erroneous way in USA. He said he did not, of course, discuss with North Vietnamese leadership NVN infiltration into SVN. However, he would like convey his own impressions. NVN, of course, denied sending men into SVN. According to Maurer's impressions, this is not quite true though we might be wrong. He knows they're sending to SVN supplies, weapons, munitions, medicine, food and possibly specialists and technicians for training. His impression is that NVN troops even if they are to be found are few. So when President Johnson speaks about obligation not to take advantage of cessation of bombardment, he is referring to things which are not based on reality and cannot be followed by NVN. For example, NVN could not cease to support struggle in SVN because struggle is going on. At any rate, US doing same thing for SVN armed forces. Maurer repeated, according his view, NVN troops as such are few if any and that during cessation of bombing, NVN would continue to supply SVN struggle with food and munitions and indeed some of the aid socialist countries give to NVN. He concluded President Johnson's formulation does not seem satisfactory as it proposes a unilateral condition.

"17. I explained our point of view and the necessity of some indication from Hanoi of reciprocity if we should cease bombardment. I cited our experience when on past occasions we had ceased bombardment NVN. Maurer showed himself well aware of our position, but said he thought more than that could be done. US a great and powerful nation and could do more with

their possibilities without risking failure. 'Possible
military disadvantage would be compensated by political
advantage.' In Maurer's opinion, there had never
before existed so many favorable conditions for reaching political settlement.

"18. ...Soviets had expressed agreement with
Romanian position saying they looked at things in
same way, but emphasized decision must remain with
Hanoi. Maurer added that moreover he had stressed to
Soviet leaders that increase in economic and military
aid by socialist countries to NVN is apt to assure
greater liberty to Hanoi. According to Romanian
judgment, this would make Hanoi less dependent on
Chinese.

"19. Maurer summed up by saying his thoughts
were very clear: negotiations would start; US would
put forward list of proposals unacceptable to NVN
and Hanoi would do likewise. Then the other nations
desirous of seeing an end to conflict would try to
push two sides together. 'This is our hope and our
desire.' Friends of both sides would compel each
to give a little here and there and both sides would
be compelled to listen to them. Thus, in end a solution could be found."

DAVIS

November 1, 1967

State responded with interest and a good many precise and exploratory
questions to the Maurer interview. State also indicated that Governor
Harriman, on his way back from Pakistan, could pursue the matter should
Bucharest desire. The questions State was interested in focused on:
(1) whether the bombing stop had to be permanent as well as unconditional;
(2) the distinction among contacts, talks and negotiations; and (3) the
authorization for the Maurer statements.

State also instructed Ambassador Davis to pursue the President's
San Antonio speech and clarify its meaning. Davis was told to say that
the speech was "not assuming North Vietnam would cut off its support to
its forces in the South while the armed struggle was continuing. At the
same time USG would feel if NVN sought to take advantage of the bombing
cessation or limitation to increase its support of its forces in the South,
to attack our forces from north of DMZ or to maintain large-scale visible
resupply efforts now impossible..."

STATE 63057 to AmEmbassy Bucharest (SECRET-NODIS),
1 November 1967, Ref: Bucharest 604:

"4. ...For example, as reported reftel, Maurer
explained Romanian position as requesting North Vietnam

12

to declare categorically that in case bombardment ceased
unconditionally and forever North Vietnam would be
willing to start negotiations for a solution within
the framework of the 1954 Geneva Accords. According
to Maurer the NVN replied in a sense which essentially
agreed with Romania, i.e., if bombardment ceased they
would be prepared to enter negotiations. The precise
wording of the reply is obviously of great significance
to the USG. Did Hanoi ask for cessation of bombardment? Did Hanoi use the words permanently or unconditionally? Did Hanoi differentiate (as it has in the
past) among contacts, talks and negotiations and which
word did they use to describe the discussions that would
take place after the stopping of the bombing? Was it
clear that the stopping of bombing would be followed
by talks within a short time? What indications were
there of the matters that would be taken up at the
talks? What was Hanoi's reaction to Maurer's request
that it 'categorically' declare its readiness to begin talks after the stopping of the bombing? FYI
Usual DRV formulation is that talk 'could' follow
bombing halt. End FYI.

"5. Other specific points on which we hope Maurer
will be willing to furnish further information include:

"a) Whether the expectation that fighting
will continue in South Vietnam concurrently with negotiations is Romanian or North Vietnamese and, if NVN,
the reasoning behind their expectation.

"b) Whether NVN agreed with Romania that
basic provisions of '54 Geneva Accords provided real
basis for discussions. If so, can Maurer provide
any specific indication of how North Vietnamese view
basic provisions?

"c) What did Hanoi indicate as its conception
of conditions under which South Vietnamese people could
decide their own destiny?

"d) What 'special ties' between South Vietnam and the US did North Vietnam see as possibly emerging as result of talks ending conflict?

What 'elasticity' in position of USG does Maurer suggest
would strengthen independent elements in North Vietnam?

"f) What further information can Maurer
provide as to North Vietnam's views on reunification
of Vietnam?

"g) To what extent did North Vietnam leaders
authorize Maurer to give report to USG?

"6. You should enquire whether, since Maurer's
conversations in Hanoi, Romanians have received any
indication of Hanoi's reaction to the President's
September 29 San Antonio formulation. In connection
with this enquiry you should state that the President
has instructed you to inform Maurer of two important
points:

"a) There can be no doubt as to the magnitude
of NVN infiltration into South Vietnam. Through the
capture of hundreds of prisoners, thousands of documents, the interrogation of numerous defectors from
the NVN army and other means of intelligence collection the USG can state categorically that there are
now in South Vietnam at least 50,000 regular soldiers
of the North Vietnamese Army formed into at least 80
battalions. Furthermore, the USG estimates on the
basis of reliable evidence that NVN infiltration has
averaged approximately 5,000 men per month over the
last two years. Finally you should note that continued
artillery and other attacks upon US positions in South
Vietnam just below the DMZ are being made solely by
regular units of the NVN army which are not included
in the figures given above.

"b) The President, in making his assumption that the North Vietnamese would not take advantage of the bombing cessation or limitation while
discussions proceed, was not assuming North Vietnam
would cut off entirely its support to its forces in
the South while the armed struggle was continuing.
At the same time USG would feel if NVN sought to take
advantage of the bombing cessation or limitation to
increase its support of its forces in the South, to
attack our forces from north of DMZ or to mount large-
scale visible resupply efforts now impossible it would
not be acting in good faith."

RUSK (Drafted by S/AH: Davidson/Isham

November 2 - 14, 1967

On 2 November in Bucharest 648, Davis said that since Maurer was
in Moscow, he had sought an appointment with Macovescu and conveyed contents

of paragraph 3, State 63057. Macovescu said that he would handle the matter with dispatch. On 4 November in State 64852, State indicated that Governor Harriman could be in Bucharest anytime from November 27 to November 30. On 3 November, in Bucharest 651, Davis requests permission to give Macovescu questions and information contained in State reftel in order to facilitate Maurer's discussions in Moscow. State concurred (State 65068) with this course of action on 4 November. On 6 November, as stated in Bucharest 668, Davis handed the paper to Macovescu. Cabling on 6 November in Bucharest 669, Davis reported that the Romanian government agreed to the Harriman visit at the end of November. On 14 November in Bucharest 712, Davis reported that Maurer had granted him an appointment for the following day.

November 15, 1967

Maurer accompanied by Macovescu had a long and very careful session with Ambassador Davis in which Maurer responded in detail to the questions contained in State 63057. While the cable is more revealing of Romanian thinking on Vietnam than on Hanoi's positions, Maurer's presentation seemed to clarify a number of points. It should be noted, however, that many of these "clarifications" were out of-whack with other signals and readings the USG was taking at the same time. Maurer's key responses were: (1) that the bombing cessation had to be permanent and unconditional before talks can start; (2) that the Romanian objective was to get negotiations started "without interrupting armed actions in SVN"; (3) that a real basis for reaching a solution existed "because essential points of NVN position are based on 1954 Geneva Accords just as essential points President Johnson's position based on Geneva"; (4) that Hanoi made "no differentiation...between contacts, talks and negotiations," and that "only reference was to discussions which would lead to solution of conflict..."; (5) that Hanoi believes there should be a "certain lapse of time" between cessation of bombardment and start of negotiations; (6) that Hanoi "understood necessity of assertion of clear stand in regard to negotiations."

Maurer made clear that Hanoi in no way authorized this report.

BUCHAREST 718 to SecState (SECRET-NODIS), 15 November 1967, Refs: State 63057 and Bucharest 668:

"1. PrimeMin Maurer received me for two hours this morning Nov 15 accompanied by Acting FonMin Macovescu and same interpreter as at first meeting. Today Maurer had before him paper which contained Romanian translation of questions embodied in paper which I had handed Macovescu on Sunday Nov 5 (Romanian translation was in script which indicates strict security control these conversations by Romanians about which PrimeMin Maurer again made special point several times during ensuing discussion).

"2. Beginning with para 4 State 63057, Maurer
proceeded to read and answer questions seriatim.

"3. To question did Hanoi ask for cessation of
bombardment, Maurer answered 'yes and no.' In explanation, he went on to say that both in his talks with
Hanoi and on other occasions, Hanoi has said that permanent and unconditional cessation of bombardment is
necessary before talks can start. This is also the
Romanian viewpoint. He left Vietnam convinced that
this was Hanoi's view. Hanoi more or less presented
this view in the statement by their FonMin in January
1966 although it was 'more hazily' expressed in this
statement and more linked with other things. Maurer
continued that objective his discussions was that
cessation of bombardment must lead to negotiations without interrupting armed actions in SVN. Obvious there
existed possibility of reaching solution because essential points of NVN position are based on 1954 Geneva
Accords just as essential points President Johnson's
position based on Geneva. Thus there is a basis for
discussions. Certainly there may be certain nuances
how one side or the other understand provisions of
Geneva Accords, but this is why talks should be held
to bring to common denominator all aspects.

"4. Maurer said this justified his first assertion that reply was 'yes.' 'But why,' Maurer asked,
'did I also say no.' Because during these discussions
there was not one single moment when the people to whom
we talked referred to this as their desire -- only a
necessity resulting from respect for international
norms, for sovereignty of NVN and it was presented
as practical possibility to bring matters to discussion.' Maurer concluded this is why his reply was
made in such 'circumstantial manner because I want
my reply to be clear and definite.'

"5. Did Hanoi use words 'permanently' or 'unconditionally'? Maurer replied, 'yes,' saying French
word 'definitivement' had been used for 'permanent.'

"6. Did Hanoi differentiate among contacts,
talks and negotiations and which word did they use
to describe discussions after stopping of bombing?
Maurer replied this was not touched upon in Hanoi.
He only touched upon subject of discussions which would
lead, if possible, to cessation of war and settlement
of conflict in Vietnam. No differentiation was made
between these words. Only reference was to discussions which would lead to solution of conflict and

16

'I did not notice any nuances' in position NVN. Goal
is political settlement based on essential point of
Vietnamese and 'as I understand it President Johnson's
viewpoint' that right of South Vietnamese people to
determine freely and of their own accord their destiny
must be recognized.

"7. Was it clear stopping of bombing would be
followed ty talks in short time? Maurer replied that
there was a rather longer discussion on this point
because NVN viewpoint was that 'certain lapse of time'
should pass between cessation of bombardment and start
of discussions. Maurer said, 'we tried to show them
that it was not quite necessary for this lapse of
time. I should like to say in this regard that my
impression is that at end our talks NVN adhered to
their original viewpoint, i.e., a certain lapse of
time should ensue. We talked quite a lot about this.
Perhaps they have certain reasons better understood
by them than by us.'

"8. Here Maurer said he would like to interject
his own opinion. Should NVN adhere to this position,
nevertheless cessation of bombing would constitute
a start of friendly actions upon NVN in order to make
this interval as short as possible. 'I think there
would be many states, not only Romania and not only
socialist countries, who would be ready to exert pressure by friendly advice on NVN to follow cessation of
bombing by something to shorten interval between this
and start of discussion.' Maurer concluded that though
this was personal reflection he wished to emphasize
that there were many socialist and other countries
who could have a certain influence on NVN.

"9. What indications were there of matters that
would be taken up at talks? Maurer answered cryptically,
'none. I avoided discussing such subjects and I continue to do so. I am not mandatory of either NVN or
USA. In doing what I did, I did not defend either
USA (which doesn't need it) or NVN (though I wish to
defend it). What made us go to Hanoi? Our friendly
relations with Hanoi are quite obvious and our friend-
ship grows greater so long as those events go on and
on. So we decided to go to Hanoi to discuss these
events as I described to you last time. We agreed
we should meet from time to time to consult each other.
Moreover, I had advantage of talks with President
Johnson and Secretary Rusk. I thought I noted something very positive in these discussions which led
me to folowing absurd conclusion.'

17

"12. . To question what was Hanoi's reaction to
Prime Minister's request that it 'categorically' declare
its readiness begin talks after stopping of bombing,
Maurer replied their discussions on this topic were
rather .long and they ended with North Vietnamese statement that it seemed to them 'Romanian point of view
as presented logical one and they would think about
it and how it could be practically implemented.'
Maurer said they had not been so punctilious about
certain words, but his idea as presented to Hanoi
was that it should state clearly that if bombing ceases
then talks would start. 'Since it and NVN said QUOTE
your stand logical one, UNQUOTE I can only understand
that such a statement must be made from NVN own words.
I did not think of formulation for such a declaration
because of nature of our discussions. Moreover, there
was no evidence that NVN had thought of formulation.
We discussed certain ideas and result is that NVN
understood necessity of assertion of clear stand in
regard to negotiations.'

"13. Re questions A through G in paragraph 5
State 63057, Maurer answered as follows:

"A. Both Romanian and NVN point of view
is that fighting will continue in SVN concurrently
with negotiations. Maurer asserted he did not discuss
reasoning for common acceptance this expectation but
remarked NVN standpoint might have some different
nuances as compared with his own. His own viewpoint
is that while easy for US to mobilize or disband great
military force in Vietnam on side NVN is completely
different. They need more than 48 hours to mobilize
or disband their forces. This was no secret. This was
not first time 'strategy' of popular war is being discussed. Maurer asserted it was quite logical that
military actions would be ended only when discussions
created for both sides certainly of mutually acceptable conditions. 'This is reason why I believe military
actions and political discussions will continue in
parallel.'

"B. Maurer stated that NVN has always
asserted that 1954 Geneva Accords provide real basis
for negotiations. This is something which constantly
appears in statements issued by leaders of NVN and
NLF. 'Deliberately we did not discuss any subject
which might be the subject of negotiations between
the two sides. This is for the Vietnamese and Americans.'

18

"C. To question what did Hanoi indicate
as its conception of conditions which SVN people could
decide their own destiny, Maurer said he did not ask
as he did not ask President Johnson about US concep-
tions. (Comment: Here for first and last time he
mentioned the name of NVN Prime Minister Phan Van Dong
as a participant in talks.)

"D. As to 'special ties' between SVN and
US emerging as result of talks, Maurer said if SVN
decided to remain separate state this would mean it
could establish not only diplomatic but economic,
cultural, etc., ties with many states of its own choosing, including USA.

He continued there
was complete unity of NVN leadership concerning securing for SVN people right to decide their own destiny
but he thought it logical there would be nuances in
their way of thinking

strengthen independent elements NVN, Maurer replied
cessation of bombing is cried out everywhere. It
would constitute an act of great political wisdom.
Maurer said he was not taking liberty of trying give
lesson to leaders USA but he thought it was good to
say what he had told US frankly and openly. He believed leaders USG have wisdom and insight to see what
in his thinking might contribute to peace and interests of US itself.

"F. To question re further information as
to NVN views on reunification Vietnam, Maurer simply
replied he had nothing to add to what he had already
said on this subject.

"G. To what extent did NVN leaders authorize
Maurer to give report to USG? Maurer replied, 'absolutely
none. It was my own exclusive responsibility.' Maurer
then explained at some length why he had done this.
Essentially because he believed there exist conditions
which can lead to political solution. Existence of
conflict, troubles, many important things in which
Romania is interested. Especially after New York
and Washington discussions, Maurer was confident USG
was $\lfloor$ garble$\rfloor$ solution. He went to Hanoi to explain
that a common basis existed for discussions to end
hostilities. He was far from thinking in Hanoi that
he would inform USG of his discussion there, but in
the end and upon further reflection he thought it
important to move this unhappy situation toward more
reasonable solution. He was not pushed by NVN but
acted solely on own initiative. It might be that
NVN would reproach him greatly for this but objectively
he believes a reasonable solution is near.

"14. Maurer stated that subsequent to his visit
in Hanoi Romanian government has not repeat not received any indication of Hanoi's reaction to President's September 29 San Antonio formulation. In
answer to my question, he stated flatly that Romanians had not participated in discussions on Vietnam
during their recent visit to Moscow."

DAVIS

November 17, 1967

In Bucharest 729, Ambassador Davis cabled his impressions from the
Maurer conversation. He believed that Maurer was frank and forthcoming,
but that the only new element which Maurer introduced was "his intimation

that there are divided councils in Hanoi and that Chinese hard stand
influence is diminishing." Davis accepted Maurer's statement of basic
Romanian policy -- "existence of conflict troubles many important things
in which Romania is interested."

November 29, 1967

In Bucharest 802, Davis reported on a discussion with Ceausescu.
Ceausescu took a very hard line in this conversation and argued, in effect,
that the "DRV and NLF represented South Vietnamese people." He further
stated that US was repeating the mistake of great powers in the past by
ignoring the opinion of others and carrying out an imperialist policy.
As to why Hanoi refused to accept the San Antonio formula, Ceausescu maintained that the formula imposed conditions, and that a formal declaration
by the US was in order.

> BUCHAREST 802 to SecState (SECRET-NODIS), 29 November
> 1967:
>
> "5. Ceausescu referred to my morning conversation
> with PrimeMin and in particular to request that PrimeMin
> try and help bring US and Vietnam together. Ceausescu's
> opinion any such attempt now would not lead to very
> 'spectacular' results until cessation of bombing.
> While Ceausescu agreed that reunification of divided
> countries should not be achieved through force, yet
> blandly argued that NLF had put forth program for re-
> unification only as long-time and peaceful development
> with which DRV agreed. He asserted that DRV could
> not wage war in South which did not have support of
> people there and suggested US policy based on incomplete
> information and incorrect assumptions. To my repeated
> questions why Hanoi had slammed door in face President's
> generous San Antonio offer and why Hanoi refused to
> say either publicly or privately what would happen
> after permanent cessation of bombing. Ceausescu took
> line we were imposing conditions; that a bombing pause
> would be only another form of ultimatum; that absence
> of formal declaration of war raised problems in inter-
> national law (i.e., bombing) not in favor of US and
> that if US would only cease bombing permanently and
> unconditionally other countries would exercise pres-
> sure on both sides to bring them to negotiating table.
> Ceausescu also argued that cessation bombing would
> be act of political wisdom."
>
> DAVIS

November 29, 1967 -- Harriman-Maurer Conversations

Maurer carried on a monologue in which he reviewed the points he had previously made in Bucharest 604 of 25 October. Maurer again focused on only one objective -- getting negotiations started "and nothing more." In this respect, he repeated that world opinion would push the two powers toward a settlement once negotiations began.

Maurer was told a very interesting story about Hanoi's view on getting discussions started. In his first meeting with Pham Van Dong, it was his impression that Hanoi did not wish to enter discussions. During the next day's talk with Dong, Hanoi's position softened. Dong took the position that North Vietnam "should enter discussions while continuing the struggle in the South as long as there is uncertainty as to the right of the SVN people to decide their destiny." Dong, expressing what Maurer considered to be the leadership position in Hanoi, desired a "rather more circumstantial" statement on Hanoi's part. "NVN was to declare that it was ready to start discussions with the US if the US declared and ceased unconditionally and permanently for all time bombardment over NVN DMZ, if US declared that it would 'never resume.'" Even in this event, Hanoi "would allow certain time to pass to enable it to test sincerity of such declaration and action."

Harriman, in response, said that what was missing from this dialogue was "any indication that Hanoi wants serious negotiations, that Hanoi says that US should stop bombing, but does not even say that they will talk." Harriman gave the impression that all we were waiting for was a message from Hanoi that they would enter "meaningful talks." Harriman also noted Hanoi's demand for a "permanent cessation."

BUCHAREST 803 to SecState (SECRET-NODIS), 29 November, 1967:

"1. After briefly touching on Middle East and Manescu's election and performance at UN,[4] I brought up Vietnam and conveyed the President's gratitude for the complete account Maurer had given Ambassador Davis. I asked Maurer if he had given full attention to the President's San Antonio speech. I told him this was as sweeping a statement as had ever been made during war and showed the President's desire for negotiated peace. I informed him that the interpretation of the 'no advantage' formulation which we had previously given him had been conveyed to Hanoi through channels then open. I told him of our disappointment at Hanoi's having turned down the offer so coldly and asked for his judgment as to why Hanoi had done so.

"2. Maurer then launched into what was virtually
a two-hour monologue out of a three hour discussion.
He said he did not know directly why San Antonio offer
had been turned down since speech was given on last
day of his talk with Pham Van Dong and neither of them
had text available.

"3. His talks with the President and the Secretary
had convinced him that primary and overriding American
goal was to guarantee right of South Vietnamese people
to determine their own destiny and only secondarily to
fulfill commitment to GVN. Based on this belief, he
advised Pham Van Dong that without ceasing military
action in South, NVN should enter into discussions
with US. He told Dong that the struggle in the South
should conclude only when US and NVN both agree on
how SVN people can define freely their own destiny.
Then as President Johnson told him categorically American troops will go home.

"4. Maurer deliberately focused on only one thing:
'The starting of negotiations and nothing more.' Maurer
believes that once discussions begun the nations of the
world will throw their influence behind reaching a successful conclusion and would put pressure both on Hanoi
and the US that would push them towards solution acceptable to both sides. US and NVN both agree that SVN people
should decide their own destiny and discussions could
work out different understandings each side may have of
this principle.

"5. At the end of the first day of conversations
with Pham Van Dong (interrupted once or twice by having
to go down to air raid shelter), Maurer concluded from
the hazy and contradictory answers he received that
Hanoi did not wish to enter discussions. Maurer decided
not to pursue the matter further. The next day Maurer
suggested that they discuss bilateral relations but
after a short morning devoted to bilateral matters
Dong brought the talks back to negotiations. Dong then
asked Maurer to allow him to present Hanoi's standpoint on the statement Maurer had asked Hanoi to make
to the effect that if bombardment would cease, they
would enter into discussions with the US.

"6. I questioned his use of 'would,' saying that
Hanoi usually uses 'could.' Maurer replied that it
is difficult for him to recall precise word but that
it didn't matter since they were talking in French,
and Dong's French is so poor that no such nuances
could be retained.

"7. Maurer continued that this time Dong's position
was very clear and logical. Dong asserted that you
(Maurer) are right. The DRV must make such a statement. It should enter discussions while continuing the
struggle in the South as long as there is uncertainty
as to the right of the SVN people to decide their destiny.

"8. Maurer and Dong then discussed details on
how such discussions could begin. Dong thought that
Hanoi's statement must be 'rather more circumstantial,
that is to mean NVN was to declare that it was ready
to start discussions with the US if US declared and
ceased unconditionally and permanently for all time
bombardment over NVN DMZ if US declared that it would
'never resume,' Hanoi would allow certain time to
pass to enable it to test sincerity of such delcara-
tion and action. Maurer asked why these conditions,
when one condition could be enough -- that the US
declare that it ceases unconditionally and for all time
and that it would not resume the bombing. Why, Maurer
asked, should there be an interval between end of
bombing and start of negotiations?

"9. Maurer apparently did not receive an answer
to his question. He indicated his personal belief
that there exists within the North Vietnamese leadership some with points of view more reserved towards
negotiations than one with which Dong finally agreed.
He thought such reserve might be the result of the
Chinese viewpoint: Maurer told me that the US should
exercise flexible judgment meant to strengthen the
Vietnamese (as opposed to Chinese) way of thinking.

"10. Maurer emphasized that the important thing
was that on the second day Pham Van Dong was expressing the opinion of the North Vietnamese leadership.
While Maurer did not see Ho, Maurer believes that
at every intermission Ho was told of the discussion.
Maurer believes that on the night of the first day,
Ho was consulted and that there might even have been
a meeting of the North Vietnamese leadership.

"14. I told him that what is missing is any indication that Hanoi wants serious negotiations, that
Hanoi says that the US should stop bombing, but does
not even say that they will talk. They ask not only
for unconditional but permanent cessation of bombing.
I pointed out that Hanoi is now attacking US forces
just below the DMZ, and that since the President will
not permit the invasion of NVN, the only way we can
slow down their attack is to hit their positions in
NVN. I mentioned the Canadian suggestion of the re-
establishment of a demilitarized DMZ and Hanoi's rejection. I said there seems to be a strange idea that
the bombing of the North is not part of the military
action of the war, but is somehow disconnected. Hanoi
is asking the US to commit itself not to resume bombing
while leaving itself free to do anything it wants. I
said it was our impression that Hanoi has no serious
intention of entering meaningful talks, for if they had,
they would send US a message either through Maurer
or other channels. If they sent US a message privately
or talked with US privately on conditions necessary
prior to beginning of negotiations, or if they told
US what they intended to do, this would be another
matter. I pointed out that we have no intention of
destroying the regime in NVN, but just want to stop
it from taking over the South by force. I told him
that I would have thought the socialist states would
be putting pressure for negotiation on Hanoi, rather
than encouraging it by escalating aid, and that I thought
the socialist countries should recognize that we are
not threatening the regime in NVN, but that we are
under treaty obligation to defend SVN against aggression from NVN. I said it was my impression that the
Soviet Union and the Eastern European states, but
not Peking, want the fighting stopped, and that if

concern exists about major confrontation, we should
get together to agree upon ending of conflict.

"15. I said we thought that the San Antonio statement, supplemented by the explanation given Maurer,
made clear a possible way to end conflict.

"16. I said I was sure that Maurer agreed that
above all the President wanted negotiations for a
peaceful settlement, and asked him if he had any doubt
about this. He replied that he had none, that if he
had any he wouldn't have talked to NVN as he did.
I asked him if he thought NVN had a right to enter
SVN, and whether he thought West Germany had a right
to enter East Germany. I recalled that we fought
in Korea because the North entered the South. I said
divided countries were unhappy situations, but the
US has agreed, and we consider that the socialist
countries have agreed, that there will be no unification by force. I told him that perhaps he hoped
reunification of Germany would never come, but that
while we hope that it will, we do not want it to come
through force. I referred to our SEATO commitment
undertaken in 1954 during the Eisenhower Administration, and said that the socialist states should realize the seriousness with which we consider our obligation and should try to induce Hanoi to terminate its
aggression.

"17. I asked Maurer how he thought the President
could contribute to a change in Hanoi's attitude.
I said a pause might be considered, though unless
Hanoi acted differently than last time, it would be
of a short duration and create a more difficult situation. I explained how Hanoi had taken advantage of
the Tet pause. I said I hoped the Soviet Union, Romania,
and other Eastern European countries would use their
influence to get talks started under conditions which
would give some hope of a successful conclusion. I
said that asking for a permanent cessation without
any indication of what might result -- perhaps nothing --
is like asking us to tie our right hand behind our
back while fighting continues. It would be different
if they said stop bombing for two weeks or a month
while we talk, but they ask for a permanent stop.
I asked how this could be taken seriously.

"18. Maurer said he 'absolutely agreed' that
bombing is a part of general military action, and said
he would go further, by saying that from the military
point of view not only could bombing be recommended,

but that the occupation of NVN as a way of destroying
the 'backyard' of SVN could be recommended. After
NVN was temporarily occupied and the war in the North
became a guerrilla one, the same military recommendation could be made concerning China, which would become
the new backyard. But, said Maurer, it would not be
justified from the political viewpoint. War is nothing
but politics conducted by other means. It is waged
to bring one side in a political conflict a decisive
advantage. This is why political considerations should
be dominant and it is why President Johnson does not
permit his troops to cross the DMZ. From the military
point of view he said the President was wrong in not
ordering the crossing of the DMZ, but from the political point of view he is correct, and that is why he
/garble/ not justified on military grounds.

"19. Maurer admitted that the cessation of bombardment involved risks that talks may not start for some
time, that negotiations may start but be unduly prolonged, or that they may not result in a solution.
But he thought that with all countries (except possibly China) exerting their influence, there would be
a settlement.

"20. I commented that the President is using limited
means because of the limited character of our objectives.
He did not want to invade NVN because he had no intention of interfering with a solialist regime which he
knows socialist states will defend. He ordered attacks
on supply routes and military targets but against the
advice of the military he has not ordered mining of
Haiphong harbor and interference with its shipping.
We have not attacked the dikes or engaged in area
bombing of population centers as was done in World
War II. The President's military advisors say the
situation in the south would become substantially
more difficult if NVN were permitted to freely move
men and supplies South. I appealed to Maurer as a
man in a strategic position who has the ear of President Johnson, of the Soviet Union, of China and Hanoi,
to advise us as to how we can bring about negotiations.
I repeated that it was impossible for the President
to stop bombing permanently, without some indication
from Hanoi as to what would happen. I said the President had made his proposal in San Antonio, and that
he would be willing to receive any other reasonable
proposal from Maurer. Maurer replied that the President might put more hope in Romanian action that was
justified. Maurer said that he believed there was
now a consensus between the US and NVN that people

of SVN should have right to decide their own destiny.
Knowing that, said Maurer, we will see what we can
do. 'There is no doubt that we will try to do something about it.'

"21. Maurer did not think it was necessary to
involve Soviet Union yet. When that time came, he
thought US was in a better position to do so than
Romania.[5]

"22. The discussion continued after lunch. I
then asked Maurer whether he had any steps in mind
now. He replied affirmatively, but said he could
not name them yet, that the subject must be thought
over and studied. I asked him to keep Ambassador
Davis informed."

DAVIS

PACKERS (RUMANIAN-NVN TRACK): NOVEMBER 1967 - FEBRUARY 1968

It was only after the Harriman-Maurer discussions in Bucharest on November 28, 1967 that the Rumanian track began to receive high level attention and priority in Washington. Maurer had recently returned from North Vietnam in an attempt to convince the DRV, so he said, to make a statement about entering discussions with the U.S. while continuing the struggle in the south. Maurer said that he stressed to Pham Van Dong that self-determination was the essence of the U.S. position.

Harriman explained the San Antonio formula to Maurer. "The North could," Harriman indicated, "continue supplying its forces to the extent it does now but that it must not increase." Harriman expressed the hope that GOR would take appropriate steps with Hanoi to explain this. Maurer said that he would take such steps under consideration. Harriman concluded that what was lacking was any "indication" or "impression" or "message" that Hanoi wanted serious negotiations.

On December 12, 1967, First Deputy Foreign Minister Macovescu and First Secretary of the GOR Embassy Iliescu (hereafter M & I) left Bucharest. They arrived in Hanoi on December 14 and stayed until the 18th. They arrived a few hours after a U.S. strike on the Doumer Bridge, which was restruck on December 17.[1]

Their schedule of meetings was as follows: (a) dinner on Friday, the 15th, with Foreign Minister Trinh, (b) a meeting with Trinh in the morning of December 16, (c) Sunday afternoon meeting with Pham Van Dong, (d) on the morning of the 18th there was a DRV Politburo meeting, (e) another meeting with Trinh after the Politburo session in which Trinh spoke to M & I from a written text. Rumanians left Hanoi on the evening of the 18th.

The Rumanian discussions with the DRV leadership were not revealed to the U.S. until M & I visited Washington on January 5, 1968. (Substance will be treated at that point in the chronology.) In other words, the Trinh statement of the DRV position made on December 29 was already public knowledge.[2]

From December 14 through 18, while M & I were in Hanoi, Ceaucescu and Maurer visited Moscow, informed the Soviets of the Harriman talks and the M & I mission. They reported that the Soviets wish success to the GOR mission in Hanoi.

On December 19, M & I visited Peking and saw Deputy Foreign Minister Gua. Gua said "it is the Vietnamese people who will have to decide."

On December 24, M & I returned to Bucharest.

On December 26, Ambassador Bogdan advised that Ceaucescu and Maurer had a message and wanted to send an emissary to the U.S. Harriman advised Bogdan that he would be glad to receive the envoy.

On December 29, Trinh spoke at a Mongolian reception. The substance of his talk was broadcast by Hanoi VNA in English on January 1. He stated, in part:

"The stand of the Vietnamese people is quite clear. That is the four-point stand of the DRV Government and the political program of the NFLSV. That is the basis for the settlement of the Vietnam question.

"The U.S. Government has unceasingly claimed that it wants to talk with Hanoi but has received no response. If the U.S. Government truly wants to talk, it must, as was made clear in our statement on 28 January 1967, first of all stop unconditionally the bombing and all other acts of war against the DRV. After the United States has ended unconditionally the bombing and all other acts of war against the DRV, the DRV will hold talks with the United States on questions concerned."

On December 29, Ambassador Bogdan informed Harriman that M would be the special envoy.

On January 3, 1968, the U.S. prohibited bombing within five miles of the center of Hanoi (JCS 6402 DTG 032158Z) until further notice (JCS 6700 DTG 062148Z).[3]

On January 5, Ambassador Harriman met with Macovescu, Bogdan, Iliescu, and Celack (Third Secretary of the Embassy).

M & I said that they had presented USG views as expressed by Harriman. These views were that the U.S. is ready to cease bombing (1) if, within a reasonable period of time, the DRV would come to serious and productive discussions/negotiations, and (2) if the DRV would not take advantage of the bombing halt to increase its infiltration. The GOR representatives said that they stressed to the DRV that they should make a "gesture" or "sign" publicly or privately that Hanoi wanted negotiations. M & I said that they repeatedly stressed that the U.S. goal for South Vietnam was self-determination.

Throughout their stay, the North Vietnamese stressed to M & I that the military situation was good for them. Hanoi leadership also repeated that they did not trust U.S. peace feelers, that the Harriman exposition was nothing new, that it was essentially as conditional as the San Antonio speech.

M & I said that they were quite pessimistic about the success of their mission until after the Politburo meeting on the morning of December 18th. It was only after that meeting that Trinh came to them with what they believed would be a responsive message. Trinh spoke from a prepared Vietnamese text and M & I, when speaking to Harriman, translated the document into French. M explained that Trinh began in even harsher terms than Pham Van Dong had the previous day. M said that he was "not going to give a presentation of all /Trinh's/ exposition, but ; I promised Trinh, I shall at least give you spirit of his document."

"It is clear that it is equally as difficult for the U.S. to put an end to the war as to broaden it. The U.S. is bound to strive to prevent the situation from getting worse and to avoid serious defeats until after the November election.

"The U.S.'s aggressive designs against Viet-Nam remain unchanged.

"The U.S. declares that it will continue its aggressive war in Vietnam. In the San Antonio speech and in other statements by the President and Rusk it is emphasized that the U.S. will stay in Vietnam in the interest of its own security and that it will abide by its commitment and that it will continue the fight. The U.S. perseveres in its double faced policy of stepping up the war while the U.S. administration feels compelled to take peaceful action to deceive and to appease public opinion.

"It is now clear that conditions are not yet ripe for peaceful settlement because the U.S. is unwilling to do so. The U.S. cannot intimidate by force the Vietnamese people nor deceive them by false maneuvers of peace. As long as the U.S. continues this aggression the Vietnamese people will fight to final victory. The position of the DRV is clear:

'The basis for settlement of the Vietnamese issue is provided by the four points of April 8, 1965; the Ministry of Foreign Affairs subsequently issued its January 28, 1967 statement. This is our position of principles on which no concession is possible.'

"Macovescu read the material in quotes twice from the paper in front of him.

"Harriman: No concession on the four points or on the January statement?

"Macovescu: No concession possible. I would ask you to note this for comment for he also gave me oral comments.

3

"He said the Harriman proposal contains nothing new. Essentially
the U.S. continues to claim reciprocity and will not stop until
specific conditions are fulfilled. The Vietnamese people will not
hold discussions under pressures or the menace of bombs. So far I
thought this was repetition of their position. But from here on
there is something which interested me and precisely because it was
near the end I paid greater attention to it.

"Foreign Minister Trinh continued reading:

'We are not against discussions but any discussions
should take place according to principle. As soon as discussion engaged in, our attitude will be serious and
responsible but it depends on attitude of the U...... whether
such discussions are fruitful.'

"Material in quotation marks was read slowly and carefully by
Macovescu.

"Here is the answer to the question that you asked Mr. Harriman.
From this point on there is a passage which in the text is in quotation marks.

'We affirm the following. If the USG really wants
discussions with the Government of the DRV it should first
unconditionally cease bombing and any other act of war
against the DRV. After the unconditional cessation of all
bombing and of any other U.S. act of war against the DRV and
at the end of an appropriate period of time the government
of the DRV will enter into serious discussions with the USG.'

"While he was reading this paragraph I stopped him and told him
comrade Minister when I mentioned cessation I said final and unconditional. Trinh looked at me and reread the sentence. I said I
mentioned 'final and unconditional cessation.' He reread the
sentence again. I interrupted for the third time. May I understand you are no longer speaking of final cessation. His answer
was that publicly we may continue to mention it but with a view
to negotiations. What I have said is our position.

"I asked him whether the Government of Romania is authorized
to pass this communication to the USG. He said yes. He repeated
it but he said to retain spirit of the message."

Harriman said that the Trinh public statement was much the same as
the M & I message, but that the M & I statement placed more emphasis on
the acceptance of the four points as a basis of negotiations. M said that
he did not establish any connection between his visit to Washington,
unknown to Hanoi, and the Trinh public statement. Harriman argued that

"there must be some connection." M responded that he did not believe
there was a contradiction between the two messages:

> "In the public statement it says the basis for negotiations
> is the four points, but in private conversation they say we will
> come with this basis but the U.S. side, we expect, will come
> with its own point of view. They especially said this."

Harriman then questioned whether it was the DRV view that discussions
will be fruitful only if we accept their four points. M responded:.

> "That is not the impression I gained from my discussions.
> They will come with their claims but would have to negotiate on
> what the U.S. puts forth. They said this specifically."

With respect to the timing of discussions, M said that Trinh stated
there could be no contacts "as long as U.S. acts of war continue,...
but as soon as bombing and other acts of aggression against North Vietnamese cease, we are prepared to receive anybody...." Trinh added: "We
shall consider these contacts as normal diplomatic activities. The
American representative will be received by our diplomats at their suggestion."

Harriman questioned further on the timing, specifically as to the
meaning of "after a suitable length of time." Here, M retreated to the
DRV text--"the appropriate and necessary period of time." M explained
this .as a period in which

> "they will try to test (I don't know by what means) the
> sincerity of your intentions--your wish to have discussions.
> I could not deduce the period, but I do not think it will be
> too long. If an understanding is reached that you stop, at a
> certain established period, discussions, not negotiations,
> will take place."

Harriman asked if the NLF had been mentioned. M responded: "Once,
by Dong...in connection with the program of the NLF and on their points
which they would like to discuss at negotiations." M reported that there
was no mention of involving the NLF in discussions but that this may have
been a slip.

Harriman specifically queried on the DRV reaction to the San Antonio
speech. M said that they would not give any assurances on 'no advantage'
because "they believe it is a condition and consequently cannot be discussed." M and Harriman then argued about whether 'no advantage' was
conditional. Harriman said: "The important thing is that they are on
notice, that taking advantage could have serious consequences." Harriman
repeated that there was a danger of talks breaking down "for physical
reasons--because of difficulty in negotiations." Harriman said that "this
is not a condition but a notice to Hanoi."

5

Harriman asked if the North·Vietnamese thoroughly understood the implications of San Antonio. M said that he could not draw conclusions, but

> "They have a political attitude towards it--no preconditions--but if you met them and discussed it at your first contact you may well find a solution which will not break down the military situation. We must not forget that through the other door the U.S. is pouring in men and supplies. Furthermore, you only stop in the North and fighting and bombing in the South will go on."

In response to a question by Daniel Davidson, Special Assistant to Harriman, M said that the period after the bombing and before talks is the same as the period after the bombing and before contacts.

M, again responding to Davidson, said that it was only his impression that military matters could be discussed at the first contacts, that Hanoi had said nothing to him on this matter.

M concluded that: "We Rumanians believe they have done it--given you the sign you wanted."

On January 6, there was another meeting by the Rumanians and Governor Harriman, with Secretary Rusk participating as well. This discussion was very general and added only a few points to the substance of the preceding day.·

Secretary Rusk said that "some of /Hanoi's leadership/ think of talks as a means of stopping the bombing while the rest of the war goes on without limitation. This is not acceptable." He added that: "The problem on our side is that the principle of reciprocity is rather important to us."

In a response to a Rusk question, M said that Hanoi would favor "private discussions." M said that he had not discussed the secrecy issue in Hanoi. M added, however, that: ·

> "There is no doubt that at the present stage, the Vietnamese side wants /contacts/ kept confidential. But after the cessation of bombing a way in which future procedures are directed towards starting 'conversations proper' will depend on your discussions through a third party."

M then read from a document:

> "As long as the US acts of war go on we cannot have any contacts with them. As soon as they cease the bombings and discontinue the acts of aggression we shall be prepared to receive any person, even a representative of the United States, who may wish to make known to us the American point of view or to get informed on our viewpoint. We shall regard these future contacts as normal diplomatic activity. The American representatives will be received by our representatives at the former's suggestion."

"Secretary Rusk and Governor Harriman met with Messrs Macovesu, Iliescu and Bodgan from 12:45 p.m. - 1:15 p.m., and the Secretary gave Macovesu two papers containing the 7 written parts and 4 oral points set forth below. At 5:15-7:15 p.m. Governor Harriman and Mr. Bundy met with the Romanians to explain further our drafts and to give them our French translation of our written points. Harriman told Macovesu we left it up to the latter's judgment as to what part and how to convey our points in Hanoi.

"U.S. Written Points

"1. The Democratic Republic of Vietnam has communicated to the United States Government this statement of the Democratic Republic of Vietnam position:

'If the United States Government really wants discussions with the Government of the Democratic Republic of Vietnam it should first unconditionally cease bombing and any other acts of war against the Democratic Republic of Vietnam. After the unconditional cessation of all bombing and of any other United States act of war against the Democratic Republic of Vietnam and at the end of an appropriate period of time the Government of the Democratic Republic of Vietnam will enter into serious discussions with the United States Government.'

The United States Government welcomes this statement.

"2. We understand that Foreign Minister Trinh has stated that 'as soon as' all bombing ceases, the Democratic Republic of Vietnam 'shall be prepared to receive' a United States representative. The United States Government will be prepared to have its representative have contacts with a representative of the Democratic Republic of Vietnam as soon as all bombing ceases. (The United States Government believes that the first contacts should take place almost immediately, perhaps one or two days, after the cessation of bombing.) The purpose of these contacts, which might be in Vientiane, Rangoon, Bucharest, or some other suitable third-country location, would be to fix the time and place of the serious discussions referred to by the Democratic Republic of Vietnam. Arrangement of the necessary modalities for the serious discussions should take no more than a few days.

"3. The United States Government takes note of the fact that a cessation of aerial and naval bombardment is easily verifiable. In fact, the act of cessation would be observed immediately internationally and become a matter of public knowledge and speculation. In these circumstances, the United States Government believes that

7

the 'serious discussions' referred to by the Democratic Republic of Vietnam should commence immediately on the conclusion of the arrangements through the contacts.

"4. Obviously it will be important at an appropriate time, in connection with the serious discussions, to accommodate the interests of all parties directly concerned with the peace of Southeast Asia. One such means is that the Democratic Republic of Vietnam and the United States Government might suggest to the two co-chairmen, and possibly to the three International Control Commission members, that they be available at the site chosen for the serious discussions in order to talk to all parties interested in the peace of Southeast Asia. This procedure could avoid the problems of a formal conference.

"5. The United States Government understands through representatives of the Romanian Government that the serious discussions contemplated by the Democratic Republic of Vietnam would be without limitation as to the matters to be raised by either side. The attitude of the United States Government toward peace in Southeast Asia continues to be reflected in the 14 points and in the Manila Communique.

"6. The United States Government draws attention to the statement of President Johnson in San Antonio on September 29 in which he said:

'The United States is willing to stop all aerial and naval bombardment of North Viet-Nam when this will lead promptly to productive discussions. We, of course, assume that while discussions proceed, North Viet-Nam would not take advantage of the bombing cessation or limitation.'

The aide memoire handed to the Romanian Government in November, 1967, which we understand was communicated to the Democratic Republic of Vietnam in mid-December, explained this statement in the following language:

'The President, in making his assumption that the North Vietnamese would not take advantage of the bombing cessation or limitation while discussions proceed, was not assuming North Viet-Nam would cut off entirely its support of its forces in the South while the armed struggle was continuing; at the same time the United States Government would feel if North Vietnam sought to take advantage of the bombing cessation or limitation to increase its support of its forces in the South, to attack our forces from north of the Demilitarized Zone or to mount large-scale visible resupply efforts, now impossible, it would not be acting in good faith.'

8

The United States Government wishes to confirm to the Democratic Republic of Vietnam that this statement remains the position of the United States Government.

"7. The United States Government would inform the Democratic Republic of Vietnam in advance of the exact date of the cessation of aerial and naval bombardment in order to enable the Democratic Republic of Vietnam to have its representative prepared to meet the representative of the United States Government.

"U.S. ORAL POINTS

"(a) The Romanian representative should be thanked for his efforts and told that we are confident that he has fully and faithfully reported the positions of both sides in these matters. We are grateful for this action and have confidence that he will continue to do so.

"(b) He should understand that the first sentence of paragraph 4 in the written message is intended to refer to the importance of the South Vietnamese Government and other interested parties being present at the site of the discussions in order to play an appropriate role.

"(c) The United States Government wishes to avoid any misunderstanding also with respect to any allegations which may be made concerning specific military actions by the United States Government against the Democratic Republic of Viet-Nam prior to cessation. In deference to the serious intent and sincere objectives of the mission of the Romanian Government, the United States Government will refrain for a limited period of time from bombing within five miles of the center of Hanoi or of Haiphong. This information is for the Romanian Government only. The United States Government states this as a fact and not as a commitment as to the future, but the United States Government would not wish the Democratic Republic of Viet-Nam to be informed of this fact for fear that, as in the past, it could be misinterpreted by them.

"(d) The United States Government awaits with interest the report of the Romanians, after consulting Hanoi, on the foregoing written and oral points.

"During the course of the January 11, 12:15 and 5:15 discussions, clarification of the USG position was given as indicated under the several headings below:

"(1) US Cessation

    "(a) Harriman stated that we 'pointed out' or 'took note'

9

that cessation would be public knowledge, but said
we hadn't thought about a public announcement and
opined that we would simply stop.

"(b) Bundy stated personally that we would probably
confirm an answer to questions that cessation was
a high-level decision without amplification and
Harriman agreed, adding that we would not mention
a time limit or condition it.

"(2) First Contacts

"(a) Timing - Harriman said 'should take place' is merely
our interpretation of 'as soon as' and not an ultimatum ('Des que' was actual French preposition used
by DRV). WAH underscored verb 'believes' as opposed
to 'insists' in same sentence 'one or two days after
cessation'.

'The maximum GOR can get us is that they will meet
us in 2 or 5 days 'after cessation' - the more you
can get of this the better but we are not asking for
those precise answers.'

"(b) Duration - Harriman noted US opinion that modalities
to be agreed on in contacts should not drag on more
than a few days, but invited DRV's different opinion
on duration.

"(3) 'Serious Discussions'

"(a) Rusk noted it will be difficult to conduct them
secretly, and if they are public many governments
and parties will feel entitled to participate.
'We could lose months'. Accordingly we suggest
'one such means' in the Para 4 that the Co-Chairman
and 3 ICC members send representatives to the location and 'any one else' could be there to discuss
with the 2 or the 5 or with each other. Peking
could be present. This procedure could avoid the
problem of a formal conference. We don't anticipate
a big meeting with 8, 12 or 15 present but the 2 or 5
could put their heads together on the possibility of
agreement.

"(b) Harriman assumed that 'all parties directly concerned
with peace in SEA' would include any socialist state
aiding DRV and SVN and the TCC's on our side. He
noted, since the DRV third point covered internal SVN
affairs, that the 'US won't talk about anything
specifically in SVN without a GVN rep being present.'

10

GVN should have an opportunity to come into
talks 'at an early point'. 'We don't want to
exclude anyone who has a legitimate right to be
present at an appropriate time.' Our para
four proposal is 'complicated' and 'quite
open to their suggestions.'

"(c) NLF - Harriman noted validity of our 13th point
that the VC 'would have no difficulty being represented and having their views presented.'

"(d) Open Agenda - Bundy said 'we would take very seriously' DRV confirmation of the wide open agenda of
'serious discussions.' Bundy and Harriman confirmed
our view that both sides could discuss their bases
for peace; ours would be reflected in the 14 pts
and Paras 25-29 of the Manila communique. We feel
both sides should be prepared to negotiate.

"(4) Bilateral US/DRV Discussions

"(a) Rusk noted that at the location of the Co-Chairman
and/or ICC members meeting 'any one else could...
discuss...with each other.'

"(b) Rusk said if talks became public, as he thought
they would 'both sides will have a serious time'
holding discussions (beyond contacts) without
other parties 'associated'. But 'this does not
mean there cannot still be bilaterals, but we
cannot have a situation where everyone else is
excluded.' If Hanoi makes that suggestion 'we will
look at it but it will be difficult.'

"(c) Harriman: 'There are many things that we can
talk to NVN about that relate to us and NVN.'

"(5) 'No advantage'

"(a) Macovescu said the spirit of our November 'promemoria'
had been given to Hanoi and he would repeat it there.'

"(b) Harriman said the President used the 'no advantage'
assumption to inform Hanoi what he would be assuming
if he stopped bombing. The US does not ask advance
DRV agreement.

11

"(c)   Harriman said we could negotiate under better
        conditions if the level of hostilities were
        reduced. The DMZ would be the easiest place to
        deescalate. The GOR may have other suggestions.

"(d)   Amb. Bogdan said the Romanians understood 'no
        advantage' is 'not a condition but a warning,'
        and Harriman said the US was not requiring Hanoi
        to agree to any conditions in advance.

"(6) Miscellaneous

"(a)   The GOR intends first to inform Hanoi, and then
        if they approve, to convey the gist of the dis-
        cussions with us to Moscow and Peking. We would
        be happy to have the Soviets informed.

"(b)   Macovesu said he left Washington, as he had left
        Hanoi, with the feeling that 'this is a new step
        towards a peaceful settlement.'"

On January 12, Ambassador Bunker was given a summary of PACKERS (State 98130).

On January 15, President Johnson sent a letter of appreciation for the Rumanian efforts to President Ceaucescu (State 98490).

On January 18, Macovescu, Iliesco and Celack left Bucharest for Hanoi via Moscow and Peking. Ambassador Bogdan informed Harriman of this trip on the 18th.

Also on January 18, Ambassador Harriman informed Bogdan that the President's January 17 State of the Union remarks "confirmed the San Antonio formula." Harriman said: "The U.S. has not changed its position."

On January 20, Bunker gave Thieu a general summation of U.S. probes of the December 29 Trinh statement--without revealing the PACKERS channel (Saigon 16501). Bunker did so in accord with his request (Saigon 16081) and cable of instruction (State 99643). Bunker was permitted to tell Thieu the explanation of 'no advantage' as given by Governor Harriman to the Rumanians. In his talk with Thieu he made "a distinction between the contacts to explore Hanoi's position and possibly to set up any 'serious discussions' and the discussions themselves." He assured Thieu that "any further decision will be a matter of full consultation with you and with our Manila allies." Thieu expressed no reservations about the U.S. approach. Thieu expressed the view that the Trinh statement was good propaganda by Hanoi. Bunker had urged permission to speak to Thieu on the basis of Bui Diem's "implication that U.S.-Hanoi contacts to bring about a negotiation would be tolerable to the GVN, provided /Thieu/ was kept informed of them

12

and given an opportunity to express his views before a rapidly moving situation becomes a fait accompli."

On January 22, Macovescu et al arrived in Hanoi. The U.S. was not informed of the results of his visit until February 12.

On February 12, Ambassador Harriman was informed of the results of the GOR visit to Hanoi by Ambassador Bogdan. Bogdan reported that Macovescu had been in Hanoi from January 22nd to the 28th, and Macovescu talked mainly with Dong and Trinh.

The GDRV asserted to Macovescu that "it did not consider the proposals of the USG an answer to the Trinh declaration of 29 December, and that San Antonio conditions remain."

At this point, Bogdan dictated the following passage:

"The position of the Vietnamese people and of the Government of the Democratic Republic of Vietnam is very clear. There are the four points of the Government of the Democratic Republic of Vietnam and the political program of the National Liberation Front of South Vietnam. This is the basis for the solution (reglementation) of the Vietnamese problem. We stated clearly: if in actuality the United States Government desires conversations, as it says it does, it must in the first place stop unconditionally the bombardment and all other acts of war against the Democratic Republic of Vietnam. After a convenient period of time, following the unconditional cessation of bombardment and all other American acts of war against the Democratic Republic of Vietnam, the Democratic Republic of Vietnam will start conversations with the United States of America on the questions of interest to the two parties /The Ambassador understands this to mean the interest of either side, not a common interest/. The convenient period of time is the time necessary to prove that the United States has really and without conditions stopped bombardment and all other acts of war against the Democratic Republic of Vietnam. After the unconditional cessation of the bombardment and all other acts of war against the Democratic Republic of Vietnam a meeting will take place between the two sides to reach an agreement on the place, the level, and the contents of the conversation. The right position and the correct attitude of the Government of the Democratic Republic of Vietnam have been warmly welcomed and supported by the peoples of the world. The attitude of the Democratic Republic of Vietnam is serious. If the conversations are leading or not to results, this depends on the United States."

Bogdan added that the GOR was ready to transmit communications to either side and that when Ambassador Davis returns to Bucharest he could obtain further details from M. Bogdan said that M was in Peking on January 31 and informed the Chinese Government of the various positions.

13

The Chinese repeated that "it was up to North Vietnam." He said that Moscow would soon be fully informed as well.

Governor Harriman took note of the continued threat to U.S. forces in the DMZ area and said that "his unofficial reaction is that Hanoi does not wish talks...."

On <u>February 24</u>, Ambassador Davis spoke to M (State 117922). M told Davis that after his discussions in Washington, Hanoi quickly responded to his travel request to Hanoi. M noted that when he reached Hanoi there was no U.S. bombing, but in accord with U.S. wishes he said nothing about this U.S. decision to the North Vietnamese.

M conveyed to Trinh the GOR belief that "minimum of conditions now created to take stride forward on road to negotiations."

KILLY

ITALION - NORTH VIETNAMESE TRACK, FEBRUARY-MARCH, 1968

The following account of Italian-North Vietnamese contacts was given on February 24, 1968 (ROME 4429).

January or February, 1967

Fanfani stated that he had been asked through a channel which he did not reveal whether he was prepared to receive an unidentified North Vietnamese. Secretary Rusk was informed and suggested that Fanfani first find out who the contact was and what authority he would have. Fanfani asked these questions, they were never answered, and he heard nothing further from this contact.

July or August 1967

Fanfani was asked by a different contact (also unspecified) whether he would be interested in sending d'Orlandi to get in touch with the North Vietnamese Ambassador in Prague. The unspecified contact was aware of the January contact. Fanfani said that there was no doubt that the initiative for the Prague meeting came from Hanoi.

September 5, 1967 - First Meeting

On instructions from Fanfani, D'Orlandi flew to Prague and met with North Vietnamese Ambassador Su. D'Orlandi asked Su why he had sought this meeting, but did not receive an answer. Su did say that he was aware of d'Orlandi's role in MARIGOLD. D'Orlandi advised Su that Hanoi should move rapidly to seize the opportunity of a trip Fanfani would make to Washington in mid-September and authorize Fanfani to transmit something new. D'Orlandi specifically requested that Hanoi set a period after the stopping of the bombing for the first contact with the U.S. D'Orlandi told Su that Fanfani would carry weight in Washington if he could present a time and place for the meeting between the DRV and the U.S. Su replied that he would be unable to obtain instructions from Hanoi prior to the Fanfani trip to Washington.

Early November, 1967 - Second Meeting

After a delay of more than 50 days, d'Orlandi returned to Prague and said to Su that he was entitled to a reply to his suggestions of September. Su said that the matter was being considered in Hanoi, but that he had not received a reply. D'Orlandi again stressed the importance of the need for Hanoi to set a time and place for negotiations after the cessation of U.S. bombing. Su said everytime Hanoi produced something in favor of negotiations the Americans backed out and showed bad faith. D'Orlandi stressed to Su a favorite theme of some substantive agreements prior to the first face-to-face contacts between Hanoi and Washington. He said the Italians would be glad to transmit such issues between the two parties. Su said that he might soon be going back to Hanoi.

Su stated that if d'Orlandi's trips to Prague became known the North Vietnamese would deny everything. Su also asked d'Orlandi not to get in touch with the DRV Prague Embassy unless it was most urgent because he would be leaving for Hanoi within a week. Su would contact d'Orlandi the moment he returned to Prague.

January, 1968 - Third Meeting

D'Orlandi flew to Prague. Su said there was general approval in Hanoi of the idea of starting negotiations. Su said that he had been authorized to talk to Fanfani. It was arranged that Su would come to Rome on February 4.

February 17, 1968

State sent out to Rome some follow-up comments of Fanfani's which had been transmitted to Secretary Rusk by Ortona on February 16. There were two main points: (a) That the Italians do not have the "impression" that San Antonio has been substantially rejected. They do believe, however, that although reciprocity is unacceptable to Hanoi, Hanoi might consider some "concession"; and (b) That a direct U.S.-NVN meeting was unlikely but that Hanoi may be interested in preliminary soundings and direct channel, possibly the Italians.

The cable also noted the Washington Post story, date of February 16, dateline Rome, which went into considerable detail on Italian-North Vietnamese conversations.[1]

State also indicated reserve with respect to this track.

The Killy slug began with this cable.

(State 117384)

Daniel Davidson, Special Assistant to Governor Harriman, was dispatched to Rome to arrive on February 20. (State 117385)

February 18, 1968

D'Orlandi was told that Su could receive him in Prague on the 21st. D'Orlandi told Fanfani that he was expected in Hanoi on the 21st and Fanfani expected him to defer his trip. Su had been expecting d'Orlandi for several days, and d'Orlandi had not given him any reason for the delay.

2

<u>February 23, 1968</u>

Davidson and Meloy met with d'Orlandi and Fanfani. Fanfani, in translating his notes from Italian to English, repeatedly made a more positive translation than was warranted by the Italian.

"Major points in his notes were:

"(A) Su (NVN Ambassador to Prague) described NLF as the representative of a great number of Southerners.

"(B) Su flatly rejected reciprocity but suggested that when contacts had been established after cessation of bombing, North Vietnamese could certainly take favorable measures and might also suggest some act of good will to the NLF. Fanfani asked if among those measures Hanoi was thinking of humanitarian measures such as liberation of PWs and received an affirmative reply. Fanfani suggested, as example, that it would be useful in order to improve atmosphere for Hanoi either before or on first day of the meetings to free PWs against previously agreed upon concessions on part of United States. Su replied that he agreed but was not authorized to answer. He did say that much will depend on attitude of US representatives at first encounter.

"(C) It is very apparent from notes that each time MARIGOLD ten points were mentioned, they were dragged in from deep left field by Fanfani. For example, initial reference to them came when Fanfani remarked that freedom of South Viet-Nam and non-intervention which North Vietnamese said should be part of settlement appeared already in the ten points 'of Tripartite Agreement of Saigon.' Fanfani asked whether Su meant to refer to those understandings and Su replied that the ten points had been bypassed by events but perhaps they can be referred to in broad outline. The only other reference to MARIGOLD occurred when Fanfani recalled that the 'three negotiators' to get around problem of reciprocity accepted Phase A-Phase B formula. Su replied that he was not authorized to discuss Tripartite contacts or current validity of the ten points but that he would submit the question to Hanoi.

"(D) Fanfani pressed Su extremely hard for the specific number of days (e.g. two days) between cessation of bombing and initiation of a dialogue between Hanoi and US. He said that it would certainly ease his task of assuring Washington that Hanoi really wanted to establish contact with it if he was given an answer. Su said he understood perfectly, would submit the question to Hanoi and might be in position to give an answer to d'Orlandi at his next meeting. Fanfani insisted on at least being assured that a specific period already existed in Hanoi's mind. Su spoke very slowly in reply and d'Orlandi is certain that following is verbatim record. 'We agree for Foreign Minister Fanfani to let it be known in communications he will make to the Government of the United States that in

3

case of unconditional cessation of the bombing, the delay of
"X" days already exists for a first meeting of representatives
of the two parties, Hanoi and Washington, with a view to.
establish contacts for serious conversation on questions concerning the two parties.'

"(E) Fanfani told North Vietnamese that they had not been
forthcoming enough to put Washington under an obligation to
reply. Fanfani asked to be put in a position to tell Washington
something about the date, place, and subject of the meeting. Su
was unresponsive.

"(F) Fanfani asked whether Hanoi was attempting contacts
through other channels or had already established a direct
channel to Washington. Su excluded this possibility. Fanfani
commented that he was astonished at flat statement that Hanoi
had no contacts with Washington. Su again gave categorical denial.
He said there were no direct contacts and although Hanoi often
received visitors they were not qualified nor in the least authorized to talk on behalf of the US Government.

"(G) North Vietnamese had suggested communique but did not
push idea very hard. Their apparent motive was to demonstrate
that they were in fact duly authorized representatives of Hanoi
and therefore in a position to release communique. When Fanfani
pointed out obvious detrimental effects of publicity, particularly predictable reaction of USG, Su quickly backed off.

"(H) Points H to J come from notes d'Orlandi made after
informal discussion during which no notes were to be kept. The
North Vietnamese took copious notes anyway. (This portion of the
notes was not read to North Vietnamese.) Both parties felt that
problem of guaranteeing an agreement was increasing to decisive
importance. Su seemed to categorically exclude the UN as a
guaranteeing agency and Fanfani and Su agreed that the ICC was
not in position to guarantee anything.

"(I) Fanfani asked if there would be any objection if he
informed Tran Van Do or even Thieu of fact that conversations
with an authorized representative of Hanoi had taken place. Su
stated he had no objections.

"(J) Su stated that declared and also real aim of Hanoi was
to have absolutely free general elections. To insure liberty of
vote, it was necessary to constitute a government with very broadly
based participation excluding only 'war criminals' (undefined).
There was discussion of various South Vietnamese personalities as
possible members of a Government. Su would raise a name and

4

d'Orlandi would comment. Su generally did not reveal his opinion but Ky was obviously unacceptable to him.

"(K) Although not reflected in notes, conversation closed with discussion of modalities of next meeting. Su suggested that d'Orlandi come to Prague on February 21 but exact date was left undetermined."

Fanfani confirmed that there was no discussion of the San Antonio formula and that they were unaware of the Clifford explanation.[2] Davidson gave Fanfani the U.S. position as contained in State 117383. (ROME 4418, Sections 1 & 2 of 2)

Also, on February 23, Davidson cabled some additional points which he had made to Fanfani and d'Orlandi. Davidson said:

"The important thing was that there must be no doubt in Hanoi's mind that it had committed itself not to take advantage of a bombing cessation by such actions as increasing its infiltration of munitions and supplies or attacking U.S. positions in the area of the DMZ."

"....I suggested that it might repeat might be sufficient if Hanoi stated that it recognized that during a period when the US was not bombing and while talks were continuing that such acts as attacks on US positions in the area of the DMZ, massive terror against the cities such as the Tet campaign or increased infiltration, would show bad faith on its part and that it, of course, would never do anything that smacked of bad faith. Hanoi could then discuss with us at the first meeting more precise definition of actions which would constitute bad faith."

Fanfani and d'Orlandi understood that this was "merely a verbal gimmick to permit Hanoi to accept all requirements of the 'not take advantage' formulation without having to actually promise 'not to take advantage'." Fanfani said that if the U.S. approves, he will dispatch d'Orlandi again to Prague. (ROME 4419)

February 24, 1968

Fanfani gave an exposition on the Italian motivation for Vietnam negotiations. He said that he was prepared to drop the matter entirely if the U.S. desired or if Hanoi did not give evidence of seriousness. He warned of escalation, and the consequences of escalation on the policy of detente with the Soviet Union. He said that an intensification of the war in Vietnam would help the communist vote in Italy. (ROME 4422)

February 26, 1968

Davidson cabled additional information on the February 22 meeting with Fanfani and d'Orlandi. After he touched on "the terrible consequences" of the U.S. stopping bombing and being forced to resume because Hanoi took advantage, Fanfani remarked that "I had used almost exactly the same expressions in discussing that contingency as Su had used." According to Fanfani, "Su told him that if the bombing stopped and then were resumed it would be 'the end of the world'."

Fanfani also discussed a coalition government-general elections issue.

"In thinking out loud of an ultimate solution, Fanfani discussed the 'hypothesis' of a government which would be composed of elements of the existing government and other forces and would have the task of preparing for free general elections. He said that the creation of such a government would avoid the problem of which elements are a majority or minority since the task of the government would be technical. He recalled that it was a non-elected Italian Government which successfully prepared the Italian elections of 1946. Fanfani said he mentioned this idea to the North Vietnamese and they didn't object to it. Su said that they thought they would win an election and that is why they want one. Fanfani mentioned that Su had asked d'Orlandi for his opinion of personalities who were clearly not rpt not part of the FLN. I asked d'Orlandi who they were and he said several professional men, members of past government, religious personalities, all in all, some 20 or 25 names. Su did not rpt not comment after d'Orlandi gave his frank evaluation of each name except to say that Foreign Minister Do was a gentleman and a man of international stature who had little internal influence. D'Orlandi said it was clear that the FLN was thinking of a government that would include people who had not rpt not fought with it but who were nonetheless patriots. I remarked that it sounded to me as if these other elements would be largely the Bogus Committees that were being set up in connection with the Tet offensive. D'Orlandi said he thought I was mistaken."[3]

Su told Fanfani that he "didn't consider any of the Eastern European channels as serious," and "Fanfani had specifically asked Su about P. M. Maurer, and the two North Vietnamese laughed as if to say that he could not rpt not conceivably be a serious channel." They also flatly ruled out the UN and the ICC in bringing about negotiations or in guaranteeing a settlement. (ROME 4440, Sections 1 & 2 of 2)

February 26, 1968

Davidson cabled urging continuation of this track. He argued that Italy was the first Western European nation to receive authorized representatives of Hanoi, and that Su had authorized Fanfani to convey his comments to the USG, and that Su had again invited d'Orlandi to Prague (d'Orlandi had been expected there by Su since February 21).

Davidson said that the press leak on the North Vietnamese visit to Rome was by a communist newspaper and "it appears that the leak did not come from the Italian Government." Davidson was sympathetic to Fanfani's explanation that he had, for political reasons, to unilaterally release a statement to the press on the visit of the two North Vietnamese representatives to discuss a basis for starting negotiations.

Davidson concluded that the U.S. had every reason to continue with the track. He noted that there was a "danger of letting d'Orlandi go to Prague" in that "he might succeed and we might face prospect of negotiations at time when the political-military situation makes negotiations undesirable." He added: "However, if Hanoi now wishes to try to force negotiations on USG, it can create other situations at least as awkward as one that might result from telling d'Orlandi that it accepts essence of San Antonio." (ROME 4441)

February 27, 1968

State agreed that "we should give a constructive response to the proposal that d'Orlandi make another visit to Prague as suggested by Ambassador Su." State added: "However, under existing circumstances, it would be unwise to suggest new formulations (as you propose para 4 Rome 4419) which might give Hanoi the idea that we were weakening on the San Antonio position."

State went on to issue guidance for the d'Orlandi-Su talk:

"However, it appears to us that Hanoi is undertaking a combined diplomatic and propaganda offensive rather than showing a serious intention to negotiate in good faith at the moment. It would be useful for the Italians to try to discover whether the North Vietnamese look upon contacts with the Italians as expressing a serious negotiating position or as part of a rather widespread exercise to impress a variety of governments.

"(c) As you suggest in 10-A Reftel 4441, it appears useful for d'Orlandi to visit Prague in order to tell Su:

"(1) his statements have been communicated to the US and after careful analysis did not seem to US Government to be any more forthcoming than public statements of Hanoi. If Hanoi has any intention of conveying anything new, Su should be requested to point it out.

"(2) D'Orlandi might on his own responsibility explore with Su anything that Su could suggest which would be more

definite on timing and particularly any statements Hanoi would
be willing to make as to their intentions relating to the military problem of 'no advantage.' D'Orlandi may draw on explanations
you have provided him as to meaning of San Antonio formula. FYI
We have been informed by French and through U Thant on information
he received from French that negotiations would start immediately
if we announced publicly unconditional cessation of bombing and
other acts of war against NVN. Therefore there is no value in
making an issue of this point through Su. END FYI.

"(3) In addition, d'Orlandi might wish to point out to
Su that since Hanoi had rejected San Antonio formula, Americans had
asked number of questions. For example, does this mean that Hanoi
feels free to move men and supplies to the South as they did during
the Tet truce last year? Would Hanoi feel free to move troops
to the DMZ area in positions to attack US forces south of the DMZ?
Would Hanoi consider it has the right to intensify artillery and
other fire across the DMZ into US positions in South Viet-Nam?

"5. If the Italians express disappointment at the lack of
detail in this message, please tell them that we are understandably
cautious because of the major military operations now in progress
or being planned by North Viet-Nam in the DMZ and the Laos Panhandle. We cannot ignore Hanoi's actions on the ground in interpreting what Hanoi's intentions may be."

(State 120937)

March 4, 1967

Report on d'Orlandi-Su meeting.

D'Orlandi met with Meloy and Davidson to report on his March 1
meeting in Prague with Ambassador Su. D'Orlandi asked Su if he were ready
to answer the question concerning the period of delay between the stopping
of the bombing and the first U.S.-Hanoi meetings? Su responded rather
lamely that he thought this contact had come to an end and, therefore, he
was not able to supply a precise answer. "He could state that the matter
of a date would be no problem. The real problem was San Antonio."

D'Orlandi said that he had dictated to Su the first portion of the
Davidson MemCon of the February 28 meeting to the North Vietnamese, but
the North Vietnamese did not comment on this.

The most important point that Su made in these talks was with respect
to "no advantage." Although he said he was speaking personally, it is
highly doubtful that he would have said the following without specific
instructions:

"....D'Orlandi then told Su that if bombing stopped and
talks began, assaulting Khe Sanh, invading or trying to detach

8

the two northern provinces of South Viet-Nam, launching a second wave of attacks against one or more cities or creating a sensation with something else like an assault on Camp Carrol, would sink the whole thing.[4] Su replied that, speaking personally and not on instructions, such thing would be out, that from the moment the two sides meet it was obvious no such thing could happen. (I questioned d'Orlandi about this remark of Su's and d'Orlandi replied that while he took no notes he is certain this is the sense of what Su said.)[5] D'Orlandi told Su that whatever he or Su thought of the effect of bombing, it is a fact that the US Government and US public opinion considers bombing of the North a most important weapon and that no President could give away such a weapon while something terrible was happening either in the DMZ or the South. Su did not respond to this comment. D'Orlandi also remarked that it might be necessary for him to go to Hanoi to receive assurances directly from the top and again Su did not reply."

Su said that he will contact d'Orlandi when he receives a reply and arrange another meeting in Rome or in Prague.

(ROME 4590)

March 5, 1968

Davidson cabled another exchange with Fanfani and d'Orlandi. Referring to a Hanoi broadcast about the North Vietnamese visit to Rome "to discuss negotiations," Fanfani argued that this was Hanoi's way of verifying that the Italian channel is the one it wishes to use.

Fanfani reviewed Su's statements about "no advantage," and told exactly the same story as he had on the previous day.

(ROME 4634)

March 14, 1968

State cabled "a slight preference for Prague as site of next meeting." (State 129885)

March 16, 1968

Lodge arrived in Rome to speak with the Italians. Nothing new was added to previous communications.

Editor's Notes

Abbreviations Used in Notes

AFP, CD Department of State, *American Foreign Policy, Current Documents*
DSB Department of State, *Department of State Bulletin*
PPP, LBJ *Public Papers of the Presidents of the United States, Lyndon B. Johnson*
PP (GRAVEL) *The Senator Gravel Edition, The Pentagon Papers*
USVN U.S. Congress, House, Committee on Armed Services, *United States–Vietnam Relations, 1945–1967* (G.P.O. Edition, The Pentagon Papers)

VI.C.1., The Seaborn Mission to Hanoi, June 1964–June 1965

1. In April 1964, right-wing forces in Laos had overthrown the remnants of the coalition government established by the 1962 Geneva Agreements (the leftist Pathet Lao had earlier withdrawn from the government). The United States had attempted to restore the coalition of neutralist and right-wing groups, even to the point of cutting off aid to the right. At the same time, faced with mounting disarray in South Vietnam and fearful of Pathet Lao gains in Laos, the Johnson administration had initiated reconnaissance flights over Laotian territory to gather information on Pathet Lao troop movements. When several American planes were shot down by ground fire, American pilots were authorized to attack hostile positions.

2. Vietcong attacks on a U.S. Army advisors barracks at Pleiku on February 6, 1965, had been the pretext for a series of retaliatory air raids on North Vietnam. The reprisals soon regularized into the ROLLING THUNDER program of sustained and systematic bombing.

3. See VI.C.1, Project MAYFLOWER—the First Bombing Pause, for the May 1965 pause.

4. The "Laos pattern of 1962" refers to the 1962 Geneva Accords on Laos, which brought left, right, and neutralist forces together in a coalition government.

5. President Charles de Gaulle of France had also recently called for a conference to restore peace to Laos, but the United States rejected all such proposals for fear a conference might sanction the gains recently made by the Pathet Lao.

6. John Moors Cabot, U.S. Ambassador to Poland, maintained sporadic contact with the Chinese Ambassador in Warsaw, a practice initiated in the 1950s and the sole avenue of direct communication between the United States and the People's Republic. For the text of Ambassador Cabot's statement, see pp. 39–40.

7. Pham Van Dong's Four Points, issued on April 8, 1965, represented the first formal statement of North Vietnamese peace terms and are discussed further in VI.C.1., Project MAYFLOWER—the First Bombing Pause. For the text of the Four Points, see p. 586.

8. Poland, along with India and Canada, was a member of the International Control Commission on Indochina established by the 1954 Geneva Agreements.

9. Up to this point, Canada had publicly supported U.S. policy, rejecting all proposals for the neutralization of South Vietnam and condemning North Vietnamese aggression. By his own account, however, Prime Minister Pearson had privately urged "caution and moderation" on Washington, and Rusk apparently feared that an American commitment to direct military intervention in Vietnam might jeopardize Canada's support and in particular its cooperative role on the ICC.

10. OPLAN 34A, put into effect on February 1, 1964, called for steadily increasing covert military actions against North Vietnam, to be conducted primarily by South Vietnamese forces and designed to weaken North Vietnam's offensive capabilities and to signal Hanoi that it could not continue to support the insurgency in South Vietnam with impunity.

11. The section deleted here most probably contains Pearson's comments about possible use of nuclear weapons in Vietnam. In the *Washington Post*, January 30, 1973, Sanford J. Ungar summarized the deleted material as follows: ". . . Lester Pearson, then prime minister of Canada and later the winner of the Nobel peace prize, had expressed support for possible American bombing of North Vietnam—during a meeting in New York with President Johnson—so long as nuclear weapons were not used."

12. From the beginning of the conflict in Indochina, Cambodia's Prince Norodom Sihanouk had attempted to maintain a neutral position. Any appeal this sort of neutrality might have had for the United States had long since dissipated, however, for in 1964 Sihanouk had veered sharply toward Peking and had become openly anti-American to the point of renouncing the American aid program. The United States indeed strongly opposed Sihanouk's appeal for an international conference to guarantee Cambodia's neutrality, fearing the impact of such a conference on South Vietnam's already precarious position.

13. The ten-point program of the NLF, originally issued December 20, 1960, and broadcast to the West in February 1961, called, among other things, for the overthrow of the "lackey" regime of South Vietnam and its replacement by a "broad national democratic coalition administration" including "representatives of all strata of people, nationalities, political parties, religious communities, and patriotic personalities." The NLF statement is printed in *USVN*, book 12, VI.B., 189–192.

14. For the Tonkin Gulf crisis, see *PP (Gravel)*, III, 183–192.

15. Reference is to the Gulf of Tonkin Resolution, August 7, 1964. For the text, see *AFP, CD-1964*, pp. 991–992.

16. The first ROLLING THUNDER strike took place on March 2, 1965, while Seaborn was in Hanoi.

17. The date here and in the heading of the cable below is obviously incorrect. The context of the message suggests that it should be May 27, 1965, instead of March 27, 1965.

18. Johnson's April 7, 1965, Johns Hopkins University speech is excerpted on p. 585. For the full text, see *PPP, LBJ-1965*, I, 394–399. The U.S. reply to the appeal of the nonaligned nations for a peaceful solution through negotiations without precondition is in *DSB* 52 (April 26, 1965): 610–611.

19. For the message of May 12, 1965, see pp. 57–58.

20. Nguyen Duy Trinh was named Foreign Minister of North Vietnam on

April 7, 1965. For further discussion of Seaborn's June 1965 mission to Hanoi, see pp. 71–73.

VI.C.1., Project MAYFLOWER—the First Bombing Pause

1. This section is taken verbatim from "The Air War in North Vietnam, February–June 1965," in *PP (Gravel)*, III, 362–381, and "Rolling Thunder Program Begins," in *USVN*, book 4, IV.C.3., pp. 106–130. The original footnotes are in *USVN*, book 4, IV.C.3., pp. 147–148.

2. Johnson's April 7 speech is excerpted on p. 585 and is printed in full in *PPP, LBJ-1965*, I, 394–399.

3. For additional details on the "UK/USSR Co-chairmen gambit," see *PP (Gravel)*, III, 325–330. The Soviets in fact initiated the move, but when the British, with American encouragement, eagerly pursued it, Moscow backed off. The statement here that consultations would be promoted under "Article 19 of the 1962 Geneva Accords" appears to be in error. The discussion cited above indicates that the British were thinking in terms of reactivating the co-chairmanship of the 1954 Geneva Accords.

4. Sarvepalli Radhakrishnan was President of India. For his cease-fire proposal, see *AFP, CD-1965*, p. 878 n.

5. Patrick Gordon Walker, British Foreign Secretary, toured Southeast Asia in early 1965 on the request of Prime Minister Harold Wilson to try to promote discussion of the Vietnam problem among the nations concerned. North Vietnam and the Peoples' Republic of China refused to receive him.

6. Phan Huy Quat, Minister for Foreign Affairs in the Khanh government, assumed the premiership of South Vietnam on February 16, 1965. His government lasted until June 11, 1965, when it was replaced by a military junta headed by Vice Air Marshal Nguyen Cao Ky.

7. Nguyen Van Binh was the Roman Catholic Archbishop of Saigon; Angelo Palmas was the nuncio, or apostolic delegate to South Vietnam.

8. Implemented during the week of May 18–24, 1965, ROLLING THUNDER 15 called for forty sorties a day against fixed military installations and lines of communication in the area between the seventeenth and twentieth parallels.

9. Attaching code names to the various peace initiatives ("slugging" in bureaucratic parlance) gave them a special classification that limited access to the cable traffic to a small number of officials. The earliest contacts seem to have been named for ships (MAYFLOWER and PINTA). The names of flowers were then used until, according to Kraslow and Loory, *Secret Search for Peace*, p. 27, some officials protested the irony in the use of flowers to designate matters connected with a bloody war. Several of the later initiatives were named for American states, after which there seems to have been no pattern.

10. Prince Norodom Sihanouk had first called for an international conference to guarantee Cambodia's neutrality. The United States had initially opposed the idea but shifted its position in 1965, apparently to demonstrate the sincerity of its commitment to peace in Southeast Asia. After a meeting with Chinese premier Chou En-lai, Sihanouk had also altered his position, indicating that he would not participate in a conference that was not restricted to discussion of Cambodia.

11. During the first four months of 1965, both Premier Souvanna Phouma

and Pathet Lao leader Prince Souphanouvong proposed that leftist, rightist, and neutralist forces meet to arrange a cease-fire in the civil war in Laos.

12. Johnson's "Three Faces of War" speech came on the first day of the bombing pause, May 13, 1965, and is printed in full in *PPP, LBJ-1965*, I, 522–526.

13. The "lesson [of] Cuba" most probably refers to the Cuban missile crisis of October 1962 when, from the American perspective, the Soviet Union backed down in the face of the superior military power of the United States. Some American officials assumed that the lesson would apply again in the case of Vietnam, but they appear to have consistently overestimated Hanoi's dependence on Moscow and underestimated the commitment of North Vietnam to objectives it regarded as essential. They seem also to have overlooked the extent to which the Sino-Soviet split limited Soviet maneuverability and increased Hanoi's leverage with both its major allies.

14. The date cited here is obviously incorrect. It should be May 12 instead of March 12.

VI.C.1., XYZ (Mai Van Bo Contacts), May 1965–February 1966

1. See VI.C.1., PINTA: The Rangoon Contact.

2. These developments are discussed at greater length on pp. 71–72.

3. Y was Paul Sturm, a retired foreign service officer who had served as consul in Hanoi, 1952–1954, and as political adviser to General J. Lawton Collins, Eisenhower's special representative to South Vietnam, 1954–1955. A scholar by training, Sturm held a Ph.D. from Yale University and had once been an instructor of French at that institution. He had taught William Bundy at Yale and was a long-time friend of George Ball.

4. Bo was most likely referring to a major search-and-destroy operation launched by U.S. Marines and ARVN forces in the Danang area in mid-August. According to U.S. estimates, nearly 700 Vietcong were killed in this first regiment-size American military action since the Korean War. During this period, the United States also intensified the bombing of North Vietnam, launching one thousand sorties in twelve days and striking staging areas across the DMZ; missile sites, dams, and power plants near Hanoi; and bridges less than twenty miles from the Chinese border.

5. Chester A. Ronning, a retired Canadian diplomat and Sinologist, went to Hanoi in March and June of 1966 on an official Canadian peace mission that had American endorsement. The Ronning missions are discussed in detail in VI.C.1., The Ronning Missions—March and June 1966. Actually, the message that talks would follow an unconditional cessation of the bombing was first conveyed to Ronning by Pham Van Dong in March.

6. The 325th division of the North Vietnamese army was a crack unit, apparently one of the first regular army units infiltrated intact into the South. Its alleged presence in South Vietnam was not only a source of controversy between North Vietnam and the United States but also a source of dispute among Americans. The Johnson administration cited the presence of the 325th in South Vietnam as justification for the dispatch of large increments of American combat forces. Critics of the administration argued that the commitment of U.S. ground forces was made before the presence of the North Vietnamese unit had been established. The matter remains unresolved, but it seems likely that North Vietnam had as many as five thousand regulars in South Vietnam by the spring of 1965.

7. Johnson's July 28, 1965, press conference was called to explain the decision to commit major combat forces to South Vietnam, although his conciliatory words seemed to catch the attention of Hanoi. The press conference is excerpted on p. 588. The full text can be found in *PPP, LBJ-1965*, II, 794–803.

8. Chinese Defense Minister Lin Piao's much publicized speech of September 1965 emphasized the inevitability of conflict between the northern industrialized parts of the world and the southern agrarian regions and avowed Chinese support for wars of national liberation. It was interpreted in the United States as heralding a new era of Chinese aggression, but a close reading indicates the emphasis Lin placed on self-reliance. For the text of the statement, see *AFP, CD-1965* pp. 732–747.

9. The text of Hanoi's May 18, 1965, communiqué is in ibid., pp. 870–871.

10. Johnson's San Francisco statement, June 25, 1965, commemorated the founding of the United Nations twenty years earlier. It is in *PPP, LBJ-1965*, II, 703–706.

11. The "Indian proposal" probably refers to Indian President Radhakrishnan's proposal of April 24, 1965, for a termination of the bombing of North Vietnam, a cessation of the fighting in South Vietnam, and the stationing of an Afro-Asian police force along the border and at critical points in the interior of South Vietnam to uphold the cease-fire. Various proposals had been advanced in 1964 and 1965 for international conferences to restore peace to Laos and guarantee Cambodia's neutrality. The United States had at first opposed all such suggestions, but as the position of the Laotian government improved and as part of the Johnson administration's effort to persuade domestic and world opinion of its commitment to peace in Indochina, it shifted its position in 1965.

12. See p. 155.

13. Ho Chi Minh established the Vietnam Fatherland Front in September 1955, apparently as a means to promote the political settlement called for by the Geneva Accords. The front's program involved a series of steps leading toward eventual unification. It encouraged temporary maintenance of the regroupment zones established by the Geneva Accords but advocated immediate restoration of normal economic, cultural, and social relations between the two zones, negotiations for integration of the armed forces, and free elections for a National Assembly. See *Viet-Nam Fatherland Front and the Struggle for National Unity* (Hanoi: Foreign Languages Publishing House, 1956), pp. 16–26.

14. The idea of a conference to guarantee the neutrality of Cambodia had originated with Prince Sihanouk and had been endorsed by a number of other nations, including, belatedly, the United States, as a possible means of promoting discussions on Vietnam by the side door. Apparently under pressure from Communist China, Sihanouk later made plain his unwillingness to participate in any conference that was not restricted exclusively to discussion of Cambodia.

15. From time to time, North Vietnamese representatives suggested that de Gaulle's Algerian settlement of 1962 could be a model for peace in Vietnam. Since there had been no third force in Algeria and de Gaulle had dealt directly

with the Algerian FLN, recognizing Algerian independence in exchange for the respect of certain French interests, U.S. officials did not regard the Evian Accords as an acceptable model.

16. Rusk's television interview of August 23, 1965, is in *DSB* 53 (September 13, 1965): 431–444.

17. The NLF's March 22, 1965, statement, which also became known as the NLF's Five Points, seems more a call to arms than a statement of political aims, although it does call for "correct" implementation of the Geneva Accords, for withdrawal of U.S. forces, and, implicitly, for the unification of the two Vietnams. For the text of the statement, with annotations showing how Hanoi softened the tones of the original proclamation issued over Liberation Radio, see Marcus Raskin and Bernard Fall (eds.), *The Viet-Nam Reader* (New York: Vintage, 1965), pp. 232–252. The statement is also printed in *USVN*, book 12, VI.B., pp. 193–198.

18. For a more complete text of the Foreign Ministry's September 23, 1965, memorandum, see *USVN*, book 12, VI.B., pp. 160–163.

19. As noted previously, Y was retired foreign service officer Paul Sturm.

20. The substance of Deptel 202/Rangoon can be found on p. 129.

21. Senator George McGovern (D-S. Dak.) was one of the earliest and most forceful critics of U.S. escalation of the war. Joseph Kingsbury-Smith was a distinguished foreign correspondent and at this time editor of the *New York Journal-American*. Sanford Gottlieb, a self-styled "professional peace advocate," was one of the founders of the National Committee for a Sane Nuclear Policy (SANE) and a leader in the peace movement of the 1960s. An organizer of the March on Washington for Peace in November 1966, Gottlieb also maintained sporadic contact with North Vietnamese and Vietcong representatives in Algiers and Paris.

22. For the U.S. "peace offensive" and the Fourteen Points, see VI.C.1. PINTA: The Rangoon Contact.

23. Alexandr N. Shelepin, Secretary of the Central Committee of the Soviet Communist Party, visited Hanoi in early January with a delegation of military experts. The United States had hoped that Shelepin might exert Soviet influence to bring about negotiations, but his purpose apparently was to demonstrate the Soviets' full support for North Vietnam. While in Hanoi, Shelepin publicly denounced American "war crimes" and "aggression" and endorsed the peace terms stated by Hanoi. He also concluded a major new agreement on Soviet economic and military assistance.

24. The statement "progressive action normally brought about reaction, as in France in 1956" appears to refer either to the Poujardist movement of 1956 or to the establishment of the Fifth Republic in 1958.

VI.C.1., PINTA: The Rangoon Contact

1. The Fourteen Points, issued in a statement by Secretary Rusk on January 3, 1966, as part of the administration's peace offensive, represented the fullest statement of the U.S. negotiating position to this point. They can be found on p. 592.

2. The Declaration of Honolulu, February 8, 1966, came at the end of a three-day meeting between President Johnson and South Vietnamese Premier Nguyen Cao Ky and their top advisers. The statement that most probably alarmed the North Vietnamese was: "We must defeat the Viet Cong and those illegally fighting with them on our soil." For the text of the declaration, see *DSB* 54 (February 28, 1966): 305–307.

3. Ambassador Goldberg's letter to the United Nations, January 4, 1966, is in ibid. 54 (January 25, 1966): 117–118. It reiterated the standard U.S. position that the United States was prepared for discussions or negotiations without any conditions and on the basis of the 1954 and 1962 Geneva Accords, although it went on to note that a "reciprocal reduction of hostilities could be envisaged" and that a cease-fire "might be the first order of business in any discussions or negotiations."

4. Undersecretary of State Walter Bedell Smith headed the unofficial U.S. delegation to the 1954 Geneva Conference. The statement quoted here was issued in lieu of formal American association with the Geneva Agreements. The quotation is accurate as far as it goes, but Smith went on to state that the United States would "view any renewal of aggression in violation of the aforesaid agreements with grave concern and as seriously threatening international peace and security." This latter statement became part of the formal American justification for escalation of the war in the 1960s.

5. *A Threat to the Peace: North Viet-Nam's Effort to Conquer South Viet-Nam* was issued by the Kennedy administration in late 1961 to justify its stepped up aid to the government of Ngo Dinh Diem. The Johnson administration issued another White Paper, *Aggression from the North*, in February 1965 as a basis for its decision to bomb North Vietnam. The pamphlet *Why Vietnam?* was released in August 1965, shortly after the decision to commit major increments of U.S. ground combat forces to the war, and contains statements by Eisenhower, Kennedy, Johnson, McNamara, and Rusk justifying and explaining the American commitment in Vietnam.

6. Rusk's Canadian Broadcasting Corporation statement is in *DSB* 54 (January 17, 1966): 86–88.

7. Ho Chi Minh's letter, dated January 24, 1966, and released on January 28, is in *AFP, CD-1966*, pp. 753–754.

8. William Bundy was scheduled to meet with top American diplomats in The Far East at Baguio, The Philippines, in March. See below, VI.C.1., The Ronning Missions—March and June 1966, note 15.

9. See above, note 2, for the Declaration of Honolulu.

10. The North Vietnamese charges of gas warfare probably refer to U.S. use of CS (initialed after the names of its discoverers, Corson and Stoughlin) and other forms of tear gas to clear tunnel complexes in which the Vietcong were entrenched. The use of such gasses was originally authorized for "humanitarian reasons," to spare women and children from explosives that would otherwise have been used to destroy the underground hideaways. Later, the gasses were used to disarm the Vietcong and make them more vulnerable to rifle fire. The charges of chemical warfare probably refer to the widespread use of herbicides and defoliants to deprive the Vietcong of cover and to destroy their food. For the controversy over the legality of such methods, see Guenter Lewy, *America in Vietnam* (New York: Oxford University Press, 1978), pp. 248–266, and Richard Falk, *The Vietnam War and International Law*, 4 vols. (Princeton: Princeton University Press, 1968–1976), IV, 190–197, 228–240, 248–252.

VI.C.1., The Ronning Missions—March and June 1966

1. Ho Chi Minh's letter of Janaury 24, 1966, is in *AFP, CD-1966*, pp. 753–754.

2. Canada had long supported the American policy of nonrecognition of the People's Republic of China and opposition to the seating of the PRC in the United Nations. Hints of a change had come as early as May 1964, however, when foreign minister Paul Martin had publicly stated that it was only a matter of time before China assumed its real position in the world and gained a seat in the United Nations, adding that these "realities" might require "some modification" of Canada's position. Canada would not in fact recognize the People's Republic until October 1970, but in late 1966 it did propose a plan that would have given Taiwan's Security Council seat to Communist China while establishing a two-China arrangement in the General Assembly.

3. The Joint Chiefs of Staff had long been advocating air strikes against North Vietnam's petroleum, oil, and lubrication supplies. Johnson finally approved the proposal sometime in late May, and the strikes began on June 29. See *PP (Gravel)*, IV, 66–113.

4. Giorgio LaPira, Italian law professor, former mayor of Florence, and close friend of Foreign Minister Amintore Fanfani, had visited Hanoi in November 1965 at Fanfani's urging and had talked with Ho Chi Minh and Pham Van Dong. According to La Pira, Ho and Pham expressed a strong desire for a peaceful solution and indicated that for negotiations to begin the United States would have to cease all belligerent operations and accept a declaration establishing the Geneva Accords as the basis for a settlement. The United States found nothing new in LaPira's report, but leakage of the details of his mission to the press in mid-December may have influenced the administration's decision to try another bombing pause and undertake a new peace offensive. For additional details on the LaPira mission, see Kraslow and Loory, *Secret Search for Peace*, pp. 126–136; Bundy Oral History Interview, Johnson Library; and correspondence printed in *USVN*, book 12, VI.B, pp. 22–23.

5. Point 13 reiterated Johnson's earlier statement that the Vietcong "would not have difficulty being represented and having their views represented if for a moment Hanoi decided she wanted to cease aggression."

6. John G. Diefenbaker, leader of the Canadian opposition, had been a consistent and unequivocal supporter of U.S. policy in Vietnam. See, for example, *New York Times*, October 27, 1965.

7. Le Duc Tho's *Nhan Dan* statement of February 3, 1966, was apparently designed to buck up waverers in North Vietnam. It warned that there was a long struggle ahead and that Hanoi must be alert for "all plots and tricks of the enemy." It chided those comrades who had developed erroneous thoughts and had made incorrect assessments of the balance of power between the "enemy and us" and the "enemy's ruses." For an English translation, see *Yearbook on International Communist Affairs-1966* (Stanford: Hoover Institution, 1967), pp. 687–691.

8. During Prime Minister Harold Wilson's February 1966 visit to Moscow, British Minister for Disarmament Lord Chalfont had spent six hours at the North Vietnamese embassy talking with a high-level delegation then also visiting the Soviet capital. Wilson later recalled that the talks were "without any results." (See Wilson, *The Labour Government*, p. 214.)

9. The conversations deleted here are briefly summarized in Ronning, *Memoir of China*, pp. 259–266.

10. The firing of General Nguyen Chanh Thi by the ruling military junta on March 10, 1966, touched off a series of demonstrations in Hue and Danang, which by April had assumed the proportions of an open revolt against the government. Led by Buddhists and strongest in central South Vietnam, the revolt also took on blatantly anti-American tones. Ky's offer to draft a new constitution and hold elections temporarily stilled the upheaval, but it would erupt again in mid-May. See below, VI.C.2., MARIGOLD, note 11.

11. The phrase "air action . . . now being pressed by DOD" refers to the plan for attacking North Vietnam's POL stores. See note 3, above.

12. Again, the reference is to the planned escalation of the air war.

13. State Department information officer Robert McCloskey issued a statement on June 3, 1966, which reaffirmed American willingness to consider stopping bombing attacks on North Vietnam if Hanoi would indicate that it would take "reciprocal action" regarding the infiltration of troops into South Vietnam. See *Washington Post*, June 4, 1966.

14. The Polish colleague was probably Januscz Lewandowski, who was already engaged in another peace initiative, later code-named MARIGOLD and discussed in VI.C.2.

15. The Baguio meeting brought together top American diplomats in the Far East, February 28–March 2, 1966. It was presided over by Assistant Secretary of State William Bundy and was held at the U.S. Embassy's summer residence near Baguio, The Philippines.

16. Davies, a junior minister in the British cabinet and later private secretary to Prime Minister Harold Wilson, had visited Hanoi numerous times, knew Ho Chi Minh well, and had written extensively about him. With Wilson's encouragement and President Johnson's approval, Davies planned a visit to North Vietnam in the summer of 1965 to explore the possibility of peace negotiations. According to Wilson, a leak of the planned visit to the press destroyed its usefulness. Davies was granted a visa to get into North Vietnam, but he was not permitted to see Ho.

17. For the "reply to the British last August," see *DSB* 53 (September 13, 1965): 444–448.

18. Trouble erupted anew in South Vietnam in mid-May. When Ky seemed to back away from his earlier pledges to resign after national elections, a new round of demonstrations began. On May 15, Ky sent troops to Danang to regain control of the city. The Buddhists responded with passive resistance and a general strike, and fighting broke out in some parts of the city. Armed resistance to the government ended by May 23, but protests continued and spread south to Saigon and north to Hue. Ky's promises to add civilians to his government appeased the opposition only briefly, and on June 7 he sent troops to Hue to quell the uprising. Order was not restored throughout South Vietnam until near the end of June.

19. Senator J. William Fulbright (D.-Ark.), chairman of the Foreign Relations Committee, had been a persistent critic of Johnson's Vietnam policies since the spring of 1965, and in early 1966 he had conducted a series of widely publicized and nationally televised hearings on the war. Columnist Walter Lippmann had been an enthusiastic supporter of Johnson's Great Society legislation and had defended the bombing attacks launched in reprisal for the

Pleiku raid, arguing that they were a necessary response to a test of America's will and would permit the President to negotiate a satisfactory settlement. By the summer of 1965, however, Lippmann had joined the opposition, arguing that Vietnam was peripheral to America's vital interests and that the United States should not get involved in full-scale war there.

20. John Finney reported in the *New York Times*, June 3, 1966, that the United States had proposed to North Vietnam through the Chinese Ambassador in Warsaw that it would stop the bombing if North Vietnam under some form of international verification would agree to stop infiltrating troops into South Vietnam. The "senatorial indiscretion," if indeed it was one, was committed by Albert Gore (D.-Tenn.).

21. As a result of Ky's earlier promise to draft a new constitution and hold elections, the government issued a decree on June 19 that provided for elections for a constituent assembly in September. The assembly would then submit a written constitution to the government within six months and the constitution was to be promulgated within sixty days.

22. The phrase "informal bilateral talks of type we had in January this year" apparently refers to the talks between Byroade and Vu Huu Binh in Rangoon.

VI.C.2., MARIGOLD

1. The "revised NLF program," drawn up in mid-August 1967 and released just prior to the September 11 elections in South Vietnam, reaffirmed the front's determination to overthrow the "U.S. puppet regime" but also stressed its own commitment to hold "free general elections" and establish a broadly representative "national unity democratic government," the latter two points an apparent shift of emphasis from earlier positions. For the text of the program, see *USVN*, book 12, VI.B., pp. 222–234.

2. The Manila Communiqué was issued at the end of President Johnson's October 24–25, 1966, meeting at Manila with the heads of state of nations contributing troops to the war in Vietnam. The most novel statement in the communiqué was a pledge to withdraw U.S. and other foreign troops from South Vietnam as soon as possible and no later than six months after "the other side withdraws its forces to the North, ceases infiltration, and the level of violence subsides." For the text, see pp. 595–599 and *PPP, LBJ-1966*, II, 1259–1265.

3. Elections for a constituent assembly to draft a new constitution were held in September 1966, and the elected delegates convened later in the year to begin their work. From the standpoint of the NLF, the U.S. statement that these processes offered the proper route to representative government in South Vietnam must have appeared a sham, since the electorate was, for all practical purposes, limited to those who supported the existing government.

4. The so-called Cultural Revolution erupted full force in China in the summer of 1966. There was some speculation at the time that the upheaval in China might encourage North Vietnam to alter its strategy in the war, but there is no clear-cut evidence to support such assertions.

5. SUNFLOWER is discussed in VI.C.3.

6. In response to American escalation of the air war against North Vietnam in June 1966, the members of the Warsaw Pact, meeting in Bucharest, issued a strong statement on July 6. The Bucharest Declaration warned that the "criminal actions" of the United States threatened world peace and pledged material and moral support to the people of Vietnam. More ominously, it proclaimed the members' readiness, "if the Government of the Democratic Republic of Vietnam requests it, to allow their volunteers to go to Vietnam in order to help the Vietnamese people in their struggle against the American aggressors." The declaration is printed in *AFP, CD-1966*, pp. 832–834.

7. In an interview with Australian journalist Wilfred Burchett on January 28, 1967, Foreign Minister Nguyen Duy Trinh stated that it was "only after the unconditional cessation of U.S. bombing and all other acts of war against the D.R.V. that there could be talks between the D.R.V. and the United States." Sources sympathetic to Hanoi described the statement as a "goodwill" gesture since, in contrast to earlier North Vietnamese statements, it did not require that the bombing be ended "finally and unconditionally" and indicated that talks "could" begin. The Trinh interview is printed on pp. 422–424.

8. The "separate study" is most probably "The Air War in North Vietnam, 1965–1968," in *PP (Gravel)*, IV, especially 102–138.

9. A partial text of Goldberg's statement of September 22, 1966, is on pp. 255–256. For the full text, see *DSB* 55 (October 10, 1966): 518–525.

10. "Faroche" was Italian Ambassador-designate to Canada, H. E. Alessandro Farace di Villapresta.

11. The relief of General Nguyen Chanh Thi from command of ARVN forces in the northern provinces had set off the political crisis of the spring of 1966. Thi was brought before a disciplinary tribunal on July 9 and was sentenced to sixty days in prison. Apparently as a result of Lodge's intercession, he was permitted to leave South Vietnam for voluntary exile in the United States "for reasons of health."

12. Throughout June and July 1966 there was much speculation in the worldwide press that private efforts to arrange peace talks might soon produce results. For specific citations, see *USVN*, book 12, VI.A., pp. 22–25.

13. The Cultural Revolution took a new turn in August when the Central Committee of the Chinese Communist Party denounced "modern revisionism" and endorsed revolutionary militance at home and abroad. Masses of young Red Guards took to the streets to root out decadence and corruption, attacking, among other things, the Soviet Embassy in Peking. Shortly after, the Peking government asked Soviet students in China to leave the country, provoking Moscow to retaliate in kind. The affair reportedly came close to bringing about a severance in diplomatic relations between the two former allies.

14. The constituent assembly elected in September was to draft a constitution which would go into effect sometime in 1967 and would lead to elections and possibly a change in the makeup of the South Vietnamese government.

15. The countries contributing troops to the war and meeting with the United States and South Vietnam in Manila were Australia, New Zealand, Thailand, The Philippines, and South Korea. For the complete text of the Manila Communiqué and Declarations, see *PPP, LBJ-1966*, II, 1259–1265.

16. According to Chester Cooper, the proposals offered here resulted at least in part from a session he and Averell Harriman had in Rome on November 2 with Italian Foreign Minister Fanfani and Ambassador to South Viet-

nam D'Orlandi. The Italians urged the Americans to come up with something substantive to offer Hanoi. Cooper claims that upon returning to Washington he and Harriman pushed very hard to get something together, and he adds that the Phase A–Phase B proposal, the really new item in the package, was something he had originally devised for the Manila Conference as a way of getting around the long-standing stalemate on mutual de-escalation. See Chester Cooper Oral History Interview, Johnson Library.

17. Johnson claims that the Manila formula on troop withdrawal originated from a conversation in which Soviet Foreign Minister Andrei Gromyko told him that previous American statements on troop withdrawals had been too vague and general (see Johnson, *The Vantage Point*, p. 248). For additional background information on this proposal, see "Evolution of the 6-Month Withdrawal Clause" and W. W. Rostow to L.B.J., October 24, 1966, in *The War in Vietnam: Classified Histories by the National Security Council* [Microfilm Collection], Reel 5, Documents #0468 and 0470.

18. British Foreign Secretary George Brown was in Moscow in November 1966. Although the documents state that MARIGOLD did not come up during his visit, Prime Minister Wilson notes in his memoirs that Brown was completely caught off guard when the Soviets asked about Lewandowski's activities, about which he had not been informed by the United States. Wilson and Brown were deeply annoyed by the Johnson Administration's refusal to take them into its confidence (see Wilson, *The Labour Government*, p. 345).

19. At this point, primary responsibility for MARIGOLD shifted from Lodge in Saigon to Ambassador John Gronouski in Warsaw. According to the highly tentative U.S. plans, Gronouski would work out the preliminary arrangements for the talks. Once direct talks with North Vietnamese representatives were set to begin, a top-level U.S. diplomat would go to Warsaw to take over.

20. According to Kraslow and Loory (*Secret Search for Peace*, pp. 63–64), the president met with McNamara, the Joint Chiefs of Staff, and Rostow at his ranch on December 6 to consider whether to go ahead with the two major air strikes set for December 13 and 14. Either before or after this meeting, Lodge, William Bundy, Katzenbach, and, apparently, Rusk and McNamara as well urged that, in light of Rapacki's warnings, the attacks should be suspended until it could be determined where MARIGOLD might lead. The President rejected all such suggestions, arguing that a cessation of the bombing had not been required by Lewandowski's formula and that a halt at this point might be interpreted in Hanoi as a sign of weakness. See William Bundy and Nicolas deB. Katzenbach Oral History Interviews, Johnson Library.

21. Goldberg's letter, actually dated December 19, 1966, was in response to Pope Paul VI's appeal for a cease-fire and U Thant's plea to heed the Pope's message. Goldberg indicated that the United States would cooperate with any effort the Secretary General might make to arrange a cease-fire. For the text, see *AFP, CD-1966*, p. 889.

22. Johnson's letter to Kosygin probably concerned the final arrangements for a nuclear nonproliferation treaty, the basic terms of which had been agreed upon in December.

23. Harrison E. Salisbury had reported in the *New York Times*, January 4, 1967, an interview in which Pham Van Dong had stated that the Four Points did not represent "conditions" for the holding of peace talks but merely formed the "basis of a settlement." The statement, along with other vague messages from Hanoi, set off a new flurry of speculation that peace negotiations might be imminent. Sometime in January, India had proposed a conference of the three members of the ICC to try to arrange peace talks. Poland had promptly rejected the proposal.

24. Kosygin was to visit England in early February.

25. Salisbury recounts his talk with Pham Van Dong in his book, *Behind the Lines: Hanoi, December 23, 1966–January 7, 1967* (New York: Harper & Row, 1967), pp. 192–205, although the formula quoted by Bundy does not appear in his account. For further discussion of the Salisbury report and the U.S. followup, see pp. 414–416.

26. Jean Sainteny had served as French High Commissioner in Indochina after World War II and had returned to Vietnam at the end of the First Indochina War in 1954. He was known to be close to Ho and Pham Van Dong, and de Gaulle sent him to Hanoi in the summer of 1966 to explore the possibilities of a settlement. Sainteny's memoir, *Ho Chi Minh and His Vietnam* (Chicago: Cowles, 1972), discusses the visit on pp. 163–166 but reveals no "formula" for peace. After his return to France, however, he told *Paris Match* that he thought North Vietnam would reduce aid to the Vietcong if the United States "made a gesture," and then commented publicly that the DRV "might accept the opening of negotiations" if the United States committed itself to a specific timetable for withdrawing its troops. Sainteny subsequently told Averell Harriman of his certainty that Hanoi was prepared to make "an important gesture" if the United States demonstrated its good faith. For Sainteny's numerous comments, see p. 414; also *USVN*, book 12, VI.A., pp. 23–24, and Chester Cooper, *The Lost Crusade* (New York: Dodd, Mead, 1970), pp. 348–349.

27. William Baggs, editor of the *Miami News* and a director of the liberal Center for the Study of Democratic Institutions, and Harry Ashmore, executive vice-president of the center, journeyed to Hanoi in early 1967 on a private peace mission, which had the State Department's approval if not exactly its blessings. For their own account of their visit, see *Mission to Hanoi: A Chronicle of Double-Dealing in High Places* (New York: Putnam 1968).

28. Wilson's "two-sentence message" does not appear in the SUNFLOWER documents nor does Johnson mention it in his memoirs. The message probably contained Wilson's request to have Johnson send someone to London before Kosygin arrived to brief him fully on U.S. policy in order to avoid, as the Prime Minister later put it, "a repetition of the Lewandowski affair." Johnson sent Chester Cooper, Harriman's top assistant, but from the British point of view SUNFLOWER turned out to be a source of greater embarrassment than MARIGOLD.

29. Tan Son Nhut airport in Saigon became the major U.S. air base in South Vietnam in the late 1960s and was frequently described during this period as the busiest airport in the world. It also housed the General Staff of the South Vietnamese armed forces.

30. Johnson's State of the Union address, delivered January 10, 1967, is in *PPP, LBJ-1967*, I, 2–14; his comments on Vietnam are on pp. 11–14.

31. Senator Robert F. Kennedy (D.-N.Y.), then on a tour of Europe, stated several times that a "critical" stage in negotiations might be near. While in Paris, Kennedy had also met with Etienne Manac'h of the French Foreign Office, who passed to him a message from Mai Van Bo that Hanoi was prepared to negotiate in return for a cessation of the bombing. Kennedy apparently missed the significance of the "signal," but a U.S. embassy official who had accompanied him picked it up and relayed it to the State Department. It was subsequently leaked to the press, which reported that Kennedy had brought home a "peace feeler." The reports and the assumption, probably incorrect, that Kennedy had been responsible for the leak, provoked an angry confrontation between Kennedy and Johnson, leading to an open break in their long-chilly relationship.

32. The reference to the leak of messages from Cairo and New Delhi is not clear. The comment may refer to reports that the DRV had made simultaneous approaches to both the United Arab Republic and India asking them to convey to the United States the word that Hanoi was ready to talk in exchange for a cessation of the bombing. Or it may refer to reports in the press in late January that the United States had made informal but direct approaches to NLF representatives in Cairo and "other capitals." See, respectively, p. 424, and *USVN*, book 12, VI.A., p. 43.

33. The "goodwill" gesture referred to by Tass is the Trinh statement of January 28, 1967. See above, note 7.

34. Wilson's remarks in Parliament, February 7, 1967, are in *Parliamentary Debates*, fifth series, vol. 740, session 1966–1967, pp. 1348–1350. In response to an observation from the floor that Hanoi had been ready to negotiate in December but had backed off because of the American air strikes, Wilson guardedly commented that "it is my view that what happened then was based on a very considerable two-way understanding, and that is why I think certain events in December occurred."

35. North Vietnam published the Johnson-Ho exchange of letters on March 21, 1967. For the text of the letters and their role in U.S.–North Vietnamese diplomacy, see VI.C.3., SUNFLOWER.

VI.C.3., SUNFLOWER

1. *New York Times* correspondent Harrison E. Salisbury was the first American journalist to be granted a visa to North Vietnam, and his reports on the destructiveness of the December bombings around Hanoi and Haiphong placed the U.S. government on the defensive and intensified international and domestic pressures for a bombing halt. For additional information on the Salisbury visit and reports, see pp. 336, 409–410, 414–415 and Salisbury, *Behind the Lines*.

2. On December 8, 1966, Pope Paul VI had appealed to the warring parties for a cease-fire and, the same day, U.N. Secretary General U Thant had urged them to heed the Pope's plea. For the text of the Pope's message, see *AFP*, *CD-1966*, pp. 844–845; for U Thant's statement, see *New York Times*, December 9, 1966.

3. Ashmore and Baggs had talked with Ho Chi Minh on January 12, 1967, and brought back the word that North Vietnam would talk in exchange for a cessation of the bombing. Largely as a result of the intervention of Senator Fulbright, President Johnson directed the State Department to assist Ashmore and Baggs in composing a reply to Ho's "overture."

4. For Johnson's February 6 or 7, 1967, letter to Wilson, see pp. 436–438.

5. Johnson's February 8, 1967, letter to Ho is on pp. 440–441.

6. The Johnson-Ho exchange of letters was in fact published by North Vietnam on March 21, 1967.

7. Johnson's second letter to Ho was dated April 6, 1967, and is printed in full in Johnson, *The Vantage Point*, p. 596.

8. U Thant's three-point program was first introduced June 20, 1966. For his statement, see *AFP, CD-1966*, p. 819.

9. For the text of Goldberg's September 22 and October 18 statements, see, respectively, *DSB* 55 (October 10, 1966): 518–525, and *AFP, CD-1966*, pp. 865–866.

10. Salisbury's dispatch was published in the *New York Times*, January 4, 1967, and immediately touched off speculation that a new flexibility in Hanoi might have brightened considerably the prospects for negotiations.

11. The Foreign Ministry statement, reported in the *New York Times*, January 7, 1967, chided Western newsmen for their overly optimistic commentary on the Salisbury interview with Pham Van Dong. It added, somewhat mysteriously, that Pham had "actually told Mr. Harrison Salisbury that the four-point stand of the North Vietnamese government constitutes the basis of a settlement of the Vietnam problem."

12. The term "slug," in bureaucratic parlance, means to attach a code name.

13. Jean Sainteny, former French High Commissioner in Indochina, had talked with top North Vietnamese officials in July 1966 and later reported to Harriman that Hanoi was prepared to make an "important gesture" once the United States stopped the bombing. The Swedish Ambassador to Peking, Lennart Petri, talked with Foreign Minister Nguyen Duy Trinh in the summer of 1966. As reported to the State Department in November, Trinh had told Petri that "we know what we will have to do" if the United States should stop the bombing. For the Petri contact, see pp. 658–661.

14. The internal struggle in China intensified in early 1967, at times assuming the proportions of full-scale civil war. The outcome at this time was quite uncertain and the implications for Chinese foreign policy and the Vietnam War quite unclear.

15. Le Chang's January 24, 1966, conversation with Kohler is on p. 139.

16. The recent "most serious escalation" referred to by Le Chang involved major ground operations in South Vietnam as well as intensification of the air war. Operation CEDAR FALLS, launched in early 1967, sent some 30,000 U.S. and ARVN troops on a search-and-destroy mission against the Iron Triangle, a Vietcong stronghold just north of Saigon. Several hundred Vietcong were reported killed, although the major body of troops escaped. The village of Ben Suc, here incorrectly called Ben Xue, is located in the northeast corner of the Triangle. It was destroyed and some 6,000 of its inhabitants were relocated. The air attacks took place during the period January 16–24, 1967. Thanhoa and Ninh Binh were rail centers south of Hanoi; Thainguyen and Viet Tri are to the north. Hanoi protested with particular bitterness the bombing of Thainguyen, which it claimed resulted in the death of 35 civilians, injury to 106, and the destruction of hundreds of homes.

17. Johnson's most recent statement on the escalation of the war probably was his affirmation in his State of the Union message on January 10 that pressure on the enemy must be increased "slowly, but inexorably" until Hanoi realized that the costs of prolonging the war exceeded any potential gains.

18. The text of the Trinh interview appeared on the front page of all North Vietnamese newspapers along with a Foreign Ministry statement indicating that it was an important document. *Nhan Dan* singled out for special emphasis Trinh's statement regarding a bombing halt and possible "talks." For Burchett's account of the interview with Trinh, see Wilfred Burchett, *At the Barricades* (New York: Times Books, 1980), pp. 237, 239–240.

19. Goldberg's speech of September 22 set forth the "standard position" that the United States was prepared to stop the bombing "the moment we are assured, privately or otherwise, that this step will be answered promptly by a corresponding and appropriate de-escalation on the other side." For the text, see pp. 255–256.

20. The constituent assembly was drafting the new constitution at this time. The government would approve its work in March and the constitution was promulgated in April. Despite Ky's statement here, the national elections would not be held until September.

21. Chester Cooper was special assistant to Ambassador-at-Large W. Averell Harriman. He went to London at this time at the special request of Prime Minister Harold Wilson to keep the British government informed on U.S. policy, thereby presumably avoiding the confusion and embarrassment that had accompanied MARIGOLD. See above, VI.C.2., MARIGOLD, note 28.

22. The idea of a presidential message to Ho Chi Minh had apparently originated sometime in January and was viewed as a sort of culmination of the Moscow channel. A number of early drafts composed before February 1 appear to have been consistent with the original Phase A–Phase B proposal offered Hanoi during MARIGOLD. Sometime between February 1 and February 8, for reasons not entirely clear, the administration's position hardened significantly.

23. The Estabrook story, February 2, 1967, concerned MARIGOLD. See pp. 342–345.

24. Apparently as a result of the intervention of Senator Fulbright, who complained to Johnson that Ashmore and Baggs had been ignored on their return from Hanoi, the State Department collaborated with the two men in drafting this response to Ho's message. The North Vietnamese subsequently indicated that no useful purpose would be served by another Ashmore-Baggs visit.

25. Wilson gives a reasonably comprehensive account of this conversation in *The Labour Government*, pp. 347–348.

26. This statement of the Phase A–Phase B formula would be the source of a minor diplomatic crisis several days later. It left quite vague the sequence in which the various acts of de-escalation would occur. From the standpoint of Cooper and Wilson in London, it seemed consistent with the plan that had already been proposed calling for the United States to stop the bombing once it had been assured that, at some later, specified time, North Vietnam would stop infiltration. To those in Washington, it seemed equally consistent with the president's letter to Ho Chi Minh, which indicated that the United States would stop the bombing once "infiltration has stopped." The source of the confusion remains unclear. Perhaps, as the State Department's Executive Secretary, Benjamin H. Read, later observed, the letter to Wilson was written "with midnight oil and without the presence of lawyers and the tense slipped." Or it is possible that policy changed after the letter to Wilson had been drafted and no one caught the contradiction. See Benjamin Read Oral History Interview, Johnson Library.

27. The precise formulation of the Phase A–Phase B scheme by Wilson at the February 7 meeting cannot be determined on the basis of available documentation. From Wilson's memoirs and other sources, it appears that he proposed that the United States would stop the bombing on assurances that Hanoi would stop "augmenting" its forces in the South. This proposal apparently included a second American concession: the United States would stop the buildup of its own forces in South Vietnam once assured that North Vietnamese augmentation would stop at the same time. The latter stipulation, according to Wilson, was intended to meet Kosygin's protests about the continuing buildup of U.S. forces (see Wilson, *The Labour Government*, pp. 350–351).

28. The point at which this stipulation became U.S. policy is not clear. According to Chester Cooper, earlier drafts of the letter to Ho contained the original Phase A–Phase B proposal, but they had not been approved by the President. Johnson may have introduced the change under pressure from the Joint Chiefs or on his own simply because he felt the original gave away too much. Or the change may have been a response to intelligence reports indicating that the North Vietnamese were planning to take advantage of the approaching Tet truce by pouring men and supplies into South Vietnam.

29. This draft of the Phase A–Phase B formula, as the documents that follow indicate, seems to have used the same sequence of actions but made implementation the partial responsibility of the United Kingdom and the Soviet Union as co-chairmen of the Geneva Conference, an approach originally suggested by Kosygin.

30. At his February 9, 1967, press conference, Rusk emphasized the large number of incidents that had occurred in the first hours of the Tet truce and added that many boats and other vessels were "dashing" along the coast to supply forces in the southern part of North Vietnam and along the DMZ. This seemed to indicate, he said, Hanoi's intention to expand rather than contract its military operations and suggested that North Vietnam was "not particularly interested in an actual ceasefire." The United States, the Secretary concluded, could not consider terminating the bombing as long as North Vietnam continued invading South Vietnam. The text of Rusk's news conference is in *DSB* 56 (February 26, 1967): 317–322.

31. For extensive excerpts from Goldberg's February 10, 1967, Howard University speech, see pp. 604–612. The complete text is in *DSB* 56 (February 26, 1967): 310–316.

32. The Chieu Hoi (Open Arms) program was designed to encourage defections from the Vietcong by grants of amnesty, financial rewards, and other incentives. In operation since 1963, it also provided for a period of "rehabilitation" after surrender.

33. At their final plenary session on the morning of Friday, February 10, Wilson once again raised the Phase A–Phase B proposal for discussion with

Kosygin. According to Wilson, Kosygin for the first time expressed real interest in it and asked to have it in writing. At Wilson's instruction, Cooper and Ambassador David Bruce proceeded to draft the proposal in collaboration with British Foreign Office officials. Cooper then asked for approval from Washington, but since this was expected pro forma, the draft was immediately passed on to Wilson, who later took it to Kosygin. Cooper claims that all of this took place on Thursday and that Washington was very lax in responding to his request for approval. Wilson's memoirs and the documents here make clear that it took place on Friday and that Washington in fact had very little time to respond.

34. When Washington finally realized, upon receipt of Cooper's February 10 message, that the proposal given to Kosygin and the letter to Ho Chi Minh differed drastically, officials phoned Cooper and made clear that prevailing policy was that infiltration must cease before the bombing would be stopped. This naturally caused an uproar in London, particularly since Kosygin was to board a train for Scotland within minutes. Wilson was able to get the message to Kosygin just as the train was preparing to leave the station, but the Prime Minister was furious and complained bitterly of the "hell of a situation" in which he had been placed.

35. Ky was apparently referring to the CEDAR FALLS campaign against the Iron Triangle, which, at least temporarily, had denied the Vietcong access to one of its major base areas.

36. On February 7, 1967, Pope Paul VI had sent parallel messages to President Johnson, Ho Chi Minh, and South Vietnamese Chief of State Nguyen Van Thieu, stating his hope that the Tet truce "may open the way to negotiations for a just and stable peace" and urging the leaders to increase their efforts for a settlement during the period of the truce. See *New York Times*, February 9, 1967.

37. Ambassador Bruce here seeks to repair at least some of the damage done by what he aptly calls "last night's imbroglio" by urging the administration to extend the Tet bombing pause until after Kosygin's departure from London, a proposal advanced earlier by Wilson.

38. For inside accounts of the "stormy session," see Wilson, *The Labour Government*, pp. 357–358; Cooper, *The Lost Crusade*, p. 363, and Cooper Oral History Interview, Johnson Library.

39. Wilson summarizes these messages and provides some excerpts in *The Labour Government*, pp. 358–360.

40. The flap over the phrase "power of attorney" derived from Wilson's statement in the letter to Johnson that he and Kosygin, each knowing the views of their respective friends, would seek a solution that each could commend to his friend, "like two solicitors seeking to settle a matter out of court, ad referendum to the two clients." The White House apparently interpreted this as a veiled request for a "power of attorney," which it peremptorily rejected.

41. The "texts" deleted here are the various Phase A–Phase B proposals made to Kosygin between February 7 and 10. The first two, in somewhat different words, call for the United States to stop the bombing after firm assurances that North Vietnamese infiltration would stop, with the United States

21. For excerpts of Trinh's interview with journalist Charles Collingwood, April 7, 1968, see *New York Times*, April 8, 9, 1968.

22. The text of the DRV's April 3, 1968, statement is in *New York Times*, April 4, 1968.

23. The "first NLF program" probably refers to the ten-point program issued on December 20, 1960. For the text, see Raskin and Fall, *Viet-Nam Reader*, pp. 216–221, or *USVN*, book 12, VI.B., pp. 189–192.

24. The GVN's Four Points, June 22, 1965, are on p. 587.

25. The Vietnam Alliance of National, Democratic, and Peace Forces was created in April 1968 by prominent non-Communist and antigovernment South Vietnamese, probably with the encouragement of and perhaps at the initiative of the NLF. Its program was almost identical with that of the front.

26. The new NLF program was actually set forth shortly before the 1967 elections in South Vietnam and was probably designed to undercut the government and draw attention away from the elections. It invited all who opposed the United States to join its ranks and also encouraged those who preferred not to join to combine forces against a common enemy. It further called for the abolition of the existing "puppet" government, for free elections to choose a "really democratic" national assembly, for the formulation of a democratic constitution, and for establishment of a government that would be independent and neutral. The new program seemed to defer resolution of the question of unification with North Vietnam. For the text, see *USVN*, book 12, VI.B., pp. 222–234.

27. The 1962 Geneva Agreements on Laos formed a coalition government composed of representatives of right, left, and neutralist groups, with the neutralists holding the majority of ministries.

28. For excerpts of Ambassador Ellsworth Bunker's "Meet the Press" interview on NBC television, November 19, 1967, see *New York Times*, November 20, 1967.

29. The National Reconciliation Program was originally conceived in Washington and was designed to erode the strength of the NLF by offering to the defectors terms that were more generous than those provided in the Chieu Hoi program. The Saigon government did not like the program, accepted it only with reluctance, and implemented it in a manner that resembled more surrender with amnesty than genuine reconciliation. See *PP (Gravel)*, II, 608.

30. For the text of Goldberg's November 2, 1967, statement to the Senate Foreign Relations Committee, see *DSB* 57 (November 20, 1967): 667–672.

31. The text of Johnson's March 31, 1968, speech is in *PPP, LBJ-1968*, I, 469–476.

32. The Fatherland Front, established by Hanoi in September 1955, called for the immediate restoration of normal economic, cultural, and social ties between the two regroupment zones established by the Geneva Accords and for negotiations to integrate the armed forces. It left considerable autonomy to each zone, however, and allowed for separate governments based on the distinctive local characteristics of the two zones. See *Viet-Nam Fatherland Front*, pp. 16–26.

33. Revolutionary Development was one of several names given the various "pacification" programs initiated by the United States and South Vietnam in the 1960s. For the implementation of the Revolutionary Development program, see *PP (Gravel)*, II, 515–623.

34. For the complete text of Johnson's February 8, 1967, letter to Pope Paul VI, see *DSB*, 56 (February 27, 1967): 319.

35. De Gaulle had frequently condemned American intervention in Vietnam and had advocated U.S. withdrawal, a return to the 1954 Geneva Agreements, and the neutralization of Indochina.

36. For the DRV January 28, 1967, statement, see pp. 422–424.

VI.C.4., OHIO

1. As noted earlier, U Thant's latest initiative was set forth on March 14, 1967, and attempted to get around the seemingly intractable issue of mutual de-escalation by calling for a "general stand-still truce" as a step toward direct talks and reconvening the Geneva Conference. The State Department's surmise about the North Vietnamese and Thant was probably correct. According to reports published at the time, the Secretary-General had met with North Vietnamese representatives in Rangoon on February 28 as a "private citizen." Immediately after returning to the United Nations, he had stated that the key to peace rested with the United States and had suggested that the best way to get talks started would be through an unconditional stoppage of the bombing. His call for a general stand-still truce conflicted with his earlier stand, and the North Vietnamese government condemned it for failing to distinguish between the aggressor and victims of aggression. See *USVN*, book 12, VI.A., pp. 54, 58.

2. For references to the Goldberg and Rusk statements, see above, VI.C.4., Vietnam Negotiations, 1967–1968, note 10.

3. For the Canadian proposal, see ibid., note 12.

4. The phrase "developments in another area" refers to the PENNSYLVANIA channel opened in Paris in late August.

5. President Johnson's speech of September 29, 1967, publicly introduced the San Antonio formula. For the text, see *PPP, LBJ-1967*, II, 876–881.

6. The increased bombing of North Vietnam in early October 1967 included attacks on a MIG base four miles from Hanoi; the Lach Tray and Thuong Ly shipyards, less than two miles from the center of Haiphong; and a missile assembly plant near Haiphong.

7. In a speech at the United Nations on October 4, 1967, Norwegian Foreign Minister John Lyng had conceded that the chances of peace would be much improved if North Vietnam would give unequivocal assurances of its willingness to negotiate once the United States had stopped the bombing. Lyng went on to insist, however, that even without such assurances the United States should stop the bombing. For a summary of the speech, see *UN Monthly Chronicle* 4 (November 1967): 70.

8. By late October 1967, the Vietnam issue had begun to place great strains on Norway's ruling coalition government. Without advance notice to Foreign Minister Lyng, a Liberal member of Parliament had proposed that the foreign ministry be instructed to forward to Washington an official Norwegian demand for a cessation of the bombing. Lyng responded that such a step was unwarranted and threatened to resign if the resolution passed. The resolution was referred to the foreign relations committee, from which it eventually emerged in greatly watered down fashion. The incident nevertheless reflected the increasingly sharp divisions within the government between the more radical wings of the Liberal party and the Conservatives, who criticized the government for not being more supportive of the United States.

9. The "unprecedented offensive" refers to the North Vietnamese/Vietcong Tet offensive launched on January 30, 1968, which included attacks on thirty-six provincial capitals, sixty-four district capitals, and five major cities, including Saigon and Hue.

VI.C.4., ASPEN

1. Rusk's rather crude historical analogies apparently refer to the closure of the Yugoslav border to Greek insurgents, a step that crippled the Greek revolution of the late 1940s, and to the Chinese Communist decisions in 1955 and 1958 to stop shelling the Nationalist-held offshore islands of Quemoy and Matsu in the face of vague American threats of nuclear retaliation.

2. Rusk refers here to the famous Ledo Road, originating at Ledo in India's Assam Province and proceeding through northern Burma to China. Designed to open an overland supply route to Nationalist China during World War II, it was constructed at great cost but was not completed until near the end of the war and never served the purpose for which it had been built.

3. Pham Van Dong's statement to *New York Times* correspondent Harrison Salisbury seemed to convey a more flexible North Vietnamese position on negotiations than had been indicated previously, but it was later qualified in a statement by the DRV Foreign Ministry. For the interview and State Department reaction to it, see pp. 409–415.

4. Sweden was at this time under considerable pressure from the East Germans to recognize East Germany and from West Germany to continue to withhold recognition. The Foreign Ministry apparently feared that steps in the direction of recognition of North Vietnam would exacerbate the already difficult "German problem."

5. Trinh is probably referring to the heavy bombing attacks on Hanoi and Haiphong in December 1966 and perhaps as well to operation CEDAR FALLS against the Iron Triangle near Saigon in January 1967.

6. The Riksdag is the Swedish parliament.

7. For the February 1967 escalation, which included resumption of the bombing, mining of coastal waters, and shelling by naval vessels and by artillery across the DMZ, see *PP (Gravel)*, IV, 148–149.

8. Johnson's February 8 letter to Ho Chi Minh is on pp. 440–441.

9. The tribunal on war crimes, sponsored by Bertrand Russell, was set to convene in Stockholm in early May. Apparently, the United States had privately urged the Swedish government not to permit the group to meet in Stockholm, but to no avail. Hence the complaint about "lack of effective action."

10. John M. Hightower's story on MARIGOLD appeared in the *New York Times* on May 9, 1967, and is printed on p. 367.

11. On April 20, 1967, U.S. aircraft bombed two power plants in Haiphong that supplied the energy for much of the city's industry, military installations, and port facilities. These were the first direct attacks on the city itself, and North Vietnamese spokesmen claimed they were responsible for one hundred civilian casualties. For the background of the April 20 raids, see *PP (Gravel)*, IV, 151–153.

12. The reference to "increasingly critical international opinion on U.S. policy" was probably based on recent anti-American demonstrations in Barcelona, Rome, London, and Paris, as well as the Russell War Crimes Tribunal, which had just concluded in Stockholm.

13. The Stockholm Viet-Nam Conference, arranged by organizations affiliated with the international peace movement and by the Swedish Society for Peace and Arbitration, opened on July 8 and was attended by 350 delegates from across the world.

14. Responding to the increasingly radical mood of the country, Sweden's ruling Social Democratic party sharpened its attacks on U.S. policy in Vietnam in the fall of 1967. Criticism of the United States was particularly heated in the party congress in October, and both Prime Minister Tage Erlander and Foreign Minister Nilsson delivered strong anti-American speeches.

15. For the new NLF program, see above, VI.C.4., Vietnam Negotiations, 1967–1968, note 26.

16. In his December 29, 1967, statement, Foreign Minister Trinh had reaffirmed North Vietnam's intention to "defend the North, liberate the South, and advance toward peaceful unification of the country." He also seemed to move a step closer to negotiations, however, stating that "if the U.S. Government truly wants to talk, it must . . . first of all stop unconditionally the bombing and all other acts of war against the D.R.V. After the United States has ended unconditionally the bombing and all other acts of war against the D.R.V., the D.R.V. will hold talks with the United States on questions concerned." The change of the verb tense from the conditional "could" to "will" was widely interpreted as signaling a more definite North Vietnamese willingness to negotiate.

VI.C.4., PENNSYLVANIA

1. The Pugwash Conferences were established in 1957 by Cyrus Eaton, Cleveland industrialist and advocate of peaceful coexistence. They brought together scientists from across the world to discuss means of preventing nuclear war and using science and technology for peaceful purposes.

2. Morris West's novel, *The Ambassador*, published in 1965, is the fictional account of an American ambassador in South Vietnam based on the actual events of 1963 during the time immediately before the overthrow of Ngo Dinh Diem. Its tone is generally critical of the United States for meddling in the internal politics of Vietnam and for trying to hold back Asian revolutions.

3. Pham Van Dong was probably referring to the U.S. Marines stationed in various bases just below the DMZ. They had been the object of heavy artillery fire and repeated attacks by North Vietnamese troops in the last half of 1967.

4. Pham refers here to Foreign Minister Trinh's January 28, 1967, interview with Wilfred Burchett. For the text, see pp. 422–424.

5. See above, VI.C.4., Vietnam Negotiations, 1967–1968, note 35.

6. The "new targets" refer to ROLLING THUNDER 57 approved by Johnson in July. They included rail yards, communication centers, and supply depots in and around Hanoi and an area along the Chinese border.

7. On August 19, 1967, McNamara ordered suspension of bombing attacks in a ten-mile perimeter around Hanoi from August 24 to September 4 to ensure the safety of Aubrac and Marcovich, test the seriousness of the contact, and demonstrate the validity of Kissinger's role as intermediary.

8. In late July 1967, North Vietnam charged that U.S. bombing and artillery fire had broken dams just north of the DMZ and cited these attacks as part of a deliberate American effort to destroy its water conservation system. Several days later, North Vietnamese officials showed foreign newsmen a site near Hanoi where dikes had been struck by U.S. bombs.

9. The bombing of North Vietnam between August 20 and 22 was particularly intensive. On August 20, the United States launched 209 missions, the heaviest raids to date. On all three days, the attacks concentrated on targets in the area of Hanoi and along the Chinese border.

10. In 1966, McNamara had proposed the establishment of a barrier across the DMZ as a means of checking North Vietnamese infiltration and as a substitute for continued escalation of the bombing. The barrier was to be composed of fences, wire, and electronic sensors, supported by aircraft, artillery, and ground troops. Some work on the project began in the spring of 1967, and McNamara, later in the year, confirmed long-standing rumors that it was being constructed. Several sections were actually completed, but the project was eventually abandoned because of its cost and perceived impracticality.

11. The attacks on Haiphong on September 11 and 12, 1967, concentrated on the bridges between the docks and the mainland.

12. The David Schoenbrun interview had been done in Bangkok and was broadcast on ABC television September 9. Reporting conversations with Pham Van Dong the preceding week, Schoenbrun indicated that the North Vietnamese leader had reiterated Hanoi's long-standing position that the bombing must be stopped unconditionally in order for talks to begin. According to Schoenbrun, Pham also affirmed that North Vietnam was prepared, if necessary, to withstand an American invasion and the aerial devastation of Hanoi and would "fight on in the mountains for as long as it can possibly take." See *Washington Post*, September 10, 1967, and *USVN*, book 12, VI.B., p. 236.

13. The escalation of North Vietnamese/Vietcong activities referred to here included sustained attacks against Marine bases at Gio Linh and Con Thien just south of the DMZ, increased terrorist activities throughout South Vietnam, and the shelling of U.S. bases at Danang and Phu Bai. American observers assumed that the escalation was designed to interfere with the South Vietnamese elections on September 11.

14. The Agence France-Presse story is reported in the *New York Times*, September 15, 1967.

15. Ronald Reagan, former movie actor and at this time Governor of California, was widely considered a presidential possibility for 1968. He had frequently criticized President Johnson for not using American military power more decisively, and he was generally regarded as the most hawkish of potential Republican candidates.

16. Campha was an auxiliary port forty-six miles northeast of Haiphong. The September attacks on Haiphong, Campha, and the port of Hongay, located between the other two ports, concentrated on wharves, docks, rail facilities, and supply depots and were designed to disrupt North Vietnamese logistics by sealing off access to the ports from the land side. These attacks were accompanied by the bombing of warehouses, rail yards, and bridges near the center of Hanoi and by raids on Vinh Linh Province just north of the DMZ.

17. In the U.N. debate of September and October 1967, British Foreign Secretary George Brown criticized North Vietnam for refusing to grasp "the many opportunities which have been offered" and said that it would be easier for the United States to stop the bombing if Hanoi would indicate a willingness to take steps of mutual de-escalation. Canadian Secretary of State for External Affairs Paul Martin had reiterated his four-stage proposal for a ceasefire. French Foreign Minister Maurice Couve de Murville, echoing the line taken by President de Gaulle, had insisted that the United States must take the "decisive initiative" to get talks underway and had called for an unconditional suspension of the bombing of North Vietnam. See *UN Monthly Chronicle* 4 (October 1967): 63–64, 70, 79.

18. By the fall of 1967, numerous signs did indicate growing American public frustration with the war. Polls showed a sharp drop in support for the war and particularly for Johnson's handling of it, and in some pre-election polls Senator Robert Kennedy led the incumbent. Businessmen began to speak out against the war, and numerous newspapers that had previously supported it began to raise questions. Criticism in the House and Senate mounted, and important Republican Senators, such as Clifford Case of New Jersey and Thruston Morton of Kentucky, publicly declared their opposition to further escalation.

19. During this period, the press issued numerous conflicting reports of North Vietnam's reactions to the latest American proposals. Most reiterated the standard position that there could be no talks until the United States stopped the bombing and all other acts of war. Other, unconfirmed reports, included the more specific indication that Hanoi was prepared to open "serious" and "significant" talks within three or four weeks after the bombing had been stopped.

20. February 28 appears to be an error. The statement most likely refers to the January 28, 1967, interview of Trinh by Australian journalist Wilfred Burchett.

21. In numerous statements between October 3 and 18, North Vietnam spokesmen dismissed the San Antonio formula as an "impudent bluff" and a "faked desire for peace" and vowed to fight on. In mid-October, North Vietnamese regulars launched another sustained attack against the U.S. Marine base at Con Thien just south of the DMZ.

VI.C.4., RUMANIA

1. For a partial text of Goldberg's September 22, 1966, speech, see pp. 255–256.

2. The Manila Communiqué is on pp. 595–599.

3. Reference is to the Bucharest Declaration of July 6, 1966. For the text, see *AFP, CD-1966*, pp. 832–834. See above, VI.C.2., MARIGOLD, note 6.

4. Rumanian Foreign Minister Corneliu Manescu was elected President of the Twenty-Second session of the United Nations General Assembly in September.

5. Throughout the 1960s, Rumania had effectively challenged Soviet economic and political dominance, developed closer ties with the West, and assumed a neutral or even pro-Chinese position in the Sino-Soviet dispute.

Hence Maurer's statement that the United States was in a better position to involve the Soviet Union than Rumania.

VI.C.4., PACKERS

1. The Longbien (Paul Doumer) Bridge spanned the Red River 1.7 miles from the center of Hanoi and was regarded as a vital link in the North Vietnamese logistics and communications network. It was first bombed on August 11 and was finally cut later in the year.

2. Trinh stated on December 29 that "after the United States has ended unconditionally the bombing and all other acts of war against the D.R.V., the D.R.V. will hold talks with the United States on questions concerned."

3. For a brief discussion of the background of this decision, see *PP (Gravel)*, IV, 232–233.

V.C.4., KILLY

1. The *Washington Post* story of February 16, 1968, reported in considerable detail Fanfani's various contacts with North Vietnamese representatives and indicated that their talks had centered on the political issues that would make up a settlement rather than on the problem of de-escalation. A recently declassified cable from the State Department to the American Embassy, Saigon, February 16, 1968, confirms that the *Post* story was essentially correct and provides some additional information about Fanfani's meetings with North Vietnamese representatives on February 5 and 6. According to the State Department, the North Vietnamese told Fanfani that the contact was serious and a sign of their good will. They reiterated that if the United States stopped the bombing North Vietnam was prepared to negotiate, but they again rejected the concept of reciprocity and affirmed that Trinh's December statement was a "clear sign which has been carefully considered and designed to resolve the conflict." The State Department saw no indication in the Fanfani conversations that Hanoi was willing to go beyond the positions it had assumed publicly and speculated that the approach, along with parallel feelers through U Thant and the government of India, may have been part of a "concerted propaganda offensive." The February 16, 1968, cable may be found in *The War in Vietnam: Classified Histories by the National Security Council* [Microfilm Collection], Reel 6, Document #0257.

2. Secretary of Defense-designate Clark L. Clifford's explanation of the San Antonio "no advantage" formula is on pp. 556–557.

3. Prior to the Tet Offensive and in connection with its new political program of the fall of 1967, the NLF had encouraged the formation of groups among anti-U.S. and antigovernment forces in South Vietnam. It apparently hoped that these "bogus committees" would isolate the Saigon government politically and might also comprise a centrist element in a coalition government. Some of these groups eventually merged into the Alliance of National Democratic and Peace Forces.

4. See above, VI.C.4., Vietnam Negotiations, 1967–1968, notes 6 and 7.

5. Although this vague statement could have been interpreted as at least a qualified acceptance of the San Antonio formula, wary U.S. officials apparently did not view it as such. A memorandum of March 25–26, 1968, "Nego-

tiating Options," prepared for the Senior Advisory Group that was to meet with the President, indicated that North Vietnam had continued to reject the San Antonio formula and went on to say that although it had sent out numerous signals in recent weeks most of these seemed to be of a "teasing nature." U.S. officials seem to have dismissed the conversations with Fanfani as merely one of "several very general statements that have been made to us through third parties—that Hanoi really understands the 'no advantage' assumptions even though it is unwilling to say so." The memorandum recommended against an immediate stoppage of the bombing as long as North Vietnam refused to go beyond the position it had assumed, but it did go on to suggest that an unconditional bombing halt even without North Vietnamese acceptance of the San Antonio formula might be worth the risk in three or four weeks. See *The War in Vietnam: Classified Histories by the National Security Council* [Microfilm Collection], Reel 8, Document #0068.

Index